Psychology A Level
Year 2

The Revision and Exam Companion

Mike Cardwell • Clare Compton • Rob McIlveen
Rachel Moody • Joseph Sparks

OXFORD
UNIVERSITY P

OXFORD
UNIVERSITY PRESS

Great Clarendon Street, Oxford, OX2 6DP, United Kingdom

Oxford University Press is a department of the University of Oxford.
It furthers the University's objective of excellence in research, scholarship,
and education by publishing worldwide. Oxford is a registered trademark of
Oxford University Press in the UK and in
certain other countries

British Library Cataloguing in Publication Data
Data available

978 019 837641 5

10 9 8 7 6 5 4 3 2 1

MIX
Paper from
responsible sources
FSC® C007785

Paper used in the production of this book is a natural, recyclable product
made from wood grown in sustainable forests.
The manufacturing process conforms to the environmental regulations of
the country of origin.

Printed in Great Britain by Bell and Bain Ltd, Glasgow.

Acknowledgements
The publishers would like to thank the following for permissions to
use their photographs:

p51: Library of Congress; p55: Skip Odonnell/iStockphoto; p85: Steve
Duck; p123: CTR Photos/Shutterstock.com; p173: Associated Press;
p313: YAY Media AS/Alamy Stock Photo.

All other photos by Shutterstock.

Cover image by: Chris Cardwell, Evoke Pictures Bristol

Although we have made every effort to trace and contact all
copyright holders before publication this has not been possible in all
cases. If notified, the publisher will rectify any errors or omissions at
the earliest opportunity.

...ledgements
The authors would like to express their gratitude to Alison Schrecker,
Sarah Flynn and Janice Chan at OUP for their enthusiasm and
continuous support for this project. Our greatest thanks go to Veronica
Wastell for her proactive approach to project management and her
impressive attention to detail. In addition, Clare Compton would like
to thank PF for his help and support. Rachel Moody is grateful for so
many inspiring and encouraging Psychology teaching colleagues, and
the joy of ATP Conferences. Joseph Sparks would like to thank Joseph
Vu for his unwavering support and Stuart Cipinko for his excellent
psychological knowledge and inspiration. He would also like to
apologise to Lynn Sparks for not managing to get one of her pets onto
the front cover! On the cover of the original version of this book we
featured Evie, an Irish Setter puppy from Bristol. A few years on, with
Evie now the proud mum of her own pups, it seems appropriate that
two of those puppies should adorn our latest edition.

Then...

...and now

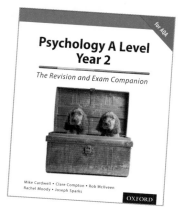

Contents

This book is part of our 'Companion' series, and shares the same aim of providing a companion to help turn your understanding of psychology into even better exam performance.

There are many features in this book that we think make it distinctive:

1. INTRODUCTION and skill practice

In the introductory section of this book we have provided activities to help you develop the skills you need in order to to perform well. You might believe that 'doing well' just means knowing the psychology, but that is only really half of the formula for success. You also have to be able to express your knowledge appropriately – i.e. know and follow the 'rules of the game'. 'Doing well', therefore, is not just knowing the content, but knowing how to use it.

2. Must know and Should know

The content in this book focuses on preparing answers to the extended writing questions worth 16 marks. If you fully understand the material AND can answer these questions, then you should be able to cope with all other kinds of questions that are asked.

We have divided this material into:

> **MUST.** For some students this will be sufficient. If you can produce this material in an exam you are likely to get a Grade C.

> Once you have mastered the 'must' content, then move on to **SHOULD**. Knowing this extra material should lift your answer to a Grade A.

> For students pushing for a high A grade, we have usually added some FURTHER EVALUATION points appropriate for 16 mark extended writing questions.

3. Activities

On the right-hand side of each spread there is a range of exam-focused activities to help consolidate your knowledge. These activities aim to help you construct better exam answers. Other activities will help you process your knowledge and enhance your understanding and memory of the material on that spread.

Answers to most activities are given at the end of this book.

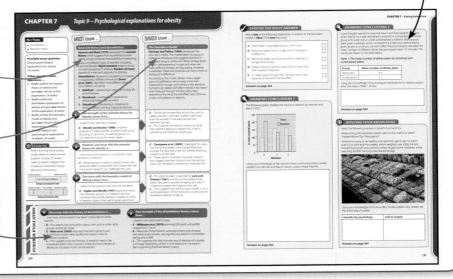

> For each topic we provide some sample examination questions. We have alternated these so sometimes these are extended writing questions and sometimes shorter questions.

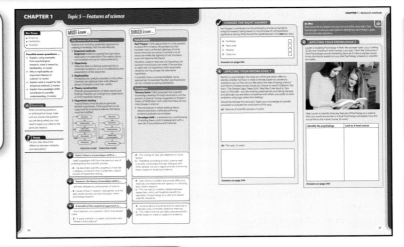

> Examiner comments are given as a form of running commentary on the answers. These indicate the strengths of the answer and offer suggestions on how it might be improved.

> We have added a final assessment, indicating the mark range for this answer and giving the reasons why this particular level would be appropriate.

> As well as providing sample questions, we have also given you sample student answers to give you an idea of what a student response to this question would look like. These are not designed to be 'model' answers to the questions, but are typically of Grade A or B standard.

On pages 12 to 17 we have included sample mock examinations, with suggested answers at the back of the book.

The A level examination

Paper 1 (7182/1) Introductory topics in psychology

Paper 2 (7182/2) Psychology in context

The content and exam information for Paper 1 and Paper 2 are covered in the Year 1 book Section B Psychopathology

Paper 3 (7182/3) Issues and options in psychology

You will have two hours to answer questions on this paper.

The paper is divided into four sections, each worth 24 marks. Section A is compulsory. For Sections B-D, you choose one topic (e.g. for Section C, you answer questions on EITHER Schizophrenia OR Eating behaviour OR Stress).

The content of the four sections is as below:

Section A	Issues and debates in psychology
Section B	Relationships
	Gender
	Cognition and development
Section C	Schizophrenia
	Eating behaviour
	Stress
Section D	Aggression
	Forensic psychology
	Addiction

Assessment objectives

The examinations assesses three separate skills, known as **assessment objectives**. These are as follows:

AO1 (description of knowledge)
AO2 (application of knowledge)
AO3 (evaluation of knowledge)

We look further at these three assessment objectives, how you can master them and how they are examined on the next few spreads. In practice, the differences between these three skills can be quite subtle, as it is a case of what you *do* with material that makes it AO1, AO2 or AO3 rather than any inherent properties of the material itself. Let's look at a (completely fictional) example from a galaxy far, far away.

'Snoke (2016) found that galactic stormtroopers behaved far more aggressively when invading other planets if they were all wearing the same military uniform rather than when they were wearing their own civilian clothes. He also found that stormtroopers were more aggressive when patrolling in large groups than when they patrolled on their own.'

Now let's look at how this material can be used as a way of responding to three very different types of question. Note that the underlying material is more or less the same in all three cases, but it has been 'tweaked' so that it is being used in either a descriptive (AO1), application (AO2) or evaluative (AO3) way.

An AO1 question

Outline the findings of one psychological study of de-individuation as an explanation of aggression. *(3 marks)*

'Snoke (2016) found that factors that increase de-individuation also tend to increase aggression. He found that galactic stormtroopers behaved far more aggressively when invading other planets if they were all wearing the same military uniform rather than when they were wearing their own civilian clothes. He also found that stormtroopers were more aggressive when patrolling in large groups than when they patrolled on their own.'

An AO2 question

Ground stewards at Grimsby United have been instructed to ban fans wearing masks and face paint and anything else that increases their anonymity. The football club believe that this will decrease violence on the terraces. Using your knowledge of de-individuation as an explanation of aggression, explain why this is likely to be the case. *(3 marks)*

'Snoke (2016) found that factors that increase de-individuation also tend to increase aggression. He found that galactic stormtroopers behaved far more aggressively when invading other planets if they were all wearing the same military uniform rather than when they were wearing their own civilian clothes. Grimsby officials believe that anonymity as a result of masks and face painting also de-individuates fans, and so would increase aggression, as it did with the stormtroopers studied by Snoke.'

An AO3 question

Explain one critical point concerning the relationship between de-individuation and aggression. *(3 marks)*

'The claim that there is a relationship between de-individuation and aggression is supported by research by Snoke (2016). He found that galactic stormtroopers behaved far more aggressively when invading other planets if they were all wearing the same military uniform rather than when they were wearing their own civilian clothes. He also found that stormtroopers were more aggressive when patrolling in large groups than when they patrolled on their own. This supports the claim that factors that increase de-individuation also tend to increase aggression.'

Training yourself to be an examiner

Throughout this book we offer you suggestions as to how to structure material for the most effective exam answers, but there is another skill that will help you understand exactly why it is necessary to do this. Knowing what the examiner is looking for and why they award marks is vital. Therefore, over the next two spreads, we'll train you to be an examiner, so you can mark your own answers. We'll start with AO1.

A01

Step 1

We have summarised the main skills an examiner looks for in the table at the bottom of the page. First, we need to determine whether the answer is **accurate** (it is in the case of the two answers below). Next, we look at the amount of **detail**. Is it overly brief and superficial or has the candidate fleshed out their answer with appropriate elaboration? The term 'appropriate' is important because not all detail adds to the quality of the answer.

Training task 1

Outline biological explanations of schizophrenia. *(6 marks)*

Answer 1

The first biological explanation is genetic factors. Twin studies are used where researchers compare identical and non-identical twins. Identical twins are genetically identical whereas non-identical twins only share 50% of their genes. Studies with twins have shown a strong genetic influence because identical twins that are schizophrenic are more likely to have a twin who is also schizophrenic. The second biological explanation is the dopamine hypothesis. This claims that schizophrenia is caused by too much activity in the brain, which leads to the abnormalities experienced by schizophrenics. A third explanation is neural correlates. This refers to the different parts of the brain that are associated with schizophrenia. For example, schizophrenics have been found to have reduced brain matter and enlarged ventricles compared to non-schizophrenics. These enlarged ventricles show that the schizophrenic has lost important brain matter.

Answer 2

Genetic explanations claim that schizophrenia is inherited biologically. Twin and family studies have shown that the closer the degree of genetic similarity with a schizophrenic patient, the greater the risk of developing the disorder. Adoption studies such as Tienari et al. (2000) have found that adopted children are more likely to develop schizophrenia if a biological parent has the disorder than if an adoptive parent has.

The dopamine hypothesis claims that schizophrenia is a consequence of dopamine receptors in the mesolimbic pathway of the brain firing too easily or too often. Drugs that block this dopamine activity also tend to reduce positive symptoms, such as hallucinations and delusions, suggesting that these symptoms are caused by excess dopamine activity. The revised dopamine hypothesis claims that the negative and cognitive symptoms found in some schizophrenics are caused by a deficit of dopamine in areas of the prefrontal cortex.

Step 2

The next skill we need to assess is how well the answer is **organised**, i.e. does it ramble around the topic in a seemingly illogical way or is it carefully structured and easy to follow? You know yourself from reading textbooks that well organised content is easier to follow and understand.

Finally we need to make a judgement about the use of specialist terminology. Has the candidate used appropriate **psychological terminology** or described the material in more general (and vague) ways?

The verdict

Answer 1 is a Level 2 response. Because the candidate has tried to cram in 3 explanations, detail is sacrificed. Some of this detail is unnecessary and doesn't add much. It is mostly clear and organised with some fairly vague terms so 4 marks.

Answer 2 is a Level 3 response. Given the time available for answer of this type, this is a very detailed answer. It is well organised (clear, coherent and logically organised). Good use of specialist terminology, so the full 6 marks.

The 'magnet effect'

Mark allocation tables such as the one on this page give information about what an answer at a particular level would look like. However, often an answer does not fit neatly into one level. For example, an answer might be 'mostly clear and organised', but also lacking in detail, so a mix of Level 2 and Level 1 criteria.

An examiner would therefore make a decision about the 'best fit' level (e.g. Level 2), but the actual mark would be drawn in the direction of the lower level (like a magnet), with the result that the examiner would award the lower of the two Level 2 marks (i.e. 3 rather than 2 marks).

Level	Marks	Knowledge	Organisation	Specialist terminology
3	5-6	Generally accurate and well-detailed	Clear and coherent	Used effectively
2	3-4	Evident with some inaccuracies	Mostly clear and organised	Some appropriate use
1	1-2	Limited and lacks detail	Lacks clarity and organisation	Absent or used inappropriately
0	0	No relevant content		

Description questions (AO1: 6 mark questions)

A02

Step 1

First, a candidate must show appropriate psychological content, i.e. they must recognise and describe the appropriate underlying psychology. Second, they must engage with the scenario outline in the stem, i.e. they must apply their psychological knowledge.

So, the first thing an examiner will be looking for is the **knowledge** shown in response to the stem. Is it **clear** and appropriate, **accurate** and **detailed**?

Training task 2

When schizophrenia patients were given drugs that lowered their dopamine levels, they showed improvement in some symptoms (e.g. hallucinations) but a worsening in others (e.g. cognitive impairment). When the same patients took psychostimulants, which raised dopamine levels, the opposite pattern emerged, with increased hallucinations but reduced cognitive impairment.

Explain how this evidence supports the dopamine hypothesis of schizophrenia. (4 marks)

Answer 1

The dopamine hypothesis claims that schizophrenia is due to an excess of the neurotransmitter dopamine in the brain. Neurons fire too often or too easily. This excess of dopamine activity in the nervous system leads to the positive symptoms of schizophrenia such as hallucinations and delusions. The revised dopamine hypothesis states that low levels of dopamine in areas of the brain such as the prefrontal cortex lead to cognitive impairments such as memory deficits.

Answer 2

Positive symptoms of schizophrenia (such as hallucinations) are caused by an excess of dopamine in mesolimbic pathways in the brain. Drugs that lowered dopamine levels in this study would have blocked dopamine transmission in these areas and so reduced these positive symptoms. Negative symptoms, such as cognitive impairment, are caused by a depletion of dopamine in the mesocortical pathways. Drugs that lowered dopamine levels would have mimicked this depletion and caused cognitive impairments. Reversing this by the use of psychostimulants would have increased positive symptoms and cognitive impairments, which is what was found in this study.

Step 2

The examiner will then look at the **application** of the material. Has it been linked effectively to the stem (i.e. has it been used to address the specific context of the question?)

An examiner will also assess whether the application of the knowledge is **appropriate** (does the knowledge actually explain the context given in the stem material?) and whether the integration of the knowledge is done **effectively** (i.e. is it clear and convincing?)

The verdict

Answer 1 is a Level 1 response. Although the knowledge is clear, accurate and detailed, it is not linked explicitly to the stem material. The 'magnet effect' would pull the answer toward Level 2, but the lack of appropriate and effective application of the knowledge would keep it in Level 1 with 2 marks.

Answer 2 is a Level 2 response.
The knowledge is also clear, accurate and detailed but this time there is an appropriate application of this knowledge to the question. So, a glance at the other criteria would tell us it is clear, coherent and makes good use of terminology. We wouldn't expect more for a 4-mark answer, so this would get all 4 marks.

Application questions (AO2: 4 mark questions)					
Level	Marks	Knowledge	Application	Organisation	Specialist terminology
2	3-4	Clear, detailed and mostly accurate	Appropriate and effective	Generally coherent	Effective use of terminology
1	1-2	Lacking accuracy and detail	Not always effective	Lacks clarity	Either absent or inappropriate
0	0	No relevant content			

Examiners are canny folk. You can't fool them by a couple of brief throwaway references to the stem material. They'll be looking closely to see if you have *really* engaged with it before they award you a mark in the higher-level band.

Training yourself to be an examiner

Step 1

Evaluation questions can come in many different forms and with many different tariffs (e.g. 2, 3, 4 or 6 marks), therefore an examiner will adjust what he or she expects in an answer. The question below asks for two evaluative points and effectively offers three marks for each. Therefore, he or she will expect a reasonable amount of clear **detail** and for the point to be made **effectively**.

Training task 3

Explain two strengths and/or limitations of the dopamine hypothesis as an explanation of schizophrenia. (6 marks)

Answer 1

Leucht et al. (2013) carried out a meta-analysis of 212 studies that had compared the effectiveness of different antipsychotic drugs (that block dopamine transmission in the brain) against a control group that received a placebo instead of the antipsychotic drugs. They found that the antipsychotic drugs were more effective than the placebo in relieving the positive symptoms of schizophrenia.

Antipsychotic drugs do not alleviate hallucinations and delusions in all schizophrenia patients. Noll (2009) found this is the case in about one-third of the people who have these symptoms. Noll also found that some people who experience hallucinations and delusions actually have normal levels of dopamine.

Answer 2

The dopamine hypothesis is supported by research evidence, e.g. Leucht et al. (2013) carried out a meta-analysis of 212 studies that compared the effectiveness of antipsychotic drugs against a placebo. They found that the antipsychotic drugs were more effective than the placebo in relieving the positive symptoms of schizophrenia. Because antipsychotic drugs block dopamine transmission this supports the claim that excess dopamine activity is a causal factor in schizophrenia.

Noll (2009) provides evidence that challenges the dopamine hypothesis explanation of schizophrenia. He found that antipsychotic drugs do not alleviate hallucinations and delusions in about one-third of the people who have these symptoms. Noll also found that some people who experience hallucinations and delusions actually have normal levels of dopamine. This suggests that dopamine cannot be the sole neurotransmitter involved in schizophrenia.

Evaluation questions (AO3: 6 mark questions)

Level	Marks	Evaluation	Organisation	Specialist terminology
3	5-6	Clear and effective	Coherent and well-organised	Used effectively
2	3-4	Mostly effective	Mostly clear and organised	Used appropriately
1	1-2	Lacks detail and/or explanation	Poorly organised	Absent or used inappropriately
0	0	No relevant content		

Step 2

Next, the examiner will look at how well the point is **organised** (does it make sense and is it a **coherent** as a strength or limitation of the topic it refers to?) Does the candidate make it clear why this is a strength or limitation?

Finally the examiner will address the question of **specialist terminology**. They are looking for evidence that a candidate is familiar with the terms that are commonly used within a particular topic, e.g. antipsychotic drugs rather than just 'drugs' and placebo rather than 'something else'.

The verdict

Answer 1 is a Level 2 response worth 3 marks. Working from the bottom level, it clearly doesn't lack detail, but the lack of explanation as to why these are strengths and/or limitations is largely absent. It is clear and organised with good use of specialist terminology (which just pushes it into Level 2) but the lack of 'effectiveness' keeps it at the bottom end of that level.

Answer 2 is a Level 3 response worth 6 marks. It is a crafted version of Answer 1, but this time with a lead-in phrase that explains the nature of the strength and/or limitation, and a conclusion that explains the significance of the critical point (i.e. making it effective).

Now we've covered the basics of marking, we're going to ramp it up a bit and stick all the constituent parts together in an essay, and even better, you get to mark it!

The question on the next page contains all three components, AO1, AO2 and AO3. In essay questions with this 'additional' AO2 component, AQA nominally assign 6 marks for AO1, 4 for AO2 and 6 for AO3. Although we would not expect the division of content to exactly reflect these weightings, there should be a proportional division that is roughly along these lines.

Using the mark allocation table at the bottom of the next page, try to work out the correct mark for this essay. We've had a go at this as well, and you can find our suggested mark on page 373.

Over to you!

Ben and his friends had gone to a music festival for the weekend. While at the festival, he was persuaded by his friends to take cocaine, a drug of abuse that elevates dopamine levels in the brain. Ben reacted badly to the drug. He started hearing voices in his head and was convinced that somebody or something that he was unable to see was following him. His reaction to the drug worried his parents because Ben's elder brother was a diagnosed schizophrenic.

With reference to Ben's psychotic reaction to the drug, discuss biological explanations of schizophrenia. (6 marks)

Answer 1

Genetic explanations claim that schizophrenia is inherited through a person's genes. For example, family studies have shown that schizophrenia is more common among biological relatives of someone with schizophrenia than among people who do not share genes with someone with the disorder. This is why Ben's parents are so concerned because his brother has schizophrenia. Also, adoption studies, e.g. Tienari et al. (2000) have shown that adopted children are more likely to become schizophrenic if their biological parents have schizophrenia than if their adoptive parents have the disorder.

The dopamine hypothesis of schizophrenia claims that the disorder is a consequence of having too much dopamine in certain areas of brain. This excess of dopamine leads to the positive symptoms of schizophrenia, such as the hallucinations and delusions typical of the disorder. Ben has an excess of dopamine in his brain because he has taken cocaine. The revised dopamine hypothesis extends the idea that dopamine is important in schizophrenia by claiming that the cognitive impairments found in schizophrenia are caused by a deficit of dopamine in pathways in the frontal lobes of the brain.

Schizophrenia has also been shown to have neural correlates, in that certain parts of the brain, such as the prefrontal cortex, have been found to correlate with schizophrenic behaviour. There is also evidence (Cannon et al., 2014) that schizophrenia is linked to a reduction in grey matter in the brain. Other research has shown that schizophrenics also have a reduction in white matter in pathways between the prefrontal cortex and the hippocampus. It is possible that both Ben and his brother have these deficits, making them more vulnerable to psychoses such as schizophrenia.

A problem for twin studies is that twins, particularly identical twins, are usually treated more similarly than children that are not twins, so it is possible that the greater likelihood of an identical twin becoming schizophrenic if the other twin is schizophrenic is more to do with this rather than any shared genes.

There are also problems for the dopamine hypothesis explanation because antipsychotics, which block dopamine transmission at dopamine receptors do not work with all schizophrenics. Noll (2009) found that about one-third of patients with schizophrenia experienced no reduction in their symptoms when taking antipsychotic medication.

Vita et al. (2012) carried out a meta-analysis of 19 studies, involving over 800 patients with schizophrenia and over 700 healthy controls. They found that the schizophrenic patients had a greater loss of grey matter than did the healthy control group.

Marking notes

Knowledge is (tick one):

Level 4   Level 1

Level 3   Level 0

Level 2

Evaluation is (tick one):

Level 4   Level 1

Level 3   Level 0

Level 2

Application is (tick one):

Level 4   Level 1

Level 3   Level 0

Level 2

Organisation is (tick one):

Level 4   Level 1

Level 3   Level 0

Level 2

Use of specialist terminology (tick one):

Level 4   Level 1

Level 3   Level 0

Level 2

Final level of Answer 1 (Circle one)

4   3   2   1   0

Final mark awarded for Answer 1

Essay questions (16 mark questions)

Level	Marks	Knowledge	Evaluation	Specialist terminology	Specialist terminology	Specialist terminology
4	13-16	Accurate and generally well-detailed	Thorough and effective	Used effectively	Used effectively	Used effectively
3	9-12	Evident with some occasional inaccuracies	Apparent and mostly effective	Appropriate. Links to knowledge not always explained	Mostly clear and organised	Mostly used effectively
2	5-8	Some knowledge is present. Lacks accuracy in places	Partly effective but mostly descriptive	Application is partial.	Lacks clarity and organisation in places	Used inappropriately on occasions
1	1-4	Limited with many inaccuracies	Limited, poorly focused or absent	Application is limited or absent	Lacks clarity and poorly organised	Either absent or used inappropriately
0	0	No relevant content				

Content checklists

Chapter 1 Research methods

I am able to...	Describe	Apply	Evaluate
Content analysis and coding			
Case studies			
Reliability and validity			
Features of science			
Probability and significance			
Statistical tests and levels of measurement			
Parametric and non-parametric tests of difference			
Tests of correlation and the Chi-Squared test			
Reporting investigations			

Chapter 2 Issues and debates

Gender bias			
Cultural bias			
Free will and determinism			
Nature–nurture debate			
Holism and reductionism			
Idiographic and nomothetic approaches to psychological investigation			
Ethical implications of research studies			

Chapter 3 Relationships

Evolutionary explanations including sexual selection and reproductive behaviour			
Physical attractiveness including the matching hypothesis			
Self-disclosure			
Filter theory			
Theories of romantic relationships			
Virtual relationships in social media			
Levels of parasocial relationship			

Chapter 4 Gender

Sex-role stereotypes. Androgyny and its measurement; Bem sex role inventory			
Role of chromosomes and hormones; Atypical chromosome patterns			
Cognitive explanations: Kohlberg's theory; gender schema theory			
Psychodynamic explanations: Freud's psychoanalytic theory			
Social learning theory and gender development			
Influence of culture and media on gender roles			
Atypical gender development			

Chapter 5 Cognition and development

Piaget's theory			
Vygotsky's theory: zone of proximal development and scaffolding			
Baillargeon's explanation of early infant abilities			
Selman's level of perspective taking			
Theory of mind and autism: Sally-Anne study			
Mirror neuron system in social cognition			

Chapter 6 Biopsychology	Describe	Apply	Evaluate
I am able to...			
Classification of schizophrenia: positive and negative symptoms			
Reliability and validity in diagnosis			
Biological and psychological explanations			
Drug, cognitive behavioural and family therapy			
Token economies in the management of schizophrenia			
An interactionist approach: the diathesis-stress model			
Chapter 7 Eating behaviour			
Evolutionary explanation for food preferences: neophobia and taste aversion			
Role of learning in food preference: social and cultural influences			
Neural and hormonal mechanisms: hypothalamus, ghrelin, leptin			
Biological explanations for anorexia nervosa: genetic and neural explanations			
Family systems theory and social learning theory			
Cognitive theory and anorexia nervosa: distortions and irrational beliefs			
Biological and psychological explanations for obesity			
Explanations for success and failure of dieting			
Chapter 8 Stress			
The physiology of stress			
Stress and illness			
Sources of stress: life changes, daily hassles and workplace stress			
Measuring stress: self-report scales and physiological measures			
Individual differences in stress			
Managing and coping with stress, including gender differences			
The role of social support in coping with stress			
Chapter 9 Aggression			
Neural and hormonal mechanisms: limbic system, serotonin, testosterone			
Genetic factors in aggression including the MAOA gene			
Ethological explanations of aggression			
Evolutionary explanations of human aggression			
Social psychological explanations			
Institutional aggression in prisons: dispositional and situational explanations			
Media influences on aggression, including the effects of computer games			
Chapter 10 Forensic psychology			
Ways of measuring crime: official statistics, victim surveys and offender surveys			
Offender profiling: top-down and bottom-up approaches			
Biological explanations of offending			
Psychological explanations of offending			
Dealing with offending behaviour			
Chapter 11 Addiction			
Describing addiction			
Risk factors in development of addiction			
Explanations for nicotine addiction			
Explanations for gambling addiction			
Reducing addiction			
Theory of planned behaviour applied to addictive behaviour			
Prochaska's six-stage model of behaviour change			

Answers are given, along with examiner comments, on pages 326 to 333.

Section A Social influence

1 Which **one** of the following did Zimbardo set up to investigate conformity? *(1 mark)*

A   a mock classroom   C   a mock prison

B   a mock courtroom   D   a mock surgery

2 Which **one** of the following did Milgram use to measure obedience in his investigations? *(1 mark)*

A   how much anxiety the participant showed

B   if the participant questioned the experimenter

C   the level of electric shocks a participant would administer to another person

D   whether a participant would respond to prods or not

3 Briefly evaluate Milgram's investigations into obedience. *(4 marks)*

4 Outline the effect of **one** situational variable on obedience. *(3 marks)*

5 Describe **one** criticism of the dispositional explanation for obedience. *(3 marks)*

6 Gina is one of team of managers. She does not agree with a policy that her company is about to introduce but at their leadership meeting she ends up voting for it.

Oliver is a new employee at this company. When he reads about the policy, he does not like it at first. However, most of his colleagues think it is an acceptable policy. After talking it through with them, Oliver begins to change his mind about it.

(a) Identify and explain the type of conformity shown by Gina. *(2 marks)*

(b) Identify and explain the type of conformity shown by Oliver. *(2 marks)*

7 A psychologist wanted to investigate whether people in their 20s conformed more than people in their 40s. She did this by using a questionnaire where participants from each age group had to respond to a number of scenarios by choosing what they would do in each situation. The questionnaire gave each respondent a score where the higher the score, the more conformist the respondent was.

(a) Name an appropriate statistical test the psychologist could use to analyse her data. Justify your choice of test. *(3 marks)*

(b) Table 1: Table of critical values

One-tailed test	0.005	0.01	0.025	0.05
Two-tailed test	0.01	0.02	0.05	0.10
$n_1 = 20$, $n_2 = 20$	105	114	127	138

Using the extract from **Table 1** (a table of critical values), identify the critical value the psychologist should select to analyse her data. Justify your choice. *(3 marks)*

8 Outline **one** explanation of resistance to social influence. *(4 marks)*

Section B Memory

9 Using your knowledge of the multi-store model:

(a) Name the store where coding is only modality specific. *(1 mark)*

(b) Name the store where capacity is unlimited. *(1 mark)*

10 A psychologist conducted a correlation to investigate the relationship between the amount of time spent on rehearsing information and how much of that information was recalled.

The data from his investigation is given in **Table 2**.

Table 2: Data showing the amount of time spent rehearsing information (minutes) and amount of information recalled (score on a memory test).

Participant	Time spent rehearsing information (mins)	Recall on memory test (%)
1	5	12
2	10	13
3	15	9
4	20	27
5	25	40
6	30	51
7	35	72
8	40	63
9	45	63
10	50	78

(a) Using the data in **Table 2**, sketch a scattergram to represent the results of the investigation. *(4 marks)*

(b) What conclusion could the psychologist draw about the relationship between rehearsal and recall? Refer to the scattergram as part of your answer. *(2 marks)*

11 Lily spent a number of weeks revising for a French mock exam. As the exam approached, she also found out that she had a mock exam for Spanish which would come first. She then began to revise intensely for this exam, although there was not much time left. She stayed in the college library for a number of evenings to revise her Spanish. When she was in the exam hall doing the Spanish exam, she found she forgot most of what she had revised – instead recalling a lot of material from French.

Discuss **at least two** explanations of forgetting. Refer to Lily's experiences of forgetting in your answer. *(16 marks)*

Section C Attachment

12 A psychologist conducted a natural experiment using a volunteer sample. He compared a group of adults who had or had not experienced separation from their main carer in the first five years of their lives. He then interviewed them to investigate whether they showed signs of poor mental health or not.

(a) Explain why the study is an example of a natural experiment. *(2 marks)*

(b) Outline **one** extraneous variable that may occur in this study. *(2 marks)*

(c) Describe **one** limitation of using a volunteer sample in this study. *(2 marks)*

13 (a) Describe the procedure and findings of **one** animal study in attachment. *(6 marks)*

(b) Outline **one** limitation of using animals studies to investigate attachment. *(2 marks)*

14 Explain how insecure-avoidant attachments are different from insecure-resistant attachments. *(3 marks)*

15 Evaluate the use of Ainsworth's 'Strange Situation' as a way of investigating attachment types. *(3 marks)*

16 Outline **two** criticisms of Bowlby's monotropic theory of attachment. *(4 marks)*

Section D Psychopathology

17 Complete the table below to show whether each of the symptoms of depression are either a behavioural, emotional or cognitive characteristic. The first one has been done as an example. *(3 marks)*

Symptom of depression	Characteristic
Sleep disruption	Behavioural
Pessimistic view of the world	
Feeling worthless	
Loss of appetite	

18 Briefly describe **one** biological explanation of OCD. *(3 marks)*

19 Give **one** strength and **one** limitation of using drugs to treat OCD. *(2 marks)*

20 Keshina has a phobia of cats which she relates back to an incident when she was a young child. She had been playing with a neighbour's cat when it suddenly attacked her by scratching her legs. It was so unexpected, that Keshina was crying for a long time afterwards and it was difficult for her parents to calm her down. Now, whenever she sees a cat, she experiences high levels of anxiety and will even cross the road to avoid one.

Discuss the behavioural approach to explaining phobias. Refer to the case of Keshina in your answer. *(16 marks)*

Answers are given, along with examiner comments, on pages 334 to 341.

Section A Approaches in psychology

1 According to the psychodynamic approach:

(a) Which **one** of the following represents our moral code? *(1 mark)*

A ego

B id

C superego

D unconscious

(b) Which **one** of the following gives the stage at which our moral code develops? *(1 mark)*

A anal stage

B genital stage

C oral stage

D phallic stage

(c) Name and outline **one** defence mechanism. *(2 marks)*

2 Olivia is a five-year-old girl who is obsessed with a cartoon character called Princess Sapphire. Olivia aspires to be like her idol and she engages in lots of role play where she quotes lines from the programmes she has seen. Princess Sapphire is popular with many young children because her dreams come true when she is kind to others. Olivia's parents are pleased that Princess Sapphire is a good role model but they are worried that their daughter is behaving like her as she expects her dreams to come true as well.

With reference to social learning theory:

(a) Explain how this item demonstrates identification. *(2 marks)*

(b) Explain how this item demonstrates vicarious reinforcement. *(2 marks)*

3 Outline and discuss the basic assumptions of humanistic psychology. Refer to the biological approach as part of your discussion. *(16 marks)*

Section B Biopsychology

4 Explain the difference between 'excitation' and 'inhibition' in relation to the process of synaptic transmission. *(3 marks)*

5 Huw was walking down a quiet lane when two of his friends jumped out on him as a joke. Huw was so shocked that he did not realise who they were until they started to laugh at him for jumping and for the fact that he was breathing heavily. Huw pointed out that they were lucky to not get hurt as his instant response was to try to hit them.

Outline what is meant by the 'fight-or-flight' response. Refer to the item above as part of your answer. *(4 marks)*

6 Look at the graph in **Figure 1** and answer the questions that follow.

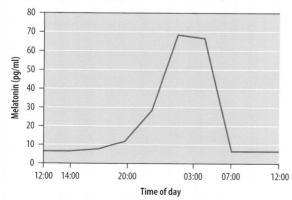

Fluctuation in melatonin levels over a 24-hour period

(a) Estimate the time of day at which melatonin levels peak. *(1 mark)*

(b) Give the period of time, to the nearest hour, when melatonin levels stay most constant. Show your working. *(2 marks)*

(c) If 1 picogram (pg) of melatonin = 10^{-12} grammes (g) of melatonin, decide whether the following statement is true or false:

$$1 \text{ pg} > 1 \text{ g}$$

Write 'True' or 'False'. *(1 mark)*

7 Evaluate **one** scanning technique used to study the brain. *(5 marks)*

8 Describe and briefly evaluate **one** piece of split brain research. *(8 marks)*

Section C Research methods

Read the item and then answer the questions that follow.

A psychologist wanted to investigate the effect of different approaches to campaigning. She compared one campaign that was based more on emotion with one that was based more on information. Fifty participants were randomly allocated to equal groups, and were exposed to one or other of the campaigns. This was done by asking both groups to read an article and watch a video recording about a charity set up for orphaned children. The psychologist measured the effect of the materials by asking each participant whether they would donate a sum of money to the charity with the options being just 'yes' or 'no'.

The results from the study are shown in **Table 1** .

Table 1: A table to show the number of people who said they would or would not donate money to a charity following either an emotion-based campaign or an information-based campaign.

	Emotion-based campaign	Information-based campaign
Money donated to charity	13	9
Money not donated to charity	12	16

9 Write a suitable hypothesis for this study. *(3 marks)*

10 Explain how the participants could have been randomly allocated to the two groups in this study. *(3 marks)*

11 Outline **one** strength and **one** limitation of using an independent groups design in this study. *(4 marks)*

12 Apart from features of the participants, outline **one** other extraneous variable that may have affected the results of this study if not controlled. *(2 marks)*

13 (a) Sketch an appropriate graph to show the data presented in Table 1. *(3 marks)*

(b) Give the percentage of all participants who said they would donate money to the charity. Show your calculations. *(3 marks)*

14 Identify the level of data used in this study. Justify your answer. *(2 marks)*

15 Table 2 shows the expected values if there was no significant difference between conditions in terms of whether people would donate to charity or not.

Table 3 shows the observed values which are the actual data from the study.

Table 2: Expected values

Cell A	Cell B
11	11
Cell C	Cell D
14	14

Table 3: Observed values

Cell A	Cell B
13	9
Cell C	Cell D
12	16

The critical value for inferential testing is given by the sum of $(O - E)^2 / E$ for each of the four cells where O = the observed value in a cell, and E = expected value in the corresponding cell.

For example, for Cell A, this would be $(13 - 11)^2 \div 11 = 0.36$

Apply this formula to Cell C, calculating the answer to 2 decimal places. Show your calculations. *(4 marks)*

16 The psychologist planned to analyse her data using $p \leq 0.1$. Explain what type of error this is likely to lead to. *(2 marks)*

17 The psychologist produced a report on her study.
  (a) Name the section of the report where she would describe her participants. *(1 mark)*
  (b) Name the section of the report where she would present her table of data. *(1 mark)*

18 The psychologist submitted her report for peer review.
  (a) State what is meant by 'peer review'. *(1 marks)*
  (b) Briefly explain the role of peer review in this study. *(3 marks)*

19 The psychologist wanted to design a study that was easy to replicate. Explain the importance of replicability in scientific investigations. *(4 marks)*

20 The psychologist used two types of media campaigns – both a written article and a video recording.

Design an experiment to investigate whether the type of medium affects people's willingness to donate to a charity. The independent variable is whether a written article or a video recording is used for a campaign, and the dependent variable is how much money (in pounds) is actually donated to the charity afterwards.

In your answer, you should provide details of:
- your sampling technique
- at least **one** control you would use
- the inferential test you would use to analyse the data
- ethical issues to be considered. *(12 marks)*

Answers to Section A are given, along with examiner comments, on pages 342 to 343.

Section A Issues and debates

1 Which **one** of the following terms describes the situation where the differences between women and men are exaggerated? *(1 mark)*

  A alpha bias
  B androcentrism
  C beta bias
  D ethnocentrism

2 Two psychologists were discussing the origins of behaviour.

Dr Mudima: I believe that you can understand almost all behaviours by going back to conception and understanding so much is programmed into an individual's DNA. For example, I am convinced we will discover a gene for autism.

Dr Young: I disagree. Yes, look for root causes for behaviour but I believe that these are a result of a series of responses to a series of stimuli. There must be triggers that autistic children have learned to respond to.

  (a) Identify and explain the type of reductionism supported by Dr Mudima. Refer to her statement as part of your answer. *(3 marks)*

  (b) Identify and explain the type of determinism supported by Dr Young. Refer to his statement as part of your answer. *(3 marks)*

3 A psychologist investigated the relative effect of heredity and environment on intelligence by carrying out a twin study. He tested seventeen pairs of genetically identical twins and found that 12/17 had IQ scores that were closely matched (differed by 5 or fewer points). He also tested thirty-four pairs of non-identical twins and found that 22/34 had IQ scores that closely matched.

  (a) Which set of twins had the highest proportion of pairs with scores that closely matched.

  Tick **one** box to show your answer. *(1 mark)*

  Identical twins ☐   Non-identical twins ☐

  (b) The psychologist concluded that an interaction of heredity and environment affected intelligence.

  Explain what this conclusion means. *(2 marks)*

4 As part of a questionnaire study, a psychologist asked participants to rate how much free will they had in everyday life. A rating of 1 represented no free will and a rating of 10 represented complete free will.

The responses to this question are shown in **Figure 1**.

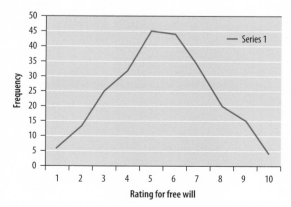

Figure 1: A line graph to show participants ratings for how much free will they believe they have in everyday life.

  (a) The psychologist concluded that the data from this question was normally distributed.

In relation to this study, explain what a normal distribution is. *(2 marks)*

  (b) Evaluate the use of a questionnaire to investigate free will. *(4 marks)*

5 Discuss the strengths of taking a nomothetic approach in psychological investigations. *(8 marks)*

Section B Topic: Relationships

6 Outline what is meant by a parasocial relationship. *(2 marks)*

7 Discuss **one** piece of research into **one** factor affecting romantic relationships. *(8 marks)*

8 A psychologist used a questionnaire to investigate the effect of age on virtual relationships.

His hypothesis was: "People aged 16-24 will attach a significantly higher value to virtual relationships compared to people aged 25–35."

  (a) Identify the independent variable in this study. *(1 mark)*

  (b) Explain whether the hypothesis is directional or non-directional. *(2 marks)*

  (c) Write **one** closed question that could be used to assess the value of virtual relationships. *(1 mark)*

9 Outline **one** limitation of the evolutionary explanation of partner preference. *(2 marks)*

10 Discuss **one** theory of romantic relationships. *(8 marks)*

Topic: Gender

6 Outline what is meant by androgyny in relation to gender. *(2 marks)*

7 Discuss **one** piece of research into **one** cognitive explanation of gender development. *(8 marks)*

8 A psychologist used a questionnaire to investigate the effect of media on gender roles.

His hypothesis was: "There will be a difference in people's perception of gender roles depending on whether they are regularly exposed or rarely exposed to TV advertisements."

  (a) Identify the independent variable in this study. *(1 mark)*

  (b) Explain whether the hypothesis is directional or non-directional. *(2 marks)*

  (c) Write **one** closed question that could be used to assess people's perception of gender roles. *(1 mark)*

9 Outline **one** limitation of the psychodynamic explanation of gender development. *(2 marks)*

10 Discuss **one** explanation of gender identity disorder. *(8 marks)*

Topic: Cognition and development

6 Outline what is meant by a mirror neuron. *(2 marks)*

7 Discuss **one** piece of research into the theory of mind. *(8 marks)*

8 A psychologist used a questionnaire to investigate the effect of age on perspective-taking.

His hypothesis was: "There will be a significant difference in the level of perspective-taking between primary school children and secondary school children."

  (a) Identify the independent variable in this study. *(1 mark)*

  (b) Explain whether the hypothesis is directional or non-directional. *(2 marks)*

  (c) Write **one** closed question that could be used to assess perspective-taking. *(1 mark)*

9 Outline **one** limitation of Balliargeon's explanation of early infant abilities. *(2 marks)*

10 Discuss **one** explanation of cognitive development. *(8 marks)*

Section C Topic: Schizophrenia

11 Discuss biological explanations of schizophrenia. Refer to psychological explanations as part of your discussion. *(16 marks)*

12 A psychologist used a questionnaire to rate levels of avolition, out of 20, in people with schizophrenia and people with depression. The higher the rating, the higher the level of avolition.

The findings from the study are shown in the table below;

	People with Schizophrenia	People with Depression
Median rating for avolition	14	14.5
Range	9	4

What conclusions would you draw from the study? Refer to **both** the medians **and** the ranges in your answer. *(4 marks)*

13 (a) Briefly outline how drug therapy is used to treat to schizophrenia. *(2 marks)*

(b) Outline **one** strength of drug therapy as a treatment. *(2 marks)*

Topic: Eating behaviour

11 Discuss biological explanations of obesity. Refer to psychological explanations as part of your discussion. *(16 marks)*

12 A psychologist used a questionnaire to rate levels of perceived autonomy, out of 30, in people with and without anorexia nervosa. The higher the rating, the higher the level of perceived autonomy.

The findings from the study are shown in the table below;

	People with Anorexia Nervosa	People without Anorexia Nervosa
Median rating for perceived autonomy	16	18
Range	5	15

What conclusions would you draw from the study? Refer to **both** the medians **and** the ranges in your answer. *(4 marks)*

13 (a) Briefly outline how learning has a role in food preferences. *(2 marks)*

(b) Outline **one** strength of using learning theories to explain food preferences. *(2 marks)*

Topic: Stress

11 Discuss self-report scales as measures of stress. Refer to physiological measures as part of your discussion. *(16 marks)*

12 A psychologist used a questionnaire to rate levels of hardiness, out of 50, in people who reported high levels of stress and people who reported low levels of stress. The higher the rating, the higher the level of hardiness.

The findings from the study are shown in the table below;

	People reporting high levels of stress	People reporting low levels of stress
Median rating for hardiness	23	26
Range	32	15

What conclusions would you draw from the study? Refer to **both** the medians **and** the ranges in your answer. *(4 marks)*

13 (a) Briefly outline how stress inoculation therapy is used to manage stress. *(2 marks)*

(b) Outline **one** strength of stress inoculation therapy. *(2 marks)*

Section D Topic: Aggression

14 Outline what is meant by 'disinhibition' in relation to aggression. *(2 marks)*

15 Explain **two** criticisms of the ethological explanation of aggression. *(6 marks)*

16 Grant knows that he can be unnecessarily aggressive but blames this on his upbringing. He believes that he got to sees his father and older brothers fighting too much, and also that they let him watch too many violent films. If anything, they encouraged him to be aggressive by cheering him on when he was.

Discuss social learning as it applies to human aggression. Refer to the case of Grant as part of your answer. *(16 marks)*

Topic: Forensic psychology

14 Outline what is meant by 'minimalisation' in relation to offending behaviour. *(2 marks)*

15 Explain **two** criticisms of biological explanations of offending behaviour. *(6 marks)*

16 Alissa has already been convicted once for robbery but still thinks she will commit similar crimes again. She has an uncontrollable urge to take anything she needs regardless of the fact that it is going to harm her victims. She admits that she has few moral standards. Alissa blames this on her childhood, and especially the fact that her parents were hardly ever around to look after her.

Discuss psychodynamic explanations of offending behaviour. Refer to the case of Alissa as part of your answer. *(16 marks)*

Topic: Addiction

14 Outline what is meant by 'tolerance' in relation to addiction. *(2 marks)*

15 Explain **two** criticisms of brain neurochemistry as an explanation of nicotine addiction. *(6 marks)*

16 Antonio knows he has a gambling addiction. He regrets his first visit to a casino where he won a significant amount of money playing a card game. He goes to the casino most nights and just when he decides it's his last time, he seems to win a sum of money. This means he cannot resist going back again to try to win even more.

Discuss learning theory as it applies to gambling. Refer to the case of Antonio as part of your answer. *(16 marks)*

KEY TERMS

- Coding
- Content analysis
- Thematic analysis

Possible exam questions ...

+ Explain what is meant by 'content analysis'. *(2 marks)*
+ Explain how observer bias might affect the findings of a content analysis. *(3 marks)*
+ Give **one** strength and **one** limitation of content analysis. *(2 + 2 marks)*
+ A researcher has collected diaries from 100 teenagers. How would the researcher carry out content analysis on this material? *(4 marks)*

 Exam tip

Research Methods questions consist of a stem, with a series of short-answer questions. You will need to apply your knowledge and make sure you link each point in your answer to the relevant parts of the study.

MUST know ...

Content analysis

Content analysis is an indirect form of observational study, analysing materials produced by people (e.g. books, films, photographs). The procedure involves:

1 Deciding on a sample (e.g. TV ads over a one-week period).
2 Coding the data using behavioural categories (e.g. men or women using household products).
3 Recording the occurrences of each coding category.

Thematic analysis

This type of qualitative content analysis summarises the data descriptively. It aims to identify underlying themes in the data, rather than spot obvious words or phrases.

 One strength of content analysis is...

...that it is based on observations of materials produced by people in their real lives.
- **E** – This includes newspapers, books, paintings, photos, films, and videos.

 Another strength of content analysis is...

...that it can be replicated.
- **E** – materials are often publically available and can be accessed by another researcher.

 A limitation of content analysis is...

...that it is affected by observer bias.
- **E** – Different observers may interpret the meaning of behavioural categories differently.

SHOULD know ...

Content analysis

In a **quantitative** analysis, the instances of each coding category are tallied, and can then be represented using descriptive statistics and graphs.

In a **qualitative** analysis, examples in each category are described.

Thematic analysis

This aims to allow themes to emerge from the data and maintain the participants' perspectives. The steps include:

1 Read and re-read the data transcripts (or watch and re-watch a video).
2 Break down the data into meaningful units.
3 Assign a label or code to each unit.
4 Combine codes into larger themes.
5 Ensure that these emerging themes represent all of the data.

- **E** – These communications can be current and relevant to a specific research question.
- **L** – This gives findings high ecological validity.

- **E** – This means that the observations can be tested for inter-observer reliability.
- **L** – If several researchers identify similar themes or occurrences of coding categories, the findings are reliable.

- **E** – The language and culture of the observer will affect their interpretation of categories and themes.
- **L** – Therefore content analysis is likely to be culture biased.

 **FURTHER EVALUATION**

 P – A criticism of thematic analysis is...

...that it is a very time-consuming and painstaking process.
- **E** – This is because it involves examining and re-examining huge amounts of data, with themes emerging iteratively.
- **E** – This enables the data to be summarised and conclusions to be drawn.
- **L** – But it is not always suitable when researchers have limited time available.

 P – A criticism of content analysis is...

...that it summarises rich qualitative data in a simplified form.
- **E** – This means that the data loses its detailed descriptive flavour.
- **E** – The observer cannot be truly objective, and may impose meaning on people's behaviour because of preconceptions.
- **L** – Therefore the coding categories may lack validity, as they do not fully represent people's understanding of their own behaviour or creative output.

CHOOSE THE RIGHT ANSWER

One piece of research carried out in the UK used content analysis to study some children's drawings, and found that children draw more complex pictures of Santa before Christmas than afterwards.

In this study, what is the complexity of the picture of Santa? (Tick **one** box only.)

A	The independent variable	☐
B	The dependent variable	☐
C	The coding category	☐
D	The sample	☐

Answers on page 344

MATCH THEM UP

Match up the terms with the explanations.

1	Coding	**A**	Indirect observation involving counting occurrences of particular behaviours
2	Sampling	**B**	How well different observers agree in their coding or tallying of the same data
3	Tallying	**C**	Indirect observation of behaviour which is summarised using examples
4	Quantitative content analysis	**D**	Counting up occurrences of each coding category
5	Qualitative content analysis	**E**	A type of content analysis which allows themes to emerge from the data
6	Thematic analysis	**F**	How well the findings represent people's real life experiences
7	Inter-observer reliability	**G**	Labelling data according to categories or themes
8	Ecological validity	**H**	Observers' coding of data may be affected by their language and preconceptions
9	Culture bias	**I**	Selecting the content which will be analysed

Answers on page 344

APPLYING YOUR KNOWLEDGE

A psychology student wants to investigate the potential gender stereotypes presented in Disney films.

(a) Suggest **three** items that could be used as coding categories in this study. *(3 marks)*

(b) Explain how the student could carry out this quantitative content analysis. *(4 marks)*

(c) Identify **one** issue of reliability in this research and describe how you could deal with it. *(3 marks)*

(d) Identify **one** issue of validity in this research and describe how you could deal with it. *(3 marks)*

(e) Explain how the procedure would differ in a qualitative content analysis. *(2 marks)*

Answers on page 344

A MARKING EXERCISE

Read the student answers to the following exam question:

A researcher analysed children's TV programmes over a period of a week to see what types of programmes were available. Explain how the researcher could have used content analysis to analyse the data he collected. What mark do you think each would get? *(4 marks)*

Robbie's answer

The researcher could create a coding system where he wrote the different kinds of programme and then mark these off. This would give the results he wants.

Anne's answer

The researcher could have predicted certain categories, e.g. comedy, cartoons, etc. based on their experience of watching children's TV, and then ticked these off on a behaviour checklist.

Pierre's answer

He could use content analysis to compare what different children watched and then decide what was the most common programme they watched. The categories are for each child.

Answers on page 344

Possible exam questions ...

+ Explain what is involved in a case study. Use examples in your answer. *(3 marks)*
+ Outline **one** strength and **one** limitation of using case studies to investigate behaviour. *(2 marks + 2 marks)*

 Exam tip

You will never be asked more than 6 marks' worth of description or 10 marks' worth of evaluation. Six marks' worth is about 150 words.

 Link

Thematic analysis is used in idiographic research, see p58.

MUST know ...

Case studies

These are a detailed study of a single individual, institution or event. A variety of research techniques can be used to gather data, such as observations, interviews, IQ or personality tests, or experiments to test the individual's cognitive abilities.

Individuals

Henry Molaison (HM) – his hippocampus was removed to reduce epileptic seizures, resulting in an inability to form new memories.

Clive Wearing – his memory was damaged by an infection.

Little Hans – Freud (1909) used him to illustrate the principles of psychoanalysis.

Phineas Gage – he survived an iron rod passing through his brain, but suffered changes to his personality.

 A strength of case studies is…

…that they provide rich, in-depth idiographic data.

- *E* – This can provide insight into the complex interaction of many factors.

 One problem with case studies is…

…they study unique individuals, who often have particular or unusual characteristics.

- *E* – For example, HM had suffered epilepsy for many years as well as the brain damage caused by the removal of his hippocampus.

 However, case studies can be used…

…to study very rare experiences which could not be generated experimentally, for practical or ethical reasons.

- *E* – For example, individuals who have suffered extreme deprivation in early childhood.

SHOULD know ...

Case studies

They provide a rich, detailed description of a person's life. Case studies can be longitudinal, following the individuals over time.

Findings are presented in a qualitative way, being organised into themes, but can also include quantitative data like scores from tests.

Events

The London riots 2011 were studied by Reicher and Stott, to re-examine explanations of 'mob' behaviour from a social psychological perspective.

Mass suicide of a cult group – Reverend Jim Jones was responsible for the deaths of 900 followers in the 1970s. This case study illustrates processes of conformity and obedience.

- *E* – This contrasts with experiments, which aim to hold variables constant.
- *L* – This means that insights overlooked by other methods are more likely to be identified in case study research.

- *E* – So we don't know how much these different factors interacted to affect his behaviour.
- *L* – This means that it is difficult to generalise from individual cases.

- *E* – The case study of David Reimer, a boy whose penis was accidentally removed and who was raised as a girl, is a fascinating example.
- *L* – In this way, it is possible to find out what happens to people who experience unusual or horrific events like accidents or extreme deprivation.

FURTHER EVALUATION

 Ethical issues

- *P* – Confidentiality and informed consent must be carefully considered in case studies.
- *E* – As many cases are unique, they may be easily recognisable, even when individuals are identified by initials or given false names.
- *E* – In addition, individuals such as HM may not have been able to give informed consent.
- *L* – So researchers should take care not to reveal personal details that enable the person to be located.

What about before?

- *P* – The interest in an individual often begins after an event, such as the brain damage to HM or Phineas Gage.
- *E* – We do not have detailed data from previously, so we cannot compare before and after.
- *E* – For example, we do not know how HM's epilepsy and previous drug treatments may have affected his brain prior to his surgery.
- *L* – This makes it difficult to draw valid conclusions.

CHOOSE THE RIGHT ANSWER

Which **one** of the following pieces of research is not a case study? (Tick **one** box only.)

A	Freud's description of Little Hans	☐
B	Research into the psychological effects of the collapse of the World Trade Towers in 2001	☐
C	The study of Little Albert by Watson and Rayner	☐
D	The memory experiments carried out on Henry Molaison by Susanne Corkin	☐

Answers on page 344

 RESEARCH ISSUES

Henry Molaison (HM) was unable to form new memories after his surgery. This meant that when the researcher came to see him, even though she had visited many times before, he did not recognise her. He could not remember giving consent, although he was always compliant and happy to be contributing to research.

How could researchers deal with the issue of informed consent in a case like HM? *(3 marks)*

Answers on page 344

An idea
Look through your Year One textbook and make a list of all the case studies you have encountered. 👍

 APPLYING YOUR KNOWLEDGE 1

Louise wishes to find out about the life of a 'typical' teenager in the UK, and asks for three volunteers at a youth club.

(a) What research methods could Louise use to find out about these teenagers' lives? Suggest how she could obtain quantitative and qualitative data for this case study. *(4 marks + 4 marks)*

Quantitative	Qualitative

(b) Louise feels these particular teenagers may not be typical, as they were highly motivated and keen to get involved. How could she carry out further research to explore whether her volunteers were representative of the population of UK teenagers? *(3 marks)*

Answers on page 344

 APPLYING YOUR KNOWLEDGE 2

David is interested in the European migrant crisis, and decides to research the 'Jungle' encampment in Calais. He wants to understand why people are hoping to come to the UK. He is considering whether to spend time with one family at the 'Jungle' and gather qualitative data for a case study, or whether to focus on a larger scale view of the issue by using statistical data gathered by aid organisations and the French police. He hopes to publish a report in the local newspaper.

Give **one** advantage and **one** disadvantage of each research method *(4 marks + 4 marks)*

Case study	Analysis of statistical data
Advantage	**Advantage**
Disadvantage	**Disadvantage**

Answers on page 344

Key Terms

- Inter-observer reliability (inter-rater reliability)
- Reliability
- Test-retest reliability

Possible exam questions ...

+ What is meant by 'reliability'? *(1 mark)*
+ How can researchers assess the reliability of their findings? *(3 marks)*
+ How can the reliability of these findings be improved? *(3 marks)*

 Exam tip

Make sure you are clear about the difference between 'reliability' and 'replicability', and learn the definitions by heart.

 Link

See page 26 for an explanation of replicability.

 Think

Think about reliability issues whenever you read about research. Do the researchers explain how they established the reliability of their measures? If not, is this a problem?

MUST know ...

Reliability is the consistency of measurements.

Reliability of observational techniques

Assessing validity
The researcher records behaviour using behavioural categories. Reliability can be **assessed** by comparing the data from two or more observers (**inter-observer reliability**).

Improving reliability
Reliability can be **improved** by making the behavioural categories clearer.

Reliability of self-report techniques

Assessing validity
These include questionnaires and interviews.

Test-retest reliability is used to **assess** reliability of self-report measures. IQ tests, personality tests and other psychological tests can also be assessed for reliability in this way. The test is repeated after a short interval, for example one week. Scores for each person are compared.

Improving reliability
Reliability can be **improved** by rewriting ambiguous questions.

Reliability of experiments

Assessing validity
The dependent variable in an experiment may be measured using a rating scale or behavioural categories. Reliability is the consistency of the way the DV is measured. In these experiments reliability is **assessed** using inter-observer or test-retest methods.

Improving reliability
Standardisation of procedures ensures that:

- Participants follow exactly the same procedure as each other.
- Other researchers can repeat the experiment.

This also **improves** reliability.

SHOULD know ...

Reliability of observational techniques

Assessing validity
Inter-rater reliability is **calculated** as a correlation coefficient between the two sets of scores from independent observers. 'Good' reliability is +.80 or more.

Improving reliability
To **improve** reliability, behavioural categories should be operationalised carefully so they are less subjective. Observers can improve by practising or being trained in choosing categories.

Reliability of self-report techniques

Assessing validity
Test-retest reliability is also **calculated** as a correlation coefficient, a measure of the consistency of scores for each individual.

Inter-interviewer reliability could also be calculated, in the same way as inter-observer reliability.

Improving reliability
If people can understand the same question in different ways, they may answer them differently the second time. So removing ambiguity **improves** reliability.

Reliability of experiments

Assessing validity
For example, in Bandura's (1963) Bobo doll study (see Year 1/AS Revision and Exam Companion and page 238 of Year 2 The Complete Companion Student Book) the DV was the aggressive behaviours of the children. This was **assessed** by controlled observation, with behavioural categories such as verbal imitation.

Improving reliability
Procedures should be standardised in any research study to **improve** reliability and replicability.

MATCH THEM UP

Match up the terms with the explanations.

1	Reliability	**A**	The extent of agreement between two researchers tallying behavioural categories
2	Inter-observer reliability	**B**	The correlation between the two sets of scores of the same participants taking the same test on two occasions
3	Test-retest reliability	**C**	Consistency of measurements
4	Inter-rater reliability	**D**	Measured by comparing answers from the same person with two different interviewers
5	Inter-interviewer reliability	**E**	Lack of clarity in questions which may confuse the participant and lead to unreliable data
6	Ambiguity	**F**	Whether two researchers allocate the same scores to the same individuals' behaviour
7	Replicability	**G**	If a study is able to be repeated using the same procedure with different participants and yield the same results

Answers on page 344

An idea 👍

Pick three key studies from your A level topics. Do you know how the researchers assessed the reliability of their measures? How might poor reliability be a problem for the findings of each study? How would this affect its support for the theory? How might the reliability be improved?

 RESEARCH ISSUES

Two psychologists watched videos of politicians in a televised debate. They assessed body language, counting instances of aggressive posture and facial expressions (Behaviours A–E). The two observers' results for one politician are given below.

Behaviour	A	B	C	D	E
Observer 1	7	5	4	12	9
Observer 2	2	5	6	6	4

(a) From these results, why are the psychologists concerned about inter-observer reliability? (*3 marks*)

(b) How could they assess the inter-observer reliability more objectively? (*2 marks*)

(c) Suggest reasons why the behavioural observations may be unreliable. (*4 marks*)

(d) What could they do to improve the reliability of the coding of behaviour? (*3 marks*)

Answers on page 344

  **APPLYING YOUR KNOWLEDGE**

Joanna is planning to research the experiences of girls in a secondary school in Uganda. She wants to collect quantitative and qualitative data. She is writing a questionnaire to find out their views of the importance of homework and helping with domestic tasks such as cooking and caring for younger siblings..

(a) Suggest a question that Joanna could ask to collect quantitative data. (*1 mark*)

(b) Write a question that would produce qualitative data. (*2 marks*)

(c) How could Joanna test the reliability of the questionnaire? (*3 marks*)

(d) Why would it matter if the reliability was low? (*3 marks*)

(e) How could Joanna improve the reliability of her questionnaire? (*4 marks*)

Answers on page 344

KEY TERMS

- Concurrent validity
- Ecological validity
- Face validity
- Mundane realism
- Temporal validity
- Validity

Possible exam questions ...

+ Explain how validity can be assessed in research. *(4 marks)*

+ How can psychologists improve the validity of their research? *(4 marks)*

 Exam tip

You will be criticising the validity of key studies within each topic you study. Learn the definitions for each type of validity, and make sure you can apply them to different kinds of research.

 Think

When you criticise the validity of a key study, think about how this affects its support for the theory. In an essay question this link is vital or your criticism won't get any marks.

MUST know ...

Internal versus external validity

Validity refers to whether an observed effect is a genuine one.

Internal validity concerns whether the researcher is measuring what they intend to, or whether the findings are affected by other factors.

External validity is how far the findings can be generalised outside the research setting, to other people (**population validity**), historical periods (historical or **temporal validity**) and settings (**ecological validity**).

Ecological validity

In an experiment, the method used to measure the DV can be quite artificial, giving poor ecological validity. This could be a lab experiment, field experiment or natural experiment. We have to consider **mundane realism** – whether a study reflects real world experiences – rather than just the location.

For example, Godden and Baddeley (1975) carried out an experiment on context-dependent forgetting. Deep sea divers learnt word lists on land or underwater, then tried to recall the words on land or underwater. The situation was 'real life' but the task was very artificial, and the divers were aware they were being studied, so may not have behaved 'naturally'.

Assessing validity

Face validity is an intuitive, common sense judgement of whether a self-report measure appears to measure what it claims to – do the questions seem to be related to the topic?

Concurrent validity compares a new measure with an existing, validated one on the same topic. The same participants take both measures and scores are compared.

Improving validity

Face validity can be improved by replacing any irrelevant questions with new items more obviously related to the topic.

Concurrent validity can also be improved by replacing items and checking whether the validity improves.

Ecological validity can be improved by giving participants more natural tasks to carry out in a more familiar environment.

If participants are sufficiently involved in the task, they may forget they are being watched, which helps to reduce demand characteristics.

SHOULD know ...

Internal versus external validity

Internal validity is affected by:

- confounding variables
- investigator effects (behaviour of the investigator that affects the participants' performance in a study)
- demand characteristics
- social desirability bias
- poor operationalisation of the dependent variable or behavioural categories.

Ecological validity

Demand characteristics can affect ecological validity if participants are aware they are being studied, so alter their behaviour to look good (social desirability bias) or to fit what they think the researcher expects. This means they are not behaving as they would in real life.

Godden and Baddeley (1980) set divers a different task, transferring nuts and bolts underwater. This had more mundane realism than the word lists, but participants were still aware of being observed, and this may have affected their behaviour.

Assessing validity

A test may be reliable (see previous spread) but lack validity if it does not actually measure the concept the researcher is aiming to measure.

For example, a stress questionnaire may give reliable results but the items may not actually relate to stress, so it lacks validity.

Improving validity

Improving research design can deal with issues such as demand characteristics and investigator effects. For example, in a double blind design, neither the participants nor the researcher who interacts with them knows the true aims of the study.

CHOOSE THE RIGHT ANSWER

A sports psychologist has written a questionnaire to find out how people's beliefs about their sporting ability affects their participation in sport. She has found a previously published questionnaire about sporting preferences, and asks participants to complete this as well as her new questionnaire.

What is she testing? (Tick **one** box only.)

A	Mundane realism	☐
B	Ecological validity	☐
C	Face validity	☐
D	Concurrent validity	☐

Answers on page 344

 A MARKING EXERCISE

Read this student answer to the following exam question:
A forensic psychologist uses cognitive tests and personality tests to assess young offenders and help to plan rehabilitation programmes for them. How could he improve the validity of the tests? *(3 marks)*

Lucy's answer

The psychologist could check the tests have been validated already, if they are published tests. He could brief the young offenders to make sure they know the psychologist is trying to help, so they can be honest with their answers and not be worried that they will be punished for 'wrong' answers. This reduces demand characteristics where they guess what the desired answers might be.

Ian's answer

They could check that the questions in the test are asking what they are meant to (face validity). They could then replace any questions that aren't. And they could take another test at the same time (concurrent validity).

What mark would you give each answer? Why would you give this mark? Explain your answer.

Student	Mark	Why you gave this mark
Lucy		
Ian		

Answers on page 344

 COMPLETE THE TABLE

Look through your Year 1 notes or Student Book. Find three different studies and assess their ecological validity by completing the table below.

Study (name and title or brief summary)	What environment was the study conducted in?	How was the DV measured?	Were the participants aware their behaviour was being studied?	Overall, how high or low is the ecological validity of this study?
Godden & Baddeley (1975) deep-sea divers	On land and underwater – natural	Recall of word lists – artificial	Yes – demand characteristics?	Low

 **APPLYING YOUR KNOWLEDGE**

You have been asked to design an experiment to test whether annoying music affects children's performance in a smartphone game. Write a suitable hypothesis. Explain how **two** issues in the research design might affect the validity of your findings.

Hypothesis *(2 marks)*	Validity issues *(4 marks)*

Answers on page 344

KEY TERMS
- Empirical
- Falsifiability
- Paradigm

Possible exam questions ...

+ Explain, using examples from psychological research, what is meant by falsifiability. *(2 marks)*
+ Why is replicability an important feature of science? *(2 marks)*
+ Explain what is meant by the 'empirical method'. *(2 marks)*
+ Explain how paradigm shifts contribute to scientific understanding. *(3 marks)*

 Exam tip

When answering questions on philosophical issues, make sure you answer the question you are being asked; you may need to apply your ideas to the particular research.

Think

Are you clear about the difference between reliability and replicability?

MUST know ...

Key features of science

Science is an evolving, systematic approach to creating knowledge, with five key features:

1 **Empirical methods**
Empirical evidence is gained through direct observation or experiment. This means claims can be tested and use to make predictions.

2 **Objectivity**
Objective data is collected systematically in controlled conditions, so it is not affected by the expectations of the researcher.

3 **Replicability**
Procedures are carefully recorded, so that other scientists can replicate them with different groups of people to test their validity.

4 **Theory construction**
Theories are explanations of observations and findings. Theories can emerge from observation or from hypothesis testing.

5 **Hypothesis testing**
A good theory must be able to generate testable hypotheses. If the hypothesis is not supported by empirical evidence, the theory must be modified.

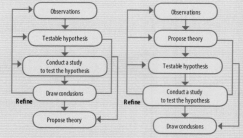

Inductive model   Deductive model

 Kuhn's theory of paradigm shift is...

...itself a paradigm shift from the previous way of understanding the scientific process.

- **E** – He described scientific progress as more like a religious conversion than a systematic, logical process of hypothesis testing.

EVALUATION *However, the theory of paradigm shift is...*

...still hotly debated by philosophers of science.

- **E** – Issues of bias in research, replicability, and the peer review process are also hot topics within psychology research.

 A benefit of the empirical approach is...

...that it teaches us to question claims that people make.

- **E** – A good scientist is a sceptic, and always asks: 'Where is the evidence?'

SHOULD know ...

Falisifiability

Karl Popper (1934) argued that it is only possible to disconfirm a theory. He pointed out that however many confirmed sightings of white swans there are, we cannot conclude that all swans are white; the sighting of just one black swan will disprove this theory.

Therefore, research tests the null hypothesis, for example 'not all swans are white'. If we are able to reject the null hypothesis (with reasonable certainty) we may accept the alternative hypothesis.

A scientific theory must be falsifiable. Some approaches, for example Freudian psychoanalysis, can be criticised as lacking falsifiability.

Paradigms

Thomas Kuhn (1962) proposed that scientific knowledge develops through revolutions, not the process of gradual change suggested by Popper's theory of falsification. Kuhn said that there are two main phases in science:

1 'Normal science', in which existing theory remains dominant, while disconfirming evidence gradually accumulates.

2 **Paradigm shift** – a revolutionary overthrowing of existing theory and its replacement with a new set of assumptions and methods.

- **E** – This change of view also depends on social factors.
- **L** – Therefore, according to Kuhn, science itself is socially constructed, through dialogue with other people, not just a logical process of evolving theory based on empirical evidence.

- **E** – Many famous studies have proved difficult to replicate, and researchers are rigorous in criticising each other's research.
- **L** – This can lead to a healthy debate between researchers, which will hopefully benefit the reputation of psychology as a valid and reliable scientific discipline.

- **E** – Good evidence should be directly observed or collected using controlled, objective methods.
- **L** – This means that we can reject pseudoscientific beliefs based on weak or subjective evidence.

✓ CHOOSE THE RIGHT ANSWER

Karl Popper's contribution to the philosophy of science has led to empirical research being based on the principle of null hypothesis significance testing. What should the hypotheses be? (Tick **one** box only.)

A Falsifiable ☐

B Replicable ☐

C Reliable ☐

D Objective ☐

Answers on page 344

⚙ APPLYING YOUR KNOWLEDGE 1

Rachel is a psychologist. She takes an online quiz which offers to identify whether her brain is male or female, based on answers to questions such as 'How do you feel about the idea of raising a family?' and 'Which of these movies would you choose to watch? (Options: 'Star Wars', 'The Twilight Saga', 'Mean Girls', 'Mad Max'.) Her result is, 'Your brain is 72% male – you like working systematically and taking the lead, and although you are able to empathise with others, you prefer to solve problems using logic rather than feelings.'

Should Rachel take this seriously? Apply your knowledge of scientific processes to evaluate the conclusions of this quiz.

(a) Features of scientific process *(3 marks)*

(b) This quiz *(3 marks)*

Answers on page 344

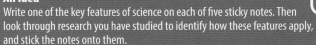

An idea

Write one of the key features of science on each of five sticky notes. Then look through research you have studied to identify how these features apply, and stick the notes onto them.

⚙ APPLYING YOUR KNOWLEDGE 2

Lauren is studying Psychology A level. Her younger sister, Lucy, is taking GCSEs and choosing A level courses. Lucy says, 'I don't like Science but I think Psychology sounds interesting because it's about people.' Lauren thinks she should explain to Lucy that Psychology is based on scientific principles.

Help Lauren to identify three key features of Psychology as a science that Lucy would encounter in A level Psychology and explain how this would link to the A level course. *(6 marks)*

Identify the psychology	Link to A level course

Answers on page 344

KEY TERMS

- Alternative hypothesis
- Null hypothesis
- Probability (*p*)
- Type I error
- Type II error

Possible exam questions ...

+ Explain what is meant by 'probability'. *(2 marks)*

+ Distinguish between a Type I and a Type II error. *(3 marks)*

+ Explain the difference between the alternative hypothesis and the null hypothesis. *(3 marks)*

+ How can the researchers be confident that they have not made a Type I error in this study? *(3 marks)*

+ Why might researchers choose to use a significance level of *p* < 0.05? *(2 marks)*

⭐ Exam tip

Hypotheses must always be fully operationalised for full marks. This means the IV and DV must be expressed in a measurable form. See the Year 1/AS Revision and Exam Companion, page 190, for further explanation.

MUST know ...

Probability

A hypothesis must be falsifiable (see previous spread). In research, we seek to falsify the null hypothesis.

As we can only test a sample of the population, we have to ask, 'What is the **probability** that the data collected came from a population where the null hypothesis is correct?'

If we are looking for a difference in the DV for two conditions of the IV in an experiment, the **null hypothesis** is 'there is no difference'. The **alternative hypothesis** is 'there is a difference'.

Samples may have small differences due to random variation or 'chance'. We test to see if any difference is likely to be due to these chance factors, or is large enough to represent a real difference in the populations from which the samples are drawn.

Type I and Type II errors

'You're pregnant.'
Type I error, false positive

'You're not pregnant.'
Type II error, false negative

SHOULD know ...

Probability

Inferential statistical tests permit us to work out how probable it is that a pattern in research data could have arisen by chance (supporting the **null hypothesis**). Alternatively, the effect may represent a real difference/correlation in the populations from which the samples were drawn (supporting the **alternative hypothesis**).

Probability levels

Psychologists generally use a **probability** level of 5% as the cut-off. This means there is a less than 5% chance of the results occurring if the null hypothesis is true, given as *p* < 0.05. So there is at least a 95% chance that the effect observed in the sample is a real one in the population.

In some studies, such as drug testing, researchers want to be more certain that effect is real. They may use a more stringent probability level of 1%, given as *p* < 0.01. This means there is less than 1% chance of the results occurring when there is no real difference/correlation between the populations from which the samples are drawn.

Type I and Type II errors

The 5% probability level gives a good compromise between Type I and Type II errors.

A **Type I error** is a false positive, in which the null hypothesis is rejected when it should have been accepted.

A **Type II error** is a false negative: the null hypothesis is accepted when it should have been rejected.

		Truth (which we will never know)	
		Alternative hypothesis H_1 true	Null hypothesis H_0 true
Test result	Reject null hypothesis	True positive	False positive **TYPE I ERROR**
	Accept null hypothesis	False negative **TYPE II ERROR**	True negative

MATCH THEM UP

Match up the terms with the explanations.

1	Null hypothesis	**A**	The null hypothesis has been wrongly accepted
2	Alternative hypothesis	**B**	A less than 5% probability that any difference has occurred by chance
3	$p < 0.05$	**C**	The null hypothesis has been wrongly rejected
4	$p < 0.01$	**D**	A testable statement of a relationship (difference, correlation, association) between variables
5	Type I error	**E**	A greater than 99% probability that the effect observed in a sample represents an effect in the population
6	Type II error	**F**	A prediction of no relationship between variables studied

Answers on page 344

 A MARKING EXERCISE

A psychologist finds their results are significant at a level of significance of $p < 0.05$. How can they be confident they have not made a Type I error in this study? Explain your answer. *(3 marks)*

Sam's answer

The probability is 5%. They have not made a type I error because a type I error is a false positive and their results are significant.

Alex's answer

There is less than 5/100 probability of a type I error. This is because $p < 0.05$ means that there is less than 0.05 chance that the effect has occurred by chance. So there is less than 5% chance of falsely rejecting the null hypothesis (a type I error).

What marks do you think these students would get? What else could you include to improve their answers?

Student	Your mark	Comment
Sam		
Alex		

Answers on page 344

 COMPLETE THE TABLE

Identify the null hypothesis and alternative hypothesis in these key studies from Year 1.

Key study	Null hypothesis	Alternative hypothesis
Bandura – Bobo dolls – imitation of violent behaviour (See Year 1/AS Revision and Exam Companion page 136.)		
Asch – conformity to group norms (See Year 1/AS Revision and Exam Companion page 22.)		
Harlow – attachment in monkeys (See Year 1/AS Revision and Exam Companion page 78.)		

Answers on page 345

 APPLYING YOUR KNOWLEDGE

Write a null hypothesis and an alternative hypothesis for each of the following research aims. *(2 marks each)*

Research aim	Null hypothesis	Alternative hypothesis
(a) To see if cats or dogs are better at solving puzzles.		
(b) To see if rats or lizards are more affectionate.		

Answers on page 345

KEY TERMS

- Calculated value
- Critical value
- Degrees of freedom
- Levels of measurement
- One-tailed test
- Significance
- Statistical test
- Test statistic
- Two-tailed test

Possible exam questions ...

+ Briefly outline the criteria used to decide if a parametric statistical test can be used with a set of data. *(3 marks)*

+ Which statistical test should the researcher use to test the significance of their findings in this study? Explain your choice. *(3 marks)*

+ Are the results significant? Explain your answer. *(3 marks)*

Link

See pages 224 and 226 of the Year1/AS Revision and Exam Companion for explanations of levels of measurement, normal distribution, skew, standard deviation.

Link

Statistical tests are used in nomothetic research – see page 58.

MUST know ...

Statistical tests

Inferential statistics allow us to find out if results are **significant** using tables of **critical values**.

Using statistical tests

Compare the calculated value of the test statistic with the critical value from the table of critical values.

To find the critical value, you need to know:

1 Significance level (using $p < 0.05$).

2 Kind of hypothesis: directional requires a **one-tailed test**, non-directional requires a **two-tailed test**.

3 Value of N, the number of participants, or the degrees of freedom (df).

There is an instruction underneath the table of critical values stating how to compare the calculated value with the critical value.

SHOULD know ...

Parametric criteria

Parametric tests (which use the mean and standard deviation to calculate the test statistic) are more powerful than non-parametric tests (which use ranked data). This means they can detect significance in some situations where non-parametric tests can't. But they should only be used if certain criteria are met:

1 The **level of measurement** is interval or better.

2 The scores (or scores of the population they represent) are **normally distributed**, and not skewed.

3 The **variances** of the two samples are similar. This is not an issue with repeated measures design. For independent groups, the variance of one sample should not exceed four times the other. (Variance is the square of the standard deviation.)

Choosing a statistical test

Sign test	⬅ related ➡	Nominal data	⬅ unrelated ➡	Chi-Squared
		⬇ Ordinal or interval ⬇		
	Pearson's r	⬅ Correlation ➡	Spearman's *rho*	
Parametric (interval data)		⬇ Tests of difference ⬇		Non-parametric (ordinal data)
	Related t-test	⬅ Related ➡	Wilcoxon	
	Unrelated t-test	⬅ Unrelated ➡	Mann–Whitney	

Note: related design includes repeated measures and matched pairs

Design	Level of measurement		
	Nominal	Ordinal	Interval
Independent groups	Chi-squared test	Mann-Whitney *U* test	Unrelated *t*-test
Repeated measures	Sign test	Wilcoxon test	Related *t*-test
Correlational	-	Spearman's *rho*	Pearson's *r*

MATCH THEM UP

Match up the terms with the explanations.

1	Test statistic	**A**	More powerful tests that can only be used on data which pass three criteria
2	Critical value	**B**	Data in categories
3	Calculated value	**C**	The name given to the value calculated using a specific statistical test, e.g. S for the sign test
4	One-tailed test	**D**	Data which is ranked or on a rating scale but without regular intervals
5	Two-tailed test	**E**	Form of test used with a directional hypothesis
6	Parametric test	**F**	The number of values that are free to vary given that the overall total values are known
7	Non-parametric test	**G**	The value of a test statistic calculated for a particular data set
8	Nominal data	**H**	The spread of data around the mean
9	Ordinal data	**I**	Form of test used with a non-directional hypothesis
10	Interval data	**J**	Data which is on a regular scale
11	Normal distribution	**K**	The value of the test statistic that must be reached to show significance
12	Skewed distribution	**L**	A symmetrical, bell-shaped distribution curve
13	Degrees of freedom	**M**	Tests that can be used on ordinal (ranked) data
14	Standard deviation	**N**	A frequency distribution in which the scores are not evenly distributed each side of the median

Answers on page 345

CHOOSE THE RIGHT ANSWER

A study is carried out asking A level students about their main areas of concern. In one question, they are asked to select from five options.

Identify the level of measurement of data collected by this question. (Tick **one** box only.)

A Nominal	☐
B Ordinal	☐
C Interval	☐
D Ratio	☐

Answers on page 345

APPLYING YOUR KNOWLEDGE

While researching stress, you have collected data measuring students' salivary cortisol level before an exam, to see whether this relates to the number of hours of sleep they had the previous night.

Which statistical test should you use? Explain why this test would be appropriate. *(4 marks)*

Choose a test	Reasons for choosing this test

Answers on page 345

COMPLETE THE TABLE

Fill in the table identifying the suitability of each statistical test. Use the decision tree on the facing page to help you. The first row is completed for you.

Test	Test statistic	Level of measurement	Parametric or non-parametric	Test of ...	Design
Chi-squared	χ^2	Nominal	–	Association or difference	Independent
Sign test	S		–		
Pearson's	r				
Spearman's	rho				
Related *t*-test	t				
Unrelated *t*-test	t				
Wilcoxon	T				
Mann-Whitney	U				

Answers on page 345

Possible exam questions …

+ Select an appropriate statistical test and explain your choice. *(3 marks)*

+ Why has the researcher chosen to analyse their data using the Wilcoxon test? *(2 marks)*

+ State whether the calculated value of *T* is significant, showing how you arrived at your answer. *(3 marks)*

 Exam tip

You are not expected to learn the formulae for calculating test statistics, but you may be given the formula and asked to use it to find the calculated value. To do this, substitute the numbers into the formula.

MUST know …

Wilcoxon test for related designs

Reasons for choosing

- The hypothesis states a **difference**.
- The two sets of data are **related**.
- The data are at least **ordinal**.

If you are given the calculated value of *T*:

1 Look at the data: is the difference in the predicted direction?

2 Find critical value of *T* from the table.

3 Compare calculated and critical values as instructed. (If the calculated value is equal to or less than the critical value, the result is significant.)

4 Report the conclusion, for example: 'As the calculated value is not significant ($p < 0.05$, one-tailed, $N = 11$), we must accept the null hypothesis and conclude that there is no difference between…'

Mann-Whitney test for unrelated designs

Reasons for choosing

- The hypothesis states a **difference**.
- The two sets of data are **unrelated**.
- The data are at least **ordinal**.

If you are given the calculated value of *U*:

1 Is the difference in the right direction?

2 Find the critical value of *U* from the table, where the two values of *N* intersect.

3 Compare calculated and critical values.

4 Report the conclusion.

SHOULD know …

How to calculate Wilcoxon *T*

1 State the hypotheses – null and alternative.

2 Place raw data in a table – two items for each participant.

3 Find the differences and rank from low to high, ignoring the signs.

If the difference is zero, omit from the ranking and reduce *N* accordingly.

If there are tied ranks, use the mean; for example, if 1 occurs five times, the ranks would be 1, 2, 3, 4, 5 – so the mean is 3.

4 Find the calculated value of *T* – the sum of the ranks of the less frequent sign.

Then follow the procedure on the left, to find the critical value and report your conclusion.

How to calculate Mann-Whitney *U*

1 State the hypotheses.

2 Place raw data in a table – separate columns for each group of participants.

3 Rank each data set, using the mean of any tied ranks.

4 Add each set of ranks, to give R_A and R_B.

5 Each column may have a different value of *N*, which are called N_A and N_B.

6 Find the calculated value of *U* using the smaller of R_A and R_B and the matching *N*, for example, $U = R_A - [N_A(N_A+1)] / 2$

Then follow the procedure on the left, to find the critical value and report your conclusion.

The Wilcoxon test is used for related samples (repeated measures or matched pairs design) and the Mann-Whitney test is used for unrelated samples (independent groups design).

To remember this: Mr and Mrs Wilcoxon are related by marriage. Mr Mann and Ms Whitney are unrelated.

✔ CHOOSE THE RIGHT ANSWER

Which **one** of these statements about the Wilcoxon test is **not** true? (Tick **one** box only.)

A It can be used for data from a matched pairs design. ☐

B It is less powerful than a *t*-test because it involves ranking data. ☐

C It can only be used for data at the ordinal level of measurement. ☐

D The value of *N* is the number of participants minus any whose scores were the same in both conditions. ☐

Answers on page 345

✎ COMPLETE THE TABLE

Compare the Wilcoxon test and the Mann-Whitney test. Fill in the table.

	Wilcoxon	Mann-Whitney
Level of measurement		
Experimental design		
Test statistic		
How to calculate test statistic		

Answers on page 345

⚙ APPLYING YOUR KNOWLEDGE 2

Calculate the value of U for the following data. The first example is worked out for you.

(a) $R_A = 131.5$, $N_A = 12$, $R_B = 99.5$, $N_B = 8$

We choose the smaller value of R to put into the formula, which is R_B.

$U = R_B - [N_B(N_B + 1)] \div 2$
$U = 99.5 - (8 \times 9) \div 2$
$U = 99.5 - 72 \div 2$
$\quad = 99.5 - 36 = 63.5$

(b) $R_A = 234$, $N_A = 15$, $R_B = 187$, $N_B = 13$

(c) $R_A = 69.5$, $N_A = 7$, $R_B = 129.5$, $N_B = 10$

Answers on page 345

⚙ APPLYING YOUR KNOWLEDGE 1

Suzi compared the recall of concrete words (e.g. cat, fish, table, cloud) with abstract words (e.g. beauty, truth, calm, fear). She used the same participants in each condition, and measured how many words each participant remembered. There were 23 participants, most of whom remembered more concrete than abstract words. Four participants remembered the same number in each condition.

(a) Write a directional hypothesis for this study. *(2 marks)*

(b) Suzi analysed the results using a Wilcoxon test. Explain why this test is suitable. *(3 marks)*

(c) The calculated value of *T* was 37. Use the table of critical values to decide if this is significant, and explain your decision. *(3 marks)*

(d) What can Suzi conclude? *(1 mark)*

▼ Table of critical vales for the Wilcoxon test.

Level of significance for a one-tailed test	0.05	0.01
Level of significance for a two-tailed test	**0.10**	**0.02**
N = 5	0	
6	2	0
7	3	2
8	5	3
9	8	5
10	11	8
11	13	10
12	17	13
13	21	17
14	25	21
15	30	25
16	35	29
17	41	34
18	47	40
19	53	46
20	60	52
25	100	89
30	151	137

Observed value of *T* must be EQUAL TO or LESS THAN the critical value in this table for significance to be shown.

Source: R. Meddis (1975). *Statistical handbook for non-statisticians*. London: McGraw Hill.

Answers on page 345

Exam tip

The table of critical values will always have an instruction at the bottom, explaining how to compare the calculated and critical values to find out if the result is significant. Look at this instruction carefully, as the comparison is different for different tests. You don't need to learn which test is which way round, just follow the instruction.

 Think

Parametric criteria:

1 Interval data
2 Normal distribution
3 Same variances

 Link

see page 30 for an explanation of how to use statistical tables.

 Link

See page 30 for more details about the parametric criteria.

 Exam tip

Remember!
Related data = repeated measures or matched pairs designs.
Unrelated data = independent groups designs.

MUST know ...

Related t-test

Reasons for choosing

- The hypothesis states a **difference**.
- The two sets of data are **related**.
- The data are **interval** level and fit the **parametric criteria**.

If you are given the calculated value of t:

1 Look at the data: is the result in the right direction? If not, the directional hypothesis is not supported so there is no need to calculate t. If your hypothesis is non-directional, miss this step.

2 Find the critical value of t from table, using $df = N - 1$. (See Topic 7.)

3 Compare calculated and critical values as instructed.

4 Report the conclusion.

For example: 'As the calculated value ($t = 1.8$) is less than the critical value ($t = 1.812$) it is not significant ($p < 0.05$, $df = 10$, one-tailed). So we must accept the null hypothesis and conclude that there is no difference between...'

Unrelated t-test

Reasons for choosing

- The hypothesis states a **difference** .
- The two sets of data are **unrelated**.
- The data are **interval** and fit the **parametric criteria**. (Variances can be assumed to be the same if participants were randomly assigned to conditions.)

If you are given the calculated value of t:

1 Is the difference in the right direction? If not, the directional hypothesis is not supported so there is no need to calculate t. If your hypothesis is non-directional, miss this step.

2 Find critical value of t from the table. Use $df = N_A + N_B - 2$.

3 Compare calculated and critical values of t.

4 Report the conclusion.

For example, 'As the calculated value of t (1.921) is greater than the critical value (1.812), it is significant ($p < 0.05$, df = 10, one-tailed). This means that we can accept the alternative hypothesis and conclude that there is a significant difference between ... and ...'.

With a directional hypothesis, this conclusion should also be stated directionally, e.g. 'participants in condition 1 did better than participants in condition 2'.

SHOULD know ...

How to calculate t for related samples

1 State the hypotheses (null and alternative).

2 Place raw data in a table – two items for each participant.

3 Find the differences (d) between each pair of scores, put these in a new column.

4 Calculate the total of the differences (Σd).

5 Add another column for the squares of the differences (d^2).

6 Calculate the total of the squares of the differences (Σd^2).

7 Find calculated value of t using the formula:

$$t = \frac{\Sigma d}{\sqrt{((N\Sigma d)^2 - (\Sigma d)^2)/N - 1)}}$$

For example, if the number of participants (N) was 10, $\Sigma d = 15$ and $\Sigma d^2 = 115$,

$$t = \frac{15}{\sqrt{(10 \times 115 - 15^2)/(10 - 1)}}$$

$$= \frac{15}{925/9}$$

$$= 0.146$$

Then follow the procedure on the left, to find the critical value and report your conclusion.

How to calculate t for unrelated samples

1 State the hypotheses (null and alternative).

2 Place raw data in a table – there may be different numbers of participants in each condition (N_A and N_B).

3 The formula is too complex to be asked in an exam. You can find an online calculator at www.socscistatistics.com/tests/studentttest/

Use this to find the calculated value of t.

Then follow the procedure on the left, to find the critical value and report your conclusion.

CHOOSE THE RIGHT ANSWER

In a cognitive psychology experiment, participants are given word lists to memorise. One group is given words of one syllable, and the other group is given words of two syllables. They are tested to see how many words they accurately recall five minutes later.

Which statistical test would be suitable for this study?
(Tick **one** box only.)

A Wilcoxon ☐

B Mann-Whitney ☐

C Related *t*-test ☐

D Unrelated *t*-test ☐

Answers on page 345

 APPLYING YOUR KNOWLEDGE

Mr Smith, the new principal of Angel College, is considering changing the times of the college day after reading that teenagers' sleep patterns are different from adults'. He conducts a one-week trial to see whether academic performance improves when students are able to sleep in for longer, starting the day at 10 am instead of 8.30 am.

Design a study that Mr Smith could carry out. Explain how he would collect data, and state an operationalised hypothesis. What experimental design is your study using? Which statistical test might be suitable to analyse the data from this study? Explain your choice.

Data collection (IV and DV)	Hypothesis and design	Statistical test + why?

Answers on page 345

 MATHS SKILLS

Leanne compared participants' ability to solve two similar visual puzzles with or without a hint. She predicted that participants would solve the puzzles more quickly with a hint than without a hint. Her data table is shown below.

Participant	Time with no hint (seconds)	Time with hint (seconds)	Difference (*d*)	*d*²
A	58	123		
B	84	68		
C	121	89		
D	82	76		
E	64	93		
F	189	115		
	Mean =	Mean =	Σd =	Σd^2 =

(a) Calculate the mean time for each condition. (*2 marks*)

(b) Calculate the differences between the times for each participant. (*2 marks*)

(c) Complete the d^2 column, and calculate Σd and Σd^2. (*2 marks*)

(d) Is the difference in the expected direction? (*1 mark*)

(e) Use the formula on the facing page to calculate *t*. (*3 marks*)

(f) The critical value for a one-tailed test with *df* = 5 at a 5% significance level is 2.015. The observed value of *t* must be EQUAL TO or GREATER THAN the critical value for significance to be shown. In this study, is the calculated value of *t* significant? (*1 mark*)

(g) What can Leanne conclude? (*2 marks*)

Answers on page 349

 RESEARCH ISSUES

In Leanne's study, she used six participants who each carried out both conditions of the experiment.

(a) What experimental design did Leanne use? Give a disadvantage of this design. (*2 marks*)

(b) While still using this design, how could Leanne improve the validity of her study? (*2 marks*)

(c) How might the sample size have affected her results? (*2 marks*)

Answers on page 345

KEY TERM

■ Correlation coefficient

Possible exam questions ...

+ Explain one advantage and one disadvantage of correlational research. *(4 marks)*

+ Use the data given in the table to sketch a scattergram of the results. *(4 marks)*

+ Which statistical test would be suitable for this study? Explain your choice. *(3 marks)*

+ State whether these findings are significant, and justify your answer. *(4 marks)*

 Exam tip

Remember! Correlation does not imply causation.

 Link

See Year 1/AS Revision and Exam Companion page 218 for more on correlations and scattergrams.

 Think

Pearson's *r* is used in calculating inter-rater reliability for observational data. Why is this interval level data?

MUST know ...

A non-parametric test: Spearman's *rho*

Reasons for choosing

- The hypothesis states a **correlation** between two variables.
- The two sets of data are **related** (pairs of scores from each person).
- The data are **ordinal**.

If you are given the calculated value of *rho*:

1 Is the correlation in the predicted direction? (The sign indicates a positive or negative correlation.)

2 **Find critical value of *rho* from the table.**

3 Compare calculated and critical values of *rho*, ignoring the sign.

4 Report the conclusion.

For example: 'As the calculated value of *rho* (−0.58) is greater than the critical value (0.564), the correlation is significant ($p < 0.05$, $N = 10$, one-tailed). This means the alternative hypothesis is supported: there is a negative correlation between… and… .'

A parametric test: Pearson's *r*

Reasons for choosing

- The hypothesis states a **correlation** between two variables.
- The two sets of data are **related** (pairs of scores from each person).
- The data are **interval** and fit the parametric criteria.

If you are given the calculated value of *r*:

1 Is the correlation in the predicted direction? (The sign indicates a positive or negative correlation.)

2 Find critical value of *r* from the table. Use $df = N - 2$.

3 Compare calculated and critical values of *r*, ignoring the sign.

4 Report the conclusion.

For example: 'As the calculated value of *r* (.372) is less than the critical value (.497), the correlation is not significant ($p < 0.05$, $N = 12$, one-tailed). This means we must reject the alternative hypothesis and conclude that there is no correlation between ... and ... '.

SHOULD know ...

How to calculate Spearman's *rho*

1 State the hypotheses (null and alternative).

2 Place raw data in a table – two scores for each participant.

3 Rank data in each column from low to high.

4 Find the difference (*d*) between each pair of ranks.

5 Square the differences and find the total, Σd^2.

6 Find calculated value of *rho* using the formula:

$$rho = 1 - \frac{6\Sigma d^2}{N(N^2 - 1)}$$

For example, if the number of participants (*N*) was 10 and Σd^2 came to 261,

$$rho = 1 - \frac{6 \times 261}{10(10^2 - 1)}$$
$$= 1 - \frac{1566}{990}$$
$$= -0.58$$

Then follow the procedure on the left, to find the critical value and report your conclusion.

How to calculate Pearson's *r*

1 State the hypotheses (null and alternative).

2 Place raw data in a table – two scores for each participant.

3 The formula is too complex to be asked in an exam. You can find an online calculator at www.socscistatistics.com/tests/pearson Use this to find the calculated value of *r*. Then follow the procedure on the left, to find the critical value and report your conclusion.

A correlation, but not significant?

Sometimes there can be a moderate or strong correlation which turns out not to be significant. This can be caused by a small sample size. The conclusion would be, 'There is not a significant correlation between…' You could suggest replicating the study with a larger sample.

On the other hand, a correlation may be weak but still significant if a very large sample is tested. For example, see the stress study by Rahe *et al* on page 202, which found a significant positive correlation between LCU scores and illness scores of +0.118 in a sample of 2664 men on US Navy cruisers.

CHOOSE THE RIGHT ANSWER

If a correlation is significant at the $p < 0.05$ level but not at the $p < 0.01$ level, what does this tell you? (Tick **one** box only.)

A There is a correlation but it is not significant. ☐

B There is between 1% and 5% chance that the correlation is due to chance factors. ☐

C There is 99% chance that the correlation is a genuine one in the population. ☐

D There is a 5% chance that the findings are due to error. ☐

Answers on page 345

 MATHS SKILLS

Calculate Spearman's *rho* for the following studies:

(a) An investigation of the association between rating on a scale of altruism and charitable giving in the last month: $N = 15$, $\Sigma d^2 = 118$ (*4 marks*)

(b) A comparison of self-report scores for attractiveness and happiness: $N = 19$, $\Sigma d^2 = 641$ (*4 marks*)

Then use the table of critical values to test the significance of these correlations, assuming there was previous research which indicated you could use a directional hypothesis, and choosing an appropriate level of significance.

▼ Table of critical values for Spearman's *rho*.

Level of significance for a one-tailed test	0.05	0.01
Level of significance for a two-tailed test	0.10	0.02
$N = 10$	.564	.648
11	.536	.618
12	.503	.587
13	.484	.560
14	.464	.538
15	.443	.521
16	.429	.503
17	.414	.485
18	.401	.472
19	.391	.460
20	.380	.447

Observed value of *rho* must be EQUAL TO or GREATER THAN the critical value in this table for significance to be shown.

Source: J.H. Zhar (1972). Significance testing of the Spearman rank correlation coefficient. *Journal of the American Statistical Association, 67*, 578–80. (Reproduced with kind permission of the publisher.)

Answers on page 345

 DRAWING CONCLUSIONS

A group of students were investigating personality traits and film preferences. Fifty participants were asked to complete questionnaires which consisted of 10 items measuring the personality trait of 'openness to experience' and 9 items rating their liking for different films, on a Likert scale. The scattergram shows the relationship between the scores for openness to experience and liking for sci-fi films, and the correlation coefficient was 0.338.

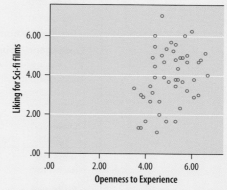

(a) What can you conclude from these findings? (*4 marks*)

(b) This correlation was tested using Spearman's *rho*, and was found to be significant at $p < 0.01$. How can the students be confident that they have not made a Type I error? (*3 marks*)

(c) Why did the students choose this test of significance? (*3 marks*)

(d) The students also hypothesised that the trait of agreeableness would be related to liking for comedy films. The correlation coefficient for these two variables was 0.291, but this was found not to be significant at $p < 0.05$ or $p < 0.01$. What can you conclude from these findings? (*4 marks*)

Answers on page 345

Topic 11 — Chi-Squared test (χ^2)

Possible exam questions ...

+ Draw a contingency table to display this data.
+ Calculate the value of Chi-Squared for this data and report whether it is significant.

MUST know ...

Chi-squared test

Reasons for choosing

- The hypothesis states a **difference** OR an **association**.
- The data in each cell are **independent**.
- The data are **nominal**.

Contingency table

The data is displayed in a table showing frequencies in each category. A 2 × 2 contingency table has two conditions of each variable, for example:

Observed values	Left handed	Right handed	Totals
Left eye dominant	12 (cell A)	3	15
Right eye dominant	32	3	35
Totals	44	6	50

If you are given the calculated value of χ^2:

1 Find critical value of χ^2, using df = (number of rows − 1) × (number of columns − 1).
2 Compare calculated and critical values of χ^2.
3 Report the conclusion, for example: 'As the calculated value of χ^2 (1.31) is less than the critical value (3.84), there is no association between handedness and eye dominance ($p < 0.05$, $df = 1$).

▼ Table of critical values for the Chi-Squared (χ^2) test

Level of significance for a one-tailed test	0.10	0.05	0.025	0.01
Level of significance for a two-tailed test	0.20	0.10	0.05	0.02
df				
1	1.64	2.71	3.84	5.41
2	3.22	4.60	5.99	7.82
3	4.64	6.25	7.82	9.84
4	5.99	7.78	9.49	11.67

Observed value of χ^2 must be EQUAL TO or GREATER THAN the critical value in this table for significance to be shown.

Source: abridged from R.A. Fisher and F. Yates (1974). *Statistical tables for biological, agricultural and medical research* (sixth edition). Longman.

SHOULD know ...

Chi-squared test

Criteria

The chi-squared test is one of the few that can deal with **nominal** (category) data. It tests **differences** between frequencies in different categories. These can also be expressed as an **association** between variables. The data must be **independent**: no item can appear in more than one cell of the contingency table.

Contingency table

There can be any number of rows and columns. A 3 × 2 contingency table would have 3 rows and 2 columns; 3 conditions of one variable, and 2 of the other.

How to calculate chi-squared

1 State the hypotheses.

In the example on the left, a non-directional alternative hypothesis could be: 'There is an association between handedness and eye dominance' OR 'There is a difference between left- and right-handed people's eye dominance'.

2 Place data (observed values, O) in contingency table and calculate totals for each row and column.

3 Calculate expected frequency (E) for each cell:

E = row × column/total

For example, for cell A, E = 15 × 44 / 50 = 13.2

Observed / Expected frequencies	Left handed	Right handed	Totals
Left eye dominant	12 / 13.2	3 / 1.8	15
Right eye dominant	32 / 30.8	3 / 4.2	35
Totals	44	6	50

4 Find calculated value of χ^2 using the formula:

$$\chi^2 = \Sigma\frac{(E - O)^2}{E}$$

For example, $\chi^2 = \dfrac{(13.2 - 12)^2}{13.2} + \dfrac{(1.8 - 3)^2}{1.8} +$

$\dfrac{(30.8 - 32)^2}{30.8} + \dfrac{(4.2 - 3)^2}{4.2}$

= 0.109 + 0.8 + 0.048 + 0.343

= 1.31

Then follow the procedure on the left, to find the critical value and report your conclusion.

An idea

Make a flow chart poster to show how to select a statistical test. You know eight different tests, and your flow chart should include decisions about level of measurement, correlation or difference, parametric or non-parametric and related or unrelated data. Add illustrations to help you remember the tests (e.g. a teapot for the Wilcoxon T, a rowing boat for Spearman's rho …)

A MARKING EXERCISE

Read this student answer to the following exam question:

Jana has researched males' and females' coffee preferences. She thinks that more females drink latte or cappuccino, and more males drink Americano or espresso.

(a) Explain why a Chi-Squared test would be appropriate for this data. (*3 marks*)

Jane should use Chi-Squared because the data is in categories. She is looking for an association between gender and coffee preference. And finally the data is independent, because they are independent groups.

What mark do you think this would get?
YOUR MARK

How could the answer be improved?

(b) Write a suitable directional hypothesis for this research. (*2 marks*)

There will be a difference between males' and females' favourite coffee type.

What mark do you think this would get?
YOUR MARK

How could the answer be improved?

Answers on page 346

MATHS SKILLS

(a) Using the data in this 3 × 2 contingency table, practise calculating χ^2 (*4 marks*)

	Condition 1	Condition 2	Totals
Category 1	13	8	21
Category 2	9	17	26
Category 3	22	5	27
Totals	44	30	74

(b) Is this significant? Explain your answer. (*3 marks*)

Answers on page 346

CHOOSE THE RIGHT ANSWER

Which **two** of these statements about the Chi-Squared test are **not** correct? (Tick **two** boxes.)

A Chi-Squared is used for any nominal data. ☐

B Chi-Squared cannot be used for ordinal data. ☐

C Chi-Squared looks for a relationship between variables. ☐

D Chi-Squared can be used to test association between variables ☐

E Chi-Squared can test differences. ☐

Answers on page 346

MATCH THEM UP

Match up the test with the appropriate type of data and hypothesis.

1 Sign test	**A**	interval, related, difference
2 Chi-Squared	**B**	interval, unrelated, difference
3 Pearson's *r*	**C**	interval, related, correlational
4 Spearman's *rho*	**D**	nominal, related, difference
5 Related *t*-test	**E**	nominal, unrelated, difference
6 Unrelated *t*-test	**F**	ordinal, related, correlational
7 Wilcoxon T	**G**	ordinal, unrelated, difference
8 Mann-Whitney U	**H**	ordinal, related, difference

Answers on page 346

Possible exam questions ...

+ Plan a study to investigate this topic. Include details of design, procedure, and how you would deal with ethical issues. *(10 marks)*
+ Outline what would be reported in the Discussion section of a journal article. *(4 marks)*
+ How should the researchers report the results of this observation? *(4 marks)*
+ Outline the sections of a journal article prepared for publication. *(6 marks)*

 Link

See Year1/AS Revision and Exam Companion for more information about peer review.

 Link

See page 60 for ethical implications of research studies and theory.

MUST know ...

Journal articles

Research studies are written up in a standard format for publication in peer-reviewed academic journals.

Abstract

A summary of the entire study in 150–200 words.

Introduction

This sets the context for the current research by reviewing previous research in the area, explaining the reasons for the current study.

Method

This generally contains four sections:

- Design: for example, 'repeated measures' or 'covert observation'.
- Participants: sampling methods, numbers and demographic details.
- Materials: how they were made or sourced.
- Procedure: including standardised instructions, environment, order of events.

Results

This section includes:

- Descriptive statistics, including tables and graphs.
- Inferential statistics.

Discussion

Here the researcher interprets the study and considers implications for future research and real-world applications.

References

All articles or books mentioned in the report are referenced in a standard format.

Ethics

Ethical issues should be considered at every stage of research. They may be mentioned in the Method section, along with how they were dealt with. They may then be examined further in the Discussion section, with any ethical implications of the findings if it is socially sensitive research.

SHOULD know ...

Journal articles

Abstract

A single sentence of each section: aims, hypothesis, procedure, sample, results and conclusions, including implications. It enables the reader to get a quick overview of the study and decide whether to read more detail.

Introduction

This is like a funnel, starting broadly and narrowing down to focus on the aims and research hypothesis of the current research.

Method

This should contain enough information for another researcher to replicate the study. Design, sampling and procedural decisions should be justified and explained. Ethical issues may also be mentioned, as well as how they were dealt with.

Results

In qualitative research, categories and themes are described along with examples from each.

Discussion

This section can include:

- Summary of the findings, with some explanation of what the results show.
- Relationship to previous research.
- Methodological criticisms and suggestions for improvement.
- Implications for theory and applications.

References

- Full references for any journal articles referred to in this Revision and Exam Companion can be found at the back of the Complete Companion Student Book Year 2. Many of the articles can be accessed online, so you can read further details of the study. If you are not able to access the full article due to a paywall, you can often read the abstract without paying.

MATCH THEM UP

Organise the journal article sections into their usual order.

1	
2	
3	
4	
5	
6	
7	
8	
9	

A	References
B	Results
C	Introduction
D	Abstract
E	Design
F	Procedure
G	Discussion
H	Participants
J	Materials

Answers on page 346

FILL IN THE BOXES

Put each key word into the box relating to the appropriate section of a research report.

inferential statistics
ethical issues
future research
scattergram
experimental design
table of findings
critical evaluation
means or medians
instructions
standard deviations
previous research
conclusions
materials
implications
sampling
applications
hypotheses
references
themes and examples
questionnaire
reason for the study
research aims

Abstract	
Introduction	
Method	
Results	
Discussion	

Answers on page 346

An idea

Select a study you know well, and write an abstract for the study in 150 words.

Include a sentence for each section:
- Abstract
- Introduction
- Method
- Results
- Discussion
using the guidance from the opposite page.

APPLYING YOUR KNOWLEDGE

Write an abstract for the Stanford Prison Experiment carried out by Zimbardo and colleagues (Haney *et al.*, 1973). Write one sentence only for each section, and keep to a maximum of 150 words. *(6 marks)*

Answers on page 346

Chapter 1 Research methods

1   Read the item then answer the questions that follow.

A cooking supplies company wanted to extend the range of their customer base, and funded a psychologist to research the way that people of different ages cook. They advertised in their shop and chose 5 younger participants (participants 1–5) and 5 older participants (participants 6–10) from those that applied. They set up a kitchen containing 100 pieces of equipment, and gave participants two different tasks.

Task 1: Participants were given recipes to follow, with free choice of cooking equipment. They were scored on how many pots and pans and other utensils they used.

Task 2: They were then asked to make a dish of their choice in 30 minutes using a selection of ingredients that were provided. These were scored by two independent raters for creativity and nutritional value, with scores on a scale of 1 to 5, where 5 is highly creative or highly nutritious. The scores in the table below are the mean of these two ratings for each participant's dish.

The following results were obtained:

Participant	Age	Task 1 score	Task 2 scores	
		number of utensils	creativity	nutrition
1	18		4	3.5
2	20		4	3
3	22		3	3
4	25		5	4.5
5	19		3	2.5
6	45		3	4
7	53		2	3.5
8	49		4	4
9	56		2.5	4
10	48		3.5	3

a) Give **one** reason why the dishes in task 2 were scored by two independent raters. *(2 marks)*

So they could work out the average, and to check for reliability of the ratings.

> This is two reasons. One + elaboration needed here.

b) Explain how the researchers could assess the reliability of the ratings for creativity and nutrition. *(2 marks)*

They could calculate the correlation of the scores from the two raters. A high correlation means a high reliability.

> Clear answer, good elaboration.

c) Write a suitable non-directional hypothesis for this investigation. *(2 marks)*

There will be no difference between the way that older and younger people cook.

> This is a null hypothesis. No marks.

d) The researchers wish to compare older and younger cooks' use of utensils. Suggest how they could use their data to compare these groups. *(2 marks)*

They could work out the average of each group and compare them to see which group used more utensils on average.

> 1 mark. They could also compare standard deviations, or they could carry out a statistical test of difference.

e) Calculate a suitable measure of central tendency for the creativity scores of older and younger cooks. Show your working. *(3 marks)*

Older: (3 + 2 + 4 + 2.5 + 3.5) / 5 = 3

Younger: (4 + 4 + 3 + 5 + 3) / 5 = 3.8

> Means are correctly calculated, with working shown. 3 marks.

f) Identify a suitable graphical display for the data from task 2, and briefly explain why this display would be appropriate. *(3 marks)*

The means could be displayed on a bar chart, with bars for each age group for creativity and nutrition. This is because they are separate categories.

> Correct chart, explanation of the bars, categories gets another mark. 3 marks.

g) What measure of dispersion could the researchers use, and what would this tell them about the data? *(3 marks)*

They could use the range. This would tell them how spread out the data are, for example the range for creativity for older people is 4 – 2 = 2.

> The range is possible, and it does tell them how spread out the data are. The calculation does not add anything – if there was a comparison with a conclusion that could get the third mark, or a comment about individual differences.

h) Name an appropriate statistical test that could be used to compare the creativity scores of older and younger participants, and explain why this would be suitable. *(4 marks)*

Mann-Whitney U test as they are independent groups and it is a test of difference, and non-parametric because the data is rating scores which are ordinal.

> Correct test and reasons.

i) The researchers found the results were not significant at p < 0.05. What is meant by 'the results were not significant at p < 0.05'? *(2 marks)*

This means that there is no significant difference between the two groups. Older and younger cooks don't differ significantly in their creativity. The difference is due to chance.

> The second sentence is a conclusion, so not answering the question. This is about probability; there is 95% probability that the difference is due to chance. 1 mark.

j) What conclusion could the researchers reach about older and younger cooks' creativity in this task? *(1 mark)*

There is no significant difference between older and younger cooks' creativity in this task.

> Correct. 1 mark.

k) The researchers are aware that their sample size was very small, and there could be a Type II error. Explain what is meant by a Type II error in this study. *(3 marks)*

The difference was not significant but there is a real difference in the population; the null hypothesis has been wrongly accepted and there should actually be a difference between older and younger cooks, but it didn't show up because the sample size was too small.

> Good answer, 3 marks. Note the 'in this study' means the concept must be applied, not just a general comment.

> The kitchen supplies company then wondered whether people's behaviour would be the same in their own home. They wanted to set up cameras in the participants' home kitchens to record their cooking behaviour.

l) Discuss ethical issues the researchers should consider in planning this observational research, and suggest how they could be dealt with. *(6 marks)*

The participants must give informed consent, so they should know that they are being observed and what is going to happen to the video recordings. Anyone else in the house must also be aware of the cameras in the kitchen and give consent, with particular concern about children or vulnerable adults. The participants must know that they can withdraw at any time, and that the video data will be destroyed. The information should be kept confidential and anonymous, so only the researchers see the videos and any published information doesn't contain the participants' names. The participants should not be harmed in the study and could be offered counselling.

> Excellent, concise answer with plenty of points relevant to this study. The last point about harm is not relevant, but still 6 marks.

> The company have persuaded two participants from each age group to take part in these observations in their home.

m) Design an observation study to investigate the differences between the cooking behaviour of younger and older participants in their own kitchens. *(12 marks)*

In your answer you should provide details of:
- The task for the participants.
- How the data can be analysed, including qualitative and quantitative analysis.

The participants should be observed cooking supper each day over one week, and the behaviour recorded on video. They should be instructed to behave as normal and not do anything special for the cameras. It might be good to put the camera in their house for 4 weeks and use 7 random days from the 4 weeks, so the participants didn't know which days they were actually being observed.

To get quantitative data, behavioural categories could be used, like 'using a pan then changing to a bigger one', 'checking the recipe', 'chatting or singing while cooking'. These would be found by watching some of the video to see what the cooks did (a pilot study).

The researchers could then tally these when they watch the sample of videos, and compare the number of times older and younger cooks do these things. Or they could just time how long it takes to make the meal, or how many pans the cook used.

To get qualitative data, the researchers could describe how happy the cook looked, or write down quotes if the cook was talking to themselves while they were cooking. They could also get the cook to make a video diary by talking to the camera about their cooking, and use quotes from this.

n) Discuss how the size and nature of the sample of participants who have agreed to take part in this observation study will affect the validity of the findings. *(4 marks)*

The participants were volunteers and had to be willing to have the camera in their kitchen for a long time, so they may not be typical. For example, many young people live in shared accommodation like student flats and the researchers would not have been able to get consent from all of the residents. And older people may have children who don't want to be observed. This means the sample is biased and not representative of the population of all older or younger cooks.

> The company then decide to survey their customers, to see what utensils they are buying. They ask every 10th customer about their cooking habits.

o) What kind of sampling is this? *(1 mark)*

Sytematic

p) Write a question that the company could use in their survey to produce qualitative data. *(1 mark)*

What is your favourite utensil, and why?

Examiner's comments

The task is well described, with a good idea about choosing a sample of 7 days from a 4-week period. The content analysis is also well explained, with appropriate, specific, measurable examples of behavioural categories, but no mention of using two observers. The qualitative data section starts well, but video diaries are a different research method so this is not relevant to an observation study. 9 marks.

This answer discusses the nature of the sample very effectively, but not the size. It is a very small sample, with only two people in each group, so the researchers won't be able to analyse quantitative data meaningfully. Population validity should be mentioned. 2 marks.

Correct.

'Why' will obtain qualitative data. 1 mark

2   Read the item then answer the questions that follow.

> Researchers are interested in the 'Macbeth effect', in which research shows that people experience an urge to cleanse their bodies when their moral integrity is threatened.
>
> In one study (Zhong and Liljenquist, 2006), participants were asked to recall an ethical or unethical deed. There were 18 participants in each group. They were then offered a choice of free gift: an antiseptic wipe or a pencil. The results are shown in the table:
>
> | | Ethical recall | Unethical recall |
> | --- | --- | --- |
> | Percentage who chose antiseptic wipes | 33.3% | 66.7% |

a) State what experimental design was used in this study. Why was this design used? *(2 marks)*

Independent groups. Because there were different participants doing each condition.

b) Should the hypothesis for this research be directional or non-directional? Explain your answer. *(2 marks)*

Directional. Because previous research has shown the Macbeth effect.

c) Explain what is meant by operationalisation. How did the researchers operationalise the IV and DV in this study? *(4 marks)*

The variables are operationalised to make them specific and measurable, as concepts like 'moral integrity' can't be directly measured. IV = which type of event they had to recall. DV = percentage choosing antiseptic wipe rather than a pencil.

1 mark for correct design. The reason is incorrect. It should be because people can't repeat the experiment as they would know what was going to happen.

Two marks.

3 marks. Good explanation. IV needs the two options, ethical or unethical. DV is correct.

d) The researchers chose to operationalise the DV in this way because they thought it had face validity. Explain what they meant by face validity. *(3 marks)*

Face validity is whether the operationalised DV intuitively makes sense as a measure of the concept, so whether taking an antiseptic wipe instead of a pencil shows that the person has an urge to clean their hands like Lady Macbeth.

> 3 marks – one for a definition, two for application in this context

e) Outline one other type of internal validity in psychological research. *(2 marks)*

Concurrent validity is whether the results for one measure match with another existing way of measuring the same concept.

> Two marks.

f) Calculate how many participants who recalled an unethical action then chose an antiseptic wipe. *(2 marks)*

66.7/100 x 18 = 12

> Correct, 2 marks.

g) State the conclusion of this study. *(2 marks)*

Recalling an unethical action increases the likelihood of choosing an antiseptic wipe rather than a pencil, compared to recalling an ethical action.

> Clear and specific, 2 marks. Note you need to compare both conditions.

h) The participants were not told in advance what the true purpose of the study was. Write a debriefing document that could be given to a participant in the 'unethical recall' group after they have taken part. *(5 marks)*

Thank you for taking part in this study. We did not tell you the true purpose of the study beforehand as it would have affected your behaviour. We were testing to see whether the recall of an event affected your choice of free gift. Some people were asked to remember an ethical action they had carried out, and others were asked to recall an unethical action. You were in the second group. You were then given a choice of an antiseptic wipe or a pencil. Previous research shows a 'Macbeth effect', where some participants who have carried out an unethical act show an urge to clean their hands. Please ask if you have any further questions. You have the right to withdraw your data at any time in the future.

> This meets the purposes of a debrief. Some mention of possible distress could also be included, but there is plenty here for 5 marks.

A group of students decided to carry out further research into morality. They wanted to see whether the seriousness of a remembered lie would relate to people's preference for cleansing products like toothpaste and mouthwash. They asked 15 participants to remember an occasion when they had lied to someone they cared about, and rate the seriousness of this lie on a 5-point Likert scale. They then asked them to evaluate some products, giving them scores for 'Would you choose to use this product?', also on a 5-point Likert scale. Products included food items as well cleansing products. The students calculated an average score for the cleansing items.

i) What graphical display could the students use for their findings from this study? *(1 mark)*

Scattergram

> Correct, as it is correlational data.

j) The students decided to analyse their findings using a Spearman's rho test. Why is this test suitable for this data? *(3 marks)*

Because it is correlational data, each person's score for the seriousness of the lie, and for preference for the cleansing products. Scores on a Likert scale are ordinal level so it is non-parametric.

> Correct answer, with the criteria for Spearman's rho applied to this data.

k) The observed value of rho was +0.467. Use the table of critical values below to state whether the result is significant, and justify your answer. *(4 marks)*

▼ Table of critical values for Spearman's *rho*.

Level of significance for a one-tailed test	0.05	0.01
Level of significance for a two-tailed test	0.10	0.02
N = 4	1.000	
5	.900	1.000
6	.829	.886
7	.714	.786
8	.643	.738
9	.600	.700
10	.564	.648
11	.536	.618
12	.503	.587
13	.484	.560
14	.464	.538
15	.443	.521
16	.429	.503
17	.414	.485
18	.401	.472
19	.391	.460
20	.380	.447
25	.337	.398
30	.306	.362

Observed value of *rho* must be EQUAL TO or GREATER THAN the critical value in this table for significance to be shown.

Source: J.H. Zhar (1972). Significance testing of the Spearman rank correlation coefficient. *Journal of the American Statistical Association, 67*, 578–80. (Reproduced with kind permission of the publisher.)

The observed value of rho was greater than the critical value rho = 0.443 (one-tailed, p < 0.05, N = 15) so the result is significant.

> Correct, with the three criteria identified. 4 marks.

l) Can the students conclude that remembering a lie causes the participants to want to buy toothpaste? Explain your answer. *(3 marks)*

This is a correlational analysis so they can't conclude that the lie has caused the toothpaste preference. An alternative explanation is that some participants scored high on all the Likert scales – a positive bias.

> This is correct; correlation does not imply causation. A possible alternative explanation is given as an elaboration. 3 marks.

3 A researcher has conducted an experiment, and is writing it up for publication. Describe the usual sections of a published journal article. *(4 marks)*

The article begins with an abstract, which is a summary of the entire paper. Then the introduction, which explains previous research in the area and the reason for this research, including the hypotheses. The Method section includes details of research design (in this case an experiment, but also explaining how the participants were organised into conditions), participants (sampling, demographics etc), materials and procedure. It should have enough detail for someone to be able to replicate the study. Then the Results section has descriptive and inferential statistics. Finally, the Discussion section where the researcher should talk about the conclusions, and any implications and applications of the research.

Examiner's comments

This is a thorough and effective description. 4 marks.

4 Explain the key features of scientific research. *(4 marks)*

Scientific research should use empirical methods, which collect objective data through direct observation. Often this means experiments, which are able to lead to conclusions about cause and effect because the IV is changed and the effect on the DV is measured. Hypothesis testing is a key feature of science, which means that you make a prediction and test it. Other people should be able to repeat your experiment, this is replicability. If the findings support the hypothesis then it can build up the theory more strongly. If not, then the theory might need to be changed.

This answer starts well and includes the main key terms that would be expected, but it appears a bit list-like at times. It loses focus in the second sentence, with too much detail about experiments: scientific research does not just include experiments. 3 marks.

5. Discuss the concept of paradigm shift in science, using examples from Psychology. (6 marks)

A paradigm is a way of understanding the world, and Thomas Kuhn said that scientific knowledge doesn't develop incrementally, but existing theories stay in place until a large body of evidence has accumulated that mean the theory needs to be thrown out. This is a paradigm shift. For example, the behaviourist psychologists were committed to experimental research and were only interested in observable behaviour, but cognitive psychology brought a paradigm shift of being able to investigate internal mental processes by inference from experimental findings. Before that, the behaviourist themselves were reacting against Freud's speculative and unfalsifiable theories by insisting that psychological research should be rigorous and based on empirical evidence. This was also a paradigm shift.

Paradigm shift depends on social psychology, with factors like persuasion and social influence being involved. For example, if a young researcher makes a new discovery and wants to challenge a theory they may have difficulty getting their research published as people tend to be resistant to change, particularly if the existing research was done by someone with high status in the research community. Publication bias is also involved with this, as peer reviewers may reject the article if it doesn't fit their paradigms. This means that paradigms are difficult to shift and the young researcher would have to be very persuasive.

A strong answer, with a good description of paradigm shift and some useful discussion points. More could be added about the revolutionary nature of paradigm shift, and the contrast between 'normal science' and paradigm shift. 5 marks

KEY TERMS

- Alpha bias
- Androcentrism
- Beta bias
- Gender bias
- Universality

Possible essay question

Discuss gender bias in psychology. *(16 marks)*

Other possible exam questions …

+ Explain what is meant by 'gender bias' in psychology. *(2 marks)*

+ Explain how androcentrism has affected psychological research. *(3 marks)*

+ Explain the difference between 'alpha bias' and 'beta bias'. *(4 marks)*

+ Outline an example of gender bias in psychological research. *(3 marks)*

Think

Issues and debates is a very theoretical topic. As you revise this topic, try to relate these theoretical ideas to the different topics that you have studied in Year 2.

MUST know …

Androcentrism, alpha and beta bias

An **alpha bias** occurs when a theory assumes that there is a real and enduring difference between males and females. There is a tendency to exaggerate the differences between men and women and therefore devalue one gender.

A **beta bias** occurs when a theory ignores or minimises the differences between males and females.

Psychology is a male-dominated subject and historically, almost all psychologists were men. Consequently, many psychological theories represent a male point-of-view, which is known as **androcentrism**.

The aim of psychology is to produce theories that have **universality** and apply to all people.

 EVALUATION

One way to reduce gender bias is…

…to take a feminist approach.

- **E** – Feminist psychology is a branch of psychology that aims to redress the imbalances in theory and research. Feminist psychology agrees that there are real biological sex differences between males and females.

EVALUATION

One criticism of gender research is…

…that the methods used are biased.

- **E** – It may not be that males and females are different, but that the methods used to test or observe them are biased.

EVALUATION

Another way to reduce gender bias is…

…to develop theories which emphasise the value of women.

- **E** – **Cornwell *et al.* (2013)** found that women are better at learning because they are more attentive, flexible and organised.

SHOULD know …

Examples of alpha and beta bias

Freud's theories reflected the culture in which he lived, where men were more powerful and typically more educated. Consequently, Freud's theory of psychoanalysis viewed femininity as a form of failed masculinity and therefore he exaggerated the differences between men and women – an **alpha bias**.

Biological psychologists examining the fight-or-flight response typically conduct research using male animals. However, recent research shows that females produce a 'tend-and-befriend' response at times of stress **(Taylor *et al.*, 2000)**. This **beta-biased** approach meant that female behaviour went undiscovered and that the stress response was not fully understood in women until recently.

- **E** – For example, Eagly (1978) claimed that women may be less effective leaders in comparison to men.
- **L** – This knowledge allows researchers to develop suitable training programmes that can help redress this gender bias.

- **E** – This could result in males and females appearing different, when they are not.
- **L** – This matters because it could reduce the validity of gender research and cause an alpha bias.

- **E** – This emphasises the value of women within the field of learning and focuses on the positive attributes of women.
- **L** – This matters because research can help challenge gender stereotypes and change people's preconceptions.

FURTHER EVALUATION

 EVALUATION **P – One issue with the beta bias is that…**

…it can draw attention away from women.

- **E** – On the one hand, the beta bias promotes equal treatment and has allowed women greater access to a range of opportunities.
- **E** – However, it also draws attention away from important differences, for example the biological demands of pregnancy and childbirth.
- **L** – Therefore, according to **Hare-Mustin and Marecek (1988)**, we should avoid the beta bias to ensure that notable differences are taken into consideration.

 EVALUATION **P – Another issue with gender research is that…**

…examples of gender bias remain unchallenged.

- **E** – Darwin's theory of sexual selection portrays women as choosy when it comes to mate selection.
- **E** – However, these views have recently been challenged and recent DNA evidence suggests that women are equally competitive and aggressive when the needs arise.
- **L** – This highlights the importance of challenging gender research, to ensure that research portrays a valid picture of women.

✓ CHOOSE THE RIGHT ANSWER

Which **one** of the following psychological approaches is the **least likely** to demonstrate androcentrism? (Tick **one** box only.)

A	Biological	☐
B	Behavioural	☐
C	Cognitive	☐
D	Psychodynamic	☐
E	Humanistic	☐

Answers on page 346

An idea

On a separate piece of paper, draw a Venn diagram. On one side write 'Gender bias' and on the other write 'Universality'.

Then list all of the theories/studies that you have encountered in Year ½ that contain gender bias on the left and list those which have universality on the right. How many can you come up with? Are there any theories/studies which overlap?

🧩 MATCH THEM UP

Match up the key terms on the left, with the definitions on the right.

1	Alpha bias	**A**	A tendency to ignore or minimise differences between men and women. Such theories tend either to ignore questions about the lives of women, or assume that insights derived from studies of men will apply equally well to women.
2	Androcentrism	**B**	Centred or focused on men, often to the neglect or exclusion of women.
3	Beta bias	**C**	A tendency to exaggerate differences between men and women. The consequence is that theories devalue one gender in comparison to the other.
4	Gender bias	**D**	The aim is to develop theories that apply to all people, which may include real differences.
5	Universality	**E**	The differential treatment or representation of men and women based on stereotypes rather than real differences.

Answers on page 346

⚙ APPLYING YOUR KNOWLEDGE

Asch's (1951) experiment examining conformity used a sample of 50 male college students, from three different American colleges. Use your knowledge to explain how Asch's research was gender biased. *(4 marks)*

Standard line   Comparison lines

Identify the psychology	Link to Asch (1951)

Answers on page 346

KEY TERMS

- Cultural bias
- Cultural relativism
- Culture
- Ethnocentrism

Possible essay question

Discuss cultural bias in psychology. *(16 marks)*

Other possible exam questions ...

+ Explain what is meant by 'cultural bias' in psychology. *(2 marks)*

+ Explain the terms 'ethnocentrism' and 'cultural relativism'. *(3 marks)*

+ Outline an example of cultural bias in psychological research. *(3 marks)*

 Exam tip

The specification only lists cultural bias and cultural relativism. Therefore, it is important that you know these two key terms explicitly. However, if you were answering a 16-mark essay on cultural bias, it would also be useful to understand the difference between alpha and beta bias.

MUST know ...

Cultural bias

Cultural bias is the tendency to judge all people in terms of your own cultural expectations. There are two types of cultural bias – alpha and beta.

An **alpha bias** is when a theory assumes that there are real and enduring differences between cultural groups. For example, assuming that individualistic cultures are less conformist, is an example of an alpha bias.

A **beta bias** is when a theory ignores or minimises cultural differences, by assuming that all people are the same. For example, using Western intelligence tests to examine intelligence (IQ) in other cultures, is an example of a beta bias.

 One strength of cultural research is...

...the development of 'indigenous psychologies'.

- **E** – Indigenous psychologies is the development of different groups of theories in different countries, for example, Afrocentrism.

 However, one issue with cultural research is...

...the development of culturally specific theories.

- **E** – The problem with findings from Afrocentric research is that they are only significant to understanding the behaviour within one culture.

 Cultural bias can be dealt with by...

...selecting samples from different cultural groups.

- **E** – **Smith and Bond (1998)** surveyed a European textbook on social psychology and found that 66% of the studies were American, 32% European and 2% from the rest of the world.

SHOULD know ...

Ethnocentrism and cultural relativism

Ethnocentrism is when you see things from your own cultural point of view. There is a tendency to see your own beliefs, customs and behaviours as 'normal'. However, ethnocentrism can lead to a beta bias, as it was previously deemed appropriate to use an American IQ test all over the world, when it wasn't.

Cultural relativism is the idea that we should study behaviour in the context of the culture in which it originates. However, cultural relativism can lead to an alpha bias. For example, **Mead's (1935)** research concluded that there were significant gender differences due to culture, when in fact there weren't.

- **E** – Afrocentrism is a movement which suggests that all black people have their roots in Africa and that theories must be African-centred.
- **L** – This matters because it has led to the development of theories that are relevant to the life and culture of African people.

- **E** – Another approach (known as 'etic') uses indigenous researchers in different cultural settings, for example **Buss's (1989)** study of mate preference, which used local researchers in 37 countries to look for universal behaviours.
- **L** – This allows researchers to develop universal theories of behaviour, while avoiding cultural bias.

- **E** – **Henrich *et al.* (2010)** calculated that a randomly selected American student was 4,000 times more likely to be a participant in a psychology study than a non-Westerner.
- **L** – This suggests that psychological research is severely unrepresentative and can be improved by simply selecting different cultural groups.

FURTHER EVALUATION

 P – One issue that can arise from culturally biased research is...

...the formation of stereotypes.

- **E** – The US Army used an IQ test before WWI which was culturally biased.
- **E** – The test showed that African-Americans were at the bottom of the scale in terms of IQ.
- **L** – The data from this test had a profound effect on the attitudes held by Americans towards other groups of people, highlighting the issue with culturally biased research.

P – One strength of psychological research today is...

...that researchers are significantly more international.

- **E** – Psychologists have an increased understanding of other cultures at a personal and professional level.
- **E** – Academics often hold international conferences, where researchers from different countries and cultures exchange ideas.
- **L** – This increased travel and exchange of ideas has helped reduce ethnocentrism in psychology and enabled a greater understanding of cultural relativism.

✔ CHOOSE THE RIGHT ANSWER

Which **one** of the following statements is **false**? (Tick **one** box only.)

A Ethnocentrism is when you use your own cultural groups as a basis for judgements. ☐

B Ethnocentrism is when you believe that your own customs and behaviours are 'normal'. ☐

C Ethnocentrism is when you consider that your own culture is different and better than another culture. ☐

D Ethnocentrism is the view that we need to understand the way in which a particular culture sees the world. ☐

Answers on page 346

🧩 MATCH THEM UP

Match up the key terms on the left, with the definitions on the right.

1	Cultural bias	**A**	The rules, customs, morals and ways of interacting that bind together members of a society or some other collection of people.
2	Cultural relativism	**B**	Seeing things from the point of view of ourselves and our social group. Evaluating other groups of people using the standards and customs of one's own culture.
3	Culture	**C**	The tendency to judge all people in terms of your own cultural assumptions. This distorts or biases your judgement.
4	Ethnocentrism	**D**	The view that behaviour cannot be judged properly unless it is viewed in the context of the culture in which it originates.

Answers on page 346

⚙ APPLYING YOUR KNOWLEDGE

Mead (1935) concluded that culture has an impact on gender roles because she found the Arapesh men and women to be gentle, responsive and cooperative, and the Mundugumor men and women to be violent and aggressive, seeking power and position. By contrast the Tchambuli exhibited gender role differences: the women were dominant, impersonal and managerial, whereas the men were more emotionally dependent.

Using your knowledge of cultural bias, identify **one** strength and **one** limitation of Mead's research. *(4 marks)*

Identify the psychology	Link to Mead

Answers on page 346

📖 RESEARCH ISSUES

Mead (1935) observed three tribal communities in New Guinea. Mead wanted to investigate whether there were differences in gender roles between the three tribes which would suggest that gender was a product of environment/culture rather than biology.

She visited three tribal communities on the island of New Guinea, including: The Arapesh (7 months); The Mundugamor (3 months); The Tchambuli (3 months).

Mead observed and recorded the behaviour of people within these groups for comparison with each other and traditional western cultures.

Identify one ethical issue that Mead should have considered in this research. Suggest how Mead could have dealt with this ethical issue. *(3 marks)*

Answers on page 346

KEY TERMS

- Determinism
- Free will
- Hard determinism
- Soft determinism

Possible essay question

Discuss free will and determinism in psychology. *(16 marks)*

Other possible exam questions …

+ Briefly explain the concept of free will. *(3 marks)*
+ Explain what is meant by 'biological determinism' and 'environmental determinism'. *(2 marks + 2 marks)*
+ Explain the difference between 'hard determinism' and 'soft determinism'. *(3 marks)*
+ Explain why science places an emphasis on causal explanations. *(3 marks)*

 Exam tip

There is a distinction between hard and soft determinism. Hard determinism is the idea that all behaviour can be predicted and humans have no free will, whereas soft determinism suggests that there is some element of free will. It's important that you understand this distinction.

MUST know …

Free will and determinism

Determinism is the view that our behaviour is governed by internal or external forces. There are many examples of determinism in psychology, including biological, environmental and psychic.

Biological determinism suggests that behaviour is governed by our genes. **Environmental determinism** suggests that our behaviour is caused by previous experience, through classical and operant conditioning. **Psychic determinism** suggests that our behaviour is caused by innate drives and early experiences.

Free will is the view that humans have complete control over their behaviour and have the ability to make a choice.

 One problem with the idea of determinism is…

…that no behaviour is completely (100%) biologically determined.

- **E** – Studies that compare identical twins typically find 80% similarity in terms of intelligence and 40% similarity for depression.

 Furthermore, another problem with the idea of determinism is…

…that no behaviour is completely (100%) environmentally determined.

- **E** – The concordance rates for intelligence and depression mentioned above, suggest that the environment is not the only factor determining behaviour.

Another issue with the idea of determinism is…

…that it provides an excuse for undesirable behaviours.

- **E** – Stephen Mobley, who killed a pizza shop manager in 1981, claimed that he was 'born to kill' due to a history of violence in his family.

SHOULD know …

Examples of free will and determinism

Research by **Hill *et al.* (1999)** found a particular gene (IGF2r) in people with high intelligence, suggesting that intelligence may be **biologically determined**.

Behavioural psychologists claim that humans develop phobias through classical conditioning – where a conditioned response can be learned if a neutral stimulus (e.g. a bee) is paired with an unconditioned stimulus (e.g. being stung), suggesting that some phobias maybe **environmentally determined**.

Humanistic psychologists, such as Maslow and Rogers, claim that humans have **free will** and that self-determination is a necessary part of human behaviour and without self-determination, self-actualisation is not possible.

- **E** – However, identical twins share 100% of their genes and even though there is an 80% similarity in terms of IQ, the results suggest that 20% is caused by other factors.
- **L** – This suggests that biological or genetic determinism cannot fully explain any behaviour.

- **E** – If identical twins show an 80% similarity in terms of IQ, this suggests that only 20% is accounted for by the environment.
- **L** – This suggests that environmental determinism is also unable to fully explain any behaviour.

- **E** – However, this argument was rejected and he was sentenced to death.
- **L** – This matters because a truly determinist position may be undesirable because it would allow individuals to 'excuse' their behaviour and could lead to all sorts of legal issues.

FURTHER EVALUATION

 P – One issue with the idea of free will is…

…that free will may just be an illusion.

- **E** – Behavioural psychologist Skinner claimed that just because we can decide between different actions does not mean that we have free will.
- **E** – While a person might 'choose' to watch a particular film, their choice is actually determined by previous reinforcement experiences.
- **L** – This suggests that our behaviour is environmentally determined and that free will is just an illusion.

 P – Another issue with the idea of free will is…

…the lack of support from cognitive neuroscience.

- **E** – **Libet *et al.* (1983)** recorded activity in motor regions of the brain, before a person had conscious awareness of the decision to move their finger.
- **E** – In other words, the decision to move the finger was a pre-determined action of the brain.
- **L** – This suggests that behavioural responses are biologically determined and that humans don't always have free will.

✔ CHOOSE THE RIGHT ANSWER

Which **one** of the following statements describes a deterministic view? (Tick **one** box only.)

A Human behaviour always has a cause. ☐

B Humans have full control over their behaviour. ☐

C Humans are not always responsible for their behaviour. ☐

D People have some choice over their actions. ☐

Answers on page 346

✎ FILL IN THE BOXES

In each box below write **one** sentence describing each type of determinism.

Biological determinism is…
Environmental determinism is…
Psychic determinism is…
OPTIONAL: Free will is…

In each box below expand the content on the left, writing another 20 words.

An example of biological determinism comes from…
An example of environmental determinism comes from…
An example of psychic determinism comes from…
An example of free will comes from…

Answers on page 347

✔ A MARKING EXERCISE

Read this student answer to the following exam question:

Using an example, explain the difference between hard and soft determinism. *(3 marks)*

Hard determinism is the idea that our behaviour is predicted and we have no free will, whereas soft determinism allows some element of free will

What mark do you think this would get?

YOUR MARK

AO1

Hint

A hint to help you decide: How many critical points have been covered? Has the answer provided an example?

Write an improved answer here…

Answers on page 347

⚙ APPLYING YOUR KNOWLEDGE

Identify the psychology

Link to Adenola

Adenola has always got his own way at school, by bullying and fighting with other children.

His older brother was excluded from school for hitting another student and last week Adenola was excluded for also hitting another student.

Using your knowledge of determinism, suggest two reasons why Adenola is aggressive. *(4 marks)*

Answers on page 347

KEY TERMS

- Environment
- Heredity
- Interactionist approach
- Nature
- Nature–nurture debate
- Nurture

Possible essay question

Discuss the relative importance of heredity and environment in determining behaviour. *(16 marks)*

Describe and evaluate the nature–nurture debate in psychology. *(16 marks)*

Other possible exam questions …

+ Explain the terms 'nature' and 'nurture'. *(4 marks)*
+ Outline one example of an interactionist approach to the nature–nurture debate. *(3 marks)*

! Think

The nature–nurture debate is one of the most well-known debates and relates to many different topics in psychology. Consider how this debate relates to one of your optional Year 2 topics. Choose from: relationships, gender, or cognition and development. Where could you use this debate in those topics?

MUST know …

Nature and nurture

Nature refers to innate (biological or genetic) influences. However, this does not just refer to characteristics present at birth, but to any characteristics determined by genes. For example, secondary sexual characteristics which appear at puberty and conditions like Huntingdon's disease are, to some extent, genetically determined.

Nurture refers to environmental influences which are acquired through interactions with the environment. This includes both the physical and social world and is often referred to as 'experience'. Nurture can affect an infant before and after birth.

 EVALUATION *One limitation of the nature–nurture debate is…*

…that the debate has become meaningless.
- *E* – Most psychologists believe that an **interactionist approach**, which considers both nature and nurture, is more suitable.

 EVALUATION *However, one strength of the nature–nurture debate is…*

…the development of the diathesis-stress model.
- *E* – The diathesis-stress model suggests that you can be born with a biological vulnerability, for example a gene for depression; however the depression will only develop if it is triggered from a stressor in the environment.

 EVALUATION *One consideration in the nature–nurture debate is…*

…the idea that nature affects nurture.
- *E* – **Plomin *et al*. (1977)** put forward the idea of 'passive influence' where parents' genes influence aspects of their behaviour, creating a certain type of environment for their children.

SHOULD know …

Examples of nature and nurture

The influence of nature includes both **genetic** and **evolutionary** influences. For example, schizophrenia has a concordance rate of 40% for MZ twins and 7% for DZ twins. This suggests that nature is a contributing factor in schizophrenia.

Behavioural psychologists suggest that certain behaviours can be explained in terms of experience alone. For example, behaviourists explain that attachment could be explained in terms of **classical conditioning** (the infant associating the mother with food) and **operant conditioning** (food reducing the discomfort of hunger), suggesting that nurture is a possible factor in the development of attachments.

- *E* – For example, the disorder *phenylketonuria* is a genetic (nature) disorder, which if discovered at birth, can be prevented from causing brain damage through a restricted diet (nurture).
- *L* – This highlights the importance of an interactionist approach in considering both nature and nurture.

- *E* – Research has found that not everyone with the gene for depression goes on to develop depression and therefore a person's nature is only expressed under certain conditions of nurture.
- *L* – This highlights the importance of taking an interactionist approach, such as the diathesis-stress model.

- *E* – For example, parents with a genetically determined mental illness may create an unsettled home environment and therefore the child's mental disorder could be the result of indirect influences.
- *L* – This highlights the interaction of nature and nurture and suggests that nature (illness) can indirectly actually affect nurture (unsettled home environment).

FURTHER EVALUATION

EVALUATION *P* – Another consideration in the nature–nurture debate is…

…the idea that nurture affects nature.
- *E* – Research which examines neural plasticity suggests that life experiences shape our biology.
- *E* – **Maguire *et al*. (2000)** found that the hippocampi (brain region involved in spatial navigation) of London taxi drivers was larger in comparison to non-taxi drivers.
- *L* – This suggests that the nurture (driving a taxi) can affect nature (the size of the hippocampi).

 EVALUATION *P* – A final consideration in the nature–nurture debate is…

…the role of epigenetics.
- *E* – Epigenetics is the material in each cell of the body, which acts as a 'switch' to turn genes on or off. Life experiences, such as nutrition or stress, control these switches.
- *E* – This explains why identical twins do not always look exactly the same.
- *L* – This provides further support to the idea that genes and the environment are much less separate than we previously thought.

✔ CHOOSE THE RIGHT ANSWER

Which **one** of the follow statements is **false**? (Tick **one** box only.)

A Nurture suggests that behaviour is the product of environmental influences. ☐

B Nurture suggests that behaviour can be explained in terms of classical and operant conditioning. ☐

C Nurture suggests that behaviour can be explained in terms of indirect learning. ☐

D Nurture suggests that behaviour can be explained in terms of inheritance. ☐

Answers on page 347

🧩 MATCH THEM UP

Match up the key terms on the left, with the definitions on the right.

1	Environment	**A**	The argument as to whether a person's development is mainly due to their genes or to environmental influences.
2	Heredity	**B**	Behaviour is a product of environmental influences.
3	Interactionist approach	**C**	Behaviour is seen to be a product of innate (biological or genetic) factors.
4	Nature	**D**	Everything that is outside our body, which includes people, events and the physical world.
5	Nature–nurture debate	**E**	With reference to the nature–nurture debate, the view that the processes of nature and nurture work together rather than in opposition.
6	Nurture	**F**	The process by which traits are passed from parents to their offspring, usually referring to genetic inheritance.

Answers on page 347

💡 DRAWING CONCLUSIONS

Researchers used a test to examine the English reading age of pairs of identical and non-identical twins. If the twins had a similar reading age, then they were said to be concordant.

The results of the experiment can be found in the graph below.

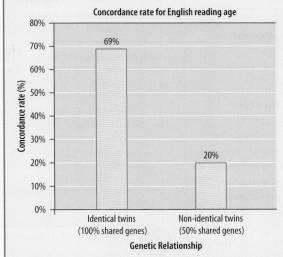

What can you conclude from the graph in relation to the nature–nurture debate? *(4 marks)*

Answers on page 347

⚙ APPLYING YOUR KNOWLEDGE

Look at the picture of the two cats. Rainbow (on the left) was cloned to produce a kitten called CC (on the right). They have identical genes but look quite different.

Using your knowledge of the nature–nurture debate, explain two reasons why CC is different to Rainbow, despite having exactly the same genes. (4 marks)

Identify the psychology	Link to CC

Answers on page 347

55

KEY TERMS

- Holism
- Reductionism

Possible essay question

Discuss holism and reductionism in psychology. *(16 marks)*

Other possible exam questions …

+ Explain what is meant by 'holism'. *(3 marks)*

+ Explain what is meant by 'levels of explanation' in relation to reductionist explanations. *(3 marks)*

+ Discuss biological reductionism in psychology. *(6 marks)*

+ Give an example of environmental (stimulus-response) reductionism from an area of psychology that you have studied. *(3 marks)*

★ Exam tip

Be careful when using the term 'reductionist', as many students often use this term incorrectly. For example, the cognitive approach is **not** reductionist because it ignores emotional and biological factors, it is simply limited. When using reductionism make sure you refer to the different types: biological, environmental or experimental.

MUST know …

Holism and reductionism

A **reductionist** approach involves breaking down complex phenomena and behaviours, into their simplest components.

A **holistic** approach suggests that we need to understand the whole experience, rather than the individual features, to fully understand complex phenomena and behaviours.

The reductionist approach suggests that explanations have three levels:

- Highest level: which includes cultural and social explanations of how social groups affect behaviour.
- Middle level: which includes psychological explanations of behaviour.
- Lower level: biological explanations, including hormone and genes.

 One issue with a reductionist approach is…

…it can lead to errors of understanding.

- **E** – Lower levels, in particular biological or behaviour levels, are taken in isolation and therefore the meaning of the behaviour might be overlooked.

 One consideration of biological reductionism is…

…the development of drug therapies.

- **E** – Drug therapies have led to treatments which have resulted in a considerable reduction in institutionalisation since the 1950s.

 One issue with environmental reductionism is…

…the experiments may not apply to human behaviour.

- **E** – The behavioural approach was developed as a result of experiments with non-human animals, but such explanations may not be appropriate for complex human behaviours.

SHOULD know …

Examples of holism and reductionism

Biological reductionism reduces complex behaviours to the actions of neurons, neurotransmitters, hormones, etc. For example, biological psychologists suggest that schizophrenia is caused by excessive activity of the neurotransmitter dopamine.

Environmental reductionism reduces behaviours to simple stimulus-response links. For example, behavioural psychologists suggest that attachment is the result of an infant associating their mother with food, through classical conditioning.

Gestalt psychology is a holistic approach which focuses on perception, suggesting that we can only understand perception by considering the whole of an image and not the individual parts, often illustrated through visual illusions.

- **E** – For example, using the drug *Ritalin* as a treatment for ADHD may ignore the true cause of the child's hyperactive behaviour.
- **L** – This matters because we do not develop an accurate understanding of human behaviour and may fail to treat the cause at issue.

- **E** – However, the success rates of drug treatments are highly variable and they treat the symptoms and not the cause.
- **L** – On the other hand, psychological treatments/therapies take into account the cause of the issue and have produced many successful therapies.

- **E** – Humans are not a scaled-up version of other animals and their behaviour is influenced by social context, intentions and so on.
- **L** – This matters because environmental reductionism ignores other possible influences such as cognition and/or emotional factors which may play a role in human behaviour.

 FURTHER EVALUATION

 P – One consideration of experimental reductionism is…

…the application of research findings to everyday life.

- **E** – The laboratory experiment of **Loftus and Palmer (1974)** provided an insight into the accuracy of eyewitness testimony; however these results have not been supported by real-life case studies.
- **E** – **Yuille and Cutshall (1986)** found eyewitness memories to be highly accurate in real-life situations.
- **L** – This suggests that experimental reductionism may have a negative effect on the application of psychological research.

P – One final consideration of the reductionist approach is…

…to consider an interactionist point of view.

- **E** – Dualists believe that there is a physical brain and a non-physical 'mind' which interact.
- **E** – Research by **Martin et al. (2001)** has found that the mind can affect our biology, as depressed patients receiving psychotherapy experience the same changes in serotonin as those receiving drugs.
- **L** – This suggests that an interactionist approach may be more appropriate than a reductionist one.

MATCH THEM UP

Match up the key levels of explanation for reductionism of the left, with the examples on the right.

1 Highest level	**A** Biological explanations of how hormones and genes etc. affect our behaviour
2 Middle level	**B** Psychological explanations of behaviour
3 Lower level	**C** Cultural and social explanations of how our social groups affect our behaviour

Answers on page 347

FILL IN THE BOXES

In each box below write **one** sentence describing each type of reductionism.

In each box below expand the content on the left, writing another 20 words.

Biological reductionism is…	An example of biological reductionism is…
Environmental reductionism is…	An example of environmental reductionism is…
Experimental reductionism is…	An example of experimental reductionism is…
OPTIONAL: Holism is…	An example of holism is…

Answers on page 347

An idea

On a separate piece of paper, draw a line, where one end is labelled 'Reductionism' and the other is labelled 'Holism'.

'Reductionism' ⟷ 'Holism'

Consider where the six key psychological approaches would fit on this continuum: behavioural, biological, humanistic, psychodynamic, cognitive and social learning theory. Write these labels in the appropriate place.

Once you have done this, you could add the key studies/theories you have encountered to your labels, e.g. Cognitive – Loftus and Palmer (1974).

Finally, you could state what type of reductionism (if any) the study demonstrates, e.g. Cognitive – Loftus and Palmer (1974) - Experimental reductionism. This would provide you with a great tool for evaluation in your Year 2 essays.

A MARKING EXERCISE

Read this student answer to the following exam question:

Explain what is meant by levels of explanation in relation to reductionist explanations. *(3 marks)*

There are three levels of explanation: high, middle and low. The highest level is the most reductionist and the lowest level is the least reductionist.

What mark do you think this would get?

YOUR MARK

AO1

Hint
A hint to help you decide: How many critical points have been covered? How much detail is there?

Write an improved answer here…

Answers on page 347

Topic 6 — Idiographic and nomothetic approaches to psychological investigations

KEY TERMS

- Idiographic approach
- Nomothetic approach

Possible essay question

Discuss idiographic and nomothetic approaches to psychological investigation. *(16 marks)*

Other possible exam questions …

+ Explain what the terms 'idiographic' and 'nomothetic' mean. *(4 marks)*
+ Describe the nomothetic approach to psychological investigation. *(4 marks)*
+ Evaluate the nomothetic approach to psychological investigation. *(6 marks)*

! Think

When you complete a personality questionnaire that predicts your personality in relation to four factors (e.g. introvert vs. extrovert and neurotic vs. emotionally stable), the data collected is using a nomothetic approach.

MUST know …

Idiographic and nomothetic approaches

The **idiographic approach** focuses on individuals and emphasises uniqueness. This approach is qualitative in nature, because the focus is on developing an in-depth insight into human behaviour. Consequently, the approach favours quality of information rather than quantity and employs methods such as unstructured interviews, case studies and thematic analysis.

The **nomothetic approach** tries to formulate general laws of behaviour and is based on the study of groups. This approach studies large numbers of people in order to make generalisations and therefore uses quantitative methods, in the same way as the scientific approach.

 One strength of the idiographic approach is…

…the focus on the individual.

- *E* – **Allport (1961)**, who was the first to use the term idiographic, argued that a drastic reorientation was needed as psychologists had lost sight of what it was to be human.

 However, one criticism of the idiographic approach is…

…that it is not scientific.

- *E* – However, some idiographic approaches, such as case studies or qualitative research, do use an evidence-based approach and seek to be objective and attempts are made to ensure validity.

 Furthermore, another criticism of the idiographic approach is…

…the inability to produce general predictions about behaviour.

- *E* – For example, to allow psychologists to develop drugs that treat mental illness. Some psychologists argue that this inability to produce general predictions is a severe limitation.

SHOULD know …

Examples of these approaches

Freud (1909) used case studies in order to understand human behaviour. The case of **Little Hans** consisted of approximately 150 pages of quotes recorded by Hans' father, plus Freud's own interpretations, which is a clear example of the idiographic approach.

Humanistic psychologists also favour the idiographic approach, as they are concerned with studying the whole person.

The biological approach takes a nomothetic approach and seeks to formulate general laws about how the body and brain work. Furthermore, behavioural psychologists produce general laws of behaviour, for example classical and operant condition, to explain learning in human and animals.

- *E* – Allport argued that it is only by fully understanding an individual that we can predict how an individual might act in a given situation.
- *L* – This matters because the idiographic approach has been responsible for refocusing psychology back on the individual.

- *E* – For example, qualitative approaches use techniques like reflexivity, where the researcher reflects critically during the research process about factors that might affect the researcher and the participants.
- *L* – Therefore, despite this criticism, the idiographic approach attempts to use evidence-based methods and techniques to ensure validity.

- *E* – Furthermore, it would be too time consuming to produce personal therapies for every unique individual.
- *L* – This suggests that the idiographic approach is not suitable for developing psychological treatments and other (nomothetic) approaches may be more useful.

 FURTHER EVALUATION

 P – **Another criticism of the idiographic approach is…**

…that it is relatively time consuming.

- *E* – While both approaches are based on large amounts of data, the idiographic approach is based on large amounts of data about one person.
- *E* – Collecting large amounts of data from a group also takes time, but is relatively quicker, because the data can be generated more easily.
- *L* – This matters because the idiographic approach is less efficient when it comes to data collection.

 P – **A final consideration of the idiographic approach is…**

…that the distinction between the idiographic and nomothetic approach is false.

- *E* – **Holt (1967)** claims that there is no such thing as a unique individual and that the approach is used for general principles.
- *E* – **Millon and David (1996)** argue that researchers should start with the nomothetic approach and can then focus on idiographic understanding.
- *L* – Consequently, researchers suggest that both approaches should be used together.

✔ CHOOSE THE RIGHT ANSWER

Which **one** of the following statements best describes the idiographic approach in psychology? (Tick **one** box only.)

A   Studying individuals and favouring qualitative methods. ☐

B   Studying individuals and favouring quantitative methods. ☐

C   Studying groups and favouring qualitative methods. ☐

D   Studying groups and favouring quantitative methods. ☐

Answers on page 347

📖 RESEARCH ISSUES

The psychologist conducting a case study on Jack (see the 'Applying your knowledge' activity) used observations and interviews with Jack and his teachers.

Identify **two** ethical issues that the researcher would need to consider in this research. *(4 marks)*

Answers on page 347

⚙ APPLYING YOUR KNOWLEDGE

Two educational psychologists decided to conduct some research in a local primary school.

One researcher chose to conduct a case study on Jack, a pupil with extreme behavioural difficulties. The other researcher chose to examine the entire student population, to formulate a general theory in relation to mathematical ability.

Using your knowledge of idiographic and nomothetic, explain how the psychologists used these two different approaches. *(4 marks)*

Identify the psychology	Link to…

Answers on page 347

✔ A MARKING EXERCISE

Read this student answer to the following exam question:

Describe the nomothetic approach to psychological investigation. *(4 marks)*

The nomothetic approach tries to develop general laws in relation to behaviour. The biological and behavioural approaches both take a nomothetic approach.

What mark do you think this would get?

YOUR MARK

AO1

Hint
A hint to help you decide:
How many critical points have been covered?
How much detail is there?

Write an improved answer here…

Answers on page 348

Key Terms

- Socially sensitive research

Possible essay question

Discuss the ethical implications of research studies and theory, including reference to social sensitivity. *(16 marks)*

Other possible exam questions …

+ Explain what is meant by 'socially sensitive research'. *(3 marks)*

+ Outline one example of research that is socially sensitive. *(3 marks)*

Think

It is important to understand how ethical implications and social sensitivity apply to research you have studied. You have encountered ethical considerations before; therefore think carefully about the idea of social sensitivity, as you encounter new research in Year 2 – is this new research socially sensitive?

MUST know …

Ethical issues during the research process

Sieber and Stanley (1988) identified four aspects of the research process at which ethical issues should be considered:

1. **The research question:** for example, the research question: 'Is homosexuality inherited?' appears to add credibility to a prevailing prejudice.
2. **The treatment of the participants:** ensuring confidentiality of information collected during and after the research process.
3. **The institutional context:** as research is often funded by private institutions, ensuring that the data is not misused.
4. **Interpretation of findings:** for example, the development of an IQ test was used to demonstrate the inferiority of certain groups of people.

 One issue with socially sensitive research is…

…the wider impact of the research itself.

- ***E*** – Even with socially sensitive research, there is the potential for an indirect impact on the participant's family and co-workers, which may not be taken into account.

 One issue with the current ethical guidelines is…

…that research may inflict harm on a group of people in society.

- ***E*** – While ethical guidelines may protect the immediate needs of the research participants, they may not deal with the other ways that research may inflict harm on people in society.

 Another issue with socially sensitive research is…

…that it may disadvantage marginalised groups in society.

- ***E*** – Many groups are often excluded from, or misrepresented in psychological research, e.g. people with disabilities.

SHOULD know …

Ethical issues in socially sensitive research

Sieber and Stanley identified ten types of ethical issue that relate to **socially sensitive research**; some of these have been examined in Year 1, including: privacy, confidentiality, valid methodology – poor methodology (and invalid findings) could shape important social policy to the detriment of those represented, deception, Informed consent, equitable treatment – ensuring that all participants are treated in an equitable manner (e.g. not withholding educational opportunities from one group), scientific freedom – scientists have a duty to engage in research, while not harming their participants, ownership of data, values, risk/benefit ratio.

- ***E*** – Therefore, it does not seem sufficient to simply safeguard the interests of the individual participants.
- ***L*** – This matters because socially sensitive research should also take into account the wider impact of the research, including the implications of the research for the wider community.

- ***E*** – For example, the current ethical guidelines do not ask researchers to consider how their research might be used by others and could form/shape social policy.
- ***L*** – This matters because Sieber and Stanley recommend that researchers should consider this within the interpretation and application of their findings.

- ***E*** – This failure to represent and research such groups creates an additional ethical issue – that these people miss out on the benefits of research.
- ***L*** – This matters because it could be argued that our understanding of human behaviour has been lessened by our misinterpretation and failure to represent different groups.

FURTHER EVALUATION

 P – **One solution to the issue of conducting socially sensitive research is…**

…to simply avoid it.

- ***E*** – Researchers could avoid researching sensitive areas like homosexuality, race, gender and addiction because the findings may have negative consequences for the participants.
- ***E*** – However, this would probably leave psychologists with nothing to research but unimportant issues.
- ***L*** – **Sieber and Stanley** argued that this is an avoidance of responsibility by psychologists, who have the duty to conduct socially sensitive research.

 P – **Another solution to the issue of conducting socially sensitive research is…**

…for researchers to engage with policy makers.

- ***E*** – In order to reduce the likelihood of misuse of data, psychologists should take responsibility for their findings.
- ***E*** – They should be aware of the possibility that their research might lead to discrimination.
- ***L*** – This matters because individual researchers should be encouraged to promote evidence-based research in a socially sensitive way and not take a neutral position.

FILL IN THE BOXES

In each box below write one sentence describing each part of the research process	In each box below expand the content on the left, writing another 20 words, related to **social sensitivity**
The research question is… .	This links to social sensitivity because… .
Conduct of research and treatment of participants refers to… .	This links to social sensitivity because… .
The institutional context refers to… .	This links to social sensitivity because… .
The application of findings refers to… .	This links to social sensitivity because… .

Answers on page 348

 MATCH THEM UP

Match up the key terms on the left, with the definitions on the right.

1	Privacy	**A**	Ensuring that suitable and good methodology is used, so that poor studies do not shape important social policy.
2	Confidentiality	**B**	Sensitive issues can arise when there is a clash between the beliefs of the scientist and the recipient.
3	Valid methodology	**C**	A participant is not told the true aims of a study and thus cannot give truly informed consent.
4	Deception	**D**	A person's right to control the flow of information about themselves.
5	Informed consent	**E**	The costs of the research should be minimised.
6	Equitable treatment	**F**	Treating all participants fairly and not withholding resources that are vital to a participants' well-being.
7	Scientific freedom	**G**	Participants must be given information about the nature and purpose of the research and their role in it.
8	Ownership of data	**H**	Researchers should be mindful over the accessibility to data, especially when research is sponsored.
9	Values	**I**	Concerns the communication of personal information from one person to another, and the trust that the information will be protected.
10	Risk/benefit ratio	**J**	Researchers have an obligation to engage in scientific research, while being mindful not to harm participants.

Answers on page 348

 APPLYING YOUR KNOWLEDGE

In a study of intelligence and social background, researchers interviewed 100 children.

They were classified in relation to their intelligence level. Twenty-five children were highly intelligent, 41 children were moderately intelligent and 34 were not very intelligent.

The researchers found that the majority of the 'not very intelligent' children attended a comprehensive sixth form college, while the majority of the other two groups attended independent schools.

Using your knowledge of social sensitivity, discuss how researcher could deal with the issues of social sensitivity in this study. *(4 marks)*

Identify the psychology	Link to social sensitivity

Answers on page 348

 RESEARCH ISSUES

1. What level of measurement is being used in the study detailed in the 'Applying your knowledge' activity? *(1 mark)*

2. Outline **one** issue with the level of measurement you have detailed in question 1. *(3 marks)*

Answers on page 348

Topic 1 Gender in psychology: Gender bias

Discuss gender bias in psychology. *(16 marks)*

Answer

A gender bias occurs when there is differential treatment or representation of men/women. Psychology has typically been a male-dominated subject and consequently, many psychological theories represent a male point-of-view, which is known as androcentrism. There are two types of cultural bias that can occur: alpha and beta bias.

An alpha bias occurs when a theory assumes that there is a real and enduring difference between males and females. Freud's theory of psychoanalysis viewed femininity as a form of failed masculinity and therefore he exaggerated the differences between men and women – an alpha bias. A beta bias occurs when a theory ignores or minimises the differences between males and females. Biological psychologists examining the fight-or-flight response typically conduct research using male animals and this beta-biased approach meant that female behaviour went undiscovered until recently. The aim of psychology is to produce theories that have universality and apply to all people.

One the main issues with psychological research/theory is that many examples of gender bias remain unchallenged. For example, Darwin's theory of sexual selection portrays women as choosy when it comes to mate selection. However, these views have recently been challenged and recent DNA evidence suggests that women are equally competitive when the needs arise. This highlights the importance of challenging gender research and reducing gender bias to ensure that research portrays a valid picture of women.

Psychologists have suggested a number of ways to reduce gender bias. One way is to develop theories which emphasise the value of women. For example, Cornwell et al., (2013) found that women are better at learning because they are more attentive and organised. This emphasises the value of women and focuses on the positive attributes of women. This matters because this type of research can help challenge gender stereotypes. Alternatively, another way to reduce gender bias is to take a feminist approach. Feminist psychology aims to redress the imbalances in theory and research. Feminist psychology agrees that there are real biological sex differences between males and females. For example, Eagly (1978) claimed that women may be less effective leaders which allows researchers to develop suitable training programmes that can help redress this gender bias in both theory and application.

However, not all psychologists agree that males and females are different and some psychologists believe that it is the methodology used in research which is biased. This could result in males and females appearing different when they are not. This matters because it could reduce the validity of gender research and cause an alpha bias. However, one way to overcome an alpha bias is to ignore or minimise these biological differences; however then you can end up with a beta bias, which on the one hand promotes equal treatment but on the other hand draws attention away from important differences, for example the biological demands of pregnancy and childbirth.

It is clear that the issue of gender bias still exists and while there are many attempts to overcome gender bias in research/theory, psychologists need to be aware of these issues when conducting research.

Level 4 (13–16 marks)

Examiner's comments: AO1: Knowledge is generally well-detailed and accurate, with specialist terminology used throughout. AO3: There is a thorough and effective evaluation which is clear and focused on the question. Additional examples/elaboration would have helped in places.

Examiner's comments

This is a good introduction which outlines many specialist terms.

The answer has outlined alpha and beta bias accurately and provided clear examples.

A thorough and effective issue is outlined and well developed.

A discussion of how to overcome gender bias is presented, drawing on research.

A second discussion is presented within the same point, drawing on further support.

Although this is a well-developed point, an example of biased research would add to it.

Further discussion of the distinction between alpha and beta bias is presented.

Topic 2 Culture in psychology: Cultural bias

Discuss cultural bias in psychology. *(16 marks)*

Examiner's comments

Answer

In psychology, a cultural bias occurs when people are judged in terms of someone else's cultural expectations. Like gender bias, there are two types of cultural bias – alpha and beta. An alpha bias is when a theory assumes that there are real and enduring differences between cultural groups, whereas a beta bias is when a theory ignores or minimises cultural differences, by assuming that all people are the same. In addition to the idea of alpha and beta bias, psychologists also make the distinction between ethnocentrism and cultural relativism.

> A good introduction to cultural bias.

> Specialist terminology is used effectively; however examples would help to illustrate this answer.

Ethnocentrism is when you see things from your own cultural point of view. With ethnocentrism there is a tendency to see your own beliefs, customs and behaviours as 'normal', whereas cultural relativism is the idea that we should study behaviour in the context of the culture in which it originates.

> Likewise, specialist terminology is used effectively; however there is a lack of knowledge presented through examples.

There are many ways that psychologists can deal with cultural bias, for example, by selecting samples from different cultural groups. Smith and Bond (1998) surveyed a European textbook on social psychology and found that 66% of the studies were American, 32% European and 2% from the rest of the world. This suggests that psychological research is severely unrepresentative and can be improved by simply selecting different cultural groups.

> An effective evaluation point that uses evidence effectively.

Furthermore, an issue that can arise from culturally biased research is the formation of stereotypes. For example, the US Army used an IQ test before WWI which was culturally biased.

> Another effective evaluation point that uses an example to elaborate the main criticism.

The test showed that African–Americans were at the bottom of the scale in terms of IQ. The data from this test had a profound effect on the attitudes held by Americans towards other groups of people, highlighting the issue with culturally biased research.

> A generally well-detailed point, linked to an evaluative comment on 'indigenous psychologies'.

Fortunately, nowadays psychologists are significantly more open-minded and well-travelled and psychologists have an increased understanding of other cultures, at both a personal and professional level. Academics often hold international conferences, where researchers from different countries and cultures exchange ideas. This increased travel and exchange of ideas has helped reduce ethnocentrism in psychology and enabled a greater understanding of cultural relativism. Furthermore, a strength of this increased understanding of culture is the development of 'indigenous psychologies' which is the development of different groups of theories in different countries, for example, Afrocentrism, which is a movement which suggests that all black people have their roots in Africa and that theories must be African-centred. This matters because it has led to the development of theories that are relevant to the life and culture of African people. However, while the development of indigenous psychologies is often seen as a strength, a problem with findings from Afrocentric research is that they are only significant to understanding the behaviour within one culture. Another approach (known as 'etic') uses indigenous researchers in different cultural settings, for example Buss's (1989) study of mate preference, which used local researchers in 37 countries in order to look for universal behaviours. This approach allows researchers to develop universal theories of behaviour, while avoiding cultural bias and is seen as a real strength of cultural research.

> An effectively used counter-argument.

> Another evaluation point based on the idea of 'etic', making a final comment about universal theories to avoid cultural bias.

Level 4 (13–16 marks)

Examiner's comments: AO1: An accurate and generally well-detailed outline. Further examples could have been used in the introduction to show further evidence of understanding. AO3: A very effective commentary, make using of numerous ideas to effectively to evaluate the ideas of cultural bias and cultural relativism.

Topic 3 Free will and determinism

Discuss free will and determinism in psychology. *(16 marks)*

Examiner's comments

Answer

The free will and determinism debate is one of the most famous debates in psychology. Determinism is the view that our behaviour is governed by internal or external forces, whereas free will is the view that humans have complete control over their behaviour.

> A good introduction providing accurate knowledge of key terms.

There are many examples of determinism in psychology, including biological, environmental and psychic. Environmental determinism suggests that our behaviour is caused by previous experience, through classical and operant conditioning. Psychic determinism suggests that our behaviour is caused by innate drives and early experiences and biological determinism suggests that our behaviour is governed by our genes. For example, research by Hill et al. (1999) found a particular gene (IGF2r) in people with high intelligence, suggesting that intelligence is biologically determined. Humanist psychologists would argue against this view, as they believe that humans have free will and self-determination, and that intelligence is not the product of biology alone.

> The answer describes the three different types of determinism accurately and provides examples to clarify understanding.

The determinism point of view has attracted a lot of criticism, mainly because psychologists generally believe that no behaviour is fully determined. For example, studies that compare identical twins typically find 80% similarity in terms of intelligence and 40% similarity in terms of depression. However, as identical twins share 100% of their genes, the results suggest that 20% is caused by other factors. This suggests that biological determinism cannot fully explain any behaviour, in particular IQ and depression. Furthermore, the same evidence suggests that no behaviour is completely environmentally determined. If identical twins show an 80% similarity in terms of IQ, this suggests that only 20% is accounted for by the environment. In addition to the lack of support from twin studies, the determinist point of view is not favoured by the criminal justice system. If behaviour is determined, then it provides a potential excuse for criminals. Stephen Mobley, who killed a pizza shop manager in 1981, claimed that he was 'born to kill' due to a history of violence in his family. However, this argument was rejected. A truly determinist position may be undesirable because it would allow individuals to 'excuse' their behaviour and could lead to all sorts of legal issues.

> The answer uses evidence effectively to refute both biological and environmental determinism.

> The answer also considers the real-world application of a deterministic point of view.

> The answer effectively criticises the free will point of view.

However, the idea of free will has attracted similar criticisms. Some psychologists argue that free will is just an illusion. Behavioural psychologist Skinner claimed that just because we can decide between different actions does not mean that we have free will. Skinner argued that our behaviour is in fact environmentally determined, but we just don't want to admit it. Furthermore, evidence from cognitive neuroscience also refutes the free will explanation. Libet et al. (1983) recorded activity in motor regions of the brain, before a person had conscious awareness of the decision to move their finger. In other words, the decision to move the finger was a pre-determined action of the brain. This suggests that behavioural responses are biologically determined and that humans don't always have free will.

> The answer draws on evidence to support these criticisms.

It is clear that psychologists do not favour a deterministic or entirely free will point of view and therefore a 'soft determinism' view that allows an element of free will is probably the most favoured.

> A nice conclusion is provided, especially as the commentary only contains criticisms.

Level 4 (13–16 marks)

Examiner's comments: AO1: An accurate and well-detailed outline which outlines the key ideas with reference to research/theory. AO3: An excellent commentary focusing on the criticisms of both free will and determinism in two detailed sections, with a final concluding comment.

Topic 4 The nature–nurture debate

Describe and evaluate the nature–nurture debate in psychology. *(16 marks)*

Examiner's comments

Answer

The nature–nurture debate is probably the most famous debate in psychology and is used when explaining a range of human behaviours.

Nature refers to innate (biological or genetic) influences. However, this does not just refer to characteristics present at birth, but to any characteristics determined by genes that may develop through our lifetime, for example Huntingdon's disease. The influence of nature includes both genetic and evolutionary influences. For example, schizophrenia has a concordance rate of 40% for MZ twins and 7% for DZ twins, suggesting that nature is a contributing factor in schizophrenia.

> A detailed and accurate account of nature, using relevant examples and research.

Nurture on the other hand refers to environmental influences which are acquired through our interactions with the environment. This includes both the physical and social world and is often referred to as 'experience'. Behavioural psychologists suggest that attachment behaviours could be explained in terms of classical conditioning (the infant associating the mother with food) and operant conditioning (food reducing the discomfort of hunger), highlighting the influence of nurture.

> Another detailed and accurate account, using further examples to explain nurture.

The nature–nurture debate has grown increasingly complex, and one argument is that nature actually affects nurture. Plomin et al. (1977) put forward the idea of 'passive influence' where a parents' genes influence aspects of their behaviour, creating a certain type of environment for their children. For example, parents with a genetically determined mental illness may create an unsettled home environment and therefore the child's mental disorder could be the result of indirect influences. This highlights the interaction of nature and nurture and suggests that nature (illness) can indirectly actually affect nurture (unsettled home environment). Equally, some psychologists suggest that nurture affects nature. Research examining neural plasticity suggests that life experiences shape our biology. Maguire et al. (2000) found that the hippocampi (a brain region involved in spatial navigation) of London taxi drivers was larger in comparison to non-taxi drivers, suggesting that nurture (driving a taxi) can affect nature (the size of the hippocampi).

> A well-detailed and effective evaluation point, with good use of examples.

> Another well-detailed and effective evaluation point, considering the other side of the argument.

Complex debates like these have led some psychologists to believe that the nature–nurture debate is now a pointless and meaningless distinction. Most psychologists believe that an interactionist approach, which considers both nature and nurture, is more suitable. For example, the disorder *phenylketonuria* is a genetic (nature) disorder, which if discovered at birth, can be prevented from causing brain damage through a restricted diet (nurture). This highlights the importance of an interactionist approach in considering both nature and nurture. Furthermore, an interactionist approach has led to the development of the diathesis–stress model. The diathesis–stress model suggests that you can be born with a biological vulnerability, for example a gene for depression, however the depression will only develop if it is triggered from a stressor in the environment. Research has found that not everyone with the gene for depression, goes onto develop depression and therefore a person's nature is only expressed under certain conditions of nurture. This highlights the importance of taking an interactionist approach, like the diathesis–stress model.

> An effective link from one evaluation point to the next.

> Introduction of more specialist terminology.

> Two effective evaluation points linked to the interactionist approach.

The interactionist approach has led to the development of theories/models that have helped develop our understanding of many physical and psychological illnesses.

> A weak/generic conclusion that doesn't add to this essay.

Level 4 (13–16 marks)

Examiner's comments: AO1: A well-detailed and accurate account of the nature–nurture debate is presented. AO3: An excellent evaluation considering in the limitations of nature–nurture while exploring the interactionist approach, using supporting research throughout.

Topic 5 Holism and reductionism

Discuss holism and reductionism in psychology. *(16 marks)*

Answer

The holism and reductionism debate centres on whether or not we should reduce complex behaviours into more simple components.

A reductionist approach involves breaking down complex behaviours and there are three types of reductionism, including: biological, environmental and experimental. Biological reductionism reduces complex behaviours to the actions of neurons, neurotransmitters, hormones, etc. For example, biological psychologists suggest that schizophrenia is caused by excessive activity of the neurotransmitter dopamine. Environmental reductionism reduces behaviours to simple stimulus–response links and experimental reductionism is concerned with reducing behaviours to isolated variables for the purpose of research.

The holistic approach suggests that we need to understand the whole experience, rather than the individual features, to fully understand complex phenomena and behaviours. Gestalt psychology is a holistic approach which focuses on perception, suggesting that we can only understand perception by considering the whole of an image and not the individual parts.

The reductionist approach has been heavily criticised. Some psychologists argue that the reductionist approach can lead to errors of understanding. For example, biological reductionism attempts to explain conditions like ADHD in terms of neurochemical imbalances, while prescribing drug therapies. However, using a drug like *Ritalin* may ignore the true cause of the child's hyperactive behaviour. This matters because we do not develop an accurate understanding of human behaviour and may fail to treat the cause of issue. Furthermore, the success rates of drug treatments are highly variable which suggest that behaviour cannot be explained by environmental reductionism alone.

Furthermore, psychologists have also criticised explanations based on environmental reductionism, as a lot of the research is conducted on non-human animals. The behavioural approach was developed as a result of experiments with non-human animals, and such explanations may not be appropriate for complex human behaviours. Humans are not a scaled-up version of other animals and their behaviour is influenced by social context, intentions, motivation, etc. This matters because environmental reductionism ignores other possible influences such as cognition and/or emotional factors which may play a role in human behaviour.

These issues with the different types of reductionism have led psychologists to consider an interactionist point of view. Interactionist ideas come from dualists who believe that there is a physical brain and a non-physical 'mind' which interact. Research by Martin et al. (2001) has found that the mind can affect our biology, as depressed patients receiving psychotherapy experience the same changes in serotonin as those receiving drugs. This suggests that an interactionist approach maybe more appropriate than a reductionist one.

Level 3 (9-12 marks) Top-end

Examiner's comments: AO1: The knowledge is accurate and generally well-detailed. Further examples of environmental and experimental determinism would have helped to develop this section. AO3: The evaluation is generally effective, although limited in the number of points. In particular, the evaluation failed to acknowledge holism and focused only on the limitations of a reductionist approach. The commentary could have explained how a holistic approach may overcome these issues. Furthermore, the answer could have explored the strengths/limitations of experimental reductionism.

Examiner's comments

This is a good description of reductionism; however examples of environmental and experimental would have been good.

This is an excellent description of holism which uses an appropriate example.

This is a good evaluation section, which focuses on the issues with biological reductionism.

There is some further evaluation; however this could have been developed to provide examples of other factors.

This is another good evaluation section; however again, examples of experiments would have enhanced this section.

This is a strong evaluation paragraph; however, the answer fails to acknowledge holism in the discussion.

Topic 6 Idiographic and nomothetic approaches to psychological investigations

Discuss idiographic and nomothetic approaches to psychological investigation. *(16 marks)*

Answer

The distinction between idiographic and nomothetic centres on whether or not we should focus on unique individual experience, or seek to create general laws that explain human behaviour.

The idiographic approach focuses on individuals and emphasises uniqueness. This approach is qualitative in nature, because the focus is on developing an in-depth understanding of human behaviour. Humanistic psychologists also favour the idiographic approach, as they are concerned with studying the whole person. Consequently, the approaches favours quality of information rather than quantity and employs methods such as unstructured interviews, case studies and thematic analysis.

The nomothetic approach tries to formulate general laws of behaviour and is based on the study of groups. Biological psychologists take a nomothetic approach. This approach studies large numbers of people in order to make generalisations and therefore uses quantitative methods.

The idiographic approach has received a lot of criticism in psychology, as the approach is unable to produce general laws/predictions about human behaviour. General predictions are useful in psychology as they allow psychologists to develop drugs that treat psychological conditions. Consequently, some psychologists argue that this inability to produce general laws is a severe limitation. This suggests that the idiographic approach is not suitable for developing psychological treatments and that the nomothetic approach may be more useful in clinical psychology.

Furthermore, many psychologists criticise the approach for being unscientific and time consuming. Methods like case studies and unstructured interviews are often seen as less rigorous because of the type of information they produce. Furthermore, the idiographic approach is based on large quantities of data about one person, which makes the approach less efficient when it comes to data collection.

However, some idiographic approaches are a lot more objective and take steps to ensure validity. For example, qualitative approaches use techniques like reflexivity, where the researcher reflects critically during the research process about factors that might affect the researcher and the participants. Therefore, despite previous criticisms, the idiographic approach attempts to use evidence-based methods and techniques to ensure validity. Furthermore, one strength of the idiographic approach is its relentless focus on the individual. Allport, who was the first to use the term idiographic, argued that a drastic reorientation was needed as psychologists had lost sight of what it was to be human. Allport argued that is only by fully understanding an individual, that we can predict how an individual might act in a given situation. This matters because the idiographic approach has been responsible for refocusing psychology back on the individual.

Despite these strengths and limitations, some psychologists believe that the distinction between idiographic and nomothetic is false. For example, Holt (1967) claims that there is no such thing as a unique individual and that the approach is used to generate general principles, while Millon and David (1996) argue that researchers should start with the nomothetic approach and can then focus on idiographic understanding. Therefore, rather than focusing on these two approaches individually, researchers suggest that both approaches should be used together in order to develop general laws that can then be focused on individuals.

Level 4 (13–16 marks)

Examiner's comments: AO1: The outline is generally well-detailed and highly accurate. Further examples could have been included to demonstrate understanding. AO3: An excellent commentary is provided, outlining both strengths/limitations as well as an effective conclusion.

Examiner's comments

A nice introduction to this approach.

A well-detailed and accurate description of the idiographic approach is provided, with examples.

A reasonable description, although further elaboration could have been included here, giving an example from the biological approach.

This is an effective evaluation point, which highlights an issue with the idiographic approach, drawing a comparison with the nomothetic approach.

This is a reasonably developed point; however, an example would have helped elaborate this section. Furthermore, the final sentence could be developed to explain why this is a problem.

The answer provides a well-detailed counter argument.

Another well-detailed and effective evaluation point.

An excellent and well-detailed final evaluation point that brings together the previous strengths/limitations.

Topic 7 Ethical implications of research studies and theory

Discuss the ethical implications of research studies and theory, including reference to social sensitivity. *(16 marks)*

Answer

The idea of ethics extends beyond the ethical implications involved when conducting research, to considerations involved at every stage of the research process.

According to Sieber and Stanley, there are four key aspects of the research process, where ethical implications should be considered, including: 1) The research question – ensuring that the research question does not add credibility to a prevailing prejudice (e.g. is homosexuality inherited?); 2) The treatment of the participants – ensuring confidentiality of information collected during and after the research process; 3) The institutional context – ensuring that data is not misused, especially when research is funded by private institutions; and 4) The interpretation of findings – ensuring that the findings have no implication for those involved. If appropriate ethical considerations are taken at every stage, then research should be socially sensitive and have no direct social consequence for the participants involved, or for the people they represent.

> While the answer has provided good knowledge about the research process, social sensitivity is only mentioned briefly.

> Further elaboration of the ethical issues involved (e.g. privacy) would have been useful here, to demonstrate understanding.

There are numerous problems associated with conducting socially sensitive research, including the potential impact of the research itself. Even with socially sensitive research, there is the potential for an indirect impact on the participant's family and co-workers, which may not have been taken into consideration. It does not seem sufficient to simply safeguard the interests of the individual participants and therefore researchers need to consider the wider implications of their research to the community. While many would argue that this is the purpose of ethical guidelines, these guidelines may not address the other ways that research may inflict harm on people in society. For example, the current ethical guidelines do not ask researchers to consider how their research might be used by others and could form/shape social public policy. Therefore, Sieber and Stanley recommend that researchers should consider this within the interpretation and application of their findings, to ensure that psychological research does not indirectly harm other members of society. Furthermore, research may disadvantage marginalised groups in society as many groups are often excluded from psychological research, including those with disabilities, the elderly or disadvantaged people, as they are not generally represented in research.

> This is a thorough evaluation point.

> This is a good evaluation point, although an example of how research might shape policy here would be useful.

> This final point is not developed and the answer should say how/why these people could be affected.

Due to the issues with conducting socially sensitive research, including those mentioned above, some psychologists suggest that we should simply avoiding conducting such research. Researchers could avoid researching sensitive areas like homosexuality, race, gender and addiction because the findings may have negative consequences for the participants. However, this would probably leave psychologists with nothing to research but unimportant issues. Another solution would be for psychologists to engage with policy makers, after the publication of their findings. This could help to reduce the likelihood that data is misused and ensure that evidence-based research is used in a socially sensitive way.

> Again, this is a good point, but would be improved with an example.

Level 3 (9–12 marks)

Examiner's comments: AO1: A generally well-detailed outline, although further information in relation to the ethical guidelines should have been presented. AO3: The evaluation is mostly effective and focused on the question, although further elaboration and examples would have improved this section.

Topic 1 Gender in psychology: Gender bias

Explain the difference between alpha bias and beta bias. *(4 marks)*

Examiner's comments

Answer

An alpha bias occurs when a theory assumes that there is a real and enduring difference between males and females. There is a tendency to exaggerate the differences between men and women and therefore devalue one gender. However, a beta bias occurs when a theory ignores or minimises the differences between males and females. For example, Biological psychologists examining the fight-or-flight response typically conduct research using male animals. However, recent research shows that females produce a 'tend-and-befriend' response which meant the female behaviour went undiscovered due to a beta-biased approach.

> The answer has provided a clear example to demonstrate explicit understanding.

Marks awarded: 3–4

Examiner's comments: AO1: This answer has accurately defined both alpha and beta biases and provided an example to further elaborate knowledge of beta bias.

Topic 3 Free will and determinism

Explain the difference between hard determinism and soft determinism. *(3 marks)*

Examiner's comments

Answer

Hard determinism takes the view that all behaviour can be predicted and that humans have no free will whatsoever. Soft determinism takes a less severe view and suggests that humans have an element of free will and although you may be 'determined' to behave in a certain way (because of your biology) we still have an element of choice. Therefore, the key difference is that hard determinism says we have no free will, whereas soft determinism says that we have an element of free will.

> The answer links back to the question succinctly to highlight understanding.

Mark awarded: 3

Examiner's comments: AO1: This answer defines all of the key terms well and reinforces the differences between hard and soft determinism, as required in this question.

Topic 5 Holism and reductionism

Give an example of environmental (stimulus-response) reductionism from an area of psychology that you have studied. *(3 marks)*

Examiner's comments

Answer

An example of environmental determinism comes from the behavioural explanation of phobias. According to behavioural psychologists, phobias can be learnt through classical conditioning, where a neutral stimulus (e.g. a dog) is associated with an unconditioned stimulus (e.g. being bitten), to form a conditioned stimulus (fear of dogs). Furthermore, this behaviour is then reinforced, as people with a fear of dogs avoid encounters with dogs, negatively reinforcing their fear. Environmental reductionism reduces the behaviour of phobias down to a simple stimulus–response (classical and operant conditioning) link.

> The answer embeds examples to highlight knowledge of key terminology.

Marks awarded: 3

Examiner's comments: This is an excellent answer which highlights a clear example of environmental reductionism from the year 1 topic, psychopathology. The answer explains the processes involved well and provides a summary link back to the question in the final sentence.

KEY TERMS

- Evolutionary explanations
- Sexual selection

Possible essay question ...

Discuss evolutionary explanations for partner preferences. *(16 marks)*

Discuss the relationship between sexual selection and human reproductive behaviour. *(16 marks)*

Other possible exam questions ...

+ Explain what is meant by 'sexual selection'. *(2 marks)*

+ Outline the sexual selection explanation of partner preferences. *(4 marks)*

+ Explain **one** limitation of the sexual selection explanation of partner preferences. *(2 marks)*

+ Briefly outline and evaluate the findings of one research study into evolutionary explanations for partner preferences. *(4 marks)*

Think

Make sure that you understand the difference between natural selection (characteristics that provide a survival advantage) and sexual selection (characteristics that provide a reproductive advantage). Quite often these two characteristics are incompatible, for example the peacock's tail.

MUST know ...

Intrasexual and intersexual selection

Darwin developed the theory of **sexual selection**, which explains the evolution of characteristics that offer a reproductive advantage. This occurs in two main ways: **intrasexual selection** and **intersexual selection.**

In intrasexual selection, individuals of the same sex (usually males) must compete with one another to gain access to members of the opposite sex. Consequently, successful individuals are able to mate and pass on their genes.

In intersexual selection, members of the same sex evolve with preferences for certain desirable qualities. Therefore, members of the opposite sex who possess these characteristics will gain a mating advantage and pass on their genes.

 One weakness of the evolutionary explanation comes from…

…research which examines cultural traditions.

- **E** – **Bernstein (2015)** points out that gender differences in mate preference might stem from cultural traditions, rather than being the result of evolved characteristics.

 Another weakness of the evolutionary explanation comes from…

…research which examines female preferences for high-status men.

- **E** – **Buller (2005)** argues that the majority of studies attempting to determine female mate preferences have been carried out on female undergraduates.

 One issue with the research examining evolutionary explanations is…

…that it might not provide a valid measure of mate choice in real life.

- **E** – Critics argue that studies such as **Buss's (1989)** survey have real issues of validity and they only provide us with an indication of expressed preferences.

SHOULD know ...

Long-term mate preferences

According to sexual selection, it pays to be choosy, as the genetic quality of a mate will determine half of the genetic quality of any offspring. By mating with an attractive, high-quality mate, offspring are more likely to be of a higher quality and an individual's genes are more likely to be passed on.

For females, this means being attracted to males who are: 1) able to invest resources in her and her children, 2) are able to physically protect them and 3) show promise as a good parent.

Males are most attracted to females who display signs of fertility, which is an indication of their reproductive value.

- **E** – **Kasser and Sharma (1999)** conducted an analysis of 37 different cultures and found that women value resources far more in cultures where their status and educational opportunities are limited.
- **L** – This suggests that we should not underestimate the role of social and economic factors in mate selection.

- **E** – It could be argued that these women expect to achieve high educational status and so have expectations of higher income levels for both themselves and their partners.
- **L** – Therefore, we may be unable to generalise these claims to non-undergraduate populations.

- **E** – However, some critics suggest that questionnaires, such as the ones used in Buss's study, are in fact a more valid measure than real-life marriage statistics.
- **L** – Therefore, we should be cautious when using the results of research examining evolutionary explanations, because the validity and generalisability of the findings is questionable.

FURTHER EVALUATION

 P – One strength of the evolutionary explanation comes from…

…research which examines mate choice during the menstrual cycle.

- **E** – **Penton-Voak *et al.* (1999)** found that the female mate choice varies across the menstrual cycle.
- **E** – Women chose a slightly feminised male face for a long-term relationship, but a more masculine face for short-term sexual relationships.
- **L** – This suggests that sexual selection favours females who pursue mixed mating strategies under certain conditions, for their own adaptive advantage.

P – Another strength of the evolutionary explanation comes from…

…human traits that serve no survival benefit.

- **E** – For example, a preference for highly creative partners.
- **E** – **Nettle and Clegg (2006)** compared a sample of British poets and artists with a control group and found that creative males had more sexual partners than non-creative males.
- **L** – This suggests that certain characteristics have evolved for sexual selection reasons which provide no survival advantage, for example being an artist.

CHOOSE THE RIGHT ANSWER

Which **one** of the following statements is **false**? (Tick **one** box only.)

A	Females are more attracted to males who show signs of fertility. ☐
B	Females are more attracted to males who are able to provide protection. ☐
C	Females are more attracted to males who show good promise as parents. ☐
D	Females are more attracted to males who are able to invest resources in them and any future offspring. ☐

Answers on page 348

An idea 👍
Here's a chance to conduct some of your own research. Using the internet, look up examples of famous couples (e.g. Catherine Zeta Jones and Michael Douglas, Bill Gates and Melinda Gates) and decide whether the evolutionary explanation of partner preferences can explain these 'selections'. Do these 'everyday' examples support the evolutionary theory?

 MATCH THEM UP

Match up the key terms on the left, with the definitions on the right.

1	Natural selection	**A**	Members of one sex display preference for desirable qualities in potential mates and those who possess these characteristics will gain a mating advantage.
2	Sexual selection	**B**	The evolution of characteristics that provide a reproductive advantage, rather than a survival advantage.
3	Intrasexual selection	**C**	The evolution of characteristics that provide an adaptive survival advantage and not necessarily a reproductive one.
4	Intersexual selection	**D**	Individuals of one sex must outcompete other members of their sex, in order to gain access to members of the opposite sex.

Answers on page 348

APPLYING YOUR KNOWLEDGE

Reuben and Tim are in Year 13 and very attracted to Ashiakia in their Psychology class.

While Ashiakia finds Reuben more attractive, once she finds out that Tim works for Waitrose and that Reuben doesn't have a job, she decides to start dating Tim.

Using your knowledge of evolutionary explanations for partner preferences, explain why Ashiakia starts dating Tim and not Reuben. *(4 marks)*

Identify the psychology		Link to Ashiakia

Answers on page 348

71

KEY TERM

- Matching hypothesis

Possible essay question …

Discuss one or more factors affecting attraction in romantic relationships, for example physical attractiveness and self-disclosure. *(16 marks)*

Other possible exam questions …

+ Explain what is meant by the 'matching hypothesis'. *(2 marks)*
+ Outline the matching hypothesis as it applies to attraction. *(2 marks)*
+ Briefly outline and evaluate the findings of one research study of the matching hypothesis. *(4 marks)*
+ Outline and evaluate the role of physical attractiveness in attraction. *(8 marks)*

 Exam tip

There are two key factors affecting attraction detailed in the specification: physical attractiveness (explained through the 'matching hypothesis') and self-disclosure. Make sure that you know that material on this page, as well as the next, in case you are asked to 'Discuss one or more factors'.

MUST know …

Physical attractiveness (part 1)

Buss's (1989) research on partner preferences demonstrates that men place great importance on physical attractiveness, as physical attractiveness is an important cue to a to a women's health, fertility and reproductive value.

While women also rely on physical attractiveness in the short term, research suggests that physical attractiveness is less important when women describe a 'serious relationship'.

The **matching hypothesis** suggests that individuals seek out partners whose social desirability approximately equals their own. To do this, partners must first assess their own 'value' and then select the best candidate, who would most likely be attracted to them.

 One issue with the claim that men value physical attractiveness comes from…

…research examining speed dating.

- **E – Eastwick and Finkle (2008)** used evidence from speed dating and a longitudinal follow-up to refute this claim. Prior to speed dating, participants demonstrated traditional sex differences in relation to the importance of attractiveness.

 One issue with the matching hypothesis is…

…the belief that matching is more complex than just physical attractiveness.

- **E –** People come into a relationship offering many desirable characteristics. For example, a person might make up for a lack of attractiveness with their charming personality, kindness, etc.

 One strength with the claim that men value physical attractiveness comes from…

…research examining marital satisfaction.

- **E – Meltzer et al. (2014)** found that objective ratings of wives' attractiveness were positively related to the level of their husbands' satisfaction.

SHOULD know …

Physical attractiveness (part 2)

By opting for partners of similar social desirability to ourselves, we can maximise our chances of a successful outcome.

While the matching hypothesis originally proposed that people would pair up with someone as 'socially desirable' as themselves, in terms of a range of assets, over time this has become synonymous with physical attractiveness alone.

Walster et al. (1966) referred to these mating choices as 'realistic' choices, because each individual is influenced by the chances of having their affection reciprocated. Therefore, in reality, people often have to settle for mating 'within their league' whether they want to or not.

- **E –** However, their ideal preferences failed to predict their actual behaviour at the event. No sex differences emerged in terms of physical attractiveness, earning prospects and romantic interest.
- **L –** This suggests that while men and women may value certain characteristics when stating their intentions, their actual behaviour may be very different.

- **E – Sprecher and Hatfield (2009)** refer to this tendency to compensate for a lack of physical attractiveness by offering other desirable traits, as 'complex matching'.
- **L –** This suggests that the matching hypothesis is not based on attractiveness alone, as people are able to attract more attractive partners, by offering compensatory assets.

- **E –** Furthermore, objective ratings of the husbands' physical attractiveness, were not related to wives' marital satisfaction.
- **L –** This supports the idea that men value physical attractiveness, as men with physically attractive wives are more content in their marriages, whereas attractiveness had no effect on females.

 FURTHER EVALUATION

 P – One issue with the matching hypothesis comes from…

…research which examines online dating.

- **E – Taylor et al. (2011)** found no evidence that daters' decisions were driven by similarity between their own and potential partners' physical attractiveness.
- **E –** Instead they found evidence of an overall preference for attractive partners.
- **L –** This suggests that people do not take their own attractiveness into account, but instead aim for someone more desirable than themselves.

P – One final criticism with the claim that men value physical attractiveness comes from…

…research examining long-term relationship satisfaction.

- **E – Pasch and Bradbury (1998)** found that both men and women desire partners who are supportive, trustworthy and warm.
- **E –** Furthermore, partners who demonstrate these qualities tend to be more satisfied with their relationship.
- **L –** This suggests that physical attractiveness is not the most important quality for males and other characteristics may play an important role.

CHOOSE THE RIGHT ANSWER

Which one of the following statements about the matching hypothesis is **false**? (Tick **one** box only.)

According to the matching hypothesis…

A Individuals seek out partners whose social desirability approximately equals their own. ☐

B Individuals must first assess their own 'value'. ☐

C Individuals will select the best available candidates, who are most likely to be attracted to them. ☐

D Individuals opt for partners with greater social desirability to maximise the chances of a successful outcome. ☐

Answers on page 348

 RESEARCH ISSUES

The researcher in the 'Drawing conclusions' activity used a questionnaire to assess partner preference.

> **Hint**
> Look at the evaluation points on the opposite page to help you.

However, the use of questionnaires in relationships is often criticised for not being a valid measure of real-life mate choice.

Outline **one** methodological and **one** ethical issue with using a questionnaire in this experiment. *(4 marks)*

Answers on page 348

 DRAWING CONCLUSIONS

A researcher used a questionnaire to assess the importance of four different qualities for partner selection, in males and females. The results are shown in the graph below.

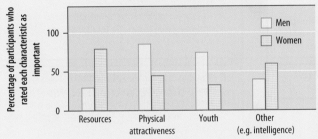

The percentages of males and females who rated four different qualities as important in a questionnaire on partner preferences

What does the bar chart show about partner preferences for men and women and how can psychology explain these findings? *(4 marks)*

Answers on page 348

 APPLYING YOUR KNOWLEDGE

John is talking about his girlfriend, Rachelle. 'We are both in the same Psychology class. She is really good at the topics, like attachment, and I am much better at research methods.

I'm always proud to be seen out with Rachelle, as other guys get really jealous when they see her. We also tell each other everything, there's no secrets in our relationship.'

Using your knowledge of the factors affecting attraction in romantic relationships explain why John and Rachelle are attracted to one another. *(4 marks)*

Identify the psychology	Link to John

Answers on page 348

KEY TERM

■ Self-disclosure

Possible essay question …

Outline and evaluate the role of self-disclosure in attraction.
(16 marks)

Other possible exam questions …

+ Explain what is meant by 'self-disclosure'. *(2 marks)*
+ Outline research into self-disclosure and its importance in attraction. *(4 marks)*

 Exam tip

There are two key factors affecting attraction detailed in the specification: physical attractiveness (explained through the 'matching hypothesis') and self-disclosure. Make sure that you know that material in this topic, as well as Topic 2 in case you are asked to 'Discuss one or more factors'.

MUST know …

Self-disclosure

The term **self-disclosure** refers to the extent to which a person reveals personal information about themselves – their intimate thoughts, feelings and experience.

Self-disclosure is an important aspect of romantic relationships, with greater disclosure leading to greater feelings of intimacy. People reveal more intimate information to those they like and also tend to like those who reveal more intimate information in return.

There is a distinction between **self-disclosure given** and **self-disclosure received** and research has shown that the level of self-disclosure received in a relationship is a better predictor of liking and loving than the level of self-disclosure given.

 One strength for the role of self-disclosure comes from…

…a meta-analysis that supports its role in the development of relationships.

- *E* – **Collins and Miller (1994)** found that people who engage in intimate disclosure tend to be liked more than people who disclose at lower levels.

 However, one issue with the role of self-disclosure comes from…

…research examining internet relationships.

- *E* – Relationships formed over the internet often involve higher levels of self-disclosure in comparison to face-to-face relationships. **Cooper and Sportolari (1997)** refer to this as the 'boom and bust' phenomenon.

 Another strength for the role of self-disclosure is…

…that self-disclosure applies beyond relationships.

- *E* – **Tal-Or and Hershman-Shitrit (2015)** showed that the relationship between gradual self-disclosure and attraction applies beyond relationships, to the liking of reality TV contestants.

SHOULD know …

Types of self-disclosure

Research has found that it is not the self-disclosure itself that predicts relationship satisfaction, but the type of self-disclosure.

Sprecher (1987) found that disclosure of personal experiences including personal disappointment, accomplishments and sexual relationships has a greater influence on relationship satisfaction, in comparison to more 'neutral' types of self-disclosure (e.g. music preferences).

There are norms about self-disclosure; for example, that we should only engage in moderate self-disclosure in the early stages of a relationship, and that we should reciprocate self-disclosure that is given to us. Furthermore, the more one person discloses to another, the more that is expected in return.

- *E* – Furthermore, they also found that the relationship between disclosure and liking was strong if the recipient believed that disclosure was shared only with them, rather than with others.
- *L* – This suggests that self-disclosure has an important role in the development and maintenance of romantic relationships.

- *E* – People reveal more about themselves which causes the relationship to get very intense (boom); however because the underlying trust is not there to support the relationship, it becomes difficult to sustain (bust).
- *L* – This research highlights the potential issues with self-disclosure and reveals the dangers of too much self-disclosure online.

- *E* – Reality TV shows like 'Big Brother' tend to be characterised by very intimate self-disclosure early on; however viewers tend to prefer characters who make more gradual disclosures.
- *L* – This supports the norms of self-disclosure and suggests that people should only engage in moderate self-disclosure in the early stages of relationships.

FURTHER EVALUATION

 P – **However, not all studies have found that…**

…self-disclosure is greater in online relationships (as suggested above).

- *E* – **Knop *et al*. (2016)** revealed that members of a social group disclose more information in face-to-face relationships, in comparison to online interactions.
- *E* – This may be due to the lack of intimacy of internet relationships as a context for self-disclosure.
- *L* – This suggests that self-disclosure is an important component of face-to-face relationships and that we should be cautious when drawing conclusions from internet research.

 P – **A final issue for the role of self-disclosure comes from…**

…cross-cultural research.

- *E* – In the West, people typically engage in more intimate self-disclosure than non-Westerners.
- *E* – Furthermore, cultural norms also shape how comfortable men and women are in self-disclosing. For example, Japanese women prefer a lower level of personal conversation, in comparison to Japanese men.
- *L* – This suggests that the importance of self-disclosure is moderated by the influence of culture and that the principles are not universal.

✔ CHOOSE THE RIGHT ANSWER

Which **one** of the following statements about self-disclosure is **false**? (Tick **one** box only.)

A	Self-disclosure is positively correlated with relationship stability.	☐
B	Neutral self-disclosure is more important than personal self-disclosure.	☐
C	Self-disclosure received is a stronger predictor of liking and loving, in comparison to self-disclosure given.	☐
D	Patterns of self-disclosure are influenced by culture.	☐

Answers on page 348

🧩 MATCH THEM UP

Match up the key terms on the left, with the definitions on the right.

1	Self-disclosure given	**A**	Revealing information about music preferences and general likes/dislikes.
2	Self-disclosure received	**B**	When you reveal your own personal thoughts, feelings and/or experiences.
3	Personal self-disclosure	**C**	Revealing information about personal disappointments, accomplishments and previous sexual relationships.
4	Neutral self-disclosure	**D**	Where you are told information about someone else's thoughts, feelings and/or experiences.

Answers on page 348

✔ A MARKING EXERCISE

Read this student answer to the following exam question: Outline research into self-disclosure and its importance in attraction. *(4 marks)*

Self-disclosure is where a person reveals intimate personal information about themselves to another person. Research suggests that people who disclose more tend to be liked more by other people.

What mark do you think this would get?

YOUR MARK

AO1

Hint
A hint to help you decide: How many critical points have been covered? How much detail is there?

Write an improved answer here…

Answers on page 348

⚙ APPLYING YOUR KNOWLEDGE

Bobby and Chelsea are on their first date. During the date, Bobby tells Chelsea about all of his previous relationships and dominates the conversation. Chelsea is a lot more reserved and only reveals a little information about herself and a recent holiday.

The next day, Chelsea is discussing her date with Jocelyn. She explains that Bobby made her feel uncomfortable and that she probably won't see him again. Likewise, Bobby is talking to his friend Blessed and says that he doesn't think that Chelsea is into him.

Using your knowledge of self-disclosure, explain why Chelsea and Bobby are unlikely to see each other again. *(4 marks)*

Identify the psychology	Link to Chelsea and Bobby
	This means that…
	This means that…

Answers on page 348

KEY TERMS

- Complementarity of needs
- Filter theory
- Similarity in attitudes
- Social demography

Possible essay question …

Discuss the filter theory of attraction in romantic relationships. *(16 marks)*

Other possible exam questions …

+ Outline the filter theory of attraction in romantic relationships. *(6 marks)*
+ Briefly outline the role of 'demography', 'similarity in attitudes' and 'complementarity' as they apply to attraction in romantic relationships. *(3 marks each)*
+ Briefly evaluate the filter theory of attraction in romantic relationships. *(4 marks)*
+ Outline **one** study of the filter theory of attraction in romantic relationships. *(6 marks)*

★ Exam tip

Filter Theory contains a number of key terms (see above) and it is important that you can describe and apply each of they key terms as they can appear as a short-answer question, in addition to an essay.

MUST know …

Filter theory

Kerckhoff and Davis's (1962) filter theory suggests that we choose romantic partners by using a series of filters that narrow down the 'field of availables' from which we might make our choice.

According to Kerckhoff and Davis, different filters are prominent at different stages of partner selection. For example, during the early stages of partner selection, demographic similarities (e.g. class and religion) are the most important factor. Thereafter, similarity of attitudes and underlying values become more important. Finally, partner compatibility and whether the individuals complement one another, is seen to be an important factor for long-term stability.

 One issue with the filter theory is…

…the lack of research support.

- **E** – **Levinger et al. (1970)** examined 330 couples who were 'steadily attached', using questionnaires to assess their relationships, in particular the idea of similarity of attitudes and complementarity of needs.

 However, one strength of filter theory is…

…its application to everyday relationships.

- **E** – According to **Duck (1973),** the filtering process allows people to make predictions about their future interactions, to avoid investing time and effort in relationships that won't work.

 Further support for the filter theory comes from…

…research examining perceived similarity in speed dating.

- **E** – **Tidwell et al. (2013)** examined the idea that perceived similarity in attitudes predicts attraction more than actual similarity does. During speed-dating, decisions about attraction are made over a shorter period of time.

SHOULD know …

The three filters

Social demography is the first filter and refers to variables such as geographical location. Social demography restricts the range of people who are realistically available and therefore we find people within our own social demography more attractive, as we have more in common.

The second filter involves psychological characteristics, specifically whether people agree on basic values. This similarity in attitudes determines whether a relationship will become stable.

Finally, people who have different needs (e.g. the need to be caring and the need to be cared for) like each other because they provide mutual satisfaction known as complementarity of needs.

- **E** – They found no evidence that either similarity of attitudes or complementarity of needs influenced progress towards permanence in relationships.
- **L** – This suggests that the filter theory is not a valid representation of relationship development and that further research and/or other theories are required.

- **E** – Duck claims that people use a variety of strategies to gather information about each other, for example provoking disagreement, to assess similarity in attitudes.
- **L** – Therefore, the filter theory exists to stop people making the wrong choice and then having to live with the consequences.

- **E** – After measuring actual and perceived similarity using a questionnaire, the researchers found that perceived but not actual similarity, predicted romantic liking in couples.
- **L** – This suggests that similarity in attitudes is an important filter in the development of romantic relationships, as outlined in the filter theory.

FURTHER EVALUATION

 P – Another issue with the filter theory is…

…the lack of research support for complementarity of needs.

- **E** – **Dijkstra and Barelds (2008)** examined 760 singles on a dating site who were looking for a long-term mate.
- **E** – The researchers found a strong correlation between the individual's own personality and their ideal partner's personality.
- **L** – This supports a 'similarity-attraction hypothesis' and not a complementarity of needs one, suggesting that this final filter might not be valid.

P – A final issue with the filter theory is…

…that it assumes that values and needs are stable over time.

- **E** – However, attitudes and needs are constantly changing over time.
- **E** – **Thornton and Young-DeMarco (2001)** found evidence of changed attitudes towards relationships in young American adults over a period of a few decades.
- **L** – This poses a problem for the filter theory which fails to take into account the role of constantly changing values, needs and preferences.

✔ CHOOSE THE RIGHT ANSWER

Which **one** of the following statements is **false**? (Tick **one** box only.)

A Filter theory suggests we use a series of filters to narrow down the 'field of availables'. ☐

B Social demography restricts the range of available people for us to meet. ☐

C A relationship will become more stable if we share similarity in attitudes. ☐

D People who have similar needs are more likely to maintain their relationship. ☐

Answers on page 349

✏ FILL IN THE BOXES

In each box below write one sentence describing each of the filters.	In each box below expand the content on the left, writing another 20 words.
Social demography is…	For example…
Similarity in attitudes is…	For example…
Complementarity of needs is…	For example…
OPTIONAL: Levinger *et al.* (1970) found…	This shows…

Answers on page 349

⚙ APPLYING YOUR KNOWLEDGE

Tommy has just joined a new school and psychology class. There are many attractive young ladies in Tommy's new group and he is delighted that he has joined this group.

With reference to the three stages of filter theory, explain how Tommy might form a relationship with someone in his new class.

(a) Identify the psychology *(2 marks)*

(b) Link to Tommy *(2 marks)*

Answers on page 349

👍 An idea

On a separate piece of paper, draw a table with three columns labelled: social demography, similarity in attitudes and complementarity of needs. Then apply each of the filters to yourself, your parents/carers, or even a friend who is in a relationship.

For example, under social demography, what type of people are you likely to meet – which area are they from, which school do they go to, what age are they, what is their social background, etc? Then do this for the other two columns.

Do you agree with the filter theory as an explanation for how we choose romantic partners and can it explain the relationships you've encountered in your life?

KEY TERM

- Social exchange theory

Possible essay question ...

Outline and evaluate the social exchange theory of romantic relationships. *(16 marks)*

Other possible exam questions ...

+ Explain what is meant by the term social exchange as it applies to romantic relationships. *(2 marks)*

+ Outline research into the social exchange theory of relationships. *(6 marks)*

! Think

One consideration of any relationship theory is whether or not it can explain different types of relationships, for example heterosexual, homosexual, arranged marriages and abusive relationships. As you consider each of the different theories in this chapter, consider whether it can explain all of the relationships mentioned above. This could also provide you with an additional evaluation point.

MUST know ...

Social exchange theory, profit and loss

Social exchange theory explains the maintenance of relationships by focusing on the rewards that partners obtain from being in a relationship, weighed against the costs that they incur. Individuals who receive favourable reward/cost outcomes are more likely to be satisfied and maintain their relationship.

According to **Thibaut and Kelley (1959)** individuals attempt to maximise their rewards and minimise their costs. Rewards that we may receive from a relationship include companionship, being cared for, sex, etc. Costs may include effort, financial investments, time, etc.

Social exchange theory stresses that commitment to a relationship is dependent on the profitability of this outcome.

 One strength of the social exchange theory comes from…

…longitudinal research examining the comparison level for alternatives.

- **E** – **Sprecher (2001)** examined 101 dating couples at a US university and found that the presence of alternatives was negatively correlated with both commitment and relationship satisfaction for males and females.

 However, one issue with the social exchange theory is…

…the definition of 'cost' and 'benefit', in terms of relationships.

- **E** – What might be considered rewarding to one person (e.g. constant attention and praise) may be punishing to another (e.g. an irritating behaviour).

 Furthermore, another issue with the social exchange theory is…

…the problem of assessing value.

- **E** – **Nakonezny and Denton (2008)** argue that individuals would need some way of quantifying the value of costs and benefits, in order to assess whether the benefits outweigh the costs.

SHOULD know ...

Comparison level

Thibaut and Kelley also suggest that we develop a comparison level (CL) – a standard against which our relationships are judged.

If we judge that the potential profit of a relationship exceeds our CL, then the relationship will be judged as worthwhile and the person will be seen as an attractive partner.

In addition, we also develop a comparison level for alternatives (CLA) where we weigh up the potential increase in rewards from a different partner, minus any costs associated with ending our current relationship. If the alternate option is more appealing, there will be temptation to leave the current relationship.

- **E** – In other words, in a relationship where the comparison level for alternatives was high, commitment to, and satisfaction with the current relationship tended to be low.
- **L** – This supports social exchange theory and the idea of the CLA, suggesting that individuals continually weigh up the costs and benefits of maintaining a relationship.

- **E** – In addition, what might be a benefit at the start of the relationship, may turn out to be a cost at a later stage of the relationship.
- **L** – This suggests that it is difficult to understand romantic relationships in terms of simple cost/benefit terms.

- **E** – Furthermore, not only is the value difficult to determine, but it is also relative to each individual.
- **L** – This suggests that social exchange theory may work for commercial and economical relationships, but the vagueness and relative value of costs and benefits, do not apply to romantic relationships.

FURTHER EVALUATION

 P – Another issue with the social exchange theory is…

…that it ignores individual differences and other factors.

- **E** – An individual's own beliefs may make them more tolerant of the relatively low ratio of benefits to costs they receive.
- **E** – They may believe that if you have committed to a relationship/marriage, you live with what it brings you.
- **L** – This suggests that the social exchange theory is limited and fails to consider individual differences and other factors.

P – A final strength of the social exchange theory is…

…its application to relationship therapy.

- **E** – Integrated Behavioural Couples Therapy (IBCT) aims to increase the proportion of positive exchanges in a relationship and decrease the proportion of negative exchanges.
- **E** – **Christensen et al. (2004)** treated 40 distressed couples using ICBT and found that two-thirds showed significant improvements.
- **L** – This highlights the positive application of social exchange theory and development of relationship therapies that can help improve troubled relationships.

✓ CHOOSE THE RIGHT ANSWER

Which **one** of the following statements in relation to social exchange theory is **false**? (Tick **one** box only.)

A Individuals attempt to maximise their rewards and minimise their costs. Furthermore, commitment is dependent on the profitability of this outcome. ☐

B If the profit of a new relationship exceeds our comparison level, then that relationship is deemed as worthwhile. ☐

C If the comparison level for alternatives is high, then the rewards of a new partner outweigh the cost of ending the current relationship. ☐

D Research has found that the comparison of alternatives is positively correlated with both commitment and relationship satisfaction. ☐

Answers on page 349

An idea 👍

On a separate piece of paper, draw a diagram to represent the three different ideas of social exchange theory: profit and loss, comparison level, and comparison level for alternatives. For example:

❤ Rewards – Costs

💡 DRAWING CONCLUSIONS

A researcher wanted to examine social exchange theory. He collected data from ten happy couples and ten unhappy couples using a questionnaire. The questionnaire assessed their commitment to their current relationship, their satisfaction and how often they considered alternate relationships (comparison to relations). The bar chart below shows their findings.

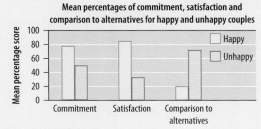

Mean percentages of commitment, satisfaction and comparison to alternatives for happy and unhappy couples

Explain what the bar chart shows, in relation to social exchange theory. *(4 marks)*

Answers on page 349

✓ A MARKING EXERCISE

Read this student answer to the following exam question: Outline research into the social exchange theory of relationships. *(6 marks)*

One study that examined social exchange theory was by Sprecher. Sprecher found that the presence of alternatives was negatively correlated with both commitment and relationship satisfaction for males and females.

What mark do you think this would get?

YOUR MARK

AO1

Hint

A hint to help you decide: How many critical points have been covered? How much detail is there?

Write an improved answer here…

Answers on page 349

KEY TERM

- Equity theory

Possible essay question …

Outline and evaluate the equity theory of romantic relationships. *(16 marks)*

Outline and evaluate the social exchange and/or equity theory of romantic relationships. *(16 marks)*

Other possible exam questions …

+ Explain what is meant by the term equity as it applies to romantic relationships. *(2 marks)*

+ Outline research into the equity theory of romantic relationships. *(6 marks)*

 Link

Many of the key ideas in the evaluation section on this page are linked to concepts explored in Chapter 2 – Issues and debates. Make sure that you understand the terms 'gender bias' and 'cultural bias', which can be used to evaluate equity theory.

MUST know …

Equity theory

Equity theory suggests that people are most comfortable when what they get out of a relationship is roughly equal to what they put in.

The central assumption of equity theory is that people are most comfortable when they perceive they are getting roughly what they deserve from any given relationship.

If people feel over-benefited, they may experience pity, guilt or shame. Whereas, if people feel under-benefited, they may experience anger, sadness, and resentment. The greater the inequity, the greater the dissatisfaction and the more likely someone is to do something about it.

 One issue with the equity theory of relationships is…

…the idea of equity sensitivity.

- *E* – **Huseman et al. (1987)** put the forward the idea of equity sensitivity, suggesting that there are three categories of people: benevolents, equity sensitives and entitleds.

 Another issue with the equity theory of relationships is…

…the idea of gender differences.

- *E* – **DeMaris et al. (2010)** point out that men and women are not equally affected by inequality in romantic relationships. Women tend to perceive themselves as more under-benefited and less over-benefited, compared to men.

 Another issue with the equity theory of relationships is…

…the idea of cultural differences.

- *E* – **Aumer-Ryan et al. (2006)** found that in all the cultures they studied, people considered it important that a relationship or marriage should be equitable.

SHOULD know …

Equity theory and marriages

Schafer and Keith (1980) surveyed married couples of all ages, noting those who felt that their marriages were inequitable, because of an unfair division of domestic responsibilities.

During the child-rearing years, wives often reported feeling under-benefited and husbands over-benefited. As a result, marital satisfaction tended to dip during these years.

However, during the honeymoon and empty-nest-stages (after children have left home), both husbands and wives were more likely to perceive equity and feel satisfied with their marriages, supporting the view that equity is linked to relationship satisfaction.

- *E* – Entitleds prefer to be over-rewarded, having the attitude that they are owed and thus entitled to receive benefits. As a result, they often feel dissatisfied unless they are over-benefiting.
- *L* – This suggests that equity theory is limited and should take into account individual differences, when examining relationships.

- *E* – **Sprecher (1992)** also found that women feel more guilt in response to being over-benefited.
- *L* – As a result, the equity theory fails to take into account these gender differences and is therefore limited in its application to both genders.

- *E* – However, people in different cultures reported differences in how fair they considered their relationship, with men and women from Jamaica claiming that their relationships were the least equitable.
- *L* – Therefore, the equity theory fails to take into account culture differences and norms and can therefore not explain romantic relationships in all cultures.

 **FURTHER EVALUATION**

 P – However, one strength of the equity theory of relationships comes from…

…research on other primates.

- *E* – **Waal (2003)** studied female capuchin monkeys and found that they became very angry if they were denied a reward.
- *E* – If another monkey unfairly received a reward instead, the capuchins grew angry and threw food at the experimenter.
- *L* – This suggests that the perception of inequity has ancient origins and supports the findings of research in human studies.

 P – A final issue with the equity theory of relationships is…

…the idea of causality.

- *E* – **Clark (1984)** argues that in most relationships, couples do not think in terms of rewards. If they do, she claims, it's a sign that their relationship is in trouble.
- *E* – According to this view, dissatisfaction is the cause of inequity and the not the consequence of inequity.
- *L* – Therefore, although inequity and dissatisfaction are linked, the nature of the cause is not clear.

CHOOSE THE RIGHT ANSWER

Which **one** of the following statements is **false**? (Tick **one** box only.)

A	People are most comfortable when the benefits of a relationship are equal to the costs.
B	The greater the inequity, the greater the dissatisfaction.
C	Equity theory takes into account individual differences in equity sensitivity.
D	Males and females place a different level of importance on equity.
E	Cultural norms play an important role in equity perception.

Answers on page 349

 WRITE YOUR OWN EVALUATION POINT

The only strength of equity theory covered here comes from research on primates by Waal (2003). However, many psychologists would argue that research on animals does not apply to humans. Write an extended burger paragraph, using Waal (2003) as a strength, but then exploring this counter-argument in the 'evaluate' section.

Point	One strength of the equity theory comes from research on primates by Waal (2003)
Evidence	[Insert results from Waal (2003)]
Explain	This shows…
Evaluate	However, there are issues with using animal studies to explain human behaviour, for example…
Link	Therefore…

Answers on page 349

 APPLYING YOUR KNOWLEDGE

Emmanuela and Chris have been married for many years and their children Winnifred and Mary have just left home.

While the children were growing up Emmanuela, who had a full-time job, did all of the chores while Chris relaxed in front of the TV every evening. Emmanuela put up with this while the children were growing up. However, now they have left home and she and Chris have retired. The situation has not changed and she is becoming increasingly dissatisfied with her marriage.

Using your knowledge of equity theory, explain why Emmanuela is becoming increasingly dissatisfied. *(2 marks)*

Identify the psychology	Link to Emmanuela

Answers on page 349

MATCH THEM UP

Many of the evaluation points on this page are using ideas explored in Chapter 2 – Issues and debates. Match up the key terms from Chapter 2, with the definitions.

1	Alpha bias	**A**	The differential treatment or representation of men and women based on stereotypes rather than real differences.
2	Beta bias	**B**	The tendency to judge all people in terms of your own cultural assumptions. This distorts or biases your judgement.
3	Cultural bias	**C**	A tendency to ignore or minimise differences between men and women. Such theories tend either to ignore questions about the lives of women, or assume that insights derived from studies of men will apply equally well to women.
4	Cultural relativism	**D**	A tendency to exaggerate differences between men and women. The consequence is that theories devalue one gender in comparison to the other.
5	Gender bias	**E**	The view that behaviour cannot be judged properly unless it is viewed in the context of the culture in which it originates.

Answers on page 349

KEY TERMS

- Commitment
- Investment
- Investment model
- Quality of alternatives/ Comparison with alternatives
- Satisfaction

Possible essay question …

Outline and evaluate the investment model of relationships. *(16 marks)*

Other possible exam questions …

+ Briefly outline the role of 'satisfaction', 'investment', 'quality of alternatives' and 'commitment' within the investment model of relationships. *(3 marks each)*

+ Outline **one** study that has investigated the investment model of relationships. *(4 marks)*

+ Briefly explain **two** criticisms of the investment model of relationships. *(4 marks)*

 Exam tip

AQA uses the term 'comparison with alternatives' whereas the original theory uses the term 'quality of alternatives'. Be aware that these two terms are interchangeable.

MUST know …

The investment model

According to the investment model, relationships persist as a result of three key factors: satisfaction, investment size and quality of alternatives.

Satisfaction is the extent to which the other person fulfils an individual's most important needs.

Investment size is a measure of all the resources that are attached to the relationship and whether or not those resources would diminish in value or be lost if the relationship were to end.

Quality of alternatives refers to the extent to which an individual's most important needs would be better fulfilled outside the current relationship.

 One strength of the investment model comes from…

…research support by **Le *et al*. (2010).**

- **E** – **Le *et al*.** analysed data from nearly 38,000 participants, in 137 studies, over a 33-year-period, to determine the key variables that predicted staying or leaving behaviours.

 However, one issue with the investment model is…

…the difficulty in measuring the different variables, for example, 'satisfaction level'.

- **E** – **Rusbult *et al*. (1998)** developed the 'Investment Model Scale' to overcome this problem, which is seen as a reliable and valid measure.

 Another strength of the investment model is…

…its application to abusive relationships.

- **E** – Victims of partner abuse experience low satisfaction, which would lead us to predict that they would leave the abusive partner, yet many stay.

SHOULD know …

Commitment level

The term commitment level is used to describe the likelihood that a relationship will continue. Commitment is usually high when partners are happy with their relationship and anticipate little gain and high levels of loss, if they were to leave the relationship.

Whereas, commitment is usually low when satisfaction levels and investment in relationship are low and the quality of alternatives is high.

Le and Agnew (2003) carried out a meta-analysis of 52 countries. They found that the correlation between satisfaction and commitment was .68; between commitment and quality of alternative was −.48; and between commitment and investment size was .46.

- **E** – They found that commitment (or lack of it) was a particularly strong predictor of whether or not a relationship would end.
- **L** – This supports the investment model as it suggests that commitment level is an accurate predictor of whether a relationship will persist or not.

- **E** – However, one problem is that the scale relies on self-report measures, which often have issues of social desirability.
- **L** – This matters because it is difficult to measure the key terms of the investment model, as the findings from questionnaires often produce biased results.

- **E** – They may stay due to the lack of alternatives or because they have too much invested in the relationship, making the dissolution too costly.
- **L** – This enables psychologists to understand the reason why many people remain in abusive relationships and develop support for victims.

FURTHER EVALUATION

 P – Another weakness of the investment model is…

…that it fails to consider future investments.

- **E** – **Goodfriend and Agnew (2008)** suggest that the notion of 'investment' should include plans that partners have made regarding the relationship.
- **E** – Consequently, some relationships might persist because of the motivation to see a cherished future plan come to fruition.
- **L** – This suggests that the original investment model is limited and that the idea of future investment should be incorporated into the model.

P – One final strength of the investment model is…

…its application to different cultures and populations.

- **E** – The idea that commitment is positively associated with satisfaction level has been found across many populations.
- **E** – Research supports the relevance of the model in different cultures (e.g. the US, the Netherlands, and Taiwan) and different types of relationship (e.g. married, non-married, gay).
- **L** – This highlights the diverse application of the model in explaining the persistence of relationships in many different populations.

COMPLETE THE DIAGRAM

Match the key terms on the right, with the diagram on the left.

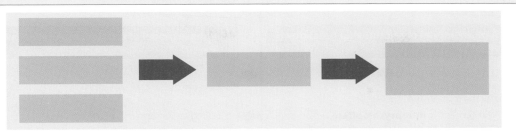

- Future stay or leave decision
- Satisfaction
- Commitment levels
- Investments
- Alternatives

Answers on page 349

 DRAWING CONCLUSIONS

Le and Agnew (2003) conducted a meta-analysis of 52 countries. Across all the studies, satisfaction level was correlated with the three aspects of the investment model. The correlation coefficients are displayed in the table below.

	Commitment	Quality of alternatives	Investment size
Satisfaction level	0.68	−0.48	0.46

Correlation coefficients

What can you conclude from the correlation coefficients displayed in the table above, in relation to the investment model? *(4 marks)*

Answers on page 349

 MATCH THEM UP

Match up the key terms on the left, with the definitions on the right.

1	Commitment	**A**	A measure of the degree to which the current partner gratifies a person's important needs.
2	Investment	**B**	A measure of all the resources attached to the relationship (e.g. financial, shared children), which would be lost if the relationship were to end.
3	Satisfaction	**C**	An individual's assessment of whether their needs might be better fulfilled by somebody other than their current partner.
4	Quality of alternatives	**D**	The likelihood that an individual will persist with their current relationship.

Answers on page 349

 A MARKING EXERCISE

Read this student answer to the following exam question:
Briefly explain two criticisms of the investment model of relationships.
(4 marks)

One issue with the investment model is that it is difficult to measure the different factors, e.g. commitment levels. Another issue is that it doesn't consider future investments.

What mark do you think this would get?

YOUR MARK

AO1

Hint
A hint to help you decide:
How many critical points have been covered?
How much detail is there?

Write an improved answer here…

Answers on page 349

KEY TERMS

- Duck's phase model of relationship breakdown
- Dyadic phase
- Grave-dressing phase
- Intrapsychic phase
- Social phase

Possible essay question …

Outline and evaluate Duck's phase model of relationship breakdown. (16 marks)

Other possible exam questions …

+ Explain what is meant by the terms 'intrapsychic phase', 'dyadic phase', 'social phase' and 'grave-dressing phase'. *(2 marks each)*
+ Give **two** criticisms of Duck's phase model of relationship breakdown. *(3 marks + 3 marks)*

! Think

Duck (1982) proposed a model of relationship breakdown that describes the different phases that people go through during the dissolution of a romantic relationship. As we saw in Topic 7, inequitable relationships create dissatisfaction which may be the first step in the eventual breakup.

MUST know …

A phase model of relationship breakdown (Part 1)

The first phase is called **breakdown**, which is where one partner becomes distressed with the way the relationship is going.

Next comes the **intrapsychic phase**, which is characterised by negativity and the thought that they might be better off out of the relationship.

In the **dyadic phase** individuals confront their partners and begin to discuss their feelings about their discontentment.

When the dissatisfaction spills over into friends and family, this is when the **social phase** begins.

Finally, if the relationship ends, the person attempts to justify their actions, which is known as the **grave-dressing phase**.

 One issue with Duck's model is…

…that it fails to acknowledge personal growth.

- **E** – Duck revised his model in 2006 and introduced a new model, with a final phase called 'resurrection processes' (Rollie and Duck, 2006).

 Another issue with Duck's model is…

…that the nature of the social phase is dependent on the type of relationship.

- **E** – For teenagers and young adults, romantic relationships are seen as more unstable and as a result, individuals may receive no real reconciliation, during the social phase.

 One strength of Duck's model comes from…

…research support for grave-dressing.

- **E** – **Monroe et al. (1999)** found that students who experienced the end of a romantic relationship for the first time, had a greater risk of developing depression.

SHOULD know …

A phase model of relationship breakdown (Part 2)

Relationships which are inequitable are more likely to create dissatisfaction, which leads to breakdown.

During the intrapsychic phase an individual may not express their dissatisfaction publically, but rather in other ways, for example social withdrawal.

Feelings of guilt and anger are likely to surface; however, the relationship might be saved if both partners are motivated to do so.

The distress is now made public and others may provide advice/support.

Here each partner must present themselves as being trustworthy and loyal, if they are to attract a new partner.

- **E** – Duck stressed that for many people, this is an opportunity to move beyond the distress associated with ending a relationship and engage in the process of personal growth.
- **L** – This suggests that the original model provided a limited account of relationship breakdown and failed to acknowledge the entire process.

- **E** – However, older people in longer-term relationships may be involved in social processes that are characterised by obvious attempts to rescue the current relationship.
- **L** – This suggests that the social phase is far more complicated than Duck originally described and that individual (in particular age) differences may play an important role.

- **E** – However, **Tashiro and Frazier (2003)** found that individuals feel better about the end of a relationship when they focus on the situation, rather than their own flaws.
- **L** – This highlights the importance of grave-dressing as the individual is able to create their own story of the breakup that doesn't affect their psychological well-being.

FURTHER EVALUATION

 P – One issue with research examining the breakdown of relationships is…

…the ethical issues involved.

- **E** – Carrying out research in this area raises issues of privacy, confidentiality, protection from harm, etc.
- **E** – This is particularly difficult when dealing with vulnerable individuals attempting to cope with the stress of a relationship breakup.
- **L** – Therefore, it is important that psychologists consider ethical guidelines and ensure that the benefits of undertaking the research outweigh the risks.

P – A final strength of Duck's model is…

…its application to relationship therapy and intervention.

- **E** – If the relationship is in the intrapsychic processes phase, repair might involve re-establishing liking for the partner and re-evaluating their behaviour in a more positive light.
- **E** – During the social phase, people outside the relationship may be able to help partners work out their differences.
- **L** – This highlights the positive application of Duck's model to help resolve relationship issues.

CHOOSE THE RIGHT ANSWER

Which **one** of the following outlines the correct sequence of breakdown, according to Duck's phase model? (Tick **one** box only.)

A Breakdown, dyadic, social, grave-dressing, intrapsychic ☐

B Breakdown, intrapsychic, social, grave-dressing, dyadic ☐

C Breakdown, intrapsychic, dyadic, social, grave-dressing ☐

D Breakdown, intrapsychic, social, dyadic, grave-dressing ☐

Answers on page 350

 APPLY YOUR KNOWLEDGE

Tola is going through a breakup with her long-term partner, Tamer.

She originally tried to talking to Tamer to explain that she was unhappy with their relationship; however, he simply didn't listen. She is now talking to her best friend Abena, who tells her to move on because: 'There's plenty more fish in the sea' and 'He was no good for you anyway'.

Which **two** of Duck's phases of relationship breakdown has Tola gone through? Justify your choice. *(4 marks)*

Identify the psychology	Link to Tola

Answers on page 350

 MATCH THEM UP

Match up the key terms on the left with the definitions on the right.

1	Breakdown	**A**	Going public; seeking support from third parties. Denigration of partner, alliance building.
2	Intrapsychic	**B**	Uncertainty, anxiety, hostility, complaints. Discussion of discontents.
3	Dyadic	**C**	Tidying up memories; making relational histories. Stories prepared for different audiences.
4	Social	**D**	Dissatisfaction with the relationship
5	Grave-dressing	**E**	Social withdrawal. Brooding on partner's faults and relational costs. Re-evaluation of alternatives.

Answers on page 350

RESEARCH ISSUES

A psychologist wanted to investigate Duck's phase model of relationship breakdown.

The psychologists recruited ten males and ten females who had recently gone through a divorce, using a volunteer sampling method. The participants were all interviewed and asked a series of questions to explore whether or not their divorce followed the stages outline by Duck.

Identify **two** ethical issues that the researcher would need to consider in this research. Suggest how the researcher could deal with each ethical issue. *(4 marks)*

Answers on page 350

Key Terms

- Gates
- Self-disclosure
- Virtual relationships

Possible essay question …

Outline and evaluate the nature of virtual relationships in social media. *(16 marks)*

Other possible exam questions …

+ Explain what is meant by the term 'virtual relationship'. *(2 marks)*
+ Outline the nature of self-disclosure in virtual relationships. *(4 marks)*
+ Outline the effect of absence of gating in virtual relationships. *(4 marks)*

! Think

In 2015, Facebook had over 1.39 billion users worldwide, with more than 890 million of these logging on every day. It could be argued that data gathered on such a large scale is a clear example of the nomothetic approach (see Chapter 2). However, is this a strength or a limitation for theories examining virtual relationships?

MUST know …

Self-disclosure in virtual relationships

Research has shown that there are differences in the way that people conduct virtual relationships, which include: higher levels of **self-disclosure** and the removal of **gates**.

Self-disclosure in the virtual world allows individuals to present an 'edited' version of themselves to others.

People feel more secure with disclosing intimate and sensitive information in private online as the anonymity of internet interactions greatly decreases the risk of self-disclosures, because people can share their inner thoughts and feelings with much less fear of disapproval and social sanctions.

 One strength of virtual relationships and social media is…

…the growing importance of the internet for romantic relationships.

- **E** – **Rosenfeld and Thomas (2012)** examined 4,000 US adults and found that individuals with internet access at home were far more likely to have partners, and less likely to be single.

 Another strength of virtual relationships is…

…that online relationships can be just as strong as offline relationships.

- **E** – It is often claimed that internet communication can only lead to superficial relationships that do not compare with the richness of face-to-face relationships.

Further support for virtual relationship comes from…

…research examining the biological basis of self-disclosure.

- **E** – **Tamir and Mitchell (2012)** found increased MRI activity in two brain regions that are associated with rewards, the nucleus accumbens and ventral tegmental area.

SHOULD know …

Absence of gating in virtual relationships

In online relationships there is an absence of barriers or 'gates' that normally limit the opportunities for less attractive, shy or less socially skilled people to form relationships.

Zhao et al. (2008) found that online social networks such as Facebook can empower 'gated' individuals to present the identities they hope to establish, but are unable to in face-to-face situations.

Furthermore, **Yurchisin et al. (2005)** interviewed 11 online daters and found that these individuals tended to give accounts of both their real and better selves in dating profiles, as a way of attracting a potential partner.

- **E** – Of these 4,000 individuals, 71.8% of those who had internet access at home had a spouse or romantic partner. For those who didn't have internet access the figure was just 35.9%.
- **L** – This suggests that the internet plays an important role in the development of romantic relationships.

- **E** – However, **Rosenfeld and Thomas (2012)** found no evidence to support this and found comparable quality in both online and offline relationships.
- **L** – This supports the role that the internet plays in the development of romantic relationships which according to Rosenfeld and Thomas are no different to face-to-face relationships.

- **E** – These areas were strongly activated when people were talking about themselves, and less so when they were talking about someone else.
- **L** – These findings suggest that the human tendency to share our personal experiences with others over social media may arise from the rewarding nature of self-disclosure.

FURTHER EVALUATION

 P – Another strength of virtual relationships is…

…that they improve the quality of relationships for shy people.

- **E** – **Baker and Oswald (2010)** surveyed 207 male and female students about their shyness, Facebook usage and the quality of their friendships.
- **E** – They found that for students who scored high for shyness, greater use of Facebook was associated with higher perceptions of friendship quality.
- **L** – This highlights the positive role of virtual relationships for shy individuals.

 P – A final strength of online relationships is…

…that they have positive consequences for offline relationships.

- **E** – **Zhao et al. (2008)** claim that relationships formed online have positive consequences for people's offline lives.
- **E** – The development of virtual relationships online allows some individuals to bypass gating obstacles and create the sort of identity that they would be unable to create in the offline world.
- **L** – This provides further support to the role of internet relationships, which may increase chances to connect to others in the offline world.

CHOOSE THE RIGHT ANSWER

Which **one** of the following statements is **false**?

A	Individuals feel more secure in disclosing sensitive information online.	☐
B	Higher levels of self-disclosure are the result of the psychological effects of anonymity.	☐
C	Gates are barriers that increase opportunities for less attractive people.	☐
D	The absence of gates enables people to project a 'socially desirable' self.	☐

Answers on page 350

 WRITE YOUR OWN EVALUATION POINT

Tamir and Mitchell (2012) provide evidence to support the biological basis of self-disclosure. They found increased MRI activity in two brain regions that are associated with rewards, the nucleus accumbens and ventral tegmental area. However, there are issues with establishing cause and effect using MRI scans. Using these key ideas, write an extended burger paragraph which includes a counter-argument in the evaluate section

Point	Support for virtual relationships comes from research examining the biological basis of self-disclosure.
Evidence	[Insert results from Tamir and Mitchell (2012)]
Explain	This shows…
Evaluate	However…
Link	Therefore…

Answers on page 350

 **APPLYING YOUR KNOWLEDGE**

Deon has just started a new sixth-form college and is rather shy. He finds it very difficult to talk to females and often says really silly things.

However, he finds it's much easier to talk to girls at college on social media and feels a lot more popular.

Using your knowledge of virtual relationships in social media, explain why Deon finds it easier to conduct his relationships online. *(4 marks)*

Identify the psychology	Link to Deon

Answers on page 350

 A MARKING EXERCISE

Read this student answer to the following exam question:
Outline the nature of self-disclosure in virtual relationships. *(4 marks)*

Self-disclosure is when a person reveals intimate information about themselves. People are often happier to disclose more intimate and sensitive information online, which makes relationships easier.

What mark do you think this would get?

YOUR MARK
AO1

Write an improved answer here…

Answers on page 350

Possible essay question …

Outline and evaluate explanations of parasocial relationships. *(16 marks)*

Other possible exam questions …

+ Explain what is meant by the term 'parasocial relationship'. *(2 marks)*
+ Outline the levels of parasocial relationships. *(4 marks)*
+ Outline the absorption addiction model of parasocial relationships. *(4 marks)*
+ Outline the attachment theory explanation of parasocial relationships. *(4 marks)*

 Think

An 18-year-old Michael Jackson fan reported that after her father left her family, Jackson became a substitute source of comfort for her. Which explanation of parasocial relationships does this support and why?

MUST know …

An attachment theory explanation

Parasocial relationships (PSRs) are one-sided relationships, where one person expends considerable emotional energy, while the other person is unaware of their existence. PSRs may function like real-life relationships in terms of attachment behaviours. **Weiss (1991)** identified three key attachment behaviours involved in PSRs:

1. Proximity seeking – the individual will attempt to reduce the distance between themselves and their attachment figure.

2. Secure base – the mere presence of the attachment figure provides a sense of security. There is little or no chance of rejection.

3. Protest at disruption – the best marker of attachment is the presence of distress following the separation of the attachment figure.

 One strength of theories explaining PSRs comes from…

…research support by **Schiappa et al. (2007).**

- **E** – **Schiappa et al.** carried out a meta-analysis that explored factors that were key in the formation of PSRs and found support for the idea that people with higher PSRs watched more TV.

 Another strength of theories explaining PSRs comes from…

…research suggesting that PSRs are linked to isolation and loneliness.

- **E** – **Greenwood and Long (2009)** found that individuals may develop PSRs as a way of dealing with feelings of loneliness or loss.

EVALUATION One strength of the absorption addiction model comes from…

…research examining personality characteristics.

- **E** – **Maltby et al. (2003)** used the *Eysenck Personality Questionnaire* to assess the relationship between PSRs and personality.

SHOULD know …

The absorption addiction model

According to the absorption addiction model, individuals can become psychologically absorbed with a celebrity which might then take on an addictive component. **Giles and Maltby (2006)** identify three levels in this process:

1. Entertainment-social – fans are attracted to their favourite celebrity and will watch them, keep up-to-date with them, and learn about their celebrity for entertainment purposes.

2. Intense-personal – this level involves a deeper level of involvement and reflects intensive and compulsive feelings about the celebrity.

3. Borderline-pathological – This level is characterised by overidentification with the celebrity and uncontrollable behaviours and fantasies about their lives.

- **E** – They also found that there was a significant positive relationship between the degree to which a person perceived TV characters as real and the tendency to form PSRs.
- **L** – This supports the idea that people in PSRs engage in proximity seeking behaviours, as outlined by Weiss (1991).

- **E** – Furthermore, **Eyal and Cohen (2006)** found evidence of a link between PSRs and loneliness experienced in a parasocial 'breakup' (e.g. the end of a TV series).
- **L** – This suggests that PSRs may not only compensate for feelings of loneliness, but their loss can also create feelings of loneliness.

- **E** – They found that the intense-personal level was associated with neuroticism (i.e. tense, emotional and moody), which is also related to anxiety and depression.
- **L** – This not only supports the absorption addiction model, but highlights a way to identify people at risk of PSRs and psychological disorders like anxiety and depression.

FURTHER EVALUATION

 P – One strength of the attachment theory of PSRs comes from…

…research investigating loss of a PSR and attachment styles.

- **E** – **Cohen (2004)** studied 381 adults and their relationships with their favourite TV character and attachment style.
- **E** – Viewers expecting to lose their favourite characters anticipated negative reactions, which were related to their attachment style, with anxious-ambivalently reacting the most negatively.
- **L** – This provides some support for the idea that PSRs can be explained though attachment theory.

 P – A final strength of theories examining PSRs comes from…

…research highlighting cultural similarities.

- **E** – **Schmid and Klimmt (2011)** investigated whether there would be differences in the PSRs formed with Harry Potter in two different cultures.
- **E** – Despite examining two different cultures, Germany and Mexico showed similar patterns of PSRs.
- **L** – This suggests that PSRs are similar in different cultures demonstrating the universal influence of mainstream media.

✔ CHOOSE THE RIGHT ANSWER

Which **one** of the following statements is **false**? (Tick **one** box only.)

A PSRs are two-way relationships where one person expends considerably more emotional energy.	☐
B PSRs typically develop with television celebrities.	☐
C PSRs give the illusion of an actual relationship through high levels of media (e.g. television and internet).	☐
D The association is so strong that the celebrity becomes a meaningful figure in the person's life.	☐

Answers on page 350

◈ MATCH THEM UP

Match up the key terms on the left, with the definitions in the centre and the examples on the right.

1	Proximity seeking	**A**	An individual will experience prolonged stress following separation or loss.	**i**	The attachment provides the individual with a 'safe haven' as there is little or no chance of rejection.
2	Secure base	**B**	The presence of the attachment figures provides a sense of security.	**ii**	An individual may collect trivia, will rearrange schedules to see them on TV.
3	Protest at disruption	**C**	An individual attempts to reduce the distance between themselves and their attachment figure.	**iii**	An individual may 'want to cry' at the loss of their favourite character on TV.

Answers on page 350

✎ FILL IN THE BOXES

In each box below write one sentence describing each process of the absorption addiction model.	In each box below expand the content on the left, writing another 20 words, by providing an example.
Entertainment-social is…	For example, …
Intense-personal is…	For example, …
Borderline-pathological is…	For example, …

Answers on page 350

✔ A MARKING EXERCISE

Read this student answer to the following exam question:

Outline the absorption addiction model of parasocial relationships. *(4 marks)*

The addiction model suggests that PSRs form through three levels. Firstly, the fan is attracted to the celebrity, secondly they will become obsessed and thirdly addicted.

What mark do you think this would get?

YOUR MARK

AO1

Hint
A hint to help you decide:
How many critical points have been covered?
How much detail is there?

Write an improved answer here…

Answers on page 350

Topic 1 Evolutionary explanations for partner preferences

Discuss evolutionary explanations for partner preferences. *(16 marks)*

Examiner's comments

Evolutionary explanations for partner preferences focus on the adaptive nature of behaviour and how/why certain partner preferences are beneficial for reproductive sexual selection.

> This is a clear introduction to evolutionary theory.

Darwin proposed the theory of sexual selection which explains the evolution of characteristics that offer a reproductive advantage. There are two main types of sexual selection, including: intrasexual selection and intersexual selection. With intrasexual selection, individuals of the same sex (usually males) must compete with one another in order to gain access to members of the opposite sex. However, in intersexual selection, members of the same sex evolve with preferences for certain desirable qualities in their mates.

> It would be beneficial to provide examples, to demonstrate further understanding.

Males and females have evolved with different preferences. Females are typically attracted to males who are: 1) able to invest resources in her and her children, 2) are able to physically protect them and 3) show promise as a good parent, whereas males are most attracted to females who display signs of fertility, which is an indication of their reproductive value. These differences are the result of different levels of investment males and females provide during the reproductive process.

> The differences between males / females has been outlined in terms of paternal investment, although further elaboration would have been useful.

Evolutionary explanations for partner preferences have received a lot of criticism, as they are unable to explain cultural differences and the research support is severely limited.

Bernstein (2015) points out that gender differences in mate preference might stem from cultural traditions, rather than being the result of evolved characteristics. Furthermore, Kasser and Sharma (1999) conducted an analysis of 37 different cultures and found that women value resources far more in cultures where their status and educational opportunities are limited. These results cannot be explained in terms of evolution alone and suggest that we should not underestimate the role of social and economic factors in mate selection.

> An effective evaluation point, using two theorists to support this criticism.

Furthermore, Buller (2005) argues that the majority of studies examining evolutionary explanations have been carried out on female undergraduates. It could be argued that these women expect to achieve high educational status and so have expectations of higher income levels for both themselves and their partners and therefore, we may be unable to generalise these claims to non-undergraduate populations. Furthermore, studies like Buller (2005) have real issues of validity, as they only provide us with an indication of expressed preferences. Therefore, we should be cautious when using the results of such studies as they only provide us with a person's intention and not their actual behaviour and we are unable to conclude that females would display these same partner preferences when it comes to selecting a real partner.

> There are two effective evaluative points here, highlighting the weaknesses of research support for evolutionary explanations.

However, despite these limitations, certain partner preferences appear to support the idea of sexual selection. For example, research has found that a preference for highly creative partners has characterised mate choice throughout evolutionary history. Nettle and Clegg (2006) found that creative males had more sexual partners than non-creative males. This suggests that certain characteristics have evolved for sexual selection reasons alone, despite their lack of survival advantage. Therefore, despite the criticisms of evolutionary research, certain behaviours are difficult to explain for any other reason and many partner preferences make intuitive sense, given the different levels of parental investment of males/females.

> The answer outlines an interesting strength linked to sexual selection and provides a good concluding sentence.

Level 4 (13–16 marks)

Examiner's comments: AO1: The answer provides a good outline, although further examples would help to demonstrate a more explicit understanding. AO3: The evaluation is thorough and effective throughout and has provided an interesting commentary, outlining the weaknesses, but also bringing in some interesting support for the idea of sexual selection.

Topic 2 Physical attractiveness

Discuss one or more factors affecting attraction in romantic relationships, for example physical attractiveness and self-disclosure. *(16 marks)*

Examiner's comments

There are two key factors affecting attraction in romantic relationships: physical attractiveness and self-disclosure.

Buss's (1989) research on partner preferences demonstrates that men place great importance on physical attractiveness, as physical attractiveness is an important cue to a to a women's health, fertility and reproductive value. While women also rely on physical attractiveness in the short-term, research suggests that physical attractiveness is less important when describing 'serious relationships'. Therefore, while physical attractiveness maybe an important factor affecting attraction for men, it is only important for women in the short term.

> Accurate knowledge in relation to attractiveness, drawing on research by Buss.

Another factor affecting attraction is self-disclosure, which is the sharing of personal/intimate information. Greater disclosure leads to greater feelings of intimacy. People reveal more intimate information to those they like and also tend to like those who reveal more intimate information in return. Therefore, the revealing of personal/intimate information appears to be an equally important factor in attraction for both males and females.

> A second factor (self-disclosure) is presented in detail, with an interesting link to males and females.

However, the claim that men value physical attractiveness has produced mixed findings in psychological research. Eastwick and Finkle (2008) used evidence from speed dating and a longitudinal follow-up to refute this claim. Prior to speed dating, participants demonstrated traditional sex differences in relation to the importance of attractiveness. However, their ideal preferences failed to predict their actual behaviour at the event. No sex differences emerged in terms of physical attractiveness and romantic interest, suggesting that while men and women may value certain characteristics when stating their intentions, their actual behaviour may be very different. On the other hand, Meltzer et al. (2014) found that objective ratings of wives' attractiveness were positively related to the level of their husbands' satisfaction, at the beginning of a marriage. Furthermore, objective ratings of the husbands' physical attractiveness, were not related to wives' marital satisfaction. This supports the idea that men value physical attractiveness, as men with physically attractive wives are more content in their marriages, whereas attractiveness had no effect on females. These results support the idea that attractiveness is not an important quality for females, both in terms of dating and marriage.

> A thorough and effective evaluation point.

> A second evaluation point is weaved into this paragraph.

> Effective evaluation, linking back to the earlier male / female distinction.

The role of self-disclosure has found more consistent results. Collins and Miller (1994) found that people who engage in intimate disclosure tend to be liked more than people who disclose at lower levels. This suggests that self-disclosure has an important role in the development and maintenance of romantic relationships.

> An effective evaluation point supporting the role of self-disclosure.

However, the role of self-disclosure is to some extent influenced by culture. In the West, people typically engage in more intimate self-disclosure. Furthermore, cultural norms also shape how comfortable men and women are in self-disclosing. For example, Japanese women prefer a lower level of personal conversation, in comparison to Japanese men. This suggests that the importance of self-disclosure is moderated by the influence of culture and that the principles are not universal.

> An interesting evaluation point drawing on cultural differences.

Therefore, while the research into attractiveness has only supported the idea that females don't value attractiveness in terms of dating/marriage, the results of research into disclosure suggest that disclosure is an important factor in relation to attraction, although it is moderated to some extent by culture.

> An excellent conclusion, drawing these two factors together effectively.

Level 4 (13–16 marks)

Examiner's comments: AO1: An interesting, accurate and well-detailed outline, drawing on two different factors with links to male/female behaviour. AO3: A balanced commentary evaluating both factors and drawing a solid conclusion to demonstrate depth of understanding.

Topic 3 Self-disclosure

Outline research into self-disclosure and its importance in attraction. *(4 marks)*

Examiner's comments

Sprecher et al. (2013) investigated whether reciprocal self-disclosure was more important in determining attraction, than one-sided self-disclosure. 156 students were placed into two-person dyads. Each dyad engaged in self-disclosure tasks over Skype. In the reciprocal condition, each member took turns in asking questions and disclosing. In the non-reciprocal condition only one person asked questions, while the other person disclosed. The researchers found that in the reciprocal condition, dyads reported more liking, closeness and perceived similarity in comparison to the non-reciprocal condition.

> This answer has provided accurate details from the study, including the number of participants and the different conditions, to demonstrate clear knowledge.

These results clearly highlight the importance of self-disclosure in attraction, as those engaging with disclosure reported more liking and closeness – two signs of attraction.

Marks awarded: 3–4

Examiner's comments: AO1: This answer has provided a detailed outline of the aim, method and results of Sprecher. Furthermore, a clear link to the question (the importance of attraction) has been drawn in the concluding sentence.

Topic 4 Attraction: Filter theory

Outline the filter theory of attraction in romantic relationships. *(6 marks)*

Examiner's comments

Kerckhoff and Davis's (1962) filter theory suggests that we choose romantic partners by using a series of filters that narrow down the 'field of availables' from which we might make our choice.

According to Kerckhoff and David, different filters are prominent at different stages of partner selection. For example, during the early stages of partner selection, the first filter is social demography, where we narrow down our selection based on variables such as geographical location. Social demography restricts the range of people who are realistically available and therefore we find people within our own social demography more attractive, as we have more in common. Thereafter, the second filter involves 'similarity of attitudes' and whether or not people agree on basic values and principles. It is this filter that determines whether the relationship will become stable. The final filter involves partner compatibility and whether the individuals complement one another (known as complementarity of needs). This filter means that people who have different needs like each other, because they provide mutual satisfaction for one another.

> The answer not only outlines the name of the stage, but provides a clear example linked to relationships.

Mark awarded: 5–6

Examiner's comments: AO1: This is an accurate answer which is generally well-detailed. All three filters are outlined with clear examples which demonstrate understanding throughout this answer. There is clarity and organisation, although a separate paragraph for each of the three filters would have made the answer easier to follow.

Topic 5 Social exchange theory

Outline and evaluate the social exchange theory of romantic relationships. *(16 marks)*

Social exchange theory attempts to explain the maintenance of relationships by focusing on reward/cost outcomes. Individuals who receive favourable reward/cost outcomes are more likely to be satisfied and maintain their relationship.

According to Thibaut and Kelley (1959) individuals attempt to maximise their rewards and minimise their costs. Rewards include things like companionship, being cared for, sex, whereas costs may include effort, financial investment, time, etc. Social exchange theory stresses that commitment to a relationship is dependent on the profitability of this outcome.

However, according to Thibaut and Kelley we also have a comparison level (CL) – a standard against which our relationships are judged. In addition, we also develop a comparison level for alternatives (CLA) where we weigh up the potential increase in rewards from a different partner, minus any costs associated with ending our current relationship. If the alternate option is more appealing, there will be temptation to leave the current relationship.

Social exchange theory has received a lot criticism and one of the main issues centres on the definitions of 'cost' and 'benefit'. What might be considered rewarding to one person (e.g. constant attention and praise) may be punishing to another (e.g. an irritating behaviour). In addition, what might be a benefit at the start of the relationship, may turn out to be a cost at a later stage of the relationship. This suggests that it is difficult to understand romantic relationships in terms of costs and benefits. In addition, some psychologists suggest that these terms are difficult to quantify. Nakonezny and Denton (2008) argue that individuals would need some way of quantifying the value of costs and benefits, in order to assess whether the benefits outweigh the costs. Furthermore, not only is the value difficult to determine, but it is also relative to each individual. An individual's own beliefs may make them more tolerant of the relatively low ratio of benefits to costs they receive, which makes this theory difficult to generalise. This suggests that social exchange theory may work for commercial and economical relationships, but the vagueness and difficulty in measuring these terms makes it difficult to apply this theory to romantic relationships.

However, one strength of the social exchange theory comes from longitudinal research examining the comparison level for alternatives. Sprecher (2001) examined 101 dating couples at a US university and found that the presence of alternatives was negatively correlated with both commitment and relationship satisfaction for males and females. This supports the social exchange theory and the idea of the CLA, suggesting that individuals continually weigh up the costs and benefits of maintaining a relationship.

Furthermore, social exchange theory has led to the development of a relationship therapy called Integrated Behavioural Couples Therapy (IBCT). IBCT aims to increase the proportion of positive exchanges in a relationship and decrease the proportion of negative exchanges. Christensen et al. (2004) treated 40 distressed couples using ICBT and found that two-thirds showed significant improvements. This highlights the positive application of social exchange theory and development of relationship therapies that can help improve troubled relationships.

Level 4 (13–16 marks)

Examiner's comments: AO1: An accurate and well detailed account of social exchange theory is presented, although further exploration of CL would have been useful. AO3: A very well-written evaluation section, weaving multiple criticisms into one paragraph effectively, before presenting two strengths. There was a missed opportunity for further evaluation, although overall this was an excellent commentary.

Examiner's comments

A good introduction, providing a basic outline.

Knowledge is evident and well-detailed. Examples are used to demonstrate understanding.

Although knowledge is clear, further explanation of the CL would have been useful.

Good knowledge of the CLA is presented.

Effective evaluation, outlining problem with defining cost/benefits.

Further evaluation embedded, outlining the issue with quantifying cost/benefits.

Even further evaluation highlighting individual differences is outlined, with a strong concluding sentence.

While this is a good evaluation point, given the previous criticisms, further evaluation of a student sample could have been included here.

An effective evaluation point highlighting the positive application of social exchange theory.

Topic 6 Equity theory

Outline research into the equity theory of romantic relationships. *(6 marks)*

Examiner's comments

One study that supports the equity theory was conducted by Schaffer and Keith (1980). They surveyed married couples of all ages, noting those who felt that their marriages were inequitable, because of an unfair division of domestic responsibilities.

During the child-rearing years, wives often reported feeling under-benefited and husbands over-benefited and as a result, martial satisfaction tended to dip during these years. However, during the honeymoon and empty-nest-stages (after children have left home), both husbands and wives were more likely to perceive equity and feel satisfied with their marriages.

These results support the equity theory as they demonstrate that when there is inequity (wives being under-benefited and husbands being over-benefited), relationship satisfaction is lower, but when there is more equity, both parties were equally satisfied with their relationship.

> The answer has divided the knowledge into clear sections, highlights the aim, methods, results and conclusion.

Mark awarded: 5–6

Examiner's comments: AO1: This is a strong answer which outlines the method and results of Schaffer and Keith in detail. Furthermore, the answer provides an excellent conclusion that explains clearly how this study supports the equity theory of relationships.

Topic 7 The investment model of relationships

Outline and evaluate the investment model of relationships. *(16 marks)*

Examiner's comments

The investment model predicts how committed people are to their relationship and the likelihood that the relationship will continue. According to the investment model, relationships persist as a result of three key factors: satisfaction, investment size and quality of alternatives.

> A strong introduction with specialist terminology used.

Satisfaction is the extent to which one person fulfils the needs of the other person. Investment size is a measure of all the resources that are attached to the relationship and whether or not those resources would diminish in value, or be lost if the relationship were to end. Quality of alternatives refers to the extent to which an individual's most important needs would be better fulfilled outside the current relationship. These three factors work together to determine how committed someone is to their relationship. Commitment is usually high when partners are happy with their relationship and anticipate little gain and high levels of loss, if they were to leave the relationship. Whereas commitment is usually low when satisfaction levels and investment in the relationship are low and the quality of alternatives is high.

> While the answer has shown excellent knowledge defining all of the key terms, real-life examples would further demonstrate this understanding.

The investment model has received a wealth of support. Firstly, Le et al. (2010) analysed data from nearly 38,000 participants, in 137 studies, over a 33-year-period, to determine key variables that predicted staying or leaving behaviours. They found that commitment (or lack of it) was a particularly strong predictor of whether or not a relationship would end. This supports the investment model as it suggests that commitment level is an accurate predictor of whether a relationship will persist or not. Furthermore, the idea that commitment is positively associated with satisfaction level has been found across many populations. Research supports the model in different cultures (e.g. the US, the Netherlands and Taiwan) and different types of relationship (e.g. married, non-married, gay, abusive, etc). This highlights the diverse application of the model in explaining the persistence of relationships in many different populations.

> Excellent use of research support to effectively evaluate the model.

> Further effective evaluation linked to cross-cultural support.

Furthermore, the investment model is able to explain different types of relationships, in particular abusive relationships. Victims of partner abuse experience low satisfaction, which would lead us to predict that they would leave the abusive partner, yet many stay. They may stay due to the lack of alternatives or because they have too much invested in the relationship, making the dissolution too costly. The investment model allows psychologists to understand the reason why many people remain in abusive relationships and develop support for victims.

While the investment model provides a good predictor of relationships, some psychologists argue that the variables, like satisfaction level, are difficult to measure. Furthermore, data is often obtained using self-report measures, which often have issues of social desirability. Therefore, it is difficult to measure the key terms of the investment model, as the findings from questionnaires may produce biased results.

Finally, the investment model does not take into account future investments. Goodfriend and Agnew (2008) suggest that the notion of 'investment' should include future plans as some relationships might persist because of the motivation to see a future plan come to fruition, which is not considered in this current model.

Level 4 (13–16 marks)

Examiner's comments: AO1: An accurate and detailed outline which uses specialist terminology throughout. Real-life examples could have been used to demonstrate further understanding. AO3: The evaluation was very effective highlighting a range of different evaluation points (both strengths and limitations) in an effective manner.

Topic 8 Relationship breakdown

Give two criticisms of Duck's phase model of relationship breakdown.
(3 marks each)

One issue with Duck's phase model is that the nature of the relationship is not taken into account. For example, older people in longer-term relationships may be involved in social processes that are characterised by obvious attempts to rescue the relationship, whereas teenage relationships are not. This suggests that the social phase is far more complicated than Duck originally described and that individual differences may play an important role.

A second issue with Duck's phase model is that it fails to take into account personal growth. Duck revised his model in 2006 and added a new final phase called 'resurrection processes'. Duck stressed that for many people, this is an opportunity to move beyond the distress associated with ending a relationship and engage in the process of personal growth, suggesting that the original model provided a limited account of relationship breakdown which failed to take into account the whole process.

Mark awarded: 5–6

Examiner's comments: AO1: This question can be treated as two three-mark questions. The answer provides two excellent evaluation points, that highlight the issue, expand and elaborate the key ideas and conclude.

Examiner's comments

Two effective points about the application of the investment model to abusive relationships and therapy.

Two evaluation points are made here, including objectivity and issues with research.

A final limitation is outlined effectively.

Examiner's comments

The first evaluation point is effective, providing an anecdotal example.

The second point is also effective, drawing on Duck's revision to the model.

Topic 9 Virtual relationships in social media

Outline and evaluate the nature of virtual relationships in social media. *(16 marks)*

The nature of virtual relationships is different from face-to-face relationships in two key ways. Firstly, there are higher levels of self-disclosure associated with virtual relationships and secondly, there are fewer 'gates', which are barriers that limit opportunities for shyer people.

Self-disclosure in the virtual world allows individuals to present an 'edited' version of themselves. People feel more secure with disclosing intimate and sensitive information online, as the anonymity of internet interactions greatly decreases the risks associated with self-disclosures, e.g. fear of ridicule.

Furthermore, in online relationships there is an absence of barriers or 'gates' that normally limit opportunities for less attractive/shy individuals. Zhao et al. (2008) found that online social networks such as Facebook can empower 'gated' individuals to present the identities they hope to establish, but are unable to in face-to-face situations.

There is growing support for virtual relationships which not only provide shyer individuals with an opportunity to meet people, but also provide relationships of a similar quality to face-to-face ones.

Rosenfeld and Thomas (2012) examined 4,000 US adults and found that individuals with internet access at home were far more likely to have partners, and less likely to be single. Of these 4,000 individuals, 71.8% of those who had internet access had a spouse or romantic partner, compared to just 35.9% for those without internet. This suggests that the internet plays an important role in the development of romantic relationships.

Furthermore, Baker and Oswald (2010) surveyed 207 male and female students about their shyness, Facebook usage and the quality of their friendships. They found that for students who scored high for shyness, greater use of Facebook was associated with higher perceptions of friendship quality. This highlights the positive role of virtual relationships for shy individuals.

Many critics argue that internet relationships lead to superficial relationships that are not the same as face-to-face relationships, however Rosenfeld and Thomas (2012) found no evidence to support this and found comparable quality in both online and offline relationships. This supports the role that the internet plays in the development of romantic relationships which according to Rosenfeld and Thomas are no different to face-to-face relationships. In addition, Zhao et al. (2008) claim that relationships formed online have positive consequences for people's offline lives. The development of virtual relationships allows some individuals to bypass gating obstacles and create the sort of identity that they would be unable to create in the offline world. This provides further support to the role of internet relationships, that may increase chances to connect to others in the offline world.

Finally, research has provided support for a biological basis of self-disclosure found in virtual relationships. Tamir and Mitchell (2012) found increased MRI activity in two brain regions that are associated with rewards, the nucleus accumbens and ventral tegmental area. These findings suggest that the human tendency to share our personal experiences with others over social media, may arise from the rewarding nature of self-disclosure.

Therefore, research highlights the positive nature of virtual relationships for not only improving the chances for individuals who are shy, but by also providing high-quality relationships to satisfy our biological needs.

Examiner's comments

A good introduction outlining key terminology for virtual relationships.

Excellent knowledge of self-disclosure, clearly linked to internet relationships.

Well-detailed knowledge using research support to demonstrate knowledge.

Effective use of research to support the idea of virtual relationships.

While this is partially effective, the final sentence could be linked explicitly to the question.

Good use of research support to compare internet and face-to-face relationships.

Further evaluation embedded highlighting the real-life impact of virtual relationships.

Interesting use of biological research. An opportunity for further discussion explaining why this is a strength would have been useful.

An interesting conclusion summarising the positive evaluation effectively.

Level 4 (13–16 marks)

Examiner's comments: AO1: An impressive essay that integrates research and theory seamlessly. AO3: While the commentary only provides strengths the answer has used these strengths to overcome various criticisms effectively.

Topic 10 Parasocial relationships

Outline the attachment theory explanation of parasocial relationships. *(4 marks)*

Examiner's comments

According to the attachment explanation of parasocial relationships (PSRs), PSRs exhibit the same properties as adult attachments. In particular, Weiss (1991) identified three key behaviours associated with PSRs, including. 1) Proximity seeking – the individual will attempt to reduce the distance between themselves and their attachment figure, for example, they may keep up-to-date with the latest news on a celebrity, or make a point of always watching their shows. 2) Secure base – the mere presence of the attachment figure provides a sense of security for the individual, allowing them to explore other relationships in a safe way. 3) Protest at disruption – the best marker of attachment is the presence of distress following the separation of the attachment figure. If the attachment figure (celebrity) is taken away from the individual, they will show clear signs of distress. These three behaviours are a clear indication of a PSR.

> The answer highlights the aspects of Weiss's attachment theory, using specialist terminology.

Mark awarded: 3–4

Examiner's comments: AO1: This is a very clear answer which outlines the three key attachment behaviours found in PSRs. The answer demonstrates understanding by providing clear examples throughout.

Topic 10 Parasocial relationships

Outline the absorption addiction model of parasocial relationships. *(4 marks)*

Examiner's comments

According to the absorption addiction model of parasocial relationships (PSRs) the preoccupation with a PSR might start to resemble a pathological addiction. Giles and Maltby (2006) identify three levels in this process: 1) Entertainment-social – fans are attracted to their favourite celebrity and will watch them, keep up-to-date with them, and learn about their celebrity for entertainment purposes. 2) Intensive-personal – this involves a deeper level of involvement and reflects intensive and compulsive feelings about the celebrity. 3) Borderline-pathological – this level is characterised by overidentification with the celebrity and uncontrollable behaviours and fantasies about their lives. It is at the third stage that the person's behaviour is showing clear signs of addiction.

> The answer outlines and describes the key aspects of Giles and Maltby's model, using specialist terminology.

Marks awarded: 3–4

Examiner's comments: AO1: This answer demonstrates accurate knowledge which is well-detailed throughout. The answer clearly understands the absorption addiction model and the three key components, using specialist terminology effectively.

KEY TERMS

- Androgyny
- Gender
- Sex
- Sex-role stereotypes

Possible essay question …

Discuss the concept of androgyny. Refer to the Bem Sex Role Inventory in your answer. *(16 marks)*

Other possible exam questions …

+ Distinguish between the terms 'sex' and 'gender'. *(2 marks)*
+ Describe one study related to sex-role stereotypes. *(4 marks)*
+ Outline the Bem Sex Role Inventory. *(4 marks)*

⭐ Exam tip

For a 16-mark question, you should aim to write about 400 words altogether. Try to balance this to match the weighting of 6 marks for AO1 and 10 marks for AO3, although your answer will be marked as a whole.

🔗 Link

See page 108 for more information about social learning theory.

MUST know…

Sex-role stereotypes

Sex-role stereotypes, or **gender stereotypes**, are a set of social norms about how men and women should behave.

Androgyny

Bem introduced the concept of **androgyny** in the 1970s. She argued that it is psychologically healthy to avoid fixed sex-role stereotypes. People should be free to adopt a variety of typically masculine or feminine behaviours.

Bem Sex Role Inventory (BSRI)

One hundred US undergraduates rated personality traits as desirable for men or women. The BSRI includes 40 items. Individuals rate themselves on a 7-point Likert scale, and scores for masculinity and femininity are calculated.

 Support for parental influence…

…comes from Smith and Lloyd (1978).

- *E* – Women played with babies differently, in line with sex-role stereotypes, depending on whether they were told they were boys or girls.

 There is research support for androgyny…

…being psychologically healthy.

- *E* – Prakash *et al.* (2010) tested 100 married women in India. Women with higher masculinity scores had lower scores for depression, anxiety, stress and physical health issues. Those with high femininity scores were less healthy.

 The BSRI has high reliability

- *E* – Test-retest reliability over a four week period ranged from .76 to .94, which is a high correlation.

SHOULD know…

Sex-role stereotypes

Children learn sex-role stereotypes from **explicit** teaching by their parents and others in society, for example 'Boys don't cry'. Children also learn **implicitly** by imitating same-sex models.

Androgyny

The **BSRI** includes items such as: 'independent', 'ambitious' (masculine items); 'compassionate', 'affectionate' (feminine items). They are rated on a scale from 'never or almost never true' to 'almost always true'.

Individuals may be categorised as masculine (high masculine score, low feminine score), feminine (high feminine score, low masculine score), androgynous (high scores for both) or undifferentiated (low scores for both).

- *E* – If they thought the baby was a boy, they encouraged more motor activity and offered stereotypically masculine toys (e.g. a squeaky hammer) rather than feminine toys (e.g. a doll).
- *L* – This supports the influence of adults on children learning sex-role stereotypes.

- *E* – Prakash used a different scale (the personal attribute scale, not the BSRI) to measure androgyny.
- *L* – This supports the psychoprotective effect of androgyny as women with masculine and feminine traits were more physically and psychologically healthy.

- *E* – A short form of the scale has been developed with just 30 items, removing less socially desirable terms such as 'gullible', which has a good correlation with the original scale.
- *L* – High reliability shows that individuals' scores for androgyny are stable over time.

FURTHER EVALUATION

Internal validity of the BSRI

- *P* – Most adjectives in the BSRI are socially desirable, so people with high self-esteem score higher overall than those with low self-esteem.
- *E* – So the scale may measure self-esteem (an intervening variable) rather than androgyny.
- *E* – In addition, positive response bias leads some people to score all their responses highly.
- *L* – Therefore the scores may be an artefact of the measurement rather than a true measure of androgyny.

Temporal validity of the BSRI

- *P* – The adjectives used in the BSRI were selected in the 1970s.
- *E* – Hoffman and Borders (2001) asked 400 undergraduates to rate the BSRI items, and only two terms were still endorsed as masculine or feminine: the words 'masculine' and 'feminine'.
- *E* – All other items failed to reach 75% agreement.
- *L* – This suggests that people's attitudes have changed and the BSRI is no longer valid.

✓ CHOOSE THE RIGHT ANSWER

Bem's sex-role inventory was developed by asking American undergraduates to rate adjectives. What were they asked? (Tick **one** box only.)

A Which traits were more masculine or feminine? ☐

B Which traits describe men or women? ☐

C Which words were used more in relation to males or females? ☐

D Which traits were more desirable for men or women? ☐

Answers on page 350

📖 RESEARCH ISSUES

The BSRI is a self-report scale to measure androgyny.

(a) What are the strengths and limitations of using a self-report scale to measure a personality trait such as androgyny? *(6 marks)*

(b) How can the reliability of a self-report scale be improved? *(3 marks)*

Answers on page 350

⚙ APPLYING YOUR KNOWLEDGE 1

Look out for examples of sex-role stereotypes in the media. For example, in films or adverts, what roles are men and women shown in? Make a flow chart to show how these models can affect people's behaviour, according to social learning theory.

Answers on page 350

⚙ APPLYING YOUR KNOWLEDGE 2

Jim and Anne have decided to bring up their child, Robin, in a gender-neutral manner, ensuring Robin did not encounter sex-role stereotypes. Robin does not identify with either gender, but happily plays with children of both sexes, enjoys a wide variety of toys such as construction bricks, dolls, and painting. Robin also dresses in unusual combinations of clothes; dresses, trousers, T shirts, and dressing up costumes. Some of Jim and Anne's neighbours are very shocked and think that Robin's parents have been neglectful by not allowing their child to follow 'normal' boy or girl behaviour.

Referring to sex-role stereotypes, explain Robin's behaviour and the neighbours' reaction to it. *(4 marks)*

Identify the psychology	Apply to Robin

Answers on page 350

KEY TERMS

- Chromosomes
- Hormones
- Intersex

Possible essay question ...

Discuss the role of chromosomes and hormones in gender development. *(16 marks)*

Other possible exam questions ...

+ Outline the symptoms and causes of Klinefelter's syndrome and Turner's syndrome. *(4 marks)*
+ Explain the role of testosterone in gender. *(4 marks)*

 Think

How do chromosomes and hormones affect behaviour? How do atypical chromosome patterns affect behaviour?

 Link

See Year 1/AS Revision and Exam Companion for information about oxytocin's role in the stress response

Link

See page 54 for the nature-nurture debate.

MUST know...

The role of chromosomes

Humans have 23 pairs of chromosomes. The sex chromosomes, XX (female) or XY (male), usually determine the sex of an individual.

Atypical sex chromosome patterns

Klinefelter's syndrome (XXY) affects 1 in 1,000 males. They have reduced testosterone, than typical males and are often infertile.

The role of hormones

Most gender development is governed by hormones. More **testosterone** is produced in male foetuses, causing genitalia to develop. The surge of testosterone during puberty produces secondary sexual characteristics (deepening voice, body hair).

Oestrogen promotes secondary sexual characteristics (breasts, body hair) in females.

Oxytocin promotes feelings of bonding and contentment.

 Males born without a penis...

...may sometimes be raised as females.

- **E** – However, Reiner and Gearhart (2004) reported that, out of 14 'intersex' males raised as females, eight had reassigned themselves by age 16.

However, genetic sex may not match external genitalia...

...and this leads to 'unpredictable' outcomes.

- **E** – For example, XX females with congenital adrenal hyperplasia (CAH) have unusually high levels of androgens and may be assigned male gender at birth.

The nature/nurture interaction....

...is also illustrated by the Batista family from the Dominican Republic.

- **E** – Imperato-McGinley *et al.* (1974) described four XY males born with female genitalia, due to androgen insensitivity, and raised as girls.

SHOULD know...

The role of chromosomes

Every foetus first develops female external genitalia. After three months, the external and internal genitalia differentiate into vulva, vagina, uterus and ovaries or penis and testes.

Atypical sex chromosome patterns

Turner's syndrome (XO, a missing X chromosome) affects 1 in 2,000 females. They have underdeveloped ovaries, so do not menstruate. They have normal intelligence and are often highly fluent verbally.

The role of hormones

Testosterone is produced by the adrenal glands in both sexes and relates to sex drive. From about three months male foetuses produce testosterone in the testes. Individuals with androgen insensitivity syndrome (AIS) may appear female.

Oestrogen is not required for development of female genitalia; these are the default option.

Oxytocin causes milk to flow in a lactating mother, and has a role in orgasm in both sexes.

- **E** – David Reimer's penis was damaged as a baby and he was raised as a girl, but he was unhappy and transitioned to a male as a teenager.
- **L** – This suggests that biological factors have a key role in gender development.

- **E** – Some people with CAH accept their assigned gender and some do not.
- **L** – Thus gender development is in part biologically determined (nature), but experience, personality and socialisation (nurture) also have a key role.

- **E** – The testosterone surge during puberty caused their male genitalia to appear, and they adjusted easily to their new male role.
- **L** – This indicates the role of culture in gender, as well as the effect of testosterone.

FURTHER EVALUATION

Real-world applications

- **P** – Intersex babies are not now treated surgically until they are older and decide themselves.
- **E** – If identified at birth, girls with Turner syndrome can be given growth hormone so they reach normal height.
- **E** – Oestrogen replacement therapy helps them develop secondary sexual characteristics, and this also benefits their heart and bone health.
- **L** – It is useful to identify atypical chromosome patterns early, so the individual can be given hormone treatments.

Do hormones affect brain development?

- **P** – Berenbaum and Bailey (2003) found that XX females exposed prenatally to androgens (because their mothers had been given male hormones) later showed more tomboyish behaviour.
- **E** – Quadagno *et al.* (1977) confirmed this experimentally; female monkeys exposed prenatally to testosterone were more aggressive.
- **E** – Although generalising from non-human animals to humans is problematic, as human behaviour is affected by expectations and choices.
- **L** – This research suggests that androgens may influence brain development.

MATCH THEM UP

Match up the abbreviations with their meanings

1	CAH	**A**	normal male sex chromosomes
2	AIS	**B**	congenital adrenal hyperplasia
3	XX	**C**	normal female sex chromosomes
4	XY	**D**	androgen insensitivity syndrome
5	XXY	**E**	sex chromosomes in Turner's syndrome
6	XO	**F**	sex chromosomes in Klinefelter's syndrome

Answers on page 351

A MARKING EXERCISE

Read this student answer to the following exam question.
Outline the role of hormones in determining gender. *(6 marks)*

Hormones are really important in determining gender, as males and females have different hormones and these produce their primary and secondary characteristics. Males have testosterone which increases hugely in puberty and produces their deep voice, muscles, and facial hair. Females have oestrogen instead, which controls their breasts and periods. If a male has less sensitivity to androgens, like the boys in the Batista family, they may not develop male genitals. This shows that the development of male genitals depends on the body's response to androgens like testosterone.

Your mark:

Your comments:

Answers on page 351

DRAWING CONCLUSIONS

Look at the image and identify the atypical chromosome pattern. *(2 marks)*

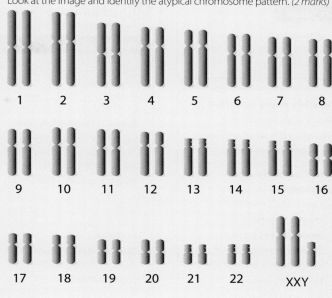

Answers on page 351

APPLYING YOUR KNOWLEDGE

Read the text and answer the question that follows.

Jolanta is 13, and her mother has taken her to see the GP as they are worried about her. She is very short compared to her friends and has not started to develop breasts. Her mother says that Jolanta talks fluently, and is doing fine at school. However, the doctor suspects that Jolanta may have Turner's syndrome.

Why does the doctor suspect Turner's syndrome, and how could she confirm this? What advice can she give to Jolanta and her mother? *(6 marks)*

Identify the psychology	Link to the doctor's advice to Jolanta

Answers on page 351

KEY TERMS

- Conservation
- Gender constancy
- Pre-operational

Possible essay question …

Describe and evaluate Kohlberg's theory of gender development. *(16 marks)*

Other possible exam questions …

+ One stage of Kohlberg's theory of gender development is called 'gender labelling'. Briefly describe **one** other stage of Kohlberg's theory. *(3 marks)*

+ Kohlberg's theory of gender development is a cognitive explanation. Explain in what way it is cognitive. *(2 marks)*

 Exam tip

Make sure you can describe each cognitive theory (Kohlberg's theory and gender schema theory) separately, but also be prepared to compare them.

MUST know...

Kohlberg's theory

Kohlberg (1966) proposed that children gradually develop the ability to think about gender, progressing through stages, as they become capable of more complex and abstract thought.

Stage 1: Gender labelling

Age 2–3 – Children label themselves and others as boy/girl/ or man/woman, based on outward appearance (clothes, hairstyle).

Stage 2: Gender stability

Age 4–7 – Children recognise that gender is stable over time (girls grow into women) but not over situations. They are still swayed by outward appearances.

Stage 3: Gender constancy

Age 6 – Children realise gender shows **conservation** across time and situations, and realise their gender will not change.

 Research evidence supports…

…Kohlberg's three stages.

- **E** – Slaby and Frey (1975) asked young children questions like: 'Were you a little girl or a little boy when you were a baby?', and found that children didn't recognise gender stability until 3–4 years old.

 However, there are methodological criticisms…

…of these studies with young children.

- **E** – Martin and Halverson (1983) re-examined the responses, concluding that the children were in 'pretend' mode.

 The ages may need adjusting…

…from Kohlberg's theory.

- **E** – Slaby and Frey found that gender constancy appeared as young as age five.

SHOULD know...

Kohlberg's theory

This is a cognitive developmental approach, like Piaget's theory of cognitive development, which proposes that brain maturation and experience interact to enable children's thinking to develop.

Stage 1: Gender labelling

Children change the labels as appearances change ('He has long hair now, so he must be a girl'). This is **pre-operational** thinking.

Stage 2: Gender stability

McConaghy (1979) found that young children thought a doll in a dress was female even when male genitals were visible.

Stage 3: Gender constancy

At this stage, children start to learn gender-appropriate behaviour by paying more attention to same-sex models.

- **E** – Also, children who scored highly on stability and constancy showed greater interest in same-sex models.
- **L** – This supports Kohlberg's developmental stages and his prediction that children who have achieved constancy will pay more attention to same-sex models.

- **E** – Bem (1989) argued that children use the cues that are most relevant in our society, such as clothes, and that many children who couldn't conserve didn't actually know what opposite-gender genitals look like.
- **L** – This weakens the validity of the findings, and their support for the theory.

- **E** – This may be because children have a lot more exposure to gender information nowadays, for example through the media.
- **L** – So, while the evidence still supports the stages, the age bands may be younger than Kohlberg proposed.

 FURTHER EVALUATION

 Gender differences

- **P** – Slaby and Frey found that boys tend to exhibit gender constancy before girls.
- **E** – This may because boys are more likely to identify with same-gender role models as men are more powerful in society.
- **E** – In addition, boys are more likely to be punished for gender-inappropriate behaviour than girls.
- **L** – Therefore, Kohlberg's theory is incomplete because principles of social learning theory are also involved.

Gender stereotypes without constancy

- **P** – Martin and Little (1990) showed that children under four display strong stereotypes about male and female behaviour.
- **E** – For example, they had strong beliefs about what boys and girls were permitted to do.
- **E** – This was before they had developed gender stability, let alone gender constancy.
- **L** – This supports gender schema theory rather than Kohlberg's theory (see next spread).

MATCH THEM UP

Match up the stages of gender development according to Kohlberg, with questions researchers could ask children to identify whether they have reached this stage.

1	Gender labelling	A	When you grow up, will you be a mummy or a daddy?
2	Gender stability	B	If you played football, would you be a boy or a girl?
3	Gender constancy	C	Are you a boy or a girl?

Answers on page 351

✔ CHOOSE THE RIGHT ANSWER

Phoenix, aged 3, is given a doll and asked, 'Is this doll a boy or a girl?'

Phoenix answers, 'A boy'.

Then a long-haired wig is placed on the doll, and Phoenix is asked again, 'Is this a boy or a girl?'

Phoenix now answers, 'A girl'.

What kind of thinking is Phoenix demonstrating? (Tick **one** box only.)

A	Pre-operational	☐
B	Consistency	☐
C	Conservation	☐
D	Constancy	☐

Answers on page 351

DRAWING CONCLUSIONS

A researcher investigated children's stage of gender development, by asking them questions. For example, he asked: 'If you played football, would you be a boy or a girl?' He then categorised the children according to the stage they had reached. A tally of the results is shown in the table below. Each number represents the age of a child who has reached that stage.

Stage	Boys	Girls
Gender labelling	2 2 2 2 2 2 2 2 3 3	2 2 2 2 3 3
Gender stability	3 3 4 4 4 4 5	2 3 3 4 4 4 4 5 5 5 6 6 6
Gender constancy	4 4 5 5 5 5 5 5 6 6	5 5 5 5 6 6 6 6

(a) What percentage of boys had reached gender stability? What percentage of girls had reached the same stage? *(2 marks)*

(b) Calculate the median ages for boys and for girls to reach gender constancy. *(2 marks)*

The researcher concludes that boys reach gender constancy earlier than girls.

(c) Comment on issues of validity in this research. *(4 marks)*

Answers on page 351

⚙ APPLYING YOUR KNOWLEDGE

Jason's father, Aison, is worried that he is not behaving like a proper boy. Aison is a soldier and wants Jason to become one too. Jason, however, likes wearing fairy dresses and prefers drawing pictures to fighting. However, Jason's mother, Polly, thinks Aison is worrying unnecessarily and Jason will grow out of this phase. Jason is 4 years old.

Based on Kohlberg's theory of gender development, what advice could you give to Jason's parents? *(6 marks)*

Identify the psychology	Link to Jason

Answers on page 351

KEY TERM

- schema

Possible essay question ...

Discuss **two** cognitive explanations of gender development. *(16 marks)*

Other possible exam questions ...

+ Outline gender schema theory as an explanation of gender development. *(6 marks)*

+ Give **one** criticism of gender schema theory. *(4 marks)*

+ Explain in what way gender schema theory is an example of the cognitive approach in psychology. *(3 marks)*

+ Explain **one** difference between Kohlberg's theory of gender development and gender schema theory. *(3 marks)*

 Exam tip

When you introduce gender schema theory the first time, put the abbreviation (GST) in brackets. You can then use the abbreviated form in the rest of your answer.

MUST know...

Gender schema theory (GST)

Martin and Halverson (1981) developed this cognitive approach, in which a child seeks to acquire information about their own gender.

Schemas are mental representations of concepts. Children learn gender schemas at about the age of three, from interaction with other children and adults, and from the media. Gender schemas relate to cultural norms, and 'appropriate' behaviour for men and women.

Ingroup and outgroup schemas: Children identify with ingroup gender schemas and actively avoid outgroup behaviours. This leads to positive evaluation of the ingroup and negative evaluation of the outgroup: 'Boys are better than girls'. This enhances self-esteem.

 Research supports gender schemas...

...being formed before gender stability is reached.

- *E* – Martin and Little (1990) found children under four had strong gender stereotypes about what boys and girls are allowed to do, despite a lack of gender stability or constancy.

 However, recent research indicates that...

...gender identity may form even earlier.

- *E* – Zosuls *et al.* (2009) observed children playing, and concluded that they were using gender labels by 19 months.

 Gender schemas are supported by....

...research showing children pictures inconsistent with stereotypes.

- *E* – For example, Martin and Halverson (1983) found children under six remembered more gender-consistent pictures (e.g. female teacher, male firefighter) than gender-inconsistent ones (e.g. female chemist, male nurse).

SHOULD know...

Gender schema theory

A key difference from Kohlberg's theory is that gender labelling is sufficient for a child to pay attention to gender-appropriate behaviours. Kohlberg claimed this did not happen until after gender constancy was established.

Resilience of gender beliefs: Children ignore information that is inconsistent with gender schemas, so it is very difficult to change stereotypes using counter-stereotypes.

Peer relationships: Children believe that same-sex peers are 'like me' and therefore more fun to play with. They also learn to avoid negative consequences of ignoring the schemas, such as being teased.

- *E* – Kohlberg's theory would require children to develop constancy before understanding gender roles, at about age six.
- *L* – This show that children have acquired information about gender roles earlier than Kohlberg suggested, supporting GST.

- *E* – However, children may show gender-typed preferences even earlier than this.
- *L* – This means that the age-related predictions of GST may be incorrect.

- *E* – Schemas even caused distortion of memories, so that children shown a boy holding a doll (inconsistent, or counter-stereotypical) described it as a girl.
- *L* – These cognitive distortions maintain ingroup schemas and this evidence supports GST.

 FURTHER EVALUATION

 Gender schemas also organise new information.

- *P* – Bradbard *et al.* (1986) told 4–9-year-olds that gender-neutral items (burglar alarms, pizza cutters) were boy or girl items.
- *E* – The children took a greater interest in items labelled as 'ingroup'.
- *E* – They also remembered more of the 'ingroup' objects a week later.
- *L* – This shows how gender schemas help children to organise new information in memory.

 Changing stereotypes

- *P* – GST explains why children are frequently highly sexist, despite efforts of parents and teachers to provide counter-stereotypes.
- *E* – However, Hoffman (1998) reported that children whose mothers work have less stereotyped views of what men do.
- *E* – This shows that children are receptive to non-stereotyped ideas of gender roles.
- *L* – This suggests practical approaches to changing stereotypes should involve direct experience of people who do not fit stereotypes.

CHOOSE THE RIGHT ANSWER

According to gender schema theory, which **one** of the following is not a benefit of ingroup identification? (Tick **one** box only.)

A	Positive evaluation of the ingroup	☐
B	Enhanced self-esteem	☐
C	Can ignore ingroup schemas and resist stereotypes	☐
D	Improve relationships with peers	☐
E	Actively seek information about ingroup behaviour	☐
F	Organises memory	☐

Answers on page 351

An idea
Make a mind-map of the different explanations of gender development. This will help you construct an organised mental schema for the topic.

 APPLYING YOUR KNOWLEDGE

Oli's parents both go out to work. Oli's mum likes doing DIY jobs at weekends, like assembling flat-pack furniture, and his dad never uses power tools but prefers to read a book. However, when Oli is shown a drill, and asked, 'Who would use this, mummy or daddy?', he replies, 'Daddy'. And when he is asked what mummy and daddy do all day, he says: 'Daddy goes to work and mummy cleans the house'.

How does gender schema theory explain Oli's answers? *(6 marks)*

Identify the psychology	Link to Oli

Answers on page 351

 DRAWING CONCLUSIONS

Children were shown pictures of male or female firefighters, teachers, nurses or chemists. There were 20 pictures of males and females in each role. A week later they were asked whether each job was being done by a man or a woman.

The results are shown in the bar chart.

Number of models whose gender was correctly remembered

(a) What do the findings show? *(4 marks)*

(b) How can gender schema theory explain these findings? *(3 marks)*

Answers on page 351

KEY TERMS

- Electra complex
- Identification
- Internalisation
- Oedipus complex

Possible essay question ...

Discuss Freud's psychoanalytic theory of gender development. *(16 marks)*

Other possible exam questions ...

+ Outline the Oedipus complex and/or the Electra complex *(4 marks)*

+ Explain how identification and internalisation are involved in a psychodynamic explanation of gender development. *(4 marks)*

 Link

See Year 1/AS Revision and Exam Companion for an outline of psychodynamic theories.

 Link

See page 48 for gender bias.

MUST know...

Freud's psychoanalytic theory

The Oedipus complex

Freud (1905) proposed that, during the phallic stage (age 3–6) boys:

1. Desire their mother and want her whole attention.

2. See their father as a rival and wish he was dead.

3. Eventually resolve the conflict by **identification** with the father, and **internalisation** of the father's gender identity (attitudes and behaviours).

The Electra complex

Jung (1913) proposed that girls:

1. Are initially attracted to their mother, but discover she doesn't have a penis.

2. Transfer their sexual desires to their father.

3. Eventually identify with the mother and internalise her gender behaviours.

 Freud supported his theory with case studies…

…such as Little Hans (Freud, 1909), who developed a fear of horses due to repressing his desires for his mother.

- **E** – Levin (1921) reported on 32 patients with bipolar disorder; 22 had unresolved Electra complex or penis envy.

 The theory lacks predictive validity.

- **E** – It predicts that children in one-parent families or with same-sex parents would have difficulty acquiring a gender identity or normal gender-role behaviour, which is not supported by evidence.

 A problem with the theory is….

…that the Oedipus and Electra complexes depend on children having an awareness of genitals.

- **E** – However, many children aged 3–5 don't know what opposite-sex genitals look like (Bem, 1989).

SHOULD know...

Freud's psychoanalytic theory

The Oedipus complex

Boys develop anxiety about their wish for their father to die. This leads to castration fear, which is repressed.

The Electra complex

Girls blame their mother for their lack of a penis, believing they were castrated. This penis envy is later converted into a wish to have a baby, resolving anger against the mother.

Unresolved phallic stage

Frustration and/or overindulgence may lead to fixation at the phallic stage, and an individual who is not capable of intimacy. Freud also claimed that fixation could be a root cause of amoral behaviour and homosexuality.

- **E** – However, these case studies are subjectively interpreted and selectively reported, to fit the researcher's expectations.
- **L** – This means that they are poor evidence, and the theories are unfalsifiable.

- **E** – Patterson (2004) found that children of lesbian parents develop gender identities in similar ways to children of heterosexual parents, and have normal social relationships.
- **L** – This means that gender development does not depend on the Oedipus or Electra complex.

- **E** – On the other hand, some research indicates a link between exposure to parental sexual activity at a young age, and teenage pregnancy and sexually transmitted infections.
- **L** – This suggests an association between early childhood experience and later sexual behaviour, but not a causal effect on gender development.

FURTHER EVALUATION

 Alternative psychodynamic explanations

- **P** – Chodorow (1994) suggested that mothers and daughters are closer because they are the same sex, whereas boys become more independent.
- **E** – This is supported by observations that mother–daughter pairs play more closely (Goldberg and Lewis, 1969).
- **E** – In addition, boys and girls attempt to identify with the father but only sons succeed.
- **L** – The advantage of this alternative explanation is that it does not predict problems in families with same-sex parents.

 Gender bias

- **P** – Feminists dismiss Freud's idea of inferior female development due to penis envy.
- **E** – In fact, Freud admitted he didn't really understand women.
- **E** – In addition, many people object to the idea that children experience sexual drives at such a young age.
- **L** – However, Lacan (1966) suggested that penis envy can be considered as a symbolic envy of male power in a male-dominated society, rather than being taken literally.

A MARKING EXERCISE

Read this student answer to the following exam question:

Describe how girls develop gender identity, according to a psychodynamic explanation. *(4 marks)*

Girls develop their gender identity by identification with their mother. Firstly, a girl desires her mother, but then switches her desire to her father. She is angry with her mother because she doesn't have a penis and thinks her mother has castrated her. This penis envy then becomes a wish to have a baby, so her anger against her mother is reduced and she can identify with her and imitate her behaviour.

Your mark:

Why did you award this mark?

Answers on page 351

 APPLYING YOUR KNOWLEDGE

Here are some key ideas from Freud's case study of Little Hans:

- At three years old, Hans was interested in his 'widdler' and liked playing with it, but his mother didn't like this behaviour and threatened to get a doctor to cut it off.
- He was very distressed by seeing a horse collapse and die in the street.
- Hans commented that horses had large 'widdlers' and assumed that his parents, being adults, must also. He was told that his mother didn't have one, and assumed she'd been castrated.
- At four, Hans developed a phobia of horses, which became generalised anxiety so that he didn't want to leave the house.
- At around the same time Hans' father started objecting to Hans climbing into his parents' bed in the morning to cuddle his mother.

Using this information, and your knowledge of Freud's psychoanalytic theory, how would Freud interpret the causes of Hans' phobia? *(8 marks)*

Little Hans	Freud's interpretation

Answers on page 352

 RESEARCH ISSUES

Explain how these issues can be used to evaluate psychodynamic explanations of gender development, by elaborating the point.

Issue	Elaboration
Based on case studies	
Gender bias	
Unfalsifiable	
Lack of predictive validity	
Non-experimental methods	

Answers on page 351

 CHOOSE THE RIGHT ANSWER

To resolve little Hans' conflict and treat his phobia, what needs to happen, according to Freud's theory? (Tick **one** box only.)

A His mother should apologise for threatening to castrate Hans, and he should forgive her.	☐
B His father should reassure Hans that he will not be castrated, and Hans should identify with his father.	☐
C Hans should be exposed to horses to desensitise him.	☐
D His mother and father should explain to Hans that it is normal for a woman not to have a penis.	☐

Answers on page 352

KEY TERM

- Social learning theory

Possible essay question ...

Discuss social learning theory as applied to gender development. *(16 marks)*

Other possible exam questions ...

+ Compare social learning theory and gender schema theory as explanations for gender development. *(8 marks)*

 Link

To remind yourself about gender schema theory, see Topic 4.

 Link

See page 242 for a discussion of Bandura's Bobo doll study.

 Link

See page 54 for the nature-nurture debate.

MUST know...

Social learning theory (SLT)

Bandura explained that we learn indirectly from other people (models) by observing and imitating their behaviour.

Indirect reinforcement

Children observe gender behaviour of others from home, school, and the media. They learn from the consequences, whether the behaviour is worth repeating (**vicarious reinforcement**). Girls **identify** with other females and are more likely to **imitate** their behaviour. Boys may also observe their mothers' behaviour at home but are less likely to imitate it.

Direct reinforcement

Reinforcement (e.g. praise) of gender behaviour increases the likelihood that a child will repeat it. Punishment reduces it.

EVALUATION | ***Research evidence supports modelling...***

...of aggressive behaviour (the Bobo doll study) and also of gender.

- ***E*** – Perry and Bussey (1979) showed children (aged 8–9 years) films of other children selecting apples or pears. The children then preferentially selected the fruit they had observed a same-sex model choosing.

EVALUATION | ***However, peers may not be important...***

...in early childhood, when gender identity is being formed.

- ***E*** – Later in childhood it seems that peer behaviour does not create gender-role stereotypes but simply reinforces existing ones.

EVALUATION | ***Direct tuition may be more effective...***

...than modelling.

- ***E*** – Martin *et al.* (1995) found that boys played with toys labelled 'boys toys' even if they saw girls playing with them. However, they didn't play with toys labelled 'girls toys' even when they saw boys playing with them.

SHOULD know...

Social learning theory (SLT)

The role of mediational processes

Bandura called SLT a social cognitive theory. Children store information about reinforcements as mental representations which create an expectancy of future outcomes. They will then display the behaviour if the expectation of reward is greater than the expectation of punishment.

Direct tuition

When children acquire linguistic skills, they learn appropriate gender behaviour through explicit instructions such as 'be ladylike'.

Self-direction

Bandura believed that people internalise gender-appropriate behaviours then actively direct their own behaviour. This is no longer dependent on external reinforcement.

- ***E*** – However, the children only imitated same-sex behaviour if it was not counter to stereotypes (e.g. a man wearing a dress).
- ***L*** – So it seems that the effects of modelling may be limited to existing stereotypes.

- ***E*** – Lamb and Roopnarine (1979) observed that reinforcement of male-type behaviour in pre-school girls was less long-lasting that reinforcement of male-type behaviour in boys.
- ***L*** – This suggests that peer reinforcement mainly acts as a reminder.

- ***E*** – However, parents' and teachers' behaviour does not always match their direct tuition, and this contradiction weakens the effect of what is being taught (Hildebrandt, 1973).
- ***L*** – This suggests that direct instruction is more important than modelling in pre-school children, but both influence behaviour.

FURTHER EVALUATION

EVALUATION | **Self-direction**

- **P** – Children learn to evaluate others' behaviour, and then their own.
- **E** – Bussey and Bandura (1992) showed children (aged 3–4 years) videos of other children playing with masculine or feminine toys.
- **E** – The younger children disapproved of others but not themselves for gender-inconsistent behaviour, whereas older children disapproved of both. These evaluations were confirmed by the children's actual choices of toys in play.
- **L** – This shows how self-regulation increases with age.

EVALUATION | **Too much emphasis on social process**

- **P** – SLT acknowledges innate, biological behaviours but doesn't include them in the explanation.
- **E** – For example, testosterone during prenatal development creates a more 'masculine' brain and behaviours.
- **E** – Also, cross-cultural research by Mead (1935) confirmed that men were more aggressive in all three societies she studied, and Buss (1989) found universal preferences in partner choice.
- **L** – These universal similarities suggest that biology plays an important role in gender.

MATCH THEM UP

Match up the researcher with the title of their study.

1	Bandura (1963)	**A**	Peer influences on sex-role development in pre-schoolers
2	Perry and Bussey (1979)	**B**	Children's gender-based reasoning about toys
3	Lamb and Roopnarine (1979)	**C**	Rules, models and self-reinforcement in children
4	Martin *et al.* (1995)	**D**	Imitation of film-mediated aggressive models
5	Hildebrandt (1973)	**E**	The social learning theory of sex differences: imitation is alive and well
6	Bussey and Bandura (1992)	**F**	Sex and temperament in three primitive societies
7	Mead (1935)	**G**	Sex differences in human mate preferences: evolutionary hypotheses tested in 37 cultures
8	Buss (1989)	**H**	Self-regulatory mechanisms governing gender development

Answers on page 352

 FILL IN THE BOXES

Three theories of gender development include some similar terms, but used in different ways. Compare social learning theory (SLT), gender schema theory (GST) and Freud's psychoanalytic theory of gender, choosing key words or phrases to summarise them.

Aspect of theory	SLT	GST	Freud's theory
Identification			
Internalisation			
Imitation			
Cognitive aspects			
How behaviour is maintained			
Key figures			
Nature/ nurture?			
Free will/ deterministic?			

Answers on page 352

 CHOOSE THE RIGHT ANSWER

According to social learning theory, older children have internalised gender-appropriate behaviours and their behaviour is no longer dependent on external rewards or punishment. What is this known as? (Tick **one** box only.)

A	Vicarious reinforcement	☐
B	Imitation	☐
C	Self-direction	☐
D	Identification	☐

Answers on page 352

 APPLYING YOUR KNOWLEDGE

Annabelle, age 16, is often told by her parents that she is not being ladylike, and that she should wear a skirt when they go out as a family, not jeans. However, her friends rarely wear skirts and seem to have lots of fun. Use social learning theory to explain how this might affect her behaviour. *(4 marks)*

Identify the psychology	Link to Annabelle's behaviour

Answers on page 352

KEY TERMS

- Culture
- Media

Possible essay question …

Describe and evaluate the influence of culture and/or media on gender roles.
(16 marks)

Other possible exam questions …

+ (Application question) Explain how cultural influences affected children's gender roles in this context.
(4 marks)

 Exam tip

You can use your knowledge of social learning theory in this topic too, as culture and media exert their influence via observational learning and vicarious reinforcement.

 Link

See page 50 for cultural bias.

MUST know...

Cultural influences

The gender rules of a culture underlie stereotypes and influence peer and parental reinforcement.

Cultural differences: People believe that women are more conformist than men, but conformity actually varies between cultures (Berry *et al.*, 2002).

Cultures can change with time, for example UK women perform more domestic duties than men but the gender gap is decreasing.

The influence of the media

Media **role models** perpetuate gender stereotypes. **Vicarious reinforcement** affects people's self-efficacy about their ability to master gender-consistent or inconsistent activities.

On the other hand, the media can present **counter-stereotypes** which reduce children's adherence to stereotypes (Pingree, 1978).

 Social role theory explains gender roles differently…

…as a product of biological differences between men and women.

- **E** – For example, women have to bear and care for children, while men are generally physically stronger.

 A problem with cross-cultural research is…

…that observers may be biased in their interpretation of behaviour.

- **E** – Freeman (1984) criticised Mead's research as invalid, as the indigenous people had told her what she wanted to hear.

EVALUATION ***Evidence for the influence of TV…***

…comes from the Notel study by Williams (1985).

- **E** – This longitudinal study compared children's stereotypes before and after the introduction of TV to their remote Canadian valley.

SHOULD know...

Cultural influences

Mead (1935) found **cultural role differences** between three social groups in Papua New Guinea: Arapesh men and women were gentle and cooperative; Mundugumor men and women were violent and competitive; whereas Tchambuli women were dominant.

The influence of the media

Usually, men are portrayed as independent and directive, whereas women are shown as dependent, unambitious and emotional (Bussey and Bandura, 1999). Men are more likely than women to be shown controlling events (Hodges *et al.*, 1981) and women in adverts are shown as more flawless and passive than men (Conley and Ramsey, 2011).

- **E** – According to social role theory (Eagly and Wood, 1999), in societies where childcare is available and work doesn't require strength, gender roles become more similar.
- **L** – This explains gender differences in roles as a product of biological differences, not just cultural stereotypes.

- **E** – However, Mead subsequently changed her conclusions, noting that there were more similarities than differences between males and females.
- **L** – This means that evidence from cross-cultural studies may be flawed, limiting the conclusions that can be drawn.

- **E** – After TV arrived, the children's views had become significantly more sex-stereotyped.
- **L** – This shows that exposure to media can have significant effects on gender attitudes.

FURTHER EVALUATION

EVALUATION **Media effects may be insignificant**

- **P** – Charlton's (2000) study looking at the effects of introducing TV to a community found no changes in aggressive behaviour.
- **E** – The researchers concluded that pre-existing community values reduced the effects of media exposure.
- **E** – However, this study concerned aggression rather than gender stereotypes.
- **L** – But it seems that the media may simply reinforce existing attitudes.

 Counter-stereotyping and backlash

- **P** – Some research has shown that counter-stereotypes can change expectations.
- **E** – However, Pingree (1978) found that pre-adolescent boys display stronger stereotypes after exposure to non-traditional models, perhaps because boys this age want to challenge adults' views.
- **E** – Additionally, gender-inconsistent messages are often mis-remembered and have no effect. (Martin and Halverson, see page 104.)
- **L** – This makes it difficult to use the media to change cultural stereotypes.

MATCH THEM UP

Match up the study and the findings.

1	Mead (1935)	**A**	Cultural role differences between three social groups in Papua New Guinea
2	Bussey and Bandura (1999)	**B**	Media counter-stereotypes reduce children's adherence to stereotypes
3	Hodges (1981)	**C**	Portrayal of men as independent and women dependent and emotional in the media
4	Conley and Ramsey (2011)	**D**	Men are more likely than women to be shown controlling events
5	Pingree (1978)	**E**	After introduction of TV, children's views became more sex-stereotyped (Notel study)
6	Williams (1985)	**F**	Children remember counter-stereotypical images less accurately than gender-consistent images
7	Martin and Halverson (1983)	**G**	Women in adverts are shown as more passive than men

Answers on page 352

 APPLYING YOUR KNOWLEDGE

A study of Harvard Law School classrooms found that in a class with a male instructor, men spoke two and a half times longer than their female classmates. However, when a female instructor led the classroom, they had 'an inspiring effect on female students,' leading women to speak three times as much as they did with a male instructor.

(a) If men spoke for a mean time of 1.5 minutes when there was a male instructor, how long was the mean time of women's comments? Show your working. *(2 marks)*

(b) There were 60 men and 40 women in the classroom. When there was a male instructor, what percentage of the time taken up by students talking were females talking? *(3 marks)*

(c) Assuming the total student talking time is the same, what percentage of student talking time was occupied by females when there was a female instructor? *(2 marks)*

(d) Suggest why the difference occurs with a female instructor, and what the effects of this could be. *(6 marks)*

Why	Effects

Answers on page 352

 RESEARCH ISSUES

Margaret Mead (1935) studied three societies in Papua New Guinea, and found evidence of cultural role differences in men's and women's behaviour between the three groups. What issues are there with validity in this research? *(4 marks)*

Answers on page 352

 DRAWING CONCLUSIONS

Sasha was researching gender stereotypes in advertising.

(a) Describe how he could carry out a content analysis to explore this topic. *(4 marks)*

He has gathered some data, shown below.

(b) Draw a suitable chart to display the data relating to advertisements for different products using male or female actors. *(4 marks)*

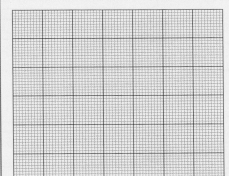

	Male	Female
Beauty product	2	15
Chocolate	4	8
Alcoholic drink	6	4
Starting a conversation	5	3
Giving information	11	3
Verbally expressing emotion	0	8

(c) What can you conclude about the roles displayed by males and females in conversation in these advertisements? *(3 marks)*

Answers on page 352

KEY TERM

- Gender identity disorder

Possible essay question …

Describe and evaluate biological and social explanations of gender identity disorder. *(16 marks)*

Other possible exam questions …

+ Explain what is meant by 'gender identity disorder'. *(3 marks)*
+ Give one criticism of biological explanations of gender identity disorder. *(3 marks)*

 Think

Make sure you are clear how to use the terms correctly. 'Atypical gender development' can include biological conditions caused by abnormal chromosomes or hormones, as well as the psychiatric condition known as gender identity disorder or gender dysphoria.

 Link

See page 52 for free will and determinism.

 Link

See page 60 for ethical issues in socially sensitive research.

MUST know…

Gender identify disorder

Gender identity disorder (GID) is a psychiatric condition involving **gender dysphoria**, discomfort with one's assigned gender.

Biological explanations

The brain-sex theory suggests that transsexuals' brains do not match their genetic sex. For example, the BSTc area of the thalamus is larger in men than women, and its size correlates with preferred gender rather than biological sex (Zhou *et al.*, 1995).

Social and psychological explanations

Overly close **mother–son relationships** could lead to greater female identification in boys. Females with poor **father–daughter relationships** could identify as males, to gain acceptance from their father. Another explanation is **childhood trauma**.

 Criticisms of the brain-sex theory…

…challenge whether differences are an effect or a cause of GID.

- *E* – Chung *et al.* (2002) noted that the BSTc is the same size in males and females until adulthood, whereas most transsexuals report gender dysphoria from early childhood.

 There is support for cross-wiring…

…from patients who have had sex organs removed.

- *E* – Ramachandran and McGeoch (2007) report that 60% of non-GID men and only 30% of GID men experience a phantom penis after penis amputation (e.g. for cancer).

 Social explanations also have some support…

…from research of boys with GID.

- *E* – For example, Zucker *et al.* (1996) found that 64% of boys with GID were also diagnosed with separation anxiety disorder, compared to 38% of boys who had some gender concerns but were not diagnosed with GID.

SHOULD know…

Biological explanations

A **'transsexual gene'**, a longer version of the androgen receptor gene, reduces sensitivity to testosterone and may under-masculinise the brain. Male to female (MtF) transsexuals are more likely to have this gene (Hare *et al.*, 2009).

Ramachandran (2008) suggested that GID is due to innate **crosswiring**, in which the sensory cortex is connected differently. So two-thirds of FtM transsexuals report the sensation of a **phantom penis**.

Some **environmental pollutants**, such as pesticides, contain oestrogens, which could affect foetal development. Vreugdenhil *et al.* (2002) found that boys with mothers who had been exposed to dioxins displayed feminised play.

- *E* – Also, people in the BSTc studies had received hormone therapy, and this could have affected their BSTc size.
- *L* – It is difficult to find consistent differences between brains of males and females, let alone people with GID, so there is inconsistent evidence for the brain-sex theory.

- *E* – In addition, only 10% of FtM patients experience phantom breasts after surgery to remove breasts.
- *L* – This suggests that some transsexual adults have differently-wired brains.

- *E* – However, Cole *et al.* (1997) studied 435 people with GID and found no greater incidence of psychiatric conditions than in a normal population.
- *L* – This suggests that the development of GID is generally unrelated to trauma or pathological family relations.

FURTHER EVALUATION

More than one explanation is needed

- *P* – Two distinct groups of MtF transsexuals have been identified.
- *E* – Furuhashi (2011) studied 27 Japanese males with GID. Some had longed to be female since childhood, and others only since adolescence.
- *E* – Blanchard (1985) also proposed two groups – 'homosexual transsexuals' and 'non-homosexual transsexuals' – who are aroused by the fantasy of themselves as a woman.
- *L* – There may be different explanations for different types of GID.

Socially sensitive research

- *P* – There are potential social consequences for individuals with GID, if causes are found.
- *E* – If a biological cause is identified, it might help society to be more accepting.
- *E* – On the other hand, a biological cause might harm individuals if it is assumed that transsexualism is inevitable. A simple cause-and-effect relationship is unlikely.
- *L* – Either way, the outcomes of research have likely consequences for individuals concerned.

MATCH THEM UP

Match up the explanation with its criticism.

1	Brain-sex theory	**A**	This does not explain FtM transsexuals
2	Childhood trauma or pathological family relations	**B**	These changes may have occurred during development, due to brain plasticity
3	A transsexual gene	**C**	No greater incidence of psychiatric conditions in people with GID than in normal population
4	Innate crosswiring	**D**	The differences are not seen until adulthood, whereas GID can appear in childhood

Answers on page 353

 CHOOSE THE RIGHT ANSWER

Which **one** of the following is **not** an example of atypical gender development? (Tick **one** box only.)

- **A** counter-stereotypes ☐
- **B** congenital adrenal hyperplasia ☐
- **C** gender identity disorder ☐
- **D** gender dysphoria ☐
- **E** intersex ☐

Answers on page 353

 APPLYING YOUR KNOWLEDGE

Carol wrote a message on a forum, 'I desperately wanted to be a boy until aged about 10 yrs, dressed as one, prayed I would wake up as one. Only did 'boys stuff', was better than my brothers at football, tree climbing etc. Aged about 13 I suddenly thought being a girl wasn't sooo bad. However, still am not 'girly'.'

Adam replied, 'I paint, love music, etc and was bullied for being intuitive and creative. It's the stereotyping we should fight!'

Becks added, 'Being tall, late developing, analytical and bossy meant I never felt properly feminine, and was surprised to discover I could produce babies!'

Using these examples, explain how sex-role stereotypes could lead to feelings of gender dysphoria. *(8 marks)*

Identify the psychology	Link to this discussion

Answers on page 353

 FILL IN THE BOXES

Summarise the genetic and hormonal causes of atypical gender development. The first row has been completed for you.

Abnormality	What is it?	Who does it affect?	Hormonal effects	Result
Klinefelter's syndrome	XXY	1/1000 males	Reduced testosterone	Less masculine appearance, infertile
Turner's syndrome				
CAH				
AIS				
'transsexual gene'				
Boys whose mothers were exposed to dioxins				
Girls whose mothers took drugs containing androgens	(Berenbaum and Bailey, see page 100)			

Answers on page 353

Gender extended answers

Discuss the concept of androgyny. Refer to the Bem Sex Role Inventory in your answer. *(16 marks)*

Androgyny means partly male and partly female. It was Bem who introduced the idea in Psychology in the 1970s, arguing that people can have personalities which have some 'masculine' and some 'feminine' characteristics. Characteristics and behaviours are only described as 'masculine' or 'feminine' because of cultural stereotypes and social norms of behaviour, and actually it is healthier to have a mixture of characteristics rather than being confined to society's idea of a 'typical' male or female.

Bem developed the Bem Sex Role Inventory (BSRI) as a way of measuring androgyny. She got 100 students to rate a list of personality traits as desirable for men or women. She then selected 40 of these to make a scale, e.g. 'ambitious' (masculine) or 'affectionate' (feminine). To take the BSRI, you rate yourself on a Likert scale and the scores for the masculine or feminine traits are added up. People can then be classified as masculine, feminine, androgynous (high scores for masculine and feminine items) or undifferentiated (low scores for both).

Bem has tested the BSRI for test-retest reliability, and it came out high. This shows that people's androgyny scores are stable over a period of time.

There is some research support for Bem's idea that it is healthy to be androgynous. Prakash tested Indian women and found that women with higher scores for masculinity had lower scores for many mental and physical health issues than the women with high femininity scores. This shows that androgyny may keep women healthier. However, Prakash used a different scale, not the BSRI so it may not be the same traits that were being measured, and also Prakash only tested married women in India so the findings can't be generalised to men, single women or women in other cultures. There could be particular reasons why married Indian women benefit from having some 'masculine' traits.

However, there is a problem with validity. The adjectives are mostly socially desirable traits, and it is a self-report scale, so people may not be totally honest about themselves. Also their view of themselves may be affected by low self-esteem. This means the scale may lack internal validity. Also, the items are dated as the original research was done in the 1970s, and attitudes have changed. In 2001 some students were asked to rate the items in the BSRI, and there were only two items that came out as consistently masculine or feminine, which were the words 'masculine' and 'feminine'. This shows that attitudes have changed so the BSRI lacks historical validity and we would have to find a different way of measuring androgyny now.

Level 3 (9–12 marks)

Examiner's comments: Overall, a clear accurate response but more detail would be useful in places.

Examiner's comments

This is a clear introduction, with a good explanation of androgyny linked to stereotyping. The question does not require a discussion of sex-role stereotypes, but this issue has been made relevant here.

This is a clear outline of how the BSRI was produced, although more detail could have been given about the Likert scale, or examples of items.

No specific data on test-retest correlation.

Accurate but lacking detail again, such as examples of mental health problems that were less frequent in androgynous women. Good evaluation of this study.

Validity issues are well discussed, but more elaboration could be given; how would low self-esteem affect scores on the BSRI?

Discuss the role of chromosomes and hormones in sex and gender. Refer to atypical sex chromosome patterns in your answer. *(16 marks)*

Chromosomes contain the genes which code for all the proteins in our bodies. Some of these proteins are hormones, neurotransmitters, receptors and enzymes which control the functioning of cells in our body and communicate between different cells and organs. Human cells have 23 pairs of chromosomes, including the sex chromosomes, which are normally XX or XY. Embryos all start off looking the same, and the sex organs are basically female to start with. After 8 weeks they start to become different; an embryo with XY develops testes, which then start to produce testosterone, the male hormone which causes the penis and testes to develop outside the body. Without that, the embryo develops as a female with uterus and ovaries inside the body and female external genitalia.

At puberty there is a rush of sex hormones, testosterone in males then produces secondary sexual characteristics like deep voice, big muscles etc. Oestrogen is produced in females and makes the secondary sexual characteristics develop, like breasts, and periods start. Females also have some testosterone and this gives them a sex drive.

Sometimes the separation of chromosomes into the sperm or egg goes wrong, then the fertilised egg (zygote) gets the wrong number of sex chromosomes. Individuals with XXY have Klinefelter's syndrome, where they look like males but they have less testosterone than they should, so they don't develop manly characteristics – they have less facial hair, broader hips and less muscles than normal males. They are also infertile.

Another possibility is Turner's syndrome, which affects females. They have XO, which means a missing X chromosome. These females' ovaries don't develop properly so they don't get periods.

As well as abnormal chromosomes, some people have an abnormality which means they don't respond normally to testosterone so they look female – androgen insensitivity syndrome, AIS.

The question is, how much of our gender identity comes from the chromosomes and hormones (nature) and how much from environmental factors like how we are treated, how we see others behaving, etc. (nurture).

Some people are 'intersex' which means they have genitals which don't match their chromosome sex. This might be because of AIS or CAH (congenital adrenal hyperplasia) where females have too much testosterone so appear to have a penis. Some people who are born like this are raised as males, and some are fine with this whereas others aren't, so it appears that gender is partly determined by biology and part by experience and how they are treated (nurture). Generally they are given hormone replacement therapy nowadays.

David Reimer had his penis removed in an accident and was raised as a girl, but always felt very unhappy about this and changed to being a boy as a teenager. This shows that you can't just allocate someone a gender arbitrarily; their biological gender will come through generally.

There was also a family in south America who had several boys who appeared to be girls when they were born, because of AIS, but suddenly grew a penis at puberty because of the extra testosterone. They adjusted fine, which shows that culture is important in gender as well as the hormones.

Level 3 (9–12 marks)

Examiner's comments: Overall, a clear essay but too much AO1 compared to AO3; the balance should be 6:10. This answer would be at the lower end of Level 3.

Examiner's comments

The description is accurate, and explains how the development of male or female sex organs is caused by chromosomes and hormones.

Here we have some more biological effects of hormones, and the answer touches on psychology too.

The question requires the consideration of atypical sex chromosome patterns, so these are important paragraphs of AO1.

The paragraph on AIS doesn't add anything here, but gives context for the discussion later.

This question begins the discussion, contextualised within the nature–nurture debate.

The discussion continues well, with a conclusion linking back to the contributions of nature and nurture. The sentence about hormone replacement isn't really adding anything.

Two relevant case studies are included, with conclusions weighing up the importance of biology in gender, but brief.

Describe and evaluate Kohlberg's theory of gender development. *(16 marks)*

Examiner's comments

Kohlberg's theory (1966) is about the cognitive development of gender understanding. He said that children develop in stages as their brains develop and they become able to think more abstractly, like Piaget's stages of cognitive development.

> The approach is introduced, with the basis in Piaget's theory.

The first stage is gender labelling, in which children find out which labels apply to men, women, boys and girls and work it out based on appearance. They use clues like long hair = girl, trousers and jacket = man. This is about age 2–3.

> Each stage is clearly outlined with explanation and ages.

Next they realise that gender is stable (so this stage is called gender stability). This means that boys grow up into men and girls grow up into women. However, they still think that gender can change if you change your clothes or get your hair cut. For example, McConaghy found that young children thought a doll in a dress was female, even when the male genitals were visible, supporting this stage. However, children this age may not know much about genitals, as Bem found that many children don't know what the genitals of someone of the other sex look like.

> This paragraph uses some research to support the description, and evaluates the research, but this is not linked explicitly enough to make it AO3.

The third stage is gender constancy, where they realise that gender is a fixed thing. This is like Piaget's conservation, where children realise that certain properties are fixed like volume and number, even if you rearrange objects. Gender constancy happens about age 6 and this is when children are more interested in same-sex models and pay them more attention, so they learn how they should behave according to their gender.

> Here is an explanation of the effect of gender constancy, how it enables children to learn gender-appropriate behaviour.

Slaby and Frey did some research which partly supports Kohlberg's theory. Children didn't recognise gender stability until they were 3–4 years, and the ones who had reached gender constancy did take more notice of same-sex models as Kohlberg predicted. However, the first criticism of Kohlberg's theory is that the ages are wrong. Slaby and Frey found that 5-year-olds could have gender constancy. Also they found that boys get there before girls, which might be because boys are punished more than girls for copying gender-inappropriate behaviour, or because males are powerful in society so it is more desirable to act like a man. So this shows that social learning and reinforcement are also involved, not just stages.

> A paragraph using Slaby and Frey's research in several ways, to support the theory and to show its limitations.

It is difficult to study children's beliefs because they may just be pretending – they are very susceptible to demand characteristics. They were asked questions like 'If you played football, would you be a boy or a girl?', which is ambiguous, and it's not clear how the children were understanding the question. This weakens the findings of Slaby's study.

> This is an excellent paragraph of evaluation, but it doesn't explain how the weakening of the findings of the study affects the theory.

There is conflicting evidence that children have strong stereotypes about what males and females are allowed to do, even before they are 4, and they haven't achieved gender stability yet. This supports gender schema theory rather than Kohlberg's theory of stages. Gender schema theory says that children learn by observation how males and females should behave, and internalise it.

> No specific evidence is given here, but gender schema theory is used as a contrast. This could have been elaborated further.

Level 3 (9–12 marks)

Examiner's comments: Overall, a Level 3 answer as not all points are linked to their effect on the theory.

Kate says, 'I really want my son George to be a proper boy, and my daughter Charlotte to be a proper girl.' Discuss why Kate says this, and how gender schema theory can help her achieve it, referring to psychological research in your answer. *(16 marks)*

Examiner's comments

According to gender schema theory, Kate will have a schema about gender, which is her understanding of what gender means, based on her experiences. She will have learned this schema and built up a mental representation of the concept of 'boy' and 'girl' from observations and interactions with her parents, friends and the media. The cultural norms she was exposed to when she was growing up have determined what she thinks of as a 'proper boy' and 'proper girl'.

> This application question requires an explanation of gender schema theory, application to Kate and her children, and evaluation using research evidence.

This is then affecting her behaviour as a mother, as she wants her children to fit the same norms and stereotypes – presumably she thinks they will be more popular or successful if they do. She probably wants them to be quite traditional in their roles, and she will reinforce this by praising them when they fit the stereotypes (active, unemotional boy; passive, compliant, affectionate girl) and punish them when they behave in ways that don't fit the stereotypes.

> The first paragraph explains how Kate acquired a gender schema, using a good range of psychological terms.

> The second paragraph explains how Kate passes on her schemas. Some comments go beyond the material in the stem – be careful not to make assumptions. We don't actually know what Kate means by a 'proper boy' and a 'proper girl'.

Our gender schemas also affect what we think of the ingroup and outgroup, so girls identify with other girls and avoid 'boy' behaviour. This enhances their self-esteem. So Kate thinks that 'proper girls', like her, are better than girls who are not proper and behave in boy-like ways. This means she will encourage Charlotte to think girls are better than boys (or tomboys, who are not 'proper girls') and she will also support George in his ingroup preferences, wanting to play with boys and boys' toys, so he doesn't get teased. This will increase the polarisation of behaviours, clothing choice etc. between the two children.

> The paragraph about ingroup/outgroup preferences is well argued and linked.

Bradbard found that young children took more notice of toys they had been told were 'boys toys' or 'girls toys' matching their ingroup, rather than the outgroup toys. They also remembered more of the ingroup toys a week later. This shows how gender schemas reinforce themselves in the memory and also affect behaviour. Kate should label toys clearly as boys or girls toys, to ensure that George and Charlotte choose the ones she thinks are suitable for their gender.

> Evidence from research is introduced at a logical point, and again linked to the stem and the question.

Martin and Little found that young children had strong gender stereotypes about what boys and girls are allowed to do, even before they got to Kohlberg's stage of gender stability, so this supports GST rather than Kohlberg's theory. If Kate wants her children to build schemas that match hers, she should expose them to TV and movies which show boys and girls in those stereotyped roles, and she should make sure they see role models in real life too.

> Further research evidence is clearly presented, linked to the theory and the stem.

Gender beliefs are very resilient to change, so if Kate believes that boys are better at sport and girls are better at baking, for example, then even if she sees counter-examples they will not change her beliefs. Martin and Halverson showed children gender-inconsistent pictures (e.g. male nurse, female firefighter) and they didn't remember them as much as gender-consistent pictures. Also, children distorted their memories to fit their schemas. This maintains ingroup schemas as predicted by gender schema theory.

> This final paragraph goes back to why Kate has gender schemas, so is not ideally placed in the argument, but is still relevant to the question.

Level 4 (13–16 marks)

Examiner's comments: Overall an excellent answer, addressing the complex demands of the question very effectively.

Discuss Freud' psychoanalytic theory of gender development. *(16 marks)*

Freud's theory is based around his idea of psychosexual stages, and the phallic stage in particular. During this stage, which is age 3–6, boys go through the Oedipus complex. They desire their mother and want to get rid of their father, as he is a rival for her love. They feel anxious about wanting their father to die, and this leads to a fear of castration. Eventually they identify with their father and internalise his gender identity. For girls, a parallel process occurs called the Electra complex. They fall in love with their father and hate their mother because she is a rival. They also think they've been castrated – this is called penis envy. Eventually they identify with their mother and the penis envy is converted into a desire to have a baby.

Another of Freud's ideas is that people can become fixated at a psychosexual stage if things don't go right. Fixation at the phallic stage could lead to immoral behaviour or homosexuality.

Freud's ideas that children experience sexual drives at a young age seem very odd to us now. Bem showed that young children age 3–5 don't even know what the genitals belonging to the opposite sex look like, so it would be impossible for girls to have penis envy. There is some research showing that girls who have been exposed to their parents having sex were more likely to become pregnant, so this could cause them some psychological problems, but that doesn't mean that their sexual drives were actually causing their gender identity to develop.

Also, Freud's theories were based on case studies which were very subjectively interpreted, like the case study of little Hans who supposedly hated his father because he was in love with his mother, but felt anxious and this turned into a fear of horses. Freud based his interpretation on evidence collected by Hans' father and didn't even meet Hans, so this is very biased and also his theories are not falsifiable so are unscientific.

Freud thought that this process was less effective for girls as women are basically inferior and no one would want to identify with them, so girls are less developed. This is a gender-biased theory and Freud admitted himself that he didn't understand women. However, it is possible to look at it metaphorically, that women are envious of male power in a male-dominated society.

If Freud was correct, children with single parents or with gay parents wouldn't be able to develop normal gender identity, but the evidence doesn't support this. Patterson found that children with lesbian parents develop normal gender identity and relationships. An alternative psychodynamic explanation by Chodorow suggests that mothers and daughters are closer because they are the same sex (identification) whereas boys become more independent. This is supported by observation; mothers play more closely with their daughters than their sons. This explanation fits better with the findings about children of gay parents developing normally.

Level 4 (13–16 marks)

Examiner's comments: Overall, an effective discussion with a good balance of description and evaluation, and interesting debate of some points.

Examiner's comments

The Oedipus complex is quite well summarised, but the Electra complex misses out some key points. However, both are linked to gender identity, which is important in answering this question.

The idea of fixation is simply summarised but could be elaborated – why would people become fixated?

Stating that Freud's ideas seem odd doesn't get any credit, but the evidence challenges his theory and this research is well linked.

A general criticism of Freud's theories and their unscientific basis is relevant. Although the very brief summary of little Hans doesn't really add anything, it could be an illustration of biased interpretation, particularly if an alternative interpretation was given. For example, little Hans could have learnt his phobia by conditioning.

The point about gender bias is clear and the balancing comment makes it more interesting as a discussion point.

Two pieces of research are woven into the argument here, and the student could have concluded that Freud's theories lack predictive validity.

Discuss social learning theory as applied to gender development. *(16 marks)*

Social learning theory (SLT) was developed by Bandura to explain how children can learn things by observing other people rather than just by direct experience and conditioning.

With gender, children learn by observing the behaviour of their parents, families, other children at school, teachers, and people on TV. If they see someone's behaviour being rewarded, they are more likely to imitate it. Girls identify with other females (SLT does not explain why, but presumably because they have labelled themselves as female, as in Kohlberg's theory) and are more likely to imitate the behaviour of other females. Boys may spend a lot of time observing their mother caring and doing housework etc. but are less likely to imitate this as they don't identify with the mother so much.

They might also then get direct reinforcement themselves. For example, if a girl wears a dress and is told 'You look pretty', that positively reinforces the behaviour and makes it more likely that the behaviour will be repeated, or if she is teased for being a tomboy because she likes climbing trees she is less likely to repeat that behaviour. Sometimes a child is given explicit instructions about how to be ladylike, or how to be a man.

Children store representations of gender behaviour and its likely outcomes (reward or punishment) and will reproduce it if they think it is beneficial. They are then able to actively direct their own behaviour without external reinforcement.

As well as Bandura's Bobo doll experiments demonstrating imitation of aggression (and more imitation of same-sex models), there is research evidence that children imitate other behaviour of same sex-models, like choosing apples or pears. However, they only imitated gender neutral behaviour, not counter-stereotyped behaviour, like a man wearing a dress, so this may just be reinforcing existing stereotypes.

However, Martin found that boys played with toys labelled 'boys toys' but not 'girls toys', even if they saw boys playing with them. So the labelling was actually more important than the modelling. This might be confusing for children when people's behaviour doesn't match what they say, so parents and teachers should try to be consistent with what they say and do in order to tackle sexism, racism etc.

Bussey and Bandura showed how children judge each other's behaviour if it is gender-inconsistent, by showing them videos of other children playing with 'boys toys' or 'girls toys'. Young children judge others but not themselves for playing with the gender-inappropriate toys. As children get older they judge themselves too and this affects their choice of toys to play with. This shows that children store information about gender-appropriate behaviour and direct their behaviour by judging whether it is appropriate or not.

A weakness of SLT is that it doesn't include any biological factors such as chromosomes and hormones, whereas there is evidence that these also affect behaviour. For example, testosterone affects the brain as well as the body and males are more aggressive than females because of this, so there are also biological factors in gender differences.

Level 4 (13–16 marks)

Examiner's comments: The AO3 is stronger than the AO1, as some key terms are missed out. But overall an effective answer.

Examiner's comments

A neat introduction with a few terms introduced. There are many important key terms in this topic, some of which are not included in this answer: imitation, vicarious reinforcement, direct tuition, internalisation, mediational processes (attention, retention, reproduction, motivation).

The brief comparison with Kohlberg's theory is an interesting AO3 point.

This explanation is clear and the effects of reinforcement on gender behaviour are illustrated with examples.

This paragraph could be elaborated with further explanation of the cognitive mediational processes.

Bandura's study can be used here as long as the relevance to gender is clear. A second study is briefly outlined.

A third study is used to support direct tuition, with an interesting implication.

A fourth study with clear linking to show how it supports SLT.

Finally a comparison with biological explanations, although assertions are made about testosterone affecting the brain and males being more aggressive, which are not supported by evidence.

Describe and evaluate the influence of culture and/or media on gender roles. *(16 marks)*

Children may learn gender roles through social learning (observation) and through acquiring gender schemas, but what they learn depends on the norms of the culture they live in. This is because they are learning from peers, parents and the media, who tend to conform to gender stereotypes which are embedded in the culture around them. There are cultural differences between expectations of male and female behaviour in different countries, so this shows that culture influences gender roles.

For example, Margaret Mead studied groups in Papua New Guinea and found that one group had gentle, cooperative men and women, another group had violent and aggressive men and women, whereas the third group had dominant women and submissive men. These cultural differences show that gender differences are not universal or innate, so they must be learned from a culture.

However, Mead's research has been criticised as she may have been biased and the people told her what they thought she wanted to hear (demand characteristics). Also, later on she changed her conclusions and decided that there were more similarities than differences between males and females.

Many people believe that women are more conformist than men, but actually conformity varies between cultures, and women in traditional, sedentary societies are more conformist than those who move about, so this shows that culture influences gender norms. Also, as societies change the norms can change, for example women in the UK do more housework than men but this gap is gradually decreasing. This means that cultural norms can change and evolve with time.

A lot of cultural influence comes via the media, which can reinforce stereotypes, or can present counter-stereotypes. Analysis of TV programmes shows that men are generally portrayed as independent and ambitious, whereas women are shown as dependent and unambitious (Bussey and Bandura). Also men are shown as controlling events whereas women are shown as passive. This reinforces gender stereotypes. The Notel study by Williams showed that children's views became more gender stereotyped after TV had been introduced, showing that media exposure can affect attitudes.

It may be possible to use the media to challenge these stereotypes, by showing adverts with women in non-traditional roles, but this doesn't always help to reduce stereotypes – Pingree found that young boys have even stronger stereotypes when they have been shown these ads. This fits with gender schema theory, which shows that schemas are very resistant to change and people's memories often distort what they see to match their schemas. So it may be possible to use the media to change cultural stereotypes, but it is not easy.

An alternative explanation is Eagly and Wood's social role theory, which looks at gender roles as a result of biological differences. Women have children and men are generally physically stronger, so traditionally there was a division of roles between men (doing physical work) and women (caring for children). Social role theory predicts that if there aren't any requirements for this division of labour any more, as jobs become less physical and childcare is available, then gender roles will get more similar. So gender differences in behaviour may be a result of biological requirements (nature) rather than culture (nurture).

Level 4 (13–16 marks)

Examiner's comments: Overall a thoughtful, well-argued answer.

Examiner's comments

A good introduction linking **how** gender roles are learnt (social learning and schemas) with **what** is learnt (cultural stereotypes) and **from whom** (peers, parents, media).

The evidence is brief but relevant and is very well linked back with a conclusion.

This research is then evaluated, although the second point is more relevant to gender differences than cultural influences.

Another relevant example of cultural differences, and how they can change.

This paragraph clearly explains the link between cultural stereotypes and the media's reinforcement, and links in some evidence.

This paragraph develops the relationship between the media and culture, examining how media can be used to challenge cultural stereotypes.

Finally a comparison with another theory allows the nature–nurture debate to be brought in.

Cal is 9 years old, and has watched a programme on TV about gender identity disorder. He feels relieved that he has now discovered an explanation for why he doesn't fit in with other boys, and has always wished he was a girl. He tells his teacher he is very unhappy as a boy and wants to become a girl, but is too scared to talk to his parents about this.

Referring to Cal's experience, discuss biological and social explanations of gender identity disorder. *(16 marks)*

Examiner's comments

Cal always felt he didn't fit in with other boys, and this could have biological explanations. One possibility is that he has a particular gene, known as the 'transsexual gene', which makes a different version of the androgen receptor and reduces sensitivity to testosterone. This would make Cal's brain develop less male characteristics, so he didn't feel he fitted in with the boys. Hare found that male to female transsexuals are more likely to have this gene than typical males.

> This answer contains two biological explanations, a social psychological and a social/cultural explanation, each with discussion and evaluation.

> The 'transsexual gene' issue is well summarised, and applied to Cal.

Another possibility is that Cal has differences in his brain, such as the thalamus being smaller than it should be for boys, or some different wiring in his sensory cortex. This could have been caused by genetic differences or by environmental pollutants like pesticides, which contain oestrogens. A researcher found that boys whose mothers had been exposed to pesticides called dioxins during pregnancy played in a more girly way. There is also evidence that the size of a particular area of the thalamus correlates with people's preferred gender rather than their biological sex, which supports this idea. However, these brain areas are the same size in girls and boys and don't become different until adulthood, so this isn't a good explanation of Cal's feelings at age 9.

> Information about the thalamus is linked to possible causes and effects, and evidence is brought in, then this is evaluated in relation to Cal. Brain wiring is not elaborated.

A social psychological explanation of Cal's experience is that he could have a poor relationship with his father and has not been able to identify with him properly, or is too close to his mother. This could explain why Cal is scared to talk to his parents about his feelings of gender dysphoria. However, Cole studied over 400 people with gender identity disorder and there wasn't any greater incidence of mental disorders than in the normal population, so this explanation isn't very good.

> The psychological explanation is also applied appropriately – be careful not to go beyond the information in the stem and make assumptions, as we don't actually know anything about Cal's family. It is not entirely clear how Cole's research relates to the theory of a poor relationship with a father, as this wouldn't necessarily cause mental disorders.

Another social explanation is that Cal doesn't fit the cultural stereotypes of boys; maybe he doesn't like sport and rough play and prefers drawing and music, for example, which are thought of as girls' activities. Or maybe the boys he knows are not very nice and the girls are more friendly and inclusive. This would affect his learning of gender schemas and his identification with the ingroup of boys. The implication is that society should work to break down restrictive stereotypes rather than seeing the problem as Cal's. The teacher may need to work at making sure children include each other and value differences rather than bullying people who are different in their preferences or behaviour.

> The paragraph about cultural stereotypes is very well argued, with practical implications applied to Cal's situation.

The whole issue of gender identity disorder is socially sensitive, as Cal could become very distressed if he thinks his feelings are not being taken seriously, or he could be encouraged to think that hormone treatments or surgery are necessary which are painful and irreversible, when actually society needs to be more accepting. He will need wise and careful guidance through this uncertain period, especially as it is not clear whether biological or social causes are the explanation of his feelings; it is probably an interaction of different factors.

> Finally, the implications of possible treatments are considered, with high-level discussion around social sensitivity and the interaction between biological and social factors.

Level 4 (13–16 marks)

Examiner's comments: Overall, clear Level 4 answer.

KEY TERMS

- Accommodation
- Assimilation
- Cognitive development
- Equilibration
- Schema

Possible essay question …

Discuss Piaget's theory of cognitive development. *(16 marks)*

Other possible exam questions …

+ Explain what is meant by the term 'schema', as used in the study of cognitive development. *(2 marks)*

+ Explain the difference between assimilation and accommodation, as used in Piaget's theory of cognitive development. *(4 marks)*

+ Outline the role played by equilibration in cognitive development. *(4 marks)*

+ Evaluate Piaget's view on the development of cognition. *(8 marks)*

 Think

Piaget's theory was based on observation of his own children's behaviour. What methodological issues might this raise?

MUST know …

Schemas

Schemas are mental structures that represent a group of related concepts. They can be behavioural (such as grasping objects) or cognitive (such as classifying objects).

Assimilation: This is the process of incorporating new information into an existing schema.

Accommodation: This occurs when a child adapts an existing schema to understand new information that doesn't seem to fit into existing knowledge.

Equilibration: The intellect strives to maintain a sense of balance (i.e. equilibrium). If an experience cannot be assimilated into existing schemas then imbalance occurs. Individuals seek to restore balance through equilibration.

 One strength of Piaget's theory is…

…its contribution to our understanding of cognitive development.

- ***E*** – Piaget's theory combines both nature (biological maturation) with nurture (experience) to explain how thinking changes with age.

 There is evidence to support…

…the existence of innate schemas.

- ***E*** – For example, Fantz (1961) found that 4-day-old infants show a preference for a human face with all its features (e.g. nose) correctly positioned, rather than a 'jumbled up' human face.

Cognitive development appears to be necessary…

…for language development.

- ***E*** – For example, Sinclair-de-Zwart (1969) found that teaching language appropriate to a task did not help children successfully complete it.

SHOULD know …

Schemas

Some schemas are innate, but new experiences lead to new schemas being developed. Schemas become more complex by assimilation and accommodation.

For example, when a baby is given a new toy car to play with, they may grasp it in the same way they grasped a rattle.

This new information cannot be assimilated into the existing schema, so the child's schema must alter to 'accommodate' new information, and so a new schema is formed.

Cognitive development is a result of these changes between existing schemas and environmental 'demands' for change (e.g. new experiences that don't fit existing schemas).

- ***E*** – It has also changed ideas about children, had an influence on educational practice, and generated much research interest.
- ***L*** – This means that it has provided many valuable insights into how children's minds develop.

- ***E*** – This preference indicates that it is the unique configuration of a face, rather than merely a complex pattern, that is important.
- ***L*** – An innate preference for faces makes sense as it is adaptive, allowing an infant to elicit attachment and caring.

- ***E*** – 90% of children given 'conservation' tasks (see page xxx) still failed them even though they had been taught appropriate verbal skills.
- ***L*** – This supports Piaget's view that cognitive maturity is a prerequisite for language, not, as some researchers believe, the other way round.

FURTHER EVALUATION

 P – Discovery learning can be…

…beneficial for children if it is used appropriately.

- ***E*** – For example, if knowledge is gained through equilibration, then true understanding only occurs if children make their *own* accommodations.
- ***E*** – Although children taught by formal methods do better in reading, maths, and English, this could be because discovery learning requires more experience on the teacher's part.
- ***L*** – Therefore it is not discovery learning that is problematical, but its application by teachers.

P – Some concepts in Piaget's theory are…

…difficult to operationalise.

- ***E*** – For example, Inhelder *et al.* (1974) argue that disequilibrium occurs when there is 'mild conflict' between what children expect to happen and what actually does happen.
- ***E*** – However, Bryant (1985) believes that disequilibrium is a more major dissonance between things.
- ***L*** – Until important concepts can be adequately operationalised, aspects of Piaget's theory cannot really be tested.

CHOOSE THE RIGHT ANSWER

Which **one** of the following best describes equilibration?
(Tick **one** box only.)

A It is a state of cognitive imbalance. ☐

B It is experienced as an unpleasant state. ☐

C It involves fitting new experiences into existing schemas without making any change. ☐

D It is a way of restoring cognitive imbalance. ☐

Answers on page 353

 FILL IN THE BOXES

In each box below, write one sentence defining each mechanism of cognitive development and provide a suitable example to illustrate your definition.

	Definition	Example
Schema		
Assimilation		
Accommodation		
Equilibration		

Answers on page 353

 APPLYING YOUR KNOWLEDGE

Mark took his two-year-old child to the park. He saw his friend Girish approaching. Girish was bald on the top of his head and had long frizzy ginger hair on the sides. As Girish approached, Mark's son shouted 'Clown, Clown!' much to Mark's embarrassment.

(a) Using your knowledge of Piaget's theory of cognitive development, explain the toddler's behaviour. *(3 marks)*

(b) Using Piaget's theory, explain how Mark could make sure that his toddler wouldn't call Girish a clown again. *(4 marks)*

Answers on page 353

 COMPLETE THE DIAGRAM

Match up the key term with the appropriate description. Write your answers in the boxes on the right.

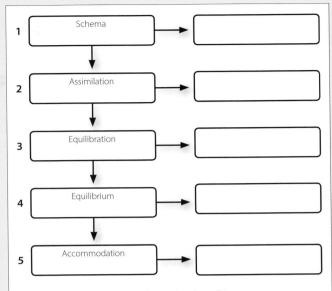

1 Schema →

2 Assimilation →

3 Equilibration →

4 Equilibrium →

5 Accommodation →

A Modifying the sucking reflex with other objects

B Dealing with experiences by assimilation

C An inbuilt sucking reflex

D Using the sucking reflex with other objects

E Seeking 'mental balance'

Answers on page 353

 MATCH THEM UP

Match up the researchers with the statement that best describes their research.

1	Bryant (1985)	**A**	'Mild conflicts' between reality and expectations are sufficient for disequilibrium.
2	Fantz (1961)	**B**	Disequilibrium is a major dissonance between reality and expectations.
3	Sinclair-de-Zwart (1969)	**C**	Language development requires cognitive development.
4	Inhelder *et al.* (1974)	**D**	There are innate schemas for faces.

Answers on page 353

 Link

See page 138 of the Year 1/AS Revision and Exam companion for a more general explanation of schemas

KEY TERMS

- Class inclusion
- Conservation
- Egocentrism
- Object permanence

Possible essay question …

Discuss research into Piaget's stages of intellectual development. *(16 marks)*

Other possible exam questions …

+ Explain what is meant by the term 'object permanence'. *(2 marks)*

+ Outline **one** study which has investigated conservation in the context of Piaget's theory of cognitive development. *(4 marks)*

+ Using an example to illustrate your answer, explain what is meant by the term 'class inclusion'. *(4 marks)*

+ Outline and evaluate research into egocentrism as the term is used by Piaget. *(6 marks)*

 Exam tip

Remember to include an example of how children behave when answering questions about this topic.

MUST know …

Sensorimotor stage (0–2 years)

The infant learns to coordinate sensory input with motor actions.

Object permanence develops at this stage. Infants assume objects no longer exist if they cannot be seen.

Pre-operational stage (2–7 years)

Conservation: Children don't understand that volume or number cannot change, even if their appearance does.

Egocentrism: Children see the world from their perspective-unaware of other perspectives.

Class inclusion: Young children can classify objects into categories, but not sub-groups.

Concrete-operational stage (7–11 years)

Children acquire the rudiments of logical reasoning.

Formal-operational stage (11+ years)

Children can now develop and test hypotheses and solve abstract problems.

EVALUATION ***One limitation of Piaget's theory is…***

…that it might be culturally biased.

- ***E*** – For example, Piaget's European background values thinking about abstract ideas.

EVALUATION ***Piaget's stage theory can be applied…***

…to education.

- ***E*** – For example, abstract mathematical calculations are difficult to teach pre-operational children.

EVALUATION ***Research shows that the effect of practice on performance is…***

…not clear.

- ***E*** – For example, Danner & Day (1977) found that practice did not improve performance, whereas Bryant and Trabasso (1971) found that it did.

SHOULD know …

Sensorimotor stage (0–2 years)

Infants repeat actions to test sensorimotor relationships.

Around eight months, they realise objects still exist even if they can't be seen.

Pre-operational stage (2–7 years)

This shows that children lack logical mental rules.

The *three mountains task (1956)* shows children find taking another's perspective difficult.

Children shown three black cows and one white cow, will say there are more black cows than cows.

Concrete-operational stage (7–11 years)

The ability to conserve is the main achievement of this stage.

Formal-operational stage (11+ years)

Children also display idealistic thinking. They can imagine how things could be.

- ***E*** – Other cultures may place greater value on concrete operational abilities, such as making things.
- ***L*** – This suggests that Piaget's theory may not be universally applicable.

- ***E*** – Piaget says this is because certain concepts can only be taught when children are 'biologically ready'.
- ***L*** – If true, this suggests that school curricula might need to be reassessed and amended.

- ***E*** – Piaget claims that if a person is not biologically ready to move to the next stage, then no amount of practice should get them there.
- ***L*** – This shows that the evidence for this aspect of Piaget's theory is equivocal.

FURTHER EVALUATION

EVALUATION ***P* – Evidence suggests that Piaget may have underestimated…**

…pre-operational children's abilities.

- ***E*** – For example, it has been argued that Piaget's tasks confuse young children, and may suffer from demand characteristics.
- ***E*** – When Hughes (1975) tried Piaget's *three mountain tasks* using familar ideas for children they did not show egocentricity.
- ***L*** – This suggests that whilst they are inventive, Piaget's methodology for studying children was flawed.

EVALUATION ***P* – Evidence suggests that Piaget may have overestimated…**

…the ability to use logic in the formal operational stage.

- ***E*** – Research clearly suggests that qualitative changes in cognitive development do occur with increasing age.
- ***E*** – However, Dasen (1994) claims only a third of adults ever reach the formal operational stage, and even then, not during adolescence.
- ***L*** – This suggests that Piaget's idea of fixed stages, which inevitably occur, may be incorrect.

CHOOSE THE RIGHT ANSWER

Which **two** of the following are **not** features of Piaget's pre-operational stage of intellectual development? (Tick **two** boxes only.)

A Class inclusion ☐
B Egocentrism ☐
C Logical thinking ☐
D Solving abstract problems ☐
E Lack of conservation ☐

Answers on page 353

 ## DRAWING CONCLUSIONS

A researcher was interested in testing the claim that pre-operational children can solve class inclusion tasks *if* the task is presented in a different way to usual. A large sample of six-year-old children were shown four toy cows, three of which were black and one white. The cows were laid on their side and the children were told they were 'sleeping'. Half of the children were asked 'Are there more black cows or more cows?' The other half were asked 'Are there more black cows or more *sleeping* cows'. The results are shown in the table below.

	Are there more black cows or more cows?	Are there more black cows or more sleeping cows?
Number of children answering correctly	25	48
Number of children answering incorrectly	75	52

(a) What level of measurement was used in this study? *(1 mark)*

(b) Identify a suitable statistical test that could be used to analyse the data in the table. Given **two** reasons why this test would be appropriate. *(3 marks)*

(c) The test showed that the null hypothesis could be rejected at $p < 0.05$. What conclusions would you draw from this study's findings? *(4 marks)*

Answers on page 353

 ## FILL IN THE BOXES

Complete the table below by identifying the approximate ages of each stage of intellectual development and **one** major characteristic of each stage.

Name of stage	Approximate age	One main characteristic of the stage
1 Sensori motor		
2 Pre-operational		
3 Concrete operational		
4 Formal operational		

Answers on page 353

 ## MATCH THEM UP

Match the concept to the statement that best describes it.

1 Object permanence	A Distinguishing between reality and appearance and understanding, for example, that quantity is not changed even when a display is transformed.
2 Hypothetico-deductive reasoning	B Understanding that objects continue to exist, even if they can't be seen.
3 Egocentrism	C The inability to see the world from another person's perspective.
4 Conservation	D Developing hypotheses and testing them to determine causal relationships.

Answers on page 353

 ## APPLYING YOUR KNOWLEDGE

Rona took her two grandchildren to her local pizza restaurant. The waiter brought Rona's pizza over first and asked her if she wanted it cut into six or eight pieces. Rona said: 'Oh, you'd better make it six, I could never eat eight pieces.' Rona's ten-year-old grandchild laughed so much he spluttered his fizzy drink all over the table. However, her six-year-old did not react to what Rona had said.

Using your knowledge of Piaget's stages of intellectual development, explain why Rona's two grandchildren reacted differently to what she said. *(4 marks)*

Identify the psychology	Link to the reactions of Rona's grandchildren

Answers on page 353

KEY TERMS

- Scaffolding
- Zone of proximal development (ZPD)

Possible essay question ...

Outline and evaluate Vygotsky's theory of cognitive development. *(16 marks)*

Other possible exam questions ...

+ Explain what is meant by 'scaffolding', as used in Vygotsky's theory of cognitive development. *(2 marks)*

+ Outline Vygotsky's concept of the zone of proximal development. *(4 marks)*

+ Give **two** limitations of Vygotsky's theory of cognitive development. *(6 marks)*

 Think

What are the similarities and differences between Vygotsky and Piaget's theories of cognitive development?

MUST know ...

Elementary mental functions

Elementary mental functions are innate, but cultural influences transform them into higher mental functions.

Children learn through problem-solving with a more competent individual (an 'expert').

Experts transmit culture to children using language.

Every function in cognitive development appears on the social level, and later on the individual level.

The **zone of proximal development (ZPD)**, where cognitive development takes place, is the region between what children can achieve alone and what they could potentially achieve with an expert's help.

Scaffolding is the process of assisting a child through the ZPD. The expert creates a scaffold which is gradually withdrawn.

 P – The role of language in cognitive development...

...is supported by research.

- *E* – Carmichael *et al.* (1932) gave participants one of two labels for certain drawings. For example, they were shown a kidney shape and told it was either a kidney bean or a canoe.

 P – Culture's role in cognitive development...

...is also supported by research.

- *E* – For example, Gredler (1992) discovered that the counting system used in Papua New Guinea is very different from our own.

 P – There is research evidence...

...for the role of the ZPD in cognitive development.

- *E* – For example, McNaughton & Leyland (1990) observed young children working with their mothers on jigsaw puzzles of increasing difficulty.

SHOULD know ...

Elementary mental funtions

Elementary mental functions are biological and a form of natural development. Higher mental functions are exclusively human.

The expert guides problem-solving but gradually the child takes over.

Language begins as shared dialogues between an expert and child, but as the skill of mental representation develops, an internal dialogue occurs.

Social experiences depend on language, enabling higher mental functions to develop.

Cognitive development must occur just beyond current development, as new challenges aren't useful if they are too far from current knowledge.

Scaffolding involves an expert responding to success or failure by providing either less, or more, explicit instructions.

- *E* – When participants were subsequently asked to draw the shape, it differed according to which label they had been given.
- *L* – This shows that words can affect the way we think about and remember things.

- *E* – Counting is done by starting on the thumb of one hand and going up the arm and down to the other fingers, ending at 29.
- *L* – This system makes it difficult to add and subtract large numbers, and shows how culture can limit cognitive development.

- *E* – The mothers offered help in line with Vygotsky's predictions. If the puzzle was easy (below the ZPD), they offered little help, but if it was difficult (beyond the ZPD), they offered more help.
- *L* – This supports Vygotsky, and shows that experts do adjust their input according to where a learner is in the ZPD.

FURTHER EVALUATION

 P – Research with non-human animals...

...can be used to support Vygotsky's claims.

- *E* – Some psychologists believe that elementary non-human mental functions can be transformed into higher mental functions by immersing them in human culture.
- *E* – Savage-Rumbaugh (1991) exposed Bonobo apes to a language-rich culture and found they can communicate using a symbol system.
- *L* – This suggests that higher mental functions (a symbol system) can be transmitted through culture.

P – The importance of the social environment...

...may have been overstated by Vygotsky.

- *E* – If social input is all that is needed to improve cognitive development, then learning would be a lot quicker than it is.
- *E* – Also, the emphasis on social factors means that biological factors were largely ignored in Vygotsky's theory.
- *L* – This suggests that there are important limitations to Vygotsky's theory of cognitive development.

✔ CHOOSE THE RIGHT ANSWER

Which **one** of the following definitions best describes the Zone of Proximal Development? (Tick **one** box only.)

A	The region between what children can do on their own and what they could potentially achieve with the help of an expert	☐
B	The region between their ideal self and their self-concept	☐
C	The region between what they can do now and what they could do next year	☐
D	The region between two stages of development	☐

Answers on page 354

⚙ APPLYING YOUR KNOWLEDGE

Beth was learning how to make cakes. At first, her mum gave her lots of help. For example, her mum gave her clear instructions on what she should do, and helped her to use the scales to weigh out the ingredients correctly. Beth enjoyed making cakes, but the more cakes she made, the less help her mum gave her. After six months, Beth's mum would get on with other things while Beth made her cakes.

Use your knowledge of scaffolding to explain why Beth's mum's behaviour changed over time. *(6 marks)*

Identify the psychology	Link to Beth's mum's behaviour

Answers on page 354

💡 DRAWING CONCLUSIONS

A researcher carried out a study in which mothers were observed helping children solve a puzzle. The researcher was interested in how much direct help was given to the children by the mothers. 'Direct help' was operationally defined as phrases such as 'Try that piece here'. Two observers recorded the amount of direct helping they saw in ten children over a one-hour-period. The results are shown in the table below.

Child	First observer	Second observer
1	5	6
2	7	6
3	7	8
4	8	7
5	12	14
6	17	15
7	14	15
8	6	5
9	2	1
10	19	18

(a) Display the findings in the table above in the form of a suitably labelled scattergram. *(4 marks)*

(b) The researcher used the scattergram to initially assess how reliable the observers were. What is the name of this method of reliability assessment? *(1 mark)*

(c) Name a parametric test that could be used to determine whether the observations are reliable or not. *(1 mark)*

Answers on page 354

KEY TERMS

- False belief
- Nativist approach
- Physical reasoning system
- Violation of expectation research

Possible essay question …

Discuss Baillargeon's explanation of early infant abilities. *(16 marks)*

Other possible exam questions …

+ Explain what is meant by the term 'violation of expectation'. *(2 marks)*
+ Outline the findings from **one** study that has investigated violation of expectation. *(4 marks)*
+ Outline Baillargeon's explanation of how infants acquire a knowledge of the physical world. *(4 marks)*
+ Give **two** limitations of Baillargeon's research into early infant abilities. *(6 marks)*

⭐ **Exam tip**

Remember! A key feature of your evaluation for this topic should be concerned with how Baillargeon's findings challenge Piaget's theory.

MUST know …

Baillargeon argues that the reason infants don't search for hidden objects is not because they lack object permanence.

Key study: Violation of expectation (VOE)

This tests for object permanence, and assumes that infants will express *surprise* at an impossible event. Baillargeon & De Vos (1991) found that three-month-olds show object permanence.

Infant's knowledge of the physical world

Infants have an *innate* **physical reasoning system (PRS)** helping them understand the physical world and learn to reason about novel physical phenomena.

Infants form an 'all-or-none' concept about physical phenomena, and then incorporate variables that affect it.

 P – One strength of Baillargeon's research is…

…her attention to certain validity issues.

- **E** – For example, she has studied children from various social classes, and not just the middle class.

 P – Baillargeon's innate 'mechanisms' are more likely…

…than Spelke *et al*.'s (1992) innate 'principles'.

- **E** – Baillargeon has been challenged by Spelke *et al*. (1992) who propose that infants are born with a core knowledge, including a basic understanding of the physical world.

 P – One weakness of Baillargeon's research is…

…that the VOE method itself might lack validity.

- **E** – For example, Smith (1999) suggests that infants may look longer at an impossible event because it is 'interesting' rather than because it violates their expectations.

SHOULD know …

Rather than lacking mental abilities, infants can't plan and execute the necessary motor actions.

Key study: Violation of expectation (VOE)

Following habituation events (to get used to the activity), infants expressed no surprise when a short object failed to appear in a high window. However, when a tall object failed to appear (the impossible event), they did.

Infant's knowledge of the physical world

Piaget did not believe an innate mechanism existed in children.

9.5-month-olds show surprise when a cover with a bulge is removed to reveal nothing. However, only 12.5-month-olds express surprise if the object is *smaller* than the bulge suggested.

- **E** – Her research also controls for the influence of parental behaviour while infants perform the tasks, and uses observers unaware of a study's purpose.
- **L** – This means that Baillargeon's research has both population and experimental validity.

- **E** – However, research findings indicate that infants do *not* show expectations about all events related to one core principle (e.g. covering objects).
- **L** – This supports Baillargeon's view that infants are born with the ability to *acquire* certain kinds of knowledge very quickly rather than with a core knowledge itself.

- **E** – Schlesinger and Casey (2003) showed that when an impossible event occurs, infants show greater perceptual interest rather than surprise.
- **L** – This suggests that the VOE method might not measure what Baillargeon says it measures.

FURTHER EVALUATION

 P – Children may not really understand…

…the principle of object permanence.

- **E** – For example, Bremner (2013) argues that demonstrating object permanence does not imply that an infant has a real understanding of it.
- **E** – For Piaget, cognitive development involves *understanding* a principle, not just acting in accordance with it, as Baillargeon's research shows.
- **L** – This suggests that Baillargeon may only have shown that Piaget underestimated children's abilities, rather than disprove his views.

P – Baillargeon's research…

…also lacks cultural validity.

- **E** – Baillargeon has not specifically studied the capabilities of very young children raised in cultures other than America.
- **E** – If there were differences in abilities related to culture, this would challenge Baillargeon's views about innate mechanisms.
- **L** – This suggests that further research is needed before we can accept Baillargeon's claims that infants' abilities are innately driven.

CHOOSE THE RIGHT ANSWER

Which **one** of the following terms refers to the idea that an infant will show surprise when witnessing an impossible event? (Tick **one** box only.)

A Physical reasoning task ☐

B Object permanence study ☐

C False belief task ☐

D Violation of expectation research ☐

Answers on page 354

 MATCH THEM UP

Match up the researchers to the statement that best describes their research.

1	Schlesinger & Casey (2003)	**A**	Infants are born with a core knowledge, including a basic understanding of the physical world.
2	Spelke *et al.* (1992)	**B**	Demonstrating object permanence in infants does not imply they have a real understanding of it.
3	Bremner (2013)	**C**	The VOE might not be a valid measure.

Answers on page 354

 APPLYING YOUR KNOWLEDGE

Charlotte had taken her five-month-old daughter to the childminder. When she picked her up, the childminder said: 'I put a on DVD called 'Larry the Lucky Lemming' to amuse her. It showed cartoon lemmings walking off a cliff and falling to earth. She got bored very quickly, so I paused the DVD. When I put the DVD back on she saw Larry the Lucky Lemming walk off the cliff but remain suspended in the air. I couldn't believe your daughter's reaction! It really grabbed her attention, but I have no idea why.'

Use your knowledge of Baillargeon's research to explain to the childminder why Charlotte's daughter behaved the way she did. *(6 marks)*

Identify the psychology	Link to Charlotte's daughter

Answers on page 354

 FILL IN THE BOXES

Use the terms below to complete the flow chart relating to Baillargeon's Violation of Expectation research.

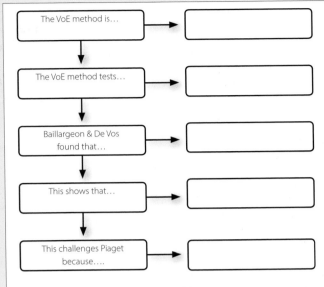

The infants were only three months old

A way of studying object permanence

Whether infants will express surprise when witnessing an impossible event

Infants do possess object permanence

Infants expressed surprise when a tall object failed to appear in a short window

Answers on page 354

 RESEARCH ISSUES

In Baillargeon's VOE research, babies are tested sitting on their mother's lap. The mothers are asked not to interact with their babies, and are additionally asked to keep their eyes shut during the task.

Explain why this apparently unusual request is made of the mothers. *(2 marks)*

Answers on page 354

KEY TERM
- Perspective-taking

Possible essay question …
Outline and evaluate Selman's levels of perspective-taking explanation of how social cognition develops. *(16 marks)*

Other possible exam questions …
+ Using examples, outline **two** stages of Selman's levels of perspective-taking. *(4 marks)*
+ Explain **two** limitations of Selman's approach to social cognition. *(6 marks)*

 Exam tip

Remember! There are five stages in Selman's theory. The first is called Stage 0 and the last is called Stage 4.

MUST know …

Selmans' perspective-taking stages

Stage 0: Undifferentiated perspective-taking (3–6 years)
Children can distinguish between self and others.

Stage 1: Social-informational perspective-taking (6–8 years)
Children are aware of perspectives that are different to their own.

Stage 2: Self-reflective perspective-taking (8–10 years)
Children view their *own* thoughts and feelings from someone else's perspective.

Stage 3: Mutual perspective-taking (10–12 years)
Children can imagine how they and others are viewed by a third, impartial party.

Stage 4: Societal perspective-taking (12–15+ years)
Personal decisions are now made with reference to social conventions.

 P – One strength of Selman's theory is…

…that research studies support it.
- *E* – For example, Cooney & Selman (1978) found that 40/48 boys made gains in their level of perspective-taking.

 P – Perspective-taking skills are key…

…in all social behaviour.
- *E* – For example, Fitzgerald & White (2003) found that maturity of perspective-taking skills was correlated with pro-social behaviour.

 P – There are real-world applications…

…of Selman's theory.
- *E* – For example, some criminals lack empathy so are more willing to harm others.

SHOULD know …

Selmans' perspective-taking stages

Stage 0: Undifferentiated perspective-taking (3–6 years)
They are governed by their own perspective.

Stage 1: Social-informational perspective-taking (6–8 years)
However, they assume that this is because others have different information.

Stage 2: Self-reflective perspective-taking (8–10 years)
They also recognise that others can do the same.

Stage 3: Mutual perspective-taking (10–12 years)
They can also consider two viewpoints simultaneously.

Stage 4: Societal perspective-taking (12–15+ years)
For example, humanely treating animals is seen as an important social convention.

- *E* – Later analysis by Gurucharri & Selman (1982) confirmed this progressive developmental sequence.
- *L* – This supports Selman's belief that perspective-taking is a progressive age-related developmental sequence.

- *E* – Also, Selman et al. (1977) found that children with poor perspective-taking skills have more difficulty forming relationships.
- *L* – This suggests that perspective-taking skills lead to important social development, and can be used to explain the lack of social development.

- *E* – Social skills training programmes encourage prisoners to learn perspective-taking skills.
- *L* – This means that they can increase their empathetic concern and hopefully this will stop them reoffending.

FURTHER EVALUATION

 P – Social experience is important in…

…the development of perspective-taking.
- *E* – For example, Fitzgerald & White (2003) found that growth in perspective-taking skills was related to parenting style.
- *E* – Children showed more growth when their parents encouraged them to take a victim's perspective.
- *L* – This shows that social experience can lead to changes in perspective-taking skills.

 P – One weakness of research in this area is…

…that much of it is correlational.
- *E* – For example, just because perspective-taking skills and social competence are correlated, does not necessarily mean that the former causes the latter.
- *E* – The latter could cause the former, *or* the two variables may be accidentally correlated.
- *L* – This means that we cannot be sure that perspective-taking skills affect social competence levels in a causal way.

CHOOSE THE RIGHT ANSWER

Which **two** of the following are **not** levels of perspective-taking in Selman's stage theory. (Tick **two** boxes only.)

A Mutually-exclusive perspective-taking ☐

B Undifferentiated perspective-taking ☐

C Self-reflective perspective-taking ☐

D Information-processing perspective-taking ☐

E Societal perspective-taking ☐

Answers on page 354

 FILL IN THE BOXES

Complete the table below by identifying each of Selman's five stages of perspective-taking and **one** major characteristic of each stage. The approximate ages for each stage have been identified for you.

Name of stage	Approximate age (years)	One main characteristic of the stage
0	3–6	
1	6–8	
2	8–10	
3	10–12	
4	12–15+	

Answers on page 354

 APPLYING YOUR KNOWLEDGE

Frank, who is 9-years-old and his 13-year-old sister, Lisa, were watching a children's TV programme. One of the children in the programme had seen a boy steal another boy's bag and run away down a busy street. The child knew he could run fast enough to catch the thief, but in an earlier scene his father had told him never to run down busy streets because of the danger from cars. The child hesitated. 'Why doesn't he chase him? said Frank. 'His dad would only get angry if he thought his son was running down the street for fun.' His sister replied, 'It's a little more complex than that, Frank. His dad won't be angry because he knows that stealing is wrong.'

Explain Frank and Lisa's different views in terms of Selman's perspective-taking stages. *(6 marks)*

Identify the psychology	Link to Frank and Lisa's different views

Answers on page 354

 DRAWING CONCLUSIONS

A psychologist was interested in studying whether experience plays a role in the development of perspective-taking. She interviewed parents about their reactions to their children hurting other children. The children of ten parents who encouraged them to see things from their victim's perspective were assessed for their perspective-taking by means of a questionnaire. Their scores on the questionnaire were compared with those of ten children whose parents did not encourage them to see things from their victim's perspective. The questionnaire scores are shown in the table below. The higher the score, the better the perspective-taking.

Parents encouraging their children to see things from their victim's perspective (Group A)	Parents *not* encouraging their children to see things from their victim's perspective (Group B)
5	4
5	4
7	5
5	1
8	2
6	7
7	3
9	3
2	3
9	1

(a) Calculate the mean perspective-taking score for each group. *(2 marks)*

(b) Calculate the median perspective-taking score for each group. *(2 marks)*

(c) Calculate the modal perspective-taking score for each group. *(2 marks)*

(d) The standard deviations for Group A and Group B are 2.2 and 1.8. What do these standard deviations suggest about the variability of performance in the two groups? *(2 marks)*

The researcher decided to see if there was a significant difference between the two sets of scores.

(e) Suggest an appropriate statistical test that could be used. *(1 mark)*

(f) Give **two** reasons why this test would be appropriate. *(2 marks)*

Answers on page 354

KEY TERMS

- Autism
- False belief
- Sally–Anne test
- Theory of mind

Possible essay question ...

Describe and evaluate theory of mind as explanation for autism. *(16 marks)*

Other possible exam questions ...

+ Explain what is meant by the term 'theory of mind'. *(2 marks)*
+ Outline the findings from **one** study which has investigated theory of mind. *(3 marks)*
+ Evaluate research into theory of mind. *(8 marks)*

 Exam tip

ToM has been used as an explanation for autism, but remember that it is something which explains **all** children's understanding that others have a separate mind to their own and therefore do not see or experience the world as they do.

MUST know ...

Theory of mind

Theory of mind (ToM) is our understanding that others have separate mental states to us.

Autistic children may find social interaction difficult as they lack a ToM.

In the **Sally–Anne test**, Sally puts her ball in a basket before leaving the room. Anne then moves the ball to a box. When Sally returns, children are asked where she will look for the ball.

High-functioning autistic adults pass the Sally–Anne test, but show poorer performance than non-autistic adults on the *Eyes Task*.

As ToM develops at a particular age and is absent in many with autism, it may be biological.

 P – Biology may not be...

...the sole determinant of ToM.

- **E** – Perner *et al.* (1994) found that ToM appears earlier in children from large families, with older siblings.

P – One weakness of ToM as an explanation for autism is...

...that not all research supports it.

- **E** – For example, studies show that not all autistic children fail the Sally–Anne test.

P – One weakness of the Eyes Task is...

...that it might not measure ToM.

- **E** – Baron-Cohen *et al.* (1997) claim that the test measures 'mindreading', which is essentially the same thing as ToM.

SHOULD know ...

Theory of mind

Social relationships require a ToM. ToM appears around age 3–4 years.

ToM is tested using **false belief** tasks (like the Sally Anne test). These measure the understanding that others may hold, and act on, mistaken (false) beliefs. Children can do these tasks successfully by age 4–6 years.

Baron-Cohen *et al.* (1985) found 20% of non-autistic children, including those with Down's Syndrome, and 80% of autistic children fail the test.

The *Eyes Task* measures the emotion expressed in people's eyes.

Baron-Cohen (1995) suggests that a ToM module (ToMM) exists. This is a specific mechanism that enables people to understand others' mental states.

- **E** – In these circumstances, a child is challenged to think about the feelings of others when resolving conflicts.
- **L** – This means that the development of ToM is probably a combination of biology and social environment.

- **E** – If ToM was a central aspect of autism, then *all* autistic children should fail the test.
- **L** – This suggests that a lack of ToM is not a complete explanation for autism.

- **E** – However, Wellman and Woolley (1990) argue that knowing someone else's internal state (mindreading) is *not* the same as knowing how they experience the world (ToM).
- **L** – This suggests that the *Eyes Task* lacks internal validity as a measure of true ToM.

FURTHER EVALUATION

 P – Research into autism suffers from...

...a cultural bias.

- **E** – For example, Baron-Cohen's research was from a very Western perspective and used only British participants.
- **E** – The higher rates of autism diagnosed in the West may be because its symptoms are not considered abnormal in other cultures.
- **L** – This means that a lack of social interaction as a key feature of autism may be a Western rather than universal perspective on the disorder.

 P – Intention may not be...

...a precursor of ToM.

- **E** – For example, Carpenter *et al.* (2001) tested autistic and non-autistic children's understanding of intention by seeing if they followed someone's gaze and looked at where they were pointing.
- **E** – 2.5–5-year-old autistic and non-autistic children behaved in much the same way.
- **L** – This suggests that understanding intentions is a separate ability to ToM.

MATCH THEM UP

Match up the researchers to the statement that best describes their research.

1	Carpenter *et al.* (2001)	**A**	ToM appears earlier in children from large families with older siblings.
2	Perner *et al.* (1994)	**B**	There is a specific mechanism which enables people to explain others' mental states.
3	Wellman & Woolley (1990)	**C**	Understanding intentions is a separate ability to ToM.
4	Baron-Cohen (1995)	**D**	The *Eyes Task* lacks internal validity as a measure of true ToM.

Answers on page 355

 RESEARCH ISSUES

In their original study using the Sally–Anne test, Baron-Cohen *et al.* (1985) also tested a group of children with Down's syndrome. They found that 12 out of 24 of the children were successful at the Sally–Anne task compared with 4 out of the 20 autistic children.

Why was the inclusion of children with Down's syndrome an important control feature of the study? *(4 marks)*

Answers on page 355

 APPLYING YOUR KNOWLEDGE

Kirsty liked to play tricks on her sisters. One day she placed some buttons into an empty sweets tube and asked her 3- and 6-year-old sisters, 'What do you think is in here?' Both of her sisters were surprised when Kirsty showed her the buttons. 'I know,' said Kirsty. 'Let's put the buttons back and ask Dad what he thinks is in the tube. What do you two think he'll say?'

What do you think Kirsty's two sisters would have said? Explain your answer with reference to ToM research. *(6 marks)*

Identify the psychology	Link to Kirsty's two sisters

Answers on page 355

 DRAWING CONCLUSIONS

A research team used the Sally–Anne test with 27 non-autistic children whose mean age was 4 years and 5 months. The test was also used with 20 autistic children whose mean age was 11 years and 11 months. The team found that 23 of the non-autistic children completed the test successfully, and 16 of the autistic children failed it.

(a) Fill in the contingency table below using the information presented in the passage above. *(4 marks)*

	Non-autistic children	Autistic children
Successful at the test		
Unsuccessful at the test		

(b) Display the findings in the contingency table above in the form of a suitably labelled bar chart. *(4 marks)*

(c) Name a statistical test that could be used to analyse the data in the contingency table. *(1 mark)*

(d) Give **two** reasons for your choice of statistical test. *(1 mark)*

(e) Explain what a Type I error is. *(2 marks)*

(f) The research team used the $p < 0.05$ significance level in their study, and found a statistically significant difference between the autistic and non-autistic children's performance on the task. What is the likelihood of a Type I error being made in this study? *(2 marks)*

Answers on page 354

KEY TERM

■ Mirror neurons

Possible essay question …

Discuss the role of the mirror neuron system in social cognition. *(16 marks)*

Other possible exam questions …

+ Explain what is meant by the term 'mirror neuron'. *(2 marks)*

+ Outline **one** study which has investigated the mirror neuron system. *(4 marks)*

+ Evaluate research into the role played by the mirror neuron system in social cognition. *(8 marks)*

 Exam tip

If you are asked to outline a study, you should include how the study was done (the procedure) and what the results were (the findings).

MUST know …

The mirror neuron

Mirror neurons (MNs) react when a person performs an action and when a person performs an action and when we see another person perform the same action.

MNs explain how imitation occurs.

MN activity is usually 'offline', so imitation usually doesn't occur because the observation-response link is 'off'. However, if the observation-response link is 'online', a behaviour is repeated immediately.

MNs in the *inferior frontal cortex* are concerned with intention.

Gallese & Goldman (1988) claim that MNs enable us to feel empathy.

MNs may play a role in language development since language acquisition involves imitation.

 Individual neurons have been found…

…which have either 'mirror' or 'anti-mirror' properties.

• **E** – For example, Mukamel *et al.* (2010) found single neurons in epileptics that were active when they performed an action and when they observed the task being performed.

 Performance deficits occur…

…when MN areas are damaged.

• **E** – For example, Tranel *et al.* (2003) found that people with damage to the *left premotor area* could not retrieve words for motor actions.

 MNs might be the cause…

…of gender differences in social sensitivity.

• **E** – Research suggests that women are generally better than men at understanding people's feelings.

SHOULD know …

The mirror neuron

Rizzolatti *et al.* (1996) first observed these neurons in the F5 area of the premotor cortex in macaque monkeys.

Imitation is important in acquiring skilled behaviours and is the beginning of the development of social cognition.

Damage to the frontal cortex (responsible for inhibitory control) leads to compulsive imitation, presumably because the link is 'on'.

These neurons are active when we see someone intending to perform a behaviour.

MNs might therefore be the mechanism for understanding another's person's perspective.

There are MNs in *Broca's area,* which is involved in speech production.

• **E** – Other neurons responded when participants performed an action but were inhibited when they observed it being performed ('anti-mirror').
• **L** – Anti-mirror neurons are important as they enable us to think about another person's actions without simultaneously performing those actions.

• **E** – However, they could identify pictures of those motor actions.
• **L** – This indicates that disruption to MN areas does cause action deficits.

• **E** – Cheung *et al.* (2009) have found physiological evidence of stronger MN activity in women than men.
• **L** – This suggests that gender differences in social sensitivity have a biological rather than a social basis.

 P – MN abnormalities might explain…

…why autistic children have difficulty copying actions.
• **E** – For example, Dapretto *et al.* (2006) found reduced brain activity in autistic children when they watched faces expressing emotion.
• **E** – The reduced activity was in the *inferior frontal gyrus,* which is known to be part of the MN system.
• **L** – This suggests that neurological differences may underpin at least some autistic characteristics.

P – However, the importance of MNs…

…may have been exaggerated.
• **E** – For example, Heyes (2009) suggests that MNs are just the outcome of associative learning (classical conditioning) rather than the result of evolutionary adaptation.
• **E** – Heyes argues that neurons become paired because they are both 'excited' at the same time or because one regularly precedes the other.
• **L** – This suggests that MNs could actually be the result of experience rather than being innate.

CHOOSE THE RIGHT ANSWER

Which **one** of the following most accurately describes mirror neurons? (Tick **one** box only.)

A Mirror neurons only respond to what people do. ☐

B Mirror neurons are not found in non-human species. ☐

C Mirror neurons are located in just one area of the brain. ☐

D Mirror neurons encode another person's activity as if the observer were performing the same activity. ☐

E Mirror neurons are more active in autistic children. ☐

Answers on page 355

RESEARCH ISSUES

Until recently, there was only indirect evidence that mirror neurons exist in humans. However, Mukamel *et al.* (2010) recorded the activity of neurons in the brains of 21 patients who were being treated for intractable epilepsy. The patients had been implanted with electrodes in order to identify the location of their seizures so that surgery could potentially be done on those areas. These electrodes were used by Mukamel *et al.* in their research. The findings seem to confirm the existence of mirror neurons in the human brain.

(a) Outline **one** ethical issue that should have been dealt with in this study. *(3 marks)*

(b) Outline **one** methodological issue arising from this research. *(3 marks)*

Answers on page 355

MATCH THEM UP

Match up the researchers to the statement that best describes their research.

1	Dapretto *et al.* (2006)	**A**	MNs might be the result of experience rather than being innate.
2	Tranel *et al.* (2003)	**B**	Neurological differences may underpin at least some autistic characteristics.
3	Cheung *et al.* (2009)	**C**	There is physiological evidence that MN activity is stronger in women than men.
4	Hayes (2009)	**D**	People with damage to the left premotor area could not retrieve words for motor actions.

Answers on page 355

DRAWING CONCLUSIONS

A researcher recorded the activity of 184 individual neurons in the F5 motor area of a macaque monkey. All of the neurons responded when the monkey performed some kind of action. Of these, 87 also responded to some type of visual stimuli. Forty-eight of the neurons that responded to visual stimuli responded only to seeing objects, and 39 responded to seeing actions. Of these 39 neurons, 12 responded when the monkey grasped an object and when it observed the researcher performing the same action.

(a) What percentage of the total number of neurons responded when the monkey grasped an object and observed the researcher performing the same action? *(1 mark)*

(b) What percentage of the number of neurons that responded to some type of visual stimuli responded only to seeing actions? *(1 mark)*

(c) What percentage of the neurons that responded to seeing actions responded when the monkey grasped an object and when it observed the researcher performing the same action? *(1 mark)*

Answers on page 355

APPLYING YOUR KNOWLEDGE

Paresh was watching the big football match on TV, with his takeaway pizza on his lap. A player was just about to shoot when an opposition player kicked him hard on the knee. Paresh winced, his leg straightened, and his pizza went flying through the air. 'What are you doing?' asked his girlfriend. 'Anybody would think it was you who'd been kicked, not some bloke on the TV.'

How could Paresh's reaction be explained to his girlfriend? *(6 marks)*

Identify the psychology	Link to Paresh's reaction

Answers on page 355

Topic 1 Piaget's theory of cognitive development

Discuss Piaget's theory of cognitive development. *(16 marks)*

Piaget says we are born with some schemas, like recognising human faces, but new schemas get developed by having new experiences such as recognising a particular face. He also says schemas become more complex by assimilation and accommodation.

Assimilation is where new information is incorporated into an existing schema, like when a baby is given a new toy to play with, they may hold it in the same way they held a rattle. Accommodation happens when an infant changes an existing schema so they can understand new information that doesn't fit their current knowledge. This new information can't be assimilated into the current schema, so the schema has to change to accommodate new information, and a new schema is formed.

If an experience cannot be assimilated into existing schemas, then imbalance occurs and this is something we don't like. This means we want to restore the balance, through a process Piaget called equilibration. Once we have done this, cognitive development happens.

There is evidence to support the existence of innate schemas. Fantz found that 4-day-old infants show a preference for a normal human face, rather than a human face with mixed up features, like eyes and a nose. This preference shows that it is the unique way a face is, rather than just a complex pattern, which is important. An innate preference for faces would be adaptive because it would allow an infant to seek out a caregiver.

Cognitive development seems to be crucial for language development. Sinclair-de-Zwart found teaching language appropriate to a task didn't help children to complete it successfully. 90% of children given 'conservation' tasks still failed them even though they had been taught appropriate verbal skills. This supports Piaget's idea that cognitive maturity is needed for language, not the other way round.

One strength of Piaget's theory is that it has helped us to understand cognitive development. It combines nature and nurture to explain how our thinking changes as we get older and it has influenced educational practice. This means it has provided many valuable insights into how children's minds develop.

Discovery learning can help children if it is appropriately used. For example, if knowledge is gained through equilibration, then real understanding is only possible if children make their own accommodations. Although children taught by formal methods generally do better in maths and English, this might be because discovery learning requires more from the teacher. This means that the problem is not discovery learning, but the way the teacher applies it.

A big problem with Piaget's theory is that some of the concepts are difficult to operationalise. Inhelder et al. argue that disequilibrium occurs when there is mild conflict between what children expect to happen and what actually does happen. However, Bryant believes that disequilibrium is a more major dissonance between things. Until these concepts are operationalised properly, we can't test bits of Piaget's theory.

Examiner's comments

> A reasonably clear opening AO1 paragraph, although defining a schema would help here.

> Again, a reasonably clear AO1 paragraph, which uses an example to illustrate the point being made.

> Reasonably clear AO1.

> This AO3 paragraph includes phrases which signal to the examiner that evaluation is now happening, such as 'evidence to support'.

> This AO3 paragraph makes use of research to support the point being made.

> An example of how Piaget's theory has influenced educational practice would make this AO3 stronger.

> Applying research to real-world examples, as has been done here, can help you to achieve AO3 marks.

> This AO3 paragraph tries to balance the commentary on Piaget's theory.

Level 4 answer (13–16 marks)

Examiner's comments: There is no wasted content and the response is detailed and accurate. The essay is organised clearly into AO1 and AO3 paragraphs.

AO1 Description of Piaget's theory is accurate and generally well-detailed. Specialist terms are used correctly and the essay is well organised.

AO3 Evaluation is effective, with a broad range of evaluative evidence in reasonable depth.

Topic 2 Piaget's stages of intellectual development

Discuss research into Piaget's stages of intellectual development. *(16 marks)*

Examiner's comments

One of the first thing an infant learns is how to match sensory input, like what they see and feel with motor actions, like hand movements. This happens in the sensorimotor stage, which is in the first two years of life and object permanence happens at this stage. Really young infants think an object no longer exists if they can't see it, so they lose interest in it. According to Piaget, we develop object permanence at eight months. This is where we realise that objects do still exist, even if we can't see them.

> This opening AO1 paragraph has potential, but lacks organisation.

Pre-operational children rely on what things look like. They don't understand that even if the appearance of something changes, its volume, number or mass can't change. They are also egocentric. This means they only see the world from their perspective and are unaware that other people may see things differently from them. While children in this stage can classify objects into categories, like animal types, they can't work out sub-groups, which are part of the wider category, like animal colour. After the age of 11, children are in the formal operational stage where they are able to solve abstract problems by developing hypotheses and testing them. They also show idealistic thinking, which means they can imagine how things might be if things were different.

> As before, this AO1 paragraph lacks organisation. Also, the concrete operational stage has been missed out entirely, so the answer lacks detail.

One problem is that some of the tasks Piaget used to test his theory confused young children. Hughes did Piaget's three mountain study, but used ideas that children were familiar with, like a naughty boy hiding from a policeman and found that the children did not show egocentric behaviour.

> This AO3 paragraph uses research to support the point, but it doesn't explain why it is a problem for Piaget's theory.

Also, Piaget may have overestimated the ability to use logic in the formal operational stage. While research suggests that changes in cognitive development do occur with age, Dasen claims only a third of adults ever reach the formal operational stage which suggests that Piaget's idea of people going through invariant stages may be wrong.

> Another issue has been identified, and some support for the issue is offered, so it can be credited as AO3.

Piaget's stage theory suggests that concepts can only be taught when children are biologically ready. For example, it may be difficult to teach abstract calculations in maths to pre-operational children. If this is true, then we might need to change the things schools teach.

> This AO3 point has not been developed at all well, and would attract limited credit.

Another problem with Piaget's theory is that it might be culturally biased. Piaget came from a Western European background, where thinking about abstract ideas is valued. This may not be true in other cultures, where there might be greater value given to concrete operational activities, like making things. This suggests that Piaget's theory may not apply to all cultures.

> Points that make reference to issues and debates can be excellent routes to AO3 provided they are used effectively.

Level 2 (9–12 marks)

Examiner's comments: Although AO1 skills are evident, important aspects of Piaget's stage theory are either absent or poorly described. There is quite a bit of AO3 material, but it has not been used in an effective way. This answer just about makes it to Level 3, but lacks the clarity and organisation that solid Level 3 answers would show.

AO1 Generally accurate and detailed, with some material used quite well.

AO3 Reasonable, but the material has not always been used effectively. Points are made and sometimes developed, but clearer expression would have allowed more credit to have been given.

Topic 3 Vygotsky's theory of cognitive development

Outline and evaluate Vygotsky's theory of cognitive development. *(16 marks)*

Examiner's comments

Vygotsky said children are born with basic mental functions, such as perception, which cultural influences change into higher mental functions like writing. Children learn through problem-solving with an expert, who is a more competent person. At the beginning, the expert is responsible for guiding the problem-solving but, gradually, this responsibility becomes the child's.

> A strong opening AO1 paragraph which gets straight to the point.

Experts teach culture using language. The language starts as conversations between the child and the expert, but an internal dialogue develops, as they learns the skill of mental representation. Every function in cognitive development appears first on a social level (between people), and then again later on an individual level. Social experiences depend on language and allow the development of higher mental functions, like writing, to happen.

> A well-focused AO1 paragraph, this time explaining the role of culture and language in Vygotsky's theory.

Cognitive development takes place in the ZPD which is the region between what the child can achieve on their own and what they can potentially achieve with an expert's help. This must take place just ahead of the child's current development. It can't be too far ahead, otherwise it's too hard.

> A concise explanation of the ZPD here, although the last sentence needs to be clearer for maximum AO1 credit.

To help, the expert creates a scaffold, which is gradually removed as the child is more able to work on their own. The expert should provide more explicit instructions if the child is struggling.

> This is a very brief explanation of scaffolding but it does include the main point, and so receives AO1 credit.

There is research support for the role of culture. Gredler discovered that counting is done by starting on the thumb of one hand and going up the arm and down to the other fingers, ending at 29 in Papua New Guinea. This system makes it difficult to add and subtract large numbers, showing that culture can limit cognitive development.

> The use of the phrase 'research support' is a good way of making an AO3 point.

The role of language in cognitive development is also supported by research. Carmichael et al. gave participants one of two labels for certain drawings. For example, they were shown a shape and told it was either a kidney bean or a canoe. When participants were later asked to draw the shape, it was different depending on which label they had been given, showing words can affect the way we think about, and remember, things.

> This AO3 paragraph follows the PEEL formula, with identification of the main point, followed by research evidence before linking back to the question. Again, though, a clearer link needs to be made to Vygotsky's theory.

McNaughton and Leyland found evidence for the ZPD when they observed young children working with their mothers on jigsaw puzzles of increasing difficulty. If the puzzle was easy, the mothers didn't offer much help, but if it was difficult, they gave more help. This supports Vygotsky's idea that experts adjust their input to help children.

> This is better, since the AO3 point is explicitly linked to Vygotsky's theory.

However, Vygotsky may have overstated the importance of the social environment. If social input is all that is needed to improve cognitive development, then learning should happen a lot quicker. Also, the focus on social factors means that biological factors are largely ignored in Vygotsky's theory, so it isn't a comprehensive theory of cognitive development.

> This final paragraph is an attempt to criticise Vygotsky's theory and would receive AO3 credit.

Level 3 (9–12 marks)

Examiner's comments: AO1 There is reasonable, and generally accurate, knowledge of Vygotsky's theory, and it is reasonably detailed. But more should have been made of scaffolding, for example.

AO3 There is plenty of evaluation in this essay, but it is not always clear what is being evaluated. While the evaluation could have been made explicit, it was sometimes implicit. This, coupled with the descriptive skills, means that this answer is a solid Level 3, which approaches, but does not quite reach, Level 4.

Topic 4 Baillargeon's explanation of early infant abilities

Discuss Baillargeon's explanation of early infant abilities *(16 marks)*

Baillargeon thought that the reason infants don't search for hidden objects isn't because they lack object permanence, but because they can't plan and carry out the motor actions they need to do it.

So she created the violation of expectation (VOE) method instead, which assumes that infants will show surprise when they see an impossible event. Baillargeon and De Vos found that three-month-olds show object permanence when they are tested with the VOE method. Infants didn't show surprise when a short object failed to appear in a high window, but they did when an impossible event happened, like when a tall object didn't appear.

Infants have an innate physical reasoning system to help understand the physical world and learn to reason about new events. They start off forming an all-or-nothing concept about something then later they incorporate variables that might affect it. For example, an infant will learn that an object can be hidden by a cover, and later they learn that the cover's appearance is affected by the object's size.

Infants are also born with mechanisms that help them understand the psychological world, such as false beliefs in others and a sense of fairness. Song and Baillargeon found infants show surprise when adults behave in a way that violates the false belief the child expects them to have.

Baillargeon controlled for the behaviour of the parents during the tasks and used observers who were unaware of the study's purpose. She also studied children from a variety of social classes, meaning her research has high population and experimental validity.

However, Baillargeon's research lacks cultural validity because she hasn't studied young children's abilities in cultures other than America. If there were cultural differences in abilities, then this would challenge the idea of innate mechanisms. This suggests further research is needed to establish if infants' abilities are innately driven.

One problem is that the VOE method itself might lack validity. Infants may look longer at something because they find it interesting, not because it violates their expectations. Schlesinger and Casey found that when an impossible event occurs, infants show greater perceptual interest rather than surprise, suggesting the VOE method might not measure what Baillargeon says it measures.

Bremner argues that demonstrating object permanence does not mean that an infant really understands it. Cognitive development involves understanding a principle, not just acting like you do.

Spelke et al. suggested that infants are born with a core knowledge, including a basic understanding of the physical world. However, research finds that infants do not show expectations about all events related to one core principle, such as covering objects. This supports Baillargeon's view that infants are born with the ability to acquire certain kinds of knowledge very quickly.

Examiner's comments

A brief, but informative opening AO1 paragraph.

This description of the VOE method earns AO1 credit.

A detailed explanation, with an example, is provided. Also creditable as AO1.

This AO1 paragraph is accurate and also includes an example, this time from research.

Using methodology to evaluate research can be an effective way to gain AO3 marks, if done effectively.

Using words such as 'however' shows the examiner that this is an AO3 paragraph.

This AO3 paragraph identifies the key point, followed by evidence and elaboration and a link-back. This is effective evaluation.

This paragraph is probably intended to be AO3, but it is mostly written as a description of a problem.

Using alternative explanations is only effective if they link back to the original explanation. As this has happened here, it's an effective final AO3 paragraph.

Level 4 (13–16 marks)

Examiner's comments: This just about makes it into Level 4. There is a sensible selection of material and specialist terms are used correctly.

AO1 Knowledge is accurate, although it could be a little more detailed in places.

AO3 There is a broad range of AO3 material. Some of this shows effective and thorough evaluation. However, not all of it does. The paragraph about Bremner, for example, fails to explain how the point raised affects Baillargeon's research, which is not effective AO3.

Topic 5 The development of social cognition: Selman's theory

Outline and evaluate Selman's levels of perspective-taking explanation of how social cognition develops. *(16 marks)*

Examiner's comments

Selman's theory is based on perspective-taking, which means being able to see a situation from someone else's perspective. When a child takes another person's perspective, it allows them to have an insight into that person's thoughts and feelings, which is important for social relations.

> Good opening AO1 paragraph that explains the nature of perspective-taking.

Selman developed an age-related model, which has five stages. Between the ages of 3–6 years, children are at the undifferentiated perspective-taking stage, so they can distinguish between themselves and other people, but are largely ruled by their own perspective. This means children believe others will feel or think the same way as they do.

> A thorough explanation of the first stage of Selman's theory, and credited as AO1.

The social-informational perspective-taking stage happens when children are 6–8 years old. Now, they are aware of other perspectives, but they assume other people have different information to them. After this is the self-reflective perspective-taking stage (8–10 years) where children view their own thoughts and feelings from someone else's perspective and realise that others can do the same.

> Appropriate and accurate description here, credited as AO1.

Then the mutual perspective-taking stage occurs, where the child can now imagine how they, and others, are viewed from the point of view of a third party and they can consider two viewpoints at the same time. The final stage is the societal perspective-taking stage, which happens after the age of 12. Personal decisions are now made with reference to social conventions, like being kind to animals, for example.

> This AO1 paragraph accurately identifies the final two stages and explains them, using a relevant example.

One strength of Selman's stage theory is that research studies like Cooney and Selman's support it. They found 40 out of 48 boys improved their level of perspective taking, and none of them went back to an earlier level. Gurucharri and Selman confirmed this progressive developmental sequence when they looked at the boys again. This supports Selman's belief that perspective-taking is a progressive age-related developmental sequence.

> Using phrases such as 'One strength of' shows that evaluation is now taking place and that you want material credited as AO3.

Perspective-taking skills are really important in all social behaviour. For example, Fitzgerald and White found that maturity of perspective-taking skills was negatively correlated with aggression. Also, Selman et al. found that children with poor perspective-taking skills found it harder to form and maintain social relationships. This suggests that a lack of perspective-taking skills may explain a lack of social development.

> Another detailed AO3 point which identifies the key issue and uses research studies to support the point, before linking back.

There are real-world applications of Selman's theory. For example, some criminals may lack empathy and perspective-taking skills, which is what makes them harm others. Social skills training encourages prisoners to learn perspective-taking skills, so they can increase their empathetic concern and hopefully stop them reoffending.

> Using real world examples can be an effective way of evaluating a theory, and earning further AO3 credit, as can be seen here.

However, a weakness is that a lot of the research is correlational. Just because perspective-taking skills and social competence are correlated, doesn't mean perspective taking causes the social competence. This means that we cannot be sure that perspective-taking skills cause social competence.

> This final AO3 paragraph identifies a problem with the research methods used and explains why it is a problem, which is also creditable as AO3.

Level 3 (9–12 marks)

Examiner's comments: A competent attempt to answer the question. The answer is mostly clear, coherent and focused, and the evaluation is reasonable throughout.

AO1 A reasonably detailed and accurate account of Selman's theory of perspective-taking.

AO3 A broad range of evidence has been used in a mostly effective way to evaluate Selman's theory, including research studies, methodology and applications to the real world.

Topic 6 The development of social cognition: Theory of mind

Outline and evaluate theory of mind as explanation for autism. *(16 marks)*

Examiner's comments

Theory of Mind (ToM) is our understanding that other people have separate beliefs and emotions to us and see the world from a different perspective. The fact that autistic children find social interaction difficult might be because they lack a theory of mind.

> A strong opening AO1 paragraph explaining both theory of mind and how this might explain why autistic children find social interaction difficult.

False belief tasks measure the understanding that others may hold, and act on, false beliefs, and are a way to test ToM. Most children can do these tasks successfully by age 4–6. A false belief task is the Sally–Anne task, where Sally puts her ball in a basket and then leaves the room. Anne then moves the ball to a box. When Sally returns, the child is asked where she will look for the ball. Baron–Cohen et al. found that 80% of autistic children, but only 15% of non-autistic children fail this test.

> A thorough explanation of the Sally–Anne task, which earns some AO1 credit, although it doesn't explain how the findings link to ToM.

High functioning adults on the autistic spectrum can pass the Sally–Anne test, so Baron–Cohen created a new test which measures the emotion expressed in people's eyes. High-functioning adults show poorer performance on this Eyes Task than non-autistic adults, showing there is a ToM impairment in autism.

> An accurate explanation of the *Eyes Task* clearly linking it to ToM, and creditable as AO1.

Baron–Cohen suggested that a theory of mind module (ToMM) exists, which is a biological mechanism which allows people to explain the mental states of other people. As theory of mind develops at a particular age and many people with autism don't have it, ToM may be biological.

> A concise, but generally accurate, description here.

However, a problem with the ToMM is that biology may not be the only cause of a theory of mind. Perner et al. found that ToM appears earlier in children from large families because they are encouraged to think about other people's feeling when resolving conflicts. This means that the development of a theory of mind is probably a combination of biology and social environment.

> The careful construction of this evaluation point is clear here. The first AO3 point links directly to the AO1 point just before it.

Studies show that not all autistic children fail the Sally–Anne test. If having a theory of mind was a main feature of autism, then we would expect all autistic children to fail the test, but they don't.

> This paragraph identifies a problem, but it doesn't say why it is an issue for ToM as an explanation for autism.

Also, intention may not be a precursor of theory of mind. Carpenter et al. tested autistic and non-autistic children's understanding of intention by seeing if they followed someone's gaze and looked at where they were pointing. They found that autistic and non-autistic children behaved in the same way, suggesting understanding intention is different to having a ToM.

> An effective piece of AO3 which makes a point, includes research evidence to support it, before linking back.

Baron–Cohen et al. claim that the Eyes Task measures 'mindreading', and they say that this is the same thing as theory of mind. But Wellman and Woolley argue that mindreading isn't the same as knowing how someone experiences the world (theory of mind).

> It is likely that this was intended as AO3 but it reads as a description and doesn't explain why this is a problem for the theory.

Research into autism has a culture bias because Baron–Cohen only used British participants in his research and it has been conducted from a very Western perspective, which means that considering a lack of social interaction as a main aspect of autism may be a Western, not a universal, perspective on the disorder.

> AO3 marks can be gained by discussing a bias in research as has been done here.

Level 3 (9–12 marks)

Examiners' comments: AO1 Description is mostly accurate, but it could have been more focused on the question in places.

AO3 Lots of points are made and are reasonably detailed. Some of the points didn't focus on the question, which means that the evaluation is not as effective as it could be.

Topic 7 The development of social cognition: The mirror neuron system

Discuss the role of the mirror neuron system in social cognition. *(16 marks)*

Mirror neurons react when a person performs an action and also when we see someone else performs the same action. This means that these neurons can explain how imitation occurs, which is important in acquiring skills and developing social cognition. Mirror neurons might play a role in language development because learning language involves imitation, and there are mirror neurons in Broca's area, which is involved in speech production.

Usually, we don't imitate someone else's behaviour because the observation-response link is 'offline'. However, if it is 'online' then we repeat someone else's behaviour immediately. The frontal cortex is responsible for inhibitory control and compulsive imitation happens if it's damaged, probably because the link is 'on'. Mirror neurons in the inferior frontal cortex are important for intentions and are active when we see someone intending to do a behaviour.

Mirror neurons mean we experience someone else's actions as our own, and empathise with them, so mirror neurons may be the biological mechanism for helping us understand someone else's perspective. Mirror neurons are more developed in humans than in other animals, making humans unique.

Individual neurons have been found which have either mirror or anti-mirror properties. Mukamel et al. found single neurons in epileptics that were active when they performed an action and when they observed the task being performed. Other neurons responded when participants performed an action, but were inhibited when they observed it being performed. These anti-mirror neurons are important as they allow us to think about another person's actions without doing them.

Performance deficits happen if mirror neuron areas are damaged. Tranel et al. found that people with damage to the left premotor area could not retrieve words for motor actions, but they could identify pictures of those motor actions. This indicates that disruption to mirror neuron areas does cause action deficits.

Mirror neurons might be the cause of gender differences in social sensitivity. Research suggests women are generally better than men at understanding people's feelings. Cheung et al. have found physiological evidence of stronger MN activity in women, suggesting that gender differences in social sensitivity have a biological basis.

Mirror neuron abnormalities might explain why autistic children have difficulty copying actions. Dapretto et al. found when autistic children watched faces expressing emotion there was reduced brain activity in the inferior frontal gyrus. This part of the brain contains mirror neurons, suggesting that neurological differences may be the reason for some autistic characteristics.

However, the importance of mirror neurons may have been exaggerated. Heyes suggests that mirror neurons are a result of classical conditioning, rather than evolutionary adaptation. She argues that neurons become paired because they are both excited at the same time. This suggests that mirror neurons could be the result of experience rather than being innate.

Examiner's comments

This opening AO1 paragraph attempts to explain the function of mirror neurons in humans.

This can be credited as AO1 as it is an attempt at describing how mirror neurons work.

Further AO1 but not clearly linked to the previous two paragraphs.

This paragraph attempts to describe why we don't always repeat an observed behaviour.

It is hard to tell if this is an AO1 or an AO3 paragraph. Remember it is important to make this clear to the examiner.

This AO3 paragraph makes use of the PEEL method for evaluating, making a point, including elaboration and research before linking back.

Another AO3 paragraph, this time linking mirror neurons to autism research.

This can be credited as AO3 because it is critical commentary of mirror neuron research.

Level 3 (9–12 marks)

Examiner's comments: AO1 A reasonably clear description of the role of mirror neurons in social cognition. AO3 There is not enough detailed AO3 for this to get top marks, even though a range of evaluative evidence has been used. Overall, this just about makes Level 3.

Piaget showed that the way children think about the world changes with age. Identify **two** stages in Piaget's theory and explain **one** way in which children's thinking would be different in each of those stages. *(4 marks)*

Examiner's comments

1 Pre-operational stage. A child at the pre-operational stage would say that there is more water in a taller glass than in a shorter glass, even if they saw the water being poured from one glass to another. This is because they don't understand that the volume does not change even if its appearance does.

> This answer has accurately compared conservation in the pre-operational stage and the concrete-operational stage.

2 Concrete operational stage. A child at this stage would say that there is the same amount of water in each glass because they can understand that even though the appearance of the glass is different, the volume of water remains the same.

Examiner's comments: AO1 This answer clearly gives two stages of Piaget's theory and explains one difference between them in sufficient detail for full marks to be awarded.

Describe **one** study that has investigated 'theory of mind'. Include details of what was done and what was found. *(4 marks)*

Baron-Cohen et al.'s Sally-Anne test involved children being told a story using puppets as props and then being asked a question at the end. The story has one puppet, Sally, putting her ball in a basket before leaving the room. The other puppet, Anne, then moves the ball from the basket to a box. When Sally comes back in, children are asked where she will look for her ball. If they have a theory of mind (ToM), then they will say the basket. If they don't have a theory of mind then they will say the box. Baron-Cohen et al. found that only 20% of autistic children could pass this test while 85% of the non-autistic children, including some with Down's syndrome, could pass this test. Baron-Cohen et al. says this shows that autistic children may lack a ToM.

> The Sally-Anne test is an ideal way to address this question.

Level 4 answer (4 marks)

Examiner's comments: AO1 The answer accurately describes one study that has investigated ToM. It is sufficiently detailed in terms of both the procedure and the results.

Explain what is meant by the term 'mirror neuron'. *(2 marks)*

A mirror neuron is a neuron that enables us to experience someone else's actions as if they were our own. A mirror neuron fires when a person performs an action themselves, but it also fires when they see someone else perform the same action.

> This is a clear explanation.

Level 2 answer (2 marks)

Examiner's comments: AO1 Accurate and appropriate answer.

KEY TERMS

- Avolition
- Delusions
- Hallucinations
- Negative symptoms
- Positive symptoms
- Schizophrenia
- Speech poverty

Possible exam questions ...

+ Explain the difference between the positive and negative symptoms of schizophrenia. *(2 marks)*
+ Outline **one** positive and **one** negative symptom of schizophrenia. *(4 marks)*
+ Identify **one** type of hallucination and **one** type of delusion that are experienced in schizophrenia. *(2 marks)*
+ Explain what is meant by 'speech poverty' and 'avolition' as used in the diagnosis of schizophrenia. *(4 marks)*

★ Exam tip

There are many symptoms associated with schizophrenia. You can only be asked about those that appear in the specification, so don't learn more than you have to!

! Think

Given that many people misunderstand what schizophrenia is, do you think the disorder needs re-naming?

MUST know ...

Classification of schizophrenia

Schizophrenia is the most common type of **psychosis**, characterised by a profound disruption of cognition and emotion and loss of contact with external reality.

Schizophrenia is characterised by 'positive' and 'negative' symptoms. **Positive symptoms** include hallucinations, delusions, disorganised speech, and grossly disorganised or catatonic behaviour.

Hallucinations are perceptual distortions or exaggerations in any sense modality. Auditory hallucinations (e.g. hearing voices) are the most common.

Delusions are firmly held, but false, beliefs caused by distortions of reasoning, or misinterpretations of perceptions or experiences. They include paranoid delusions and delusions of grandeur.

Disorganised speech reflects problems in organising thoughts appropriately.

Grossly disorganised or catatonic behaviour includes being unable or unmotivated to initiate or complete a task. Catatonic behaviours involve reduced reaction to the immediate environment.

Negative symptoms include speech poverty, avolition, affective flattening, and anhedonia. People are often unaware of these symptoms and less concerned by them than others are.

Speech poverty (alogia) is characterised by deficits in verbal fluency and productivity, and less complex syntax.

Avolition is a reduction of self-initiated involvement in interests and desires, and an inability to begin and persist with tasks.

Affective flattening is a reduction in the range and intensity of different forms of emotional expression.

Anhedonia is a loss of interest/pleasure in physical (e.g. bodily contact) or social (e.g. interpersonal situations), or a lack of reactivity to normally pleasurable stimuli.

Diagnosing schizophrenia

In the USA, schizophrenia is diagnosed using DSM-V.

DSM-V requires a person to show two or more Criterion A symptoms: delusions, hallucinations, disorganised speech, grossly disorganised or catatonic behaviour, negative symptoms.

DSM-V also requires the person to display social/occupational dysfunction in one or more major areas of functioning. These are Criterion B symptoms.

Criterion C symptoms refer to duration. Continuous signs of disturbance must have persisted for at least six months.

SHOULD know ...

Classification of schizophrenia

Schizophrenia is most often diagnosed between the ages of 15 and 35. Men and women are equally liked to be diagnosed as schizophrenic.

'Positive' symptoms appear to reflect an excess or distortion of normal functions.

Other types of hallucination include visual (seeing things) and olfactory (smelling things).

Paranoid delusions involve the belief that a person is being conspired against (e.g. being followed by MI5). Delusions of grandeur involve inflated beliefs about the person's power and importance (e.g. believing oneself to be Jesus Christ).

In 'derailment', the individual shifts from topic to topic as new associations arise, and fails to form coherent and logical thoughts.

These symptoms lead to difficulties in daily living (e.g. lack of personal hygiene). Catatonia is characterised by rigid postures or aimless motor activity.

Negative symptoms appear to reflect a reduction or loss of normal functions, and weaken a person's ability to cope with everyday life.

Speech poverty is believed to reflect slowing or blocked thoughts. In timed verbal fluency tests, schizophrenics typically produce fewer words belonging to particular categories despite knowing as many words as non-schizophrenics.

Schizophrenics will sit for hours on end doing nothing.

During speech, schizophrenics may show a deficit in *prosody*, the non-linguistic features such as intonation, which give listeners cues about emotional content.

Social anhedonia overlaps with disorders like depression, whereas physical anhedonia doesn't.

Diagnosing schizophrenia

In the UK and elsewhere, ICD-10 is more commonly used to diagnose schizophrenia.

Only one Criterion A symptom is required if delusions are 'bizarre', or hallucinations involve a voice offering a running commentary about the person, *or* two or more voices in conversation.

These include work, interpersonal relations, and self-care.

The six month period must include one month or more of Criterion A symptoms.

CHOOSE THE RIGHT ANSWER

Which **two** of the following are positive symptoms of schizophrenia? (Tick **two** boxes only.)

A Alogia ☐

B Affective flattening ☐

C Disorganised speech ☐

D Anhedonia ☐

E Grossly disorganised or catatonic behaviour ☐

Answers on page 355

 FILL IN THE BOXES (1)

The **positive symptoms** of schizophrenia are those which apparently reflect an excess or distortion of normal functions. The specification could ask you specifically about hallucinations and delusions. Fill in the boxes below to summarise these two examples of positive symptoms. *(6 marks)*

	Definition	Example
Hallucinations		
Delusions		

Answers on page 355

 FILL IN THE BOXES (2)

The **negative symptoms** of schizophrenia are those which appear to reflect a reduction or loss of normal functions. The specification could ask you directly about speech poverty and avolition. Fill in the boxes below to summarise these two examples of negative symptoms. *(6 marks)*

	Definition	Example
Speech poverty		
Avolition		

Answers on page 355

 COMPLETE THE TABLE

For a diagnosis of schizophrenia, DSM-V requires a person to display Criterion A, B and C features. For each criterion, select a key term or phrase to help you outline DSM's approach to diagnosing schizophrenia. Some of the boxes have been completed for you.

	Key word/phrase	Key word/phrase
Criterion A		Delusions, hallucinations
Criterion B	Dysfunction	
Criterion C		

Answers on page 355

 APPLYING YOUR KNOWLEDGE

Will and Sarah were looking at some old letters they found at a car boot sale. 'Look at this one,' said Will. 'What do you think this is all about?' Will read out the letter. 'Blimey,' said Sarah. 'You'd be a bit worried if you were his mum and that came through your letter box.'

Dear Mother,

I am writing on paper. The pen which I am using is from a factory called 'Perry & Co.' The factory is in England. I assume this. Behind the name Perry & Co., the city of London is inscribed, but not the city. The city of London is in England. I know this from my schooldays. Then, I always liked geography. My last teacher in that subject was Professor August A. He was a man with black eyes. There are also blue and grey eyes and other sorts too. I have heard it said that snakes have green eyes. All people have eyes. There are some, too, who are blind. These blind people are led about by a boy. It must be terrible not to be able to see. There are people who can't see and, in addition, can't hear. I know some people who hear too much. One can hear too much.

Using your knowledge of the symptoms of schizophrenia, identify and describe **two** symptoms that are evident in the letter Will and Sarah found. *(6 marks)*

Answers on page 355

 Link

Topic 2 looks at the issues of reliability and validity that surround the classification and diagnosis of schizophrenia.

KEY TERMS

- Co-morbidity
- Culture
- Gender bias
- Reliability
- Symptom overlap
- Validity

Possible essay question

Discuss issues relating to reliability **and** validity in the diagnosis **or** classification of schizophrenia. *(16 marks)*

Other possible exam questions ...

+ Give **one** example of gender bias in the diagnosis **and/or** classification of schizophrenia. *(2 marks)*
+ Explain what is meant by the terms 'co-morbidity' and 'symptom overlap' in the context of the diagnosis of schizophrenia. *(4 marks)*
+ Outline how culture might influence the diagnosis of schizophrenia. *(4 marks)*
+ Evaluate research relating to the reliability **and/or** validity of the diagnosis and classification of schizophrenia. *(8 marks)*

★ Exam tip

'Reliability' and 'validity' are key terms, so it's important not to get them the wrong way round in your answer!

MUST know ...

Reliability and validity

Reliability is the consistency of a diagnosis across repeated measurements. Two types of reliability are test-retest reliability and inter-rater reliability.

Validity is the extent to which a diagnosis reflects an actual disorder (i.e. whether a diagnostic system such as DSM-V measures what it says it measures).

Co-morbidity is the extent to which two or more conditions occur simultaneously in a person.

Culture influences the diagnostic process, and there is significant variation between cultures in the diagnosis of schizophrenia.

Gender bias occurs when the accuracy of a diagnosis depends on a person's gender.

Symptom overlap occurs when the symptoms of one disorder occur in another disorder.

 Inter-rater reliability is a major issue...

...in the diagnosis of schizophrenia.

- **E** – Perfect agreement between clinicians yields a kappa score of 1, whereas 0 indicates complete disagreement.

 A diagnosis of schizophrenia tells us little...

...about a person's chances of improvement.

- **E** – For example, research indicates that whilst some schizophrenics show an improvement from the disorder, others don't.

Co-morbidity can have negative consequences...

...for people diagnosed with schizophrenia.

- **E** – For example, Weber *et al.* (2009) found that schizophrenia was co-morbid with medical problems such as hypertension and asthma.

SHOULD know ...

Reliability and validity

Test-retest reliability refers to the consistency of measurements taken by a single clinician at several points in time. *Inter-rater reliability* refers to the consistency of measurements between different clinicians at the same time.

Reliability is a pre-condition for validity. A diagnosis cannot be valid if it is not reliable.

Conditions that are co-morbid with schizophrenia include substance abuse and anxiety.

British and American psychiatrists differ in their diagnoses of schizophrenia (Copeland, 1971). There also appears to be cultural, especially racial, differences in schizophrenia diagnosis (Barnes, 2004).

Broverman *et al.* (1970) found that American clinicians equated mentally healthy 'adult' behaviour with mentally healthy 'male' behaviour, meaning that women tended to be perceived as less mentally healthy.

Some of the symptoms in schizophrenia occur in depression and bipolar disorder.

- **E** – Whaley (2001) and Regier *et al.* (2013) reported kappa scores of 0.11 and 0.46 respectively when diagnoses of schizophrenia were made.
- **L** – Since a kappa score of 0.7 or greater is considered good, this suggests that schizophrenia is not reliably diagnosed by clinicians.

- **E** – About 10% of schizophrenics show a lasting and significant improvement, but 30% show some improvement with intermittent relapses.
- **L** – This shows that a diagnosis of schizophrenia itself has little predictive validity in terms of a person's likelihood of recovering from the disorder.

- **E** – The researchers also found that being diagnosed with a psychiatric disorder was associated with a lower standard of medical care.
- **L** – This means that co-morbidity adversely affects the prognosis for patients with schizophrenia.

FURTHER EVALUATION

 P – The prognosis for ethnic minority groups may be more positive...

...than for majority group members.

- **E** – Brekke & Barrio (1997) found that non-white minorities (Afro-Americans and Latinos) were *less* symptomatic than majority (white Americans) group members.
- **E** – The 'ethnic culture' hypothesis proposes that minorities have better protective characteristics and social structures than majority group cultures.
- **L** – This supports the view that minorities experience less distress with mental disorders, and have a better prognosis.

 P – Research suggests there is a gender bias...

...in the diagnosis of schizophrenia.

- **E** – For example, Loring & Powell (1988) found that a case described as 'male' was more likely than the same case described as 'female' to be diagnosed as schizophrenic.
- **E** – However, this bias was more evident in male than in female clinicians.
- **L** – This suggests that diagnosis can be influenced by a clinician's gender as well as a person's gender.

✔ CHOOSE THE RIGHT ANSWER

Which **one** of the following statements about the relationship between reliability and validity is true? (Tick **one** box only.)

A If a diagnosis is valid, it doesn't have to be reliable. ☐

B If a diagnosis is reliable, it means that it is valid ☐

C A reliable diagnosis is a necessary, but not sufficient, condition for a valid diagnosis. ☐

D A reliable diagnosis is a sufficient, but not necessary, condition for a valid diagnosis. ☐

E A reliable diagnosis is neither necessary nor sufficient for a valid diagnosis. ☐

Answers on page 356

🧩 MATCH THEM UP

Match up the following terms with their appropriate definitions.

1	Intra-rater reliability	A	The extent to which a diagnosis reflects an actual disorder.
2	Inter-rater reliability	B	The extent to which a clinician reaches the same diagnosis about a person at different points in time.
3	Validity	C	The extent to which several clinicians reach the same diagnosis about a single person.
4	Predictive validity	D	The extent to which we can gauge a person's likely outcome following a diagnosis.

Answers on page 356

✏ FILL IN THE BOXES

The specification says that you need to be familiar with co-morbidity, culture bias, gender bias, and symptom overlap, and you could be asked specifically about any, or all, of these. Fill in the boxes below to summarise these four concepts.

	Explanation	Elaboration
Co-morbidity		
Culture bias		
Gender bias		
Symptom overlap		

Answers on page 356

🔗 Link

See pages 16–19 for an explanation of assessing and improving reliability and validity.

💡 DRAWING CONCLUSIONS

 A researcher asked a class of her students to present themselves to psychiatric hospitals claiming to be hearing voices saying 'empty', 'hollow' and 'thud'. All of the students were psychologically healthy. In the first part of the study, 14 out of 20 were admitted and diagnosed as schizophrenic. In the second part of the study, the hospitals were told to be aware that other students would be trying to gain admission, and they should be on the look out for these 'imposters'. However, the researcher did not send any more students. Of 35 people who were genuinely disturbed and sought admission, 12 were not diagnosed as schizophrenic.

(a) Use the data above to complete the following contingency table. *(4 marks)*

	Genuinely schizophrenic	**Not schizophrenic**
Schizophrenia diagnosed		
Schizophrenia not diagnosed		

(b) What percentage of the total number of people studied were genuinely schizophrenic? *(1 mark)*

(c) What percentage of those who were genuinely schizophrenic were not diagnosed as schizophrenic? *(1 mark)*

(d) What percentage of those who were not schizophrenic were correctly diagnosed? *(1 mark)*

Answers on page 356

⚙ APPLYING YOUR KNOWLEDGE

Chrissy and Slimane were discussing social class differences in schizophrenia. 'You seem to be much more likely to be diagnosed as schizophrenic if you're from the most deprived social class than if you're from the "elite" or "established" middle class,' said Chrissy. 'It's just an illusion,' said

Slimane. 'There's no real social class difference, but if you're from a higher social class, you drift downwards in the class system because of your disorder,' he continued. 'Maybe,' said Chrissy, 'but I think it's got more to do with the validity of diagnosis from established middle-class psychiatrists.'

Explain Chrissy's concerns about the validity of diagnosis. *(4 marks)*

Answers on page 356

KEY TERMS

- Biological explanations
- Dopamine hypothesis
- Genetics
- Neural correlates

Possible essay question
Outline and evaluate **one or more** biological explanations for schizophrenia (e.g. genetics, the dopamine hypothesis and neural correlates). *(16 marks)*

Other possible exam questions …

+ Outline research into the role played by genetic factors in schizophrenia. *(4 marks)*
+ Evaluate the dopamine hypothesis as a explanation for schizophrenia. *(4 marks)*
+ Briefly outline and evaluate neural correlates as an explanation of schizophrenia. *(8 marks)*

 Think

The methodologies used to study the genetics of schizophrenia are the same as those used to study, for example, the genetics of aggression. Do you think that the methodological criticisms of this kind of research are the same no matter what aspect of behaviour is being studied?

MUST know …

Genetic factors

Family studies show the risk of someone developing schizophrenia is higher if a family history of it.

Twin studies show that MZ twins (sharing 100% of their genes) are more concordant for schizophrenia than DZ twins (sharing 50%).

Adoption studies show adopted children with schizophrenic biological mothers are more likely than adopted children with non-schizophrenic biological mothers to develop the disorder.

The dopamine hypothesis

The original dopamine hypothesis claimed that positive symptoms are caused by an excess of dopamine.

David & Kahn's (1991) revised hypothesis proposes that the positive symptoms are due to an excess of dopamine in the *mesolimbic pathway*.

Neural correlates

Cognitive symptoms of schizophrenia result from deficits within PFC and connections with other brain areas.

Individuals with schizophrenia have reduced volume of grey matter and reduced white matter pathways.

EVALUATION · *A weakness of family studies is…*

…the influence of environmental factors.

- **E** – Findings from family resemblance studies are limited by the fact that families typically share environments as well as genes.

EVALUATION · *The higher concordance rate in MZ twins…*

…may be the result of environmental as well as genetic factors.

- **E** – Twin studies assume that MZ and DZ environments are equivalent.

EVALUATION · *Support for the dopamine hypothesis…*

…comes from drug therapy for schizophrenia.

- **E** – Antipsychotic drugs reduce activity in the neural pathways that use dopamine.

EVALUATION · *Support for grey matter deficits…*

…being significant in schizophrenia.

- **E** – Schizophrenia patients showed significant grey matter loss over time (Vita et al., 2012).

EVALUATION · *There are implications for treatment…*

…that arise from finding neural correlates.

- **E** – Early detection and intervention may prevent development of the disorder.

SHOULD know …

Genetic factors

Risk is higher the closer genetic relatedness to a schizophrenic (Gottesman, 1991)

Joseph (2004) reports 40.4% concordance for MZs, but only 7.4% for DZs.

Tienari *et al.* (2000) found 6.7% of children whose mothers were schizophrenic developed the disorder compared with 2% whose mothers weren't.

The dopamine hypothesis

Schizophrenics have an excess of D_2 receptors on receiving neurons, resulting in more dopamine binding and more neurons firing.

The negative and cognitive symptoms are believed to be due to a *deficit* of dopamine in the *mesocortical pathway*.

Neural correlates

Hippocampal dysfunction correlates with cognitive impairments in schizophrenia (Mukai *et al.*, 2015)

Individuals who convert to schizophrenia show steeper rate of grey matter loss (Cannon *et al.*, 2014) and reduced white matter in PFC connection with hippocampus (Du *et al.*, 2013)

- **E** – Joseph (2004) believes that parents who adopt children of schizophrenic parents differ from those who adopt children of non-schizophrenic parents.
- **L** – This means that family resemblance and adoption studies might not tell us much about the role of genetic factors in schizophrenia.

- **E** – However, MZs are treated more similarly than DZs in several ways, e.g. being treated as 'the twins' rather than two separate individuals.
- **L** – This means that it is difficult to assess the relative contribution of genes and environmental factors as causes of schizophrenia.

- **E** – Leucht *et al.'s* (2013) meta-analysis showed that all antipsychotics are significantly more effective than placebo in reducing schizophrenic symptoms.
- **L** – This supports the idea that dopamine plays an important role in schizophrenia.

- **E** – Grey matter reduction was mostly in frontal, temporal and parietal lobes.
- **L** – This supports the link between these brain areas and schizophrenia.

- **E** – Hallucinations and delusions also present in some people despite normal dopamine levels.
- **L** – This suggests other neurotransmitters beside dopamine must be involved.

CHOOSE THE RIGHT ANSWER

Which **two** of the following statements about the role played by the dopamine hypothesis and neural correlates in schizophrenia are **false**? (Tick **two** boxes only.)

A Deficits in the prefrontal cortex are linked to the cognitive symptoms of schizophrenia. ☐

B The positive symptoms of schizophrenia are caused by a deficiency of the neurotransmitter dopamine. ☐

C People with schizophrenia have been found to have an excess of grey matter in their brain. ☐

D The negative and cognitive symptoms are believed to be due to a excess of dopamine in the mesocortical pathway. ☐

E Schizophrenia is linked to a reduction of white matter pathways. ☐

Answers on page 356

 FILL IN THE BOXES (1)

Research into the role played by genetic factors in schizophrenia uses three methodologies. For each of the methodologies in the table below, outline **one** finding which suggests that genetic factors are involved in schizophrenia and **one** finding which challenges that suggestion.

	One finding that suggests genetics are involved	One finding that challenges the view that genetics are involved
Family studies		
Twin studies		
Adoption studies		

Answers on page 356

 RESEARCH ISSUES

When rats are given substances which deplete dopamine in the prefrontal cortex, they show cognitive impairment (e.g. memory deficits). These impairments can be reversed using *olanzapine*, an atypical antipsychotic drug thought to have beneficial effects on the negative symptoms of schizophrenia in humans.

What is the major limitation of using non-humans such as rats to study the causes of schizophrenia? *(2 marks)*

Answers on page 357

APPLYING YOUR KNOWLEDGE

'If you look at the evidence from MZ twin studies, it's hard to argue that schizophrenia isn't genetic,' said Fabio. 'Rubbish!' said Roy. 'MZ twins are raised in the same environment, so you don't know how much of their similarity in behaviour is due to genes or the environment. There's only one 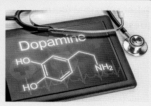 way you might get me to believe that twin studies tell us anything about the genetics of schizophrenia, and even then I'd have my doubts.'

What kind of evidence would Fabio need to try to change Roy's views, and why do you think Roy would still be doubtful? *(6 marks)*

Answers on page 357

 FILL IN THE BOXES (2)

There are two versions of the dopamine hypothesis, the 'original' and the 'revised' version. For each of these versions, write one or two sentences which summarise what the hypotheses say, and outline one finding which supports each hypothesis and one finding which challenges each hypothesis.

	The cause of schizophrenia	One finding which supports the hypothesis	One finding which challenges the hypothesis
The original dopamine hypothesis			
The revised dopamine hypothesis			

Answers on page 356

 Link

Dopamine appears to play a role in several behaviours. Two of these are addiction and anorexia nervosa. Dopamine has also been implicated in OCD, which you studied in Year 1.

KEY TERMS

- Cognitive explanations
- Dysfunctional thought processing
- Family dysfunction

Possible essay question

Discuss **one or more** psychological explanations for schizophrenia (e.g. family dysfunction, cognitive explanations). *(16 marks)*

Other possible exam questions ...

+ Explain what is meant by the term 'dysfunctional thought processing'. *(2 marks)*
+ Outline family dysfunction as an explanation for schizophrenia. *(4 marks)*
+ Evaluate **one or more** cognitive explanations for schizophrenia. *(8 marks)*

★ Exam tip

A good way of evaluating an explanation is to compare it with another one. For example, you could compare psychological and biological explanations. You must always signal that this is what you are doing by using an appropriate phrase.

MUST know ...

Family dysfunction

Schizophrenia is caused by abnormal family communication patterns. Bateson *et al's*. (1956) **double bind theory** says that parents predispose their children to schizophrenia through contradictory communications.

Expressed emotion (EE) is a communication style whereby family members talk about a schizophrenic critically (*high* EE) or non-critically (*low* EE).

High EE levels are associated with high relapse rates.

Cognitive explanations

These emphasise the role of **dysfunctional thought processing**, especially in delusions and hallucinations.

Delusions occur when a person relates irrelevant information to themselves, and consequently draws false conclusions.

Hallucinations occur because the person attributes a *self-generated* auditory experience to an *external source*.

 The evidence for double bind theory is...

...mixed, at best.

- **E** – For example, Berger (1965) found evidence of more double bind statements in families of schizophrenics than non-schizophrenics.

 Schizophrenics differ in their...

... vulnerability to the influence of high EE.

- **E** – For example, Altorfer *et al.* (1998) found that 25% of schizophrenics showed no physiological responses to stressful comments from relatives.

Positive and negative symptoms...

...can be explained in terms of faulty cognitions.

- **E** – For example, schizophrenics with positive symptoms, like hallucinations and delusions, show biases in information processing.

SHOULD know ...

Family dysfunction

A mother tells her son she loves him but then turns away when he approaches her for affection. Such contradictions invalidate each other, preventing an internally coherent construction of reality from developing.

High EE family members may be emotionally overly involved or concerned with the person and their behaviour.

Schizophrenics may have a lower tolerance for environmental stimuli, leading to stress beyond a manageable level.

Cognitive explanations

Schizophrenics process information *differently* to non-schizophrenics.

Irrelevant muffled voices might be interpreted as criticism. The inability to recognise distortions and substitute more realistic explanations is called 'impaired insight'.

The voice is experienced as coming from an external source because the person doesn't *check* its actual source.

- **E** – However, Liem (1974) reported no differences in communication patterns in families of schizophrenics and non-schizophrenics.
- **L** – This suggests that double bind theory is not a useful way of explaining schizophrenia's causes.

- **E** – It has been suggested that whether EE behaviour is stressful or not depends on how the schizophrenic *perceives* it.
- **L** – This shows that not all schizophrenics are equally vulnerable to high levels of EE in their family environment.

- **E** – Schizophrenics with negative symptoms display dysfunctional thought processes such as having low expectations of pleasure.
- **L** – This means that cognitive dysfunction offers a comprehensive explanation of schizophrenia.

FURTHER EVALUATION

 P – Findings relating to CBT for psychosis (CBTp)...

...also support cognitive explanations of schizophrenia.

- **E** – For example, NICE (2014) found that CBTp was more effective than anti-psychotic drugs in reducing symptom severity and improving social functioning.
- **E** – CBTp focuses on changing cognitions about delusions and hallucinations, rather than altering biochemistry.
- **L** – This supports the view that faulty cognitions are the cause of schizophrenia.

P – Family relationships may interact with...

...genetic factors on the development of schizophrenia.

- **E** – Tienari *et al*. (1994) found biological children of schizophrenics were more likely to develop the disorder even if adopted.
- **E** – However, this was only true if the adoptive family itself was rated as 'disturbed'.
- **L** – This suggests that genetic vulnerability alone is not sufficient for schizophrenia to develop.

FILL IN THE BOXES

For the two psychological theories based on family dysfunction identified below, outline what each explanation says. Then outline **one** strength and **one** weakness of each explanation.

	Double bind	Expressed emotion
Basic outline		
One strength		
One weakness		

Answers on page 357

Link

See the Year 1/AS Revision and Exam Companion, page 138, for more general evaluative issues relating to the cognitive approach.

APPLYING YOUR KNOWLEDGE

Bonnie and Delaney were discussing cognitive explanations of schizophrenia. 'I get the idea that schizophrenia is a result of dysfunctional thought processes, and that schizophrenics process information differently from non-schizophrenics,' said Bonnie. 'But I just don't think I could say anything about how they explain specific symptoms.' 'OK,' said Delaney. 'I've drawn a table to help you. First of all, describe each symptom, then use your revision guide to find the appropriate cognitive explanation.'

Complete the table.

	Description	Cognitive explanation
Hallucinations		
Delusions		
Anhedonia		

Answers on page 357

 DRAWING CONCLUSIONS

In some families, the family members are frequently hostile towards each other, critical of each other, and over-involved and over-concerned with each other's lives. These families are said to be high in expressed emotion (high EE). Other families do not show these characteristics and are said to be low in expressed emotion (low EE).

The table below shows the results from four studies conducted in different countries.

	Study location	Number of participants	Follow-up period (months)	Percentage relapse rate in high EE participants	Percentage relapse rate in low EE participants
Vaughn and Leff (1976)	South London	37	9	50	12
Vaughn *et al.* (1984)	Los Angeles	54	9	56	28
Cazzullo *et al.* (1989)	Milan	45	9	58	21
Barrelet *et al.* (1990)	Geneva	41	9	32	0

(a) Calculate the overall average percentage relapse rates in the high and low EE participants. *(2 marks)*

(b) What do the differences in relapse rates between the high and low EE participants suggest? *(2 marks)*

(c) What do the differences between the ranges for the high and low EE participants suggest? *(2 marks)*

(d) What do the findings for the two continental European countries combined indicate compared with the findings for the British study and the American study? *(4 marks)*

Answers on page 357

KEY TERMS

- Atypical antipsychotics
- Drug therapy
- Typical antipsychotics

Possible essay question

Discuss the use of typical **and/ or** atypical antipsychotics as treatments for schizophrenia. *(16 marks)*

Other possible exam questions …

+ Distinguish between typical and atypical antipsychotics. *(2 marks)*
+ Outline the use of typical or atypical antipsychotics in the treatment of schizophrenia. *(4 marks)*
+ Evaluate drug therapy as a treatment for schizophrenia. *(8 marks)*

 Exam tip

Since both typical and atypical antipsychotics are named on the specification, you could be asked to write about either or both of them. Don't learn one without learning the other!

Think

Would you be able to explain the distinction between how 'effective' a therapy is and how 'appropriate' it is to your teacher? Do you think it matters if a therapy is inappropriate as long as it is effective?

MUST know …

Antipsychotics

There are two types of **antipsychotic** medication used to treat schizophrenia. They are called **typical** and **atypical antipsychotics**.

Typical antipsychotics

These are dopamine *antagonists*. They bind to dopamine receptors, but do not stimulate them, reducing dopamine's effects. An example is *chlorpromazine*.

They significantly reduce hallucinations and delusions within a few days.

Atypical antipsychotics

These also block D_2 receptors. However, they rapidly dissociate from the receptors, allowing normal dopamine transmission. An example is *clozapine*.

Atypical antipsychotics have a stronger affinity to serotonin receptors than to dopamine receptors, and lead to different effects from typical antipsychotics.

EVALUATION **P – One strength of antipsychotics is…**

…that they are effective in treating schizophrenia.

- **E** – For example, Leucht *et al.* (2012) meta-analysed 65 studies comparing relapse rates for antipsychotics and placebos.

EVALUATION **P – One weakness of typical antipsychotics is…**

…the side effects they produce.

- **E** – For example, more than 50% of schizophrenics experience movement problems (extrapyramidal side effects) resembling Parkinson's disease.

EVALUATION **P – Atypical antipsychotics have advantages over…**

…typical antipsychotics.

- **E** – For example, drugs like *olanzapine* and *quetiapine* have fewer side effects, especially those involving extrapyramidal symptoms.

SHOULD know …

Antipsychotics

Antipsychotics are usually the initial treatment method for schizophrenia, and are later combined with psychological therapy to manage the disorder.

Typical antipsychotics

They particularly affect D_2 receptors in the mesolimbic pathway. However, they also affect D_2 receptors in other areas, leading to extrapyramidal side effects.

Other positive symptoms (e.g. thought disturbances) take longer to be reduced.

Atypical antipsychotics

They have a lower risk of extrapyramidal side effects, possibly because they have little effect on dopamine systems controlling movement.

They also have beneficial effects on negative symptoms and cognitive impairment, and are used with treatment-resistant schizophrenics.

- **E** – 64% of patients whose antipsychotic medication was replaced by a placebo relapsed, whilst only 27% of those who remained on their medication relapsed.
- **L** – This shows that antipsychotics significantly reduce the likelihood of relapse in schizophrenics.

- **E** – Extended use of typical antipsychotics leads to tardive diskinesia, a serious and permanent movement disorder affecting the tongue, face, and jaw.
- **L** – These side effects can lead to schizophrenics stopping their medication, and hence reducing their chances of improving.

- **E** – Consequently, patients are more likely to continue taking their medication.
- **L** – This means that improvement is more likely with atypical than typical antipsychotics.

FURTHER EVALUATION

P – Although atypical antipsychotics have fewer side effects than typical antipsychotics…

…they do not seem to be more effective in reducing symptoms.

- **E** – For example, Crossley et al. (2010) meta-analysed 15 studies of the efficacy and side-effects of typical and atypical medication.
- **E** – Although atypical antipsychotics had fewer side effects, they did not differ from typical antipsychotics in terms of their efficacy.
- **L** – This suggests that the only advantage of atypical antipsychotics is their side-effect profile.

P – There are important ethical issues…

…in treating schizophrenia with typical antipsychotics.

- **E** – For example, they have side effects, psychosocial consequences, and may even cause death.
- **E** – Critics say that when these factors are taken into account, a cost-benefit analysis of typical antipsychotics would probably be negative.
- **L** – This means that researchers need to discover effective and ethically sound treatment methods which produce a positive cost-benefit analysis.

CHOOSE THE RIGHT ANSWER

Which **one** of the following statements about typical and atypical antipsychotics is true? (Tick **one** box only.)

A Typical antipsychotics bind to dopamine receptors and stimulate them. ☐

B Atypical antipsychotics affect both dopamine and GABA. ☐

C Typical antipsychotics have few side effects. ☐

D Atypical antipsychotics have a lower risk of extrapyramidal side effects. ☐

E Atypical antipsychotics are only effective in treating the positive symptoms of schizophrenia. ☐

Answers on page 357

 DRAWING CONCLUSIONS

In a study designed to compare the relative effectiveness of different antipsychotic drugs, a researcher randomly assigned 100 schizophrenics who had not been previously treated to one of four groups. Each group were given one of four typical antipsychotics. The researcher asked a colleague who was familiar with antipsychotic medication to rate the participants in terms of how much they had improved on a 7-point scale (1 = no improvement, 7 = large improvement). The table below shows the mean ratings of improvement in each of the four groups.

	Drug A	Drug B	Drug C	Drug D
Mean improvement rate	4.6	3.8	5.9	6.2

(a) Identify the independent and dependent variables in this study. *(2 marks)*

(b) The researcher's colleague was 'familiar with antipsychotic medication'. Explain **one** weakness of using this colleague to make the ratings. *(2 marks)*

(c) The researcher concluded that all of the drugs were effective in treating schizophrenia. Explain why this conclusion is not justified. *(3 marks)*

(d) The researcher wanted to know if Drug C and Drug D had significantly different effects. Name a statistical test that she could have used, and give **three** reasons for choosing this test. *(4 marks)*

Answers on page 357

 FILL IN THE TABLE

Test your knowledge of the differences between typical and atypical antipsychotics by placing the terms below into the appropriate box.

	Typical antipsychotics	Atypical antipsychotics
The drug works by…		
An example of the drug is…		
The drug significantly reduces…		
One side-effect of the drug is…		

- the positive symptoms of schizophrenia
- weight gain
- blocking dopamine receptors, but rapidly dissociate from them, allowing normal dopamine transmission
- chlorpromazine
- extrapyramidal effects, such as tardive dyskinesia
- both the positive and negative symptoms of schizophrenia
- binding to dopamine receptors, but not stimulating them
- clozapine

Answers on page 357

 APPLYING YOUR KNOWLEDGE

Carmen and Martin were discussing the use of placebos in assessing the effectiveness of drug therapies. 'The problem you've got,' said Martin, 'is that antipsychotics have side effects.   If a person was assessing whether someone was showing an improvement, they'd know they'd been given a placebo because they wouldn't be showing any side effects. That would bias their judgement.' 'You're right,' said Carmen. 'That means comparing drugs with placebos is never going to tell us anything about how effective drugs are.'

Explain one way in which it might be possible to overcome the problem Martin has pointed out about placebos. *(4 marks)*

Answers on page 357

 Link

See page 130 for a discussion of the role played by dopamine in schizophrenia, and how this is related to the action of antipsychotic drugs.

KEY TERMS
- Cognitive behavioural therapy

Possible essay question
Discuss the use of cognitive behavioural therapy in the treatment of schizophrenia. *(16 marks)*

Other possible exam questions ...
+ Outline how cognitive behavioural therapy can be used to treat schizophrenia. *(4 marks)*
+ Explain **two** limitations of using cognitive behavioural therapy to treat schizophrenia. *(6 marks)*
+ Evaluate cognitive behavioural therapy as it is used in the treatment of schizophrenia. *(8 marks)*

 Exam tip

We identify six phases in CBTp. You wouldn't need to write about all of these in an 'outline' question, so try to use the material presented here to construct an outline of CBTp you can remember easily.

 Think

If schizophrenia has a biological cause, is it appropriate to use psychological therapies like CBTp to treat it?

MUST know ...

Cognitive behavioural therapy for psychosis (CBTp)

CBTp assumes that feelings and behaviour are negatively influenced by distorted beliefs. It aims to identify and correct these beliefs.

CBTp is usually delivered one-to-one for at least 16 sessions.

The phases in CBTp are:

Assessment: The therapist discusses the person's current symptoms and their origins.

Engagement: The therapist empathises with the person's distress.

The ABC model: This is used to challenge the person's beliefs.

Normalisation: Placing the person's own psychotic experiences on a continuum with normal experiences.

Critical collaborative analysis: Gentle empathetic and non-judgemental questioning helps the person understand their false beliefs.

Developing alternative explanations: Enables healthier explanations for behaviour.

 P – It is difficult to assess...

...how effective CBTp is.
- **E** – NICE's (2014) review of research indicates that CBTp is more effective in reducing symptom severity than antipsychotic medication alone.

 P – Most meta-analytic studies of CBTp's effectiveness...

...may be seriously flawed.
- **E** – For example, studies have typically failed to allocate participants randomly to treatment conditions.

 P – Methodologically sound meta-analyses of CBTp's effectiveness...

...suggest it actually has little therapeutic benefit.
- **E** – For example, Jauhar *et al.* (2014) found that CBTp has only a small effect on reducing hallucinations and delusions.

SHOULD know ...

Cognitive behavioural therapy for psychosis

By monitoring thoughts, feelings, and behaviours schizophrenics are better able to consider alternative explanations for why they occur.

CBTp can also be delivered in groups.

Once these are known, realistic therapeutic goals are set.

Emphasis is placed on how the therapist and person will work together.

This involves rationalising, disputing, and, ultimately, changing the person's beliefs.

If the person is told their experiences are actually common, they will feel less alienated and stigmatised.

This takes place in an atmosphere of trust.

The therapist helps with this if the person has difficulty.

- **E** – However, CBTp is typically used in *conjunction* with antipsychotic medication.
- **L** – This means that it is difficult to assess CBTp's effectiveness independent of antipsychotic medication.

- **E** – However, meta-analyses fail to take an individual study's quality into account.
- **L** – This means that claims about CBTp's effectiveness may be biased by methodologically weak research studies.

- **E** – However, even this small effect disappears when assessment of improvement is done by 'blind' judges.
- **L** – This suggests that the usefulness of CBTp in the treatment of schizophrenia may be overstated.

FURTHER

 P – CBTp's appropriateness and effectiveness appears to depend on...

the stage of a schizophrenic's disorder.
- **E** – For example, Addington & Addington (2005) say that CBTp is inappropriate in the initial acute phase of schizophrenia.
- **E** – CBTp is more appropriately used following stabilisation of symptoms with antipsychotic medication.
- **L** – This means that CBTp should be used in conjunction with drug therapy rather than as a 'first choice' therapy.

 P – CBTp is not yet an established therapy in...

...the treatment of schizophrenia.
- **E** – For example, in the UK, CBTp is only available to 10% of people who could benefit from it.
- **E** – Even when it is available, many who are offered CBTp either refuse it or fail to attend therapeutic sessions.
- **L** – This means that if CBTp *is* beneficial, more needs to be done to raise its availability and uptake.

CHOOSE THE RIGHT ANSWER

Which **one** of the following statements about CBTp is **false**? (Tick **one** box only.)

A CBTp's aim is to identify and correct distorted beliefs. ☐

B CBTp is usually delivered on a one-to-one basis for at least 16 sessions. ☐

C CBT is never used in association with other forms of therapy. ☐

D CBTp can be delivered in groups. ☐

E CBTp assumes that feelings and behaviour are negatively influenced by distorted beliefs. ☐

Answers on page 358

 RESEARCH ISSUES

Meta-analysis is a method for systematically combining data from different studies. The aim is to produce a single conclusion that is stronger than the conclusion drawn by any of the individual studies. It is a useful technique when lots of studies have been done on a topic but have produced conflicting results. However, there are several weaknesses associated with meta-analysis. An important question to ask of any meta-analysis is whether the studies that have been combined are all similar in type.

Explain why meta-analytic studies of CBTp's effectiveness should be treated with caution. *(2 marks)*

Answers on page 358

 Link

See page 116 of the Year 1/AS Revision and Exam Companion for other applications of cognitive behavioural therapy to the treatment of mental disorders.

 COMPLETE THE DIAGRAM

In each box below, write one sentence describing what happens in the phases of CBTp.

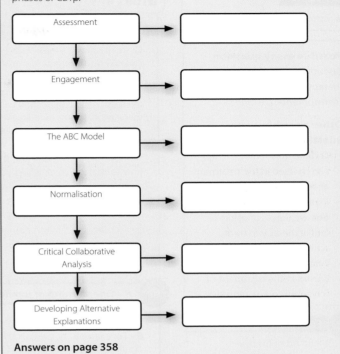

Answers on page 358

 APPLYING YOUR KNOWLEDGE

Jack was reading a case study of a schizophrenic who claimed that he knew what people were going to say before they said it. 'Wow!' said Jasper, 'that's some ability.' 'Don't be daft,' said Jack. 'He couldn't really. He just believed that he could. They used CBTp to show him that he didn't really have that ability.' 'Really?' said Jasper. 'How did they do that?'

Using your knowledge of the aims of CBTp, suggest a way in which the schizophrenic's false beliefs could have been challenged. *(4 marks)*

Answers on page 358

KEY TERMS

- Family therapy

Possible essay question

Discuss the use of family therapy as a treatment for schizophrenia. *(16 marks)*

Other possible exam questions …

+ Outline how family therapy can be used in the treatment of schizophrenia. *(4 marks)*
+ Explain **one** strength and **one** weakness of using family therapy to treat schizophrenia. *(6 marks)*
+ Evaluate family therapy as it is used in the treatment of schizophrenia. *(8 marks)*

 Exam tip

As with other therapies, 'comparative' evaluation is another way of earning AO3 marks. Family therapy could be compared with other psychological therapies (e.g. CBTp or token economy) or with biological therapy (antipsychotic drugs).

Think

We've mentioned the apparent economic benefits of family therapy in this spread. Are a therapy's economic benefits more important than any other benefits it may have?

MUST know …

Family therapy

Family therapy is based on the finding that families can play an important role in affecting the course of schizophrenia.

Therapy lasts for 3–12 months over at least ten sessions, in conjunction with antipsychotic medication. It aims to reduce levels of expressed emotion (EE) and stress. An alliance is formed with family members using several strategies:

(1) Providing knowledge about schizophrenia and how to deal with it (*psychoeducation*).

(2) Reducing the emotional climate (e.g. anger and guilt) within the family, and the burden of care (e.g. expectations about the schizophrenic's behaviour).

(3) Encouraging family members to set appropriate limits while maintaining some degree of separation when needed.

EVALUATION **P – One strength of family therapy is…**

…that is has economic benefits.

- **E** – For example, NCCMH (2009) found there were significant cost savings when family therapy was combined with antipsychotic medication.

EVALUATION **P – The main benefit of family therapy…**

…may simply be that it increases medication compliance.

- **E** – For example, Pharoah *et al.* (2010) found that family therapy had *some* effect on mental state, social functioning, and relapse and readmission rates.

EVALUATION **P – There are methodological issues…**

…in studies of family therapy's effectiveness.

- **E** – For example, Pharoah *et al.'s* (2010) meta-analysis of 53 studies indicated that many of them failed to allocate participants randomly to treatment conditions.

SHOULD know …

Family therapy

'Family' includes a schizophrenic's parents, siblings, and partner.

By reducing EE levels and increasing family members' ability to anticipate and solve related problems, schizophrenics will hopefully be less likely to relapse.

(1) Knowledge helps families to support the schizophrenic and resolve practical problems.

(2) If practical, the schizophrenic is involved during the sessions and encouraged to talk about their family, the support they find helpful, and what makes things worse.

(3) Family therapy improves household relationships as members are encouraged to listen to each other, openly discuss problems, and negotiate solutions.

- **E** – Although family therapy initially adds cost, this is offset by a reduction in rehospitalisation due to lower relapse rates during therapy.
- **L** – Reduced relapse rates *following* therapy mean that the economic benefits of family therapy may be even higher.

- **E** – However, it also had an effect on how likely schizophrenics were to take their antipsychotic medication.
- **L** – This suggests that the reason schizophrenics show an improvement is because of antipsychotic medication rather than family therapy *per se*.

- **E** – Additionally, over 20% of studies failed to use observers 'blind' to what treatments patients were receiving.
- **L** – These methodological deficiencies mean that drawing conclusions about family therapy's effectiveness is difficult.

 FURTHER EVALUATION

EVALUATION **P – Carers lower in EE might be just as effective as…**

…family therapy.
- **E** – For example, Garety *et al.* (2008) found that family therapy and having a carer without family therapy were both associated with lower relapse rates compared with a 'no carer' condition.
- **E** – Most of the carers showed relatively low levels of EE.
- **L** – This suggests that family therapy might not be any more effective than a good standard of care.

EVALUATION **P – The benefits of family therapy to family members…**

…has yet to be shown.
- **E** – For example, Lobban *et al.* (2013) found that in 60% of studies, family therapy had a significant positive impact on at least one outcome category for relatives (e.g. family functioning).
- **E** – However, the studies reporting these beneficial effects were methodologically poor.
- **L** – This means that we cannot draw any firm conclusions about the benefits of family therapy to family members of schizophrenics.

CHOOSE THE RIGHT ANSWER

Which **one** of the following is associated with family therapy? (Tick **one** box only.)

A The use of tokens as rewards. ☐

B Increasing the burden of care for family members. ☐

C Avoiding the use of therapeutic drugs. ☐

D Reducing levels of expressed emotion and stress. ☐

E Increasing the emotional climate within the family setting. ☐

Answers on page 358

MATCH THEM UP

Match up the researchers to the statement that best describes their research.

1	Pharoah *et al.* (2010)	**A**	Family therapy and having a carer without family therapy are both associated with lower relapse rates compared with a 'no carer' condition.
2	NCCMH (2009)	**B**	In 60% of studies, family therapy has a significant positive impact on at least one outcome category for relatives (e.g. family functioning).
3	Lobban *et al.* (2013)	**C**	Family therapy has some effect on mental state, social functioning, and relapse and readmission rates.
4	Garety *et al.* (2008)	**D**	There are significant cost savings when family therapy is combined with antipsychotic medication.

Answers on page 358

APPLYING YOUR KNOWLEDGE

Elizabeth and Mary were talking about family therapy for people with schizophrenia. Elizabeth said that as far as she was concerned, family interventions are an important and valid approach to treating schizophrenia. 'I agree that research studies show that family therapy is effective,' Mary said, 'but there are far too many things that can limit its effectiveness.'

Using your knowledge of the processes involved in family therapy, outline **three** practical issues that could limit its effectiveness. (6 marks)

Answers on page 358

DRAWING CONCLUSIONS

A researcher wanted to know if family therapy could reduce the relapse rate for schizophrenic family members. One hundred high-stress families were identified. Half of the schizophrenic family members received standard after-care therapy, whilst the other half received supportive family therapy. This therapy encourages the family to convene a family meeting whenever an issue arises, in order to discuss and specify the exact nature of the problem, to consider alternative solutions, and to select and implement the consensual best solution. A year after the study began, the researcher identified which schizophrenic family members had been readmitted to hospital and which had not. The findings are shown in the table below.

	Number readmitted to hospital	Number not readmitted to hospital
Standard after-care therapy	53	47
Supportive family therapy	9	91

(a) Draw a suitably labelled bar chart of the data in the above table. *(4 marks)*

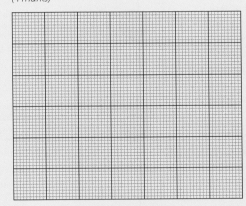

(b) The researcher decided to analyse the results using a statistical test. Identify a suitable test that could have been used. Give **two** reasons for your choice of test. *(3 marks)*

(c) The researcher set the significance level at p < 0.05. What is the likelihood of a Type I error being made? *(1 mark)*

(d) The statistical test showed that the null hypothesis could be rejected. What conclusion would be drawn about the effectiveness of supportive family therapy as compared with standard after-care therapy? *(3 marks)*

Answers on page 358

Link

Family therapy is clearly linked to the psychological explanations of schizophrenia that were discussed on page 132.

KEY TERMS

- Token economy

Possible essay question

Discuss the use of token economies in the management of schizophrenia. *(16 marks)*

Other possible exam questions ...

+ Explain what is meant by the term 'token economy'. *(2 marks)*

+ Outline how token economies are used in the management of schizophrenia. *(4 marks)*

+ Explain **one** strength and **one** weakness of using token economies in the management of schizophrenia. *(6 marks)*

+ Evaluate the use of token economies as a way of managing schizophrenia. *(8 marks)*

★ Exam tip

This topic lends itself well to AO1. However, do not get carried away with your outline/description. On 16-mark questions, there are more marks awarded for AO3. Your evaluation should therefore always be proportionately greater than your outline/description.

MUST know ...

Token economy (TE)

A **TE** is a behavioural therapy which uses operant conditioning principles, particularly positive reinforcement.

Initially, a plastic token is repeatedly *paired* with something the schizophrenic values, such as a sweet. The token is called a *secondary reinforcer*.

The clinician then sets target behaviours (e.g. getting dressed) and uses tokens whenever they are performed, to ensure the target behaviour is learned.

For a TE to be effective, tokens must be given immediately after performance of the target behaviour.

When tokens can be exchanged for various primary reinforcers, they are called *generalised reinforcers*. TEs are less effective when the time interval between the token being given and it being exchanged increases (Kazdin, 1977).

 P – One strength of the TE is...

...that it seems to be effective in managing schizophrenic behaviour.

- **E** – For example, Dickerson *et al.* (2005) reviewed 13 studies which used the TE in therapeutic settings.

 P – One weakness of the TE is...

...that tokens may not be the reason for behavioural improvements.

- **E** – To show that tokens improve behaviour, a control group not on a TE system has to be compared with an experimental group who are.

 P – There are ethical issues...

...about using TEs therapeutically.

- **E** – For example, clinicians exercise control over important reinforcers such as food.

SHOULD know ...

Token economy (TE)

TE is a way of decreasing negative symptoms (e.g. social withdrawal) and increasing more positive behaviours.

This pairing leads to the token acquiring the same properties as the thing the schizophrenic values. The valued thing is called *a primary reinforcer*.

At first, tokens are exchanged frequently for reinforcers so that target behaviours increase in frequency.

If there is a delay, then some other, possibly negative, behaviour which occurred after the target behaviour would be reinforced instead.

Tokens that can be exchanged for various primary reinforcers produce *higher* rates of responding from schizophrenics (Sran & Borrero, 2010).

- **E** – They found that 11 of these reported beneficial effects could be directly attributable to the TE.
- **L** – This suggests that the TE can increase the target behaviours of schizophrenics.

- **E** – Most TEs involve all schizophrenics in an institution, so improvement can only be compared with their *past* behaviour.
- **L** – Consequently, it is possible that things like increased staff attention, rather than tokens, are actually causing behavioural improvements.

- **E** – However, all humans have certain basic rights, such as access to food.
- **L** – Because these rights should not be violated, TEs may not be an appropriate way of managing schizophrenic behaviour.

FURTHER EVALUATION

 P – The TE may only be effective...

...within an institutional setting.

- **E** – Schizophrenics in institutions receive 24-hour care, and are monitored and rewarded appropriately.
- **E** – However, outpatient schizophrenics living in the community are only seen for a few hours a day.
- **L** – Given the need for reinforcement to be given immediately after a target behaviour has been performed, TEs are unlikely to be effective for outpatient schizophrenics.

 P – Randomised trials are the best way of...

...assessing the effectiveness of TEs.

- **E** – However, TEs have fallen out of use in much of the developed world precisely because of the absence of such trials.
- **E** – Developing countries may hold the key to how effective TEs are, since they are still used therapeutically.
- **L** – Randomised trials would enable the question of whether TEs actually work to be addressed conclusively.

CHOOSE THE RIGHT ANSWER

Which **two** of the following statements about token economy are true? (Tick **two** boxes only.)

A	Token economy is based on the principles of classical conditioning.	☐
B	Token economy involves pairing a neutral stimulus with a target behaviour.	☐
C	For a token economy to be effective, tokens must be given immediately after the performance of a target behaviour.	☐
D	Tokens are initially exchanged frequently for reinforcers so that target behaviours increase in frequency.	☐
E	A token economy is more effective when the time interval between the token being given and it being exchanged increases.	☐

Answers on page 358

 MATCH THEM UP

Match up the concept to the statement that best describes it.

1	Secondary reinforcer	**A**	Something which is valued by the schizophrenic.
2	Positive reinforcer	**B**	Something, such as a token, which can be exchanged for various primary reinforcers.
3	Primary reinforcer	**C**	A token which is repeatedly paired with something the schizophrenic values.
4	Generalised reinforcer	**D**	Something which causes a behaviour to increase in frequency because it has a desirable consequence.

Answers on page 358

 APPLYING YOUR KNOWLEDGE

Simon was taking Matt to the football match, but needed to fill his car with petrol. 'You drove past a petrol station five minutes ago!' said Matt. 'I know,' said Simon, 'but I have to drive to the next one, because I get points on my reward card there.' Simon promptly ran out of petrol. As they walked to the next station Matt said, 'They really ought to have called it a "reinforcement card" not a "reward card".' 'What's the difference?' said Simon.

Using your knowledge of reinforcement and its role in token economies, explain to Simon the difference between a reinforcer and a reward. *(4 marks)*

Answers on page 358

 DRAWING CONCLUSIONS

A researcher wanted to investigate the effectiveness of a token economy system on the behaviour of eleven schizophrenics. He initially identified a number of target behaviours and counted how many times these occurred over the course of a week. A token economy system was then introduced. After two weeks, the number of times the target behaviours occurred was counted again. The researcher predicted that there would be an increase in the production of target behaviours following the introduction of the token economy system. For one of the schizophrenics, the number of target behaviours remained the same. For two, the number of target behaviours decreased. The remaining eight showed an increase in the number of target behaviours. A Sign test was chosen to analyse the data. Part of the table of critical values for 'S' for a one-tailed hypothesis is shown below.

N	0.05	0.01
10	1	1
11	2	1
12	2	2
13	2	2

To be significant, the calculated/observed value must be equal to or less than the critical/table value

(a) What is the calculated value of the Sign test statistic 'S'. Explain your answer. *(2 marks)*

(b) Using the table above, state whether the findings of the study are significant at $p < 0.05$. Explain your answer. *(3 marks)*

(c) What conclusion would be drawn from the findings of this study? *(2 marks)*

(d) Name a parametric test that could have been used instead of the Sign test. *(1 mark)*

(e) What is meant by the term Type II error? *(2 marks)*

(f) Why is a Type II error less likely if a parametric rather than a non-parametric test is used? *(3 marks)*

Answers on page 358

 Link

See page 134 of the Year 1/AS Revision and Exam Companion for more information on operant conditioning.

KEY TERMS

- Diathesis-stress model

Possible essay question

Discuss the diathesis-stress model as an explanation for schizophrenia. *(16 marks)*

Other possible exam questions ...

+ Outline the diathesis-stress model of schizophrenia. *(4 marks)*

+ Explain why it is important to take an interactionist approach in explaining **and/or** treating schizophrenia. *(6 marks)*

+ Evaluate the diathesis-stress model of schizophrenia. *(8 marks)*

 Exam tip

This topic has an obvious link with biological explanations for schizophrenia. Remember, though, to focus on the diathesis-stress model and don't get carried away with a lengthy outline and/or evaluation of biological explanations!

 Think

How does the diathesis-stress model relate to the nature–nurture debate?

MUST know ...

An interactionist approach

The **diathesis-stress model** proposes that schizophrenia is the result of an *interaction* between biological and environmental influences.

People differ in their biological vulnerability ('diathesis') to schizophrenia and in terms of how much stress they experience in their lives.

Relatively minor stressors may lead to schizophrenia in people who are highly vulnerable. A major stressful life event may lead to schizophrenia in those with low vulnerability.

Tienari *et al.* (2004) found that women who were born to schizophrenic mothers and adopted as children were significantly less likely to develop schizophrenia if they were raised in a 'healthy' adoptive family (low stress) than a 'less healthy' adoptive family (high stress).

 P – Genetic vulnerability is not the only diathesis...

...that increases the risk of developing schizophrenia.

- *E* – For example, birth complications are associated with an increased risk of schizophrenia.

 P – Urban environments are not necessarily more stressful...

...than rural environments.

- *E* – For example, Romans-Clarkson *et al.* (1990) found no urban-rural differences in mental health among women in New Zealand.

 P – Knowledge of different diatheses...

...can possibly help to prevent schizophrenia.

- *E* – For example, Borglum *et al.* (2006) found that women infected with the cytomegalovirus during pregnancy were more likely to have a child who developed schizophrenia.

SHOULD know ...

An interactionist approach

The model can explain why not all people with a genetic vulnerability to schizophrenia develop the disorder.

People with a family history of schizophrenia have a *high vulnerability*. Stressors includes childhood trauma and living in densely populated urban environments.

The model assumes that diathesis and stress add together in some way to cause schizophrenia.

In women who were born to non-schizophrenic mothers and adopted as children, the 'healthiness' of the family environment did not affect the likelihood of schizophrenia developing. These 'low' biologically vulnerable women were also less likely to develop schizophrenia than the women with 'high' biological vulnerability.

- *E* – Verdoux *et al.* (1998) estimate the risk to be four times greater for people who experience birth complications.
- *L* – This means that vulnerability should not be defined in terms of genetic influences alone.

- *E* – Paykel *et al.* (2000) found that urban-rural differences disappeared when socioeconomic differences between the two groups were taken into account.
- *L* – This suggests that living in densely populated urban environments may not actually be a significant stress factor for schizophrenia.

- *E* – However, this was only the case if both the mother and child had a particular gene deficit.
- *L* – This suggests that anti-viral medicine during pregnancy may prevent schizophrenia in the offspring of women known to have the gene defect.

FURTHER EVALUATION

 P – There are methodological issues...

...with Tienari *et al's* (2004) study.

- *E* – For example, family functioning was only measured once.
- *E* – This fails to reflect developmental changes in family functioning over time.
- *L* – This means that it isn't definitively known whether genetic factors moderate susceptibility to environmental risks associated with adoptive family functioning.

P – There are difficulties in...

...determining the causal diathesis in diathesis-stress models.

- *E* – For example, ineffective ways of coping with stress early in life can influence responses to later stressful life events, and increase their future susceptibility to developing schizophrenia.
- *E* – Hammen (1992) believes that ineffective coping skills in childhood may increase their vulnerability.
- *L* – This suggests that it may be a lack of resistance to stress that triggers schizophrenia, rather than genetic vulnerability.

CHAPTER 6 · *Schizophrenia*

 CHOOSE THE RIGHT ANSWER

Which **one** of the following is **not** a claim made by the diathesis-stress model? (Tick **one** box only.)

A	Environmental stressors include childhood trauma and living in a densely populated urban environment.	☐
B	Schizophrenia is a result of an interaction between biological and environmental influences.	☐
C	Relatively minor stressors can lead to schizophrenia in people with a high biological vulnerability to the disorder.	☐
D	Diathesis and stress add together in clearly known ways to cause schizophrenia.	☐
E	How biologically vulnerable a person is can be measured in terms of their family history of schizophrenia.	☐

Answers on page 358

 MATCH THEM UP

Match up the researchers to the statement that best describes their research.

1	Borglum *et al.* (2006)	**A**	There are no urban-rural differences in schizophrenia when socioeconomic differences between these groups are taken into account.
2	Hammen (1992)	**B**	Women infected with the cytomegalovirus during pregnancy were more likely to have a child who developed schizophrenia.
3	Tienari *et al.* (2004)	**C**	Ineffective coping skills in childhood can increase vulnerability to schizophrenia.
4	Paykel *et al.* (2000)	**D**	Women born to schizophrenic mothers and adopted as children are significantly less likely to develop schizophrenia if raised in a 'healthy' adoptive family.

Answers on page 358

 Link

See pages 48-49 of the Year 2 Complete Companion for further reading on the interaction between nature and nurture.

APPLYING YOUR KNOWLEDGE

The diagram below is a hypothetical illustration of the diathesis-stress model. 'Biological vulnerability' has been measured in terms of a person's family history of schizophrenia, whilst 'stress' has been measured in terms of life events that a person can experience.

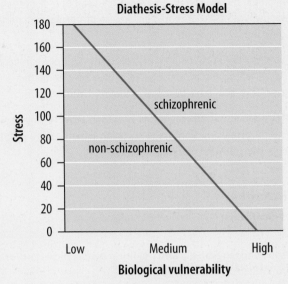

On the 'biological vulnerability' axis, 'low' indicates that a person has no family history of schizophrenia, 'medium' indicates that one of their parents is schizophrenic, and 'high' indicates that both of their parents are schizophrenic. On the stress scale, being overdrawn at the bank has a stress value of 50, going away to university has a stress value of 75, and being made unemployed has a stress value of 100.

Adrian has one schizophrenic parent and is overdrawn at the bank. Both of Barry's parents are schizophrenic, and he has recently been made unemployed. Chris has no family history of schizophrenia, but he is overdrawn at the bank and has just gone away to university. Dave has one schizophrenic parent and has just gone away to university. Six months into his course, Dave's bank manager tells him that he has reached his overdraft limit. To make matters worse, Dave he has lost his job at the local burger bar.

Using the diagram above, distinguish between the four characters in terms of whether they are likely to be schizophrenic or, in one case, likely to develop schizophrenia.

Answers on page 358

Outline **one** positive and **one** negative symptom of schizophrenia. *(4 marks)*

Positive symptoms mean there is an excess or distortion of normal functions. 'Negative' symptoms appear to reflect a reduction or loss of normal functions, and weaken a person's ability to cope with everyday life.

One positive symptom is hallucinations, especially auditory hallucinations. They include hearing a voice telling the person how to behave or commenting on their behaviour. Schizophrenics can also have visual or olfactory hallucinations.

One negative symptom of schizophrenia is speech poverty. This is where the schizophrenic has trouble with producing words and speaking fluently, showing that people with schizophrenia have slow or blocked thoughts.

Level 4 (4 marks)

Examiner's comments: AO1 Detailed enough for full marks given the injunction.

Examiner's comments

This paragraph is not relevant.

Symptom identified and outlined.

Symptom identified and outlined.

Discuss issues relating to reliability **and** validity in the diagnosis **and/or** classification of schizophrenia. *(16 marks)*

Reliability in diagnosis means the consistency of a diagnosis across repeated measurements. Test-retest reliability is if the same psychiatrist makes the same diagnosis at several points in time. Inter-rater reliability means if different psychiatrists make the same diagnosis at the same time. Validity is whether a schizophrenia diagnosis actually reflects schizophrenia, so this could be seeing if the DSM-V measures what it says it measures. A diagnosis cannot be valid if it is not reliable.

Culture influences diagnosis, and there is significant variation between cultures in the diagnosis of schizophrenia. Copeland found that British and American psychiatrists differ a lot when asked to diagnose a patient. Also, there are racial and gender differences in the diagnosis of schizophrenia. American psychiatrists are more likely to mean healthy male behaviour when they say healthy adult behaviour which means women are seen as less mentally healthy.

Inter-rater reliability is a big problem when diagnosing schizophrenia. Perfect agreement between clinicians gets a kappa score of 1, while 0 means complete disagreement. Whaley and Regier reported kappa scores of 0.11 and 0.46 when diagnoses of schizophrenia were made. A kappa score of 0.7 or greater is considered 'good', so this suggests that schizophrenia is not reliably diagnosed by clinicians.

One problem is that a diagnosis of schizophrenia doesn't tell us much about how likely someone is to improve. Research suggests that about 10% of schizophrenics show a lasting and significant improvement from the disorder, but 30% show some improvement, but they sometimes relapse. This shows that a diagnosis of schizophrenia itself isn't a valid way to predict how likely someone is to recover from it.

Examiner's comments

AO1 paragraph with a reasonably detailed and accurate explanation of reliability and validity.

Another AO1 paragraph, this time focusing on reliability of diagnosis across cultures. Note that this could easily be made into AO3 if necessary.

The inclusion of 'suggests' at the end of the paragraph indicates that it can be credited as AO3.

This is a little muddled and can receive only limited AO3 credit.

Brekke and Barrio found that non-white minority group members, such as Afro-American and Latinos, showed fewer symptoms than the majority group of white Americans. This can be explained by the ethnic culture hypothesis that says ethnic minority groups have better social structures and protective characteristics. This supports the idea that mental disorders lead to lower levels of distress being experienced by those from ethnic minorities, and that they have a better prognosis.

> This is a potentially relevant AO3 point, but it is muddled and in desperate need of clarification.

There is a gender bias when it comes to diagnosing schizophrenia. Loring and Powell found that if a case was described as 'female' then it was less likely to be diagnosed as schizophrenic than if the same case was described as 'male'. This bias was more obvious in male psychiatrists than female psychiatrists suggesting that diagnosis can be influenced by the gender of the patient and the psychiatrist.

> A reasonably effective AO3 point, but it should be more detailed.

Level 2 (5–8 marks)

Examiner's comments: AO1 Some relevant knowledge has been presented but the description of the issues is basic.

AO3 In places, the evaluation is unclear and therefore only effective some of the time. Only a restricted range of evidence has been used, and the answer lacks organisation.

Outline **one** biological explanation for schizophrenia *(4 marks)*

Examiner's comments

The original dopamine hypothesis claimed that the positive symptoms of schizophrenia are caused by an excess of dopamine. Dopamine transmitting neurons fire too easily or too often. Schizophrenics are believed to have an excess of D2 receptors on receiving neurons, resulting in more dopamine binding and more neurons firing. David and Kahn created the revised dopamine hypothesis which says that the positive symptoms of schizophrenia are due to an excess of dopamine in the mesolimbic pathway. The negative and cognitive symptoms are believed to be due to a deficit of dopamine in the mesocortical pathway.

> There are only 4 marks on offer, so only a limited amount of information is needed for full marks.

Level 4 (4 marks)

Examiner's comments: AO1 This answer has chosen the dopamine hypothesis as the biological explanation of schizophrenia, and has explained it accurately and in detail.

Discuss **one or more** psychological explanations for schizophrenia (e.g. family dysfunction, cognitive explanations). *(16 marks)*

Examiner's comments

Bateson et al.'s double bind theory says that by communicating with their children in contradictory ways, parents predispose them to schizophrenia. For example, a mother might tell her son she loves him, but turn away when he wants a hug. As these behaviours contradict each other, the child doesn't develop a coherent construction of reality, and schizophrenia develops.

> A detailed AO1 paragraph explaining the double bind theory of schizophrenia.

Another family communication style is expressed emotion. This is where family members talk about a schizophrenic in a critical or hostile way, known as high expressed emotion. Low expressed emotion is where there is non-hostile communication. High expressed emotion families are also overly involved or concerned with the individual and their behaviour. High expressed emotion levels are associated with high relapse rates, which might be because schizophrenics have a lower tolerance for environmental stimuli, which means they end up feeling more stress than they can cope with.

> A reasonably clear explanation of expressed emotion, gaining AO1 credit.

Alternatively, schizophrenia may be caused by dysfunctional thought processes, as schizophrenics process information differently to non-schizophrenics. Delusions happen because someone relates irrelevant information to themselves, leading to false conclusions. Similarly, hallucinations happen because the voice is experienced as coming from an external source and the person doesn't check its real source like most people do.

> This AO1 paragraph accurately describes how dysfunctional thought processes can be used to explain hallucinations and delusions.

Double bind theory research findings are mixed. Berger found evidence of more double bind statements in families of schizophrenics than non-schizophrenics. However, Liem reported no differences in communication patterns, suggesting that double bind theory is not a useful way of explaining the causes of schizophrenia.

> A concise, but effective AO3 paragraph

Altorfer et al. found that a quarter of schizophrenics showed no physiological responses to stressful comments from relatives. So whether expressed emotion behaviour is stressful or not, seems to depend on how it is perceived. Not all schizophrenics are equally vulnerable to high levels of expressed emotion, suggesting that this is not a good explanation of schizophrenia.

> Using phrases like 'suggesting that' is an excellent way to link an AO3 point back to the question being asked, although the evaluation point itself could be more detailed.

The cognitive dysfunction explanation can explain both the positive and the negative symptoms of schizophrenia. The positive symptoms can be explained by biases in information processing, like a lack of reality testing, while the negative symptoms can be explained by dysfunctional thought processes like having low expectations of pleasure. This means that cognitive dysfunction offers a comprehensive explanation of schizophrenia.

> Another appropriate AO3 paragraph, which makes a point, elaborates it, and links back at the end.

A strength of cognitive explanations for schizophrenia is that CBT for psychosis (CBTp), which is based on this explanation, is effective. NICE found that CBTp was more effective than drugs in improving social functioning. CBTp focuses on changing people's thinking about where delusions and hallucinations come from, supporting the view that faulty cognitions cause schizophrenia.

> Arguing that the explanation has led to effective therapies, lends support to the explanation itself, and is creditable as AO3.

Family relationships may interact with genetic factors in the development of schizophrenia. Tienari et al. found that the biological children of schizophrenics were still more likely to develop the disorder even if they are adopted. However, this was only true if the adoptive family itself was rated as 'disturbed'. This suggests that genetic vulnerability alone is not enough for schizophrenia to develop and families also play a role.

> Offering an alternative explanation, such as an interactionist approach, can be an excellent way of gaining AO3 marks.

Level 4 (13–16 marks)

Examiner's comments: AO1 A 'breadth' approach has been taken here, and three explanations are presented in a detailed and accurate way.

AO3 Evaluation is effective, if not always thorough, throughout the answer. There is just enough here for this to be awarded a Level 4 mark.

Evaluate the use of typical **and/or** atypical antipsychotics as treatments for schizophrenia.
(8 marks)

Examiner's comments

One strength of antipsychotics is that they have been shown to be effective in treating schizophrenia. Leucht et al.'s meta-analysis of 65 studies compared relapse rates for antipsychotics and placebos. They found that when patients' antipsychotic medication was replaced by a placebo 64% of them relapsed. But only 27% of patients who stayed on their medication relapsed, showing that antipsychotics reduce the chance of schizophrenics relapsing.

> A strong opening AO3 paragraph that makes good use of research.

But one weakness of typical antipsychotics is that they have side effects. More than half of schizophrenics experience movement problems resembling Parkinson's disease. Using typical antipsychotics for a long time also leads to tardive dyskinesia, which is a permanent movement disorder affecting the tongue, face, and jaw. These side effects can stop schizophrenics taking their medication and this means that their chances of improving are lower.

> This identifies the critical point, gives evidence to support it and draws a conclusion from it. An effective piece of AO3.

Atypical antipsychotics have advantages over typical antipsychotics because they have fewer side effects, especially those involving movement. This means that patients are more likely to continue taking their medication, so improvement is more likely with atypical than typical antipsychotics.

> Some effective evaluation here, which contrasts the typical and atypical antipsychotics.

Although atypical antipsychotics have fewer side effects than typical antipsychotics they do not seem to be more effective in reducing symptoms. Crossley et al.'s meta-analysis compared the efficacy and side-effects of typical and atypical drugs. Although atypical antipsychotics had fewer side effects, they were no more or less effective than typical antipsychotics. This suggests that the only reason atypical antipsychotics are better is because they have fewer side effects.

> This paragraph uses a research study to offer commentary on the effectiveness of drug therapy and so receives AO3 credit.

Because typical antipsychotics have so many serious side effects, there is an ethical issue with giving these drugs to schizophrenics. When you take these side effects into account and balance them with the benefits of the treatment, the cost-benefit analysis would be negative. This means that researchers need to discover effective and ethically sound treatment methods which produce a positive cost-benefit analysis.

> Evaluating the ethical issues surrounding therapy can be an effective way to gain AO3 marks, as can be seen here.

Level 4 (7–8 marks)

Examiner's comments: AO3 This is an effective answer which shows planning and organisation. A range of specialist terms has been used effectively and a range of evaluation points have been addressed. Each point is made thoroughly and effectively, making this a top level answer.

Discuss the use of cognitive behavioural therapy in the treatment of schizophrenia. *(16 marks)*

Examiner's comments

Cognitive behavioural therapy for psychosis (CBTp) aims to identify and correct feelings and behaviours that are negatively influenced by distorted beliefs. The idea is that by monitoring their thoughts and behaviours, schizophrenics are more able to find alternative explanations for why their symptoms occur. CBTp has various phases and these start with assessment, where the person's current symptoms are discussed with the therapist and some realistic goals are set.

> This is an effective AO1 paragraph, describing the rationale behind CBTp.

Then the therapist empathises with the person's distress and highlights how they will work with the schizophrenic. The faulty beliefs are challenged by rationalising and disputing them. Normalisation is when the person's own psychotic experiences are placed on a continuum with normal experiences. The idea is that if someone is told that their experiences are common, then they feel less alienated.

> Further AO1, which shows sound knowledge and understanding of how CBTp is used.

Gentle questioning is also used to help them to understand their false beliefs and the person is encouraged and helped by the therapist to find healthier explanations for their behaviour.

> This AO1 paragraph seems incomplete. An example would be useful here.

It is hard to work out how effective CBTp is. NICE's review of the research suggests that CBTp is more effective in reducing symptom severity than drugs alone, but CBTp is usually used as well as drug therapy, so it is hard to see how effective CBTp is independent of antipsychotic medication.

> Although creditable as AO3, this point needs clarification for its importance to be appreciated.

Studies of CBTp's effectiveness can't allocate participants to treatment conditions randomly. But the meta-analytic studies of CBTp's effectiveness that use these studies don't take into account the quality of each study. This means that claims about CBTp's effectiveness may be biased by methodologically weak research studies.

> The same comment applies here. This AO3 point would benefit from clarification.

Also, when methodologically sound meta-analyses of CBTp's effectiveness have been done, they show it has very little therapeutic benefit. Jauhar et al. found that CBTp only has a very small effect on the positive symptoms, like hallucinations and delusions. They also found that when assessment of improvement is done by 'blind' judges, this small effect disappears, suggesting that CBTp's usefulness may be overstated.

> This is an effective AO3 paragraph, which strengthens the point made in the previous paragraph.

Addington and Addington say that CBTp is inappropriate in the initial acute phase of schizophrenia, but it is more appropriately used following stabilisation of symptoms with antipsychotic medication. This means that CBTp should be used in conjunction with drug therapy rather than as a 'first choice' therapy.

> A short, but effective AO3 paragraph discussing the appropriateness of CBTp.

CBTp isn't an established therapy for treating schizophrenia, and in the UK CBTp is only available to 10% of people who could benefit from it. Even when it is available, many who are offered CBTp either refuse it or fail to attend therapeutic sessions. This means that if CBTp is beneficial, more needs to be done to raise its availability and uptake.

> This final paragraph is also creditable as AO3.

Level 3 (9–12 marks)

Examiner's comments: AO1 Although this answer is characterised by accurate description, there are occasions on which more detail is necessary.

AO3 There is plenty of evaluation in this answer, and some of it is extremely effective. However, it is only effective some of the time. This is a clear Level 3 answer, which approaches, but does not quite reach, Level 4.

Discuss the use of family therapy as a treatment for schizophrenia. *(16 marks)*

Examiner's comments

Family therapy is offered for up to a year over at least ten sessions, and is used in conjunction with antipsychotics. It aims to reduce levels of expressed emotion and stress. If expressed emotion levels are reduced and if family members are more able to anticipate and solve problems, then relapse rates should, hopefully, be lower.

> A reasonably clear introductory paragraph, which receives AO1 credit.

Family therapy provides knowledge about schizophrenia and how to deal with it to the family members and this helps them to support the schizophrenic. It also helps to reduce emotions like anger and guilt within the family and tries to manage their expectations about the schizophrenic's behaviour. Family members are encouraged to set appropriate limits but also keeping some degree of separation.

> This AO1 paragraph amplifies the first paragraph, and is accurate and detailed.

If possible, the schizophrenic is involved in these sessions because talking to their family about their needs and what they feel makes things better or worse is important. Family therapy improves relationships within the family too because they are encouraged to listen to each other, discuss problems and negotiate.

> Also creditable as AO1.

One strength of family therapy is that is has economic benefits. NCCMH found there were significant cost savings when family therapy was combined with antipsychotic medication. Family therapy is initially expensive, but because it reduces rehospitalisation, it works out cheaper in the long run. Also, reduced relapse rates following therapy mean that the economic benefits of family therapy may be even higher.

> Making the link between psychology and the economy is valid as AO3. The point has been made coherently.

The main benefit of family therapy may simply be that it means schizophrenics actually take their medication. Pharaoh et al. found that family therapy had some effect on things like social functioning and relapse rates, but it also had an effect on how likely schizophrenics were to take their medication. This suggests that the reason schizophrenics show an improvement is because of antipsychotic medication rather than family therapy.

> This is an effective AO3 point, suggesting an interesting explanation for family therapy's effectiveness.

Studies which look at family therapy's effectiveness have methodological issues, because many of them don't allocate participants to conditions randomly. Also, a lot of studies didn't use observers 'blind' to what treatments patients were receiving. These methodological problems mean that it is difficult to tell how effective family therapy is.

> This is a reasonable AO3 point, but would benefit from more detail, so that the point about 'blind' assessment is made more powerfully.

It may be that having carers who are low in expressed emotion may be just as effective as family therapy. Garety et al. found that family therapy and having a carer without family therapy were both associated with lower relapse rates compared with a 'no carer' condition. Most of the carers showed relatively low rates of expressed emotion, meaning that family therapy might not be any more effective than a good standard of care.

> This is an important AO3 point, as it suggests that family therapy's benefits may be the result of lower expressed emotion.

Level 4 (13–16 marks)

Examiner's comments: AO1 Knowledge of family therapy is accurate and generally well-detailed. There is a good choice of relevant material, although slightly more detail would help.

AO3 Evaluation is effective, and a broad range of evaluative evidence has been offered in reasonable depth. The answer has been planned and organised effectively. Overall, a response that satisfies the Level 4 descriptors.

Discuss the use of token economies in the management of schizophrenia. *(16 marks)*

Examiner's comments

Token economy uses operant conditioning and uses positive reinforcement where a behaviour happens more often if it is followed by a desirable consequence. Token economies are a way of decreasing negative symptoms like social withdrawal and increasing positive behaviours.

> Although this is AO1 material, it isn't particularly clear, and would benefit from more examples.

To start with, a plastic token is repeatedly paired with something the schizophrenic values, such as a sweet. This pairing leads to the token acquiring the same properties as the sweet the schizophrenic values.

The clinician then sets target behaviours, such as getting dressed, and uses tokens whenever the target behaviour happens, so the target behaviour is learnt. At first, tokens are exchanged frequently for reinforcers so that target behaviours increase and are given immediately after the behaviour. If there is a delay, then the token might reinforce the wrong behaviour. Tokens can be exchanged for a variety of things, producing higher response rates.

> The second and third AO1 paragraphs offer a reasonably clear description of how token economy is used with schizophrenics.

Token economies seem to be effective in managing schizophrenic behaviour. When Dickerson et al. reviewed 13 studies that used token economy in therapeutic settings they found that 11 of them reported beneficial effects, suggesting that the adaptive behaviour of schizophrenics can be increased by token economy.

> This paragraph uses research evidence to make an AO3 point about the effectiveness of token economy.

One problem for token economy is that tokens may not be the reason that behaviour improves. It is possible that things like increased staff attention, rather than tokens, are actually causing behavioural improvements. To show that it is tokens, a token economy system has to be compared to a control group who aren't using a token economy system. But it's hard to do this because most token economies involve all schizophrenics in an institution, so improvement can only be compared with their past behaviour.

> This is a very interesting AO3 point, which explores the possibility that token economy may be effective for reasons other than those proposed by the learning approach.

Using token economies in a therapy setting raises some serious ethical issues. This is because therapists have control over important reinforcers, which include things like food. People have a basic human right to access food, and these rights should not be violated. Token economies may not, therefore, be an appropriate way of managing a schizophrenic's behaviour.

> The ethical issues surrounding any therapy is a good way of questioning a therapy's appropriateness, and earns AO3 credit.

Token economies may only be effective within an institutional setting. Schizophrenics in institutions receive 24-hour care, and are monitored and rewarded appropriately. Outpatient schizophrenics living in the community, on the other hand, are only seen for a few hours a day. Given the need for reinforcement to be given immediately after a target behaviour has been performed, TEs are unlikely to be effective for outpatient schizophrenics.

> Another important AO3 issue with psychological therapies concerns the extent to which their benefits transfer to the 'real world'.

Token economies have fallen out of use in much of the developed world precisely because of the absence of randomised trials. Developing countries may hold the key to how effective token economies are, since they are still used therapeutically. Randomised trials in those countries would enable the question of whether token economies actually work to be conclusively addressed.

> This final AO3 point could have been linked to the earlier commentary on meta-analysis and the reasons why token economy is effective.

Level 4 (13–16 marks)

Examiner's comments: AO1 Knowledge and understanding of token economy is generally accurate and well-detailed.

AO3 Evaluation is thorough and mostly effective. The answer is clear, coherent and focused, showing good evidence of planning and organisation. A Level 4 mark is appropriate here.

Discuss the diathesis-stress model as an explanation for schizophrenia. *(16 marks)*

Examiner's comments

The diathesis–stress model says that schizophrenia is the result of an interaction between biological and environmental influences. It explains why not all people with a genetic vulnerability to schizophrenia develop the disorder. This is because people differ in their biological vulnerability to schizophrenia. The model assumes that diathesis and stress add together in some way to cause schizophrenia.

> This an AO1 paragraph, but does not describe the model especially clearly.

People with a family history of schizophrenia have a high vulnerability, while those with no family history of the disorder have a low vulnerability. Also, the stress that people experience in their lives is different, and includes things like childhood trauma and living in densely populated areas.

> This is also AO1, but perhaps its impact would have been greater if it was integrated with the first paragraph.

Relatively minor stressors may lead to schizophrenia in people who are highly vulnerable and a major stressful life event may lead to schizophrenia in people with a low vulnerability.

> Again, the AO1 seems a little out of place, and these first three paragraphs would benefit from better organisation.

Tienari et al. found that women who were adopted as children and born to schizophrenic mothers were significantly less likely to develop schizophrenia if they were raised in a healthy adoptive family, which was considered to be low stress, than a less healthy adoptive family, considered to be high stress. In women who were adopted as children and born to non-schizophrenic mothers, the healthiness of the family environment did not affect the likelihood of schizophrenia developing. These 'low' biologically vulnerable women were also less likely to develop schizophrenia than the women with 'high' biological vulnerability.

> This attempt at AO3 illustrates the need to organise material. The whole paragraph highlights the importance of planning an answer.

Genetics are not the only biological vulnerability that increase the risk of schizophrenia. Verdoux et al. claim there is an increased risk of developing schizophrenia if you have a complicated birth. This means that vulnerability should not be defined in terms of genetic influences alone.

> A reasonably effective AO3 point, using the PEEL technique.

Knowledge of different biological vulnerabilities can possibly help to prevent schizophrenia. Borglum et al. looked at women who were infected with the cytomegalovirus during pregnancy. They found the women were more likely to have a child who developed schizophrenia, but only if both the mother and child had a particular gene deficit. This suggests that anti-viral medicine during pregnancy may prevent schizophrenia in the offspring of women known to have the gene defect.

> Another AO3 point that would receive some credit but needs to be made more clearly to be considered effective.

It is hard to determine which vulnerability is causing the disorder. Ineffective methods of coping with stress in early life can influence how we cope with stress later on, making it more likely that we might develop schizophrenia. Hammen believes that ineffective coping skills in childhood may make life generally more stressful for a person, and increases their vulnerability. This suggests that it may be a lack of resistance to stress that triggers schizophrenia rather than genetic vulnerability.

> Yet another potentially effective AO3 point. However, once again, the material has not been used as well as it should have been.

KEY TERMS

- Evolutionary explanations
- Food preference
- Neophobia
- Taste aversion

Possible essay question

Discuss the evolutionary explanation for food preferences. *(16 marks)*

Other possible exam questions …

+ Explain what is meant by the terms 'neophobia' and 'taste aversion'. *(2 marks + 2 marks)*
+ Briefly outline the role of neophobia in food preferences. *(3 marks)*
+ Briefly outline and evaluate the role of taste aversion in food preferences. *(8 marks)*

 Think

In order to understand the problems faced by our ancestors, we must consider the environment in which they lived. The **environment of evolutionary adaptation (EEA)** refers to the environment in which our species first evolved.

MUST know …

The evolution of food preference

Evolutionary explanations of food preference focus on the adaptive benefits that certain foods would have offered to our ancestors.

Preference for **fatty foods** would have been adaptive, because the conditions in the EEA meant that energy sources were vital to stay alive.

Furthermore, a preference for a **meat diet**, full of nutrients, would have provided the catalyst of growth for the brain, allowing humans to evolve into the intelligent creatures they became.

Finally, a preference for **sweetness** found in ripe fruit, would have provided vitamins and minerals that were necessary for bodily functions and growth, which were particularly valuable in the EEA.

 EVALUATION *One issue with the evolutionary explanation for food preferences is…*

…that not all food preferences are the product of evolution.

- **E** – **Kerb (2009)** points out the 'mismatch' between evolved preferences (e.g. fatty and sweet foods) and modern environments.

 EVALUATION *However, one strength of the evolutionary explanations for food preference comes from…*

…support for the preference of sweet foods.

- **E** – **Grill and Norgen (1978)** reported that newborn infants show an acceptance response the first time they taste something sweet, which is an innate response.

 EVALUATION *Another strength of the evolutionary explanation for food preferences comes from…*

…the application of taste aversion to chemotherapy.

- **E** – Evidence: Some cancer treatments, such as chemotherapy, can cause gastrointestinal illness. Unfortunately, when this illness is paired with food consumption, taste aversion can result.

SHOULD know …

Taste aversion and neophobia

Taste aversion is a learned response to eating toxic, spoiled or poisonous food. The development of taste aversion would have helped our ancestors to survive because, if they survived eating poisoned food, they would be unlikely to make the same mistake again.

Food neophobia is characterised by a reluctance to consume new or unusual foods and helps protect animals from the risk of being poisoned by consuming something that is potentially harmful. In humans, food neophobia is particularly strong in relation to animal products, rather than non-animal products. This is likely to have evolved because of the greater threat of illness posed by, for example, rotting meat.

- **E** – For example, a trait that is beneficial today (e.g. the consumption of low cholesterol food) would not have evolved because of its beneficial effects for our ancestors.
- **L** – This suggests that the evolutionary explanation of food preferences is limited and cannot explain modern day food preferences.

- **E** – Furthermore, **Bell et al. (1973)** reported that the Inupiat people from Northern Alaska had no experience of sweet foods, but accepted sweet food when it was later introduced from other cultures.
- **L** – These studies provide support for the evolutionary preference of sweet foods that would have been beneficial to our ancestors.

- **E** – Research has led to the 'scapegoat technique' where cancer patients have novel food along with familiar food, prior to the chemotherapy. Consequently, the patients form an aversion to the novel food and not the familiar food.
- **L** – This highlights the positive application of evolutionary theory to helping patients with cancer.

 FURTHER EVALUATION

 EVALUATION **One strength of the evolutionary explanation for food preferences comes from…**

…support for the heritability of food neophobia.

- **E** – **Knaapila et al. (2007)** measured food neophobia in 468 adult female twin pairs.
- **E** – The heritability estimate for food neophobia in this sample was 67%, suggesting that two thirds of the variation in food neophobia is genetically determined.
- **L** – This provides support for the view that neophobia evolved to protect humans from harmful foods.

EVALUATION **However, one issue with the evolutionary explanation for food preferences is…**

…that food neophobia is also maladaptive.

- **E** – Neophobia poses a problem for individuals who may restrict their diet to foods with poor nutritional quality.
- **E** – **Perry et al. (2015)** found that neophobia was associated with poor dietary quality among children.
- **L** – This suggests that food neophobia may no longer provide an advantage and may be a maladaptive response in modern society.

CHOOSE THE RIGHT ANSWER

Which **one** of the following statements is **false**? (Tick **one** box only.)

A Sweet foods provide vitamins and minerals that are necessary for bodily functions. ☐

B Sweet foods are associated with a high concentration of sugar/calories, necessary for energy levels. ☐

C Sweet foods are innately preferred in children. ☐

D Sweets foods are avoided by cultures that have no experience of sweet tasting food. ☐

Answers on page 359

An idea 👍

On a separate piece of paper, plan the following essay: **Discuss the evolutionary explanation for food preferences. (16 marks)**
This is a tricky essay, as there is a lot you could write about. What six points are you going to make to obtain your AO1 marks? Remember that for each point you need to explain how/why your point is an 'evolutionary advantage'. Furthermore, you will need five key evaluation points. How are you going to remember your five key evaluation points? Plan the essay, condensing all of the information onto just one side of A4.

 FILL IN THE BOXES

In each box below state one evolutionary food preference.	Then explain the adaptive advantage of each chosen food preference.
Food preference 1:	
Food preference 2:	
Food preference 3:	
Taste aversion is…	

Answers on page 359

 APPLYING YOUR KNOWLEDGE

Identify the psychology

Link to Abigail

Abigail recently went to France for a family holiday.

While at a restaurant, her family decided to try frogs' legs. She felt very strongly about the sight and smell of the frogs' legs, but after a lot of persuasion she decided to try one.

The next day, she was ill and decided that she would never eat frogs' legs again.

Using your knowledge of the evolutionary explanation for food preferences, outline two key explanations for Abigail's behaviour. *(4 marks)*

Answers on page 359

KEY TERMS

- Food preference
- Learning

Possible essay question …

Discuss the role of learning in food preference. *(16 marks)*

Other possible exam questions …

+ Briefly describe the role of social influences in food preference. *(4 marks)*

+ Explain the role of cultural influences in food preference. *(4 marks)*

+ Outline research findings relating to social and/or cultural influences in food preference. *(6 marks)*

 Exam tip

The specification mentions 'social influences' and 'cultural influences'. Questions might ask for either of these separately, or be phrased more generally, for example 'The role of learning in food preferences'. In this latter type of question, you could include either or both of these different types of influence.

MUST know …

Social influences

Learning explanations focus on cultural and environmental influences. According to these explanations, we learn what food is good to eat and what food should be avoided from significant others in our life.

Parental influences

One way in which children acquire their food preferences is by observing their parents. Parents also exercise control over the availability of food, either as a reward or because of the perceived health benefits.

Peers

Social learning theory emphasises the impact of observing other people; the behaviour of same-age peers has been found to have a powerful influence on food preferences.

 One limitation of the learning explanation for food preferences comes from…

…the limited research into the role of parental influences.

- ***E*** – Many of the studies in this area have been small-scale and typically use white American samples.

 Another issue with the learning explanation for preferences is…

…that not all parental influences are equally effective.

- ***E*** – **Russell *et al.* (2015)** interviewed parents of children aged 2–5 years old and found that not all methods they used influenced their children's food preference.

 However, one strength of the learning explanation for food preferences comes from…

…research supporting the role of media influences.

- ***E*** – **Boyland and Halford (2013)** found that exposure to food advertising on television influenced food preferences and actual food intake in children.

SHOULD know …

Cultural influences

Media effects

Social learning can also explain the role of television and other media on food preferences. While the media may have a major impact on what people eat and their attitudes towards certain food, eating behaviour may also be limited by personal circumstances, such as age and income.

The context of meals

In certain societies, like the US and UK, the desire for convenience foods is growing increasingly common. People learn to rely on takeaway meals as a way of feeding themselves. Research has also found that eating more 'informally' leads to a learned preference for quickly prepared snack-foods, rather than more elaborate meals.

- ***E*** – **Robinson *et al.* (2001)** examined 800 children from a range of different backgrounds and found a complex association between the behaviour of parents and food preferences.
- ***L*** – This suggests that the role of parents is more complex than originally thought and children do not simply learn by observing their parents.

- ***E*** – Parental modelling and food exposure were found to be effective, whereas forcing consumption or restricting food access were ineffective.
- ***L*** – Although this supports the idea that children do learn food preferences from their parents, some approaches were more effective than others.

- ***E*** – The relationship was further supported by the fact that children who had the greatest preference for high-carbohydrate and high-fat foods were the ones who watched the most television.
- ***L*** – This suggests that media influences play an important role in shaping food preferences, while highlighting the negative effects of advertising unhealthy foods.

FURTHER EVALUATION

 Another strength of the learning explanation for food preferences is…

…the real-world application to television advertising.

- ***E*** – **Cairns *et al.* (2013)** suggest that television is the dominant medium for children's exposure to food marketing, especially for unhealthy foods.
- ***E*** – This had led to many countries developing regulations concerning the advertising of unhealthy foods.
- ***L*** – This matters because it limits the negative impact of the media on food preferences and promotes healthy eating behaviours in children.

A final strength of the learning explanation for food preferences comes from…

…research examining cultural influences.

- ***E*** – **Chen and Yang (2014)** examined Twitter feeds in Columbus, Ohio.
- ***E*** – They found an association between healthy food choices and the number of local high-quality grocery stores.
- ***L*** – These results show that cultural influences do have an effect on learned food habits and that people can resist unhealthy habits, if there are healthy alternatives available locally.

CHOOSE THE RIGHT ANSWER

Which **two** of the following are cultural factors that affect food preferences? (Tick **two** boxes only.)

A Children acquire their eating behaviour by observing their parents.	☐
B Children acquire their eating behaviour from same age peers.	☐
C Children acquire their eating behaviour through social learning and the media.	☐
D Children acquire their eating behaviour due to an overreliance on takeaway meals.	☐

Answers on page 359

💡 DRAWING CONCLUSIONS

A psychologist conducted a study on the effect of advertising on food preferences. He recruited 20 primary school boys and girls and made half watch a series of fast-food adverts, while the other half were not exposed to any adverts. He then asked each of the participants what they wanted for their dinner that evening. The percentage of participants who wanted fast-food is shown in the graph below.

The effect of advertising on desire to eat unhealthy food

☐ Males
☐ Females

y-axis: 0, 10, 20, 30, 40, 50, 60, 70, 80, 90
x-axis: No advertising, Advertising

Advertising vs. No advertising

What does the bar graph show about the effects of advertising?

Answers on page 359

⚙ APPLYING YOUR KNOWLEDGE

Jamie Oliver was determined to change the eating habits of children.

Using your knowledge of social and cultural influences, outline two ways in which Jamie Oliver could influence the eating behaviour of children. *(4 marks)*

Identify the psychology	Link to Jamie

Answers on page 359

A MARKING EXERCISE

Read this student answer to the following exam question:

Outline the role of cultural influences in food preference. *(4 marks)*

A person's culture can influence their food preferences, as the culture of a person's parents may determine the food they eat. Likewise, the culture of a person's friends may also have an effect.

What mark do you think this would get?

YOUR MARK

AO1

Hint
A hint to help you decide:
How many critical points have been covered?
How much detail is there?

Write an improved answer here…

Answers on page 359

KEY TERMS

- Ghrelin
- Hypothalamus
- Leptin

Possible essay question ...

Discuss the neural and hormonal mechanisms involved in the control of eating behaviour. *(16 marks)*

Other possible exam questions ...

+ Outline the role of the hypothalamus, ghrelin and leptin in the control of eating behaviour. *(3 marks each)*
+ Briefly outline the neural mechanisms involved in the control of eating behaviour and give one criticism of their role. *(4 marks)*
+ Briefly outline the hormonal mechanisms involved in the control of eating behaviour. *(6 marks)*

⭐ Exam tip

The specification lists three specific mechanisms that you need to be aware of, including: hypothalamus (neural), ghrelin, and leptin (hormonal). You should be prepared to answer a question on any of these specific mechanisms, or a more general question on 'neural and hormonal mechanisms'.

MUST know ...

Homeostasis

Homeostasis is the mechanism by which an organism maintains a steady internal environment.

Glucose levels play an important role in producing feelings of hunger. Hunger increases as glucose levels decrease.

For example, a decline in glucose levels activates a part of the brain called the **lateral hypothalamus**, resulting in feelings of hunger. This causes the individual to search for and consume food, which raises the level of glucose. This rise in the level of glucose activates the **ventromedial hypothalamus**, which leads to feelings of satiation, which in turn stops us from eating.

 One limitation of the homeostatic explanation of eating behaviour is...

...that the explanation is incompatible with evolutionary theory.

- **E** – If the homeostatic hunger mechanism was truly adaptive, it should anticipate and prevent energy deficits, not just react to them.

 One limitation with the role of the lateral hypothalamus (LH) is...

...that this brain region controls more than just eating.

- **E** – Damage to the LH causes deficits in other aspects of behaviour (e.g. thirst and sex), and not just hunger.

 However, support for the role of the ventromedial hypothalamus (VMH) comes from...

...early brain damage research.

- **E** – Lesions or damage to the VMH can result in hyperphagia and obesity in a number of different species, including humans.

SHOULD know ...

Hormonal mechanisms in the control of eating

There are two main hormones involved in the control of eating: **ghrelin** and **leptin**.

Ghrelin

Ghrelin is realised in the stomach and stimulates the **hypothalamus** to increase appetite. Ghrelin levels determine how quickly we feel hungry, as they go up drastically before we eat and then down for about three hours after a meal.

Leptin

Leptin (from the Greek *leptos*, meaning 'thin') is a hormone that plays a crucial role in appetite and weight control. It is normally produced by fat tissue and secreted into the bloodstream, where it travels to the brain to decrease appetite.

- **E** – The theory that hunger and eating are triggered only when energy resources fall below their desired level is incompatible with the harsh reality in which the system would have evolved.
- **L** – This matters because the homeostatic explanation provides a limited explanation of eating behaviour and fails to take into account evolution.

- **E** – Furthermore, recent research has found that eating behaviour is controlled by neural circuits in the brain, not just the hypothalamus.
- **L** – While the LH may be linked to the control of eating behaviour, it is not the brain's 'eating centre', as originally thought.

- **E** – Furthermore, studies have shown that compared to lesions in other brain areas, animals with VMH lesions ate substantially more and gained more weight.
- **L** – This supports the role played by the VMH in the control of eating.

FURTHER EVALUATION

 Support for the role of ghrelin in appetite control comes from...

...research by **Wren *et al*. (2001).**

- **E** – Wren gave participants an intravenous ghrelin or a saline infusion and measured their appetite in terms of the amount of food consumed at a free-choice buffet.
- **E** – The results revealed that the ghrelin condition consumed on average 28% more than the saline condition.
- **L** – This supports the role of ghrelin in appetite control, as ghrelin acts as an important signal which stimulates food intake.

 One consideration for the role of leptin comes from...

...cases where people develop leptin resistance.

- **E** – Some people develop resistance to leptin and so it fails to control their appetite and weight gain.
- **E** – Leptin resistance is often found in overweight and obese people, making it harder for them to lose weight.
- **L** – This provides an important insight into the role of leptin and the possible application of this research to helping people with weight problems/obesity.

COMPLETE THE DIAGRAM

Using the key terms below, complete the flow chart to outline the neural mechanisms involved in the control of eating.

- Satiety
- Ventromedial hypothalamus is turned on
- Lateral hypothalamus is turned on
- Hunger
- Decrease in blood glucose

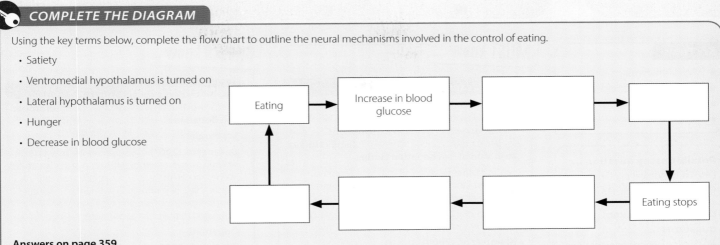

Answers on page 359

CHOOSE THE RIGHT ANSWER

Which **one** of the following statements is **false**? (Tick **one** box only.)

A Ghrelin is released in the stomach and stimulates the hypothalamus to decrease appetite. ☐

B Leptin is produced by fat tissue and secreted into the bloodstream, where it travels to the brain to decrease appetite. ☐

C The ventromedial hypothalamus is activated by a rise in glucose levels and leads to feelings of satiation. ☐

D The lateral hypothalamus is activated by a decrease in glucose levels and leads to feelings of hunger. ☐

Answers on page 359

MATCH THEM UP

Match up the key terms on the left, with the definitions on the right.

1	Ghrelin…	**A**	…is produced by fat tissue and secreted into the bloodstream, where it travels to the brain to decreases appetite.
2	Leptin…	**B**	…is released in the stomach and stimulates the hypothalamus to increase appetite.
3	Ventromedial hypothalamus…	**C**	…is activated by a decrease in glucose levels and leads to feelings of hunger.
4	Lateral hypothalamus…	**D**	…is activated by a rise in glucose levels and leads to feelings of satiation.

Answers on page 359

A MARKING EXERCISE

Read this student answer to the following exam question:

Briefly outline the hormonal mechanisms involved in the control of eating behaviour. *(6 marks)*

Ghrelin and leptin are the two main hormones involved in eating. Ghrelin increases appetite before we eat, whereas leptin controls weight.

What mark do you think this would get?

YOUR MARK

AO1

Hint
A hint to help you decide:
How many critical points have been covered?
How much detail is there?

Write an improved answer here…

Answers on page 359

KEY TERMS

- Anorexia nervosa
- Biological explanations
- Genetic explanations
- Neural explanations

Possible essay question …

Discuss biological explanations for anorexia nervosa. *(16 marks)*

Other possible exam questions …

+ Outline genetic explanations for anorexia nervosa. *(4 marks)*

+ Outline neural explanations for anorexia nervosa. *(4 marks)*

+ Briefly outline **one or more** biological explanations of anorexia nervosa and give **one** limitation of these explanations. *(6 marks)*

★ Exam tip

The specification details both genetic and neural explanations for anorexia and therefore you should be prepared to answer a specific question on either of these two explanations, as well as a more general question on 'biological explanations'.

MUST know …

Genetic explanations

Recent research has highlighted the importance of biological factors in anorexia nervosa (AN), which include **genetic** and **neural explanations**. Support for genetic explanations comes from **family studies**, **twin studies** and **adoption studies**.

Family studies have found that first-degree relatives of individuals with AN are ten-times more at risk of developing AN.

Wade *et al.* (2000) found a heritability rate of 58% for AN, when examining female MZ twins.

Klump *et al.* (2009) assessed other eating disorders and found heritability estimates ranged from 59–82%, with non-shared environmental factors accounting for the remaining difference.

 One issue with the genetic explanation of AN is…

…the inconsistent estimates of heritability in twin studies.

- ***E*** – **Fairburn *et al.* (1999)** point out that twin studies examining AN have given widely contrasting heritability ranges. Furthermore, many studies also violate the 'equal environments assumption'.

 One strength of the biological approach to AN is…

…the real-world application to providing treatments.

- ***E*** – In many US states, the treatment of AN is restricted under insurance plans, because AN is not considered a biological disorder.

 One issue with the serotonin explanation of AN is…

…that drug treatments involving serotonin are ineffective.

- ***E*** – Drugs which alter levels of serotonin, for example selective serotonin reuptake inhibitors (SSRIs), are ineffective when used with some AN patients.

SHOULD know …

Neural explanations

Neural explanations consider the role of **serotonin** and **dopamine**.

Serotonin

Bailer *et al.* (2007) measured serotonin activity in women recovering from different types of anorexia, in comparison to healthy controls. They found higher levels of serotonin in women recovering from binge-eating/purging type anorexia, compared to the other two groups.

Dopamine

Kaye *et al.* (2005) used PET scans to examine dopamine activity in patients recovering from AN. They found overactivity of the dopamine receptors in the basal ganglia, which play an important role in the interpretation of harm and pleasure.

- ***E*** – Many of the studies assume that MZ and DZ twins experience similar environments. However, research suggests that MZ twins are treated more similarly compared to DZ twins.
- ***L*** – This suggests that the heritability estimates of AN are not a valid representation of the genetic influences of AN.

- ***E*** – However, biological research (including genetic and neural research) has created a case for insurance companies to consider AN as a biological disorder and provide treatment.
- ***L*** – This highlights the positive application of biological research to providing treatment for patients with AN in the US.

- ***E*** – **Ferguson *et al.* (1999)** found no difference in the symptom outcomes for patients with AN for those taking SSRIs and those who were not.
- ***L*** – This suggests that the serotonin explanation of AN does not provide a valid account of AN.

FURTHER EVALUATION

 One strength of the dopamine explanation of AN comes from…

…research examining 'eye-blink'.
- ***E*** – Increased eye-blink is indicative of higher levels of dopamine activity in the brain.
- ***E*** – **Barbato *et al.* (2006)** found a significant correlation between blink rate and the duration of AN.
- ***L*** – This suggests that there is a relationship between dopamine and AN and that AN symptoms develop over time.

 A final strength of the biological explanation of AN is…

…that it reduces the stigma associated with AN.
- ***E*** – Explanations based on the biological approach challenge the belief that AN is somehow the patient's fault.
- ***E*** – Furthermore, they also offer the possibility of treating AN by regulating the brain areas involved in the behaviours associated with the disorder.
- ***L*** – This matters because the biological approach has helped improve the lives of many individuals suffering from AN.

✔ CHOOSE THE RIGHT ANSWER

Which **one** of the following statements is **false**?

A Anorexia nervosa (AN) is five-times higher in first-degree relatives. ☐

B The heritability of AN is approximately 58% in MZ twins. ☐

C Increased levels of serotonin are associated with AN. ☐

D Increased dopamine activity is associated with AN. ☐

Answers on page 359

🎯 WRITE YOUR OWN EVALUATION POINT

Ferguson *et al.* (1999) pose a problem for the serotonin explanation of AN; however, there are numerous advantages with the biological explanation. Write an evaluation paragraph, where you explain the issue outlined by Ferguson, but bring in a counter-argument within your evaluation point.

Point	One issue with the serotonin explanation of AN is that drug treatments involving serotonin are ineffective.
Evidence	[Insert results from Ferguson et al. (1999)]
Explain	This shows…
Evaluate	However, there are numerous advantages with the biological explanation…
Link	Therefore…

Answers on page 359

✔ A MARKING EXERCISE

Read this student answer to the following exam question:
Outline neural explanations for anorexia nervosa. *(4 marks)*

There are two neural explanations for AN, including serotonin and dopamine. In both cases an increased activity in serotonin or dopamine can lead to AN.

What mark do you think this would get?

YOUR MARK

AO1

Hint
A hint to help you decide:
How many critical points have been covered?
How much detail is there?

Write an improved answer here…

Answers on page 359

🧩 MATCH THEM UP

Match up the key study, with the biological factor and with the findings.

1 Wade *et al.* (2000)	**A** Adoption study	**i** They assessed other eating disorders and found heritability estimates ranged from 59–82%, with non-shared environmental factors accounting for the remaining difference.
2 Klump *et al.* (2009)	**B** Serotonin	**ii** They found a heritability rate for AN of 58% when examining female MZ _____.
3 Bailer *et al.* (2007)	**C** Twin study	**iii** They used PET scans to examine _____ activity in patients recovering from AN. They found overactivity of the _____ receptors in the basal ganglia, which play an important role in the interpretation of harm and pleasure.
4 Kaye *et al.* (2005)	**D** Dopamine	**iv** They found higher levels of _____ in women recovering from binge-eating/purging type anorexia, compared to the other two groups.

Answers on page 359

177

KEY TERMS

- Autonomy
- Control
- Enmeshment
- Family system theory

Possible essay question

Outline and evaluate family systems theory as an explanation for anorexia nervosa. *(16 marks)*

Other possible exam questions …

+ Explain what is meant by 'enmeshment', 'autonomy' and 'control' in the context of family systems theory. *(2 marks each)*

+ Briefly outline family systems theory as an explanation for anorexia nervosa and give one criticism of this explanation. *(6 marks)*

 Exam tip

You may, on occasion, be asked to 'describe research' into family systems theory. The studies in Topic 5 have been used to provide you with AO3 evaluation. However, if you simply describe the findings without any critical commentary, they could be used as AO1 research.

MUST know …

Family systems theory

Family systems theory suggests that individuals cannot be understood in isolation, but rather as part of their family, as the family is an emotional unit.

Minuchin *et al.* (1978) put forward the psychosomatic family model, which states that the prerequisite for the development of anorexia nervosa (AN) is a dysfunctional family occurring alongside a physiological vulnerability. There are three characteristics of a psychosomatic family, including **enmeshment, autonomy** and **control**.

Enmeshment family members are overly-involved with each other and lack boundaries. Enmeshment stifles the development of children to deal adequately with social stressors and makes the development of AN more likely.

 One strength of the family systems theory comes from…

…research support for the idea of enmeshment.

- *E* – **Manzi *et al.* (2006)** found that enmeshment was rooted in manipulation and control, whereas family cohesion was indicative of supportive family interactions.

 However, one limitation of the family systems theory is…

…the lack of research support for the psychosomatic family model.

- *E* – **Kog and Vandereycken (1989)** failed to find the characteristics predicted by the psychosomatic family model in families of individuals with AN.

 One strength of the family systems theory is…

…the development of successful treatments for AN.

- *E* – Family-focused therapies have shown that families are a key part in the recovering process for individuals with AN.

SHOULD know …

Enmeshment, autonomy and control

Enmeshed families are not allowed to become independent and develop **autonomy**.

Furthermore, psychosomatic families are characterised by overprotective **control**. Overprotectiveness can delay an individual's beliefs regarding the extent to which they are in control of their own lives. Consequently, an individual may rebel against this control by refusing to eat.

There are two other characteristics of a psychosomatic family, which include **rigidity** and a **lack of conflict resolution**. Rigid families show a lack of flexibility in their adaption to new situations and a low tolerance for conflict and difficulty in acknowledging and resolving problems.

- *E* – Furthermore, Mazi found that cohesion was linked to positive outcomes, whereas enmeshment had the opposite effect.
- *L* – These findings support Minuchin's ideas that enmeshed families show a lack of autonomy and high degree of control that could contribute to AN.

- *E* – Furthermore, there is growing evidence that families in which someone has an eating disorder are a diverse group in terms of the nature of family relationships and the emotional climate.
- *L* – This suggests that the psychosomatic family model is not an accurate predictor of AN.

- *E* – **Carr (2009)** concluded that there is compelling evidence for the effectiveness of family interventions for adolescents with AN.
- *L* – This highlights the positive application of family systems theory for the development of successful, family-based treatments for individuals with AN.

FURTHER EVALUATION

 Another issue with the family systems theory is…

…that the focus is mainly on mother–daughter relationships.

- *E* – **Gremillion (2003)** argues that although any family member can contribute to enmeshment, it is usually seen as maternal in origin.
- *E* – As a result, therapy to reduce enmeshment usually focuses on reforming the mothers.
- *L* – This matters because the theory and subsequent treatment shows a clear gender bias and ignores the contribution of fathers to an enmeshed family.

 A final strength of the family systems theory comes from…

…research support for the idea of conflict resolution.

- *E* – **Latzer and Gaber (1998)** examined conflict resolution in 40 families of daughters with AN and 40 matched families.
- *E* – They found that families with daughters with AN had more difficulty discussing topics of disagreement, without returning to or mentioning food.
- *L* – This supports Minuchin's claim that avoidance of conflict is a property of families where one member has AN.

✓ CHOOSE THE RIGHT ANSWER

Which **one** of the following is **not** a characteristic of a psychosomatic family? (Tick **one** box only.)

A	A family which is overly-involved and lacks boundaries.	☐
B	A family which shows a low degree of tolerance for conflict.	☐
C	A family which exercises large influence over its members.	☐
D	A family which is able to adapt to new situations.	☐
E	A family which does not allow it members to determine their own actions.	☐

Answers on page 360

MATCH THEM UP

Match the key characteristics of the 'psychosomatic family' on the left, with the definitions on the right.

1 Autonomy		**A**	A family characterised by parents who are over-emotionally involved with their children and dismissive of their emotional needs.
2 Control		**B**	A family which shows a low tolerance for conflict and difficultly resolving problems.
3 Enmeshment		**C**	When someone directs or exercises influence over our events and behaviour.
4 Rigidity		**D**	A family which shows a lack of flexibility in their adaptation to new situations.
5 Lack of conflict resolution		**D**	The freedom to make decisions and determine actions without constraint.

Answers on page 360

📖 RESEARCH ISSUES

A psychologist investigated the relationship between enmeshment, autonomy and control with anorexia nervosa.

The psychologist decided to conduct interviews with patients experiencing AN and their immediate family members in their own homes.

Identify two ethical issues the researcher would need to consider in this research.

Suggest how the researcher could deal with these ethical issues.
(4 marks)

Answers on page 360

⚙ APPLYING YOUR KNOWLEDGE

Demelza has anorexia. Her family are extremely close and her mother insists on knowing everything about her children and has even been known to read their diaries. Whenever Demelza has a problem at school, her Mum will often turn up at the school to complain, without consulting Demelza first.

Furthermore, her father is very protective towards her and her sisters. He insists on dropping them off and picking them up whenever they go out with their friends and will often call multiple times to check that they're okay.

Identify the psychology		Link to Demelza
	Using your knowledge of family systems theory, explain two factors that might have contributed to Demelza's AN. *(4 marks)*	

Answers on page 360

KEY TERMS

- Media
- Modelling
- Reinforcement
- Social learning

Possible essay question

Outline and evaluate the social learning theory explanation of anorexia nervosa. *(16 marks)*

Other possible exam questions …

+ Briefly explain the role of modelling, reinforcement and media in the context of anorexia nervosa. *(3 marks each)*

+ Give two criticisms of the social learning theory explanation of anorexia nervosa. *(3 + 3 marks)*

Link

The key ideas found in Topic 6 are all aspects of social learning theory, first examined in Year 1. While revising it would be useful to first review social learning theory. See Year 1/AS Revision and Exam Companion, Topic X, Approaches in psychology, on page xxx.

MUST know …

Social learning theory, modelling and reinforcement

According to **Bandura (1977)** people learn by observing the behaviour of others and from the outcome of their behaviour.

Children pay particular attention to **role models** in their life and observe their attitudes and behaviours. Models can be parents or peers, or 'symbolic' models, such as someone portrayed in the media. These models provide examples of attitudes to food, or dieting behaviour that can be observed by the individual and imitated.

If an individual imitates a behaviour and receives **positive reinforcement** (e.g. comments like 'Wow, you've lost weight!'), they are more likely to continue imitating this behaviour in the future.

 One issue with the social learning explanation of anorexia nervosa (AN) is…

…that research findings do not always produce consistent results.

- **E** – **Pike and Rodin (1991)** found that there was no evidence for daughters imitating the weight concern of their parents.

 One strength of the social learning explanation of AN comes from…

…research support for peer influences.

- **E** – **Costa-Font and Jofre-Bonet (2013)** investigate the effect of peer weight on the likelihood of an individual developing AN.

 However, one issue with the social learning explanation of AN comes from…

…research examining peer influence and teasing.

- **E** – While Jones and Crawford (see above) found that overweight girls and underweight boys were more likely to be teased, other research has found different results.

SHOULD know …

Peer and media influences

Peer influences

Peer reinforcement is particularly important during adolescence and a specific mechanism of peer influence is teasing. **Jones and Crawford (2006)** found that overweight girls and underweight boys were most likely to be teased by their peers, suggesting that through teasing, peers serve to enforce gender-based ideals.

Media influences

The media is a major source of influence for body image in Western adolescents. The portrayal of thin models on television and in magazines is a significant factor contributing to body image concerns, which drive a desire for thinness in Western adolescent girls.

- **E** – Furthermore, **Ogden and Steward (2000)** found that although mothers and daughters were similar in their weight and BMI, there was no association for their restrained eating.
- **L** – These findings do not support the modelling hypothesis and social learning explanation of AN.

- **E** – They found that individuals who had peers with a larger BMI had a lower likelihood of developing eating disorders, including AN.
- **L** – This suggests that having peers with a lower than average BMI makes individuals more prone to developing AN, highlighting the potential influence of peers.

- **E** – **Cash (1995)** found that it was the perceived severity of the teasing that was linked to body image, rather than just the presence or absence of teasing.
- **L** – This suggests that peer influence isn't as significant as Jones and Crawford originally highlighted and that only severe teasing during adolescence has an effect on body image.

FURTHER EVALUATION

 Another strength of the social learning explanation of AN comes from…

…research support for media influences.
- **E** – Eating attitudes and behaviours were studied among adolescent Fijian girls, following the introduction of TV in 1995.
- **E** – After exposure to TV, the girls stated a desire to lose weight in order to become more like Western television characters.
- **L** – This suggests that the media can have a powerful effect on the development of eating disorders.

 However, one issue with the social learning explanation of AN is…

…that not all media influences have the same effect.
- **E** – **Harrison and Cantor (1997)** found no association between television exposure and eating disorders.
- **E** – However, they did find an association between reading fitness magazines and dieting.
- **L** – This suggests that not all media influences affect eating behaviours in the same way and that further research into the different types of media is required.

CHOOSE THE RIGHT ANSWER

Which **two** of the following are **not** part of the social learning explanation for AN? (Tick **two** boxes only.)

A Modelling ☐

B Positive reinforcement ☐

C Irrational thoughts ☐

D Maternal role models ☐

E Media influences ☐

F Psychosomatic family ☐

Answers on page 360

DRAWING CONCLUSIONS

A psychologist examined the influence of the media before the introduction of the television on a remote island (1995) and three years after (1998). The results can be found in the table below.

Table 1: The mean BMI score for males and females, before the introduction of the TV (1995) and after (1998).

	1995		1998	
	Females	**Males**	**Females**	**Males**
Mean BMI	22.5	23.8	19.8	22.2
Standard Deviation	2.2	1.4	4.8	5.6

What do the results suggest about the influence of the media?

Why is standard deviation a useful measure for psychologists?

Answers on page 360

DRAW A GRAPH

Sketch an appropriate graph for the data in Table 1.

Answers on page 360

APPLYING YOUR KNOWLEDGE

Denise is obsessed with fitness magazines and often reads magazines for diet tips and fitness strategies.

She has recently started going to the gym seven days a week and often skips meals to ensure that she is controlling her calories. Her boyfriend Fayaz keeps telling her how great she looks and giving her lots of attention. However, her family are concerned that she is developing an eating disorder.

Using your knowledge of social learning, explain why Denise is showing signs of an eating disorder. *(4 marks)*

Identify the psychology	Link to Denise

Answers on page 360

KEY TERMS

- Cognitive theory
- Distortions
- Irrational beliefs

Possible essay question

Outline and evaluate the cognitive theory explanation of anorexia nervosa. *(16 marks)*

Other possible exam questions ...

+ Explain what is meant by the term' irrational beliefs' in the context of the cognitive theory of anorexia nervosa. *(2 marks)*

+ Explain what is meant by the term 'distortions' in the context of the cognitive theory of anorexia nervosa and give one example of such a distortion. *(2 + 2 marks)*

 Think

Be aware that there is no one definitive 'cognitive theory' that applies to AN, but rather there are a number of different theories that constitute a cognitive 'approach'.

MUST know ...

Cognitive theory and anorexia nervosa

Cognitive theories of anorexia nervosa (AN) focus on how individuals think differently about themselves and their social world.

Cognitive theories consider the role of **distortions** and **irrational beliefs**.

Cognitive distortions are errors in thinking that cause an individual to develop a negative body image. These can occur because of comparison with others (e.g. from exposure to models in the media) which lead to a misperception that they're overweight and feelings of self-disgust.

A typical **irrational belief** in an individual suffering from AN is that they must be thin for others to like them, or blaming themselves for their social exclusion.

 One strength of the cognitive explanation of AN comes from…

…research support for the role of cognitive factors.

- *E* – **Lang et al. (2015)** compared the performance of 41 children and adolescents diagnosed with AN, compared to 43 healthy control participants.

 Another strength of the cognitive explanation of AN comes from…

…research using the Stroop test.

- *E* – Garner and Bemis found that patients with AN showed selective attention towards stimuli that are related to body fatness and fattening food.

 Further support for the cognitive explanation of AN comes from…

…the success of cognitive behavioural therapy in treating AN.

- *E* – **Fairburn et al. (2015)** compared the effectiveness of CBT-E with interpersonal psychotherapy (IPT), an alternate treatment with no cognitive element.

SHOULD know ...

A cognitive behavioural model of AN

Garner and Bemis (1982) put forward a cognitive behavioural model of AN. They suggest that individuals with AN have a number of characteristics in common. They tend to be high-achieving perfectionists, introverted and full of self-doubt.

When these characteristics are combined with cultural ideals of thinness, an individual develops irrational beliefs that losing weight will reduce their distress and make them more attractive to others.

Finally, losing weight becomes self-reinforcing for the individual because of the sense of achievement and the positive comments (reinforcement) from others.

- *E* – The individuals with AN displayed a more inflexible and inefficient cognitive processing style and were less able to overcome previously held beliefs, in the face of new information.
- *L* – This suggests that inefficient cognitive processing is an underlying characteristic of AN.

- *E* – **Ben-Tovin et al. (1989)** used a 'food Stroop' test and discovered that patients with AN found it harder to colour-name words that were relevant to weight concerns.
- *L* – This suggests that patients with AN have a selective preoccupation with information related to body fatness and fattening food, supporting the idea of distorted thinking.

- *E* – They found that after 20 weeks, two-thirds of the CBT-E patients had met the criteria for remission compared with just one-third of the IPT patients.
- *L* – These findings suggest that CBT-E is an effective treatment for individuals with eating disorders, which reinforces the cognitive aspect of AN.

 One issue with the cognitive explanation of AN is…

…the over-reliance on self-report measures of cognitive processing.

- *E* – **Viken et al. (2002)** criticise self-report measures as a tool for assessing cognitive processing, especially as many measures are taken retrospectively.
- *E* – Consequently, many cognitive scientists reject this approach in favour of performance-based measures that sample cognitive processing directly.
- *L* – This suggests that our understanding of cognitive distortions is limited because of the limited methodology used.

A final issue with the cognitive explanation of AN comes from…

…the lack of empirical research.

- *E* – **Cooper (1997)** claims that cognitive models of AN are largely the result of clinical observation, rather than empirical research.
- *E* – Furthermore, she also points out that there has been comparatively little research carried out that tests the hypotheses derived from the different models of anorexia.
- *L* – Consequently, Cooper suggests that the cognitive approach of AN has lagged behind the development of cognitive explanations in order disorders, like depression.

✔ CHOOSE THE RIGHT ANSWER 1

Which **one** of the following characteristics is **not** associated with AN? (Tick **one** box only.)

A Perfectionism	☐
B High-achieving	☐
C Extroverted	☐
D Full of self-doubt	☐

Answers on page 360

✔ CHOOSE THE RIGHT ANSWER 2

Which **one** of the following evaluative comments is **false**? (Tick **one** box only.)

A A strength of the cognitive approach is that it has contributed to the development of successful treatments.	☐
B A strength of the cognitive approach comes from the use of self-report data from questionnaires.	☐
C A strength of the cognitive approach comes from research supporting the idea of cognitive distortions in patients with AN.	☐
D A weakness of the cognitive approach is the reliance on retrospective data.	☐

Answers on page 360

📖 RESEARCH METHODS (CALCULATIONS)

A psychologist used the 'food Stroop' test to examine cognitive distortions. The results are shown in Table 1.

Table 1: The time taken to state food and non-food words on a 'food Stroop' test for ten patients with AN

	Time taken for food related words	Time taken for non-food words
1	3	1
2	3.2	1.2
3	4.1	1.8
4	2.9	1.9
5	2.8	1.5
6	3.6	2.5
7	3.8	1.6
8	2.7	1.7
9	2.5	1.3
10	4	2
Mean		

1 Calculate the mean score for both conditions.

2 What can the psychologist conclude from the results?

Answers on page 360

✔ A MARKING EXERCISE

Read this student answer to the following exam question:

Explain what is meant by the term 'distortions' in the context of the cognitive theory of anorexia nervosa and give **one** example of such a distortion. *(2 + 2 marks)*

A distortion is an error of thinking that causes an individual to develop a negative body image. For example: 'I ate a bag of sweets at the cinema this evening which is why I'm so fat.' This thought has led to a misconception that the individual is fat, just from eating one bag of sweets, which is clearly distorted.

What mark do you think this would get?

YOUR MARK

AO1

Hint
A hint to help you decide:
How many critical points have been covered?
How much detail is there?

Write an improved answer here, or if you think this is a full-mark answer, write an answer to this alternate question: Explain what is meant by the term 'irrational thinking' in the context of the cognitive theory of anorexia nervosa and give **one** example of an irrational thought. *(2 + 2 marks)*

Answers on page 360

KEY TERMS

- Biological explanations
- Genetic explanations
- Neural explanations

Possible essay question

Discuss biological explanations for obesity. *(16 marks)*

Other possible exam questions …

+ Briefly explain and give **one** criticism of genetic explanations of obesity. *(6 marks)*

+ Briefly explain and give **one** criticism of neural explanations of obesity. *(6 marks)*

 Think

Biological explanations also include evolutionary theories/explanations. Neel (1962) proposed the 'thrifty gene' hypothesis which suggests that the ability to hold reserves of body fat would have been an adaptive advantage for our ancestors, which may explain why obesity still exists in modern society today, as those ancestors with the 'thrifty gene' survived and passed on this gene to future generations.

MUST know …

Genetic explanations for obesity

Biological explanations of obesity focus on **genetic** and **neural explanations**.

Explanations that emphasise genetic inheritance use twin and adoption studies as evidence.

Twin studies

Maes et al. (1997) conducted a meta-analysis and found heritability estimates for BMI of 74% in MZ twins and 32% in DZ twins, highlighting a large genetic component.

Adoption studies

Stunkard et al. (1989) examined 540 adult adoptees. They found a strong relationship between the weight category of adopted individuals and their biological parents, but no significant relationship with their adoptive parents, also suggesting a strong genetic link.

 One issue with the genetic explanation of obesity is…

…that genetic influences vary with age.

- **E** – Research suggests that BMI is not stable across a person's lifetime. **Elks et al. (2012)** found that heritability estimates varied according to the age group of individuals studied.

 Another issue with the genetic explanation of obesity is…

…that obesity rates vary at different times and in different cultures.

- **E** – For example, in 1993, 13% of UK males were classified as obese, but this figure rose to 26% in 2013.

 One strength for the role of leptin in explaining obesity comes from…

…research support in human patients.

- **E** – **Montague et al. (1997)** reported on two severely obese cousins of Pakistani origin, who had low levels of leptin despite their elevated fat levels.

SHOULD know …

Neural explanations for obesity

Neural explanations for obesity focus on the **hypothalamus** and **leptin**.

The hypothalamus

Research has identified a part of the hypothalamus called the **arcuate nucleus** which appears to play a role in appetite and obesity. The arcuate nucleus monitors sugar levels and acts when energy levels are low, producing the desire to eat. Any malfunction in the area can lead to overeating.

Leptin

Leptin is a hormone secreted by fat cells and acts to decrease feeding behaviour and promote energy expenditure. Leptin inhibits food intake and **Bates and Myers (2003)** found that disruption to leptin signalling, can result in obesity.

- **E** – They found that heritability was highest during childhood and then decreased during adulthood.
- **L** – This shows that gene expression is greatest during childhood and that genetic contributions decrease with age and environmental contributions increase with age.

- **E** – Furthermore, obesity rates vary within one culture. In China, the overall rate of obesity rate is below 5% in the countryside, but higher than 20% in some cities.
- **L** – These differences in time and location cannot be explained by genetic factors alone and are likely to be the result of psychological factors.

- **E** – Furthermore, **Gibson et al. (2004)** reported on another obese child from the same region, who after four years of treatment with leptin injections, displayed dramatic effects on appetite, metabolism and weight.
- **L** – These studies support the role of leptin in regulating appetite and its link to obesity.

FURTHER EVALUATION

 Another strength of biological explanation for obesity is…

…that they reduce the stigma associated with being obese.

- **E** – Biological explanations offer theories of obesity that are perceived as being out of the individual's control and therefore less stigmatising.
- **E** – Furthermore, biological explanations also offer treatments based on remedial leptin injections, which offer individuals some hope.
- **L** – This matters because the biological explanation can offer suitable treatments and help reduce the stigma of being obese.

One issue with the evolutionary explanation for obesity (see Think box) is…

…that the majority of humans should have inherited the 'thrifty gene'.

- **E** – If Neel's theory is correct then the majority of people should be obese.
- **E** – However, **Ng et al. (2014)** found that more than half of the world's 671 million obese people live in just ten countries,
- **L** – This suggests that the high levels of obesity found in these cultures can be explained by cultural factors and not evolutionary ones.

CHOOSE THE RIGHT ANSWER

Which **one** of the following statements is **false**? (Tick **one** box only.)

A Genetic explanations suggest that obesity is inherited.	☐
B Adoption studies suggest that obesity runs in the family.	☐
C Neural explanations suggest that damage to the hippocampus can lead to obesity.	☐
D Hormonal explanations suggest that a disruption of leptin signalling can result in obesity.	☐
E Evolutionary explanations focus on the adaptive advantage of obesity in modern society.	☐

Answers on page 360

DRAWING CONCLUSIONS

A researcher examined the obesity rates in the UK for males and females in 1993 and 2013. The results can be found in the graph below.

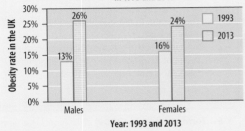

The obesity rates in the UK for males and females in 1993 and 2013

1 What does the bar chart show about obesity? *(4 marks)*

2 Briefly outline two biological causes of obesity. *(4 marks)*

Answers on page 360

KEY TERMS

Select key terms to help you remember the different biological explanations for obesity. Some have been done for you.

Key term	Key point	Key point
Genetic: Twin studies	Maes et al. (1997)	74% MZ twins, 32% DZ twins
Genetic: Adoption studies		
Neural: Hypothalamus		
Neural: Leptin		
Evolution	The 'thrifty gene' hypothesis	

On a separate piece of paper, use your key terms to answer the following exam question: Briefly outline **one** neural explanation of obesity. *(2 marks)*

Answers on page 360

APPLYING YOUR KNOWLEDGE

Daniel has always had a problem with his weight.

His Mum, Dad and sister are also overweight and he has given up trying to lose weight because he believes that his weight problem is 'not his fault'.

Using research, outline **two** biological explanations that could support Daniel's claim that his weight problem is not his fault. *(4 marks)*

Identify the psychology	Link to Daniel

Answers on page 360

KEY TERMS

- Disinhibition
- Restraint theory

Possible essay question

Discuss psychological explanations for obesity. *(16 marks)*

Other possible exam questions ...

+ Briefly outline the restraint theory of obesity and give **one** criticism of this explanation. *(6 marks)*

+ Briefly outline the disinhibition explanation of obesity and give **one** criticism of this explanation. *(6 marks)*

+ Briefly outline the boundary model of obesity and give **one** criticism of this explanation. *(6 marks)*

+ Outline research into psychological explanations of obesity. *(6 marks)*

★ Exam tip

When outlining the boundary model, either as a short-answer question or essay, it's always useful to sketch a diagram first, to help you remember the key elements of this theory.

Hunger boundary		Satiation boundary
	Zone of biological indifference	

Normal (unrestrained) eater

Hunger boundary	Diet boundary	Satiation boundary

Dieting (restrained) eater

MUST know ...

Restraint theory and disinhibition

Herman and Mack (1975) developed the **restraint theory** which suggests that any attempt to avoid eating, actually increases the probability of overeating.

There are different types of restraint, including: rigid and flexible. **Rigid restraint** presents an all-or-nothing approach, whereas **flexible restraint** represents a less strict approach to dieting.

Disinhibition represents a tendency to overeat in response to different stimuli and **Bond et al. (2001)** identified three different types of disinhibition, including:

1. **Habitual** – overeating in response to daily life circumstances.

2. **Emotional** – overeating in response to emotional states, such as stress.

3. **Situational** – overeating in response to environmental cues (e.g. special occasions).

 One strength of the restraint theory for obesity comes from…

…support from laboratory studies.

- **E** – **Wardle and Beales (1988)** randomly assigned 27 obese women to either a diet group (focusing on restraint), an exercise group or a non-treatment group for seven weeks.

 However, one issue with the restraint theory for obesity is…

…that most of the research is conducted under laboratory conditions.

- **E** – While laboratory research typically shows that restrained eaters overeat after they violate their diet more recent research has challenged this view.

 One issue with the boundary model of dieting comes from…

…research that questions the 'what the hell effect'.

- **E** – **Ogden and Wardle (1991)** argue that rather than passively giving in to a desire to eat, the individual may actively decide to overeat as a form of rebellion against their self-imposed restrictions.

SHOULD know ...

The boundary model

Herman and Polivy (1984) developed the boundary model. This model takes into account biological influences and suggests that food is regulated along a continuum. When energy levels are low, we experience hunger and when we have sufficient energy, we stop eating. However, in-between these two extremes we have a 'zone of biological indifference'.

According to the model, dieters have a larger zone of indifference which means that their threshold for hunger and fullness is less sensitive. Furthermore, dieters will often impose a 'boundary' and if they go through this boundary, they experience the 'what the hell effect' and continue to eat until satiation or beyond.

- **E** – The results showed that at both four and six weeks, women in the diet condition ate more than the women in the exercise and non-treatment groups.
- **L** – This supports the restraint theory, as rather than restraint leading to weight loss, it led to overeating and potential weight gain.

- **E** – **Tomiyama et al. (2009)** challenged this view and found that dieters who tracked their food (outside the laboratory) did not overeat following violations of their diet.
- **L** – These results contradict the earlier research and suggest that diet violations and the restraint theory do not lead to overeating in everyday life.

- **E** – This idea has been supported by **Loro and Orleans (1981)** who found that obese binge eaters frequently reported bingeing as a way of 'unleashing resentment' against their diet.
- **L** – This suggests that the boundary model is not a valid explanation of the motivation underlying the breakdown/failure of dieting.

FURTHER EVALUATION

 One issue with the theory of disinhibition is…

…that most of the research has been conducted on white women.

- **E** – This means that conclusions about men and/or other racial groups cannot be made.
- **E** – **Atlas et al. (2002)** reported that both restraint and disinhibition scores were significantly lower in African American students.
- **L** – This suggests that the findings of research need to be considered within their cultural context and that theories of dieting do not apply to all cultures equally.

One strength of the disinhibition theory comes from…

…research into attachment styles.

- **E** – **Wilkinson et al. (2010)** examined 200 adults whose BMI ranged from 17 to 41.
- **E** – Measures of disinhibition and attachment style showed that attachment anxiety was significantly linked to disinhibition eating and to BMI.
- **L** – This supports the idea that one way of dealing with anxiety is through overeating, which in time leads to an increase in BMI, supporting the disinhibition theory.

CHOOSE THE RIGHT ANSWER

Which **one** of the following statements, in relation to the boundary model, is **false**? (Tick **one** box only.)

A Food intake is regulated along a continuum.	☐
B Restrained eaters have a larger zone of biological indifference.	☐
C Restrained eaters are more sensitive to feelings of hunger and fullness.	☐
D Dieters impose a 'diet boundary' that is lower than their situation threshold.	☐
E If a dieter goes through their diet boundary, they experience the 'what the hell effect'.	☐

Answers on page 361

 DRAWING CONCLUSIONS 1

The following graph displays the results of research by Herman and Mack (1975).

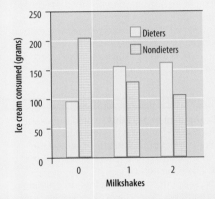

Using your knowledge of the restraint theory and/or boundary model, explain how Herman and Mack's results support these theories.

Answers on page 361

 DRAWING CONCLUSIONS 2

A psychologist wanted to examine how much food people consume when they're on a diet (restrained condition) in comparison to another group who were not on a diet (unrestrained condition). Both groups were given a preload, which consisted of a small snack, before being given access to an all you can eat buffet. The psychologists recorded the mean number of different dishes the participants ate in 15 minutes. The results are shown in the table below.

Table 1: The mean number of dishes eaten by restrained and unrestrained eaters.

Group	Mean number of dishes eaten
Restrained	8.4
Unrestrained	3.1

Using your knowledge of psychological explanations for obesity, explain what the data in Table 1 shows.

Answers on page 361

 APPLYING YOUR KNOWLEDGE

Note: The following scenario is based on a true story.

While writing this textbook Joseph went to the cinema to watch 'Independence Day: Resurgence'.

While he is trying to be healthy and resist the urge to eat, he spent over £5 on pick-and-mix sweets, which weighed over 400g! He tells himself that he will save some for when he gets home. However, while watching the film he consumes the entire bag.

Using your knowledge of the boundary model, explain why Joseph ate the entire bag of sweets. *(4 marks)*

Identify the psychology	Link to Joseph

Answers on page 361

KEY TERM

- Dieting

Possible essay question

Outline and evaluate **one or more** explanations for the success and/or failure of dieting. (16 marks)

Other possible exam questions …

+ Outline research into the success and/or failure of dieting. (6 marks)

+ Briefly outline **one** explanation for the success and/or failure of dieting and give **one** criticism of this explanation. (6 marks)

 Think

An interesting theory of dieting suggests that as we try to suppress our thoughts about food and see certain foods as 'forbidden', this will only serve to increase our preoccupation with the very food we are trying to avoid – known as 'ironic processes of mental control'.

MUST know …

A theory of hedonic eating

Stroebe (2008) argued that restrained eaters (dieters) are more sensitive to the hedonic (i.e. pleasurable) properties of food. As a result of this increased sensitivity, the perception of attractive food triggers the desire to eat.

Mischel and Ayduk (2004) put forward a second process that also makes it difficult for dieters to resist the temptation of attractive food – **attention allocation**. Once food has triggered pleasurable thoughts, restrained eaters find it difficult to withdraw their attention from the attractive food item.

The failure of dieting can therefore be considered in two phases:

1 exposure to attractive food
2 selective attention.

 One strength of the ironic processes of mental control theory (see Think box) comes from…

…experimental support by **Soetens et al. (2006)**

- **E** – They divided a group of participants into restrained and unrestrained eaters, and then subdivided the two groups into high or low disinhibition.

 One strength of the hedonic theory of dieting comes from…

…research examining physiological and affective reactions to the perception of food.

- **E** – The presence or even smell of palatable food induces more salivation in restrained eaters than in unrestrained eaters.

 One strength of research examining theories of dieting is…

…the real-world application and development of healthy eating programmes.

- **E** – These programmes emphasise regulation of body hunger and satiety signals and the prevention of inappropriate attitude to food (e.g. comfort eating).

SHOULD know …

The key to a successful diet

Redden (2008) claims that the key to a successful diet lies in the attention we pay to what is being eaten.

Redden suggests that people like experiences less as they repeat them, therefore when it comes to dieting this makes it harder to stick to a particular diet.

In order to overcome this, Redden suggests that we need to think about the details of a meal (e.g. rocket, tomato, etc.), rather than considering the meal as a whole (e.g. 'not another salad'). By focusing on the specific details, we get bored less easily and are more likely to maintain a diet.

- **E** – The disinhibited restrained group (those who tried to eat less, but who would often overeat) used more thought suppression than the other groups.
- **L** – This shows that restrained eaters who tend to overeat, try to suppress thoughts about food more often, but then think more about food afterwards.

- **E** – **Brunstorm et al. (2004)** tested the salivary reactivity in 40 females who were in close proximity to hot pizza. Participants who were dieting showed a greater salivary response than those who were not dieting.
- **L** – This supports the hedonic theory of dieting suggesting that dieters have an increased sensitivity to food.

- **E** – A meta-analysis of participation in these programmes was associated with improvements in both eating behaviour, psychological well-being and weight stability.
- **L** – This highlights the positive application of dieting research to developing programmes that improve both eating behaviour and psychological well-being.

FURTHER EVALUATION

 One issue with research examining the success and failure of dieting is…

…the overreliance on anecdotal evidence.

- **E** – Anecdotal evidence is often used to justify claims concerning particular dieting strategies.
- **E** – However, anecdotal evidence is not based on objective, scientific data collection methods, which creates a problem for the reliability of such evidence.
- **L** – This matters because much of the evidence is made without proper control over extraneous variables and randomised controls, which makes the findings less valid.

 A final consideration with research examining the success and failure of dieting is…

…the idea of free will vs. determinism.

- **E** – It is likely that a number of genetic factors exert an influence on weight.
- **E** – For example, research has discovered a gene that codes for lipoprotein lipase (LPL), an enzyme produced by fat cells to help store calories. If too much LPL is produced the body will efficiently store calories.
- **L** – This suggests that some people will struggle to lose weight because of their genes, regardless of their intention to do so.

CHOOSE THE RIGHT ANSWER

Which **one** of the following statements is **true**? (Tick **one** box only.)

A Restrained eaters (dieters) are less sensitive to the hedonic (i.e. pleasurable) properties of food.	☐
B Restrained eaters find it easy to withdraw their attention from an attractive food item.	☐
C The key to a successful diet is paying less attention to what is being eaten.	☐
D Dieters fail because they get bored of the diet/regime.	☐

Answers on page 365

MATCH THEM UP

Match up the key psychologists on the left, with their ideas on the right.

1	Stroebe (2008)	**A**	…claimed that the key to a successful diet lies in the attention we pay to what is being eaten.
2	Mischel and Ayduk (2004)	**B**	…provided experimental support for the hedonic theory of dieting.
3	Redden (2008)	**C**	…put forward the theory of attention allocation; the idea that once food has triggered pleasurable thoughts, restrained eaters find it difficult to withdraw their attention from the attractive food item.
4	Soetens *et al.* (2006)	**D**	…argued that restrained eaters (dieters) are more sensitive to the hedonic (i.e. pleasurable) properties of food.
5	Brunstorm *et al.* (2004)	**E**	…provided experimental support for the theory of ironic processes of mental control.

Answers on page 365

An idea 👍

On a separate piece of paper, draw a line, where one end is labelled 'Free will' and the other is labelled 'Determinism'.

Free will ←————————————————→ Determinism

Then consider each of the explanations found in the different topics encountered in this chapter (e.g. evolutionary explanations of food preference, the role of learning in food preference, etc). For each section in this chapter, decide whether you think the theory is suggesting that humans have free will, or whether our behaviour is determined and plot your answers on your continuum.

APPLYING YOUR KNOWLEDGE

Identify the psychology		Link to Jasmine

	Jasmine is becoming increasingly frustrated with her weight. She has tried several diets that she has found in women's magazines and each has failed within two weeks.

Using your knowledge of the success and failure of dieting, explain why Jasmine's diets fail and provide a strategy that Jasmine could use to be more successful. *(4 marks)* | |

Answers on page 365

Topic 1 The evolutionary explanation for food preference

Discuss the evolutionary explanation for food preferences. *(16 marks)*

Examiner's comments

The evolutionary explanation for food preference focuses on why humans have evolved to prefer certain foods, due to their adaptive advantage for our ancestors. Food preferences that helped our ancestors survive would have been passed onto future generations, which is why we have these same preferences today.

> This is a strong introduction that demonstrates clear understanding of evolutionary theory.

For example, the preference for fatty foods would have been adaptive, because fatty foods would have provided our ancestors with energy that would help keep them alive. Furthermore, the preference of a meat diet which is full of nutrients would have provided our ancestors with the catalyst of growth required by the brain, allowing humans to evolve into the intelligent creatures they are today. Finally, a preference for sweetness found in ripe fruit, would have provided our ancestors with essential vitamins and minerals that were necessary for bodily functions and growth.

> This section provides three clear examples of different food preferences, plus their adaptive advantage.

In addition, humans have also developed taste aversion and food neophobia, which is a learned response to eating toxic, spoiled or poisonous food and the avoidance of unfamiliar food. The development of taste aversion would have helped our ancestors to survive because, if they survived eating poisoned food, they would be unlikely to make same mistake again.

> This section provides evident knowledge of taste aversion; however, further expansion of food neophobia is required.

There is a lot of support for the evolutionary explanation of food preference. For example, Grill and Norgen (1978) reported that newborn infants show an acceptance response the first time they taste something sweet, which is an innate response. This study provides support for the evolutionary preference of sweet foods, as humans have an innate acceptance reaction to sweet foods, that would have been beneficial for our ancestors.

> This is a reasonably effective evaluation point; however, the answer should say why this is beneficial.

Furthermore, there is support for the idea of taste aversion, which has been applied to patients undergoing chemotherapy. Some cancer treatments, such as chemotherapy, can cause gastrointestinal illness. Unfortunately, when this illness is paired with food consumption, taste aversion can result. Research has led to the development of the 'scapegoat technique' where cancer patients are given a novel food along with familiar foods, prior to the chemotherapy. Consequently, the patients form an aversion to the novel food and not the familiar food. This highlights the positive application of evolutionary theory to helping patients with cancer overcome their taste aversion.

> This is an effective evaluation point, highlighting the positive application of evolutionary theory.

In addition, another strength comes from support for the heritability of food neophobia. Knaapila et al. (2007) measured food neophobia in 468 adult female twin pairs. The heritability estimate for food neophobia in this sample was 67%, suggesting that two thirds of the variation in food neophobia is genetically determined. This provides some support to the view that neophobia evolved to protect humans from harmful foods.

> Another effective evaluation point, linked to food neophobia. However, the answer could explain the implication of a 67% concordance rate.

However, despite the support for evolutionary explanations, not all food preferences are the product of evolution. Kerb (2009) points out the 'mismatch' between evolved preferences (e.g. fatty and sweet foods) and modern environments. For example, a trait that is beneficial today (e.g. the consumption of low-cholesterol food) would not have evolved because of its beneficial effects for our ancestors. This suggests that the evolutionary explanation of food preferences is limited and cannot explain modern day food preferences.

> Another effective evaluation point, highlighting a modern day limitation.

Level 4 (13–16 marks)

Examiner's comments: The knowledge section is accurate and well-detailed. There is arguably too much AO1 in this essay and therefore the answer should aim to condense the quantity of AO1, maybe by only outlining two food types (fatty and meat). AO3: There is a range of effective evaluation points considered, highlighting both strengths and limitations. A conclusion would have reinforced the points, however due to the over-detailed AO1, the answer missed out on a concluding paragraph.

Topic 2 The role of learning in food preference

Outline and evaluate the role of learning in food preference. (*16 marks*)

Examiner's comments

Learning explanations focus on cultural and environmental influences and include: parental influences, peers and the effects of the media.

> There is good knowledge of parental influences here, although a real-life example would demonstrate this understanding further.

One way in which children acquire their food preferences is by observing their parents. Parents also exercise control over the availability of food, either as a reward, or because of the perceived health benefits. However, although parents have a large influence over their children, social learning emphasises the impact of peers. The behaviour of same-age peers has been found to have a powerful influence on food preferences, as research suggests that children are more likely to identify with models who are the same sex and similar in age.

> Good use of specialist terminology.

In addition to parents and peers, the media can also have a profound effect on food preferences. Social learning can also explain the role of television and other media on food preferences and the social learning explanations of anorexia focus on the portrayal of food, weight and dieting in the media.

> A nice link to anorexia, although an example related to food preference would have been stronger.

There is a range of research support for the learning explanation of food preferences, which focuses on real-world application, cultural differences and psychological research. For example, Boyland and Halford (2013) found that exposure to food advertising on television influenced food preferences and actual food intake in children. The relationship was further supported by the fact that children who had the greatest preference for high-carbohydrate and high-fat foods were the ones who watched the most television. This suggests that the media plays an important role in shaping food preferences, while highlighting the negative effects of advertising on unhealthy food consumption. This has resulted in many countries developing regulations concerning the advertising of food. Research by Cairns et al. (2013) suggested that television is the dominant medium for children's exposure to food marketing, especially for unhealthy foods. Consequently, many countries have introduced legislation to prevent the advertising of unhealthy foods, which limits the negative impact of the media on food preferences and promotes healthy eating behaviours in children.

> The answer has integrated two pieces of research to support the idea of media influences.

> While this is a very good point, an example of food legislation would have been useful here to demonstrate further knowledge.

While the role of the media has received a lot of research support, the influence of parents is less conclusive. For example, Robinson et al. (2001) examined 800 children from a range of different backgrounds and found a complex association between the behaviour of parents and food preferences. This suggests that the role of parents is more complex than originally thought and children do not simply learn by observing their parents. Furthermore, Russell et al. (2015) interviewed parents of children aged 2-5 years old and found that not all of the methods they used influenced their children's food preference. Parental modelling and food exposure were found to be effective, whereas forcing consumption or restricting food access were ineffective. Although this supports the idea that children do learn food preferences from their parents, some approaches were more effective than others.

> Effective evaluation examining the role of parents.

> Further effective evaluation for the role of parents.

The research suggests that the learning explanation of food preference is certainly powerful when it comes to the media, and the research has resulted in the reduction of advertising, highlighting the positive application of psychology. However, the findings of parental influences are less conclusive and highlight a complex interaction between parents and food preferences, suggesting that learning theory may not explain parental influences equally well.

> This is a very strong conclusion which reiterates the main points of the argument.

Level 4 (13–16 marks)

Examiner's comments: AO1: A well-detailed account of the different types of learning is presented, although further real-life examples would have demonstrated better understanding. AO3: A range of thorough and effective evaluation is presented with a strong conclusion to reiterate the argument.

Topic 3 Neural and hormonal mechanisms

Discuss the neural and hormonal mechanisms involved in the control of eating behaviour. *(16 marks)*

Examiner's comments

Neural mechanisms of eating focus on the role of the hypothalamus, whereas hormonal mechanisms focus on the role of ghrelin and leptin.

Glucose levels play an important role in producing feelings of hunger. A decline in glucose levels activates a part of the brain called the lateral hypothalamus (LH), resulting in feelings of hunger. This causes the individual to search for and consume food, which raises the level of glucose. This rise in the level of glucose activates the ventromedial hypothalamus (VMH), which leads to feelings of satiation, which in turn stops us from eating. This cycle demonstrates how the hypothalamus is involved in the control of eating, by responding to changes in the level of glucose in the body.

> There is excellent knowledge of the hypothalamus which is explicitly linked to the control of eating.

The hormone ghrelin is realised in the stomach and stimulates the hypothalamus to increase appetite. Ghrelin levels determine how quickly we feel hungry, as they go up drastically before we eat and then down for about three hours, after a meal. Leptin on the other hand plays a crucial role in appetite and weight control. It is normally produced by fat tissue and secreted into the bloodstream, where it travels to the brain to decrease appetite.

> While the answer describes these hormones, a more explicit link to the question and the control of eating could have been made.

There are mixed conclusions about the role of the hypothalamus and support comes from research on brain-damaged patients. Lesions or damage to the VMH can result in hyperphagia and obesity in a number of different species, including humans. Furthermore, studies have shown that compared to lesions in other brain areas, animals with VMH lesions eat substantially more and gain more weight. These two findings support the role played by the VMH in the control of eating. However, research examining the LH has found that this brain region controls more than just eating. Damage to the LH causes deficits in other aspects of behaviour (e.g. thirst and sex), and not just hunger. Furthermore, recent research has found that eating behaviour is controlled by neural circuits in the brain, not just the hypothalamus. While the LH may be linked to the control of eating behaviour, it is not the brain's 'eating centre', as originally thought.

> An effective evaluation point that draws on two pieces of research.

> A good counter-evaluation in terms of the LH.

There is some research support for the role of ghrelin and leptin. Wren et al. (2001) gave participants an intravenous ghrelin or a saline infusion and measured their appetite in terms of the amount of food consumed at a free-choice buffet. The results revealed that the ghrelin condition consumed on average 28% more than the saline condition. This supports the role of ghrelin in appetite control, as ghrelin acts as an important signal which stimulates food intake.

> Effective use of research support for the role of ghrelin.

Research has also found that some people develop a resistance to leptin and therefore have an inability to control their appetite and weight gain. Leptin resistance is often found in overweight and obese people, making it harder for them to lose weight. This provides an important insight into the role of leptin and the possible application of this research to helping people with weight problems/obesity.

> A nice evaluation point, highlighting the positive application of research.

Level 4 (13–16 marks)

Examiner's comments: AO1: There is a generally well-detailed outline which is accurate. The answer could have provided more explicit links in terms of the role of hormones. AO3: The evaluation provides a range of well-supported points that evaluate both of the explanations provided.

Topic 4 Biological explanations for anorexia nervosa

Briefly outline **one or more** biological explanations of anorexia nervosa and give one limitation of these explanations. *(6 marks)*

Examiner's comments

Biological explanations include genetic and neural explanations. There are two neurotransmitters implicated in anorexia nervosa (AN), including: serotonin and dopamine. Bailer et al. (2007) measured serotonin activity in women recovering from different types of anorexia, in comparison to healthy controls. They found higher levels of serotonin in women recovering from binge-eating/purging type anorexia, compared to the other two groups, suggesting that higher levels of serotonin may cause certain types of AN.

> This introductory sentence is not required. The answer could go straight into the serotonin explanation.

However, one issue with the serotonin explanation is that drug treatments involving serotonin are not always effective. Drugs which alter levels of serotonin, for example selective serotonin reuptake inhibitors (SSRIs), are ineffective with some AN patients. Ferguson et al. (1999) found no difference in the symptom outcomes for patients with AN, for those taking SSRIs and those who were not. This suggests that the serotonin is not the only factor involved in the development AN, as the drugs treatments are not 100% effect.

> This answer provides an excellent evaluation, drawing on research evidence.

Mark awarded: 5–6

Examiner's comments: It's worth approaching these questions in two parts: 1) outlining one or more biological explanations (AO1); 2) outline one limitation (AO3). This answer provides a detailed outline of one explanation (serotonin) using research to provide a detailed and accurate account. Furthermore, the answer highlights one issue effectively, drawing on further research to highlight this limitation.

Topic 5 Family systems theory and anorexia nervosa

Briefly outline family systems theory as an explanation for anorexia nervosa and give **one** criticism of this explanation. *(6 marks)*

Examiner's comments

Minuchin et al. (1978) put forward the psychosomatic family model, which states that the prerequisite for the development of anorexia nervosa (AN) is a dysfunctional family occurring alongside a physiological vulnerability. There are three characteristics of a psychosomatic family, including enmeshment, autonomy and control. Enmeshment family members are overly-involved with each other and lack boundaries and as a result, family members are not allowed to develop autonomy. Furthermore, psychosomatic families are characterised by overprotective control. Overprotectiveness can delay an individual's beliefs regarding the extent to which they are in control of their own lives. Consequently, an individual may rebel against this control by refusing to eat.

> This is a very detailed explanation of family systems theory and while it's good to explain all of the elements, too much detail can reduce the time spent on longer questions later.

One issue with the family systems theory is that the focus is mainly on mother-daughter relationships. Gremillion (2003) argues that although any family member can contribute to enmeshment, it is usually seen as maternal in origin. As a result, therapy to reduce enmeshment usually focuses on reforming the mothers. This matters because the theory and subsequent treatment shows a clear gender bias and ignores the contribution of fathers to an enmeshed family.

Mark awarded: 5–6

Examiner's comments: Like the previous question, it is worth approaching questions like this in two parts. 1) Outline the family systems theory (AO1); 2) outline one limitation (AO3). This answer provides a good outline of family systems theory, although further links to AN with each aspects of the theory could have been made. The evaluation is effective, using research evidence to highlight one limitation.

Topic 6 Social learning theory and anorexia nervosa

Outline and evaluate the social learning theory explanation of anorexia nervosa. *(16 marks)*

Social learning theory attempts to explain the development of anorexia nervosa (AN) through reinforcement, while taking into account the role of peers and media influences.

According to Bandura (1977) people learn by observing the behaviour of others and from the outcome of their behaviour. Children pay particular attention to role models in their life and observe their attitudes and behaviours. Models can be parents, peers, or 'symbolic' models, such as someone portrayed in the media. These models provide an example of attitudes to food, or dieting behaviour that can be observed by the individual and later imitated. If an individual imitates a behaviour and receives positive reinforcement (e.g. comments like 'Wow, you've lost weight!'), they are more likely to continue imitating this behaviour in the future, which could lead to the development of AN. Furthermore, the media is a major source of influence for body image in Western adolescents. The portrayal of thin models on television and in magazines is a significant factor contributing to body image concerns.

While research examining the social learning explanation has not always produced consistent results (in particular in relation to parental influence), evidence examining the effect of the media and peers has provided some support. For example, Costa-Font and Jofre-Bonet (2013) investigate the effect of peer weight on the likelihood of an individual developing AN. They found that individuals who had peers with a larger BMI had a lower likelihood of developing eating disorders, including AN. This suggests that having peers with a lower than average BMI makes individuals more prone to developing AN, highlighting the potential influence of peers. While peers appear to have some effect, Pike and Rodin (1991) found that there was no evidence of daughters imitating the weight concerns of their parents. Furthermore, Ogden and Steward (2000) found that although mothers and daughters were similar in their weight and BMI, there was no association for their restrained eating. These findings do not support the modelling hypothesis and social learning explanation of AN, in terms of parental influences.

Research examining the media can also take advantage of countries which until recently didn't have television. Fiji introduced TV in 1995, which gave psychologists an opportunity to examine the effect of this exposure. Becker et al. (2002) found that after exposure to TV, the Fijian girls stated a desire to lose weight in order to become more like Western television characters. This suggests that the media can have a powerful effect on the development of eating disorders. However, there are many other variables that could have contributed to these results and Harrison and Cantor (1997) found no association between television exposure and eating disorders. However, they did find an association between reading fitness magazines and dieting which suggests that not all media influences affect eating behaviours in the same way and that further research into the different types of media is required. Furthermore, it could be that only motivated individuals (those concerned with reading fitness magazines) are influenced by the media, suggesting that the media has a more profound effect on individuals who have a motivation towards fitness and appearance.

Examiner's comments

> A good introduction, outlining the different factors.

> Good use of specialist terminology.

> A good outline of SLT, linked to the development of AN.

> Good use of research support to highlight the influence of peers.

> Excellent use of two studies to evaluate the effect of parental influences.

> The evaluation point is good, but could have been more effective. How does it show this contribution?

> Excellent further evaluation, looking at specific media types, with additional commentary at the end.

Level 4 (13–16 marks)

Examiner's comments: AO1: An excellent outline of SLT is provided, examining a range of different influences. AO3: A well-developed commentary, providing a range of strengths/limitations specifically looking at the different aspects of the theory.

Topic 7 Cognitive theory and anorexia nervosa

Outline and evaluate the cognitive theory explanation of anorexia nervosa.
(16 marks)

Examiner's comments

There are many different aspects of the cognitive explanation for anorexia nervosa (AN). However, they all centre on how individuals with AN think differently about themselves and their social world.

Cognitive theories consider the role of distortions and irrational beliefs. Cognitive distortions are errors in thinking that cause an individual to develop a negative body image. These can occur because of comparison with others (e.g. from exposure to models in the media) which lead to a misperception that they're overweight and feelings of self-disgust. A typical irrational belief in an individual suffering from AN is that they must be thin for others to like them, or blaming themselves for their social exclusion.

> A good outline highlighting clear knowledge of distortions and irrational beliefs.

Garner and Bemis (1982) suggest that individuals with AN have a number of characteristics in common. They tend to be high-achieving perfectionists, introverted and full of self-doubt. When these characteristics are combined with cultural ideals of thinness, an individual develops irrational beliefs that losing weight will reduce their distress and make them more attractive to others.

> Good use of theory to support the assumptions of the cognitive approach.

There is a wide range of support for the cognitive explanation, drawing on research evidence and the effectiveness of treatments. Lang et al. (2015) compared the performance of 41 children and adolescents diagnosed with AN, compared to 43 healthy control participants. The individuals with AN displayed a more inflexible and inefficient cognitive processing style and were less able to overcome previously held beliefs, in the face of new information. This suggests that inefficient cognitive processing is an underlying characteristic of AN. Furthermore, Garner and Bemis found that patients with AN showed selective attention towards stimuli that is related to body fatness and fattening food. Ben-Tovin et al. (1989) tested this idea using a 'food Stroop' test and discovered that patients with AN found it harder to colour-name words that were relevant to weight concerns. This suggests that patients with AN have a selective preoccupation with information related to body fatness and fattening food, providing further support to the idea of cognitive distortions.

> Effective evaluation, using research support.

> A second study is used effectively to reinforce the first point.

Furthermore, cognitive treatments have been successful in the treatment of AN. Fairburn et al. (2015) compared the effectiveness of CBT-E with interpersonal psychotherapy (IPT), an alternate treatment with no cognitive element. They found that after 20 weeks, two-thirds of the CBT-E patients had met the criteria for remission compared with just one-third of the IPT patients. These findings suggest that CBT-E is an effective treatment for individuals with eating disorders, which reinforces the cognitive explanation of AN.

> Evidence for the effectiveness of CBT-E has been used effectively.

Despite the wide range of support, some researchers criticise the over-reliance of self-report measuring when examining AN to support the cognitive approach. Viken et al. (2002) criticise self-report measures as a tool for assessing cognitive processing, especially as many measures are taken retrospectively. Consequently, many cognitive scientists reject this approach in favour of performance-based measures that sample cognitive processing directly. This suggests that our understanding of cognitive distortions is limited because of the limited methodology used. However, although this criticism is a valid argument, the wide-range of supporting evidence highlights the strength of this explanation and its positive application to treatments.

> A good criticism of the methodology is presented.

> A nice concluding sentence, although this could have been developed more.

Level 4 (13–16 marks)

Examiner's comments: AO1: An accurate and detailed outline of the cognitive explanation is presented with plenty of examples. AO3: The evaluation provides a thorough and effective range of strengths as well as some limitations of the approach and is focused on AN throughout.

Topic 8 Biological explanations for obesity

Discuss biological explanations for obesity. (16 marks)

Examiner's comments

Biological explanations for obesity include both genetic explanations and neural explanations.

Genetic explanations suggest that obesity is determined by a person's genetic makeup and is the result of inheritance. Consequently, genetic explanations use twin studies to support their claim, For example, Maes et al. (1997) conducted a meta-analysis and found heritability estimates for BMI of 74% in MZ twins and 32% in DZ twins, highlighting a large genetic component for obesity.

> The answer has used twin studies to demonstrate knowledge of genetic explanations.

There is a lack of research support for genetic explanations as genetic influences vary with ages and there are different rates of obesity in different cultures. Firstly, research suggests that BMI is not stable across a person's lifetime. Elks et al. (2012) found that heritability estimates varied according to the age group of individuals studied. They found that heritability was highest during childhood and then decreased during adulthood. This shows that gene expression is greatest during childhood and that genetic contributions decrease with age and environmental contributions increase with age. This highlights that genes only play a part in the development of obesity and environmental influences also have a significant impact, especially as we get older.

> This is a very effective evaluation point, explaining a complex criticism of genetic explanations.

Secondly, obesity rates vary at different times and in different cultures. For example, in 1993, 13% of UK males were classified as obese, but this figure rose to 26% in 2013. Furthermore, obesity rates vary within one culture. In China, the overall rate of obesity is below 5% in the countryside, but higher than 20% in some cities. These differences in time and location cannot be explained by genetic factors alone and are likely to be the result of environmental factors.

> Another effective evaluation point, highlighting another issue with genetic explanations.

Neural explanations focus on the hypothalamus and the hormone leptin. Research has identified a part of the hypothalamus called the arcuate nucleus which appears to play a role in appetite and obesity. Any malfunction in the area can lead to overeating. Leptin is a hormone secreted by fat cells and acts to decrease feeding behaviour and promote energy expenditure. Leptin inhibits food intake and Bates and Myers (2003) found that disruption to leptin signalling, can also result in obesity.

> Excellent use of specialist terminology.

> Further knowledge is presented on hormonal explanations well.

The role of leptin has received some support. Montague et al. (1997) reported on two severely obese cousins of Pakistani origin, who had low levels of leptin despite their elevated fat levels. Furthermore, Gibson et al. (2004) reported on another obese child from the same region, who after four years of treatment with leptin injections, displayed dramatic effects in terms of appetite, metabolism and weight. These studies support for the role of leptin in regulating appetite and its link to obesity.

> Evidence to support the role of leptin is presented effectively.

Finally, one strength of the biological explanation is that it reduces the stigma associated with being obese. Biological explanations offer theories of obesity that are perceived as being out of the individuals control and therefore less stigmatising. Furthermore, biological explanations also offer treatments based on remedial leptin injections, that offer individuals some hope. This matters because the biological explanation can offer suitable treatments and help reduce the stigma of being obese.

> Two evaluation points in relation to general strengths of the biological approach.

Level 4 (13–16 marks)

Examiner's comments: AO1: This is a well-presented essay which is structured clearly. The answer divides the essay in half, outlining and evaluating genetics and hormones separately, before providing a general strength in the conclusion. AO3: The evaluation is always thorough and effective and the use of specialist terminology is impressive.

Topic 9 Psychological explanations for obesity

Briefly outline the boundary model of obesity and give **one** criticism of this explanation. *(6 marks)*

Examiner's comments

Herman and Polivy (1984) developed the boundary model. This model takes into account biological influences and suggests that food is regulated along a continuum. According to the model, dieters have a larger zone of indifference which means that their threshold for hunger and fullness is less sensitive. Furthermore, dieters will often impose a 'boundary' and if they go through this boundary, they experience the 'what the hell effect' and continue to eat until satiation or beyond. Therefore, as a result of this larger zone of indifference and the 'what the hell effect' many dieters will overeat which can lead to obesity.

> This is an excellent outline, which provides three key elements to the boundary model.

One issue with the boundary model of dieting comes from research that questions the 'what the hell effect'. Loro and Orleans (1981) found that obese binge eaters frequently reported bingeing as a way of 'unleashing resentment' against their diet, rather than passively giving into a desire to eat. This suggests that the boundary model is not a valid explanation of the motivation underlying obesity and that obesity is caused by resentment rather than a lack of willpower.

> This is an effective evaluation point, drawing on research support.

Marks awarded: 5–6

Examiner's comments: This is a very good answer, as the answer links the boundary model, which is a theory of dieting/overeating, to obesity. Furthermore, the answer has effectively evaluated the boundary model based on the underlying assumption of the 'what the hell effect', using psychological research to reinforce the answer.

Topic 10 Explanations for the success and failure of dieting

Briefly outline **one** explanation for the success and/or failure of dieting and give **one** criticism of this explanation. *(6 marks)*

Examiner's comments

One theory that explains the failure of dieting is known as the theory of hedonic eating. Stroebe (2008) argued that restrained eaters (dieters) are more sensitive to the hedonic (i.e. pleasurable) properties of food. As a result of this increased sensitivity, the perception of attractive food triggers the desire to eat and as a result their diets fail. Furthermore, Mischel and Ayduk (2004) suggested that dieters also experience attention allocation, which makes it even more difficult for them to withdraw their attention away from attractive food.

> This outline draws on two pieces of research, which demonstrates excellent knowledge.

One issue with research (or the lack of research) on the failure of dieting is the overreliance on anecdotal evidence. Anecdotal evidence is often used to justify claims concerning particular dieting strategies. However, anecdotal evidence is not based on objective, scientific data collection methods, which creates a problem for the reliability of such evidence. This matters because much of the evidence is made without proper control over extraneous variables and randomised controls which makes the findings less valid.

Marks awarded: 5–6

Examiner's comments: The answer has provided an accurate and detailed explanation of hedonic eating, highlighting the key elements of this theory using specialist terminology. Furthermore, despite the lack of criticisms, the answer has used the idea that of anecdotal evidence effectively, elaborating on key points well.

KEY TERMS

- Adrenaline and noradrenaline
- Cortisol
- General adaptation syndrome
- Hypothalamic pituitary-adrenal system
- Sympathomedullary pathway

Possible essay question

Discuss research into the general adaptation syndrome. *(16 marks)*

Other possible exam questions ...

+ Outline the main features of the hypothalamic pituitary-adrenal system. *(3 marks)*
+ Outline the main features of the sympathomedullary pathway. *(3 marks)*
+ Explain the role played by cortisol in stress. *(3 marks)*
+ Describe the main features of the general adaptation syndrome. *(6 marks)*

⭐ **Exam tip**

You might find it easier to use some abbreviations in your answers to questions on this topic. The hypothalamic pituitary-adrenal system can be abbreviated to HPA and the sympathomedullary pathway can be abbreviated to SAM.

MUST know ...

General adaptation syndrome (GAS)

The body's response is the same to all stressors. Selye's (1936) three stages to the **GAS** response:

1 The **alarm reaction** involves two simultaneous processes. The immediate short-term response is the **sympathomedullary pathway (SAM)**. The **hypothalamus** activates the **sympathetic branch (S)** of the **autonomic nervous system. Adrenaline (A)** and **noradrenaline** are released by the **adrenal medulla (M)**.

The slower long-term response is the **hypothalamic pituitary-adrenal system (HPA)**. The **hypothalamus (H)** activates the **pituitary gland (P),** stimulating the **adrenal cortex (A)** to release **cortisol**.

2 In the **resistance stage**, the body *appears* to be coping with the stressor's demands.

3 In the **emergency stage**, the body's functioning is impaired. The immune system is suppressed.

 P – Selye's GAS is supported by...

...findings from both non-human and human research studies.

- **E** – For example, research shows that both non-human and human bodies produce the same physiological responses to any stressor.

 P – A weakness of Selye's GAS is...

...its proposal that infections and illnesses occur because stressors deplete resources.

- **E** – Research indicates that 'resources' such as sugars, neurotransmitters, hormones, and proteins are *not* depleted even under conditions of extreme stress.

P – The fight-or-flight response is inappropriate for many of today's stressors...

...because stressors like exam revision don't actually require energetic levels of physical activity.

- **E** – The fight-or-flight response is only adaptive when a stressor requires energetic behaviour.

SHOULD know ...

General adaptation syndrome (GAS)

The GAS response enables the body to cope with extreme stress, but can lead to stress-related illnesses.

Adrenaline and noradrenaline cause physiological responses including increased heart rate and muscle tension. These prepare us to deal with the stressor. (**The fight-or-flight response**).

The hypothalamus uses **corticotrophin releasing hormone (CRH)** to activate the pituitary gland. The pituitary gland activates the adrenal cortex using **adrenocorticotrophic hormone (ACTH)**.

However, as sugars, hormones, and neurotransmitters are depleted, the immune system becomes less effective.

The adrenal glands may be damaged. Stress-related illnesses and mental impairments may occur.

- **E** – These findings support Selye's 'doctrine of specificity', which says that there is a non-specific response of the body to any demand made on it.
- **L** – This indicates that the physiological responses to stressors are extremely well understood.

- **E** – Sheridan & Radmacher (1992) found that it is more likely to be increases in the activity of hormones such as cortisol which lead to stress-related illness.
- **L** – This means that Selye was wrong to explain stress-related illnesses in terms of a depletion of the body's 'resources'.

- **E** – Repeated activation of the stress response for stressors that don't require energy to be expended can lead to cardiovascular problems and immunosuppression.
- **L** – This means that the way the our bodies react to today's stressors may be *impairing* some of the processes designed to protect us.

FURTHER EVALUATION

P – There are gender differences in...

...the body's response to stressors.

- **E** – Stressed female rats release oxytocin. This increases relaxation, reduces fearfulness, and inhibits the fight-or-flight response.
- **E** – Taylor *et al*. (2000) argue that 'tend and befriend' is a more adaptive response for women, because it evolved in the context of being their child's primary caregiver.
- **L** – This suggests that the standard description of the SAM and HPA is a gender-biased account of the stress response.

 P – Purely physiological accounts of the stress response are not sufficient...

...to explain how we respond to stressors.

- **E** – Lazarus found that participants expecting a film to be 'exciting' for the actors, showed less physiological activity than those expecting the film to be 'painful' for the actors.
- **E** – Lazarus & Folkman's (1984) **transactional model** proposes that cognitive appraisal moderates our body's response.
- **L** – This suggests that cognitive factors must be considered when explaining the body's response to stress.

CHOOSE THE RIGHT ANSWER

Which **three** of the following are associated with the general adaptation syndrome? (Tick **three** boxes only.) *(3 marks)*

A Resistance stage ☐

B Alarm response ☐

C Exhaustion reaction ☐

D Alarm reaction ☐

E Resistance response ☐

F Exhaustion stage ☐

Answers on page 361

MATCH THEM UP

Match up the key terms with the appropriate descriptions.

1	Cortisol	A	Released by the pituitary gland, and activates the adrenal cortex
2	Adrenocorticotrophic hormone (ACTH)	B	Used by the hypothalamus to activate the pituitary gland
3	Adrenaline and noradrenaline	C	Activation of the sympathetic branch of the autonomic nervous system
4	Corticotrophic releasing hormone	D	A hormone which impairs cognitive performance and lowers the immune response
5	Fight-or-flight response	E	Released into the bloodstream by the adrenal medulla

Answers on page 361

APPLYING YOUR KNOWLEDGE

You might have seen a version of the 'Scary Michael Jackson' video on YouTube. If you haven't, a version can be found at https://www.youtube.com/watch?v=UBr6wxRvJHc. YouTube user 'hugsandkisses5' recorded her own reaction to one of the versions, which you can see at https://www.youtube.com/watch?v=ON2spSqVYqU.

Explain how hugsandkisses5's body responded to seeing the 'ghost' in terms of what you know about how the body responds to stress. Use the terms 'sympathomedullary pathway', 'sympathetic branch of the autonomic nervous system' and 'parasympathetic branch of the autonomic nervous system' in your explanation. Why did her body continue to react for a while even though she only saw the 'ghost' for a very brief period of time?

Answers on page 361

DRAWING CONCLUSIONS

On the day of their A level examinations, a psychologist asked 24 students to complete a questionnaire measuring how much stress they perceived themselves to be experiencing. A measure was also taken of how much adrenaline their bodies were producing compared with a baseline measurement taken before they started their revision. A scattergram of the findings is shown below:

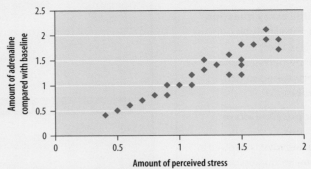

(a) Explain why the data in this study is primary data rather than secondary data. *(2 marks)*

(b) Explain one strength of primary data compared with secondary data. *(3 marks)*

(c) What kind of relationship is shown in the above scattergram? *(2 marks)*

(d) Identify **one** statistical test that could be used to determine the strength of the relationship between the two variables. Give **two** reasons for your choice. *(3 marks)*

(e) The researcher concluded that high levels of perceived stress were causing higher levels of adrenaline to be produced. Explain why this conclusion cannot be justified. *(2 marks)*

Answers on page 361

KEY TERMS

- Cardiovascular disorder
- Immunosuppression

Possible essay question

Using research studies, discuss the role of stress in immunosuppression *and* cardiovascular disorders. *(16 marks)*

Other possible exam questions ...

+ Outline what is involved in immunosuppression. *(3 marks)*
+ Describe **one** study into the relationship between stress and immunosuppression. *(4 marks)*
+ Describe **one** study into the relationship between stress and cardiovascular disorders. *(4 marks)*
+ Evaluate research into the role of stress in immunosuppression *and* cardiovascular disorders. *(8 marks)*

⭐ Exam tip

If you are asked to 'describe' a study, you should write about what was done (procedure) and what was found (results).

❗ Think

What other illnesses does research suggest are linked with stress?

MUST know ...

Stress and cardiovascular disorders

High adrenaline levels *increase* heart rate, constrict blood vessels, and dislodge plaque on blood vessel walls.

Williams *et al.* (2000) found that of 13,000 initially healthy people, the highest scorers on an anger scale were 2.5 times more likely to have had a heart attack six years later compared with those with the lowest scores.

The role of stress in immunosuppression

One effect of cortisol is to *reduce* the body's immune response (immunosuppression).

Kiecolt-Glaser *et al.* (1984) found that natural killer cells were less active in students while they were revising than before they started. This suggests that ongoing stressors reduce immune system functioning.

 P – The role of stress in cardiovascular disorders is supported by...

...studies on people with ischaemia (reduced blood flow to the heart).

- **E** – Sheps *et al.* (2002) found that ischaemics with erratic heartbeats when doing public speaking were more likely to die from cardiovascular disorders than those with stable heartbeats..

 P – Self-report measures need to be treated cautiously...

...when interpreting research into the relationship between stress and cardiovascular outcomes.

- **E** – People who remember more unpleasant than pleasant events are likely to score more highly on stress measures and cardiovascular outcomes.

 P – The relationship between stress and illness is not simple...

...and it is difficult to show that stressors cause a change in health.

- **E** – For example, Lazarus (1992) says that health is fairly stable and slow to change.

SHOULD know ...

Stress and cardiovascular disorders

This causes the heart to work harder, increases blood pressure, and blocks arteries. This can lead to coronary heart disease, hypertension, and strokes.

Even people with 'moderate' anger scores were more likely than the lowest scorers to experience a coronary event, suggesting that adrenaline level increases are closely associated with cardiovascular disorders.

The role of stress in immunosuppression

Immunosuppression increases the chances that someone will become ill because invading bacteria and viruses are not attacked by the immune system.

The researchers also found that those students who reported experiencing other life stressors, and had small social networks, were those with the lowest natural killer cell activity levels.

- **E** – This shows that psychological stress dramatically increases the risk of death in at least some people with poor coronary artery circulation.
- **L** – This supports many other studies in showing that there is a very strong link between stress and cardiovascular disorders.

- **E** – This could lead to an exaggerated score on both measures.
- **L** – This means that self-report measures might produce stronger, but unjustified, correlations between higher perceived stress and cardiovascular symptoms.

- **E** – We would need continuous health measurements to show that stress was directly responsible for ill-health. However, this would be both expensive and impractical.
- **L** – This highlights an important difficulty in this area of research and a limitation in drawing conclusions from studies.

FURTHER

 P – Some stressors might enhance the immune system...

...rather than impair it.

- **E** – Evans et al. (1994) found lower levels of an antibody protecting against infection with a chronic stressor, but higher levels of that antibody when the stress was acute.
- **E** – Segerstrom & Miller's (2004) meta-analysis also shows that acute stressors promote the body's ability to fight infection.
- **L** – This means that stress may sometimes be beneficial to the body's immune system.

 P – Individual differences modify the effects of stress...

...on the cardiovascular and immune systems.

- **E** – Age, how reactive the sympathetic branch of the ANS is, and gender can all modify a stressor's effects.
- **E** – For example, women show more adverse immunological/hormonal changes when stress is caused by marital conflict.
- **L** – Therefore, individual differences must be considered before we can talk about how stress affects the cardiovascular and immune systems.

CHOOSE THE RIGHT ANSWER

Which **two** of the following are associated with immunosuppression? (Tick **two** boxes only.)

A Blocked arteries (atherosclerosis) ☐

B Constriction of blood vessels ☐

C Production of cortisol ☐

D Restricted blood flow to parts of the brain ☐

E Decreased natural killer cell activity ☐

Answers on page 361

RESEARCH ISSUES

Interleukin-b is a protein which is produced soon after tissue injury and regulates the remodelling of the connective tissue in wounds and the rate of production of collagen, the tough fibrous tissue in scars. A researcher decided to investigate whether stress affected how quickly wounds heal. Groups of participants agreed to undergo a small skin biopsy on their arms. A non-stressed control group were compared with a group who were caring for an elderly relative with dementia. It was hypothesised that the wounds would take longer to heal in the group caring for an elderly relative. The mean time for the biopsy wounds to heal are shown below.

	Participants not caring for a relative	Participants caring for a relative
Mean time for wound to heal (days)	54	63

The researcher used a Mann-Whitney U test to analyse the data. The difference in wound healing time was significant at p < 0.05.

(a) Was the hypothesis directional or non-directional? Give **one** reason for your answer. *(2 marks)*

(b) Give **two** reasons why the researcher chose the Mann-Whitney U test to analyse the data. *(2 marks)*

(c) The Mann-Whitney U test is a non-parametric statistical test. Identify a parametric alternative to the Mann-Whitney U test. *(1 mark)*

(d) The researcher set the significance level at p < 0.05. What is a Type I error, and what is the probability of a Type I error being made in this study? *(2 marks)*

(e) The researcher concluded that caring for relatives with dementia is stressful, and stress suppressed the immune system which caused the difference in wound-healing times. Give one criticism of the conclusion the researcher drew. *(2 marks)*

Answers on page 361

MATCH THEM UP

Match up the researchers to the statement that best describes their research.

1	Williams *et al.* (2000)	**A**	Higher levels of an antibody protecting against infection are produced when an acute stressor is experienced.
2	Kiecolt-Glaser *et al.* (1984)	**B**	Natural killer cell activity is lowered when students revise for an important examination.
3	Evans *et al.* (1994)	**C**	Psychological stress dramatically increases the risk of death in at least some people with poor coronary artery circulation.
4	Sheps *et al.* (2002)	**D**	Adrenaline levels are closely associated with cardiovascular disorders.

Answers on page 361

APPLYING YOUR KNOWLEDGE

In a study of supporters of Premiership football teams, researchers analysed the results of hundreds of games played by Sunderland. They looked at the results of each match and at how many deaths from heart attacks and strokes occurred in the health authority area on the days that Sunderland played. They found that male death rates increased by 66% when Sunderland lost on their home ground. Although there was an increase when the team lost and were playing away from home, it was much less than when they lost at home. There was no increase in female deaths irrespective of how well the team did.

Use your knowledge of the relationship between stress and illness to explain these findings, and suggest a reason why defeats on their own ground led to a greater increase in supporters' death rates than defeats on other grounds. *(4 marks)*

Answers on page 361

KEY TERMS

- Life changes
- Life change units (LCUs)

Possible essay question

Discuss research into life changes as a source of stress. *(16 marks)*

Other possible exam questions ...

+ Explain what is meant by the term 'life changes' as used in research into sources of stress. *(2 marks)*
+ Outline **one** study which has investigated life changes as a source of stress. *(4 marks)*
+ Evaluate research studies into life changes as a source of stress. *(8 marks)*

 Exam tip

You can use your knowledge of the limitations of correlation and self-report methods in this topic.

 Think

Can you think of a better way of measuring life changes than the scale devised by Holmes and Rahe?

MUST know ...

Life changes

Life changes are events that require major adjustment in some aspect of our life, and are believed to be significant sources of stress.

The stress of life changes can be measured using the **Social Readjustment Rating Scale (SRRS)**. This consists of 43 life events, each of which has a **Life Change Unit (LCU)** score associated with it. 'Death of a spouse' is listed 'most stressful' and scores the maximum of 100 LCUs.

Rahe *et al.* (1970) used a modified SRRS, called the **Schedule of Recent Experiences (SRE)**, to study the relationship between stress and illness in naval personnel. SRE scores were positively correlated with scores on a measure of *ill-health*.

 P – Life changes research has provided important insights... .

...into the possible causes of physical and psychological problems.

- **E** – For example, Heikkinen & Lonnqvist (1995) found that life changes such as family discord, loss, financial troubles, and unemployment were associated with suicides in Finland.

 P – However, the SRRS is a very simplistic measure...

...which ignores the fact that the same life changes may be more stressful for some than others.

- **E** – For example, the death of a spouse may be more stressful if it is untimely than if it occurs after a long and painful illness.

 P – An important methodological issue in life changes research is...

...that it relies on peoples' memories of events.

- **E** – For example, Rahe (1974) found that the recall reliability depends on the time interval between test and re-test.

SHOULD know ...

Life changes

Life changes may be positive *or* negative, such as marriage or bereavement. Change requires effort to adapt, and this may affect our health.

A person identifies which of the 43 life events has occurred within some time period (e.g. a year). The scores for each event are added up to give a total LCU score.

Since the SRE included both positive *and* negative events, it seems it is change, rather than the negativity of change, that requires effort to adapt and creates stress. Other studies (e.g. Cohen, *et al.*, 1993) have also shown that higher LCU scores are associated with increased likelihood of illness.

- **E** – These life changes may even have been *causal* factors in the suicides.
- **L** – This suggests that this kind of research can be valuable in understanding important human behaviour.

- **E** – The SRRS assigns the same score to an event regardless of how it is perceived by a person.
- **L** – This means that a better measure of life changes would take individual differences in the perception of stressors into account.

- **E** – However, Hardt *et al.* (2006) found moderate to good reliability of recall for most childhood experiences.
- **L** – Since most findings are similar to Hardt *et al.*'s, this suggests that reliability levels for retrospective reports of life events *are* good.

FURTHER EVALUATION

P – Major life changes are relatively rare...

...and 'daily hassles' are the most significant source of stress for most people.

- **E** – DeLongis *et al.* (1988) found that life changes and health were not significantly correlated, but 'hassles' and next-day health problems were.
- **E** – Bouteyre's (2007) study of the hassles associated in transitioning from school to university replicated this finding.
- **L** – This suggests that research emphasis should be on 'daily hassles' rather than life events.

 P – Life changes research is correlational...

...and doesn't allow causal relationships to be inferred.

- **E** – Life changes and illness may be accidentally correlated because both are causally related to another variable.
- **E** – People with high anxiety levels are likely to be more prone to illness *and* more likely to report negative life events, so the causal variable is high anxiety.
- **L** – This means that significant correlations between life changes and illness might be due to intervening variables.

CHOOSE THE RIGHT ANSWER

Which **two** of the following are examples of life changes as identified on the SRRS? (Tick **two** boxes only.)

A Bereavement ☐

B Being late for an appointment ☐

C Home maintenance ☐

D Son or daughter leaving home ☐

E Relating well with friends ☐

Answers on page 362

 FILL IN THE BOXES

In each box below, write a word or phrase that completes the sentence.

Life changes can be defined as...	An example of a life change is...
The researchers who devised the SRRS are...	The number of life changes on the SRRS is...
A life change unit is...	The life change which has the highest life change unit is...
An alternative to the SRRS is...	Researchers who used this scale in their study are...

Answers on page 362

 APPLYING YOUR KNOWLEDGE

Munya and Nadia were discussing the SRRS. 'I'm going to say what a good way of measuring how stressful your life it is if a question comes up on it,' said Nadia. 'I'm not,' said Munya. 'It's way too simplistic, doesn't apply to students like us, and it relies on you having a really good memory, which I don't!' he continued. 'Those sound like three very good evaluation points for the exam. If only I knew what you were talking about,' said Nadia. Using your knowledge of research into life changes as a source of stress, how would you explain Munya's three evaluation points to Nadia? *(6 marks)*

Answers on page 362

 RESEARCH ISSUES

An A level student decided to investigate for herself the relationship between stress and ill-health. She placed an advertisement in her local shop asking for people to take part in her study. Each of the 12 people who took part in the study completed the SRRS and estimated the number of days they had taken off through sickness in the previous year. A scattergram of the data she collected is shown below:

(a) Write an operationalised directional hypothesis for this study. *(2 marks)*

(b) It has been claimed that the SRRS has internal validity. What is meant by the term 'internal validity'? *(1 mark)*

(c) Name the sampling method used by the student. *(1 mark)*

(d) Outline **one** limitation of this sampling method. *(2 marks)*

(e) The student used Spearman's rho test to analyse her data. Give **two** reasons why this test was used. *(2 marks)*

(f) Name a parametric alternative to Spearman's rho test. *(1 mark)*

(g) The student found a correlation of +.27 with the alternative test and had set her significance level as p < 0.05. Use the relevant table in your textbook to decide if there is a significant correlation between the two variables. Explain how you reached your decision. *(3 marks)*

Answers on page 362

KEY TERMS

- Daily hassles
- Daily uplifts

Possible essay question

Discuss research into daily hassles as a source of stress. *(16 marks)*

Other possible exam questions …

+ Explain what is meant by the term 'daily hassles' as used in research into sources of stress. *(2 marks)*
+ Using examples, outline the difference between life changes and daily hassles. *(3 marks)*
+ Outline **one** study which has investigated daily hassles as a source of stress. *(4 marks)*
+ Evaluate research studies into daily hassles as a source of stress. *(8 marks)*

 Exam tip

Remember that you can use also use life changes research findings as a way of evaluating daily hassles (and *vice versa*).

 Think

What are the ten most frequently occurring hassles in your everyday life? How does your list compare with the hassles your fellow students identify?

MUST know …

Daily hassles

Kanner et al. (1981) define daily hassles as 'the irritating, frustrating, and distressing demands that to some degree characterise everyday transactions with the environment'.

Kanner et al. studied 100 participants aged 45–67 and found a negative correlation between the frequency of reported daily hassles and psychological well-being. Importantly, daily hassles were also a better predictor of well-being than life changes were.

Lazarus' (1999) explanation for the effects of daily hassles is that an **accumulation** of them creates persistent irritations, frustrations, and overloads, which cause more serious stress reactions such as anxiety and depression.

 P – Daily hassles are more stressful than life changes…

…according to some research findings.

- **E** – For example, Ruffin (1993) found that daily hassles were linked to greater physical and psychological dysfunction than major life changes were.

 P – One limitation of most daily hassles research is…

…that it is correlational and does not allow causal conclusions to be drawn.

- **E** – For example, the negative thinking that occurs in depression might cause people to report higher severity of hassles.

 P – There are gender differences…

…in perceptions of what constitutes a 'hassle'.

- **E** – For example, Miller *et al.* (1992) found that for men, pets are associated with hassles such as the money needed to care for them.

SHOULD know …

Daily hassles

These include everyday work concerns and issues arising from family life.

Daily hassles were measured using the *Hassles and Uplifts Scale (HSUP)*. Psychological well-being was measured using the *Hopkins Symptom Checklist* and the *Bradburn Morale Scale*.

An alternative explanation is that chronic stress due to major life changes make us more vulnerable to daily hassles. The latter's presence may *amplify* the stress caused by the former. Major life changes might also *deplete* a person's resources making them less able to cope with daily hassles than usual.

- **E** – Additionally, Flett *et al.* (1995) reported that life changes are associated with greater seeking of social/emotional support from significant others.
- **L** – This means that daily hassles could be more stressful because other people provide less social/emotional support for them than for life changes.

- **E** – Consequently, it could be that depression is causing the hassles rather than the other way round.
- **L** – This means that we need to be cautious when interpreting correlational research findings in this area.

- **E** – However, for women, pets are associated with uplifting feelings such as a lack of psychological pressure.
- **L** – This shows that it is difficult to define something as a 'hassle' objectively because of individual differences in how things are perceived.

FURTHER EVALUATION

 P – The validity of daily hassles findings is threatened…

…by its use of self-report studies.

- **E** – For example, social desirability bias is always possible when data are collected using self-reports.
- **E** – People may be embarrassed to admit that certain things (e.g. looking after their children) are hassles for them, and so do not report these to researchers.
- **L** – This means that we need to exercise caution when drawing conclusions from research which uses self-report as its methodology.

 P – Retrospective reporting of daily hassles…

…also threatens the validity of research findings.

- **E** – For example, peoples' recall of events that happened a month ago may not always be accurate.
- **E** – Charles *et al.* (2013) found that keeping a daily diary of hassles led to a more accurate record of events than retrospective recall.
- **L** – This suggests that there are methodologies available which may avoid the problems of retrospective recall, and provide more valid data.

CHOOSE THE RIGHT ANSWER

Which **two** of the following are examples of daily hassles? (Tick **two** boxes only.)

A Getting enough sleep ☐

B Christmas ☐

C Home maintenance ☐

D Having too many things to do ☐

E Pregnancy ☐

Answers on page 362

 ## MATCH THEM UP

Match up the researchers to the statement that best describes their research.

1	Ruffin (1993)	A	Daily hassles were linked to greater physical and psychological dysfunction than were major life changes.
2	Miller *et al.* (1992)	B	Daily hassles were a better predictor of well-being than life changes.
3	Charles *et al.* (2013)	C	Pets are associated with hassles, such as the money needed to care for them.
4	Kanner *et al.* (1981)	D	Keeping a daily diary of hassles led to a more accurate record of events than retrospective recall.

Answers on page 362

 ## APPLYING YOUR KNOWLEDGE

Liza has had a cold that she can't seem to shake off, and frequently has to see the college nurse because of headaches and problems with sleeping. Liza has a Twitter account, and updates her followers daily about the good and bad things that have happened to her. Sasha is a devoted follower of Liza and sent the following tweet: '@Liza Have you noticed that when you moan about how rubbish the day's been you don't go to college next day?' Liza replied: '@Sasha But if I have a good day, I'm OK for school. What's that all about?'

Using your knowledge of psychology, send a tweet to @Liza telling her 'what it's all about'. You have a maximum of 140 characters, so this is an exercise in being succinct yet informative, a good skill to have for questions which ask you to 'Outline…'. *(3 marks)*

Answers on page 362

 Link

Other limitations of self-report studies can be found on page 216 of the Year 1/AS Revision and Exam Companion.

 ## RESEARCH ISSUES

A research team asked 20 students (10 males, 10 females) to wear headcams for the whole of their first day at college. Two of the researchers used content analysis to identify the number of hassles each student experienced during the day. They predicted that male and female students would differ in the number of hassles they experienced.

(a) What is 'content analysis'? *(2 marks)*

(b) Explain how the researchers could have carried out content analysis to find the information they wanted. *(4 marks)*

(c) Explain how the researchers could have assessed the reliability of their content analysis. *(3 marks)*

(d) Was the researchers' prediction directional or non-directional? Explain your answer. *(2 marks)*

(e) Identify a non-parametric test that could have been used to analyse the results. Give **two** reasons why you chose this test. *(3 marks)*

(f) The researchers found a significant difference between the number of hassles experienced by the males and females. The difference was significant at p < 0.02. Explain why the researchers did not think that they had made a Type I error in relation to the difference they found. *(2 marks)*

In a follow-up study, the researchers asked each student to rate how stressful they had found the day. They used a Spearman's rho test to discover if daily hassles and stress were significantly correlated. For males, the correlation was .66, whereas for females it was .63.

(g) Use the relevant table in your textbook to decide if the two correlation coefficients are significant at p < 0.02. Explain your answer. *(4 marks)*

Answers on page 362

KEY TERMS

- Job control
- Workload
- Workplace stress

Possible essay question

Using research studies, discuss the effects of workload **and** control on workplace stress. *(16 marks)*

Other possible exam questions ...

+ Explain what is meant by the terms 'workload' and 'control' as used in research into workplace stress. *(2 marks)*

+ Outline **one** study which has investigated the effects of workload on workplace stress. *(4 marks)*

+ Outline **one** study which has investigated the effects of control on workplace stress. *(4 marks)*

+ Evaluate research studies into workplace stress. *(8 marks)*

★ Exam tip

Evaluating a study doesn't just mean criticising it. Some of the research has told us really interesting things about workplace stress, and what could be done to reduce it.

MUST know ...

Workload and control

Workload is defined as the amount of activity involved in a job, while **control** is the extent to which people feel they can manage aspects of their work, such as meeting deadlines.

Marmot *et al*'s (1997) study of over 10,000 civil servants found that low job control and high workload was strongest among the younger workers, and was not reduced by high levels of social support.

Johansson *et al*'s (1978) study of 28 manual labourers at a Swedish sawmill found that workers with a high workload and low control (high-risk group) had higher adrenaline levels and illness rates than those with a low workload and high control (low-risk group).

 P – The job-strain model of workplace stress has support...

...from some studies of workplace stress.

- **E** – For example, Kivimaki *et al.* (2002) found that Finnish workers with a high workload and low control were twice as likely to die from CHD as those with a low workload and high control.

 P – 'Work underload' can also be a factor...

...in creating workplace stress.

- **E** – For example, Shultz *et al.* (2010) found that employees who reported work underload also reported low job satisfaction and significant absenteeism due to stress-related illness.

 P – There are wide individual differences...

...in the way people react to, and cope with, workplace stressors.

- **E** – For example, Schaubroek *et al.* (2001) found that some workers are actually less stressed by having no control or responsibility, and have better immune system functioning.

SHOULD know ...

Workload and control

The *job-strain model* of workplace stress proposes that the workplace causes stress when a person has a *high* workload and *low* job control.

Senior grade staff have a *high* workload and *high* control, while junior grade staff have a *low* workload and *low* control. Stress is therefore experienced by both grades, but for different reasons. Coronary heart disease (CHD) was associated with *low* job control, but not with *high* workload.

The high- and low-risk groups were matched on factors like education and job experience. A self-report measure showed that the high-risk group also reported a greater sense of social isolation.

- **E** – However, neither workload nor control on their own were associated with death from CHD.
- **L** – This suggests that high workload or low control may not always be stressful but, as the job-strain model predicts, a combination of them is.

- **E** – This suggests that work underload ('*rust out*') can cause similar problems to those associated with work overload ('*burn out*').
- **L** – The stressful nature of work underload suggests that the job-strain model may be an oversimplification.

- **E** – Lazarus' (1995) 'transactional model' proposes that whether a workplace stressor is perceived as stressful depends largely on a person's coping abilities.
- **L** – This offers additional support for the view that the job-strain model is an oversimplification.

FURTHER EVALUATION

 P – Questionnaires may not be the best methodology...

...to study the influence of workplace stressors.

- **E** – For example, Dewe (1989) suggests that through things like social desirability bias, questionnaires may distort the importance of factors.
- **E** – Keenan & Newton (1989) found that interviews could identify stressors, like interpersonal conflicts, not typically identified in questionnaire studies.
- **L** – This suggests that interviews may be a more valid way of assessing the impact of workplace stressors.

 P – Workplace stress does not directly cause depressive illness...

...but it can make depression more likely when combined with other problems.

- **E** – For example, home difficulties or daily hassles may lead to poorer mental health when combined with workplace stressors.
- **E** – Warr (1987) argues that low levels of certain aspects of work, such as a job's variety, may contribute to poor mental health.
- **L** – This suggests that while work is generally seen as good for our mental health, aspects of it can be harmful when combined with other stressors.

CHOOSE THE RIGHT ANSWER

Which **one** of the following is **not** an example of a workplace stressor? (Tick **one** box only.)

A Having too much work to do ☐

B Doing work that isn't challenging ☐

C Feeling that aspects of the job cannot be managed ☐

D Having a high degree of job satisfaction ☐

E Doing a job that exceeds your abilities ☐

Answers on page 362

 ## RESEARCH ISSUES

Workplace stressors such as overload and control have been linked with potentially harmful behaviour in those affected by them. Chen & Spector (1992) gave 400 employees questionnaires about job stressors, frustration, satisfaction, and potentially harmful behaviours including sabotage, theft, and substance abuse. The researchers wanted to see if job stressors were correlated with any of the potentially harmful behaviours.

Identify **one** ethical issue the researchers needed to address, and suggest a way they could have dealt with it. *(3 marks)*

Answers on page 362

 ## APPLYING YOUR KNOWLEDGE

Homer and Moe were discussing their jobs.

'I think being a Nuclear Safety Inspector is too hard for me. I'm worried something will go wrong and I won't be able to deal with it,' said Homer.

'I wish I had a job like yours,' said Moe. 'At least it would stimulate me. Serving beer all day is just so boring, but at least I'm my own boss, unlike you!'

Lenny and Karl walked in. 'Sorry we're late,' said Karl, 'but I've just had way too much to do and not enough time to do it in.'

'I'm late because I fell asleep,' said Lenny. 'I've been sitting at my desk with nothing to do at all.'

Using your knowledge of workplace stress, identify the kind of workplace stressors the four employees are experiencing (e.g. work overload). *(4 marks)*

Employee	Stressor
Homer	
Moe	
Karl	
Lenny	

Answers on page 362

 ## RESEARCH METHODS

Twenty employees in a small company were divided into those that had a low degree of control in the workplace and those that had a high degree of control. Each employee was asked to rate how stressed they felt at work using a 10-point rating scale, where 1 = not at all stressed and 10 = extremely stressed. The raw data are shown below.

Low degree of control employees	High degree of control employees
8	4
7	5
8	3
6	3
1	2
6	2
6	3
8	5
6	5
9	2

(a) Calculate the means for the two groups of participants. *(2 marks)*

(b) Identify **one** weakness of using the mean to describe the stress reported by the low degree of control employees. *(2 marks)*

(c) Name **two** alternative measures of central tendency that could have been used instead of the mean. *(2 marks)*

(d) Identify **one** measure of dispersion that could have been used to describe the variability in the ratings of stress given by the participants. *(1 mark)*

(e) Identify a parametric test of difference that the researcher might have considered using to analyse the data. *(1 mark)*

(f) Identify a suitable non-parametric alternative to the test you identified in (e) above. *(1 mark)*

(g) At what level of measurement are the ratings provided by the participants? *(1 mark)*

Answers on page 362

KEY TERMS

- Hassles and Uplifts Scale (HSUP)
- Physiological measures of stress
- Skin conductance response
- Social Readjustment Rating Scale (SRRS)

Possible essay question

Discuss the use of self-report scales **and** physiological measures of stress. *(16 marks)*

Other possible exam questions ...

+ Outline how any **one** self report scale (e.g. Social Readjustment Rating Scale, Hassles and Uplifts Scale) has been used to measure stress. *(4 marks)*

+ Outline how the skin conductance response is used to measure stress. *(4 marks)*

+ Explain **one** limitation of using **either** self-report scales **or** physiological measures in stress research. *(4 marks)*

★ Exam tip

You are already familiar with the self-report scales described here from the pages on life changes and daily hassles. The evaluative points on this page could legitimately be used as part of your answer to a question on those topics.

MUST know ...

Social Readjustment Rating Scale (SRRS: Holmes & Rahe, 1967)

Consists of 43 life events, each associated with a Life Change Unit. Adding up the LCUs for each event experienced in some time period gives a total score.

Hassles and Uplifts Scale (HSUP: Kanner *et al.*, 1980)

Consists of 117 'hassles' and 135 'uplifts', relating to work, health, family, friends, the environment and practical considerations.

Skin conductance response

Adrenaline and noradrenaline cause sweating. The electricity the skin conducts increases with sweat production. The index and middle fingers have 0.5V applied across them, and the current that flows gives a skin conductance measure.

EVALUATION

P – One weakness of the SRRS is…

…that the same event may have a different meaning for different people.

- **E** – For example, 'divorce' may be stressful if a marriage was happy, but less stressful if it was unhappy.

EVALUATION

P – One weakness of the HSUP scale is…

…that it is time-consuming for participants to complete.

- **E** – The scale consists of 252 items (117 hassles and 135 uplifts) and participants may not maintain thoughtful, focused attention when completing it.

EVALUATION

P – One strength of physiological measures is…

…that they avoid some of the problems associated with self-report measures.

- **E** – For example, physiological measures are not liable to social desirability bias and response set.

SHOULD know ...

Social Readjustment Rating Scale (SRRS: Holmes & Rahe, 1967)

Initially, 400 participants rated each event on a scale of 1–100 having been told that 'marriage' is 50 LCUs. Events requiring more adjustment have higher than 50 LCUs.

Hassles and Uplifts Scale (HSUP: Kanner *et al.*, 1980)

Each 'hassle' is rated on a 3-point scale as 'severe', 'moderately severe' or 'extremely severe'. Each 'uplift' is rated on a 3-point scale as 'somewhat often', 'moderately often', or 'extremely often'.

Skin conductance response

The palms of the hands contain glands which are partly responsive to emotional stimuli, and produce a strong sweat response. Skin conductance is measured in microSiemens.

- **E** – The SRRS doesn't take individual differences in the perception of an event into account.
- **L** – This means that the SRRS's use of a fixed LCU for each event may be unrepresentative of how stressful an event is.

- **E** – This is supported by low test-retest correlations (.48 on the hassles scale and .60 on the uplifts scale).
- **L** – Low reliability coefficients mean that the validity of the scale as a measure of hassles and uplifts is questionable.

- **E** – However, as Lazarus' (1990) 'transactional model' argues, stress is more than just a physiological response.
- **L** – This means that despite avoiding some of the problems of self-report measures, physiological measures are not perfect measures of stress.

FURTHER EVALUATION

P – Stress is not the only stimulus…

…that causes an increase in activity in the sympathetic branch of the ANS.

- **E** – For example, Oshumi and Ohira (2010) found that fear, anger, surprise, sexual arousal, temperature, and medication all increase physiological activity and produce an increased skin conductance response.
- **E** – Cognitive perception can also affect skin conductance.
- **L** – This means that skin conductance might not be a valid measure because of the influence of other factors.

P – A further weakness of the SRRS is…

…that some of the life events only apply to adults.

- **E** – For example, events like 'retirement' and 'son or daughter leaving home' are not relevant for younger age groups.
- **E** – Itula-Abumere (2013) has found that younger populations have different perceptions of what constitute the most stressful life events.
- **L** – This shows that using the SRRS with inappropriate age groups could yield uninformative data about how much stress they are experiencing.

CHOOSE THE RIGHT ANSWER

Which **two** of the following statements are **true** about self-report and physiological measures of stress? (Tick **two** boxes only.)

A   The HSUP consists of over 250 items. ☐

B   Skin conductance decreases with increasing stress. ☐

C   The preferred measure of skin conductance is microSiemens. ☐

D   Items on the HSUP are rated on a 5-point scale. ☐

E   The SRRS is a 50-item multiple choice questionnaire. ☐

Answers on page 363

FILL IN THE BOXES

Complete the following boxes, which relate to the SRRS and HSUP self-report scales. You may need to refer to pages 184 and 186 to complete parts of the table.

Scale	Total number of items	How the scale is completed	One strength of the measure	One weakness of the measure
SRRS				
HSUP				

Answers on page 363

APPLYING YOUR KNOWLEDGE

Mitzi and Daniel were revising for their exams.

'I know what reliability and validity are,' said Daniel, 'so I'll be OK if they ask that in the examination. But I hate it when they ask me to describe a way in which reliability and validity can be assessed. I haven't got a clue how to answer that.'

'It's easy,' said Mitzi, 'just remember my little slogan: Do it and do it again, then do it with something else.'

'Thanks,' said Daniel, 'but I really don't know what you are talking about.'

Using your knowledge of how reliability and validity can be assessed, explain to Daniel what Mitzi's slogan means. *(6 marks)*

Answers on page 363

DRAWING CONCLUSIONS

An A level student was interested in how much stress staff and students at her school were experiencing. Every member of the teaching and administrative staff, along with the students at the school, was asked to complete the HSUL self-report measure. The mean scores for each group are shown in the table below.

Group/Measure	Hassles score	Uplifts score
Teaching staff	210	45
Administrative staff	150	60
Students	105	270

(a) Which group has the highest hassles and lowest uplifts scores? *(1 mark)*

(b) Which group were neither highest nor lowest on both measures? *(1 mark)*

(c) Which group has a hassles score two-and-a-half times its uplifts score? *(1 mark)*

(d) Draw a suitably labelled bar chart of the data in the above table. *(4 marks)*

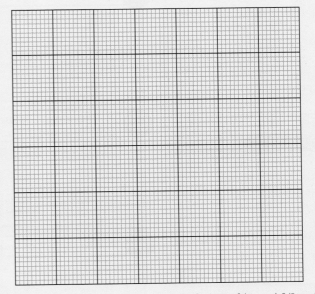

(e) What conclusions can be drawn from the findings of this study? *(3 marks)*

Answers on page 363

Link

Ways of assessing and improving reliability are discussed on pages 16–19 of The Complete Companion Student Book, Year 2.

KEY TERMS

- Type A
- Type B
- Type C

Possible essay question

Discuss research into the Type A, B, and C personalities as individual differences in stress. *(16 marks)*

Other possible exam questions ...

+ Explain the difference between Type A and Type B as individual differences in stress. *(2 marks)*
+ Explain what is meant by 'Type C' in relation to individual differences in stress. *(2 marks)*
+ Outline **one** study which has investigated the role of Type A and Type B behaviour. *(4 marks)*
+ Evaluate research studies into the Type A, B, and C personalities in stress. *(8 marks)*

⭐ Exam tip

Exams are very stressful (!), and stress leads to cognitive impairment. You'd be amazed at how many students write 'insecurely attached' and 'securely attached' when asked about Type A, B, and C personalities. Make sure you're not one of them!

MUST know ...

Personality

The **Type A** personality is made up of three characteristics:

(1) competitiveness and achievement striving

(2) impatience and time urgency

(3) hostility and aggressiveness.

Type Bs are patient, relaxed, and easygoing.

Friedman & Rosenman (1959, 1974) used interviews to classify men as either Type A or B. After an interval of nearly nine years, 12% of Type As had experienced a heart attack compared with only 6% of Type Bs.

The **Type C** personality strongly suppresses negative emotions and is an unassertive and likeable person who rarely gets into arguments and is generally helpful to others.

Morris *et al.* (1981) found that women with cancerous breast lumps were more likely than women with non-cancerous lumps to have Type C personalities.

 P – Research studies of women...

...suggest that they can have Type A personalities too.

- *E* – For example, Friedman *et al.* (1986) found that both men and women with CHD reduced their risk of further problems when given Type A counselling alongside cardiac counselling.

 P – The original claims about Type A behaviour and stress... .

...have been challenged by more recent research findings.

- *E* – For example, Ragland & Brand (1988) conducted a 22-year follow-up of the participants originally studied by Friedman and Rosenman.

 P – The concept of Type C...

...has been challenged by some research studies.

- *E* – For example, Giraldi *et al.* (1997) found no association between emotional suppression and cancer progression.

SHOULD know ...

Personality

Friedman and Rosenman believed these characteristics lead to increased blood pressure and stress hormone levels, both of which are linked to CHD.

These characteristics are believed to *decrease* a person's risk of stress-related illness.

The sample consisted of over 3,000 initially healthy Californian men aged 39–59. Friedman and Rosenman found that the Type As also had higher blood pressure and cholesterol levels, and twice as many Type As actually *died* from heart attacks.

Type Cs cope with stress in a way that ignores their own needs in order to please others. This behaviour has been linked to cancer, possibly because of its effects on the immune system.

The sample consisted of 75 women who were interviewed about their Type C behaviour by an interviewer 'blind' to initial cancer diagnoses.

- *E* – Cardiac counselling alone was only half as effective as a combination of cardiac counselling and Type A counselling for both men and women.
- *L* – This suggests that Friedman and Rosenman were wrong to focus their original research only on men with Type A personalities.

- *E* – The results showed there was little evidence of a relationship between Type A and mortality.
- *L* – Although the Type A participants may have modified their behaviour, the lack of a relationship challenges the claim that Type A is a significant risk factor in CHD.

- *E* – However, a link was found between stressful life events and a cancer diagnosis.
- *L* – This suggests that environmental variables (life events) may be more important than the Type C personality in causing some of the negative effects of stress.

 FURTHER EVALUATION

 P – The three characteristics of the Type A personality...

...don't appear to contribute equally to its negative effects.

- *E* – Myrtek's (2001) meta-analysis identified 'hostility' as the key characteristic of Type A and the development of CHD.
- *E* – There was no association between 'time pressure' and 'competitiveness' and the development of CHD.
- *L* – This suggests that it is 'hostility' alone that is contributing to CHD rather than the Type A personality.

 P – Some research suggests a *direct* link...

...between aspects of personality and illness.

- *E* – For example, Nemeroff & Musselman (2000) studied blood platelets, which increase the risk of heart attack, in people suffering from depression.
- *E* – Blood platelets were reduced as much by a *placebo* drug as by an anti-depressant (Prozac).
- *L* - This suggests that mood itself can exert a *direct* effect on the body's physiological systems.

CHOOSE THE RIGHT ANSWER

Which **two** of the following statements apply to Type A personalities?
(Tick **two** boxes only.)

A They are easy-going, relaxed, and patient.	☐
B They are characterised by extreme emotional suppression.	☐
C They experience constant time pressure.	☐
D Their behaviour has been linked to cancer.	☐
E They are easily frustrated by other people.	☐

Answers on page 363

🔑 **KEY WORDS**

For each of the Type A, B, and C personalities, select two key terms or phrases that will help you to remember the differences between them

Personality type	Key term 1	Key term 2
Type A		
Type B		
Type C		

Now try to write an answer to the exam question below using the key terms/phrases:

Exam question: Distinguish between the Type A, B, and C personalities as identified by researchers into personality differences in stress. *(6 marks)*

Answers on page 363

 DRAWING CONCLUSIONS

The table below shows the data obtained by the Western collaborative group study into the relationship between personality and coronary heart disease (CHD)

Nature of CHD	Percentage Type A	Percentage Type B
Heart attacks	12.8	6.0
Recurring heart attacks	2.6	0.8
Fatal heart attacks	2.7	1.1

What do these findings show about the Type A and B personalities and CHD? *(4 marks)*

Answers on page 363

 APPLYING YOUR KNOWLEDGE

Ben, Sanya and Oliver were discussing their forthcoming exams. Ben had devised a detailed revision timetable which identified what subject he should be revising, on what day, at what time, and for how long. He set the alarm on his phone to remind him when he should stop revising one subject and switch to another. Sanya liked to please his fellow psychology students, and so he had helped Ben construct his timetable, even though he hadn't made his own yet. Oliver wasn't worried about revision. After all, the exams were a month away. That would be plenty of time to revise for his exams.

(a) Which student is most likely to be Type A? *(1 mark)*

(b) Which student is most likely to be Type B? *(1 mark)*

(c) Which student is most likely to be Type C? *(1 mark)*

After the exams, the three students met up for a game of pool in their local leisure centre.

(d) Which student probably wouldn't care if he won or lost? *(1 mark)*

(e) Which student would probably be unhappy if he lost, but would hide his disappointment from the other two? *(1 mark)*

(f) Which student would probably try hardest to win? *(1 mark)*

Answers on page 363

KEY TERM

- Hardiness

Possible essay question

Discuss research into hardiness as an individual difference in stress. *(16 marks)*

Other possible exam questions ...

+ With reference to hardiness, outline what is meant by 'challenge', 'commitment' and 'control'. *(3 marks)*

+ Outline **one** study which has investigated the role played by hardiness in stress. *(4 marks)*

+ Evaluate research into the role played by hardiness as an individual difference in stress. *(8 marks)*

 Exam tip

You could be asked to select an area of psychology and explain how it benefits the economy. 'Hardiness' research is a good topic to use in this respect.

MUST know ...

Hardiness

The three characteristics of the hardy personality are:

(1) Challenge (seeing change as a challenge rather than a threat)

(2) Commitment (seeing a role as being meaningful rather than meaningless)

(3) Control (being in control of events rather than being controlled by the circumstances).

Kobasa (1979) found that 'highly stressed' American male executives who were not often ill scored high on measures of the three Cs, whereas those who reported frequent illness were low scorers on those measures.

Kobasa's findings have been replicated by Maddi (1987) and Lifton *et al.* (2006), and are therefore reliable.

 P – There may be a physiological basis...

...for the hardiness concept.

- **E** – For example, Maddi (1999) found that people high in hardiness have lower blood pressure than people low in hardiness.

 P – People can be trained...

...to improve their hardiness.

- **E** – For example, Maddi *et al.*'s (1998) training programmes have been used to increase self-confidence and a sense of control.

 P – The measurement of hardiness...

...has been problematical for researchers.

- **E** – For example, early research used lengthy and awkwardly-worded questionnaires to measure challenge, commitment, and control.

SHOULD know ...

Hardiness

These characteristics enable people to resist, and cope with, the negative effects of stress. The characteristics are called the '3 Cs'.

Kobasa measured stress using the SRRS, and illness using self-report measures. 86 participants were identified as high stress/low illness and 75 as high stress/high illness.

Maddi studied employees at an American telephone company. Lifton *et al.* studied American university students who either completed their courses or 'dropped out' without graduating.

- **E** – Additionally, Contrada (1989) discovered that hardy Type Bs had the lowest blood pressure of all.
- **L** – This suggests that the characteristics of hardiness and Type B might both directly affect autonomic nervous system activity and reduce responses leading to CHD.

- **E** – Hardiness training is more effective than relaxation/meditation and placebo/social support in increasing job satisfaction and decreasing self-reported illness.
- **L** – This indicates that hardiness training programmes can have beneficial real-world applications.

- **E** – More specific scales, such as Maddi's (1997) *Personal Value Survey*, have addressed some of the issues with the original questionnaires.
- **L** – However, issues like low internal reliability of new measures have not yet been fully resolved.

 FURTHER EVALUATION

 P – Negative affectivity (NA) may be a simpler way...

...of describing the hardy personality.

- **E** – For example, High NA individuals are more likely to report distress and dissatisfaction, dwell more on their failures, and focus on negative aspects of themselves and the world.
- **E** – These characteristics correlate reasonably well with low hardiness levels.
- **L** – This suggests that hardy individuals might simply be those people who are *low* in NA.

P – The three characteristics of the hardy personality...

...do not seem to be equally important in contributing to hardiness.

- **E** – For example, both Cohen *et al.* (1993) and Kim *et al.* (1997) have argued that 'control' is the most important contributor to hardiness.
- **E** – Both researchers found that people who perceive themselves to be in control of their lives were much less susceptible to the negative effects of stress.
- **L** – This suggests that challenge and commitment might not actually make much of a contribution to hardiness.

CHOOSE THE RIGHT ANSWER

Which **two** of the following statements are **not** characteristics of hardiness? (Tick **two** boxes only.)

A Seeing yourself as being in control of your life. ☐

B Suppressing negative emotions and being unassertive. ☐

C Seeing change as an opportunity for development. ☐

D Displaying hostility and aggressiveness. ☐

E Being involved with the world around you and having a sense of purpose. ☐

Answers on page 363

 APPLYING YOUR KNOWLEDGE (1)

A local company makes an annual profit of £1 million a year. However, the £100,000 cost of absenteeism must be deducted from this profit. The company asks an occupational psychologist if there is any way in which absenteeism could be reduced. The psychologist recommends that the company hires an expert to try and increase the employees' hardiness. The expert guarantees to reduce absenteeism by at least 50%, but says that his fee for his hardiness training course will be £25,000. The company's budget officer has never spent more than £500 on courses for the employees, and refuses to hire the expert.

Did the budget officer make the right decision? Use the mathematical skills you have gained during your study of psychology to explain your answer. *(4 marks)*

Answers on page 363

 APPLYING YOUR KNOWLEDGE (2)

Two college lecturers were discussing their jobs.

One of them said: 'I've been here ten years teaching my subject and next year they want me to teach a subject I've never taught before. It's outrageous! Where I work you don't get a choice in which classes you teach, you just have to teach the classes you've been given. We got an open day coming up, but if the management think I'm going to give up my Saturday morning to go into work, they've got another think coming.'

His colleague replied: 'You need to change! I love working at my college and I'm happy to teach more than I have to, and I don't mind doing it for free. I want our college to be the best! It's great the way I'm allowed to just get on with my job, and not feel that people are watching me all the time. If they wanted me to teach a new course, I'd jump at the opportunity!'

Using your knowledge of hardiness, explain how the two lecturers differ in terms of the three Cs. Who is the hardiest of the two? *(8 marks)*

Answers on page 363

 RESEARCH METHODS

In a study investigating hardiness and absenteeism from work, a researcher classified 100 participants as either being low or high scorers on a measure of the three Cs, and whose absence from work either was or wasn't a cause for concern for the company. The researcher hypothesised that there would be an association between scores on the three Cs and whether the company was concerned or not about the employees' absenteeism. The results are shown in the table below.

	Low score on the three Cs	High score on the three Cs
Absence a cause for concern	6	43
Absence *not* a cause for concern	39	12

(a) Is the researcher's hypothesis one- or two-tailed? Explain your answer. *(2 marks)*

(b) Write a suitable null hypothesis for this study. *(2 marks)*

(c) At what level of measurement is the data in this study? *(1 mark)*

(d) What is the most appropriate measure of central tendency to use in this study? *(1 mark)*

(e) Suggest a suitable statistical test that could be used to analyse the data in this study. *(1 mark)*

(f) A questionnaire was used to measure the three Cs. Explain **one** disadvantage of using a questionnaire in this study. *(2 marks)*

(g) Participants were led to believe that the questionnaire they completed was part of their annual appraisal. Identify **one** ethical issue this study raises, and explain how it could be dealt with. *(3 marks)*

Answers on page 363

🔗 **Link**

The importance of control in the workplace is discussed on page 188.

KEY TERMS

- Benzodiazepines
- Beta blockers

Possible essay question

Outline and evaluate research into drug therapy (e.g. benzodiazepines, beta blockers) as a way of managing and coping with stress. *(16 marks)*

Other possible exam questions ...

+ Explain how benzodiazepines differ from beta blockers as ways of managing and coping with stress. *(4 marks)*

+ Outline research into benzodiazepines as drug therapy for stress. *(4 marks)*

+ Outline research into beta blockers as drug therapy for stress. *(4 marks)*

+ Evaluate drug therapy as a way of managing and coping with stress. *(8 marks)*

 Exam tip

If you are asked to explain the difference between two terms or concepts, don't just outline them, otherwise you will not gain full credit. Remember to do what the question asks you to do!

MUST know ...

Benzodiazepine anti-anxiety drugs (BZs)

BZs (e.g. *Librium, Diazepam*) reduce stress by slowing down central nervous system activity and inducing feelings of relaxation. They enhance the activity of GABA, a neurotransmitter which quietens neural activity by making it harder for neurons to be stimulated by other neurotransmitters.

Beta blockers (BBs)

BBs target the sympathetic nervous system and block receptor sites activated by adrenaline and noradrenaline. Heart rate, blood pressure, breathing rate, and sweating do not increase, and the person feels calmer and less anxious without the brain or alertness being affected.

 P – Drugs therapies are effective...

...in managing the negative effects of stress.

- **E** – For example, Kahn *et al.* (1986) found that BZs were significantly more effective than a placebo for the treatment of anxiety and stress.

 P – Two advantages of drug therapies are...

...that they require little effort from users and work quickly.

- **E** – For example, drugs require users to do nothing other than remember to take their medication.

P – One disadvantage of BZ anti-anxiety drugs is...

...that they produce biological dependence.

- **E** – For example, people who take BZs show marked withdrawal symptoms when the drugs are discontinued.

SHOULD know ...

Benzodiazepine anti-anxiety drugs (BZs)

BZs also reduce the activity of serotonin, a neurotransmitter that has an arousing effect in the brain.

Beta blockers (BBs)

BBs bind to beta-receptors in the heart and other organs, and reduce adrenaline and noradrenaline's effects. BBs have been used to reduce 'stage fright', and in sports where hand–eye co-ordination is important. However, their use is banned by the International Olympics Committee.

- **E** – Lockwood (1989) found that BBs were effective in reducing stress in a study of American orchestral musicians. The drugs also seemed to increase their confidence and performance.
- **L** – These findings suggest that drug therapies can be beneficial, at least when the stressor is a short-term one.

- **E** – Psychological therapies require time, effort, and motivation if they are to be effective.
- **L** – Therefore, it isn't surprising that some people prefer a quick and effort-free therapy to a slow and effortful therapy to manage their stress.

- **E** – Even low doses of BZs are associated with biological dependence.
- **L** – This suggests that BZs are not appropriate as a treatment method for people suffering from 'everyday stress'.

FURTHER EVALUATION

 P – A further disadvantage of BZ anti-anxiety drugs is...

...that they have serious side effects.

- **E** – For example, BZs produce increased agitation or panic as well as aggressiveness and cognitive side effects.
- **E** – Cognitive side effects include memory impairment, especially the ability to store acquired knowledge in long-term memory.
- **L** – This also suggests that BZs are not an appropriate way of treating 'everyday stress'.

 P – Drug therapies only treat the symptoms of stress...

...and do not address its causes.

- **E** – Although drugs are effective, stress reduction occurs only for as long as the drug is being taken.
- **E** – Whatever caused the stress in the first place still remains.
- **L** – This means that psychological methods may be more preferable since they address the source of the stress and not just the symptoms it produces..

CHOOSE THE RIGHT ANSWER (1)

Which **two** of the following statements is true about benzodiazepine anti-anxiety drugs? (Tick **two** boxes only.)

A They target the sympathetic nervous system. ☐

B They block sites which are normally activated by adrenaline. ☐

C They enhance the action of GABA. ☐

D They bind to receptors in the cells of the heart and other organs. ☐

E They target the central nervous system. ☐

Answers on page 363

CHOOSE THE RIGHT ANSWER (2)

Which **two** of the following statements is true about beta blockers? (Tick **two** boxes only.)

A They prevent adrenaline from having a strong effect. ☐

B They reduce serotonin activity. ☐

C They enhance the action of dopamine. ☐

D They increase the flow of chloride ions into post-synaptic neurons. ☐

E They are also used in the treatment of coronary heart disease. ☐

Answers on page 363

FILL IN THE BOXES

Below are six questions relating to drug therapy. Each of the questions can be turned into an AO3 point. This can either be a strength or weakness of drug therapy, depending on how the question is answered. Write 'yes' or 'no' in each box for benzodiazepines (BZs) and beta blockers (BBs)

	BZs	BBs
Is the drug effective in reducing stress?		
Does the drug require time/effort from the user?		
Does the drug lead to biological dependence?		
Does the drug have unpleasant side effects?		
Does the drug only address the symptoms of stress rather than its causes?		
Is the drug widely available and relatively inexpensive?		

Answers on page 364

RESEARCH ISSUES

A randomised control trial (RCT) is a study in which people are allocated at random to receive one of several clinical interventions. One of these interventions is the standard of comparison or control. The control may be a standard practice, a placebo (sugar pill), or no intervention at all. RCTs seek to measure and compare the outcomes after the participants receive the interventions. Because the outcomes are measured, RCTs are quantitative studies.

Explain what is meant by the terms 'demand characteristics' and 'investigator effects', and why RCTs help to overcome these. *(6 marks)*

Answers on page 363

APPLYING YOUR KNOWLEDGE

Chris had always suffered from 'nerves'. When he was told he had an interview for a university place, he knew he'd need to be at his best, but he also knew that the stress and anxiety he'd experience would affect how well he did. His brother advised him to tell his doctor and ask him to prescribe some drugs. However, when he told his mother he was going to do that she got very angry with him and said she wouldn't be happy if he did that.

Using your knowledge of drug therapies, what would your advice be to Chris? The table in the 'Fill in the boxes' activity could be the basis for your advice. *(6 marks)*

Answers on page 364

KEY TERM

- Stress inoculation therapy

Possible essay question

Outline and evaluate the use of stress inoculation therapy as a way of managing and coping with stress. *(16 marks)*

Other possible exam questions …

+ Outline how stress inoculation therapy could be used to manage a stressor. *(6 marks)*

+ Evaluate stress inoculation therapy as a way of managing stress. *(8 marks)*

 Exam tip

A good way to evaluate SIT is to compare its strengths and weaknesses with drug therapy. For example, a weakness of SIT is that it can be time-consuming, whereas drug therapy is not. However, a strength of SIT is that unlike drug therapy it does not have side-effects.

MUST know …

Stress inoculation therapy (SIT)

SIT aims to change how people *think* about stressors. The three phases in SIT are:

(1) Conceptualisation: The therapist and client investigate the client's sources of stress. The client is taught to see perceived threats as problems to be solved, and to break down global stressors to specific components that can be coped with.

(2) Skill acquisition, rehearsal, and consolidation: Coping skills are taught and rehearsed in the clinic using imagery, modelling, and role play. After this, they are gradually rehearsed in real life.

(3) Application and follow-through: Finally, the client applies the coping skills in increasingly stressful situations.

 P – SIT is effective…

…in treating a variety of different stressors.

- **E** – For example, Jay & Elliott (1990) found SIT reduced the stress experienced by parents whose children were undergoing medical procedures.

 P – One advantage of SIT is…

…that it isn't just a 'one-off' treatment for a current stressor.

- **E** – For example, skills acquisition provides long-lasting effectiveness so that people are less adversely affected by future stressors.

 P – One disadvantage of SIT is…

…that it can be time-consuming and requires high motivation.

- **E** – For example, Meichenbaum (2007) says that some clinical disorders may need follow-up sessions for as long as a year.

SHOULD know …

Stress inoculation therapy

SIT is a form of cognitive behavioural therapy (CBT) developed by Meichenbaum (1985) specifically to manage stress.

The client is helped to recognise the maladaptive strategies they use to deal with stress and what can be changed about these. This helps them to 'reconceptualise' stressors.

These skills match the client's preferred coping method and include positive thinking, time management, and self-statements such as: 'Relax – you're in control. Take a slow breath.'

It is important for the client to learn to anticipate situations where it may be difficult to apply the skills and rehearse coping responses.

- **E** – The therapy has also been successfully applied to academic stress, the stress of public speaking, and anxiety reduction in phobics.
- **L** – This suggests that SIT is a useful psychological alternative to biological approaches to managing stress.

- **E** – This compares favourably with biological therapies which only address current symptoms rather than underlying causes.
- **L** – This offers additional support for the view that SIT is a useful alternative to biological approaches to stress management.

- **E** – Some people might not want to invest this amount of time and/or might not want to change their way of thinking.
- **L** – This means that, although it is effective, SIT might not be suitable for everyone.

 P – SIT suffers from…

…the hello–goodbye effect.

- **E** – For example, people might initially exaggerate their problems in order to receive SIT ('hello') and then minimise their problems afterwards to please the therapist ('goodbye').
- **E** – Therapies such as SIT depend on subjective reports from the people who undertake them.
- **L** – This means that assessing SIT's effectiveness can be difficult.

 P – Some elements of SIT may be more important…

…than others in having a beneficial effect on stress.

- **E** – For example, SIT might be effective just because people learn to relax, which reduces activity in the sympathetic nervous system.
- **E** – Some activities could be making no contribution at all to reducing stress.
- **L** – This means that it might be possible to reduce the processes in SIT without reducing its overall effectiveness.

✔ CHOOSE THE RIGHT ANSWER

Which **two** of the following are **not** phases in SIT? (Tick **two** boxes only.)

A   Conceptualisation ☐

B   Cognitive dissonance ☐

C   Application and follow-through ☐

D   Unconscious operant conditioning ☐

E   Skill acquisition, rehearsal, and consolidation ☐

Answers on page 364

FILL IN THE BOXES (1)

Identify in which of the three phases in SIT the following are used.

Technique	Phase a feature in
Using imagery, modelling, and role play	
Investigating the person's sources of stress	
Teaching the person to see perceived threats as problems to be solved	
Applying coping skills in increasingly stressful situations	
Using self-statements such as: 'Relax – you're in control. Take a slow breath'	
Learning to anticipate situations where it may be difficult to apply the skills and rehearsing coping responses	

Answers on page 364

🔗 Link

SIT has also been applied to anger management. This is discussed on pages 278–279 of The Complete Companion Student Book, Year 2.

FILL IN THE BOXES (2)

This activity uses the same six questions that were asked about drug therapy, but this time applied to SIT. As we noted previously, each of the questions can be turned into an AO3 point as either a strength or weakness of SIT depending on how the question is answered. First, transfer the 'yes' or 'no' responses you gave for **either** BZs **or** BBs and put these into the boxes. Now, write 'yes' or 'no' in each of the boxes for SIT. When you have done that, head straight for the 'Applying your knowledge' activity!

	BZs *or* BBs	SIT
Is the therapy effective in reducing stress?		
Does the therapy require time/ effort from the user?		
Does the therapy lead to biological dependence?		
Does the therapy have unpleasant side effects?		
Does the therapy only address the symptoms of stress rather than its causes?		
Is the therapy widely available and relatively inexpensive?		

Answers on page 364

APPLYING YOUR KNOWLEDGE

Our nervous student, Chris, listened to what you told him about the strengths and weaknesses of drug therapy as a treatment for stress. He can't make up his mind about whether to go to his doctor or not, and wonders if there are any other therapies available. He has heard about SIT, and wonders if it might be an alternative to drug therapy.

What would your advice be to Chris? The table you completed in the 'Fill in the boxes (2)' activity will help you allow Chris to weigh up the relative strengths and weaknesses of the two forms of therapy. *(6 marks)*

Answers on page 364

KEY TERM

- Biofeedback

Possible essay question

Discuss biofeedback as a way of managing and coping with stress. *(16 marks)*

Other possible exam questions ...

+ Outline how biofeedback is used to help people manage and cope with stress. *(4 marks)*

+ Evaluate biofeedback as a way of managing stress. *(8 marks)*

 Exam tip

Think about using alternative methods of managing and coping with stress as a way of evaluating Biofeedback.

 Think

Which of the three methods of managing and coping with stress do you think is the most effective?

MUST know ...

Biofeedback

In biofeedback, a person learns to exert voluntary control over involuntary (autonomic) behaviours. The four processes in biofeedback are:

(1) Learning relaxation techniques: These reduce sympathetic nervous system activity and activate parasympathetic activity.

(2) Feedback: Aspects of sympathetic activity (e.g. sweating) are measured by machines (e.g. skin conductance response), while the person relaxes. The machines give *feedback* about *biological* activity using light or sound.

(3) Operant conditioning: Lowering physiological activity is rewarding and reinforces the behaviour that caused it.

(4) Transfer: The newly acquired learning is applied to the real world whenever stressors are encountered.

 P – One strength of biofeedback is…

…that research studies have demonstrated its effectiveness.

- **E** – For example, Bradley (1995) found that biofeedback users had significantly fewer muscle-tension headaches than people using relaxation alone.

 P – A second strength of biofeedback is…

…that it has advantages over other stress management approaches.

- **E** – For example, it is not invasive like drugs are, and can be used when drugs or SIT would be inappropriate (e.g. with children).

 P – Biofeedback is a popular stress reduction technique…

…for a whole range of disorders.

- **E** – For example, as well as stress, biofeedback has been used to treat migraine and asthma.

SHOULD know ...

Biofeedback

Biofeedback combines biological (physiological activity) and psychological (operant conditioning) approaches.

Since adrenaline and noradrenaline are no longer produced, stress symptoms are reduced.

Other measures include EEG (heart rate), EEG (brain activity) and EMG (muscle tension). The aim is to use the feedback to change physiological activity.

Because it is reinforcing, the behaviour becomes more likely to be repeated.

Biofeedback has been used to treat PTSD, a disorder that sometimes develops when a person experiences a traumatic event.

- **E** – Additionally, Lemaire *et al.* (2011) found that doctors reported less stress after using biofeedback daily for a one-month period.
- **L** – These findings suggest that biofeedback can be successful at managing the negative effects of stress.

- **E** – Unlike drugs, biofeedback also offers a long-lasting way of managing stress.
- **L** – This means that biofeedback is a useful alternative when other methods cannot be used.

- **E** – The technique has also been used in a variety of populations from children to military personnel.
- **L** – The popularity of biofeedback would seem to be because it is a versatile technique for managing and coping with stress.

FURTHER EVALUATION

 P – Biofeedback has several limitations…

…compared with other stress management techniques, such as drugs.

- **E** – For example, it is a relatively lengthy treatment, typically lasting more than a month.
- **E** – It also requires some effort from the person undertaking it, and uses expensive equipment, which requires supervision.
- **L** – This means that alternative approaches may be more preferable if time and effort are important factors in stress reduction.

P – Unconscious operant conditioning may be irrelevant…

…in biofeedback's success as a stress management technique.

- **E** – For example, relaxation or the placebo effect could explain why biofeedback has beneficial outcomes.
- **E** – Relaxation is sufficient to reduce sympathetic nervous system activity, and the presence of specialised equipment might make people *believe* the technique will be effective.
- **L** – This means that the theoretical reason for biofeedback's success might be completely mistaken.

CHOOSE THE RIGHT ANSWER

Which **two** of the following are **not** features of biofeedback? (Tick **two** boxes only.)

A Combines biological and psychological processes ☐

B Involves learning to exert voluntary control over involuntary processes ☐

C Leads to an increase in physiological activity ☐

D Is based on the principles of classical conditioning ☐

E Involves the use of relaxation techniques ☐

Answers on page 364

 DRAWING CONCLUSIONS

A researcher wanted to see if the high levels of sympathetic nervous system activity seen in PTSD sufferers could be reduced by biofeedback training. A hundred military personnel were randomly allocated to either an experimental group (who received biofeedback training) or a control group (who received no training). The physiological activity of all of the participants was measured before the study began. After the study was over, physiological activity was measured again. The results of the study are shown in the table below.

	Experimental group (Biofeedback training)	Control group (No biofeedback training)
Number showing a decrease in physiological activity	36	18
Number showing no change or an increase in physiological activity	14	32

State **one** findings from the study and draw **one** conclusion. (State what the findings show.) *(2 marks)*

Finding 1

Conclusion 1

Answers on page 364

 Link

Operant conditioning is discussed further as part of the behaviourist approach. You can read about this on pages 126–127 of The Complete Companion Student Book, Year 1 /AS.

 FILL IN THE BOXES

For the very last time, we need to return to an activity that you've done previously. As before, the table below has the same six questions that were asked about drug therapy and SIT. We now have an extra column headed 'Biofeedback'. Transfer your 'yes' and 'no' answers for drug therapy and SIT to the relevant boxes, and complete the boxes for biofeedback. You now have a table that allows you to offer comparative evaluation for all three of the therapies you need to know about. Once you've completed the table, head for the Applying your knowledge activity where Chris is waiting for you!

	BZs *or* BBs	SIT	Biofeedback
Is the therapy effective in reducing stress?			
Does the therapy require time/effort from the user?			
Does the therapy lead to biological dependence?			
Does the therapy have unpleasant side effects?			
Does the therapy only address the symptoms of stress rather than its causes?			
Is the therapy widely available and relatively inexpensive?			

Answers on page 364

 APPLYING YOUR KNOWLEDGE

Chris now knows about a biological approach to managing stress (drugs) and a psychological approach (SIT). He is still undecided about which therapy he should use, so asks you if there is any form of therapy which combines biological and psychological processes. You describe what is involved in biofeedback to him, and he seems to be impressed by its potential. However, he really can't decide which of the three to choose.

Based on the table in the 'Fill in the boxes' activity, what are you going to advise Chris to do? *(6 marks)*

Answers on page 364

KEY TERMS

- Emotion-focused coping
- Problem-focused coping
- Tend-and-befriend response

Possible essay question

Discuss research into gender differences in coping with stress. *(16 marks)*

Other possible exam questions ...

+ Outline **one** study which has investigated gender differences in coping with stress. *(4 marks)*

+ Evaluate findings from research studies into gender differences in coping with stress. *(8 marks)*

★ Exam tip

In a 16-mark extended writing question, the maximum number of AO3 marks available is 10. If you aim for 25–30 words per mark, your evaluation will need to be around 250–300 words in total.

❗ Think

If there are significant physiological and psychological gender differences, should we have written separate books for male and female students?

MUST know ...

Physiological differences

Although there are similarities in how men and women respond to stress, there are important differences. For example, testosterone levels increase in men when confronted with a stressor.

Testosterone dampens oxytocin, a hormone that promotes bonding feelings. So, while men respond to stress by becoming aggressive, women 'tend' (to their offspring) and 'befriend' (other group members for mutual defence) because their oxytocin is unsuppressed.

Psychological differences

It has been claimed that men adopt a 'problem-focused' (PF) and women an 'emotion-focused' (EF) coping style in response to stressors (Peterson *et al.*, 2006).

These coping differences may occur because men and women typically face different kinds of stressor.

 P – Women do not always 'tend-and-befriend'...

...when confronted by a stressor.

- **E** – For example, females behave aggressively in situations requiring defence, such as threats to their offspring.

 P – One problem with research into coping styles is...

...that it relies on potentially unreliable self-report measures.

- **E** – For example, men and women may differ in their willingness to reveal the emotional side of their coping.

P – The claim that men and women use different coping styles is...

...not supported by much research.

- **E** – For example, Hamilton & Fagot (1988) found no differences in coping styles used by male and female undergraduates.

SHOULD know ...

Physiological differences

Similarities include increased adrenaline, noradrenaline, cortisol, and oxytocin.

Taylor *et al.* (2000) propose that 'tend-and-befriend' is a more adaptive response for women because of differential parental investment in the offspring: such behaviour maximises their own, and their offspring's, survival chances.

Psychological differences

PF coping involves tackling the problem itself, whereas EF coping involves tackling the symptoms of stress, such as the anxiety that accompanies it.

Men identify relationship, finance and work-related events as most stressful, whereas women identify family and health-related issues. The former require PF and the latter EF strategies (Matud, 2004).

- **E** – Also, females whose offspring are mobile shortly after birth flee rather than stay huddled together.
- **L** – This shows that females adopt a variety of strategies to defend against stressors, rather than only 'tending-and-befriending'.

- **E** – Women may be more, and men less, willing to report their emotional difficulties.
- **L** – This means that reported differences in coping style may be a reflection of social desirability responding.

- **E** – Other research (e.g. Peterson *et al.*, 2006) has found that some men use EF rather than PF coping.
- **L** – This means that the simple division of men as users of PF, and women as EF, coping styles is far too simplistic.

 P – Social support may be a confounding variable...

...in research into coping styles.

- **E** – For example, women are more likely than men to receive social support when confronted by a stressor.
- **E** – Social support is extremely effective in reducing how much stress people experience.
- **L** – This means that women may use a different coping style because they experience less stress than men do.

P – Lifestyle differences may play a role...

...in gender differences in coping style.

- **E** – For example, it has been argued that men experience more job-related stress than women do.
- **E** – However, Frankenhauser (1986) found that women in non-traditional gender roles (e.g. bus drivers) show higher stress hormone levels than women in traditional roles.
- **L** – This suggests that coping styles may be a consequence of the different types of stressors to which men and women are traditionally exposed.

CHOOSE THE RIGHT ANSWER

Which **one** of the following physiological activities only occurs in men in response to a stressor? (Tick **one** box only.)

A Increase in adrenaline output ☐

B Increase in the production of cortisol ☐

C Increase in the production of oxytocin ☐

D Increase in testosterone production ☐

E Increase in noradrenaline output ☐

Answers on page 364

 FILL IN THE BOXES

Complete the sentences in columns two, three, and four.

	This can be defined as…	An example is…	The gender this is typically seen in is…
Problem-focused coping style			
Emotion- focused coping style	This can be defined as…	An example is…	The gender this is typically seen in is…

Answers on page 364

 MATCH THEM UP

Match up the researchers to the statement that best describes their research.

1	Frankenhauser (1986)	A	Male and female undergraduates do not differ in their coping styles.
2	Hamilton & Fagot (1988)	B	The type of coping style used depends on which events men and women identify as most stressful.
3	Peterson *et al.* (2006)	C	Women in non-traditional gender roles show higher stress hormone levels than women in traditional roles.
4	Matud (2004)	D	Some men use emotion-focused coping styles.

Answers on page 364

 RESEARCH ISSUES

One way in which research into coping styles has been studied is through the use of self-report scales. Although gender differences in coping styles have been discovered, self-report scales may lack validity. Explain what is meant by validity, and why self-report scales may lack validity. *(4 marks)*

Answers on page 364

APPLYING YOUR KNOWLEDGE

Kitty and Charlie were preparing for their psychology exams. Charlie threw his file down on the floor and exploded with rage. 'There's too much of this stuff for me to learn,' he screamed. Kitty agreed that there was, but said that she was going to spend time with her friends, and probably have an evening at the cinema.

Using your knowledge of gender differences in coping with stress, explain Kitty and Charlie's different reactions to the stress of revising for exams. *(6 marks)*

Answers on page 364

Link

Gender bias in psychology is discussed on pages 42 and 43 of The Complete Companion Student Book, Year 2.

KEY TERMS

- Emotional support
- Esteem support
- Instrumental support

Possible essay question

Discuss the role played by **one or more** types of social support in coping with stress. *(16 marks)*

Other possible exam questions …

+ Explain what is meant by 'esteem social support'. *(2 marks)*
+ Distinguish between instrumental and emotional social support. *(2 marks)*
+ Outline **one** study which has investigated the role of social support in coping with stress. *(4 marks)*
+ Evaluate research into two different forms of social support. *(8 marks)*

 Exam tip

Remember that there are three types of social support. You could be asked to explain what they involve or to distinguish between them. If you are asked to distinguish between them you must do more than just explain what each is in order to gain full credit.

MUST know …

Types of social support

Social support is the help we receive from people during stressful times.

Instrumental support is when direct aid and material sources are offered.

Emotional support involves focusing on the anxiety a person is feeling, and trying to reduce it.

Esteem support involves increasing a person's sense of self-worth so that they can feel more confident about coping with both instrumental and emotional issues.

The **buffering hypothesis** proposes that social support protects people from stress because it helps them to think about stress differently.

 P – The effectiveness of social support…

…has been demonstrated in some research studies.

- **E** – For example, Kamarck *et al.* (1990) studied participants attempting a stressful mental task either alone or with a close same-sex friend for company.

 P – There are gender differences…

…in the type of social support used by men and women.

- **E** – For example, Lucknow *et al.* (1998) found that women are more likely than men to use emotional social support.

 P – There are cultural differences…

…in the type of social support people use.

- **E** – For example, Bailey & Dua (1999) found that participants from individualistic cultures (e.g. Anglo-Australian) preferred instrumental social support.

SHOULD know …

Types of social support

Nabi *et al.'s* (2013) research suggests that perceptions of social support are directly correlated with the number of friends we have.

The focus is on *doing* something, such as providing money, and is a problem-focused approach.

This includes listening or offering advice, and is an emotion-focused approach.

Typically, this involves someone in a close relationship making a person feel better about themselves.

This kind of support is instrumental, because it is problem-focused.

- **E** – Those attempting the task with a friend showed lower physiological reactions (e.g. heart rate) compared with those attempting the task alone.
- **L** – This shows that social support can have a direct physiological effect and lower activity of the autonomic nervous system.

- **E** – However, men are more likely than women to use instrumental social support.
- **L** – This suggests than when social support is needed, men prefer it to be more problem- than emotion-focused.

- **E** – However, participants from collectivist cultures (e.g. Asian) use emotional support more.
- **L** – These findings probably reflect differences in how interconnected their societies are.

FURTHER EVALUATION

 P – Social support may be neither important nor beneficial…

…in managing the negative effects of stress.

- **E** – For example, Kobasa *et al.* (1985) found that social support was much less important than hardiness in reducing stress levels.
- **E** – Kiecolt-Glaser & Newton (2001) found that social support was not always beneficial when stress was the result of strained friendships or relationships.
- **L** – This suggests that social support might be over-valued as a way of coping with stress.

P – Pets may be just as good as humans…

…as a form of support.

- **E** – For example, Allen (2003) found that pets were beneficial in reducing children's blood pressure and cardiovascular risks in the elderly.
- **E** – Even talking to pets can be more effective than talking to people in reducing stress!
- **L** – This suggests that we should value our pets, as much as we value our friends, as forms of support in coping with stress.

CHOOSE THE RIGHT ANSWER

Which **one** of the following is not a **type** of social support?
(Tick **one** box only.)

A Providing direct aid and material sources. ☐

B Increasing a person's sense of self-worth. ☐

C Protecting people from stress because it helps
them to think about stress differently. ☐

D Focusing on the anxiety a person is feeling, and
trying to reduce it. ☐

Answers on page 364

FILL IN THE BOXES

Define, and give an example of, each of the three types of social
support identified below.

Social support type	Definition	Example
Emotional support		
Esteem support		
Instrumental support		

Answers on page 364

APPLYING YOUR KNOWLEDGE

Bruce, from Australia, and Ravi,
from India, were about to take their
psychology exam. Lou-Anne, from
America, and Steve, from England,
joined them in the cafeteria. All four
students were nervous. 'What we need
is help from other people to calm us
down,' said Bruce.

'You mean social support?' said Steve.

'Yes, but there are different types of social support.' said Ravi.

'I think we'll differ in the kind of support we prefer.' said Lou-Anne.

Using your knowledge of gender and culture differences in social
support, identify the different kinds of social support each student is
likely to have sought. *(4 marks)*

Student	Social support sought
Bruce	
Steve	
Ravi	
Lou-Anne	

Answers on page 364

RESEARCH ISSUES

A student researcher measured 'perceived social support' in 13 members
of her psychology class who had Facebook accounts. As in Nabi *et
al.* (2013), perceived social support was measured using the 12-item
Multidimensional Scale of Perceived Social Support devised by Zimet *et
al.* (1988). This includes statements such as 'My family really tries to help
me', which are rated on a 7-point scale. Participants were also asked how
many Facebook friends they had. The student then drew a scattergram,
which is shown below.

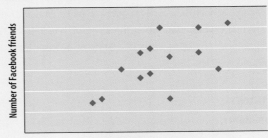

Perceived social support

(a) The student was hoping to replicate Nabi *et al.*'s findings. Explain
why her experimental hypothesis is likely to have been one-tailed.
(2 marks)

(b) What kind of correlation does the scattergram show? *(1 mark)*

(c) The student wanted to use Pearson's 'r' to determine whether
the correlation was significant. Identify **two** criteria for using a
parametric test of correlation. *(2 marks)*

(d) What test of correlation could the researcher have used if the criteria
for using Pearson's test were not met? *(1 mark)*

(e) The researcher set her significance level at $p < 0.05$. She found a
correlation of .30. Using the table on page 30 of The Complete
Companion Student Book, Year 2, explain whether the correlation is
statistically significant or not. Remember, you will also need to know
the sample size and whether the experimental hypothesis was one-
or two-tailed. *(3 marks)*

Answers on page 364

Outline the main features of the sympathomedullary pathway. *(4 marks)*

In the sympathomedullary pathway, the hypothalamus activates the sympathetic branch of the autonomic nervous system. Adrenaline and noradrenaline are released into the bloodstream by the adrenal medulla, producing the fight-or-flight response. Adrenaline and noradrenaline target organs like the heart, causing it to beat faster. Increases in heart rate, blood pressure, and muscle tension prepare us to deal with the stressor. The body returns to its normal resting state when the stressor has passed. However, this occurs relatively slowly, and so our body stays in a state of arousal for a while even though the stressor has passed.

> This student has worked really hard to impress the examiner, and has been very successful!!

Level 4 (4 marks)

Examiner's comments: AO1 The answer provides clear knowledge of the sympathomedullary pathway. It is accurate and detailed, and uses specialist terminology throughout.

Evaluate research into the role of stress in immunosuppression **and/or** cardiovascular disorders. *(8 marks)*

The role of stress in cardiovascular disorders is supported by studies on people with reduced blood flow to the heart. Sheps et al. found that people who showed erratic heartbeats when asked to do a public speaking test were significantly more likely to die from cardiovascular disorders than those whose heartbeats remained stable.

> This paragraph describes a relevant study's findings, but doesn't use the findings in an evaluative way.

A lot of this research uses self-report methods, like questionnaires. This means that we need to be careful when we interpret the results because self-report measures might produce stronger, but unjustified, correlations between higher perceived stress and cardiovascular symptoms.

> This is more evaluative, but needs a relevant study to illustrate the point being made.

Some stressors might actually improve the immune system rather than make it worse. Segerstrom and Miller's meta-analysis of research says that acute stressors promote the body's ability to fight infection. This means that in some situations stress may be beneficial to the body's immune system.

> Again, this is relevant. However, the point needs to be be more detailed.

Level 2 (3–4 marks)

Examiner's comments: AO3 The AO3 in this answer isn't particularly effective. Some appropriate material has been selected, but more could have been made of it. This answer highlights the need to use what you know rather than merely regurgitate it.

Discuss research into daily hassles **and/or** life changes as a source of stress. *(16 marks)*

Daily hassles include everyday work concerns and issues arising from family life. Kanner et al. studied 100 participants aged 45–67 and found a negative correlation between the frequency of reported daily hassles and psychological well-being. They found daily hassles were also a better predictor of well-being than life changes were.

One explanation for the effects of daily hassles is that when a lot of them happen it builds up and causes constant frustration and overload, which cause serious stress reactions like anxiety and depression.

Life changes may be positive or negative, such as marriage or bereavement. Change requires effort to adapt, and this may affect our health. Chronic stress due to major life changes make us more vulnerable to daily hassles, which may make the stress caused by the life changes worse. Major life changes might also use up a person's resources so they can't cope with daily hassles as well.

The stress of life changes can be measured using the Social Readjustment Rating Scale (SRRS). This is made up of 43 life events each of which has a LCU score. The 'Death of a spouse' life event is the most stressful and scores 100 LCUs. A person says which of the life events has occurred in the last year and the scores are added up to give a total LCU score.

A strength of life changes research is that it has provided important insights into the possible causes of physical and psychological problems. Heikkinen and Lonqvist found that life changes such as family problems and financial troubles were associated with suicides in Finland. This suggests that this kind of research can be valuable in understanding important human behaviour.

A major weakness of research into both life changes and daily hassles is that it is correlational and doesn't allow causal relationships to be established. The negative thinking in depression might cause people to report higher severity of hassles, so it could be that depression is causing the hassles not the other way round. Also, Brown suggests people with high anxiety levels are more likely to be both more prone to illness and more likely to report negative life events. This means that we need to be cautious when interpreting correlational research findings in this area.

There are individual differences in perceptions of stressful events. For example, Miller et al. found that men associate pets with hassles, while women associate them with uplifting feelings. Also, the SRRS ignores the fact that some life changes can be more stressful for some people than others, as it gives the same score. This means that it is difficult to measure life changes and daily hassles objectively.

An important methodological issue in life changes and daily hassles research is that it relies on peoples' memories of events. Rahe found that the recall reliability depends on the time interval between test and retest. However, Hardt et al. found moderate to good reliability of recall for most childhood experiences and Charles et al. found that keeping a daily diary of hassles led to a more accurate record of events than retrospective recall. Since most findings are similar to Hardt et al.'s, and there are methodologies that avoid the problem of retrospective recall, this suggests that we can gain valid data.

Level 4 (13–16 marks)

Examiner's comments: AO1 Detailed, accurate and well organised. This answer earns top AO1 marks.

AO3 The evaluation is thorough and a broad range of evidence has been used effectively. This is a clear Level 4 response to the question.

Examiner's comments

Using a research study can be an effective way to gain AO1 marks.

This AO1 paragraph is short, but successfully explains how daily hassles might cause stress.

Another clear and detailed AO1 paragraph, this time focusing on life changes.

Good, clear and accurate description of the SRRS, and credited as AO1.

A clear AO3 paragraph that makes some good use of research to support the AO1.

Another clear AO3 paragraph, this time focusing on the issues raised by correlational research.

This AO3 point follows the PEEL route, identifying the point, giving evidence to support it, followed by elaboration and a conclusion.

Using methodology is an effective way to gain AO3 credit, as long as it is clearly explained, as it is here.

Outline findings from research into the effects of workload **and/or** control on workplace stress. *(6 marks)*

Examiner's comments

The job-strain model of workplace stress proposes that the workplace causes stress when a person has a high workload and low job control. Marmot et al.'s study of civil servants found low job control and high workload was strongest among the junior grade workers, and wasn't reduced by high levels of social support. The study also found that coronary heart disease (CHD) was associated with low job control, but not with high workload so the junior staff were most affected.

> A clear outline of Marmot and his colleagues' findings.

Johansson et al. studied manual labourers at a Swedish sawmill and found that workers with a high workload and low control had higher adrenaline levels and illness rates than those with a low workload and high control. Both groups were matched on important factors like education and job experience, and the workers with the high workload and low control also reported more social isolation.

> These findings are also outlined accurately.

Level 4 (6 marks)

Examiner's comments: AO1 The findings of two relevant studies have been outlined accurately. The answer clearly demonstrates sound knowledge and understanding of the findings of research in this area.

Discuss drug therapy **and/or** stress inoculation therapy as a way of managing and coping with stress. *(16 marks)*

Drugs such as BZs reduce stress by slowing down central nervous system activity and make people feel relaxed. They increase the activity of GABA, which makes it harder for neurons to be stimulated by other neurotransmitters. Serotonin has an arousing effect on the brain and BZs reduce serotonin activity.

> A clear AO1 paragraph explaining how BZs work to reduce stress.

Betablockers work on the sympathetic nervous system so the person feels calmer and less anxious because their heart rate, blood pressure and breathing rates don't increase. Betablockers bind to receptors in the heart and other organs, reducing adrenaline and noradrenaline's effects.

> Another AO1 paragraph, this time focusing on betablockers.

Stress inoculation therapy is a type of CBT so helps change how people think about stressors and is made up of three parts. First the therapist and client find out what is causing the stress and the client is taught to see threats as problems to be solved. They also recognise the maladaptive strategies they use to deal with them. Then they are taught coping skills and these are rehearsed in the therapy session. After this, they apply their coping skills in increasingly stressful situations in the real world.

> A reasonably well-constructed AO1 paragraph on stress inoculation therapy

Kahn et al. found that BZs were much more effective than a placebo at treating anxiety and stress, and Lockwood found that betablockers were effective in reducing stress. These findings suggest that drug therapies can be beneficial, at least when the stressor is a short-term one.

> A concise AO3 paragraph relating to the strengths of drug therapy.

Examiner's comments

Two advantages of drug therapies are that they require little effort from users and work quickly. Drugs require users to do nothing other than remember to take their medication, whereas psychological therapies, like SIT, require time, effort and motivation. This explains why some people prefer a quick and effort-free therapy to a slow and effortful therapy to manage their stress.

> Comparing therapies can be an effective way to gain AO3 marks.

Drug therapies only treat the symptoms of stress not the underlying causes of it. The drugs only work as long as you keep taking them, and whatever caused the stress in the first place doesn't go away. This means that psychological methods may be preferable since they address the source of the stress and not just the symptoms it produces.

> This AO3 paragraph needs further elaboration.

One disadvantage of SIT is that it can be time-consuming and can take up to a year for some clinical disorders. Some people may not want to spend this much time and they may not want to change their way of thinking. This means that, although it is effective, SIT might not be suitable for everyone.

> Again, creditable as AO3, but in need of clarity and elaboration.

SIT is effective in treating a variety of different stressors and Jay and Elliott found SIT reduced the stress experienced by parents whose children were undergoing medical procedures. The therapy has also been successfully applied to academic stress, the stress of public speaking, and anxiety reduction in phobics, suggesting that SIT is a useful psychological alternative to biological therapies, like drugs.

> An AO3 paragraph which follows the PEEL formula, but the strengths of SIT would have been better placed before its limitations.

Level 3 (9–12 marks)

Examiner's comments: AO1 This answer adopts the 'breadth' approach and describes both drug therapy and SIT. Appropriate material has been selected, and the answer is generally accurate and reasonably detailed.

AO3. There is some reasonable evaluation, although better organisation would have made this more effective than it was. Specialist terms are used appropriately. This answer is at the top end of Level 3, but with better organisation would have made Level 4.

Discuss biofeedback as a way of managing and coping with stress. *(16 marks)*

Biofeedback combines biological and psychological approaches to get someone to have voluntary control over involuntary behaviour. First, the client learns relaxation techniques which reduce sympathetic nervous system activity and activates parasympathetic activity. This reduces stress symptoms because adrenaline and noradrenaline aren't being produced.

> A reasonably clear opening AO1 paragraph explaining the nature of biofeedback.

Next, machines measure aspects of sympathetic activity, like sweating by using things like skin conductance response while the client relaxes. The machines give feedback about the biological activity by using either light or sound. The machine could also measure heart-rate or brain activity, but the point is to use the feedback to change the biological activity.

> Development of the opening paragraph, creditable as AO1.

Lowering the physiological activity is rewarding and so it reinforces the behaviour that causes it, which means it is more likely that that behaviour will be repeated in the future. After this has been done, the new learning is applied to the real world at stressful times.

> Further description gaining AO1 credit.

One strength of biofeedback is that research studies have demonstrated it is effective. Bradley found that biofeedback users had significantly fewer muscle-tension headaches than people using relaxation alone. Also, Lemaire et al. found that doctors reported less stress after using biofeedback every day for one month. These findings suggest that biofeedback can successfully manage the negative effects of stress.

> Using phrases such as 'one strength of' shows the examiner that this is intended as AO3.

A second strength of biofeedback is that it has advantages over other stress management techniques. For example, it is appropriate to use with children, unlike drugs or SIT. Unlike drugs, biofeedback is non-invasive and offers a long-lasting way of managing stress. This means that biofeedback is a useful alternative when other methods can't be used.

> Comparing one therapy with another therapy can be an effective way to gain AO3 marks, as can be seen here.

However, biofeedback has several limitations compared with other stress management techniques, like drugs. It takes a long time to complete, usually lasting more than a month, and it requires some effort from the client. This means that alternative approaches may be more preferable if time and effort are important factors in stress reduction.

> This AO3 point clearly explains one problem with biofeedback.

Unconscious operant conditioning may be irrelevant in biofeedback's success and it could be that relaxation might be why biofeedback is beneficial, because relaxing will reduce sympathetic nervous system activity. It might also be the placebo effect, where the presence of specialised equipment might make people believe the technique will be effective. If either of these are true, then it means that the theoretical reason for biofeedback's success might be completely wrong.

> Another clear AO3 point, identifying the point, elaborating on it and then linking back to the original point.

Level 4 (13–16 marks)

Examiner's comments: AO1 Accurate and generally well-detailed description of biofeedback, making good use of specialist terminology.

AO3 Clear and effective evaluation, with all the points elaborated appropriately. A clear Level 4 answer.

Discuss research into gender differences in coping with stress. *(16 marks)*

Men and women respond to stress in similar ways, including increased adrenaline, noradrenaline, cortisol, and oxytocin. However, there are also important physiological differences, for example, testosterone levels increase in men when confronted with a stressor.

> A good opening AO1 paragraph explaining how men and women physiologically respond to a stressor.

Testosterone reduces oxytocin, a hormone that promotes bonding feelings. This means that while men tend to respond aggressively to stress, women tend to their offspring and befriend other group members for mutual defence, because their oxytocin has not been reduced by testosterone. Taylor et al. suggests that because women have greater parental investment, 'tend-and-befriend' is a more adaptive response for them because it maximises the chances of them, and their offspring, surviving.

> Another good AO1 paragraph, this time linking hormones to behaviour.

Men tend to adopt a 'problem-focused' coping style in response to stress, while women adopt an 'emotion-focused' style of coping, showing that there are psychological differences, too. Problem-focused coping involves addressing the problem itself, whereas emotion-focused coping tackles the symptoms of stress, like the anxiety that comes with it. This might be because men and women face different types of stressors. According to Matud, men identify relationship, finance and work-related events as most stressful, which require problem-focused coping strategies, while women identify family and health-related issues, which require more emotion-focused coping strategies.

> A clear explanation, using examples, of problem-focused and emotion-focused coping, gaining AO1 credit.

One problem with research into coping styles is they rely on unreliable self-report measures. Men and women may differ in their willingness to reveal the emotional side of their coping, with women being more willing to report their emotional difficulties than men. This means that any differences in coping style may reflect social desirability, rather than a genuine gender difference.

> Evaluating the methodology used in research is an effective way to gain AO3 credit, as long as it is clearly explained, as it is here.

There is not much research support for the claim that men and women use different coping styles. For example, Hamilton and Fagot found no differences in coping styles used by male and female undergraduates and other research (e.g. Peterson et al.) has found that some men use emotion-focused rather than problem-focused coping. This means that saying men use problem-focused, and women use emotion-focused, coping styles is far too simplistic.

> This AO3 point identifies the point, giving evidence to support it, followed by elaboration and a conclusion.

A confounding variable in research into coping styles may be social support. This support is extremely effective in reducing how much stress people experience and women are more likely than men to receive social support when confronted by a stressor. This means that women may use a different coping style because they experience less stress than men do.

> Suggesting an alternative explanation for behaviour is also an effective way to gain AO3 credit.

Level 3 (9–12 marks)

Examiner's comments: AO1 There is a lot of detailed AO1 in this answer, demonstrating good knowledge and understanding of the topic.

AO3 Evaluation here is thorough and effective, but there are not many points made. For a Level 4 mark, we would expect to see more AO3 points.

Discuss the role played by **one or more** types of social support in coping with stress. *(16 marks)*

Social support is the help we receive from people during stressful times and Nabi et al.'s research suggests that perceptions of social support are directly correlated with the number of friends we have. There are different types of social support, for example, instrumental support is when direct help and material sources, such as money, are offered. It takes a problem-focused approach because the focus is on doing something. The buffering hypothesis focuses on instrumental support because it says that social support protects people from stress because it helps them to think about stress in a different way.

Emotional support, on the other hand, is an emotion-focused approach. It involves focusing on anxiety someone is feeling and trying to reduce it by offering advice or listening. Esteem support involves someone close to you making you feel better about yourself. It tries to increase your sense of self-worth, so you can feel more confident about coping with things.

The effectiveness of social support has been demonstrated in some research studies. Kamarck et al. studied participants attempting a stressful mental task either alone or with a close same-sex friend for company. Those attempting the task with a friend showed lower physiological reactions, compared with those attempting the task alone. This shows that social support can have a direct physiological effect and lower the activity of the autonomic nervous system.

There are gender differences in the type of social support used by men and women. For example, Lucknow et al. found that women are more likely to use emotional social support and men are more likely to use instrumental social support. This suggests that when social support is needed, men prefer it to be more problem-focused than emotion-focused.

There are cultural differences in the type of social support people use. For example, Bailey and Dua found that participants from individualistic cultures preferred instrumental social support, while participants from collectivist cultures use emotional support more. These findings probably highlight the fact that collectivist cultures are more interconnected than individualistic cultures.

Social support may not be important or beneficial in managing the negative effects of stress. For example, Kobasa et al. found that social support was much less important than hardiness in reducing stress levels. Kiecolt-Glaser and Newton found that if the cause of someone's stress was strained friendships or relationships, then social support wasn't always beneficial. This research suggests that social support might be over-valued as a way of coping with stress.

Examiner's comments

This AO1 paragraph accurately and clearly describes the role of social support, making good use of research.

Another clear AO1 paragraph, this time focusing on emotional and esteem support.

A detailed AO3 paragraph that makes use of research to support the AO1.

AO3 marks can be gained by discussing cultural differences, or gender differences, in social support, as has been done in this and the following paragraph.

Detailed and effective AO3, making a point before elaborating on it and linking back.

Examiner's comments

Pets may be just as good as humans as a form of support. For example, Allen found that pets reduced children's blood pressure and lowered cardiovascular risks in the elderly. Even talking to pets can be more effective than talking to people in reducing stress, suggesting that we should consider our pets, as much as we value our friends, as forms of support in coping with stress.

A clear and well explained AO3 point with an appropriate conclusion makes this an effective piece of evaluation.

Level 4 (13–16 marks)

Examiner's comments: AO1 The answer is detailed, accurate and well organised.

AO3 A broad range of evaluative points have been used in reasonable depth, and specialist terms are used effectively.

KEY TERMS

- Limbic system
- Serotonin
- Testosterone

Possible essay question …

Discuss the role of neural **and/or** hormonal mechanisms in aggression. *(16 marks)*

Other possible exam questions …

+ Outline the role of the limbic system in aggression. *(4 marks)*
+ Outline the role played by serotonin in aggression. *(4 marks)*
+ Outline testosterone's role in aggression. *(4 marks)*
+ Evaluate the role played by **one** neural and **one** hormonal mechanism in aggression. *(8 marks)*

 Exam tip

Remember that 'neural influences' include both brain structures and neurotransmitters. You could write about either, or both, of these in your answer.

 Think

This topic suggests that aggressive behaviour is determined by our biology. To what extent does the evidence support this perspective?

MUST know …

Neural influences

Limbic System: Coordinates behaviour that satisfies emotional and motivational urges.

Amygdala: Evaluates sensory information and prompts a response. If certain areas are stimulated, animals respond aggressively.

Hippocampus: Involved in forming long-term memories. If one animal encounters another it has previously been attacked by, it responds aggressively.

Serotonin: Exerts a calming, inhibitory effect on neuronal firing in the amygdala. When serotonin levels are low, aggression is more likely.

Hormonal influences

Testosterone: Produces male characteristics, including aggression. Testosterone acts on brain areas involved in controlling aggression.

 P – The amygadala's role is backed by…

…research into studies into human aggression.

- **E** – For example, Pardini *et al.* (2014) carried out a longitudinal study of 56 male participants, with varying histories of violence.

 P – The role of the hippocampus in aggression is supported by…

…MRI scans of hippocampal asymmetry.

- **E** – For example, Raine *et al.* (2004) found that the hippocampus in the right and left hemispheres were different in size in convicted violent criminals but not in unconvicted violent criminals.

 P – There is some support for the serotonin deficiency hypothesis…

…to explain human and non-human aggression.

- **E** – For example, Duke *et al's.* (2013) meta-analysis of 175 studies found a small, inverse relationship between serotonin levels and human aggression.

SHOULD know …

Neural influences

Limbic system: The amygdala and hippocampus are associated with aggression.

Amygdala: Removing these areas of the amygdala eliminates the aggressive response.

Hippocampus: Impaired functioning stops the nervous system putting stimuli into context. This may cause inappropriate aggressive responses. Habitually violent offenders, show impaired hippocampal functioning (Boccardi *et al.* 2010).

Serotonin: Drugs which deplete serotonin levels, are associated with increases in aggression in men, but *not* in women (Mann *et al.* 1990).

Hormonal influences

Testosterone: Removing testosterone reduces aggression. Reinstating normal levels leads to aggressive behaviour returning (Sapolsky, 1998).

- **E** – MRI scans showed that those with lower amygdala volumes exhibited higher levels of aggression and violence.
- **L** – This suggests that the amygdala plays a key role in evaluating sensory information; lower volume makes aggression more likely.

- **E** – Hippocampal asymmetry possibly arises early in brain development.
- **L** – These asymmetries might impair the ability of the hippocampi and amygdala to work together, leading to incorrect processing of emotional stimuli and inappropriate responses.

- **E** – Raleigh *et al.* (1991) and Rosado *et al.* (2010) found lower serotonin levels were associated with increased aggression in monkeys and dogs respectively.
- **L** – This suggests that low levels of serotonin could be a causal factor in aggression.

 FURTHER EVALUATION

 P – The role of testosterone in human aggression is seemingly supported…

…by a large number of research studies.

- **E** – For example, Dabbs *et al.* (1987) measured salivatory testosterone in violent and non-violent criminals.
- **E** – They found that those with the highest testosterone levels had a history of primarily violent crimes whereas those with the lowest levels had committed only non-violent crimes.
- **L** – This suggests that testosterone does play a role in human aggression.

P – However, the role of testosterone has been challenged…

…by studies failing to show a relationship between it and human aggression.

- **E** – For example, some research has shown *no* correlation between testosterone and *actual* violence in male prison inmates.
- **E** – Mazur (1985) suggests that testosterone may actually promote status-seeking behaviour, of which aggression is just one type.
- **L** – This suggests that the relationship between testosterone and aggression in humans might be more complex than has been suggested.

✓ CHOOSE THE RIGHT ANSWER

Which **two** of the following brain structures are believed to play a role in aggression? (Tick **two** boxes only.)

A	Amygdala	☐
B	Cerebellum	☐
C	Medulla	☐
D	Hippocampus	☐
E	Pons	☐

Answers on page 364

📖 RESEARCH ISSUES

Pardini *et al.* (2014) conducted a longitudinal study of 56 males, from childhood to adulthood. A longitudinal study is an observational research method in which data is gathered for the same subjects repeatedly over a period of time. Longitudinal research projects can extend over years or even decades. Pardini *et al.* found that those with lower amygdala volumes exhibited high levels of aggression and violence. The researchers believe that the amygdala plays an important role in evaluating the emotional importance of sensory information, and that lower amygdala volume compromises this ability and makes violent behaviour more likely.

Outline **one** strength and **one** limitation of using longitudinal studies in psychological research such as Pardini *et al*'s. *(4 marks)*

Answers on page 364

🔗 Link

See pages 140 and 141 of the Year 1/AS Revision and Exam Companion for an explanation of the way neurotransmitters, such as serotonin, and hormones, such as testosterone, work.

💡 DRAWING CONCLUSIONS

A researcher was interested in studying the effects of testosterone on the brain's threat response in males. She placed an advertisement in a local newspaper inviting healthy young men to take part in the study. The 16 participants were randomly allocated to either a control condition or an experimental condition. The control group participants were given a placebo, while the experimental group participants were given testosterone. During the study, all participants were given a drug that suppressed their own testosterone to ensure that the participants had similar levels during the study. Consequently, those who received testosterone only received enough to return their levels to the normal range. The researchers found that, compared with the control group, the experimental group participants showed increased reactivity of the amygdala when they viewed angry facial expressions.

(a) Name the sampling method used by the researcher. *(1 mark)*

(b) Outline **one** limitation of this sampling method. *(2 marks)*

(c) Why were the participants randomly allocated to the control and experimental groups? *(2 marks)*

(d) Identify **one** other important control that was applied in this study. *(1 mark)*

(e) Identify a statistical test that could have been used to analyse the results. Give **two** reasons for choosing this test. *(3 marks)*

Answers on page 364

⚙ APPLYING YOUR KNOWLEDGE

In August 1966, Charles Whitman killed his wife and mother before making his way to the University of Texas campus. Once there, he killed 15 people he did not know and wounded another 24 before being killed himself by the police. Whitman was apparently aware of his aggressiveness since, just before he embarked on the killing, he wrote a note:

'I don't quite know what compels me to type this letter… Lately I have been a victim of many unusual and irrational thoughts… I talk[ed] with a doctor once for about two hours and tried to convey to him my fears that I felt overcome by overwhelming violent impulses… After my death I wish that an autopsy would be performed on me to see if there is any visible physical disorder.'

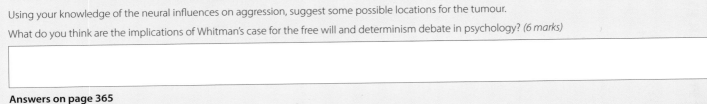

An autopsy revealed a small tumour in Whitman's brain. However, the wounds caused by the police gun fire made it difficult to establish the tumour's precise location.

Using your knowledge of the neural influences on aggression, suggest some possible locations for the tumour.

What do you think are the implications of Whitman's case for the free will and determinism debate in psychology? *(6 marks)*

Answers on page 365

KEY TERMS

- Genetic factors
- MAOA

Possible essay question ...

Outline and evaluate the role of genetic factors, including the MAOA gene, in aggression. *(16 marks)*

Other possible exam questions ...

+ Outline the findings from **one** study into genetic factors in aggression. *(4 marks)*

+ Explain how the MAOA gene might be involved in aggression. *(3 marks)*

+ Evaluate research findings into the role played by the MAOA gene in aggression. *(8 marks)*

 Exam tip

This topic is full of potential AO3 material. You'll need to think very carefully about how you organise your evaluation so that it is effective.

 Think

Are people who inherit a gene for a particular behaviour responsible for their actions, or is there nothing they can do to prevent the behaviour occurring?

MUST know ...

Genetic factors in agression

Twin studies: Monozygotic (MZ) twins share 100% of their genes, so should be more alike, in terms of their aggressive behaviour than dyzygotic (DZ) twins, who only share 50% of their genes.

Adoption studies: If an adoptee's aggressive behaviour correlates more with its biological parents than its adoptive parents, then a genetic influence is implied.

The role of MAOA: A gene responsible for producing an enzyme called monoamine oxidase A (MAOA) is associated with aggression. MAOA regulates serotonin metabolism.

MAOA-L: This variant (the 'warrior gene') is associated with *low* MAOA levels. It occurs in about two-thirds of people in populations with a history of warfare.

 P – One issue with this area of research is...

...that most studies have focused on people convicted of violent crime.

- **E** – However, convicted violent criminals form only a small sample of those who actually commit violent crime.

 P – It is difficult to establish genetic contributions...

...to aggressive behaviour.

- **E** – For example, more than one gene usually contributes to a behaviour, and there are many environmental influences on aggressive behaviour.

 P – There are methodological issues....

...with the measurement of aggressive behaviour.

- **E** – For example, Miles and Carey's (1997) meta-analysis found that the method of assessing aggression was a significant moderator of aggressive behaviour.

SHOULD know ...

Genetic factors in agresssion

In adult twins, about 50% of the variance in aggression towards others is due to genetics (Coccaro *et al.*, 1997).

Hutchings & Mednick (1975) found that a significant number of adopted boys with criminal convictions had convicted *biological* parents.

Many male members in one family who were particularly aggressive, showed abnormally low MAOA levels and a defect in this gene (Brunner *et al.*, 1993).

People with the MAOA-H variant (high MAOA levels) displayed *less* indirect aggression than those with the L variant. The latter were more likely to behave anti-socially as adults, but only after childhood maltreatment.

- **E** – Additionally, offenders designated as 'violent' on the basis of a court conviction are not necessarily the most persistent or most serious offenders.
- **L** – This might explain why many studies have found little, or no, evidence of heritability for violence.

- **E** – Genetic and environmental factors may also interact with each other.
- **L** – This means that the connection between genetic factors and aggression is far from straightforward.

- **E** – Genetic factors explained a large proportion of the variance in aggressive behaviour in self-report method studies, but observational studies showed significantly less genetic influence, and more environmental influence.
- **L** – These inconsistencies from different measurements make assessing the relative contributions of genetic and environmental factors difficult.

 **FURTHER EVALUATION**

 P – The role of the MAOA gene in serious violent behaviours is...

...supported by research studies.

- **E** – For example, Tiihonen *et al.* (2015) found that extremely violent behaviour in Finnish prisoners was associated with the MAOA-L gene in combination with the CDH13 gene.
- **E** – There was no substantial evidence for either of these genes in non-violent offenders, showing that this genetic combination is specific to violent behaviour only.
- **L** – This suggests that MAOA does play a role in some types of aggression.

 P – Gender differences in aggressive behaviour...

...might be explained by the MAOA gene.

- **E** – For example, the MAOA gene is linked to the X chromosome, of which men have one whereas women have two.
- **E** – In women, an unaffected second X chromosome with a 'normal' MAOA gene may prevent the expression of an abnormal version of it.
- **L** – This could explain why males are typically more aggressive than females.

CHOOSE THE RIGHT ANSWER

Which **one** of the following has not been investigated in the study of genetic factors in aggression? (Tick **one** box only.)

A Pairs of twins raised together ☐

B Families ☐

C Similarities between MZ and DZ twins ☐

D MAOI ☐

E Adopted children ☐

Answers on page 365

 DRAWING CONCLUSIONS

Twin studies assess the role of genetic factors by using the *concordance rate*. This is defined as the probability that a second twin will display a behaviour given that the first twin already displays it. To calculate the concordance rate, we find the number of twin pairs who both display a behaviour and divide it by the total number of twins we have studied.

A student conducted a very simple, small scale study on twin pairs in his school. He found five pairs of MZ twins and five pairs of DZ twins. The first twin in each of the pairs had been rated by his peers as aggressive (it was a very unusual school!). He asked one of his friends to observe the other twins and decide whether they were 'aggressive' or 'not aggressive'. The results are shown below:

MZ twin pair no.	First twin	Second twin	DZ twin pair no.	First twin	Second twin
1	Aggressive	Aggressive	1	Aggressive	Not aggressive
2	Aggressive	Aggressive	2	Aggressive	Aggressive
3	Aggressive	Not aggressive	3	Aggressive	Aggressive
4	Aggressive	Not aggressive	4	Aggressive	Not aggressive
5	Aggressive	Aggressive	5	Aggressive	Not aggressive

(a) Calculate the concordance rate for the MZ twins. *(1 mark)*

(b) Calculate the concordance rate for the DZ twins. *(1 mark)*

(c) What do the concordance rates for the MZ and DZ twins suggest about the role played by genetic factors in aggression? *(3 marks)*

Answers on page 365

 APPLYING YOUR KNOWLEDGE

Sara had read a really unusual report in a newspaper about a family in America. She told her friend Maia: 'A guy called Freeman May had a grandfather who was really aggressive. The grandfather used to beat both his wife and children with a belt. One of his sons, Landon May, was so aggressive he actually murdered a woman. The really strange thing is that *his* son ended up on death row in the same prison as him after he murdered one of his friend's parents. It just goes to prove it: some people really are 'natural born killers'. There just has to be a gene for aggression, and if you inherit it you're aggressive whether you want to be or not.'

Maia wasn't so convinced: 'Well, you might be right, but it's actually very difficult to work out what is a product of our genetic inheritance.'

Suggest three reasons Maia could have given to Sara as to why it is difficult to determine the role played by genetic factors in aggression. *(6 marks)*

Answers on page 365

🔗 **Link**

The issue of free will and determinism is discussed on pages 46 and 47 of *The Complete Companion Student Book, Year 2*.

KEY TERMS

- Ethological explanation
- Fixed action pattern
- Innate releasing mechanism

Possible essay question …

Discuss the ethological explanation of aggression. Include reference to innate mechanisms **and** fixed action patterns in your answer. *(16 marks)*

Other possible exam questions …

+ What are innate releasing mechanisms? *(2 marks)*
+ What are fixed action patterns? *(2 marks)*
+ Outline the ethological explanation of aggression. *(4 marks)*
+ Using research studies, evaluate the ethological explanation of aggression. *(6 marks)*

 Exam tip

If a question only requires evaluation (AO3), the marks awarded gives you an indication how much elaboration is required. With 6-mark questions, you would be expected to offer two or three elaborated points.

 Think

What are the issues with using research with stickleback fish to explain human aggression?

MUST know …

The ethological explanation

Aggression occurs when a very specific stimulus (a **sign stimulus**), triggers an **innate releasing mechanism (IRM)**. This IRM activates ('releases') a **fixed action pattern (FAP)**, which is an innate, stereotyped, behaviour produced by every member of a species.

The energy needed for this is called the **action specific energy (ASE)**. After each FAP, ASE must build up again.

The FAP can also be released if there is no sign stimulus, but the ASE is high enough.

Some aggressive behaviour is **ritualised** in the form of **threat displays**. This makes actual aggression less likely.

Predator species have instinctive inhibitions preventing them from using their natural weapons (e.g. strong teeth) against conspecifics.

 P – Ritualised aggression is seen in humans…

…and has the same benefits as for non-humans.
- **E** – For example, Hoebel (1967) found that Inuit Eskimos use song duels to settle grudges and disputes.

 P – Fixed action patterns are not simply innate…

…and can be modified by environmental factors.
- **E** – Lehrman (1953) says learning and experience interact with innate factors in complex ways.

 P – Lorenz's idea of 'instinctive inhibitions' is…

…not supported by evidence.
- **E** – Lorenz believed that predators with powerful natural weapons have instinctive inhibitions against using them on members of their own species.

SHOULD know …

The ethological explanation

In male stickleback fish, their red underbelly is a sign stimulus that triggers an IRM which activates the FAP of aggression.

In Lorenz's 'hydraulic model', ASE is like 'fluid' in a 'reservoir'. As it builds, it places pressure on a spring (the IRM) which is also being pulled by weights (the sign stimulus). When the ASE is high enough, and the sign stimulus is present, the FAP is released. In this case, spontaneous aggression occurs.

Gorillas pound their chests to intimidate a rival, and make their opponent back down.

Non-hunting species without natural weapons have not developed the same inhibitions.

- **E** – Ritualised displays are also seen in cultures where aggression is common, such as the Yanamomö people of South America.
- **L** – These examples show that even in highly aggressive cultures, ritualised aggression is used to prevent conflicts from escalating into dangerous physical aggression.

- **E** – Research also shows that there are subtle differences between conspecifics in the production of aggressive behaviour.
- **L** – This shows that aggressive behaviour patterns are not as 'fixed' as Lorenz claimed.

- **E** – However, male lions and chimpanzees routinely kill members of their own species.
- **L** – This suggests that killing conspecifics is not as rare as Lorenz believed.

FURTHER EVALUATION

 P – One weakness of Lorenz's hydraulic model is…

…that research studies contradict its claims.
- **E** – For example, the model says that aggressive behaviour cannot be performed again until the ASE that caused the FAP has built up again.
- **E** – However, Von Holst (1954) showed that performing an aggressive behaviour can increase rather than decrease the likelihood of further aggression.
- **L** – This suggests that Lorenz was wrong to claim that performing a FAP leads to a reduction in action-specific energy and the likelihood of further aggression.

 P – A human FAP of aggression is…

…no longer adaptive.
- **E** – Human behaviour is more flexible than that of non-humans, and we can respond to environmental challenges more effectively.
- **E** – Non-humans rely on stereotypical fixed patterns of behaviour to respond to environmental challenges.
- **L** – This means that while non-humans may respond aggressively to specific sign stimuli, human behaviour is far more varied and less predictable.

✓ CHOOSE THE RIGHT ANSWER

Which **one** of the following statements is true of ritualised aggression? (Tick **one** box only.)

A Ritualised aggression is never seen in humans. ☐

B Ritualised aggression involves costly and dangerous physical aggression. ☐

C Ritualised displays enable an individual to assess its relative strength before deciding to escalate a conflict. ☐

D Ritualised displays involve intimidation followed by aggression. ☐

Answers on page 365

MATCH THEM UP

Match up the ethological term to the correct description of it.

1	Innate releasing mechanism	**A**	A very specific stimulus that triggers an innate releasing mechanism.
2	Sign stimulus	**B**	The energy needed for an innate releasing mechanism to release a fixed action pattern.
3	Action specific energy	**C**	An innate, stereotyped, behaviour produced by all members of the same species.
4	Fixed action pattern	**D**	A neural network that is stimulated by a sign stimulus and activates the fixed action pattern associated with that sign stimulus.

Answers on page 365

⚙ APPLYING YOUR KNOWLEDGE

Tom was telling Duncan about a TV programme he'd recently seen. In it, two rival groups regularly met at a pre-arranged battle ground and then used bows to fire arrows at each other. However, the arrows had no flights on them, so where the arrow landed was a matter of luck.

'For a culture steeped in the knowledge and experience of birds, and who know the importance of feathers, they must be pretty stupid not to use feathers to make their arrows fly true,' said Tom. 'Not at all,' said Duncan. 'Thanks for telling me that. You've just given me a brilliant AO3 point for a question on the ethological explanation of aggression.'

What AO3 point do you think Duncan was going to make from the description Tom had given him? *(4 marks)*

Answers on page 365

💡 DRAWING CONCLUSIONS

A researcher investigated how aggressively a pair of male and female fish behaved under different living conditions. In one condition, the fish were kept in isolation from other fish. In the second condition, they lived with other fish in a communal tank. In the third condition, the fish were kept behind a glass screen that allowed them to see the fish in the other section of the tank. The number of aggressive behaviours seen is shown in the table below:

	Living in isolation	Living in a community	Living behind glass
Average frequency of chasing attacks by both fish	47	9	17

(a) Draw a suitably labelled bar chart of the data in the above table. *(4 marks)*

(b) What is the main conclusion that can be drawn from the findings of this study? *(2 marks)*

(c) How could the concept of action specific energy be used to explain the aggression that was seen when the fish lived in isolation? *(3 marks)*

Answers on page 365

🔗 Link

The nature–nurture debate is discussed on pages 48 and 49 of The Complete Companion Student Book, Year 2.

KEY TERM

- Evolutionary explanations

Possible essay question ...

Discuss evolutionary explanations of human aggression. *(16 marks)*

Other possible exam questions ...

+ Outline what is meant by an 'evolutionary explanation' of human aggression. *(3 marks)*
+ Give **two** limitations of evolutionary explanations of human aggression. *(6 marks)*
+ Evaluate evolutionary explanations of human aggression. *(8 marks)*

 Exam tip

Remember that 'discuss' requires you to demonstrate both your AO1 skills and your AO3 skills.

 Think

Given its unfalsifiable nature, do you think evolutionary psychology can be considered scientific?

MUST know ...

Evolutionary explanations

Humans have evolved adaptations designed to harm others. These adaptations are fundamental and universal components of human nature.

Sexual Competition: Males use aggression to eliminate competition for females. This results in reproductive success, and a genetically transmitted tendency for males to be aggressive towards other males.

Sexual Jealousy: Men are constantly at risk of cuckoldry, as they cannot be certain of their paternity. So aggression is an adaptive strategy to deter a mate from sexual infidelity.

Warfare: This is costly, but any behaviour associated with warfare would have evolved because of its adaptive benefits for the individual and their offspring.

 P – There is support for the idea...

...that aggression and status are linked.

- **E** – For example, Daly and Wilson (1988) found that many tribal societies give higher status to those who have committed murder.

 P – One potential problem for evolutionary explanations is...

...explaining the apparent maladaptiveness of aggression.

- **E** – For example, violent behaviour can result in social ostracism, injury, or even death.

 P – Evolutionary explanations of aggression fail to explain...

...the levels of cruelty found in human conflicts.

- **E** – For example, they don't explain the wide scale slaughter of whole groups, such as in the Rwandan genocide of 1994.

SHOULD know ...

Evolutionary explanations

Aggression would have helped early humans solve adaptive problems. This would enhance survival and reproductive success.

Puts (2010) argues that male traits, such as aggression, seem to imply competition with other men did take place among ancestral males.

Buss (1988) identifies several 'mate retention' strategies, including violence towards both a partner and a perceived rival. Dobash and Dobash (1984) found that, in domestic violence cases, women cite extreme sexual jealousy as the main cause of violence against them.

Chagnon (1988) found that male warriors in traditional societies tend to have more sexual partners and more children.

- **E** – Even in industrialised societies, such as the USA, the most violent gang members often have the highest status among their peers.
- **L** – This suggests aggression is an important way of gaining status among males.

- **E** – This apparent maladaptiveness can only be explained if the benefits of aggression outweighed the costs, relative to other strategies, in our evolutionary past.
- **L** – If this is the case, then natural selection would favour the evolution of aggression, despite its apparent maladaptiveness.

- **E** – They also don't tell us why humans torture or mutilate their enemies when they have been defeated and thus are no longer a threat.
- **L** – This suggests that human cruelty in warfare may be more a consequence of de-individuation (see page xx) than of evolutionary adaptations.

FURTHER EVALUATION

P – Sex differences in aggressive behaviour...

...may be due to socialisation not evolution.

- **E** – Smetana (1989) found parents are likely to explain why misbehaviour was wrong to girls, but to punish boys physically, which might increase male physical violence.
- **E** – As girls learn they aren't as strong as boys, they might adopt more socially acceptable forms of aggression.
- **L** – This questions the claim that only males have evolved aggression: females might simply have evolved a different *form* of aggression.

 P – Evolutionary explanations for aggression in warfare are gender biased...

...and do not adequately reflect the behaviour of women in warfare.

- **E** – For example, female 'warriors' are almost unheard of, and women's participation in war is rare.
- **E** – This is fundamental to women's exclusion from warfare, as women simply do not increase their reproductive fitness as much as men do.
- **L** – Therefore, our understanding of the physically aggressive displays found in warfare is limited to the behaviour of males only.

✔ CHOOSE THE RIGHT ANSWER

Which **one** of the following is **not** an adaptive problem that could be solved through the use of aggression? (Tick **one** box only.)

A Intimidating rivals for females	☐
B Gaining resources	☐
C Deterring a partner from sexual infidelity	☐
D Maximising the risk of cuckoldry	☐

Answers on page 365

📖 RESEARCH ISSUES

One way of measuring sexual jealousy is Buss and Shackelford's (1997) *Mate Retention Inventory* (MRI). On this, participants are asked to indicate how often their partner has performed a particular behaviour in the past year, using scales ranging from 0 (never) to 3 (often). Statements on the scale include: 'I didn't take her to a party where other males would be present' and 'He became angry when I flirted too much'.

(a) Outline **one** ethical issue researchers would need to consider before using the MRI. *(2 marks)*

(b) Outline **one** limitation of the MRI as a self-report measure of sexual jealousy. *(2 marks)*

Answers on page 365

🔗 Link

See page 132 of The Complete Companion Student Book, Year 1/AS, for an explanation of the evolutionary approach to psychology.

⚙ APPLYING YOUR KNOWLEDGE

Nicholas had taken a fancy to Denise, but Denise never paid him much attention. One day when Nicholas knew Denise would be able to see him, Nicholas picked a fight with a group of other men who had done nothing to provoke him. 'How can she resist me now?' he thought. 'What an idiot,' thought Denise.

What does the above scenario suggest about evolutionary explanations of aggression? *(4 marks)*

Answers on page 365

💡 DRAWING CONCLUSIONS

A researcher studied ten members of a gang well known for its aggression. Each gang member was rated by his peers in terms of how violent they were considered to be. The researcher also asked each gang member to rate themselves and the others in terms of how much status each had in the gang's hierarchy (1 = highest, 10 = lowest). The researcher then ranked each gang member in terms of the two variables. Based on Campbell's (1993) research, it was predicted that there would be a positive correlation between how violent the gang members were and their status within the gang. The results are shown in the table below.

Gang Member	Ranking on the violence measure	Ranking on the status measure
A	3	6
B	4	7
C	1	1
D	8	8
E	10	9
F	7	4
G	9	5
H	5	3
I	2	2
J	6	10

(a) State a null hypothesis for this investigation. *(3 marks)*

(b) Was the hypothesis one- or two-tailed. Explain your answer. *(2 marks)*

(c) Give **two** reasons why Spearman's rho was used to analyse the data. *(2 marks)*

(d) The calculated value for Spearman's rho is .61. Is the correlation between the two variables significant at p < 0.05? Explain your answer. Use the table on page 31 of The Complete Companion Student Book to help you. *(3 marks)*

(e) The researcher concluded that aggression causes gang members to have a higher status within the gang. Why is this conclusion not justified? *(3 marks)*

Answers on page 365

KEY TERM

- Frustration–aggression hypothesis

Possible essay question …

Discus the frustration-aggression hypothesis as a social psychological explanation of human aggression. *(16 marks)*

Other possible exam questions …

+ Outline how the frustration-aggression hypothesis explains human aggression. *(4 marks)*

+ Outline **one** strength and **one** weakness of the frustration-aggression hypothesis. *(4 marks)*

+ Using psychological research, evaluate the frustration-aggression hypothesis of aggression. *(8 marks)*

 Exam tip

When you are asked to make a critical point (such as outlining a strength or weakness), the number of marks available indicates how much elaboration you are expected to give.

 Think

Do you think Berkowitz's revised Frustration–Aggression Hypothesis improves Dollard's original version?

MUST know …

The frustration-aggression hypothesis

Frustration is anything that prevents someone reaching a goal. The frustration-aggression hypothesis claims that frustration always leads to aggression.

Frustration leads to the arousal of an aggressive drive, which can be *relieved* through aggression.

Pastore (1952) argued that unjustified frustration produces the most aggression.

Aggression can be displaced if it isn't possible to behave aggressively towards the source of frustration.

Berkowitz (1989) argues that many unpleasant experiences can lead to aggression. Anything that prevents our goal being reached creates negative affect, and this, not frustration, leads to aggression.

 P – One strength of the frustration-aggression hypothesis is…

…that it can be used to explain mass killings.

- **E** – For example, Staub (1996) proposed that mass killings are often due to frustration caused by socio-economic difficulties, leading to 'scapegoating' and then aggression towards the 'scapegoat'.

 P – The frustration–aggression hypothesis can also explain…

…violent behaviour in football fans.

- **E** – For example, Priks (2010) used Swedish football teams' changed position in the league as a measure of frustration and the number of objects thrown during matches as a measure of aggression.

 P – A major weakness of the frustration-aggression hypothesis is…

…that not all is aggression is caused by frustration.

- **E** – For example, Reifman et al. (1991) found that as temperatures increased, so did the likelihood that pitchers would be aggressive to batters.

SHOULD know …

The frustration-aggression hypothesis

Although Dollard *et al.* claimed that frustration was a necessary condition for aggression, they also believed that contextual factors, such as the threat of punishment, can sometimes inhibit aggression.

This reduction is called **catharsis.**

Pastore found that people said they would be angrier if a bus they were waiting for simply didn't stop (unjustified) than if it didn't stop but had an 'out of service' sign clearly displayed (justified).

Displacement involves finding a 'scapegoat' in order for catharsis to occur.

For Berkowitz, the nature of the frustrating event is less important than how negative the resulting affect is.

- **E** – Goldhagen (1996) argued that ordinary Germans condoned the violence towards Jews after WW1, seeing as them being responsible for Germany's loss and subsequent plight.
- **L** – This shows that widespread frustration can have violent consequences for a 'scapegoat', especially when manipulated by propaganda.

- **E** – He found that when their team performed worse than expected, the fans threw more objects onto the pitch, and were more likely to fight with opposition supporters.
- **L** – This suggests that fans became more aggressive when expectations of good performance were frustrated, which supports the frustration–aggression hypothesis.

- **E** – Other aversive events, such as pain and noxious stimuli, can also lead to aggression.
- **L** – This does, however, support Berkowitz's revision of the frustration–aggression hypothesis and its claim that experiences which create negative affect increase the likelihood of aggression.

 P – The concept of catharsis…

…has little research support.

- **E** – For example, Bushman (2002) found that behaving aggressively is likely to lead to *more* aggression in the future.
- **E** – Dollard et al. claimed that aggression reduces arousal, and makes people *less* likely to behave aggressively.
- **L** – This means that Bushman's finding directly contradicts one of the central claims made by the frustration–aggression hypothesis.

 P – The frustration-aggression hypothesis has been challenged…

…by social learning theorists.

- **E** – They say that frustration produces generalised arousal, but aggressive behaviour depends on whether someone has seen it being either directly, or vicariously, reinforced
- **E** – Rather than frustration always leading to aggression, people *learn* to produce aggression and the circumstances it is most likely to be successful in.
- **L** – This means that aggression is not an automatic consequence of frustration.

CHOOSE THE RIGHT ANSWER

Which **one** of the following is **not** a claim made by the original frustration-aggression hypothesis? (Tick **one** box only.)

A	All aggression is a result of frustration.	☐
B	Frustration always leads to aggression.	☐
C	Contextual factors can inhibit aggression in some situations.	☐
D	Frustration is neither necessary nor sufficient for aggression.	☐
E	Frustration is caused when people are prevented from getting something they want.	☐

Answers on page 365

 RESEARCH ISSUES

In a study conducted by Mallick and McCandless (1966), one group of children were prevented by a confederate, who directed sarcastic comments towards them, from completing a series of simple tasks for monetary reward (the frustration group). The confederate did not prevent a second group of children from completing the tasks (the control group). When the children were given the opportunity to behave aggressively towards the confederate, the group that were frustrated were significantly more aggressive.

Mallick and McCandless concluded that the results offered clear support for the view that frustration causes aggression. However, there is a potentially confounding variable in this study. Identify the variable and explain how it might affect the validity of the results. *(4 marks)*

Answers on page 365

 APPLYING YOUR KNOWLEDGE

Toby and Izzy were discussing a newspaper article about train delays.

'I don't mind waiting for a train that's been delayed if there's a good reason for it, like the train having to stop because a passenger has been taken ill,' said Izzy. 'But what really frustrates me is when they come up with all these daft excuses like the wrong kind of snow or leaves on the line.'

'I agree,' said Toby. 'It says in this newspaper that yesterday's trains were delayed because of "strong sunlight". I'd probably punch someone who told me I was going to be late because the sun was shining!'

Using your knowledge of the frustration–aggression hypothesis, explain why some reasons for delayed trains are more likely than others to lead to an aggressive reaction from people. *(4 marks)*

Answers on page 366

 DRAWING CONCLUSIONS

A researcher conducted a field experiment to test the frustration–aggression hypothesis. A male research assistant was instructed to push into a queue waiting to be served at a busy ticket office. In one condition, the assistant pushed in front of the person who was second in line. In another condition, the assistant pushed in front of the person who was twelfth in line. The research assistant did this ten times in each condition.

The researcher assumed that how close a person is to reaching their goal has a strong effect on how much frustration they experience. She predicted that people who were second in line would feel more aggressive than those who were twelfth in line. After each person had bought their ticket, they were asked to rate how aggressive they felt towards the research assistant on a 7-point scale (1 = not at all aggressive, 7 = extremely aggressive). The mean ratings are shown in the table below.

	2nd in line	12th in line
Mean rating	5.9	2.4

(a) Was the researcher's hypothesis one- or two-tailed. Explain your answer. *(3 marks)*

(b) Outline one strength and one limitation of conducting field experiments in psychology. *(4 marks)*

(c) Name a non-parametric statistical test that could have been used to analyse the data. Give two reasons for choosing this test. *(3 marks)*

(d) The researcher wrote a report of her investigation and submitted it to a peer-reviewed journal. Explain what is meant by peer review. *(2 marks)*

(e) Write a suitable Abstract for this investigation. You should make reference to an aim/hypothesis, method, results, and conclusion in your answer. *(6 marks)*

Answers on page 365

KEY TERM

- Social learning

Possible essay question ...

Discuss the social learning theory explanation of human aggression. *(16 marks)*

Other possible exam questions ...

+ Outline how social learning theory explains human aggression. *(4 marks)*
+ Outline and evaluate **one** study into the role played by social learning in human aggression. *(4 marks)*
+ Evaluate social learning theory as an explanation for human aggression. *(8 marks)*

 Exam tip

Exam questions on this topic are likely to ask you to focus on social learning theory. Writing all about Bandura's Bobo Doll study won't allow you to gain many marks, unless you explicitly link it to the theory.

MUST know ...

Social learning theory (SLT)

Children learn to be aggressive if they are *directly rewarded* for it. Aggression is also learned *indirectly* by seeing someone else being rewarded for behaving aggressively.

Children learn the consequences of aggression by watching others being rewarded or punished for it *(vicarious reinforcement)*.

For social learning to happen, the child forms **mental representations** of events. Behaviour will be imitated if the expectancy of reward is greater than that of punishment.

Children develop confidence in their own abilities to be aggressive. These are called **self-efficacy expectancies**.

Bandura *et al.* (1961) found that children physically and verbally imitate aggression they have seen.

 P – One strength of SLT is that it can explain inconsistencies…

…in people's use of aggression.

- **E** – For example, a child may be aggressive when out with friends, but not when at home.

 P – SLT can also be used to explain…

…cultural differences in aggression.

- **E** – For example, aggression is very rare in the children of the !Kung San of the Kalahari desert.

 P – There are real-life applications…

…of SLT's views about aggression.

- **E** – For example, if aggression is learned, then it can also be modified. The American Psychological Association's intervention programme (ACT Against Violence) aims to educate parents about the dangers of providing aggressive role models.

SHOULD know ...

Social learning theory (SLT)

Learning occurs through *observing* a *role model*, with whom children *identify*, and then *imitating* their behaviour.

Children learn (through observation) if a behaviour is worth repeating (through vicarious reinforcement).

SLT includes a type of schema called a **script**. Children learn scripts about aggression from other people. Scripts are internalised and aggression can become the norm.

Children who haven't been very good at aggressive behaviour in the past have *low* self-efficacy expectancies, and may resolve conflict in other ways.

One group saw an adult 'model' behave aggressively towards a 'Bobo' doll. The other group witnessed non-aggressive behaviour.

- **E** – SLT says that reinforcement for aggression is more likely in some situations than others.
- **L** – This suggests that the expectation of rewarding consequences determines whether aggression will be displayed: when expectancies are high, aggression is more likely.

- **E** – Parents do not use physical punishment with their children, and aggressive postures are avoided by adults and devalued by society as a whole.
- **L** – This shows that the absence of either direct or vicarious reinforcement means that there is little motivation for the !Kung San children to learn aggressive behaviours, just as SLT suggests.

- **E** – Weymouth and Howe (2011) found that after completing the programme, parents discontinued their use of physical punishment.
- **L** – This shows that the power of social learning can be used to decrease aggressive behaviour.

**FURTHER EVALUATION**

 P – One major issue for SLT is…

…methodological issues in the research supporting it.

- **E** – For example, in Bandura *et al.'s* (1961) study, aggression was shown toward a Bobo doll, not an actual person.
- **E** – Bandura found that when children watched a film of someone hitting *a live* clown, they *still* imitated the aggressive behaviour that they had seen.
- **L** – Even so, this kind of research lacks the realism of aggression seen in everyday life.

 P – However, there is some real-world support…

…for SLT's predictions.

- **E** – For example, Gee and Leith (2007) analysed penalty records from hockey games. North American born players were more likely to be penalised for aggressive play than European born players.
- **E** – North American born players were more likely to have been exposed to aggressive models who were less likely to have been punished for their behaviour.
- **L** – This supports SLT's claim that aggressive behaviour can be acquired by seeing the consequences of other people's behaviour.

✓ CHOOSE THE RIGHT ANSWER

Which **one** of the following is **not** a feature of social learning theory? (Tick **one** box only.)

A Scripts ☐

B Vicarious reinforcement ☐

C Catharsis ☐

D Self-efficacy ☐

E Imitation ☐

Answers on page 366

📖 RESEARCH ISSUES (1)

The following is an extract from an account of Bandura *et al's* (1961) study:

The stated aim of Bandura and his colleagues' study was to increase aggressive tendencies in young children by exposing them to aggressive role models. Bandura and his colleagues obtained consent from the teachers of the children before the study began. After the study, films of the children's imitative behaviour were published and widely circulated.

Outline **three** ethical issues raised in the passage above. *(6 marks)*

Answers on page 366

📖 RESEARCH ISSUES (2)

Bandura *et al.* (1961) needed to match pairs of children in each condition of the experiment so that the groups were equivalent in terms of their everyday behaviour. They also needed to ensure that the observer's rating of the children's behaviour was reliable.

Explain **one** way in which the children could have been matched, and **one** way in which the reliability of the observers' ratings could have been assessed. *(3 + 3 marks)*

Answers on page 366

🔗 Link

See pages 136 and 137 of the Year 1/AS Revision and Exam Companion for an explanation of social learning theory.

✓ A MARKING EXERCISE

Read this student answer to the following exam question:

Explain **one** strength and **one** limitation of social learning theory as an explanation of human aggression. *(3 + 3 marks)*

> One strength of using social learning theory as an explanation for aggression is that it can explain cultural variations in aggression. The !Kung San of the Kalahari desert do not physically punish their children and aggression is not rewarded. This means that there is little motivation for the !Kung San children to learn to be aggressive, so they aren't aggressive, which is what SLT says should happen.
>
> One limitation of using social learning theory as an explanation for aggression is that Bandura's study was a laboratory study and the task was artificial. The Bobo doll isn't a real person and doesn't hit back and all extraneous variables were controlled. This means that it isn't very true to real life.

This answer was awarded full marks for the first paragraph and no marks for the second paragraph. Why do you think the second paragraph was awarded no marks? Write an improved second paragraph.

Answers on page 366

⚙ APPLYING YOUR KNOWLEDGE

Daria and Hafsat were walking through their local park, where some children were playing rugby and others were playing football.

'Isn't it amazing, how the kids playing football are always arguing with the referee, while the kids playing rugby just do what the referee tells with them without any argument,' said Hafsat.

'Yes,' said Daria, 'it's all because of vicarious reinforcement.'

Using your knowledge of social learning theory, explain how vicarious reinforcement can be used to explain differences in the children's behaviour. *(4 marks)*

Answers on page 366

KEY TERM

- De-individuation

Possible essay question ...

Discuss de-individuation as a social psychological explanation of human aggression. *(16 marks)*

Other possible exam questions ...

+ Explain what is meant by the term 'de-individuation'. *(2 marks)*
+ Give **one** criticism of the de-individuation explanation of human aggression. *(3 marks)*
+ Briefly outline and evaluate **one** study related to the de-individuation explanation of human aggression. *(4 marks)*
+ Evaluate de-individuation as a social psychological explanation for human aggression. *(8 marks)*

 Exam tip

Remember that de-individuation, social learning theory, and the frustration-aggression hypothesis are all examples of 'social psychological' explanations of human aggression. A general question requiring, say, an outline of one social psychological explanation, gives you the freedom to write about the one you are most confident with.

MUST know ...

De-individuation

De-individuation is when people lose their personal identity and inhibitions about violence. when they join crowds or large groups.

Zimbardo believes that being in a large group gives people a 'cloak of anonymity' that diminishes personal consequences for their actions.

Being anonymous has the psychological consequence of reducing inner restraints and increasing behaviours that are usually inhibited.

De-individuation diminishes our fear of being negatively evaluated and leads to a reduced sense of guilt.

Zimbardo (1969) found that de-individuated participants inflicted more severe electric shocks on a learner than participants who were identifiable. This study shows that anonymity, a key component in de-individuation, increases aggressiveness.

 P – There is research support...

...for Zimbardo's concept of de-individuation.

- **E** – For example, Rehm et al. (1987) observed games of handball in Germany where one team wore the same coloured shirts and the other team all wore different coloured shirts.

 P – The baiting crowd is...

...a real-world illustration of de-individuated behaviour.

- **E** – Mann (1981) analysed 21 instances of suicide leaps and found that in 10 of the 21 cases where a crowd had gathered, baiting had occurred.

 P – There is anthropological support...

for the concept of de-individuation.

- **E** – Watson (1973) collected data on warriors in 23 societies and whether they changed their appearance before going to war, and whether they killed, tortured, or mutilated their victims.

SHOULD know ...

De-individuation

Factors contributing to de-individuation include anonymity and altered consciousness, due to alcohol or drugs.

De-individuation has been used to explain mindless football hooliganism and social atrocities such as genocide.

People normally refrain from acting aggressively because of social norms against such behaviour and because they are easily identifiable.

Conditions that increase anonymity have the same effect.

The de-individuated participants wore bulky lab coats with no name tags, hoods that hid their faces, sat in separate cubicles, and were never referred to by name. The identifiable participants wore their usual clothes, had name tags, could see each other, and were introduced to each other.

- **E** – The orange-shirted teams showed significantly more aggressive acts than the other teams.
- **L** – This supports the idea that de-individuation through increased anonymity leads to more aggressive behaviour being displayed.

- **E** – This baiting behaviour tended to happen at night, when the crowd was large and some distance from the jumper.
- **L** – Since these features are likely to produce a de-individuated state, this suggests that de-individuation does occur in real-world settings.

- **E** – Warriors who significantly changed their appearance, through costumes or war paint, were more likely to be highly aggressive towards their victims compared with those who did not.
- **L** – This lends support to the idea of anonymity inducing a de-individuated state, leading to aggression.

 FURTHER EVALUATION

P – There are gender differences...

...in how people respond under de-individuated conditions.
- **E** – Cannavale et al. (1970) and Diener et al. (1973) found that in de-individuated situations, there was an increase in aggression in the all-male groups, but not in the all-female groups.
- **E** – Men tend to respond to provocation in more extreme ways than women do.
- **L** – This suggests that responses to provocation may be magnified under de-individuated conditions.

 P – Disinhibition and anti-social behaviour are not more common...

...in large groups and anonymous settings.
- **E** – For example, Postmes and Spears' (1998) meta-analysis of de-individuation studies showed that an increase in people's responsiveness to situational norms is the most common effect.
- **E** – De-individuation could lead to *either* pro- *or* anti-social behaviour, depending on the situation.
- **L** – This suggests that the evidence for de-individuation is not as strong as researchers claim.

CHOOSE THE RIGHT ANSWER

Which **two** of the following factors do **not** contribute to creating a de-individuated state? (Tick **two** boxes only.)

A Anonymity ☐

B Sensory underload ☐

C Alcohol ☐

D Drugs ☐

E Increased personal responsibility ☐

Answers on page 366

 DRAWING CONCLUSIONS

The table below shows the results obtained by Watson (1973) in his study of the extent to which warriors in 23 societies changed their appearance prior to going to war and the extent to which they killed tortured, or mutilated their victims.

	Did not change their appearance	Changed their appearance
Low levels of killing, torture, and mutilation	7	3
High levels of killing, torture, and mutilation	1	12

The data in the table above could be analysed using a 2 x 2 Chi-Squared test. Calculate the value of Chi-Squared using the step-by-step procedure on page 32 of The Complete Companion Student Book. Alternatively, the calculation can be done for you at the following address: http://www.socscistatistics.com/tests/chisquare/

(a) State a two-tailed hypothesis for Watson's study. *(2 marks)*

(b) Is the value of Chi-Squared significant at $p < 0.05$? Use the table on page 32 of The Complete Companion Student Book to explain your answer. *(4 marks)*

(c) State a conclusion based on the outcome of the statistical test. *(2 marks)*

Answers on page 366

 Link

In some countries, de-individuation has been accepted as grounds for extenuating circumstances in murder trials. You can read more about the free will and determinism debate on pages 46 and 47 of The Complete Companion Student Book, Year 2.

 RESEARCH METHODS

In Diener *et al*.'s (1973) 'trick-or-treat' study, 27 houses in Seattle were monitored on Halloween. 1,352 children entered the houses, some alone and some in groups. Sometimes, the child was asked by the host for their name, and sometimes they were not. Just inside the door were two bowls, one filled with candy bars and the other filled with small coins. The host told the children to take one candy bar each, but not to touch the money. The host then said that she had to go back to doing her work in another room. However, the host secretly looked through a peep-hole in the door to see if the children stole anything.

The results are shown in the bar chart below.

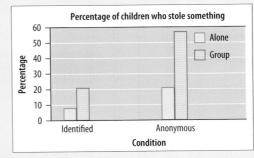

Outline **two** findings and **two** conclusions that you might draw from this bar chart. *(4 marks)*

Finding 1:

Conclusion 1:

Finding 2:

Conclusion 2:

Answers on page 366

 APPLYING YOUR KNOWLEDGE

Miki was reading an article on football crowds. A researcher called Adrian Aveni had found that the majority of people who go to football matches are with one or more friends. 'That's interesting,' thought Miki. 'I'm going to add that to my list of AO3 points on the de-individuation topic. I think I can use that to challenge what Zimbardo has to say about being in a crowd.'

Using your knowledge of de-individuation theory, explain how Miki could have used the article she had read to challenge Zimbardo's views about being in a crowd. *(6 marks)*

Answers on page 366

KEY TERMS

- Dispositional explanations
- Institutional aggression
- Situational explanations

Possible essay question ...

Discuss dispositional **and** situational explanations of institutional aggression in the context of prisons. *(16 marks)*

Other Possible exam questions ...

+ Explain **one** limitation of the situational explanation for institutional aggression in the context of prisons. *(4 marks)*

+ Evaluate **one** dispositional explanation of institutional aggression in the context of prisons. *(8 marks)*

+ Briefly explain what is meant by the term 'institutional aggression' in the context of prisons. *(2 marks)*

 Exam tip

If a question asks you to explain the difference between situational and dispositional explanations of institutional aggression, remember to draw a comparison, rather than just describing each one.

 Think

What other kinds of 'institutions' are there in which aggression occurs?

MUST know ...

Situational explanation: The deprivation model

Institutional aggression is influenced by prison-specific variables rather than by prisoners. Sykes (1958) calls these 'deprivations'. They include the loss of liberty, autonomy, and security.

One way inmates cope with these deprivations is to behave aggressively against other prisoners or staff.

Dispositional explanation: The importation model

Inmates bring their violent pasts to prison, and use them as coping mechanisms. Normative systems in the outside world, such as violence, are 'imported' into the prison.

Gang membership is consistently related to prison violence and other forms of anti-social behaviour, and is a strong predictor of institutional aggression.

EVALUATION **P – There is research support...**

...for the importation model.

- **E** – For example, Mears *et al.* (2003) found that a 'code of the street' belief system affects inmate violence.

EVALUATION **P – There is research support...**

...for the deprivation model.

- **E** – For example, McCorkle *et al.* (1995) found situational factors, such as overcrowding and a lack of meaningful activity, significantly influenced the amount of aggression inmates displayed.

EVALUATION **P – The deprivation model can be used...**

...to reduce aggression in prisons.

- **E** – For example, if most violence occurs in overheated, noisy and overcrowded environments, then decreasing these factors should reduce aggression.

SHOULD know ...

Situational explanation: The deprivation model

Other prison characteristics associated with prisoner aggression include overcrowding, heat and noise, and density.

Kimmel and Martin (2002) found that prison violence can be a way of avoiding the risk of appearing weak or being vulnerable to exploitation.

Dispositional explanation: The importation model

Dispositional characteristics include anger, anti-social personality, impulsivity, and low self-control.

Drury and DeLisi (2011) found that gang members were significantly more likely to engage in murder, hostage taking, and assault whilst in prison.

- **E** – This effect is especially noticeable in prisoners who lacked family support and were involved in gangs before they were imprisoned.
- **L** – This suggests that inmate behaviour stems in part from the cultural beliefs inmates import with them into prison.

- **E** – This includes both inmate-on-inmate assaults and inmate-on-staff assaults.
- **L** – This suggests that peer violence is used to relieve the deprivation experienced in prisons.

- **E** – Wilson (2010) did this at HMP Woodhill and found a large reduction in assaults on prison staff and other inmates.
- **L** – This provides substantial support for the idea that situational variables are the main cause of prison violence, and can be successfully applied to reduce prison violence.

 FURTHER EVALUATION

EVALUATION **P – The importation model's claims about pre-prison gang membership...**

...has been questioned.

- **E** – DeLisi *et al.* (2004) found prisoners with prior street gang involvement were no more likely than others to behave aggressively in prison.
- **E** – This could, however, be explained by the fact that prisons tend to isolate violent gang members from the other prisoners.
- **L** – This might explain why we do not always see aggressive behaviour from pre-prison gang members in the prison itself.

 EVALUATION **P – The link between aggression and situational factors...**

...has not always been supported by research.

- **E** – For example, Harer and Steffenmeier (1996) collected data from American prisons, including importation variables, such as race, criminal history, and deprivation variables, such as staff-to-prisoner ratios and security levels.
- **E** – They found that only the importation variables were significant predictors of prison violence.
- **L** – This shows that the deprivation model may not be an adequate predictor of institutional aggression.

CHOOSE THE RIGHT ANSWER

Which **one** of the following is **not** a prison characteristic associated with prisoner aggression? (Tick **one** box only.)

A Overcrowding	☐
B Loss of autonomy	☐
C High temperatures	☐
D Low population density	☐
E Loss of security	☐

Answers on page 366

FILL IN THE BOXES

Put the terms below into the appropriate box.

	Factors influencing aggression	First example of a factor	Second example of a factor	Main reason for prisoner aggression
Deprivation model				
Importation model				

Loss of autonomy

Dispositional characteristics

Impulsivity

Coping with the need for respect and fairness

Loss of liberty

Prison specific variables

Using violent pasts as coping mechanisms

Anti-social personality

Answers on page 366

APPLYING YOUR KNOWLEDGE

Under the heading 'Prisoners live in luxury', a national newspaper reported the following:

Dozens of photos uploaded to Facebook show prisoners boasting of a cushy prison lifestyle with access to TVs showing champion's league football, gaming consoles and gyms, while eating food that includes curries, kebabs, birthday cakes and crisps.

The article attracted the following comment from a reader:

Send them to Penal Colony 43 in Moscow, −40C and no luxuries there.

Linz burst out laughing at this comment. 'Why are you laughing?' said Fay. 'It's exactly what should happen to people who are put in prison.'

'Don't be ridiculous,' said Linz. 'There's actually a very good reason for prisoners having access to all that stuff.'

Using your knowledge of research into institutional aggression in prison, explain what the 'very good reason' might be. *(4 marks)*

Answers on page 366

 A MARKING EXERCISE

Read this student answer to the following exam question:

Briefly explain **one** limitation of the dispositional explanation and **one** limitation of the situational explanation of aggression in prisons. *(2 + 2 marks)*

One limitation of the dispositional explanation of aggression is that it is not supported by research. DeLisi *et al.* found that inmates who were in a gang before they went to prison were no more likely to behave aggressively in prison than the other prisoners.

One limitation of the situational explanation for aggression is that it has no research support. There is no evidence that people behave aggressively in prisons because of the situation they are in.

This answer was awarded full marks for the first paragraph and no marks for the second paragraph. Why do you think the second paragraph was awarded no marks? Write an improved second paragraph here…

Answers on page 366

KEY TERM

■ Media influences

Possible essay question …

Discuss research into the effects of computer games on aggression. *(16 marks)*

Other Possible exam questions …

+ Outline and briefly evaluate **one** study into the effects of computer games on aggression. *(4 marks)*
+ Evaluate research into the effect of computer games on aggression. *(8 marks)*
+ Give **two** criticisms of research into media influences on aggression. *(6 marks)*
+ Evaluate research into media influences on aggression. *(8 marks)*

 Exam tip

You could be asked a specific question on the effects of computer games on aggression as the specification uses the word 'including'. A more general question on media influences would allow you to write about TV and films as well, if you wanted to.

 Think

Some people can play violent computer games, or watch violent films, but they are not aggressive themselves. Why do you think this is?

MUST know …

Violent films and TV

Experiments show that those who watch violent scenes have more aggressive thoughts and behaviour.

Longitudinal studies show that exposure to violent TV in childhood predicts higher levels of adult aggression.

Bushman & Huesmann's (2006) meta-analysis found exposure to media violence significantly affected aggressive behaviour.

Violent computer games

Experiments show short-term increases in physiological arousal and hostility, following violent game play.

Children with high exposure to violent games became more verbally and physically aggressive over time (Anderson *et al.*, 2007).

Greitemeyer & Muuge's (2014) meta-analysis indicated a small increase in aggressive behaviour following exposure to violent games.

 P – The relationship between media violence and aggressive behaviour…

…has been overstated.

- **E** – For example, Ferguson and Kilburn (2009) found that in studies where aggression was measured, the relationship between media violence exposure and aggression is almost zero.

 P – There are methodological problems…

…in studying media influences on aggression.

- **E** – For example, Livingstone (1996) found that most research is American and has used unrepresentative samples such as male students.

 P – Other causal variables may be involved…

…in computer game aggression.

- **E** – For example, Ferguson et al. (2009) claim that research rarely controls for other variables that increase aggression.

SHOULD know …

Violent films and TV

Bjorkqvist (1985) found children who watched a violent film scored higher on aggression measures.

This relationship persisted even when parenting style was controlled for (Huesmann *et al.*, 2003).

Short-term effects were greater for adults than children, whilst the reverse was true for long-term effects.

Violent computer games

Participants behaved more aggressively after playing a violent game, compared with a non-violent game (Anderson and Dill, 2000).

However, the link between violent computer games and aggression may be due to their competitive nature (Adachi and Willoughby, 2013).

Pro-social games were linked to an increase in pro-social behaviour.

- **E** – Other studies that have found a relationship has typically reported only small-to-medium effect sizes.
- **L** – This shows that the link between exposure to media violence and violent behaviour may not be as strong as has been claimed.

- **E** – The findings from this research may not generalise to other cultures and populations.
- **L** – This suggests that better methodologies are needed before firm conclusions can be drawn about media influences on aggression.

- **E** – When these variables are controlled for, the effects of violent media content on aggression disappear.
- **L** – This suggests that it is the other risk factors which are the primary cause of aggression, not exposure to media violence.

FURTHER EVALUATION

P – A major issue in this area of research…

…concerns the measurement of aggression.

- **E** – Artificial measures of aggressive behaviour, such as administering noise blasts to other participants, are typically used as dependent variables.
- **E** – Longitudinal studies can measure both short- and long-term real-life aggression, but cannot control for exposure to other forms of media violence.
- **L** – Unless these issues can be resolved, strong claims about media influences on aggression can never be made.

 P – Game difficulty and mastery may be more important variables…

…in causing aggressive behaviour.

- **E** – Przybylski *et al.* (2014) suggest it's the player's experience of frustration and failure during the game, not the violent storyline, that causes aggressive behaviour
- **E** – They found that in both violent and non-violent games it was game difficulty that led to frustration and aggression.
- **L** – This suggests the link between computer games and aggression is more complicated than some research suggests.

CHOOSE THE RIGHT ANSWER

Which **one** of the following methods of studying media influences on aggression involves the use of secondary data? (Tick **one** box only.)

A	Experiment	☐
B	Questionnaire	☐
C	Meta-analysis	☐
D	Observation	☐

Answers on page 366

DRAWING CONCLUSIONS

Bushman & Anderson (2002) randomly assigned participants to play either a violent (e.g. Duke Nukem) or a non-violent (e.g. Austin Powers) computer game for 20 minutes. The participants then read a story, and were asked to list 20 thoughts, feelings, and actions about how they would respond if they were the character in the story. One of the stories was about 'Todd':

Todd was on his way home from work one evening when he had to brake quickly for a yellow light. The person in the car behind him must have thought Todd was going to jump the light because he crashed into the back of Todd's car, causing a lot of damage to both vehicles. Fortunately, there were no injuries. Todd got out of his car and surveyed the damage. He then walked over to the other car.

The researchers found that participants used responses like 'Call the guy an idiot' and 'This guy's dead meat', although the extent to which these phrases were used depended on whether they had played a violent or non-violent game, as shown in the bar chart below:

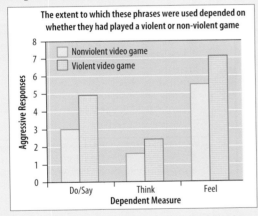

(a) What is the main conclusion that can be drawn from this study? *(3 marks)*

(b) Identify **one** non-parametric statistical test that could be used to determine whether the 'violent' and 'non-violent' groups differ in terms of the number of aggressive responses they used? *(1 mark)*

(c) Give **two** reasons for selecting this test. *(2 marks)*

Answers on page 367

 RESEARCH ISSUES

A researcher wanted to investigate whether men or women are more likely to be the victims in 'slasher' films. He content analysed ten 'slasher' movies, but found no evidence of a systematic bias in the deaths of victims as a function of gender.

Outline **one** strength and **one** weakness of using content analysis in studies of media influences. *(4 marks)*

Answers on page 366

 MATCH THEM UP

Match the researchers to the statement that best describes their research.

1	Anderson *et al.* (2007)	**A**	Exposure to violent TV in early childhood predicts higher levels of adult aggression in both boys and girls, a relationship which persisted even when variables such as socio-economic status and parenting style were controlled for.
2	Przybylski *et al.* (2014)	**B**	Children who had higher exposure to violent games became more verbally and physically aggressive over time.
3	Huesmann *et al.* (2003)	**C**	In studies where aggression towards another person has been measured, the relationship between media violence exposure and aggression is close to zero
4	Ferguson and Kilburn (2009)	**D**	In both violent and non-violent games it is game difficulty and lack of mastery, rather than the violent storyline, which leads to frustration and aggression.

Answers on page 367

 APPLYING YOUR KNOWLEDGE

Sasha was watching one of her brothers playing 'Carmageddon', a particularly violent computer game. As he played, he got more and more aggressive, until she had to stop him playing the game. Her other brother was playing 'Super Hexagon', which is not violent, but has been described as a 'devilishly simple treat'. Much to Sasha's surprise, her brother behaved even more aggressively when he played this game.

Using your knowledge of media influences on aggression, explain why non-violent computer games may also be associated with aggressive behaviour. *(4 marks)*

Answers on page 367

🔗 **Link**

This topic is clearly linked with explanations of media influences. These are discussed on pages 246 and 247 of The Complete Companion Student Book, Year 2.

KEY TERMS

- Cognitive priming
- Desensitisation
- Disinhibition

Possible essay question ...

Outline and evaluate **one or more** explanations of media influences on aggression. *(16 marks)*

Other Possible exam questions ...

+ Outline desensitisation as an explanation of media influences on aggression. *(4 marks)*

+ Outline how disinhibition explains media influences on aggression, and give **one** criticism of this explanation. *(4 marks)*

+ Outline cognitive priming as an explanation of how the media might influence aggression and give **one** strength and **one** weakness of this explanation. *(6 marks)*

⭐ Exam tip

When you are given the option of writing about 'one or more' explanations (for example), you can write about one in detail or several in proportionately less detail. This is called a 'depth versus breadth trade-off'.

MUST know ...

Media influences

Desensitisation: Under normal conditions, anxiety about aggression inhibits its use. Media violence, however, may lead to aggression by removing this anxiety. The more violence that is watched, the more acceptable aggression becomes.

Disinhibition: Watching or playing violent media may change our usual standards of what is considered acceptable behaviour. Exposure to violent media can legitimise the use of violence because it undermines usual inhibitory social sanctions.

Priming: This is a temporary increase in the accessibility of thoughts and ideas. Constant exposure to violent media activates aggressive thoughts/ideas about violence, which then 'prime' other aggressive thoughts through their associations in memory pathways.

EVALUATION P – There is research support...

...for the desensitisation explanation of media influences.

- **E** – For example, Carnagey *et al.* (2007) found that playing violent computer games produces physiological desensitisation in the form of reduced physiological arousal.

EVALUATION P – The disinhibition effect depends on other factors...

...such as the individual or the context.

- **E** – Younger children are more likely to be affected as they are less likely to consider the motives or consequences of the violence (Collins, 1989).

EVALUATION P – There is some research support...

...for cognitive priming.

- **E** – For example, Bushman (1998) found that participants who watched a violent film had faster reaction times to aggressive words than those who watched a non-violent film.

SHOULD know ...

Media influences

Linz *et al.* (1989) found a decrease in physiological arousal (e.g. heart rate) when people were exposed to real violence after being repeatedly exposed to media violence.

This can have immediate- and longer-term effects. In the short term, media violence triggers physiological arousal which increases the likelihood of aggression. In the longer term, prolonged exposure to violent media gives the message that violence is acceptable, and we feel less inhibited about behaving aggressively.

Zelli *et al.* (2005) found that priming by aggressive stimuli influenced individuals to make hostile attributions about the behaviour of others. These hostile attributions, in turn, increased the likelihood of aggressive behaviour.

- **E** – Participants who played a violent computer game had a lower heart rate and skin conductance response while viewing a 10-minute clip of real-life violence than those who played a non-violent game.
- **L** – This shows that physiological desensitisation can occur following exposure to violent media.

- **E** – The disinhibition effect is greater in families where children experience physical punishment from their parents than in households with strong norms against violence (Heath *et al.*, 1989).
- **L** – This demonstrates that the relationship between media violence and disinhibition is not a straightforward one.

- **E** – However, Atkin (1983) found that increased aggression only resulted when more realistic, or realistically perceived, violence was viewed.
- **L** – These studies suggest that exposure to media violence primes memories related to aggression, but only if the violence is realistic and intense.

FURTHER EVALUATION

EVALUATION P – Disinhibition is less likely...

...in situations where violent behaviour has negative consequences.

- **E** – Goranson (1969) showed people a boxing match film that either had no apparent consequences or resulted in the loser dying.
- **E** – Participants who did not see the negative consequences were more likely to behave aggressively afterwards than those who did.
- **L** – This suggests that disinhibition may be more likely when the negative consequences of violent media are not seen by viewers.

EVALUATION P – Desensitisation to aggression...

...can be maladaptive for some people, but adaptive for others.

- **E** – Bushman and Anderson (2009) found that desensitisation to violent media can reduce helping behaviour.
- **E** – However, desensitisation can be adaptive for people, such as soldiers, who are more professionally effective if they become desensitised to the horrors of combat.
- **L** – This means that although it can cause people to become 'comfortably numb', desensitisation can also be adaptive under certain circumstances.

CHOOSE THE RIGHT ANSWER

Which **two** of the following are **not** explanations of media influences on aggressive behaviour? (Tick **two** boxes only.)

A	Desensitisation	☐
B	Cognitive priming	☐
C	Systematic desensitisation	☐
D	Disinhibition	☐
E	Primacy and recency	☐

Answers on page 367

 ## RESEARCH ISSUES

In Goranson's (1969) study, participants were shown a film of a boxing match. For one group, the loser was depicted as dying. The other group saw no apparent consequences. Afterwards, participants undertook another task in which their aggressiveness was measured using the Buss-Durkee 'aggression machine' technique. This uses a machine which supposedly delivers electric shocks of varying intensity to another participant, who is actually a confederate of the experimenter.

Outline **one** ethical issue that arises using this method of measuring aggression, and explain **one** way in which this issue could be dealt with. *(4 marks)*

Answers on page 367

FILL IN THE BOXES

Write a definition of each of the three explanations of media influences on aggression in the first column. One explanation accounts for why people behave aggressively immediately after exposure to violent media, but return to 'normal' shortly afterwards. One explains why peoples' behaviour changes over the long-term, and one applies to both. Decide whether the explanation applies to immediate, long-term, or both, and write your answers in the second column.

	Definition	Application
Desensitisation		
Disinhibition		
Cognitive priming		

Answers on page 367

 ## MATCH THEM UP

Match the researchers to the statement that best describes their research.

1	Bushman (1998)	**A**	Playing violent computer games produces physiological desensitisation in the form of reduced physiological arousal.
2	Carnagey *et al.* (2007)	**B**	Participants who watched a violent film had faster reaction times to aggressive words than those who saw a non-violent film.
3	Heath *et al.* (1989)	**C**	There is a decrease in physiological arousal when people are exposed to real violence after being repeatedly exposed to media violence.
4	Linz *et al.* (1989)	**D**	The disinhibition effect is greater in families where children experience physical punishment from their parents.

Answers on page 367

 ## APPLYING YOUR KNOWLEDGE

Emily had read about a study in which young adults played either a violent or non-violent video game for 25 minutes. After the game, the participants had been asked to look at neutral pictures, such as a man on a bike, or violent pictures, such as a man with a gun. The researchers had found that when shown a violent image, those who had played the violent game showed a smaller brain response than those who had played the non-violent game. Emily could not understand why these findings were important.

Using your knowledge of desensitisation, explain why these findings are important. *(4 marks)*

Answers on page 367

 Link

This topic links back to media influences on aggression which are discussed on page 244 and 245 of The Complete Companion Student Book, Year 2.

Topic 1 Neural and hormonal influences

Evaluate the role of neural **and/or** hormonal mechanisms in aggression. *(8 marks)*

Examiner's comments

The role of the amygdala in aggression is supported by studies of human aggression. Pardini et al. carried out a longitudinal study of 56 male participants, with varying histories of violence. MRI scans showed that those with a smaller amygdala showed higher levels of aggression and violence, even after controlling for confounding variables. This suggests that the amygdala plays an important role in evaluating sensory information's importance, and a smaller amygdala can't do this as efficiently, which makes aggression more likely.

> Given the question, it is important to evaluate from the beginning. There is no unnecessary AO1 here.

The hippocampus' role in aggression is supported by MRI scans of hippocampal asymmetry. Raine et al. found that the hippocampus in the right and left hemispheres were different sizes in convicted violent criminals but not in unconvicted violent criminals. Hippocampal asymmetry possibly happens early in brain development. These asymmetries might stop the hippocampus and amygdala working together, which would mean emotional stimuli may not be processed properly, leading to aggression.

> This AO3 paragraph makes use of the PEEL formula, identifying an example, elaborating on it and then linking back.

There is some support for the serotonin deficiency hypothesis as an explanation for aggression. For example, Duke et al.'s meta-analysis of 175 studies found a small, inverse relationship between serotonin levels and some aspects of human aggression. Research has also found lower serotonin levels were associated with increased aggression in monkeys and dogs, suggesting that low levels of serotonin could be a reason for aggression.

> This AO3 paragraph begins well discussing the role of serotonin in human aggression, but then changes to talking about non-humans with no clear reason for doing so.

The role of testosterone in human aggression seems to be supported by a lot of research studies. Dabbs et al. measured testosterone levels in the saliva of violent and non-violent criminals and found that those with the highest testosterone levels had a history of violent crimes. Those with the lowest levels had committed non-violent crimes, suggesting that testosterone does play a role in human aggression.

> Using phrases like 'is supported by' indicates to the examiner that this is meant to be read as AO3.

However, the role of testosterone has been challenged because lots of studies don't show a relationship between this hormone and human aggression. For example, some research has shown no correlation between testosterone and violence in male prison inmates. Mazur suggests that testosterone may actually promote status-seeking behaviour, and aggression is only one type of this. This suggests that the relationship between testosterone and aggression in humans is more complicated than we think it is.

> Another effective and thorough AO3 paragraph, with reasonable depth.

Level 4 (7–8 marks)

Examiner's comments: AO3 In this answer, the candidate has chosen to take a breadth approach, and write about **both** neural and hormonal influences. The evaluation is thorough and effective throughout.

Topic 2 Genetic factors in aggression

Outline the findings from **one** study into genetic factors in aggression. *(4 marks)*

Examiner's comments

Caspi et al. studied the role played by the MAOA gene. There are two variants of this gene. One is associated with high levels of MAOA (MAOA-H) and one with low levels of MAOA (MAOA-L). They discovered that children with the MAOA-L variant of the MAOA gene were significantly more likely to grow up and behave antisocially, but only if they had been treated badly when they were children. Children with the MAOA-H variant of the MAOA gene who were badly treated, and those with the MAOA-L variant of the gene who were not treated badly, didn't display anti-social behaviour.

This answer describes the findings of Caspi's research in reasonable detail.

Level 4 (4 marks)

Examiner's comments: AO1 An accurate and reasonably clear description of the findings of Capsi's study.

Topic 3 The ethological explanation of aggression

Discuss the ethological explanation of aggression. Include reference to innate mechanisms and fixed action patterns in your answer. *(16 marks)*

Examiner's comments

Aggression happens when a sign stimulus triggers an innate releasing mechanism (IRM). This IRM releases a fixed action pattern (FAP), which is an innate behaviour produced by all members of the same species. For example, when a male stickleback fish enters another's territory, its distinctive red underbelly is a sign stimulus that triggers an IRM, which activates the FAP of aggression. The energy needed for an IRM to release a FAP is called the action specific energy (ASE). After each FAP, the ASE needs to build up again before the FAP can be released.

Clear and accurate AO1 paragraph detailing the process by which aggression happens according to the ethological explanation.

In the hydraulic model, ASE is seen as being like a fluid in a reservoir. As it builds up, it places pressure on a spring (the IRM) which is also being pulled by weights (the sign stimulus). When the ASE is high enough, and the sign stimulus is present, the FAP is released.

Another accurate AO1 paragraph, this time explaining the hydraulic model.

The FAP can also be released if the ASE is high enough, even if there is no sign stimulus. In this case, spontaneous aggression occurs. Some aggressive behaviours are ritualised in the form of threat displays. These allow individuals to assess their relative strength and are intended to make an opponent back down. For example, gorillas beat their chests to intimidate a rival to make them submit and leave, making aggression less likely. Lorenz believed that predator species have instinctive inhibitions that stop them from using their natural weapons, like their strong teeth, against their own species.

Using examples of ritualised aggression has enhanced this AO1 paragraph.

Research has found ritualised aggression has the same benefits for humans as for non-humans. For example, Hoebel found that Inuit Eskimos use song duels to settle disputes. Ritualised displays are also seen in cultures where aggression is common, such as the Yanamomö people of South America, showing that in very aggressive cultures, ritualised aggression is used to stop conflicts turning into dangerous physical aggression.

Real life examples can be an excellent way to gain AO3 marks, if they are explicitly linked to the theory, as they are here.

Fixed action patterns aren't just innate, but can be modified by environmental factors. Lehrman says learning and experience interact with innate factors in complex ways. Research also shows there are subtle differences between members of the same species in the production of aggressive behaviour. This shows that aggressive behaviour patterns are not as fixed as Lorenz claimed.

An effective AO3 paragraph that identifies the key point and elaborates upon it before linking back.

One weakness of Lorenz's hydraulic model is that research studies contradict its claims. For instance, the model says that aggressive behaviour cannot be performed again until the ASE that caused the FAP has built up again. However, Von Holst showed that performing an aggressive behaviour can increase rather than decrease the likelihood of further aggression. This suggests that the idea that performing a FAP leads to a reduction in biological energy and the likelihood of further aggression is wrong.

> Phrases such as 'One weakness of' show the examiner that this is intended to be read as AO3.

A human FAP of aggression is no longer adaptive. Human behaviour is more flexible than non-human behaviour, and we can respond to environmental challenges more effectively. Non-humans rely on stereotypical fixed patterns of behaviour to respond to environmental challenges. This means that while non-humans may respond aggressively to specific sign stimuli, human behaviour is far more varied and less predictable.

> Whether a theory can be applied to human aggression is an important point to consider, leading to AO3 credit here.

Level 4 (13–16 marks)

Examiner's comments: AO1 Detailed and clear description of how ethology explains aggression, making excellent use of specialist terminology.

AO3 Evaluation is thorough and effective throughout the response, making use of a reasonably broad range of evaluative points.

Topic 4 Evolutionary explanations of human aggression

Evaluate evolutionary explanations of human aggression *(8 marks)*

Examiner's comments

There is support for the idea that aggression and status are linked. For example, Daly and Wilson found that many tribal societies give higher status to those who have committed murder. Even in industrialised societies, such as the USA, the most violent gang members often have the highest status among their peers. This suggests aggression is an important way of gaining status among males.

> Phrases such as 'There is support for' show the examiner that this is an AO3 paragraph.

Evolutionary explanations say that aggression is an adaptive behaviour. However, one problem for evolutionary explanations is explaining the apparent maladaptiveness of aggression. For example, violent behaviour can result in injury, or death. This maladaptiveness can only be explained if the benefits of aggression outweighed the costs, relative to other strategies, in our evolutionary past. If this is the case, then natural selection would favour the evolution of aggression, despite its apparent maladaptiveness.

> An effective piece of AO3 which makes a point, includes research evidence to support it, before linking back.

Evolutionary explanations of aggression also fail to explain the cruelty found in human conflicts. For example, they don't explain the Rwandan genocide where there was a large scale slaughter of people. They also don't tell us why humans torture or mutilate their enemies when they have been defeated and so are no longer a threat. This suggests that human cruelty in warfare may be because of social psychological factors such as de-individuation rather than because it is adaptive.

> Using real life examples, as has been done here, can allow for effective AO3.

Differences in aggressive behaviour between the sexes may be due to socialisation not evolution. For example, Smetana found parents are more likely to explain why a behaviour was wrong to girls, but to physically punish boys, which could increase male physical violence. As girls learn they aren't as physically strong as boys, they might adopt more socially acceptable forms of aggression, such as reducing someone's self-esteem. This questions the claim that only males have evolved aggression as a way to deal with rivals: females might have just evolved a different type of aggression.

> Suggesting an alternative explanation for a behaviour can be an excellent way of gaining AO3 marks, as long as it is done clearly.

Evolutionary explanations for aggression in warfare are gender biased and don't explain the behaviour of women in warfare. Women's participation in war is rare. According to evolutionary explanations, this is because in war women don't increase their reproductive fitness as much as men do. Therefore, our understanding of the physically aggressive displays in warfare can only explain the behaviour of males.

Level 4 (7–8 marks)

Examiner's comments: AO3 There is no wasted content in this answer. Every paragraph is clear and effective, putting this firmly into the top mark band.

> AO3 marks can be gained by discussing a bias in research, in this case, a gender bias.

Topic 5 The frustration–aggression hypothesis

Discuss the frustration–aggression hypothesis as a social psychological explanation of human aggression. *(16 marks)*

Examiner's comments

Frustration is the result of any event that stops someone getting what they want. The frustration–aggression hypothesis says all aggression is the result of frustration and that frustration always leads to aggression. Dollard et al. said frustration was a necessary condition for aggression, but they also believed that situational factors can sometimes stop aggression happening. Frustration leads to the arousal of an aggressive drive, which behaving aggressively relieves because it has a cathartic effect on the individual. It is not always possible to behave aggressively towards the source of our frustration, so aggression is displaced onto something else. Displacement involves finding a scapegoat, like kicking the dog.

> This AO1 paragraph explains the original theory using specialist terminology well.

There is a difference between justified and unjustified frustration. Unjustified frustration usually produces more aggression. Pastore found people said they would be angrier if a bus they were waiting for didn't stop, which they would consider to be unjustified, than if it didn't stop and had an 'out of service' sign, which was considered a justified reason. This shows that only some kinds of frustration lead to aggression.

> Using research studies is an effective way to gain AO1 marks

Frustration isn't the only unpleasant experience that leads to aggression. Anything that stops us reaching an anticipated goal creates a negative affect in the individual. Berkowitz's revised frustration–aggression hypothesis says it is this negative affect that leads to aggression, and the frustrating event is less important.

> A reasonably detailed AO1 paragraph, this time explaining Berkowitz's revised frustration-aggression hypothesis.

The frustration–aggression hypothesis can explain mass killings, which often happen because of frustration caused by socio-economic difficulties. This leads to scapegoating, leading to aggression towards the scapegoat. Goldhagen claimed ordinary Germans overlooked the violence towards Jews because they saw them as responsible for Germany's problems. This shows that widespread frustration can have violent consequences for a scapegoat.

> Showing how a theory can explain real world situations can be an effective way of earning further AO3 credit, as can be seen here.

This theory can also explain violent behaviour in football fans. For example, Priks found that when their team performed worse than expected, the fans threw more objects onto the pitch, and were more likely to fight with opposition supporters. This suggests that fans became more aggressive when expectations of good performance were frustrated, which supports the frustration–aggression hypothesis.

> Another detailed AO3 point using the PEEL method to identify, elaborate and link back to the question.

Dollard et al. claimed that aggression is cathartic, and reduces arousal, making people less likely to behave aggressively, but there is not much research evidence to support this idea. Bushman found that behaving aggressively is likely to lead to more aggression in the future which directly contradicts one of the main claims made by the frustration–aggression hypothesis.

> It seems that two AO3 points have been made here, but neither of them are very well developed.

The frustration-aggression hypothesis has been challenged by social learning theory. Whether a person behaves aggressively depends on if aggression has been seen to be rewarding. Instead of frustration always leading to aggression, people learn to be aggressive, which means that aggression is not an automatic consequence of frustration, as the frustration-aggression hypothesis suggests.

> Using an alternative explanation can be an effective way to gain AO3 credit, as long as it is linked to the original explanation.

Level 3 (9–12 marks)

Examiner's comments: AO1 This is a reasonably detailed and accurate explanation of the frustration–aggression hypothesis. Berkowitz's revised version could have been explained more clearly.

AO3 A reasonably broad range of AO3 has been included and the answer is coherent and focused, allowing for some effective AO3 to take place.

Topic 6 Social learning theory

Discuss the social learning theory explanation of human aggression. *(16 marks)*

Examiner's comments

Social learning theory (SLT) says that aggression can be learned indirectly by seeing someone else being rewarded for behaving aggressively. Learning happens through observing a role model and then imitating their behaviour. Children learn the consequences of aggression by watching others being rewarded or punished for displaying it and learn if the behaviour is worth repeating.

> A strong AO1 paragraph explaining the key features of SLT and linking it to aggressive behaviour.

For social learning to happen, the child must form mental representations of events in their social environment, so SLT includes scripts. Children learn scripts about how and when to be aggressive from other people.

> An example to illustrate the point being made would help here.

Bandura et al. found that both boys and girls physically and verbally imitate aggression they have seen adults perform. In the Bobo doll study, one group of children saw an adult 'model' behave aggressively towards a Bobo doll. The other group saw the adult behaving non-aggressively and, when given the opportunity, the children imitated the behaviour they had seen.

> Making use of a research study, as has been done here, is an effective way to gain AO1 marks, as long as the focus remains on the question.

One strength of SLT is that it can explain inconsistencies in people's use of aggression. For example, a child may be aggressive when they're with their friends, but not when they are at home. SLT says that reinforcement for aggression is more likely in some situations, like with friends, than others, like at home. This suggests that the expectation of rewarding consequences determine whether aggression will be displayed: when expectancies are high, aggression is more likely.

> This AO3 paragraph includes phrases which signal to the examiner that evaluation is now happening, such as 'One strength of'.

SLT can also be used to explain cultural differences in aggression. Aggression is very rare in the children of the !Kung San. Parents do not use physical punishment and aggression is devalued by society as a whole. This shows that the absence of vicarious reinforcement means that there is little motivation for the !Kung San children to learn aggressive behaviours, just as SLT suggests.

> AO3 marks can be gained by discussing a theory's application across cultures, as has been done here.

There are real-life applications of SLT's views about aggression. For example, if aggression is learned, then it can also be changed. The American Psychological Association's intervention programme educates parents about the dangers of providing aggressive role models. Weymouth and Howe found that after completing the programme, parents didn't use physical punishment anymore. This shows that SLT can be used to help decrease aggressive behaviour.

> Using real-world applications can be an effective way of evaluating a theory, and earning further AO3 credit.

One major issue for SLT is methodological issues in the research which supports it. For example, in Bandura et al.'s study, aggression was shown toward a Bobo doll rather than an actual person. However, Bandura also found that when children watched a film of someone hitting a live clown, they still imitated the aggressive behaviour that they had seen. Having said that, this kind of research lacks the realism of aggression that is seen in everyday life.

> Using methodology to evaluate research can be an excellent way to gain AO3 marks, if done effectively.

However, there is some real-world support for SLT's predictions. Gee and Leith analysed penalty records from 200 games of the National Hockey League. North American players were more likely to be penalised for aggressive play and fighting than players born in European countries. They were also more likely than the Europeans to have been exposed to un-punished aggressive models, supporting SLT's claim that aggressive behaviour can be learned by seeing the consequences of other people's behaviour.

> An effective piece of AO3 which makes a point, includes research evidence to support it, before linking back.

Level 4 (13–16 marks)

Examiner's comments: AO1 A clear and accurate explanation of SLT and how it explains human aggression.

AO3 A broad range of evaluative points have been used and these have generally been used effectively.

Topic 7 De-individuation

Outline de-individuation as a social psychological explanation of human aggression. *(6 marks)*

Examiner's comments

De-individuation is when people lose their personal identity and their inhibitions about violence. It is a psychological state which happens when people join crowds or large groups. Anonymity and altered consciousness, due to alcohol or drugs, are factors that might lead to de-individuation.

> A clear AO1 paragraph that defines de-individuation and highlights some of the factors that might cause it to occur.

Zimbardo believes that being in a large group makes people feel anonymous and this lowers personal consequences for their actions. Being anonymous reduces inner restraints and it increases behaviours that are usually inhibited. De-individuation has been used to explain mindless football violence and atrocities such as genocide.

> This AO1 paragraph makes use of some real-life examples to help illustrate the point being made.

People usually don't behave aggressively because there are social norms that say this behaviour is wrong and also because they can be identified easily. But de-individuation reduces our fear of being judged negatively by others and leads us to feel less guilty.

Zimbardo found that de-individuated participants inflicted more severe electric shocks on a learner than participants who were identifiable. This study shows that anonymity, an important component in de-individuation, increases aggressiveness. The de-individuated participants wore bulky lab coats with hoods that hid their faces, sat in separate cubicles, and were never referred to by name. The identifiable participants wore their own clothes, could see each other, and were introduced to each other.

> Making use of a research study, as has been done here, is an effective way to gain AO1 marks.

Level 4 (6 marks)

Examiner's comments: AO1 The answer provides clear knowledge of de-individuation as an explanation for human aggression, and it is accurate and detailed. The answer is well structured and makes use of specialist terminology.

Topic 8 Institutional aggression in prisons

Discuss situational explanations of institutional aggression in the context of prisons. *(8 marks)*

Examiner's comments

One situational explanation for institutional aggression is called the deprivation model. This says that aggression is influenced by prison-specific variables rather than by prisoners themselves. Sykes calls these variables 'deprivations' and they include the loss of liberty, autonomy, and security. Other prison characteristics associated with prisoner aggression include overcrowding, heat and noise, and density. This explanation claims that one way inmates cope with these deprivations is to behave aggressively. Kimmel and Martin found that prison violence can be a way of avoiding the risk of appearing weak or being vulnerable to exploitation. They found that most prison violence was because of a need for respect and fairness.

> A strong AO1 paragraph explaining the deprivation model and how it explains institutional aggression.

There is research support for the deprivation model. For example, McCorkle et al. found situational factors, such as overcrowding and a lack of meaningful activity, significantly influenced the amount of aggression inmates displayed. This aggression was both on staff and on other prisoners. This suggests that violence is used to relieve the deprivation experienced in prisons.

> Using phrases such as 'There is research support' indicates to the examiner that this is intended as AO3.

One strength of the deprivation model is that it can be used to reduce aggression in prisons. If most violence occurs in overheated, noisy and overcrowded environments, then decreasing these factors should reduce aggression. Wilson did this at HMP Woodhill and found a large reduction in assaults on prison staff and other inmates. This gives a lot of support for the idea that situational factors are the main cause of prison violence, and can be successfully applied to reduce prison violence.

> An effective piece of AO3 which makes a point, includes research evidence to support it, before linking back.

However, the link between aggression and situational factors has not always been supported by research. Harer and Steffenmeier collected data from 24,000 inmates from 58 American prisons, including importation variables, such as race and criminal history, as well as deprivation variables, such as staff-to-prisoner ratios and security levels. They found that only the importation variables were significant predictors of prison violence. This shows that the deprivation model may not be an adequate predictor of institutional aggression.

> An issue has been identified, and some support for the issue is offered, so it can be credited as AO3.

Level 4 (7–8 marks)

Examiner's comments: AO1 This answer is accurate and explained in detail.

AO3 The evaluative points included in this answer are thorough, leading to effective AO3.

Topic 9 Media influences on aggression

Give **two** criticisms of research into media influences on aggression. *(4 marks)*

Examiner's comments

One criticism of research into media influences on aggression is that a lot of the time extraneous variables are not controlled for in the research. Things like trait aggression, family violence and mental health can all increase aggression, so if they aren't controlled for, then we can't be sure that it is exposure to media violence that increases aggression.

Another criticism of research is that most research is done in America, using male students. As this is not a representative sample, we cannot generalise the results to other cultures or populations. This means that we cannot make any real conclusions about media influences on aggression.

> Both identify a criticism and explain why it is a criticism for this area of research.

Level 4 (4 marks)

Examiner's comments: AO3: Two detailed evaluation points have been made.

Topic 10 Explanations of media influences

Two students were discussing a computer game which had recently been released. They were both shocked by the amount of violence in it. The main point seemed to be to kill as many people as possible. The person playing the game could evidently do this without any fear of punishment at all.

Discuss **one or more** explanations of media influences on aggression. Refer to the features of the computer game in your answer. *(16 marks)*

Examiner's comments

Normally, anxiety about aggression stops it happening. Media violence, however, may lead to aggression by removing this anxiety. This is called desensitisation. So, the more times you play the computer game, the more acceptable the violence within it becomes. Linz et al. found a decrease in physiological arousal when people were exposed to real violence after being repeatedly exposed to media violence.

> This AO1 paragraph explains desensitisation and applies the scenario in the question to it reasonably well.

Disinhibition theory says that watching or playing violent media may change our usual standards of what acceptable behaviour is. Exposure to aggressive media can legitimise the use of violence because it undermines things that would usually stop us, like punishments. So the gamer would be able to kill the people in the game without fearing any punishment. Their standards of acceptable behaviour have changed because of the time they spend watching the violence as they play the game. Research shows that prolonged exposure to violent media over time sends the message that violence is acceptable, and we feel less inhibited about behaving aggressively.

> A thorough AO1 paragraph about disinhibition and makes some excellent use of the scenario in the stem of the question.

Another explanation for media influences on aggression is cognitive priming. This says that constant exposure to violent media activates aggressive thoughts about violence, which then prime other aggressive thoughts through their associations in memory pathways. So killing as many people as possible in the computer game acts as a cognitive prime for physical fighting.

> A short, but reasonably effective, AO1 paragraph explaining how the computer game may act as a prime for real-life aggression.

There is research support for the desensitisation explanation. Carnagey et al. found that playing violent computer games produces desensitisation by reducing physiological arousal. Participants who played a violent computer game had a lower heart rate and skin conductance response while viewing a ten minute clip of real-life violence than those who played a non-violent game. This shows that physiological desensitisation can happen after watching violent media.

> Using phrases such as 'There is research support for' indicates to the examiner that this is intended to be read as AO3.

Desensitisation to aggression can be maladaptive for some people, but adaptive for others. For example, Bushman and Anderson found that desensitisation to violent media can reduce helping behaviour. But desensitisation can be adaptive for some people, such as soldiers, who are more effective in their role if they become desensitised to the violence of war. This means that although it can be maladaptive, desensitisation can also be adaptive sometimes.

> Applying psychological theories to real life situations can be an effective way to gain AO3 marks.

The disinhibition effect depends on other factors such as the individual or the context. Younger children are more likely to be affected as they don't consider the motives or consequences of the violence as much. Heath et al. found the disinhibition effect is greater in families where children experience physical punishment from their parents than in households with strong norms against violence. This demonstrates that the relationship between media violence and disinhibition is not straightforward.

> Another strong AO3 paragraph that identifies the key point and explains it thoroughly before linking it back to the question.

There is some research support for cognitive priming. For example, Bushman found that participants who watched a violent film had faster reaction times to aggressive words than those who saw a non-violent film. However, Atkin found that increased aggression only happened when more realistic violence was viewed. These studies suggest that exposure to media violence primes memories related to aggression, but only if the violence is realistic.

> This AO3 paragraph makes effective use of the PEEL technique.

Level 4 (13–16 marks)

Examiner's comments: AO1 This is an application question, so every point of theory has to be applied to the scenario in the stem. This answer has done this well, allowing it to reach Level 4.

AO3 The evaluative points are thorough and well made, allowing for effective AO3 to take place.

KEY TERM

- Crime

Possible essay question

Discuss ways of measuring crime. *(8 marks)*

Other possible exam questions ...

+ Discuss two problems of defining crime. *(4 marks)*

 Think

Discussions of explanations of crime are often focussed around whether criminal tendencies are innate or acquired – the nature–nurture debate. Keep this debate in your mind as you study this chapter, and think how to apply it to each topic.

MUST know ...

Defining crime

A **crime** is any act that violates the law and results in punishment by the state.

Measuring crime

Official statistics In the UK, the Home Office publishes annual crime statistics for England and Wales, based on incidents reported to or discovered by the police.

Victim surveys

The *Crime Survey* uses confidential interviews about attitudes to crime and specific crimes committed against participants in the last year, whether or not they were reported.

Offender surveys

The *Offending, Crime and Justice Survey* (OCJS) was a longitudinal study from 2003–2006 in England and Wales, studying 5,000 people aged 10–25.

 There is universal agreement...

...about the unacceptability of some behaviours.

- **E** – For example, murder, rape and theft are illegal in every country.

 Official statistics under-represent...

...certain types of crime.

- **E** – This is because victims may not report a crime if they don't feel the police will do anything, if they wish to avoid stigma, or if they are unaware a crime has been committed.

 Victim surveys also have validity issues....

...as people may not be honest, and samples may be unrepresentative.

- **E** – The sampling is biased as only 75% of those contacted take part, and people without a postal address are excluded.

SHOULD know ...

Defining crime

There are **cultural differences** as laws vary between countries. Also a country's laws change over time, e.g. homosexuality was illegal in the UK until 1969, and remains illegal in some countries (e.g. Egypt, Saudi Arabia). So the definition of crime is a **social construction**.

Measuring crime

Official statistics have been collected since 1805, so trends can be tracked.

Victim surveys use a representative sample of the population, for example the *Crime Survey* interviews adults from 50,000 households selected randomly from postal addresses.

Offender surveys aim to identify causes and contexts of offending, anti-social behaviour and drug use.

- **E** – However, there are still cultural variations in how these are treated, such as the French concept of 'crime passionnel' resulting in more lenient sentencing.
- **L** – So cultural attitudes may influence how crimes are defined and dealt with by legal systems.

- **E** – Walker *et al.* (2006) found that only 42% of crimes reported in the *British Crime Survey* were reported to the police.
- **L** – This means that official statistics miss the 'dark figure' of unreported crime, although general trends tend to agree with other kinds of statistics.

- **E** – Also, people can only report five crimes per year, whereas victims of some crimes such as domestic abuse may have experienced more than five incidents.
- **L** – So, although victim surveys may provide information about the 'dark figure' of unreported crime, they may still result in an underestimate.

FURTHER EVALUATION

 Offender surveys

- **P** – Surveys of offenders also rely on self-report methods.
- **E** – People are likely to underplay their involvement in crime and drug use.
- **E** – However, the OCJS report that participants said they were honest in their answers.
- **L** – It is difficult to assess how accurate these data are. A combination of different survey methods probably gives the most accurate picture.

Crime statistics in other countries

- **P** – The UNICR (United Nations Interregional Crime and Justice Research Institute) monitor crime statistics from around the world.
- **E** – Most governments publish annual reports.
- **E** – However, some countries do not publish crime statistics; for example, China and Burma.
- **L** – These statistics allow some comparisons between countries, although with caution as laws and definitions of crime vary.

DRAWING CONCLUSIONS

The responses to two questions in the Crime Survey for England and Wales, 2013–2014 are summarised below.

A	Did you experience any crime in the previous 12 months?	Not a victim of crime	29819
		Victim of crime	5532
B	How worried are you about being attacked because of skin colour, ethnic origin or religion?	Very worried	348
		Fairly worried	546
		Not very worried	2522
		Not at all worried	5021

(a) What percentage of respondents said they had been a victim of crime during that year? *(2 marks)*

(b) What percentage of respondents had some degree of worry about being attacked because of skin colour, ethnic origin or religion? *(2 marks)*

(c) Draw an appropriate chart to display the data for question (b). *(3 marks)*

Refugees and migrants from war-torn countries are particularly vulnerable to homelessness, and would therefore be unrepresented in a survey of households.

(d) How might this reduce the validity of the data collected in response to question (b)? *(3 marks)*

Answers on page 367

CHOOSE THE RIGHT ANSWER 1

Which way of measuring crime is likely to omit the 'dark figure' of unreported crime? (Tick **one** box only.)

A Home Office Statistics ☐

B The *Crime Survey for England and Wales* ☐

C An offender survey, such as the *Peterborough Adolescent and Young Adult Development Study* ☐

Answers on page 367

RESEARCH ISSUES

The *Crime Survey* selects a random sample of 50,000 UK households from the Royal Mail list of addresses. People aged 16 or over are asked to participate.

However, only 75% of people agreed to take part in 2005.

(a) How will this affect the representativeness of the sample? *(1 mark)*

The average household size is 2.3 people. 20% of people in the UK are under 16.

(b) Calculate how many people took part in the 2005 survey. *(2 marks)*

The *Crime Survey* asks participants about crimes that they have experienced directly as victims.

(c) Suggest a type of crime that will not be measured by this survey, and explain your answer. *(2 marks)*

The interviews take place in people's homes, with other family members present.

(d) How might this lead to under-reporting of certain types of crime? *(1 mark)*

The sample does not include people living in accommodation such as halls of residence or hostels, or homeless rough sleepers.

(e) How might this affect the validity of the data? *(2 mark)*

Answers on page 367

CHOOSE THE RIGHT ANSWER 2

Which **one** of the following would **not** be defined as a crime in the UK? (Tick **one** box only.)

A Driving at 40mph in a 30mph speed zone ☐

B Failing to pay for a TV licence ☐

C Selling a faulty phone to a customer and refusing to replace it ☐

D Selling a kitchen knife to a customer aged 17 ☐

Answers on page 367

KEY TERMS

- Disorganised type of offender
- Offender profiling
- Organised type of offender
- Top-down approach

Possible essay question

Describe and evaluate the top-down approach to offender profiling. *(16 marks)*

Other possible exam questions ...

+ Distinguish between an organised and a disorganised type of offender. *(4 marks)*

+ Briefly explain how the top-down approach is used to create an offender profile. *(4 marks)*

Think

'Top-down' and 'bottom-up' are psychological terms used in the topic of perception. In this context, top-down processing involves the brain's use of contextual and existing knowledge to interpret new inputs, whereas bottom-up processing is data-driven, and begins with the actual sensory input.

MUST know ...

The top-down approach

A way of narrowing down potential suspects by creating a profile of the most likely offender.

1. **Profiling inputs** Data is collected including a detailed description of the crime scene, the crime, and background information about the victim. Possible suspects must not be considered, to avoid bias.

2. **Decision process models** The profiler organises the data into patterns, considering issues such as murder type (mass, spree or serial), time and location factors.

3. **Crime assessment** The crime is classified as being committed by an **organised** or **disorganised type of offender**.

 Top-down profiling can be useful...

...for opening up new avenues of investigation.

- **E** – Copson (1995) questioned 184 US police officers; 82% said the technique was useful and 90% said they would use it again.

 However, the method is based on flawed data...

...from interviews with 37 dangerous sexual killers.

- **E** – These individuals can be highly manipulative and unreliable.

 Top-down approaches can be harmful...

...as profiling could mislead investigations.

- **E** – Top-down analysis is not based in scientific evidence, and has been dismissed by courts as 'junk science', with ambiguous descriptions which could fit many individuals.

SHOULD know ...

The top-down approach

Types of crime and offender

- **Organised** – planned, targeted victim, violent fantasies may be acted out. The offender is usually intelligent, socially and sexually competent.

- **Disorganised** – unplanned, random selection of victim. The offender usually leaves evidence at the crime scene like blood, semen, fingerprints and the weapon.

4. **Criminal profile** Hypotheses about the offender's background, habits and beliefs are used to work out a strategy for the investigation.

5. **Crime assessment** People matching the profile are evaluated.

6. **Apprehension** If a suspect is caught, the process is reviewed to check that conclusions at each stage were valid.

- **E** – The approach was developed by the FBI to solve bizarre and extreme murder cases.
- **L** – It involves an intuitive application of a profiler's prior knowledge, and can offer investigators a different perspective, which can help prevent wrongful conviction.

- **E** – This data was used to identify the key characteristics that police use to 'read' a crime scene.
- **L** – These killers may have a different approach to 'typical' killers, so the classification of crimes and criminals may not be generalisable.

- **E** – In addition, smart offenders could deliberately try to deceive profilers by providing misleading clues.
- **L** – So police and courts must take care not to be convinced by the believability of profiles which appear to be a good match.

 Accuracy of top-down profiling

- **P** – For profiling to be useful, the profile should closely match the actual offender's characteristics.
- **E** – However, Alison *et al.* (2003) showed that police officers made poor judgments of accuracy.
- **E** – They rated a profile as equally accurate a match to a description of the genuine offender as to a fabricated offender.
- **L** – This shows that profiling leads to unreliable judgements of its own usefulness.

 A false dichotomy

- **P** – There is more likely to be a continuum than two distinct categories of offender.
- **E** – Canter *et al.* (2004) analysed murders by 100 US serial killers, finding no clear division between the two types of offender.
- **E** – Instead they found several subsets of organised-type crimes, and little evidence for disorganised types.
- **L** – This suggests that the categories may not be very useful for profiling serial killers.

DRAWING CONCLUSIONS

A study (Alison *et al.*, 2001) investigated whether police officers were prepared to perceive offender profiles as accurate descriptions of offenders. Group A were given a description of the real offender, and Group B were given a fabricated account of an offender with very different characteristics. They were both told that the offender had confessed when he was caught. Both were given the same profile, and asked to rate it for accuracy on a 7-point Likert scale (1 = very inaccurate, 7 = very accurate). The mean accuracy ratings are shown in the table.

	Group A (genuine offender)	Group B (fabricated offender)
Mean accuracy rating	5.3	5.3
Standard deviation	0.89	1.3

(a) What do the results show about accuracy ratings of the profile by the two groups? *(3 marks)*

(b) What can you conclude from these findings about the usefulness of offender profiles? *(3 marks)*

(c) The median scores for each group were 6. What does this tell you about the distribution of scores? *(2 marks)*

Answers on page 367

 RESEARCH ISSUES

Forensic psychologists generally publish their theories and research evidence in journals or books, so that other professionals can learn from them. What ethical issues might arise from the publication of details of effective offender profiling techniques? *(3 marks)*

Answers on page 367

APPLYING YOUR KNOWLEDGE 1

Saga and Henrik are investigating a series of murders in Malmö and Copenhagen which seem to have some common features, such as the bodies being staged after death to look like artworks in a gallery. How could the investigators make use of top-down profiling techniques to help them locate and apprehend the murderer? *(6 marks)*

Identify the psychology	Link to this investigation

Answers on page 367

APPLYING YOUR KNOWLEDGE 2

Luke works as a psychiatrist in a high-security prison, and wants to collect some data to test the hypothesis that serial killers can be divided into two groups; organised or disorganised. He decides to carry out semi-structured interviews of convicted serial killers, and analyse these along with the court transcripts and police reports relating to the crimes.

(a) Explain how Luke could analyse the content of the interview transcripts and other materials to test this hypothesis. *(4 marks)*

(b) Why might there be discrepancies between the different sources? *(2 marks)*

Answers on page 368

KEY TERMS

- Bottom-up approach
- Geographical profiling
- Investigative psychology

Possible essay question

Discuss the bottom-up approach to offender profiling. *(16 marks)*

Other possible exam questions …

+ Explain what is meant by 'geographic profiling'. *(2 marks)*
+ Compare the top-down and bottom-up approaches to offender profiling. *(4 marks)*
+ Explain how investigative psychology is used to create an offender profile. *(4 marks)*

 Exam tip

If you are asked to distinguish between two approaches, you must select directly comparable aspects and say how they are different.

MUST know …

Investigative psychology

This data-driven approach was developed by David Canter. Three features are:

1. Interpersonal coherence assumes that people are consistent in their behaviour, so there will be correlations between the crime and their everyday life, although there may be changes over time.

2. Forensic awareness: Rapists who conceal fingerprints often have a previous conviction for burglary.

3. Smallest space analysis: A statistical technique which explores correlations between crime scene details and offender characteristics from large numbers of similar cases. This can identify themes or categories of offender, such as instrumental opportunistic, instrumental cognitive or expressive impulsive murderers.

 The bottom-up approach is more scientific…

…because it uses statistical analysis of objective data from offenders.

- **E** – However, it doesn't include data from unsolved crimes.

 Investigative psychology can be useful…

…and Canter's first attempt at profiling led to the successful conviction of a serial killer and rapist in 1986.

- **E** – This led to police interest, and Copson (1995) found that 75% of police officers surveyed had found profilers' advice useful.

 Circle theory has limitations

- **E** – Canter and Larkin (1993) studied 45 sexual assaults, and found 91% of offenders were marauders and the rest were commuters.

SHOULD know …

Geographical profiling

Geographical profiling analyses locations and connections between crime scenes.

Circle theory: Canter also proposed that most offenders have a spatial mindset, committing crimes within an imaginary circle. Marauders commit crimes within a defined radius of their home; commuters travel to another area to commit crimes.

Criminal geographic targeting (CGT) is a computerised system developed by Rossmo. The formula uses data about time, distance and movement, and produces a map called a 'jeopardy surface', showing likely closeness to the offender's residence.

- **E** – Also, the assumptions about where offenders are most likely to commit crimes, and formulae calculating jeopardy surfaces may be incorrect.
- **L** – This means that bottom-up approaches have the potential to be objective and systematic, but in practice are biased.

- **E** – However, only 3% said the profiling helped them identify the actual offender, and profiling was only used in 75 cases across 48 police forces.
- **L** – This suggests that it only gives a slight benefit in catching offenders, but this is still valuable.

- **E** – However, in cities people's ranges may not be circular due to transport links.
- **L** – Circle theory can be useful for narrowing down searches, but could lead police to look in the wrong place.

FURTHER EVALUATION

 Geographic profiling is limited

- **P** – The geographic approach can help prioritise house-to-house searches or DNA testing.
- **E** – However, geographic profiling is limited to spatial behaviour; it ignores any personality characteristics of offenders.
- **E** – This means it is unable to distinguish between multiple offenders in an area.
- **L** – So there may not be any advantage over the traditional method of sticking pins in a map to see where a group of crimes were committed.

 Offender profiling should be used with caution

- **P** – Profiling can help police narrow down the field of possibilities.
- **E** – The danger lies in being restricted by profiling.
- **E** – For example, in the murder of Rachel Nickell, a psychologist's profile led to the wrong suspect, as the actual murderer was taller than described in the profile.
- **L** – This can lead to police wasting time trying to convict the wrong person, or even wrongful convictions.

CHOOSE THE RIGHT ANSWER

An assumption of bottom-up offender profiling is that people tend to behave consistently, so that the way they interact with victims is similar to how they interact with people generally. Which term is used to describe this? (Tick **one** box only.)

A Interactional consistency ☐

B Instrumental opportunistic ☐

C Interpersonal coherence ☐

D Decision process models ☐

Answers on page 368

 COMPLETE THE TABLE

If you are asked to explain the difference between top-down and bottom-up offender profiling, you need to give direct comparisons between aspects of each. Complete the summary table to help you think this through.

Aspect of the approach	Top-down	Bottom-up
Developed by		
Starts with	All details about crime scene, no info about suspects	
How the profile is developed		Predictions based on empirical data
Assumptions	Offender's characteristics match the crime: organised/disorganised	
Research basis		Court and police records of hundreds of prisoners.
Usefulness		Can be useful in hard-to-solve cases
Criticisms		
Conclusion relating to both approaches	Can narrow down suspects, BUT may lead to police focussing on the wrong suspect.	

Answers on page 368

 DRAWING CONCLUSIONS

Criminal geographic targeting (CGT) can be used to locate the residence of a criminal by analysing the locations of crime sites. The graph below shows the relationship between the number of crime sites available for analysis and the 'hit percentage' produced by this model. The lower the hit percentage, the more successful the model.

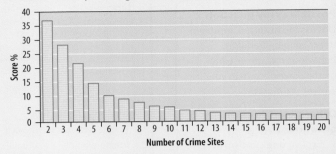

(a) How many crime locations are required to produce hit percentages of less than 10%? *(1 mark)*

(b) What can we conclude from this about the validity of the CGT model? *(2 marks)*

(c) This model assumes that the offender is not a commuter. Explain what this means. *(1 mark)*

Answers on page 368

 APPLYING YOUR KNOWLEDGE

Saga and Henrik have decided to take a more scientific approach to their investigation in Malmö and Copenhagen (see previous spread). How could the investigators make use of bottom-up profiling techniques? *(6 marks)*

Identify the psychology	Link to this investigation

Answers on page 368

KEY TERM

- Atavistic form

Possible essay question

Discuss the historical approach to explaining offending behaviour. Include research on the atavistic form in your answer. *(16 marks)*

Other possible exam questions ...

+ Explain **one** criticism of the historical approach to explaining offending behaviour (atavistic form). *(4 marks)*

+ Outline the atavistic form as an explanation of offending behaviour. *(4 marks)*

 Exam tip

Although these historical approaches were biological explanations of crime, in answering an exam question about biological explanations it would be better to focus on more current theories (see next spread). But you could be asked specifically about the theory of atavistic form, as this is in the specification.

 Link

See page 52 for free will and determinism.

Link

See page 48 for gender bias.

MUST know ...

Atavistic form

Lombroso (1876) proposed that offenders possess similar physical characteristics to lower primates, such as a large jaw and excessively long arms. They are throwbacks to an earlier stage of evolution, which causes them to become criminals. He linked specific features to different crimes, like an aquiline nose in murderers, and produced an *Atlas of criminal types*.

He identified three types:

- Born criminals – the atavistic type
- Insane criminals – mentally ill
- Criminaloids – offenders whose mental characteristics predisposed them to criminal behaviour under the right circumstances

 Lombroso brought science to a study of crime,...

... based on empirical observation and detailed measurement.

- **E** – However, he didn't compare prisoners with non-prisoners, so there was no control group.

 The theory is deterministic ...

... as it proposes that biological factors cause criminality, sometimes interacting with environmental factors, but still outside the control of the individual.

- **E** – Before this, criminals were believed to have a free choice to commit crimes and should be deterred by harsh punishments.

 The theory is gender biased ....

...as Lombroso believed that women are less evolved than men.

- **E** – He didn't study women directly, but believed that women are naturally passive, low in intelligence and maternal, and therefore unlikely to become criminals.

SHOULD know ...

Atavistic form

Lombroso gathered **empirical evidence** from post-mortem examinations of over 50,000 criminals and measurements of the faces of living criminals. In a study of 383 convicted Italian criminals, he found that 21% had just one atavistic feature and 43% had at least five.

Later, Lombroso recognised that inherited atavistic form (nature) interacts with **environment** (nurture).

Somatotypes

Sheldon (1949) linked body types to temperaments: mesomorphs (athletic, active and assertive), ectomorphs (tall and thin, restrained and nervous) or endomorphs (round, relaxed and sociable). He studied 200 young adults, concluding that delinquents tended to be mesomorphs.

- **E** – Goring (1913) compared 3,000 convicts with non-convicts, and the only difference was that convicts were slightly smaller.
- **L** – Although Lombroso's methods and conclusions can be criticised, he did raise the possibility of scientific studies of the criminal mind.

- **E** – Lombroso believed that biology and environment may remove free will, so criminals should be treated humanely.
- **L** – This view of criminal behaviour allowed for a consideration of the interaction between biological and environmental factors, and a more humane response.

- **E** – He also believed that those women who did become criminals had masculine traits which would be beneficial in a man but made women 'monsters'.
- **L** – These androcentric views were fairly typical in the nineteenth century and were not developed from empirical evidence.

 FURTHER EVALUATION

 Evidence relating to somatotypes

- **P** – There is some evidence supporting a link between body type and criminality.
- **E** – For example, Glueck and Glueck (1970) found that 60% of delinquents were mesomorphs.
- **E** – However, a correlation with body type does not imply a causal relationship.
- **L** – This means that the relationship between body type and criminal behaviour may not give any useful information for identifying or treating offenders.

 Identifying criminal types

- **P** – Although the theory of atavistic form has been rejected, we still try to identify criminal types.
- **E** – For example, Eysenck's theory looks at personality types and criminality.
- **E** – In addition, research into genetic causes of criminality (see next spread) implies that some people have an innate disposition to commit crimes.
- **L** – So Lombroso's later ideas, of an interaction between biological and environmental factors, have similarities with current theories.

✓ CHOOSE THE RIGHT ANSWER

The theory of atavistic form is deterministic because…
(Tick **one** box only.)

A It suggests that criminals will have an ugly appearance. ☐

B It proposes that biological factors are responsible for offending behaviour. ☐

C It is androcentric. ☐

D It studied correlations between facial features and different crimes. ☐

Answers on page 368

📖 RESEARCH ISSUES

(a) Identify strengths and limitations of Lambroso's research methods. *(4 marks)*

Strengths	Limitations

(b) Overall, how scientific was his approach to collecting data? *(2 marks)*

(c) Why were there problems with the validity of his conclusions? *(3 marks)*

Answers on page 368

MATCH THEM UP

Match up the term with its description

1	Atavistic form	**A**	Tall, thin body shape, nervous temperament
2	Aquiline	**B**	Athletic body shape, assertive personality
3	Criminaloid	**C**	Nose shaped like an eagle's beak
4	Ectomorph	**D**	Similar characteristics to lower primates
5	Mesomorph	**E**	Having mental characteristics that predispose to crime in certain conditions
6	Endomorph	**F**	Round shape, relaxed and sociable temperament

Answers on page 368

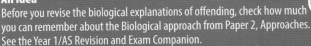

An idea

Before you revise the biological explanations of offending, check how much you can remember about the Biological approach from Paper 2, Approaches. See the Year 1/AS Revision and Exam Companion.

On a piece of paper, make a mind map, including key ideas: genes, genotype, phenotype, nervous system, neurons, neurotransmitters, hormones.

⚙ APPLYING YOUR KNOWLEDGE

Count Dracula by Bram Stoker contains this description of Dracula, a murderous vampire:

His face was a strong, a very strong, aquiline, with high bridge of the thin nose and peculiarly arched nostrils … His eyebrows were very massive, almost meeting over the nose, and with bushy hair that seemed to curl in its own profusion. The mouth, so far as I could see it under the heavy moustache, was fixed and rather cruel-looking, with peculiarly sharp white teeth. These protruded over the lips … his ears were pale, and at the tops extremely pointed. The chin was broad and strong … his hands … were rather coarse, broad, with squat fingers. Strange to say, there were hairs in the centre of the palm.

How does this description fit the theory of atavistic form? *(6 marks)*

Identify the psychology	Link to Dracula

Answers on page 368

KEY TERMS

- Epigenetics
- Genetic explanations
- Neural explanations

Possible essay question

Discuss genetic and/or neural explanations of offending behaviour. *(16 marks)*

Other possible exam questions ...

+ Outline neural explanations of offending behaviour. *(4 marks)*

+ Describe **one** study that has investigated genetic explanations of offending behaviour. *(4 marks)*

 Exam tip

The nature–nurture debate can be applied very effectively to this topic, as the diathesis-stress model explains how a genetic susceptibility can interact with adverse experiences to produce criminal tendencies. See page 54 for nature-nurture and page 52 for determinism.

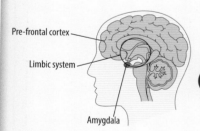

Pre-frontal cortex
Limbic system
Amygdala

MUST know ...

Genetic explanations

Genes may predispose individuals to criminal behaviour.

A faulty **MAOA** gene was found by Brunner *et al.* (1993) in 28 violent males in a Dutch family.

Tiihonen *et al.* (2015) estimated that 5–10% of violent crime in Finland is caused by abnormal MAOA or **CDH13** genes.

Neural explanations

Differences in **brain structures** may be innate or acquired. 60% of US prisoners have had a brain injury, compared with 8.5% of the general population (Harmon, 2012).

Neurotransmitter differences:

- When **serotonin** levels are low, the pre-frontal cortex is unable to inhibit impulsive aggressive urges. **Dopamine** hyperactivity may enhance this effect.

- High **noradrenaline** is associated with sympathetic nervous system activation: the fight-or-flight response.

 Twin and adoption studies...

...support genetic explanations of offending behaviour.

- **E** – Raine (1993) reviewed research on the delinquent behaviour of twins, and found 52% concordance rate for MZ twins (with identical DNA) and 21% for DZ twins (with 50% of the same genes).

 Non-violent crimes are more difficult...

...to link to biological explanations.

- **E** – There is evidence from twin studies (e.g. Blonigen *et al.*, 2005) that the personality trait of psychopathy is inherited, which causes lack of empathy, increasing the likelihood that the psychopath will commit crimes.

 Biological explanations are deterministic....

...and lawyers have used them to excuse crime.

- **E** – They imply that a person may be unable to control their criminal urges.

SHOULD know ...

Genetic explanations

Environmental factors 'switch' genes on or off. This is an **epigenetic** effect, changing the phenotype but not the genotype.

Caspi *et al.* (2002) found that 12% of men with low MAOA expression had experienced childhood maltreatment, but were responsible for 44% of violent convictions.

Neural explanations

Raine (2004) reviewed 71 brain imaging studies, showing that violent criminals have reduced functioning in the **pre-frontal cortex**, an area associated with control of impulses.

Raine *et al.* (1997) found that murderers had abnormalities in their **amygdala**, an area of the limbic system linked to emotion and motivation.

- **E** – In addition, Mednick *et al.'s* (1987) study of 14,000 adoptees found that 15% of boys adopted by a criminal family became criminals themselves, compared to 20% with biological parents who were criminals.
- **L** – Taken together, these findings suggest that inherited factors are marginally more significant than environmental influences.

- **E** – However, offending behaviour includes a broad range of behaviours such as fraud, drug use and bigamy, and Findlay (2011) points out that crime is a social construction.
- **L** – This means it is difficult to explain such a range of behaviours in terms of genes.

- **E** – However, not everyone with the defective gene in Tiihonen's study became an offender, and Caspi's study supports a diathesis-stress model.
- **L** – It may be hard for some men with genetic predispositions and adverse experiences to avoid criminal violence.

FURTHER EVALUATION

Real-world applications

- **P** – Differences in neurotransmitter levels could be treated with drugs or dietary interventions.
- **E** – For example SSRIs can increase serotonin levels.
- **E** – However, the relationship could be spurious; childhood experiences could have caused both criminal behaviour and also changes in the structure of the brain or neurotransmitter levels.
- **L** – Drugs may help some individuals, particularly if they also suffer mental illnesses.

Non-human animal research

- **P** – Much research on neurotransmitters relies on non-human animals.
- **E** – These studies, and much of the human research, investigate aggressiveness rather than criminal behaviour.
- **E** – Also, there is not 100% correspondence with any brain area or neurotransmitter.
- **L** – This means the data cannot be used to predict who may become an offender, and research can't be generalised to non-violent crimes.

MATCH THEM UP

Match up the term with the explanation.

1	Monoamine oxidase A (MAOA)	A	A gene found in abnormal form in Finnish offenders
2	Cadherin 13 (CDH 13)	B	Brain structures including the thalamus and amygdala, linked to emotion and motivation
3	Epigenetics	C	A gene for an enzyme involved in neurotransmitter metabolism
4	Prefrontal cortex	D	Genes can be switched on or off by environmental factors
5	Limbic system	E	High levels of this neurotransmitter are linked to aggression
6	Serotonin	F	Region of the brain responsible for decision making and control of impulses
7	Noradrenaline	G	Low levels of this neurotransmitter are associated with impulsive aggression

Answers on page 368

CHOOSE THE RIGHT ANSWER

Which **two** of the following may be associated with a propensity to violent crime? (Tick **two** boxes only.)

A   Having an MAOA gene ☐

B   Brain damage in the prefrontal cortex ☐

C   High levels of serotonin in the brain ☐

D   Having an identical twin who is a violent criminal ☐

Answers on page xxx

RESEARCH ISSUES 1

Twin studies have shown higher concordance rates for delinquent behaviour in monozygotic twins than dizygotic twins. For example, 52% concordance for MZ and 21% for DZ.

(a) What can you conclude from this about genetic causes of delinquency? *(3 marks)*

(b) A criticism of these studies is that there is an assumption that MZ and DZ twins only differ in their genetics. Why might this assumption not be correct? *(2 marks)*

(c) Why might the classification of twins as MZ or DZ been inaccurate in early studies? How might this problem be avoided using modern techniques? *(2 marks)*

Answers on page 368

RESEARCH ISSUES 2

Adoption studies aim to separate out the effect of genes and the environment, by comparing adopted children's criminal behaviour with that of their biological and adopted parents. The assumption is that similarities with biological parents are due to heredity, while similarities with adoptive parents are caused by environmental influences.

(a) One criticism of adoption studies is that children are not all adopted at birth. How might this affect the findings of the studies? *(2 marks)*

(b) Adoption agencies often try to match children and adoptive parents on key characteristics. How might this affect the validity of conclusions of these studies? *(2 marks)*

(c) How might the adoption process itself influence outcomes for children? Consider the effect of attachments to caregivers. *(2 marks)*

Answers on page 368

APPLYING YOUR KNOWLEDGE

Alana has discovered that her estranged lover, the father of her son, has been arrested for murder. In his trial, his lawyer presents evidence that he has two genes, variants of MAOA and CHD13, which together make it very difficult for him to resist violent behaviour. Alana is very worried that her son, Alan, will also become a murderer.

Use your knowledge of research into genetic explanations of offending behaviour to examine this possibility. *(6 marks)*

Identify the psychology	Link to Alan

Answers on page 368

KEY TERMS

- Extraversion
- Neuroticism
- Psychoticism

Possible essay question

Describe and evaluate Eysenck's theory of the criminal personality. *(16 marks)*

Other possible exam questions …

+ Briefly outline Eysenck's theory of the criminal personality. *(4 marks)*

+ Give **one** criticism of Eysenck's theory of the criminal personality. *(3 marks)*

Exam tip

Eysenck's theory proposes a genetic basis to personality, but adult personality is determined by learning experiences too. You can use the nature–nurture debate to discuss this interaction.

MUST know …

Eysenck's theory of personality

Character traits cluster along three normally distributed dimensions:

- Extraversion – introversion
- Neuroticism – stability
- Psychoticism – normality

Link to criminal behaviour

Extraverts seek more arousal and therefore engage in dangerous activities. Neurotics are unstable and may over-react to situations of threat. Psychotic individuals are aggressive and lack empathy.

Criminality develops from an interaction between innate traits and environmental factors such as conditioning. People who are high in extraversion and neuroticism are less easily conditioned, and do not learn to avoid anti-social behaviour.

 Research support for personality types…

…comes from twin studies.

- **E** – Zuckerman (1987) found a +.52 correlation for neuroticism in MZ twins but only .24 for DZ twins. For extraversion, MZ twins had +.51 and DZ had +.12 correlation, and results for psychoticism were similar.

 A criticism of personality traits is…

…that it assumes personality is consistent.

- **E** – However, many psychologists support a situational perspective; someone may be calm and relaxed at home but neurotic at work.

 Personality tests lack validity…

…because they depend on self-reported data.

- **E** – People may tend towards socially desirable answers, so their answers may not be truthful. Lie scales are included to try to eliminate dishonest responders.

SHOULD know …

Biological basis

Eysenck (1982) claimed each trait has a biological basis and 67% of the variance for the traits is due to genetic factors.

Extraversion is related to cortical arousal level. Extraverts seek external stimulation to increase arousal. Introverts are innately over-aroused and seek to avoid stimulation.

Neuroticism relates to reactivity in the sympathetic nervous system. A neurotic person is unstable and gets easily upset. A stable personality has a less reactive nervous system and is calm under pressure.

Psychoticism is related to higher testosterone levels, so men are more likely to be at this end of the spectrum.

- **E** – However, a correlation of +.50 means that about 40% of variance in this trait is due to genes.
- **L** – This indicates some genetic factor is involved in personality traits, as MZ twins have higher concordances than DZ, but it is not as high as Eysenck suggested.

- **E** – Mischel and Peake (1982) asked family, friends and strangers to rate 63 students in a variety of situations and found almost no correlation between traits displayed.
- **L** – This shows that the notion of a fixed criminal personality is flawed, as people behave differently in different situations.

- **E** – The Eysenck Personality Questionnaire (EPQ) consists of forced-choice items, such as 'Are you a worrier?' which must be answered with 'yes' or 'no' – there is no option for 'sometimes'.
- **L** – This means the findings of the EPQ may not represent reality.

Personality and criminal behaviour

- **P** – Criminals score higher for the personality traits of extraversion and psychoticism than non-criminals.
- **E** – Dunlop *et al.* (2012) found that these traits, and high scores on the lie scale, were good predictors of delinquency.
- **E** – However, participants were students and their friends, and only minor offences were assessed, reducing the generalisability of these findings.
- **L** – So there is some support for a link between personality traits and criminal behaviour.

Applications

- **P** – It is difficult to know how the information about personality and criminality can be used.
- **E** – Although the three traits are predictors of delinquency, they are not good enough to detect who is likely to become an offender.
- **E** – One possibility is to modify the socialisation experiences and conditioning of children who have the potential to become offenders.
- **L** – So personality trait theory could have some applications in preventing or treating offending behaviour.

MATCH THEM UP

Match up the trait with the description.

1	Extraversion	**A**	Angry, anxious or depressed
2	Neuroticism	**B**	Calm under pressure
3	Psychoticism	**C**	Outgoing, positive, easily bored
4	Introversion	**D**	Conscientious, empathetic
5	Stability	**E**	Quiet, seeking to reduce stimulation
6	Normality	**F**	Egocentric, aggressive, impulsive

Answers on page 369

 RESEARCH ISSUES

The Eysenck Personality Questionnaire (EPQ) is one of the best-known psychological tests. A number of shorter versions have been developed including the EPQ-BV ('BV' stands for brief version). Sato (2005) assessed this new scale in terms of test–retest reliability and concurrent validity.

(a) Explain how test–retest reliability is calculated. *(3 marks)*

(b) If the reliability was low, explain how this could be improved. *(2 marks)*

(c) Explain what is meant by 'concurrent validity'. *(1 mark)*

(d) Concurrent validity was calculated by comparing the current scale and the original scale. A figure of .88 was produced. Explain what this value means in the context of concurrent validity. *(2 marks)*

(e) Name **one** other method that could be used to assess the validity of a questionnaire/psychological test and explain how it could be used here. *(3 marks)*

(f) Describe **two** factors that threaten the validity of psychological tests such as the EPQ. *(4 marks)*

Answers on page 369

 **APPLYING YOUR KNOWLEDGE**

Luca is an energetic, lively teenager who loves partying and is the class clown. He is getting into trouble at school because he can't seem to sit still, and when a teacher tells him to calm down he becomes rude and stroppy. What his friends don't know is that, when he is at home on his own, he can feel really low and anxious. His usual solution is to go online and get into some banter, or to get out of the house to be with his friends laughing and joking, climbing up statues or over fences and walls, and adding his tag on bridges. How might Luca score on the Eysenck Personality Questionnaire, and how does this relate to his anti-social behaviour? *(6 marks)*

Luca's personality traits	Luca's anti-social behaviour

Answers on page 369

KEY TERMS

- Cognitive distortion
- Hostile attribution bias
- Minimalisation
- Moral reasoning

Possible essay question

Discuss **one or more** cognitive explanations of offending behaviour. *(16 marks)*

Other possible exam questions …

+ Explain what is meant by 'hostile attribution bias'. *(2 marks)*

+ Explain how cognitive distortions can be used to explain offending behaviour. *(4 marks)*

+ Evaluate moral reasoning as an explanation for offending behaviour. *(6 marks)*

 Link

Read more about Kohlberg's theory of moral development on page 42 of The Complete Companion Student Book

---

MUST know …

Cognitive distortions

Irrational or inaccurate thinking which can allow an offender to rationalise their behaviour.

Hostile attribution bias is a negative interpretation of events, attributing malicious intentions to other people's behaviour. For example, if someone smiles you perceive them as mocking.

Minimalisation is underplaying the consequences of an action to reduce negative emotions such as guilt. For example, a burglar may think that stealing from a wealthy family doesn't affect them.

Levels of moral reasoning

In England and Wales the 'age of criminal responsibility', when children are considered to be able to understand principles of right and wrong, is ten years old.

 Research support for hostile attribution bias…

…comes from studies of violent offenders in prison.

- ***E*** – Schönenberg and Aiste (2014) found that offenders were more likely than matched controls to interpret pictures as expressing aggression.

 Research support for minimalisation…

…comes from sex offenders' own accounts of their crimes.

- ***E*** – Kennedy and Grubin (1992) found that offenders downplayed their behaviour, often suggesting that the victim's behaviour was responsible for the crime, or denying that a crime had been committed.

 Research into levels of moral reasoning….

…supports a universal sequence of stages.

- ***E*** – Gudjonsson and Sigurdsson (2007) found that 38% of male juvenile offenders did not consider the consequences of their actions, suggesting they were at Kohlberg's pre-conventional level of moral reasoning.

SHOULD know …

Levels of moral reasoning – Kohlberg's theory

Pre-conventional level: Children under ten years old accept the rules of authority and judge actions by their consequences. Criminals are likely to be at this level, believing that breaking the law is justified if the rewards outweigh the risks of punishment.

Conventional level: Most adults believe that conformity to social rules is desirable, as it maintains social order and positive relationships. They may break the law in order to protect a family member.

Post-conventional level: 10% of adults reach this stage, defining morality by abstract moral principles rather than compliance to norms.

- ***E*** – The pictures were emotionally ambiguous and showed varying intensities of angry, happy and fearful emotions.
- ***L*** – This misinterpretation of facial expressions may explain some aggressive behaviours in individuals who perceive these non-verbal cues as aggressive.

- ***E*** – However, Maruna and Mann (2006) suggested that this is fairly normal behaviour, as we try all to blame external factors or other people, to protect ourselves.
- ***L*** – Therefore, sex offenders do use minimalisation, but this mechanism is not especially deviant.

- ***E*** – Chen and Howitt (2007) found, in Taiwanese male adolescent offenders, that those with more advanced reasoning were less likely to be involved in violent crimes.
- ***L*** – This research supports the relationship between moral reasoning and offending behaviour.

FURTHER EVALUATION

Limitations of Kohlberg's theory

- ***P*** – Kohlberg's theory concerns moral thinking rather than behaviour.
- ***E*** – Krebs and Denton (2005) found that people are motivated by factors like financial gain and only use moral principles to justify behaviour retrospectively.
- ***E*** – Also, Kohlberg's theory was based on research in men and boys, so is gender biased.
- ***L*** – So the theory is limited in its ability to explain causes of offending behaviour, and particular in relation to women.

Real-life application of cognitive explanations

- ***P*** – Cognitive explanations can be used in treatment of offenders.
- ***E*** – Heller *et al.* (2013) used cognitive behavioural techniques (CBT) to reduce cognitive distortions in young men in Chicago.
- ***E*** – Participants who had attended 13 one-hour sessions had a 44% reduction in arrests compared to a control group.
- ***L*** – So, although it is not possible to identify potential criminals by their cognitive distortions, CBT can help rehabilitate people.

CHOOSE THE RIGHT ANSWER

A campaigner for animal rights has broken into a research lab and released 25 experimental rats, who are now running for the woods. The campaigner has been arrested for criminal damage and theft. Which stage of moral reasoning is he likely to be at? (Tick **one** box only.)

A Pre-conventional ☐

B Conventional ☐

C Post-conventional ☐

Answers on page 369

An idea 👍
Before you revise this spread, make sure you are clear about the cognitive approach to psychology generally. Make a mind map of key ideas and assumptions on a separate piece of papers. You can also link in the cognitive explanation of depression which you covered in Psychopathology.

 Link

See Year 1/AS Revision and Exam Companion, page 138 and p114, for the cognitive approach and the cognitive explanation of depression.

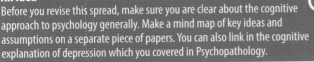 **APPLYING YOUR KNOWLEDGE 1**

In Heller *et al*.'s CBT intervention with Chicago youth, the first activity is the 'Fist Exercise'. High school students are divided into pairs; each student in turn has 30 seconds to get his partner to open his fist. Almost all try to use physical force to open their partners' fists. The group leader then asks them to explain what they tried and how it worked, pointing out that almost no one has asked their partner to open their fist. When youth are asked why, they usually provide responses such as: 'He wouldn't have done it,' or 'He would have thought I was a punk.' The group leader will then ask: 'How do you know?'

(a) What cognitive distortions are the young people displaying? *(2 marks)*

(b) How does the intervention try to address these? *(2 marks)*

(c) The researchers predict that the intervention will increase high school graduation rates by about 10%. What might the economic benefits of this intervention be? *(3 marks)*

Answers on page 369

 APPLYING YOUR KNOWLEDGE 2

In his investigation of levels of moral reasoning in young males, Kohlberg used scenarios such as this:

Heinz's wife was dying from a particular type of cancer. Doctors said a new drug might save her. The drug had been discovered by a local chemist and Heinz tried desperately to buy some, but the chemist was charging ten times the money it cost to make the drug and this was much more than the Heinz could afford.

Heinz could only raise half the money, even after help from family and friends. He explained to the chemist that his wife was dying and asked if he could have the drug cheaper or pay the rest of the money later.

The chemist refused, saying that he had discovered the drug and was going to make money from it. The husband was desperate to save his wife, so later that night he broke into the chemist's and stole the drug.

Then Kohlberg asked: 'Should Heinz have stolen the drug?'

(a) How would a person at each level of moral reasoning have answered? *(3 marks)*

(i) Pre-conventional:

(ii) Conventional:

(iii) Post-conventional:

(b) What issues of validity are there with this research? *(3 marks)*

Answers on page 369

MATCH THEM UP

Match up the level of reasoning to the justification for crime.

1	Pre-conventional level	A	It was important to do this in order to protect my friend.
2	Conventional level	B	It was OK to do this as there was little chance of being caught.
3	Post-conventional level	C	It was worth doing this as there are bigger ethical principles at stake.

Answers on page 369

KEY TERM

- Differential association theory

Possible essay question

Discuss **one or more** psychological explanations of offending behaviour. *(16 marks)*

Other possible exam questions …

+ Briefly outline differential association theory as an explanation for offending. *(2 marks)*

+ Describe and evaluate differential association as an explanation for offending. *(16 marks)*

 Exam tip

An exam question may ask for a biological and/or psychological explanation of offending, and you can choose which you write about. If you are asked for 'one or more' explanations, it may be best to focus on one so you can explain it effectively in the time available.

MUST know …

Differential association theory

Sutherland (1939) proposed that offending behaviour can be explained entirely by social learning.

What is learned?

A child learns attitudes towards crime, and which crimes are acceptable or desirable, as well as methods of committing crimes.

Who is it learned from?

Family, peers and the local community may model criminal behaviour or may show acceptance of deviant attitudes.

How is it learned?

Sutherland did not specify this, but it is likely to be direct reinforcement (operant conditioning), and observation; if role models are successful this provides vicarious reinforcement. Social norms are also involved.

 The theory made a major contribution

…to understanding causes of crime as being social, not just blaming individuals.

- **E** – In this theory, crime could be explained in terms of people's social experiences, rather than labelling them as 'mad' or 'bad'.

 Supporting evidence comes from…

…family studies and peer group studies.

- **E** – Osborne and West (1979) found that 40% of sons of fathers with a criminal conviction had committed a crime before age 18, compared to 13% of sons of non-criminal fathers.

 An issue with this research is…

…that it is correlational.

- **E** – So it is possible that offenders seek out other offenders, rather than being influenced by them to become offenders.

SHOULD know …

Key principles

1 Criminal behaviour is learned rather than inherited,

2 …through *association* with…

3 …intimate personal groups.

4 Techniques and attitudes are learned.

5 Learning is directional – for or against crime.

6 If favourable attitudes outweigh unfavourable ones, then a person becomes an offender.

7 Learning experiences (differential associations) vary in frequency and intensity.

8 Criminal behaviour is learned through the same processes as any other behaviour.

9 General 'need' (e.g. for money) is not a sufficient explanation for crime because not everyone with those needs turns to crime.

- **E** – Sutherland also introduced the concept of 'white collar crimes', committed by middle class, respectable people, such as fraud, corruption, forgery and copyright infringements.
- **L** – This has important applications, as we can try to change social learning environments, whereas genes cannot be changed.

- **E** – Akers *et al.* (1979) surveyed 2,500 US adolescents, finding that peers were the greatest influence on drinking and drug-taking.
- **L** – Family studies can't separate out the effects of genes and environment, but peer studies show that young people are being influenced by their peers, supporting differential association theory.

- **E** – Some critics also argue that the theory is untestable because of the interaction between learned and inherited factors, and it is unclear what ratio of favourable to unfavourable influences would tip the balance.
- **L** – This means that we cannot conclude cause and effect, and we cannot test the theory experimentally, so its validity is unclear.

FURTHER EVALUATION

 Different types of crime

- **P** – Social learning probably influences smaller crimes most, rather than violent impulsive ones like rape and murder.
- **E** – Although non-violent crimes are much more common so this influence is still useful to understand.
- **E** – Also, 40% of offences are carried out by people under 21, which is better explained by a desire for risk-taking.
- **L** – So differential association only gives a partial explanation of offending behaviour.

 The role of biological factors

- **P** – This explanation ignores biological factors.
- **E** – There may be innate genetic factors or early experiences which affect brain development.
- **E** – There is clear evidence that biological factors are also important in the development of anti-social and violent behaviour.
- **L** – This means that a diathesis-stress model may offer a better account by combining social factors with biological predispositions.

MATCH THEM UP

Match up the evaluation point with its elaboration

1	Major contribution to understanding causes of crime as social	A	In 2,500 US adolescents, peers were the greatest influence on substance abuse
2	There is research evidence	B	So we can't conclude cause and effect
3	The research is correlational	C	So it only gives a partial explanation of offending behaviour
4	Social learning doesn't explain serious violent crime	D	This has practical applications as we can change social environments but not genes
5	The explanation ignores biological factors	E	A diathesis-stress model may offer a fuller account of offending behaviour.

Answers on page 369

CHOOSE THE RIGHT ANSWER

Which **one** of the following is **not** true of differential association theory? (Tick **one** box only.)

A It is supported by experimental evidence. ☐

B It is a sociological theory. ☐

C It can explain how people's attitudes become less favourable to particular crimes. ☐

D It involves learning processes such as reinforcement. ☐

E It does not incorporate the contribution of inherited susceptibilities. ☐

Answers on page 369

COMPLETE THE TABLE

Practise remembering Sutherland's nine key principles by completing the table from memory, then check against the list on the opposite page. We have given you some hints in the left hand column.

Practise several times until you can remember them fluently.

Criminal behaviour is…	
(How?)	
(Who?)	
(What?)	
Learning is…	
If…. then…	
Learning experiences vary in…	
(learning processes)	
General 'need' is not…	

APPLYING YOUR KNOWLEDGE

Lauren's mother and father divorced and Lauren and her mother had to move to the rough part of town to find cheaper accommodation. Initially Lauren found it difficult to make friends but then started hanging out with the 'bad girls' in the neighbourhood, many of whom have been excluded from school. Lauren's behaviour seems to go from bad to worse, and the visits from the police soon start after she is found to be selling stolen property at school.

How can we explain Lauren's behaviour in terms of differential association theory? *(6 marks)*

Identify the psychology	Link to Lauren's behaviour

Answers on page 369

KEY TERMS

- Affectionless psychopathy
- Maternal deprivation
- Psychodynamic explanation
- Superego

Possible essay question

Describe and evaluate psychodynamic explanations of offending behaviour. *(16 marks)*

Other possible exam questions ...

+ Briefly outline **one** psychodynamic explanation of offending behaviour. *(3 marks)*

+ Outline **one** study related to the psychodynamic explanations of offending behaviour. Include details of what the researchers did and what was found. *(4 marks)*

 Link

See page 106 for an explanation of identification with the same-sex parent.

 Link

See page 48 for more on gender bias.

MUST know ...

Maternal deprivation theory

Bowlby (1951) was a Freudian psychiatrist. He proposed that prolonged separations between a mother and child would have long-term emotional consequences. There was most risk if the separation was before the age of about two and a half years and there was no substitute mother-person, with continuing risk up to age five years.

The long-term consequence is **affectionless psychopathy**; lack of empathy, shame or sense of responsibility.

Bowlby (1944) studied 44 delinquent children attending his clinic. 39% of all thieves, and 12 out of 14 classified as affectionless, had experienced frequent separations.

 Bowlby's theory has important applications…

…in the care of young children.

- **E** – Bowlby, with the Robertsons, demonstrated that children could cope with separations from parents as long as alternative emotional care was provided.

 However, the research does not allow causal conclusions…

…as separation was not manipulated.

- **E** – There could be other explanations of the association between separation and emotional problems, such as the effect of disrupted home life.

 Freud's theory is gender biased…

…as he proposed that women develop a weaker superego than men.

- **E** – This is partly because Freud believed there was little reason for anyone to identify with a woman because of her lower status, so girls' identification with their mother was weaker.

SHOULD know ...

The superego

In Freud's psychoanalytic theory, the id operates according to the pleasure principle, and the superego is a moral compass, causing guilt when rules are broken. The ego acts as the reality principle and mediates between the id and superego.

A child whose parent is absent develops a weak superego, and acts impulsively to gratify the id.

A child with a strict parent develops a harsh superego, with excessive guilt and anxiety. Committing crime and receiving punishment may relieve these feelings.

A child with a criminal parent will identify with them and adopt the same deviant superego.

- **E** – It is difficult to treat emotional problems in adolescent delinquents, and much better to prevent them by avoiding early separations.
- **L** – Social policies and childcare provision have been influenced enormously by Bowlby's work on attachment and maternal deprivation.

- **E** – It is even possible that the child's affectionless personality caused the separations in some cases, as the mother could not cope.
- **L** – This means Bowlby's 44 thieves study should be used with caution to support his theory.

- **E** – If Freud's views were correct, women should be more likely to become criminals than men. This is not the case.
- **L** – This means that the alpha bias in Freud's theory devalues women and leads to incorrect predictions, so the theory is not supported by evidence.

FURTHER EVALUATION

Consideration of emotion

- **P** – The psychodynamic is the only explanation of offending which considers emotional factors.
- **E** – Unlike cognitive theories, it takes into account the involvement of feelings of anxiety or rejection in offending behaviour.
- **E** – It also recognises the role of innate drives and early childhood experiences in moulding adult personality.
- **L** – So psychodynamic explanations address multiple factors and offer some useful insights into the effect of childhood experiences on adult behaviour.

 ### Complex set of factors

- **P** – There are many factors that interact to cause offending.
- **E** – Farrington *et al.* (2009), in a 40-year longitudinal study in London, identified the most important risk factors at age 8–10 for later offending.
- **E** – They include: family history of criminality; risk-taking personality; low school attainment; poverty; poor parenting.
- **L** – This shows that a combined approach (biological, personality, cognitive and psychodynamic) can give a fuller picture of the causes of offending.

An idea
Before revising this section, make sure you remember the key features of the psychodynamic approach (Paper 2 – Approaches) and Bowlby's theory of maternal deprivation (Paper 1 – Attachment). Make a mind map on a large piece of paper, and add on some links to show how these theories explain delinquent behaviour.

 Link
See page 82 of the Year 1/AS Revision and Exam Companion for an explanation of Bowlby's theory of attachment.

 Link
See page 142 of the Year 1/AS Revision and Exam Companion for an explanation of the psychodynamic approach.

 MATCH THEM UP

Match up the problem with its consequence.

1	Criminal same-sex parent	A	Harsh superego
2	Overdeveloped superego	B	Weak superego
3	Underdeveloped superego	C	Affectionless psychopathy
4	Maternal deprivation	D	Uncontrolled impulses
5	Absent parent	E	Excessive guilt and anxiety
6	Strict parent	F	Deviant superego

Answers on page 370

 RESEARCH ISSUES

Bowlby's study of 44 thieves at a London clinic included a comparison group of 44 adolescents who had been referred to the clinic for emotional issues but had not yet committed any crime.

(a) What sort of sampling did Bowlby use? What are the limitations of this type of sample? *(3 marks)*

(b) Bowlby diagnosed some as having affectionless psychopathy. He also carried out the clinical interviews to collect data about separations, and knew which young people had committed thefts and which had not. How could this affect his findings? *(2 marks)*

(c) The number of separations experienced was measured by asking the young people to remember their early childhood. How might this affect validity? *(1 mark)*

Answers on page 370

 COMPLETE THE TABLE

Summarise all the psychological explanations of offending behaviour by completing the table.

	Eysenck's theory	Cognitive	Differential association	Psychodynamic
Consists of:	Personality traits – genetic + learned			
Link to criminal behaviour		Hostile attribution bias, minimalisation Pre-conventional level of moral reasoning		
Applications			Improving social environments to reduce crime	
Research support				Bowlby's 44 thieves – separations associated with affectionless psychopathy and delinquency
Criticisms	Personality may not be consistent, self-report tests not valid			

Answers on page 370

Key Terms

- De-individuation
- Recidivism

Possible essay question

Discuss research on custodial sentencing and its effects on recidivism. *(16 marks)*

Other possible exam questions …

+ Explain what is meant by 'recidivism'. *(2 marks)*
+ Outline the aims of custodial sentencing. *(4 marks)*
+ Outline the psychological effects of custodial sentencing. *(4 marks)*

 Think

In the UK in 2015 there were 80,000 men and 4,000 women in prison. 46% of adults and 67% of under 18-year-olds are reconvicted within one year of release. The cost to the economy of this recidivism (re-offending) is at least £9.5 billion per year.

 Link

See de-individuation and the Stanford Prison Study on page 244

 Link

See page 274 for an explanation of differential association theory.

MUST know …

Aims of custodial sentencing

A custodial sentence requires an offender to be held in a prison or secure psychiatric hospital. Aims include:

1. **To protect the public - incapacitation:** necessary with violent offenders or psychopaths.
2. **To punish an offender and prevent recidivism:** a behaviourist approach, aiming to decrease the likelihood of the behaviour being repeated.
3. **To deter others:** a social learning approach, learning from the consequences of others' behaviour.
4. **To atone for wrongdoing - retribution:** the offender should pay for what they have done.
5. **To rehabilitate offenders:** providing therapy or education to prevent further criminal behaviour.

 Punishment is ineffective…

…in preventing recidivism or acting as a deterrent.

- ***E*** – At least 50% of the prison population re-offend within a year of release, and even severe punishments do not work as deterrents; murder rates in US states with the death penalty are no lower.

 Incapacitation, retribution and rehabilitation…

…are also limited in their benefits.

- ***E*** – Incapacitation only applies to a small number of dangerous prisoners, rehabilitative therapy cannot be forced on someone, and retribution can be better achieved in other ways.

 Prison may even increase re-offending…

…by acting as a training ground for crime.

- ***E*** – Sutherland's differential association theory suggests that spending time with other criminals will normalise pro-criminal attitudes and provide learning opportunities for how to be successful at committing crimes.

SHOULD know …

Psychological effects of custodial sentencing

De-individuation: loss of individual identity, leading to increased aggression

Depression, self-harm and suicide: Offenders may feel hopeless and helpless. Young men are at highest risk of suicide in the first 24 hours of imprisonment.

Overcrowding and lack of privacy: 25% of prisoners are in overcrowded accommodation, with two people in a cell designed for one. Overcrowding causes stress, aggression and illness.

Effects on the family: parents in prison experience guilt and separation anxiety, and their children suffer financially and psychologically.

- ***E*** – This may because of the long gap between offending and sentencing, so the offender sees the sentence as a punishment for being caught.
- ***L*** – This means punishment does not work, as offenders may learn that they should avoid being caught.

- ***E*** – For example, restorative justice offers the chance for offenders to make amends to victims, while changing their attitudes to offending.
- ***L*** – This means that many of the aims of custodial sentencing could be better achieved by other types of sentencing or treatment.

- ***E*** – Latessa and Lowenkamp (2006) found that placing offenders at low risk of recidivism with high-risk offenders makes it more likely that low-risk offenders will re-offend.
- ***L*** – So imprisonment may reinforce pro-criminal attitudes and encourage increased criminal behaviour on release.

FURTHER EVALUATION

 Individual differences

- ***P*** – Custodial sentences may be more effective with some offenders than others.
- ***E*** – For example, Walker *et al.* (1981) found that length of sentence didn't affect the recidivism rate of habitual offenders.
- ***E*** – Young people are more likely to re-offend, and those committing theft or burglary are twice as likely to re-offend as drug or sex offenders.
- ***L*** – Thus, sentencing should be targeted in different ways with different groups of offenders.

 Non-custodial sentencing

- ***P*** – Prison care is expensive and ineffective in reducing crime, so alternatives should be considered.
- ***E*** – These include probation, fines, electronic monitoring, community service and anti-social behaviour orders.
- ***E*** – Evidence shows that cautions are more effective deterrents than arrests (Klein *et al.*, 1977), and non-custodial sentences avoid the psychological problems of imprisonment.
- ***L*** – Other forms of sentencing, such as community sentences, are especially suitable for new or non-violent offenders.

MATCH THEM UP

Match up the aim of custodial sentencing with its explanation and its evaluation point

1	Incapacitation	**A**	To atone for wrongdoing	**i**	Desire for change is important – therapy can't be forced on someone
2	Punishment	**B**	To protect the public	**ii**	Can be better achieved through restorative justice
3	Deterrence	**C**	To prevent recidivism	**iii**	Only relevant for dangerous prisoners
4	Retribution	**D**	To treat or educate	**iv**	Not effective in reducing recidivism
5	Rehabilitation	**E**	To discourage others from crime	**v**	Murder rates no lower in US states with death penalty so even harsh sentences are ineffective

Answers on page 370

 A MARKING EXERCISE

Read this student answer to the following exam question.

Outline the psychological effects of custodial sentencing. *(4 marks)*

One effect is depression, as prisoners often feel hopeless and helpless. This leads to high rates of self-harm and suicide. Also there is often overcrowding in prisons and 25% of prisoners have to share a cell.

This answer was awarded 2 out of 4 marks.

Why do you think it was awarded this mark?

What would you need to add to improve this answer?

Answers on page 370

 APPLYING YOUR KNOWLEDGE

Brigitte had a difficult childhood with an alcoholic mother, and was taken into care at age 13. As a teenager she was cautioned by the police for shoplifting to fund her drug habit, but managed to get work in hotel when she was 17 and kept on the right side of the law. She started medication for depression and anxiety, which she still takes. When she was 22 she fell in love with Ethan, who was good to her, and treated her to new clothes and foreign holidays, but turned out to be a drug dealer. Brigitte and Ethan now have a 13-month-old baby. After a police raid, Brigitte was arrested and has been found guilty of supplying heroin in her local city.

What factors should the judge consider in deciding whether to give Brigitte a custodial sentence for her crime? *(6 marks)*

Identify the psychology	Link to Brigitte

Answers on page 370

 DRAWING CONCLUSIONS

Women only represent 5% of the prison population, but their characteristics differ from male prisoners, as shown in the table below.

Social characteristics of male and female prisoners		
Characteristic	**Men**	**Women**
Have experienced emotional, physical or sexual abuse	27%	53%
Committed their offence in order to support the drug use of someone else	22%	48%
Serving a prison sentence for a non-violent offence	71%	81%
Have no previous convictions	12%	26%
Have spent time in local authority care	24%	31%
Have symptoms indicative of psychosis	15%	25%
Have attempted suicide at some point	21%	46%

(a) In October 2015 there were 3,948 female prisoners. How many of these had committed their offence in order to support the drug use of someone else? *(1 mark)*

(b) What percentage of female prisoners were serving sentences for violent crimes? *(1 mark)*

(c) Using data from the table, describe the psychological differences between male and female prisoners. *(3 marks)*

Answers on page 370

KEY TERMS

- Behavioural modification
- Operant conditioning
- Token economy

Possible essay question

Describe and evaluate the use of behaviour modification in custody as a means of dealing with offender behaviour. *(16 marks)*

Other possible exam questions ...

+ Explain how behaviour modification can be used to deal with offending behaviour. *(3 marks)*
+ Give **one** limitation of behaviour modification as a way of dealing with offending behaviour in custody. *(3 marks)*

 Exam tip

When answering questions on this topic, it is easy to lapse into a general description of operant conditioning and token economy systems without making reference to their use in prison. Marks will be awarded to the extent that your answers are focused on offending behaviour.

MUST know ...

Token economy

Prisoners are rewarded with tokens when they perform desirable behaviours, such as obeying orders. These can be exchanged for treats like cigarettes, food or TV time.

This **reinforcement** increases the likelihood that the behaviour will be repeated (**operant conditioning**).

The treats are primary reinforcers and the tokens become secondary reinforcers through **association** (classical conditioning).

Target behaviours and rewards must be clearly defined in advance, with a hierarchy of rewards for different behaviours.

Punishment can also be used by removing tokens for undesirable behaviour.

Shaping works progressively towards longer-term objectives and more complex behaviours.

 Token economy can be effective...

...and is easy to implement.

- **E** – It provides a means of controlling unmanageable behaviour and improving the prison environment for staff and prisoners, without needing input from psychologists.

 It is less successful in prisons...

...than in schools or for dealing with people with autism.

- **E** – It was used widely and was effective in US prisons in the 1970s, increasing socially acceptable behaviours and reducing crime (Milan and McKee, 1976).

 It doesn't affect re-offending rates...

...or behaviour outside of the prison.

- **E** – This is because token economy only has short-term effects while the rewards are available, and once they cease the stimulus-response link is extinguished.

SHOULD know ...

Key study: Hobbs and Holt (1976)

A token economy was introduced in a school for delinquent boys to try to reduce inappropriate social behaviour.

How? 125 boys were observed in four cottages over 14 months. One was a control group with no tokens.

Two supervisors observed each boy and recorded behaviours in six categories such as following instructions or completing chores. Boys were told daily how many tokens they had earned, and exchanged them weekly for treats, or saved them for off-campus activities.

Showed? Social behaviours increased by an average of 27% in boys who were included in the programme, with no increase in the control group.

- **E** – For it to work well, the token economy needs careful pre-planning and consistent application by staff.
- **L** – So, as long as the token economy is clear and consistent, it can provide a simple way of improving prison life.

- **E** – However, good results did not persist, and use in the UK was limited to young offenders' institutes.
- **L** – Token economy has fallen out of favour in prisons, but is still used in some special schools for young people with behavioural difficulties or autism.

- **E** – Furthermore, the behaviours learned in prison may not apply in the real world, such as walking in a straight line.
- **L** – So token economy can improve behaviour in the prison environment, but this doesn't have a long-term effect on prisoners once they return to their natural environment.

 FURTHER EVALUATION

 Individual differences

- **P** – Some people respond better to operant conditioning than others.
- **E** – For example, juvenile delinquents who had been trained with a token economy system were less likely to re-offend after one year (Cohen and Filipcjak, 1971).
- **E** – Whereas 50% of violent offenders treated using token economy in a maximum security psychiatric hospital re-offended (Rice *et al.*, 1990).
- **L** – So it seems that young offenders may be more responsive to a token economy programme.

Ethical issues

- **P** – Token economy systems can violate human rights as individuals are being manipulated, not always with their agreement.
- **E** – This can be overcome by agreeing procedures and goals between prisoners and staff.
- **E** – However, it is unethical to make basic needs (food or visiting rights) dependent on tokens, or to take away tokens as a punishment.
- **L** – These ethical issues contributed to the loss of popularity of token systems in prisons.

CHOOSE THE RIGHT ANSWER

In a token economy system, tokens are given when prisoners perform desirable behaviours, and these can be exchanged for desirable goods such as chocolate.

Choose **one** of the items below to answer **each** question. Write a letter in each box.

1 In this system, what role is the chocolate playing? ☐

2 What role is the token playing? ☐

3 Tokens can be taken away for undesirable behaviour. What is this consequence called? ☐

4 If prisoners were given electric shocks every time they swore, this might reduce swearing, but would also be unethical. Which consequence is this? ☐

A Primary reinforcer

B Secondary reinforcer

C Negative reinforcement

D Negative punishment

E Positive punishment

Answers on page 370

 A MARKING EXERCISE

Read this student answer to the following exam question:

Outline **one or more** research studies into use of token economy in custody. *(4 marks)*

Hobbs and Holt used token economy in a young offenders' school in Alabama. They had three cottages with the token economy system and one without, total 125 boys. The supervisors observed the boys every day and gave them tokens if they had behaved well, then the boys could buy treats with their tokens. The researchers found that the behaviour improved with the token economy.

How many marks would you give this answer?

What does it need to improve it?

Answers on page 370

📖 **RESEARCH ISSUES**

In the study by Hobbs and Holt, data was gathered by recording behaviour on a daily chart. Two supervisors recorded each boy's behaviour in five categories, such as following rules, following instructions and walking in a straight line. The boys' behaviour was compared before and after they were awarded tokens.

(a) Identify the independent and dependent variables. *(2 marks)*

(b) Explain why this study might be classed as a natural experiment. *(2 marks)*

Two supervisors recorded the behaviour for each boy.

(c) Why were two supervisors used? *(2 marks)*

Reliability was calculated by comparing the observations of each boy by the two supervisors. Calculations of reliability ranged from 70–100%.

(d) How could the reliability be improved in this study? *(2 marks)*

(e) After the research programme finished, the token economy programme gradually deteriorated. Suggest why this might be. *(2 marks)*

(f) Hobbs and Holt comment that there is no evidence to show whether behaviours learned at the school were transferred to real life when the boys left. Using your knowledge of operant conditioning, explain why the boys were unlikely to continue these behaviours after release from the programme. *(4 marks)*

Answers on page 370

 APPLYING YOUR KNOWLEDGE

Mrs Cole is the Headteacher at a school for teenagers with behavioural difficulties who have been excluded from mainstream school. She wants to try a token economy system to improve the young people's behaviour. Using your knowledge of token economy systems, what recommendations can you make to Mrs Cole about how to set this up, and what benefits might there be for her school? *(6 marks)*

How to set it up	Benefits

Answers on page 370

KEY TERMS

- Anger management
- Cognitive behaviour therapy (CBT)

Possible essay question

Discuss anger management as a method of dealing with offender behaviour. Refer to evidence in your answer. *(16 marks)*

Other possible exam questions …

+ Identify **one** method of dealing with offending behaviour, and briefly outline its aims. *(3 marks)*

+ Explain **one** strength and **one** weakness of using anger management to deal with offending behaviour. *(4 marks)*

⭐ Exam tip

SIT is a type of cognitive behaviour therapy (CBT), but you need to ensure you explain specifically how it is used to manage anger, and how this can reduce future offending behaviour, in order to get the marks in a question in this topic.

MUST know …

Anger management

Anger management programmes use a **cognitive approach** to reduce aggression in prisons as well as rehabilitating offenders and reducing recidivism.

Key aims

Novaco (2011) identified three aims:

- Cognitive restructuring – greater self-awareness and control of angry thoughts.
- Regulation of arousal – control of the physiological state of anger.
- Behavioural strategies – problem solving, strategic withdrawal and assertiveness.

Example

Ireland (2004) compared baseline and post-treatment assessments for 50 young offenders who had 12 hours of anger management therapy. They were assessed by self-report and by prison officers. She found significant improvements in this group, with no change in an untreated control group.

 Anger management programmes are successful…

…in reducing anger generally.

- **E** – Taylor and Novaco (2006) report 75% improvement rates based on six meta-analyses.

 A methodological issue is…

…that the studies are difficult to compare.

- **E** – Some are brief and intense, and some last for years; some are run by psychologists, and others by prison staff.

 These programmes have limitations…

…as many offenders drop out of the programmes.

- **E** – This may be because they find it difficult to talk about their thoughts and feelings, and to make the effort to change their attitudes and behaviours.

SHOULD know …

Stress inoculation therapy (SIT)

A CBT model developed by Novaco (1975), used with groups in prison or on probation.

1. **Cognitive preparation:** learning about anger and analysing their own patterns of anger.
2. **Skill acquisition:** learning skills like self-regulation, cognitive flexibility and relaxation, and how to resolve conflicts assertively without getting angry.
3. **Application training:** applying skills in role play with feedback from group members, then in real-world settings.

Example

Trimble *et al.* (2015) studied 105 offenders on probation. They had nine two-hour anger management sessions, which significantly reduced the anger the offenders experienced or expressed compared to pre-treatment scores.

- **E** – However, findings of studies with offenders are inconsistent; meta-analyses show only moderate benefits of anger management programmes (Howells *et al.*, 2005).
- **L** – This means it is difficult to draw clear conclusions about the effectiveness of anger management programmes for offenders.

- **E** – Also, anger is assessed through self-report or observations by prison staff, both of which are subject to bias. Prisoners often want to be helpful in showing that the therapy worked; the 'hello–goodbye effect'.
- **L** – This means that meta-analyses are not comparing like with like, so findings are inconsistent.

- **E** – It helps to measure 'readiness to change' before the start of a programme.
- **L** – This way programmes can be focussed on the offenders who will complete the course and benefit most from it.

FURTHER EVALUATION

Short- versus long-term goals

- **P** – Most studies focus on short-term goals of reducing aggression in prison.
- **E** – Effects on recidivism are harder to measure as individuals are difficult to follow up.
- **E** – However, McGuire (2008) found that some programmes did reduce re-offending after one year.
- **L** – Anger management programmes are more likely to be successful long-term in combination with general therapeutic support for people on probation.

Anger and aggression

- **P** – Anger management programmes assume that treating anger will reduce aggression and violent crime.
- **E** – However, Loza and Loza-Fanous (1999) found no difference between violent and non-violent offenders' anger levels.
- **E** – This may be because violent offenders mask their anger, or offenders may blame their violent behaviour on anger to avoid personal responsibility.
- **L** – Howells *et al.* (2005) concluded that much violence can take place without anger being a prominent feature.

An idea

Make up a mnemonic to help you learn the stages of the stress inoculation model:

Cognitive Preparation	C
	P
Skill Acquisition	S
	A
Application Training	A
	T

CHOOSE THE RIGHT ANSWER

Which **two** of the following are **not** stages in the stress inoculation model of anger management therapy? (Tick **two** boxes only.)

- **A** Cognitive preparation ☐
- **B** Skill acquisition ☐
- **C** Reciprocal inhibition ☐
- **D** Application training ☐
- **E** Counter conditioning ☐

Answers on page 370

APPLYING YOUR KNOWLEDGE

Dexter is a regular in the local magistrates' court. He frequently gets into fights when he goes out to town for the evening and has a bit of a reputation in the bars and clubs around town as a 'hard man'. After he is arrested for fighting yet again, the magistrate decides that Dexter has 'anger issues' and recommends that he take part in anger management treatment. Suggest an appropriate anger management programme suitable for Dexter and explain how this treatment would proceed. *(6 marks)*

Identify the psychology	Link to Dexter

Answers on page 370

DRAWING CONCLUSIONS

A secure training centre for young offenders aged 12–17 has been running 10-week anger management classes. The summary table below shows how self-report anger ratings changed over the 10-week period in 17 young people who took this programme.

Group	Anger ratings decreased	Anger ratings increased	Anger ratings stayed the same
Completed programme	14	2	1
Control group	8	6	5

A sign test can be used to test the significance of the data.

(a) What is the calculated value of the sign test statistic 'S' for the group who completed the programme? Explain your answer. *(2 marks)*

▼ Table of critical values of *S*.

Level of significance for a one-tailed test	0.05	0.01
Level of significance for a two-tailed test	0.10	0.02
N		
10	1	1
11	2	1
12	2	2
13	3	2
14	3	2
15	3	3
16	4	3
17	4	4
18	5	4
19	5	4
20	5	5

(b) Using the table of critical values of 'S' above, state whether the findings of the study are significant at p < 0.05. Explain your answer. *(2 marks)*

(c) The control group consisted of young people who have signed up for this course but are currently on a waiting list. Why was this a suitable control group? *(2 marks)*

(d) What conclusions can you draw from the results of the control group? *(3 marks)*

(e) How could the validity of the anger ratings be criticised? *(2 marks)*

Answers on page 370

KEY TERM

- Restorative justice

Possible essay question

Describe and evaluate restorative justice programmes. (16 marks)

Other possible exam questions …

+ Explain what is meant by 'restorative justice'. (3 marks)
+ Outline what is involved in a restorative justice programme. (4 marks)
+ Briefly evaluate restorative justice programmes. (4 marks)

MUST know …

Restorative justice

Restorative justice enables offenders to repair the harm they have done, often by meeting with victims and a mediator, or by letter.

Aims of restorative justice

Rehabilitation of offenders: The victim explains the impact of the crime. The offender can understand the victim's perspective, and take responsibility. This should affect their future behaviour.

Atonement for wrongdoing: Offenders may offer compensation (money or community service) and show their remorse. The victim can express their distress; this helps the offender develop empathy.

Victim's perspective: The victim feels less powerless, as they have a voice. They may understand the offender's story better, reducing their sense of victimisation.

 EVALUATION *Victims find restorative justice beneficial…*

…and this is supported by evidence.

- *E* – The UK Restorative Justice Council (2015) report 85% satisfaction from victims after face-to-face meetings with offenders.

 EVALUATION *Re-offending rates are reduced…*

…by 14% overall by restorative justice programmes.

- *E* – Sherman and Strang (2007) reviewed 20 studies of face-to-face meetings in three countries, and found reduced re-offending in all cases.

EVALUATION *Restorative justice also has other advantages…*

…compared to custodial sentencing.

- *E* – It is much less expensive, reduces exposure to criminal attitudes in prison, and promotes offender accountability.

SHOULD know …

A theory of restorative justice

Wachtel and McCold (2003) propose that the focus should be on restoring relationships, rather than punishment. Three stakeholders must be involved for fully restorative justice; the victim seeking reparation, the offender taking responsibility, and the community aiming to maintain a healthy society.

Peace circles have been set up in communities with high crime levels, supporting victims and welcoming offenders into the circle to enable mutual understanding. A 'talking piece' is passed round to allow each person to talk without interruption. A 'keeper' helps to maintain an atmosphere of respect and develop constructive solutions.

- *E* – Dignan (2005) found that victims were more satisfied by this process than when cases go through court.
- *L* – This research shows that, for a large range of crimes, from theft to violent crime, restorative justice benefits victims.

- *E* – For example, one study found an 11% re-offending rate compared to 37% in matched controls who served prison sentences.
- *L* – This shows that restorative justice is also successful in its aim of reducing crime rates.

- *E* – Facing a victim may still be sufficiently unpleasant to act as a punishment and a deterrent to future crime.
- *L* – Overall, restorative justice meets many of the aims of custodial sentences while also addressing the needs of victims.

FURTHER EVALUATION

EVALUATION Not a global solution

- *P* – The system isn't able to apply to all crimes committed.
- *E* – Firstly, the offender has to admit to the crime.
- *E* – Secondly, some crimes may not have a direct victim, and some victims may decline the offer.
- *L* – This means that restorative justice can't be a global solution to dealing with all offending behaviour.

EVALUATION Ethical concerns

- *P* – We should consider possible harmful effects on the victim and the offender.
- *E* – One concern is whether the victim may feel worse afterwards.
- *E* – Also, sometimes the victims can abuse their position of power over the offender, who may be young or vulnerable, and may try to shame them.
- *L* – So restorative justice programmes must be carefully managed to ensure benefit to both victim and offender.

✓ CHOOSE THE RIGHT ANSWER 1

What percentage of reduction in re-offending rates does restorative justice achieve, according to the UK Restorative Justice Council (2015)? (Tick **one** box only.)

A 11%	☐
B 12%	☐
C 14%	☐
D 20%	☐

Answers on page 370

✓ CHOOSE THE RIGHT ANSWER 2

What is the main ethical concern in restorative justice initiatives? (Tick **one** box only.)

A The victim may express how distressed they were by the crime.	☐
B The victim may forgive the offender.	☐
C The offender may feel better afterwards.	☐
D The victim may feel worse afterwards.	☐

Answers on page 370

⚙ APPLYING YOUR KNOWLEDGE 1

Anwar works as a community support worker in the centre of Bristol. Over the last 12 months, there has been a spate of crimes such as car theft and burglary. This has created considerable tension between residents of the community and the relatively small number of young men who are responsible for most of the crimes. Having studied forensic psychology at university, Anwar would like to implement a restorative justice programme in the community in an attempt to reduce this tension.

What sort of restorative justice programme might Anwar introduce and how would this help to reduce tensions within the community? *(6 marks)*

Answers on page 370

💡 DRAWING CONCLUSIONS

A survey was carried out by the Restorative Justice Council in March 2016, to find out what restorative justice (RJ) programmes were being offered in different parts of the UK.

- 215 organisations were providing RJ services.
- 193 offered face-to-face victim/offender meetings.
- 132 providers reported that they had delivered a total of 2,638 face-to-face interventions.
- 96 providers reported they had facilitated letter exchanges in a total of 2,179 cases.
- 90 providers reported they had facilitated shuttle mediation in a total of 2,124 cases.

(a) What percentage of organisations were offering face-to-face victim/offender meetings? *(1 mark)*

(b) What percentage facilitated letter exchanges? *(1 mark)*

(c) What was the average number of face-to-face interventions? *(1 mark)*

(d) What was the total number of RJ interventions (direct and indirect) delivered in the last year by survey respondents? *(2 marks)*

Answers on page 371

⚙ APPLYING YOUR KNOWLEDGE 2

Nick's twin brother, was murdered in a local park by a 16-year-old called Craig who lost control of his anger while beating him up to try and get his credit card PIN number. Craig was arrested and sent to prison. Sixteen years later, Nick took the opportunity to meet Craig for  restorative justice when Craig applied for parole. Nick said later that, 'Restorative justice helped me understand that all people can make a serious mistake in their life and be given a second chance – even murderers, even the murderers of my twin brother.'

What was the purpose of this meeting, and how could it benefit Craig and Nick? *(4 marks)*

Identify the psychology	Link to Craig and Nick

You can read Nick's story, and others, on www.restorativejustice.org.uk.

Answers on page 371

Topic 1 Defining and measuring crime

Homosexuality was a crime in the UK until 1969, but remains illegal in many countries; for example, in Saudi Arabia and Iran homosexual activity can be punished with a death penalty.

Referring to the statement above, explain **two** problems in defining crime. *(4 marks)*

Examiner's comments

Crime is often defined as an act that violates the law and results in punishment by the state. A problem with this is that different countries have different laws. For example in the UK homosexuality is not a crime now, whereas in Saudi Arabia and Iran it is. This reflects cultural differences in attitudes to homosexuality.

Secondly, laws can change with time as social attitudes change. This shows that definitions of crime are not fixed but are a social construct.

Examiner's comments: Two problems are clearly presented but only one is appropriately applied to the stem. 3 marks.

> Remember to explicitly link each point to the relevant material from the stem – here, the change in homosexuality laws with time.

Discuss ways of measuring crime. *(8 marks)*

Examiner's comments

Crime can be measured in three ways: Home Office statistics (incidents reported to the police), victim surveys and offender surveys.

Home Office statistics cover all incidents reported to the police or which the police have investigated, and have been collected for 200 years so they are useful for tracking trends in different types of crimes, although the definitions of crime have changed in that time so that makes some of it difficult to make valid comparisons. Another problem is that some crimes don't get reported, maybe because people didn't trust the police to do anything about it, so there is a 'dark figure' of unreported crime.

Victim surveys like the Crime Survey of England and Wales interview a representative sample of the population, to find out what crimes they have experienced in the last year. The advantage of this is that it covers crimes that victims didn't bother reporting. However, people may not be honest. For example victims of domestic abuse may not report it if the abuser is present and they would be scared of the consequences, so they are still an underestimate of crime incidence. Also, the sample is chosen randomly, but 25% of people don't want to take part so the actual sample ends up biased.

Surveys of offenders can be longitudinal surveys of groups of people, and this can help to identify social factors associated with crime as well as numbers of incidents, which is useful. However, people may not be honest about certain crimes like child abuse because of stigma or fear of consequences which might mean they are under-reported.

So in conclusion it's probably best to use a combination of different survey methods to get a fuller picture of crime.

Examiner's comments: This is a brief description of offender surveys with no examples given of particular surveys or their findings. Overall, this is enough material for Level 4 in an 8-mark answer.

> The introduction is not necessary but the student probably wrote this to help them plan their answer.

> The three ways of measuring crime are each described and evaluated in a separate paragraph, with evaluation points, positive and negative, for each one. Definitions of crime are relevant, as the point has been linked in to validity of measures.

> The examples are appropriate and well linked, and so are the evaluation points. More details could be given about the sample size for victim surveys.

> The concluding sentence makes a relevant point, so adds a thoughtful end to the answer.

Topic 2 and Topic 3 Offender profiling: The top-down approach AND The bottom-up approach

Describe and critically compare the top-down and bottom-up approaches to offender profiling.
(16 marks)

Offender profiling aims to narrow down possible suspects in order to catch the offender. Top-down profiling takes an intuitive approach, based on the profiler's experience and hunches, and has been described as an art-form, whereas bottom-up profiling takes a more scientific, data-driven approach.

The top-down approach starts with collection of all possible details about the crime scene, background information about the victim, and anything else that might be relevant, however trivial. The profiler looks for patterns particularly if it is a serial murder. They then classify the crime as organised or disorganised, assuming that will match the personality of the offender. A profile is then produced, with hypotheses about the offender's background and behaviour, which will help the investigators to plan a strategy for their investigation. People who match this profile are then interviewed.

Bottom-up profiling starts with data from similar crimes, and analyses it statistically to make predictions. For example, smallest space analysis looks at correlations between crime scene details and offender characteristics, and identifies themes or types of offender. Geographical profiling tries to work out where the criminal lives; circle theory is based on the idea that people either commit crimes near where they live (marauders), or they travel somewhere else to commit crimes (commuters), but they have a spatial mindset so they are likely to live within a radius of the crime area. Criminal geographic targeting is similar but produces a map with contours showing how likely the criminal is to live in particular areas.

The bottom-up approach uses objective data and statistical analyses, rather than just hunches, so it can be more scientific than top-down. But it only uses information about criminals who have been caught, so unsolved crimes don't get taken into account. And it is still based on assumptions which may not be true, such as the idea that people are consistent in their behaviour between their everyday life and how they behave when committing a crime, which may not be valid.

Surveys of police have found that they think offender profiling can be useful. For example 75% thought the bottom-up profile was useful, but only 3% said it actually helped them catch the criminal. Similarly, 82% of US police said top-down profiling was useful, but courts can be dismissive of evidence based on profiling as it is not scientific. This suspicion may be justified, as research by Alison showed that police are very bad at recognising which offender is described by a profile – profiles can be ambiguous descriptions which could fit many individuals, like horoscopes.

There is a problem with both types of profiling, which is that they may mislead investigators. Some offenders may deliberately leave confusing clues if they know how profiling is done, which is a particular problem with top-down profiling. Bottom-up profiling does take into account the forensic awareness of some offenders, who may know how to avoid leaving clues because they have previous convictions, or have spent time in prison and learned from other criminals. However, it still carries the risk that profiling can lead investigators down the wrong path and they miss the actual offender, and waste time trying to convict the wrong person just because they match the profile.

Level 4 (13–16 marks)

Examiner's comments: Overall, very well organised, answering the question effectively with high-level evaluation points.

Examiner's comments

The first paragraph gives a comparison of the basis of the approaches, which is a useful place to start.

There is a clear description of each approach, with some detail of the steps involved, although there could be more explanation of organised or disorganised offenders.

This paragraph starts with a good general description then gives details of several techniques used, and includes correct terminology.

Critical comparison can include similarities as well as differences, and needs to be evaluative rather than just comparing the processes. Here the student has compared the basis of the approaches, and criticised the 'scientific' validity of bottom-up processing.

Usefulness is another good point of comparison, and is critically evaluated effectively.

Finally the answer compares the ways each approach can mislead investigators, and finishes with the consequences of this – why it is a problem.

Topic 4 and Topic 5 Biological explanations of offending behaviour: A historical approach AND Genetic and neural

Discuss biological approaches to explaining offending behaviour, including reference to historical explanations as well as genetic and neural explanations. *(16 marks)*

The historical explanation of atavistic form is a biological approach, as Lombroso thought that criminals are throwbacks to an earlier stage of evolution. They have physical features like apes, such as hairiness, large jaws and long arms, and their behaviour is also less evolved.

Lombroso collected evidence to support his claims by examining over 50,000 criminals, alive or post-mortem, and found that many of them had features he had identified as atavistic. However, there is a methodological issue with this as he didn't compare with non-criminals so there wasn't a control group. Goring (1913) compared criminals with non-criminals and the only difference was that criminals were a little smaller.

Another criticism of Lombroso's theory is that it was gender biased. He believed that women are less evolved than men, and should naturally be passive and maternal, but women who have masculine traits could become monsters and commit crimes. This is not based on any evidence but just his prejudices.

Genetic explanations aim to identify particular genes linked to criminal behaviour. The MAOA gene is an example – a faulty one has been linked to violent behaviour. It affects the amounts of neurotransmitters linked to aggression. Brunner found this in 28 violent males in a Dutch family. However, this is only a case study so can't be generalised, and it could be that the men learned their behaviour via social learning.

The role of MAOA is supported by Caspi, who found that the MAOA gene variant, along with experience of abuse in childhood, gave a much higher chance of convictions for violent crimes. This was a longitudinal study on 1,000 people so has much more generalisability. This shows that there is an interaction between innate, genetic factors (nature) and experiences (nurture), which is a diathesis-stress model.

Neural explanations relate to brain abnormalities or neurotransmitter imbalances. Criminals may have brain damage from an accident or physical abuse, which could cause problems in their pre-frontal cortex (PFC). The PFC is responsible for rational behaviour and control of emotional impulses which come from the limbic system, so if this is damaged the person may not be able to control their violent behaviour. 60% of US prisoners have a brain injury, compared to 9% of the whole population. Also Raine looked at MRI images of criminals' brains and found that they have abnormal PFC and amygdalas. This supports the brain injury idea, although this is correlational data so it may be that the people's environment caused them to learn criminal behaviour and also led to brain damage, rather than the brain damage causing the behaviour.

Another neural explanation is neurotransmitter differences, like low serotonin, which has been linked to aggression as well as depression. This could lead to useful treatments like SSRIs to reduce aggressive behaviour, which is a practical application. However, it doesn't explain non-violent crime.

Biological explanations are deterministic as they say that criminals can't help behaving that way because of their genes or neural differences. This means that they could avoid

Examiner's comments

This questions requires a brief description of three explanations, which has been well covered in this answer. The structure is sensible in this case, evaluating each explanation as it goes along, and then a general point about biological explanations at the end.

There is an appropriate balance between AO1 and AO3, as there are 6 marks for AO1 and 10 for AO3, so this gives an idea of the proportions to aim for, although the answer is marked as a whole.

There are some well-explained methodological criticisms of studies and the logical argument is clear, for example the progression from criticising Brunner's study as not generalisable, to the Caspi study on a much larger sample.

Information is accurate and concise, with good use of psychological terms and enough details of findings of studies.

criminal responsibility, and lawyers have used this as a defence. It can't be the case as not everyone with the MAOA gene variant becomes a criminal, so a diathesis-stress model gives a better explanation.

Level 4 (13–16 marks)

Examiner's comments: To improve this answer, the links could be expressed more explicitly; AO1 merges into AO3 at times, and conclusions of studies are not always linked back to explain how they support the theory.

However, it is a very competent Level 4 answer.

Topic 6 Psychological explanations of offending behaviour: Eysenck's theory

Briefly outline Eysenck's theory of the criminal personality. *(4 marks)*

Examiner's comments

Eysenck's personality theory measures traits on three dimensions: extravert/introvert, psychotic/normal and neurotic/stable, which are measured using the EPQ – Eysenck Personality Questionnaire. Criminals are likely to be high on extraversion as they need more stimulation and are likely to get into risky behaviour. They will be high on neuroticism as they can be unstable and reactive or stressy. This can be an over-sensitive fight-or-flight system. They will also be high on psychoticism as these people lack empathy and can be aggressive and impulsive and anti-social. This might relate to testosterone levels, which are higher in men than women. All these factors are mainly due to genes.

Examiner's comments: Still, enough for 4 marks.

This outline clearly explains the dimensions of Eysenck's theory and how each one links to criminal behaviour, via biological mechanisms. It also identifies the genes as a factor, but does not explicitly state that this is a biological approach.

Topic 7 Psychological explanations of offending behaviour: Cognitive

Evaluate levels of moral reasoning as an explanation for offending behaviour. *(6 marks)*

Examiner's comments

Criminals are likely to be at the pre-conventional level of moral development, thinking that crime only matters if you get caught, or that the rewards of crime outweigh the risks of getting caught. This is supported by research by Gudjonsson who assessed young male offenders using a questionnaire, and found that about a third of them didn't think about the consequences of being caught or didn't think they would be caught. This supports the idea that they are at the pre-conventional level.

However, people at higher levels could also commit crimes for different reasons; for example if they are at the conventional level they might think it's worth committing a crime in order to help someone, like the Heinz dilemma. And if they're at the post-conventional level they might think there's a higher good, like animal rights activists breaking into research labs and releasing animals.

Also, Kohlberg's stages were about moral reasoning, and it's not clear whether people actually behave this way in real life. He used theoretical scenarios and in real life people's decisions are much more complicated. And his research was all on males, so it is gender biased as females develop a different sense of morals based on caring.

Examiner's comments: A fluent and effective answer. 6 marks.

This answer gives a brief explanation of levels of moral development, but just enough to be able to evaluate them, which is the focus of the question. There is supporting research which is well linked, and several criticisms which are well organised.

Outline how cognitive distortions can explain offending behaviour, and discuss practical applications of this theory. *(8 marks)*

Examiner's comments

Cognitive distortions are irrational or biased thoughts. Hostile attribution bias is when someone thinks that other people hate them, or when you see someone looking at you, you assume they are challenging you. This can make people aggressive in reaction to what they have perceived as rude or aggressive behaviour even if it wasn't really. Criminals also use minimalisation, which is when they say what they did wasn't so bad, or it hasn't affected anyone. This makes the criminal not feel bad about what they did.

These cognitive distortions can be changed by CBT so that criminals think more accurately about what's going on. They might learn to challenge their negative thoughts about other people, thinking instead that maybe people are just looking randomly rather than challenging you. CBT has worked in criminals and reduced re-offending rates, and it is used in anger management therapies to help offenders not get so angry.

Examiner's comments: The practical application section is brief but appropriate, and there is brief comment about the effectiveness, though without any specific research support. This needed more elaboration for an effective discussion. Level 3 answer.

> There is reasonable use of theory and psychological terminology, although the writing style is unclear. The student would do better to refer to 'offenders' or 'people' rather than 'you' or 'they'.

Topic 8 Psychological explanations of offending behaviour: Differential association

Briefly outline and evaluate differential association theory as an explanation for offending. *(4 marks)*

Examiner's comments

The main idea is that people learn the behaviour from people around them – family, peers and communities; it is a social learning theory, so it is learned behaviour. Crime is learned, so it is nurture not nature. People learn attitudes about crime from other people (social norms) and also how to successfully commit crimes.

As this theory is about social contexts where people learn behaviour, rather than personality factors which make them bad people, it is a more useful theory than biological ones as we can actually change social contexts and reduce crime. However, there is evidence that people can have a genetic predisposition to aggression (the MAOA gene) so a diathesis–stress model is probably better, where people have an innate tendency plus some experiences which help to make them criminals.

Examiner's comments: A very good answer for 4 marks.

> The description is a little repetitive, but an accurate summary of the key ideas. The evaluation contains two key points, which are well explained and based around the nature–nurture debate.

Topic 9 Psychological explanations of offending behaviour: Psychodynamic

Describe and evaluate a psychodynamic explanation of offending behaviour. *(8 marks)*

Examiner's comments

Freudian psychoanalytic theory describes how the psyche develops through childhood, because of the innate drives. Boys have to go through the Oedipus complex, where they desire their mother and hate their father and want him to die, before they identify with their father and develop a superego to balance the id (pleasure principle) and ego. If the superego is weak then the boy is impulsive and just lives to gratify his impulses and desires (the id). If the superego is too strong they may commit crimes because they already feel guilty and want to be punished. For girls, the Electra complex is similar but they end up identifying with their mother. Freud believed women have a weaker identification with their parent because women are low status and so no one really wants to be a woman.

> Mostly accurate description of Freud's theory, although some confusion (the ego develops to balance the id and the superego). The student explains how the superego can be too strong or too weak, resulting in criminal behaviour.

This leads to the first criticism. Freud's theory predicts that women have a weaker superego than men, which should mean they commit more crimes, but this is not the case, as 3 times as many men as women are convicted of crimes.

Also, Freud's theory would predict that children brought up by single parents or same-sex couples would have poorly developed superegos, but this is not true as Patterson showed that children from these families develop normal gender identity.

On the other hand, Freud's theory led to Bowlby's maternal deprivation theory, and this does have supporting evidence, for example his 44 thieves study. He found that 86% of affectionless thieves had experienced separations from their mother when they were a young child, compared to only a few of the other thieves.

So early childhood experiences may be a factor in developing offending behaviour, but there are many other factors too, such as family history, personality, and poverty (Farrington).

Examiner's comments: The answer is quite well balanced between AO1 (3 marks available) and AO2 (5 marks available).

The first criticism is well explained, but the second is more relevant to gender development than criminality – it has not been linked in to this, losing some focus. Overall just Level 3.

> Bowlby's theory is not explained at all but the study is briefly summarised, and the final paragraph adds some further evaluation.

Topic 10 Dealing with offending behaviour: Custodial sentencing and recidivism

Read the item and then answer the question below.

Susan is a 35-year-old mother of two young children, whose brother, Clive took part in an armed robbery on the village post office. Over the following six months, she allowed him to visit her house; she helped him disguise himself and supplied clothes, money and his passport. Susan denied to the police having had any contact with Clive. She has been found guilty in court of aiding and abetting a criminal and lying to the police. This is her first offence but the judge is considering whether to give her a six-month prison sentence, as a deterrent, for this serious crime.

Referring to the aims of custodial sentencing, discuss issues the judge should consider in sentencing Susan. *(8 marks)*

Examiner's comments

Custodial sentencing has several possible aims, and the judge should consider whether these aims will be met by giving Susan a custodial sentence. Sometimes it is necessary to put an offender in prison or a secure psychiatric hospital if they would be a danger to the public, but this doesn't apply to Susan. Secondly prison sentences are meant to be a punishment, to make sure the person doesn't repeat offend. This may be applicable to Susan, to make sure she isn't tempted to help her criminal brother again in the future. Also it will be in the news and may make other people realise what a serious offence it is to help a criminal and lie to the police, so this would act as a deterrent. Another reason for imprisoning people is so that victims feel the offender has paid for their crime, but Susan's crime doesn't have direct victims as such, so this is not really relevant.

The final reason is for rehabilitating an offender, with therapy or education in prison. This doesn't seem relevant for Susan as her offence was very specific and she wouldn't need a prison sentence to learn that it was wrong.

On the other hand, the judge should think about the psychological effects on Susan and her children. Spending time in prison could be really bad for her as a young mother; she won't get to see her young children much, and that could make her depressed and also it is bad for the children as they will be separated from their mother for so long, and will see her in prison which would be traumatic. And while she is in prison she would be mixing with criminals – this is her first offence and she might get corrupted by other criminals, taking on their attitudes by differential association, so this is a reason to give her a different sort of sentence like community service, for example.

Examiner's comments: The AO1 and AO2 are well done, but the question asked for a discussion, and the student has not discussed whether custodial sentencing achieves its aims. This makes it a Level 3 answer.

> This is an application question, so every point of theory has to be applied to the scenario in the stem. This answer has achieved this very successfully. The psychological effects of custodial sentences are also discussed – in fact this could have been the bulk of the answer, with research forming part of the evaluation.

Topic 11 and Topic 12 Dealing with offending behaviour: Behaviour modification in custody AND Anger management

Discuss **two** ways of dealing with offending behaviour in custody. *(16 marks)*

Examiner's comments

Two ways that offenders' behaviour can be dealt with in custody are behaviour modification by token economy (a behaviourist approach) and anger management (a cognitive approach).

> This question requires two ways of dealing with offending behaviour **in custody**, so these are the two to go for.

Token economy is based on the principles of operant conditioning. Prisoners are given tokens as a reward for desirable behaviours. They can swap the tokens for things they want, like cigarettes or chocolate, and this reinforces the good behaviour. The treats are a primary reinforcer and the tokens become a secondary reinforcer by association. The idea is that the reinforcers will increase the chance of good behaviour. It is important that the prisoners are really clear about the system of rewards in advance, and that it is applied consistently by staff, for it to work.

> The introductory paragraph usefully states which approach the two ways come from.

Token economy has some support from research. Hobbs and Holt saw it being used in a school for delinquent boys in the 1970s. The token economy was set up in three houses and the social behaviours increased in all three houses, but not in the control house where there wasn't a token economy. This supports that token economy can be useful in improving social behaviour in custody, in young people at least.

> The answer is then fairly balanced between the two, although the description of token economy is more detailed, with more use of psychological terms.

However, the system didn't last long after the study finished and other studies have found that it tends to die out as staff become inconsistent and it doesn't work long term. Also the behaviours are very specific and depend on reinforcement, so they don't continue once the offender has been released back into the community. For example, one Hobbs and Holt programme was trying to get the boys to do things like walking in a straight line, which might be useful in the school but not in real life. So this reduces its ecological validity.

> Research support for token economy is used effectively, and the other discussion points are clear. However, the comment about ecological validity is irrelevant – the skill was valid in the context where it was learnt, but not transferable.

Anger management is a type of cognitive behaviour therapy (CBT) and aims to help offenders change their thought patterns so they don't react so aggressively to things that annoy them. The stress inoculation model has three steps. First, clients learn about anger and analyse what makes them angry. Secondly, they learn skills to deal with anger in different ways rather than attacking people, for example how to talk about things calmly, and they practise relaxation skills to calm their bodies down. Thirdly, they apply these skills.

> SIT is briefly described; the steps are accurate but it seems the student forgot to learn the names of the steps.

Research shows that anger management courses are effective. Young male offenders improved a lot after anger management in Ireland. Meta-analyses generally show that people's anger scores reduce when they have anger management training. However, these are self-report scores so they may not be accurate. They may just be saying they're less angry because they want to get early release.

> The research support is very brief, lacking details, but the evaluation of self-report is good.

A limitation of anger management is that some offenders may find it difficult to talk about their thoughts and feelings in a group, and it is hard work to change thought patterns and behaviours. The offenders have got to be willing to change, rather than just signing up for a course in order to try and get early release. Also it's not clear how the skills learnt in prison would apply to aggressive behaviour in real life after release, and whether the programmes actually reduce re-offending rates.

> The limitations are clear and concise.

Level 3 (9–12 marks)

Examiner's comments: Overall a good answer, but more detail needed in some places. Level 3.

Topic 13 Dealing with offending behaviour: Restorative justice programmes

Describe and evaluate restorative justice programmes. *(16 marks)*

Examiner's comments

Restorative justice (RJ) programmes have been set up as an alternative to prison, and have grown in their impact over the last 20 years, and the EU has now made it a law that victims have to be given information about restorative justice.

The aims of RJ are for rehabilitation of offenders, and giving them an opportunity to atone for their crimes. This generally takes place in face-to-face meetings between the offender and their victim(s), with a facilitator there to help keep everyone calm. Alternatively, it could be indirect, with an exchange of letters between the offender and victim. The victim explains how the crime has affected them, and this helps the offender to understand the personal impact of what they did, which hopefully will put them off re-offending. This is the rehabilitation. The offender may pay compensation to the victim, or may show their guilt and remorse and this helps the victim to feel less victimised and move on.

> The aims of RJ are clearly explained, although what 'atone for their crimes' means could be unpacked more.

> The process is described and linked to the aims.

Wachtel and McCold wrote about the theory of RJ. Ideally the offender, victim and community are involved. This can be seen in peace circles, where members of a community meet up and the victims and offenders are all able to talk and listen to each other, to increase mutual understanding.

> The theory is briefly described, and an application to peace circles is explained.

RJ is successful in achieving its aims, as 85% of victims feel satisfied with the process. This is better than victims whose cases go through the court system, where they don't get a chance to meet the offender and the impact of the crime on the victim is not really heard. This shows that victims feel that offenders have atoned for their crime to some extent via RJ. Also RJ reduces re-offending. The Restorative Justice Council report that there is 14% reduction in re-offending compared to prison sentences. This is clearly achieving the aim of rehabilitating offenders so they don't commit more crimes.

> The evaluation then addresses how successful RJ is in achieving its aims, so the logic of this answer continues into the AO3 section.

Other aims of custodial sentences include deterrence, punishment and protecting the public by locking up dangerous prisoners. The RJ process can be really unpleasant for offenders, who have to face their victims and hear how much trauma they've experienced, so this can act as a deterrent to further crime, although maybe not to first-time offenders. It can also count as a punishment for the same reason. It doesn't lock up dangerous prisoners, but if they have been truly rehabilitated then they wouldn't need locking up. However, it may be more suitable for some crimes than others.

> There is some useful comparison with custodial sentences, and other aims of sentencing.

> The point about different crimes could be elaborated more.

RJ is only possible if the victim agrees to it, so this limits its application. Also there are ethical considerations, as victims may end up feeling worse, or may gang up on a vulnerable offender and make them feel terrible, which isn't the aim of RJ. So these ethical issues need to be carefully considered in planning how RJ is going to work, and the facilitator needs to protect victims and offenders from further harm.

> Limitations are discussed extremely briefly, although ethical issues are explained, giving further evaluative commentary.

Level 4 (13–16 marks)

Examiner's comments: This is a well-structured answer, with a good balance of AO1 and AO3.

Overall a clear, logical answer although some evaluation points could be elaborated further, Level 4.

KEY TERMS

- Addiction
- Physical dependence
- Psychological dependence
- Tolerance
- Withdrawal syndrome

Possible exam questions ...

+ Explain what is meant by the terms 'physical dependence', 'psychological dependence', 'tolerance' and 'withdrawal'. *(2 marks each)*

+ Explain the nature of physical dependence, psychological dependence, tolerance and withdrawal as they apply to addiction. *(4 marks each)*

 Exam tip

There are four key terms listed in the specification, including physical and psychological dependence, tolerance and withdrawal. While you are unlikely to be asked to evaluate any of the information on this page, you should be prepared to answer a short answer knowledge (AO1) or application (AO2) question and therefore it's vital that you know how to apply these terms. (See application of knowledge task on facing page.)

 Think

Researchers often shy away from the term 'addiction' when discussing smoking, gambling and drinking and use the term problem instead. However, the key is to consider whether the behaviour has the characteristics outlined on this page.

MUST know...

Physical and psychological dependence

Physical dependence

Physical dependence can occur with the long-term use of many drugs. This can include drugs of abuse, such as nicotine, but also many prescription drugs (e.g. anti-anxiety drugs). People who are physically dependent have to take the drug in order to feel 'normal'.

Physical dependence can be demonstrated through **withdrawal symptoms** (e.g. shaking or anxiety) and the person will use the drug to remove these negative withdrawal symptoms.

Finally, physical dependence often leads to increased **tolerance** to the drug, where the user requires an increased dose in order to obtain the same effect.

Psychological dependence

Psychological dependence can occur when a drug becomes part of an individual's thoughts. It is often demonstrated by a strong urge to use the drug, despite being aware of the harmful effects.

Psychological dependence can be demonstrated through **cravings**, which is an increased desire to repeat the experience associated with a particular drug or activity. If a person's cravings are not met, then they will start to feel very anxious which can lead to relapse.

Psychological dependence can occur with non-physical addictions (e.g.gambling).

What causes psychological dependence?

People often experience a difference between what they think and feel. This can be explained by two different information-processing systems: 1) rational and 2) experiential. The rational system operates according to rules and is conscious and analytical. The experiential system is preconscious, automatic and strongly associated with emotion. The experiential system drives us to behave in a particular way, based on how we feel.

Each system can contribute to behaviour in various ways and one system can completely dominate the other. If a person acts in an irrational way (which is very common in cases of psychological dependence) it means that their experiential system has taken priority over their rational system.

SHOULD know...

Tolerance and withdrawal

Tolerance

When drugs are used for a long time **tolerance** can develop. This means that larger and larger doses are required in order for the drug to have the same effect. There are three types of tolerance:

1 **Metabolic tolerance:** where the enzymes metabolising the drug become more efficient.

2 **Changes in receptor density:** where prolonged drug use changes the receptor density which reduces the response to a 'normal' dose of the drug.

3 **Learned tolerance:** where the user experiences a reduced effect to the drug, because they have learned to function normally under the influence of the drug.

Isbell *et al.*, (1955) demonstrated the effect of tolerance in a group of prisoners who were given the same amount of alcohol over a 13-week period to keep them in a state of intoxication. After a few weeks, the men no longer appeared drunk, despite receiving the same amount of alcohol. This was due to increased metabolic tolerance and learned tolerance, where they learned to cope with being drunk.

Withdrawal symptoms

Withdrawal symptoms can occur when a user stops taking a drug. When the effect of the drug wears off, the user may experience: anxiety, shakiness/trembling, insomnia, irritability, loss of appetite and headaches.

While the withdrawal symptoms for different drugs are not the same, they all share negative effects which may result in the person taking the drug, in order to relieve these symptoms.

While tolerance is the consequence of the body adjusting to chronic drug use, withdrawal symptoms are the consequence of the body reacting to the cessation of drugs.

The two phases of withdrawal

Acute withdrawal begins just hours after someone stops taking a drug. During this stage the physical cravings are intense and persistent, as the body begins to adjust to the loss of the drug.

Post-acute withdrawal can last for months or even years. During this stage a person might experience emotional or psychological turmoil, as the brain begins to re-organise itself.

CHOOSE THE RIGHT ANSWER

Which **one** of the following statements about tolerance is **false**?
(Tick **one** box only.)

A Tolerance is where an individual requires larger and larger doses of a drug to experience the same effect. ☐

B Tolerance can occur when the enzymes which metabolise the drug become less efficient. ☐

C Tolerance can occur when there are changes in receptor density which reduce the response to the drug. ☐

D Tolerance can occur when an individual learns to function normally under the influence of the drug. ☐

Answers on page 371

An idea 👍
On a separate piece of paper, draw a mind map related to addiction. Research different types of addiction, both substance and behavioural (e.g. heroin and gambling) and list the characteristics in terms of physical dependence and psychological dependence, as well as the withdrawal symptoms associated with these addictions.

 MATCH THEM UP

Match up the key terms with the definitions.

Physical dependence	Is evident when an individual needs to take the drug in order to feel 'normal'. It can be demonstrated by the presence of withdrawal symptoms if the individual abstains from the drug.
Psychological dependence	Can occur when a drug on which an individual is physically dependent is discontinued. In such situations, withdrawal symptoms, such as shaking and anxiety, can occur, as the body attempts to deal with the absence of a drug's effects.
Tolerance	Occurs when a drug becomes a central part of an individual's thoughts, emotions and activities, resulting in a strong urge to use the drug.
Withdrawal syndrome	Means that an individual no longer responds to a drug in the same way, with the result that larger and larger doses are needed in order to experience the same effects as before.

Answers on page 371

 APPLYING YOUR KNOWLEDGE

Identify the psychology		Link to Joseph
	While writing this Revision and Exam Companion, Joseph drinks at least eight cups of coffee a day.	
	If he goes more than an hour without a coffee, he starts to feel nauseous and anxious and has to get another cup as soon as possible. He claims that he now needs this much coffee in order to feel the effect and stay awake.	
	Using your knowledge of dependence, tolerance and withdrawal symptoms, explain the example of addiction described above.	

Answers on page 371

KEY TERMS

- Genetic
- Personality
- Stress

Possible essay question ...

Outline and evaluate the role of two or more risk factors in the development of addiction. *(16 marks)*

Other possible exam questions ...

+ Outline the role of genetic vulnerability as a risk factor in the development of addiction. *(4 marks)*

+ Outline the role of stress as a risk factor in the development of addiction. *(4 marks)*

+ Briefly outline and evaluate the role of personality as a risk factor in the development of addiction. *(6 marks)*

Link

For your exam you could be required to outline the role of five different risk factors, including: genetics, stress, personality, family influences and peers. All of these are detailed in the specification, so make sure that you review the next section on family influences and peers.

MUST know...

Genes, stress and personality

Some people appear to be born with a **genetic vulnerability** to substance abuse. **Vike *et al.* (2005)** examined 1,572 Dutch twin pairs and found that 44% of smoking initiation was explained by genetic factors.

Stress is a risk factor which is often associated with substance abuse. People often deal with stressful life events by engaging in a variety of behaviours that make them feel better or forget their stress, for example alcohol.

Finally, **personality** also appears to play an important role in predicting the development of addiction and traits like **sensation seeking** and **impulsivity** are commonly associated with addiction.

 One limitation of the genetic explanation of addiction is...

...the inconsistent findings reported in women.

- *E* – While studies of male alcoholics have consistently support the role played by genetic factors, research examining women has produced inconsistent findings.

 Support for the idea of stress as a risk factor comes from...

...research which examines coping strategies.

- *E* – **Matheny and Weatherman (1998)** found a strong relationship between use of coping resources and the ability to maintain abstinence from smoking, once they had given up.

 However, one limitation of the stress explanation for addiction is...

...the inconsistent research findings.

- *E* – While some research has established a link between stress and drug relapse **(Dawes *et al.* 2000)** other findings are less consistent.

SHOULD know...

Examples of genes, stress and personality

Blum and Payne (1991) suggest that a decreased ability to activate dopamine receptors in the reward centres of the brain results in a vulnerability to addiction. This means that anything which increases the level of dopamine, produces strong feelings of euphoria.

The **self-medication model** suggests that individuals intentionally use different forms of pathological behaviour (e.g. alcohol or drugs) to 'treat' psychological symptoms they experience because of everyday stressors.

Finally, research highlights a relationship between addiction and personality disorder. **Verhheul *et al.* (1995)** found an overall prevalence of personality disorders which was 44% in alcoholics and 70% for cocaine addicts.

- *E* – **McGue (1997)** found that only two out of four adoption studies have reported a significant correlation between alcoholism in female adoptees and their biological parents.
- *L* – This matters because it suggests that genetic factors may be less important in the development of alcoholism in women, in comparison to men.

- *E* – This suggests that if addiction is a consequence of stress, then effective coping strategies should reduce the need for addictive behaviours.
- *L* – This matters because it highlights the positive application of stress coping resources (such as problem solving and tension control) as a tool for reducing addictive behaviour.

- *E* – **Arevalo *et al.* (2008)** found evidence of an association between stress and illicit drug use, but no association between stress and alcohol addiction.
- *L* – This suggests that researchers need to be cautious when generalising the findings from stress research, as stress is not a risk factor for every type of addiction.

FURTHER EVALUATION

 P – **Support for the idea of personality as a risk factor comes from...**

...longitudinal research by **Labouvie and McGee (1986)**.

- *E* – They found that adolescents who progressed to heavier levels of alcohol abuse tended to score higher on impulsivity.
- *E* – Furthermore, they also found that impulsivity was linked to a wide range of other health-risk behaviours (e.g. illicit drug use).
- *L* – This provides support for the idea that personality is a risk factor for addictive behaviours.

P – **One strength of identifying personality as a risk factor is...**

...the positive application of research to help improve lives.

- *E* – By identifying vulnerable individuals in advance (e.g. people who are likely to become alcoholics), help can be provided to stop their behaviour.
- *E* – This could potentially prevent the development of a range of substance disorders.
- *L* – This matters because it will help reduce the personal cost to those individuals and the cost to society.

CHOOSE THE RIGHT ANSWER

Which **one** of the following statements is **false**? (Tick **one** box only.)

A Addiction is linked to genetic vulnerability. ☐

B Addiction is linked to increased activation of dopamine receptors. ☐

C Addiction is the result of self-medication, where individuals use pathological behaviours to treat stress. ☐

D Addiction is linked to personality traits like sensation seeking and impulsivity. ☐

Answers on page 371

 MATHS SKILLS (1)

A psychologist wanted to investigate the link between impulsivity and alcohol addiction. She tested ten participants who were alcoholics (Group A) and ten participants with no addictive behaviour (Group B). Each participant was given a questionnaire that measured impulsivity. The scores are shown in the table below.

Table 1: Impulsivity scores for 10 participants who were alcoholics and 10 participants with no addictions.

Group A (Addicted to alcohol)	Score on impulsivity questionnaire	Group B (No addictive behaviour)	Score on impulsivity questionnaire
1	65	1	16
2	69	2	18
3	70	3	25
4	75	4	24
5	66	5	26
6	62	6	21
7	71	7	18
8	63	8	17
9	72	9	19
10	66	10	14
Mean		**Mean**	

1. Calculate the mean score for the two groups. *(2 marks)*

2. Why did the psychologist use the mean rather than the median/mode? *(2 marks)*

Answers on page 371

 MATHS SKILLS (2)

Sketch a suitable graph for the results displayed in Table 1 (see 'Maths skills' activity). *(4 marks)*

Answers on page 371

 APPLYING YOUR KNOWLEDGE

Chris comes from a family of smokers; both of his parent's smoke and so does his younger brother Adam.

Chris began smoking at an early age and now he is in his twenties. He has tried to stop and is finding it very difficult, especially when his job as a teacher is particularly stressful.

Using your knowledge of risk factors, outline two risk factors relevant to Chris's behaviour.

Identify the psychology	Link to Chris

Answers on page 371

KEY TERM
- Peers

Possible essay question …

Discuss risk factors in the development of addiction. *(16 marks)*

Other possible exam questions …

+ Outline the role of family influences as a risk factor in addiction. *(4 marks)*
+ Explain one limitation of family influences as a risk factor in addiction. *(2 marks)*
+ Outline research findings relating to the role of peers as a risk factor in the development of addiction. *(6 marks)*

 Link

For your exam you could be required to outline the role of five different risk factors, including: genetics, stress, personality, family influences and peers. All of these are detailed in the specification, so make sure that you review the previous section on genetics, stress and personality.

MUST know...

Family influences and peers

According to **social learning theory**, behaviours are learned through observation of people that we have social contact with, including family and peers.

Parents can influence addictive behaviours in two ways: firstly, they act as a social model for their offspring and secondly, through their parenting style. Authoritative parents help their children to develop resilience to addictive behaviours.

Peer pressure is the direct or indirect encouragement from one's own age group and is often linked to risky behaviours such as smoking or substance abuse. This can be explained through social identity theory where people engage with addictive behaviours to be accepted.

 Support for the role of family and peers as a risk factor comes from…

…research which examines parental attitudes.
- **E** – **Bahr et al. (2005)** found that tolerant parental attitudes were strongly associated with an increased prevalence of binge drinking, smoking and drug use.

 However, one criticism for the role of family as a risk factor comes from…

…research which examines a lack of parental influence.
- **E** – **Stattin and Kerr (2000)** suggest that a lack of parental monitoring may result from adolescents disclosing too much information about their substance abuse.

Finally, another criticism for the role of family as a risk factor comes from…

…the lack of research into the role of siblings.
- **E** – Most family intervention strategies target only the parents, rather than siblings, which some psychologists feel is an issue.

SHOULD know...

Family influences and peers research

Reith and Dobbie (2011) demonstrated the importance of family in the initiation of gambling behaviours. From interviews they found that gambling knowledge and behaviour was passed on through everyday life and that individuals who watched and heard family members engaging with and talking about gambling, eventually joined them.

Latkin et al. (2004) found that the probability of drug abuse was related to the number of members within an individual's social network who used drugs. By modelling behaviours such as alcohol use, members of social networks represent such behaviours as positive and socially acceptable, which contributes to the development of certain addictions.

- **E** – Furthermore, they also found that adolescents with parents who were tolerant were more likely to interact with peers who smoke, drank or used illicit drugs.
- **L** – This suggests that family and peer influences are two risks factors which are not independent and in fact affect one another.

- **E** – Therefore, the parents' inability to deal with this information may cause them to stop monitoring their offspring, who they believe are 'beyond their control'.
- **L** – This suggests that a lack of monitoring and control is an important risk factor and not direct family influences.

- **E** – **Feinberg et al. (2012)** claim that this failure to address sibling influences is likely to hinder efforts to reduce early substance use and later substance dependence.
- **L** – This matters because it undervalues the role of sibling influences which could be the main source of influence for adolescents.

FURTHER EVALUATION

 P – Support for the role of peers as a risk factor comes from…

…research on social media.
- **E** – **Litt and Stock (2011)** found that teenagers who viewed peers' Facebook profiles that portrayed alcohol use were more likely to drink themselves.
- **E** – Furthermore, after exposure to these profiles, these teenagers reported a greater willingness to use alcohol.
- **L** – This supports the role of peers as a risk factor for addiction and highlights the importance of social media in addiction.

 P – However, one criticism for the role of peers as a risk factor comes from…

…research which examines friendship selection.
- **E** – **De Vries et al. (2006)** found that smoking behaviour among adolescents is more likely to be a consequence of friendship selection than a cause.
- **E** – For example, smokers befriend other smokers, rather than smokers influencing non-smokers.
- **L** – This matters because it challenges the role of peers as a risk factor and suggests that the role of peers may be overstated.

CHOOSE THE RIGHT ANSWER 1

Which **one** of the follow statements about parents is **false**? (Tick **one** box only.)

A Parents can influence addictive behaviours through social learning theory.	☐
B Parents can influence addictive behaviours by acting as a role model/social model.	☐
C Parents can influence addictive behaviour through an authoritative parental styling.	☐
D Parents can influence addictive behaviour through too much parental monitoring.	☐

Answers on page 371

CHOOSE THE RIGHT ANSWER 2

Which **one** of the following statements about peers is **false**? (Tick **one** box only.)

A Peers can influence addictive behaviour directly and/or indirectly.	☐
B Peer influence can be explained through social identity theory, where a person adopts a behaviour to be socially accepted as part of an out-group.	☐
C Peer influence is stronger if there is a larger number of peers in a social group who engage in an addictive behaviour.	☐
D Peer influence can be indirect through social media, such as Facebook.	☐

Answers on page 371

APPLYING YOUR KNOWLEDGE

Tola is seventeen-years-old and has recently started smoking.

Most of her friends smoke and she believes that smoking will help her to fit in with the group of popular girls at school, who also smoke.

Furthermore, Tola has recently told her parents that she regularly smokes and they believe that she is beyond their help and refuse to get involved.

Use your knowledge of risk factors (family influences and peers) and discuss how family and peers are contributing to Tola's addiction.

Identify the psychology	Link to Tola

Answers on page 371

A MARKING EXERCISE

Read this student answer to the following exam question:

Outline the role of family influences as a risk factor in addiction. *(4 marks)*

Family influences are a risk factor in addiction for three reasons: firstly, social learning theory; secondly, by acting as a role model and thirdly, due to an authoritative parenting style.

What mark do you think this would get?

YOUR MARK

AO1

Hint
A hint to help you decide:
How many critical points have been covered?
How much detail is there?

Write an improved answer here…

Answers on page 371

KEY TERMS

- Dopamine
- Neurochemistry
- Nicotine

Possible essay question ...

Outline and evaluate the brain neurochemistry explanation of nicotine addiction. *(16 marks)*

Other possible exam questions ...

+ Outline the brain neurochemistry of nicotine addiction. *(6 marks)*
+ Outline the role of dopamine in nicotine addiction. *(4 marks)*
+ Explain **one** limitation of the brain neurochemistry explanation of nicotine addiction. *(6 marks)*

 Exam tip

Many students worry about biological psychology and there are a lot of biological terms on this page. Remember that you will only ever need to provide up to 6 marks worth of description (AO1) in your exam, so bear this in mind when revising.

MUST know...

Nicotine, dopamine and the brain's reward pathways

Nicotine is the main active ingredient in tobacco and can have a range of different effects, including: tranquillisation, increased alertness and even improved cognitive function.

On average, a smoker takes in 1–2 mg of nicotine per cigarette which reaches its peak levels in the bloodstream and brain within 10 seconds.

Nicotine attaches to neurons in the **ventral tegmental area (VTA)**. These neurons trigger the release of **dopamine** from the **nucleus accumbens (NAc)**. Nicotine also stimulates the release of **glutamate**, which triggers the release of even more dopamine. Dopamine produces pleasure and a desire to repeat the behaviours again.

 Support for the link between nicotine and dopamine comes from...

...research examining drugs for epilepsy.

- ***E** – **Paterson and Markou (2002)** found that GVG (an epilepsy drug) reduces the surge of dopamine in the NAc that occurs after taking nicotine.

 Support for the link between glutamate and nicotine comes from...

...research examining nicotine-dependent rats.

- ***E** – **D'Souza and Markou (2013)** blocked the transmission of glutamate which resulted in a decrease in nicotine intake in rats, which is consistent with the role of this neurotransmitter.

 Further support for the link between nicotine and dopamine comes from...

...patients with Parkinson's Disease (PD).

- ***E** – PD is characterised by a gradual loss of dopamine producing nerve cells, causing symptoms of PD to appear.

SHOULD know...

Glutamate, GABA and the development of nicotine addiction

To explain why dopamine levels remain high after the direct nicotine stimulus ends, researchers have focused on **glutamate** and **GABA**.

Glutamate speeds up the activity of neurons, whereas GABA slows down neuron activity.

Nicotine causes glutamate to speed up dopamine release, but it also prevents GABA from slowing it down after the dopamine levels have raised. This combination amplifies the effect of dopamine and the rewarding properties of nicotine.

Because the effects of nicotine disappear within a few minutes, this creates a need to continue taking in nicotine through the day, resulting in tolerance, dependence and ultimately addiction.

- ***E** – This reduces the addictive tendencies of nicotine and other drugs that boost dopamine levels in the brain.
- ***L** – This matters because it highlights the link between dopamine and nicotine and provides a method of treating nicotine addiction, which has fewer side effects than most smoking treatments.

- ***E** – This is because glutamate enhances the dopamine-releasing effects of nicotine, so blocking it would decrease the effects of dopamine for longer.
- ***L** – This matters because it highlights the link between glutamate and nicotine, allowing researchers to devise treatments based on blocking the transmission of this neurotransmitter.

- ***E** – Research suggests that smokers are less likely to get PD, suggesting that nicotine may have a neuroprotective function against the development of PD.
- ***L** – This provides further support for the link between nicotine and dopamine, while also providing some insight into possible treatments for PD.

FURTHER EVALUATION

 P – One implication for the role of nicotine is...

...its adverse effects on brain neurochemistry.

- ***E** – **Khaled *et al*. (2009)** found that the incidence of depression was highest in long-term smokers and lowest in those who had never smoked.
- ***E** – **Luk and Tsoh (2010)** found similar results in a Chinese study, where smoking was associated with a greater risk of depression.
- ***L** – This highlights the negative implications of nicotine in terms of both addictive effects and possible links to depression.

 P – A final consideration for the role of nicotine is...

...the different effects found in men and women.

- ***E** – **Cosgrove *et al*. (2014)** studied the brains of men and women using PET scans, while smoking.
- ***E** – For women there was a strong dopamine effect in the **dorsal putamen**, whereas men had a strong effect in the **ventral striatum**.
- ***L** – These results suggest that men and women smoke for different reasons, men for the nicotine effect and women to relieve stress.

COMPLETE THE DIAGRAM

Match the key terms below, with the diagram on the left.

Dopamine reward pathway

Dopamine release

Stimulation of nicotine receptors

Nucleus accumbens

Prefrontal cortex

Ventral tegmental area

Nicotine enters the brain

Answers on page 371

CHOOSE THE RIGHT ANSWER

Which **one** of the following statements is **false**? (Tick **one** box only.)

A Nicotine attaches to neurons in the prefrontal cortex. ☐

B Neurons in the ventral tegmental area trigger the release of dopamine. ☐

C Nicotine stimulates the release of the neurotransmitter glutamate. ☐

D Glutamate triggers the release of dopamine. ☐

E Dopamine produces feelings of pleasure and a desire to repeat behaviours again. ☐

Answers on page 371

An idea

Draw a flow chart to outline the effect of nicotine on the brain's reward pathways. Your flow chart should have four key stages.

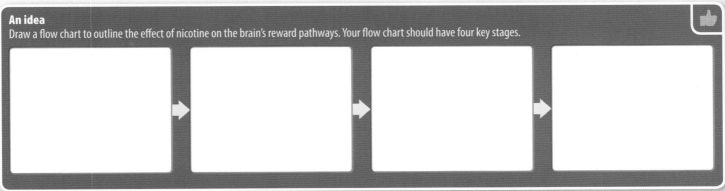

A MARKING EXERCISE

Read this student answer to the following exam question:

Explain **one** limitation of the brain neurochemistry explanation of nicotine addiction. *(4 marks)*

One problem with the neurochemistry explanation of nicotine addiction is the fact that nicotine has a different effect on men and women. This means that the reason why men and women smoke is different, which is not taken into account in this explanation.

What mark do you think this would get?

YOUR MARK

AO1

Hint
A hint to help you decide:
How many critical points have been covered?
How much detail is there?

Write an improved answer here…

Answers on page 371

KEY TERMS

- Cue reactivity
- Learning theory

Possible essay question …

Outline and evaluate the learning theory explanation of nicotine addiction. *(16 marks)*

Other possible exam questions …

+ Briefly explain the learning theory explanation of nicotine addiction. *(4 marks)*
+ Give **two** criticisms of the learning theory of nicotine addiction. *(3 marks)*
+ Outline the role of cue reactivity in nicotine addiction. *(3 marks)*

 Link

The key ideas found on this page are all aspects of the behaviourist approach, first examined in Year 1. While revising it would be useful to review the behaviourist approach, for the approaches in psychology topic (see Year 1/AS Revision and Exam Companion, page xxx), as well as explanations for the development of phobias, in the psychopathology topic (see Year 1/AS Revision and Exam Companion, page xxx).

MUST know…

Initiation

Addiction can be explained in terms of **learning theory,** as the pleasure from a particular behaviour, such as smoking, is reinforced, making it more likely that the person will repeat this behaviour in the future.

Social learning theory can explain why young people begin smoking, through the **observation** of social models who smoke (e.g. family and peers). Furthermore, **vicarious reinforcement** causes young people to expect positive consequences from smoking, thus leading to the initiation of an addiction. Finally, as addictive substances are immediately rewarding, the behaviour is **positively reinforced** through the principles of **operant conditioning**.

 Support for the role of SLT in the initiation of smoking comes from…

…research which examines peer group influences.
- *E* – **DiBlasio and Benda (1993)** found that peer group influences were the primary encouragement for adolescents who experimented with smoking.

 Support for the role of negative reinforcement in addiction comes from…

…research which examines people trying to quit smoking.
- *E* – **Shiffman and Waters (2004)** found that sudden increases in negative moods, rather than slow changes in stress levels, were associated with relapse.

 Support for the role of classical conditioning in addiction comes from…

…research which examines cue reactivity.
- *E* – **Wiers et al. (2013)** found that smokers showed a significant approach bias towards smoking related cues, compared to ex-smokers and non-smokers.

SHOULD know…

Maintenance and relapse

A person may maintain their smoking addiction and repeat a behaviour many times because of the positive consequences, for example 'looking cool' **(positive reinforcement)**. However, many people maintain their smoking habit to avoid negative withdrawal symptoms and therefore smoking provides relief **(negative reinforcement)**.

When a person stops smoking, the urge to smoke again can persist long after their withdrawal symptoms disappear. This can be explained in terms of **classical conditioning**, as regular smokers associate specific moods, situations and environmental factors with the rewarding effects of nicotine and therefore these cues can trigger a relapse.

- *E* – Furthermore, **Karcher and Finn (2005)** found that if a person's parents smoke they are 1.88 times more likely to smoke. However, this figure rose to 2.64 times for siblings and 8 times for close friends.
- *L* – This suggests that the closer the social model, the higher the chance of initiation.

- *E* – Furthermore, there is even evidence that changes in negative moods can increase nicotine cravings.
- *L* – This suggests that negative reinforcement contributes to the maintenance and relapse of smoking and people are more likely to smoke when they experience a negative mood.

- *E* – This approach bias was positively correlated with their cravings scores, which was not the case for ex-smokers and non-smokers.
- *L* – This suggests that smoking cues are present in heavy smokers and that classical conditioning plays a significant role in the relapse of nicotine addiction.

FURTHER EVALUATION

 P – One limitation of the learning theory of addiction is…

…the different patterns of behaviour displayed in men and women.
- *E* – **Lopez et al. (1994)** found that women tend to start smoking later in life than men.
- *E* – Other research has found that women are more likely to light up in stressful situations and experience withdrawal effects sooner than men.
- *L* – This matters because the learning theory of addiction is unable to account for these differences and therefore other explanations may be more suitable.

 P – One strength of the learning theory of addiction is…

…its application the development of effective treatments.
- *E* – **Drummond et al. (1990)** proposed a treatment based on the idea that cues are associated with smoking.
- *E* – Cue exposure therapy (CET) involves presenting the cues without the opportunity to engage in the smoking behaviour, which leads to the association being extinguished.
- *L* – Therefore, the learning theory has led to the development of successful treatments for patients with addictions.

COMPLETE THE DIAGRAM

Match the key terms with the diagram below to explain the relapse of smoking.

Smoking-related stimuli (e.g. cigarette smoke)

Nicotine activates brain reward pathways

Brain restores equilibrium by lowering DA levels

Smoking-related stimuli (e.g. cigarette smoke)

Brain restores equilibrium by lowering DA levels

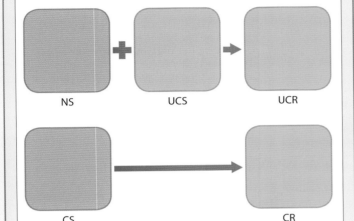

NS + UCS → UCR

CS → CR

Answers on page 372

 MATCH THEM UP

Match up the key terms with the examples.

Classical conditioning	When young people smoke because they expect to receive a positive outcome from smoking.
Positive reinforcement	When young people begin smoking as a result of observing social models.
Negative reinforcement	When smoking is repeated because it removes any unpleasant outcome (e.g. withdrawal symptoms).
Vicarious reinforcement	When a regular smoker associates specific moods, situational and environment factors with the rewards effects of nicotine.
Social learning theory	When smoking is repeated because it leads to a rewarding outcome.

Answers on page 372

✓ **CHOOSE THE RIGHT ANSWER**

Which **one** of the following is **not** part of the learning theory of addiction? (Tick **one** box only.)

A Social learning theory ☐
B Classical conditioning ☐
C Operant conditioning ☐
D Cue reactivity ☐
E Social identity theory ☐

Answers on page 372

 APPLYING YOUR KNOWLEDGE

Identify the psychology

Nico has recently given up smoking, but is really struggling.

When he used to smoke, he had to stand outside the front of his work building.

Now he has given up, every time he leaves work, especially after a stressful day, he has an overwhelming urge to smoke.

Using your knowledge of learning theory, explain why Nico is finding it hard to resist the urge to smoke.

Link to Nico

Answers on page 372

KEY TERMS

Learning theory
- Partial reinforcement
- Variable reinforcement

Possible essay question ...

Outline and evaluate the learning theory explanation of gambling addiction. *(16 marks)*

Other possible exam questions ...

+ Explain what is meant by the terms 'partial reinforcement' and 'variable reinforcement' in the context of gambling. *(2 + 2 marks)*

+ Give **two** criticisms of the learning theory explanation of gambling addiction. *(3 + 3 marks)*

 Link

In this chapter you will explore the role of learning theory in addiction. Why not use this as an opportunity to review the behaviourist approach in the approaches in psychology topic and the behaviourist explanation of phobia in the psychopathology topic.

MUST know...

Learning theory explanations of gambling addiction

According to learning theory, gambling can be explained in terms of operant conditioning and reinforcement.

Griffiths (2009) suggests that gamblers playing slot machines may become addicted because of different types of rewards (positive reinforcement), including: physiological rewards (e.g. the buzz from winning); psychological rewards (e.g. the near misses); social rewards (e.g. peer praise); as well as financial rewards if they win.

However, as gamblers generally lose, their behaviour can be explained in terms of **partial reinforcement**, where wins follow some bets, but not all. Consequently, these behaviours are harder to extinguish due to the uncertainty of the reinforcement.

 One issue with the learning explanation of gambling is...

...that it can't explain all forms of gambling.
- ***E*** – The principles of operant conditioning are difficult to apply to different types of gambling, for example scratch cards and sports betting.

 Another issue with the learning explanation of gambling is...

...that it can't explain why relatively few people become addicts.
- ***E*** – While many people may gamble at some time during their lives and experience reinforcement, relatively few become addicts.

 One strength of the learning explanation of gambling comes from...

...research which supports the idea of partial reinforcement.
- ***E*** – **Horsley et al. (2012)** tested the idea of partial reinforcement, among high- and low-frequency gamblers, using either partial or continuous reinforcement.

SHOULD know...

Variable reinforcement, gambling and its rewards

Casinos use a form of partial reinforcement, called variable reinforcement. Gambling machines use **variable-ratio reinforcement**, where wins occur after an unpredictable number of responses and it's this unpredictable nature which keeps people gambling.

There are three other examples of 'rewards' to gamblers: The **'big win' hypothesis –** where gamblers will continue to gamble to repeat a 'big win' they have previously experienced. The **'near miss'** – a near miss creates a brief moment of excitement that can also encourage further gambling. Finally, the casino environment can act as a continued stimulus, creating feelings of excitement.

- ***E*** – Scratch cards have a short time-period between the behaviour and consequence, whereas sports betting has a much longer period.
- ***L*** – This matters because the learning theory is unable to explain why both types of gamblers continue to gamble, despite these differences in reinforcement.

- ***E*** – If the learning explanation was the only cause of gambling, then it would be reasonable to assume that a higher proportion of people may become addicts.
- ***L*** – This matters because it suggests that there must be other factors involved in the formation of gambling addictions.

- ***E*** – They found that after partial reinforcement, high-frequency gamblers continued to respond to a gambling situation for longer, in comparison to low-frequency gamblers.
- ***L*** – This supports the idea that partial reinforcement is likely to contribute to the maintenance of gambling, especially in high-frequency gamblers.

 FURTHER EVALUATION

***P* – Another strength of the learning explanation of gambling comes from...**

...research examining 'big wins'.
- ***E*** – **Sharpe (2002)** claimed that the placement of early 'big wins' could lead to irrational thoughts about gambling machines.
- ***E*** – For example, an early big win may give the gambler the belief that they can control the outcome of the machine and win.
- ***L*** – This supports the idea of 'big wins' and shows that the overestimation of winning and underestimation of losing, encourages persistent gambling.

 ***P* – However, one limitation of the learning explanation of gambling comes from...**

...the different pathways of gambling addicts.
- ***E*** – Some gamblers are behaviourally conditioned and start gambling because of role models or peer groups.
- ***E*** – Other addicts gamble to relieve adverse emotional states (e.g. depression or anxiety).
- ***L*** – This suggests that the learning theory can only explain some types of gambling, in particular those that are behaviourally conditioned.

✔ CHOOSE THE RIGHT ANSWER

Which **one** of the following statements about variable reinforcement is **correct**? (Tick **one** box only.)

Only some responses are reinforced, for example every 5th response.	☐
All responses are reinforced.	☐
No responses are reinforced.	☐
Only some responses are reinforced, however the reinforcement is unpredictable.	☐

Answers on page 372

🧩 MATCH THEM UP

Match up the key terms with the examples.

Partial reinforcement	Kate knows that if she continues betting on the slot machines she will win, because she always wins after a certain amount of tries, although she doesn't know exactly how many.
Variable reinforcement	Lynne continues to do the National Lottery, because five months ago, she had four numbers and the bonus ball, and if she'd had one more number, she would have won the jackpot.
The 'big win' hypothesis	Joseph is hooked on fruit machines, as he wins following some bets, but not all
The 'near miss'	John finds going to the casino very exciting – the thrill of the roulette table is what keeps him returning.
The gambling environment	Stephanie keeps doing the National Lottery every week, because she can remember that she won £5,000 on the very first ticket she purchased.

Answers on page 372

🎯 WRITE YOUR OWN EVALUATION POINT

Evidence from Horsley *et al.* (2012) supports the idea that people become addicted due to partial reinforcement. However, some psychologists argue against this as not everyone who gambles becomes addicted. Using these two ideas, write an extended burger paragraph that outlines the research support for Horsley *et al.* (2012), but provides a counter-argument in the 'evaluate' section.

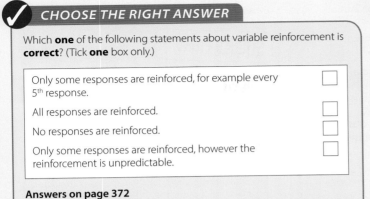

Point	One strength of the learning explanation of gambling comes from Horsley *et al. (2012)*
Evidence	[Insert methods and results]
Explain	This shows…
Evaluate	However…
Link	Therefore…

Answers on page 372

⚙ APPLYING YOUR KNOWLEDGE

Identify the psychology		Link to Gareth
	 Gareth has recently started a new job, which is very dull. On his way home from work, he calls into a betting shop. Gareth has a few wins in the first week and finds the atmosphere very exciting. He is now visiting the betting shop most days and spending over half of his wages on gambling. Using your knowledge of learning theory, outline two reasons for Gareth's addiction.	

Answers on page 372

KEY TERM

- Cognitive biases

Possible essay question …

Discuss research relating to the cognitive theory explanation of gambling addiction, including the role of cognitive biases. *(16 marks)*

Other possible exam questions …

+ Explain what is meant by the term 'cognitive biases' in the context of the cognitive theory of gambling addiction. *(2 marks)*

+ Outline the findings of **one** study relating to the cognitive theory explanation of gambling addiction. *(4 marks)*

Link

They key ideas found on this page are all aspects of the cognitive approach, first examined in Year 1. While revising it would be good to review the cognitive approach, for the Approaches in psychology topic, as well as explanations for the development of depression, in the Psychopathology topic. See Year 1/ AS Revision and Exam Companion pages XX and xx.

MUST know…

The role of cognitive biases

According to the cognitive approach, the development and maintenance of gambling is the result of **irrational beliefs** and **distorted thinking patterns**, known as **cognitive biases**.

There are four types of cognitive bias, including:

1 **The gambler's fallacy:** The belief that completely random events are somehow influenced by recent events.

2 **Illusions of control:** The overestimation of personal ability to influence the outcome of random events.

3 **The 'near miss' bias:** Where gamblers see near misses as motivation, as they are not losing they are 'nearly winning'.

4 **The recall bias:** The tendency to remember and overestimate wins, while forgetting about losses.

 One strength of the cognitive explanation of gambling comes from…

…research examining the idea of cognitive biases.

- *E – **Ladouceur et al., (2002)** found that 80% of the verbalisations made by problem gamblers seeking treatment, were classified as irrational.

 Another strength of the cognitive explanation of gambling comes from…

…the development of successful treatments.

- *E – Interventions such as cognitive behaviour therapy (CBT) aim to reduce the cognitive biases associated with gambling addicts.

 However, one issue with the cognitive explanation of gambling is…

…that not all types of gambling are explained by cognitive biases.

- *E – **Lund (2011)** examined irrational beliefs and gambling preferences in nearly 5,000 adults, to determine the link between cognitive biases and types of gambling.

SHOULD know…

Griffiths (1994) – Cognitive bias in fruit machine gambling

Aim: To discover whether regular gamblers think and behave differently to non-regular gamblers, when playing fruit machines.

Procedure: Griffiths compared 30 regular (fruit machine) gamblers, with 30 non-regular gamblers. Each participant was given £3 to spend on a fruit machine. Griffiths was interested in examining the gamblers' verbalisations, to provide an insight into their cognitive biases.

Findings: The regular gamblers believed they were more skilful than they actually were and made more irrational statements.

Finally, subsequent interviews revealed that 26 out of 30 gamblers believed that the game was due to skill, in comparison to none of the non-regular gamblers.

- *E* – However, research examining recreational gamblers (those who gamble occasionally and only for pleasure) has not found the same level of cognitive biases.
- *L* – This provides support to the idea that irrational beliefs are an important factor in the development of gambling addictions.

- *E* – **Echeburua et al. (1996)** found that CBT was a particularly effective treatment in preventing the relapse of gamblers who played slot machines.
- *L* – This highlights the positive application of the cognitive approach to help treat people with gambling addictions.

- *E* – Lund found that cognitive biases were more likely in gamblers who preferred gambling machines and internet gambling, in comparison to sports betting and horse racing.
- *L* – This matters because the cognitive explanation does not explain all types of gambling and therefore other explanations are required to explain different types of gambling.

FURTHER EVALUATION

 P – **However, one issue with the cognitive explanation of gambling is…**

…that increased knowledge does not decrease cognitive biases.

- *E* – **Benhsain and Ladouceur (2004)** found no differences on a gambling-related cognition scale in university students trained in statistics and those not trained in statistics.
- *E* – Furthermore, **Delfabbro et al. (2006)** found that gamblers were just as accurate as non-gamblers, in estimating the odds of winning.
- *L* – This suggests that other factors may play an important role in the development of gambling addictions.

 P – **A final issue with the cognitive explanation of gambling is…**

…that gambling may have a biological basis.

- *E* – **Clark et al. (2014)** identified a brain region (the insula) that appears to play a role in distorted thinking.
- *E* – Furthermore, researchers have found that if this brain region is damaged then people become immune to cognitive biases.
- *L* – These findings suggest that cognitive biases may have a biological bias and are not just the result of irrational thinking.

✔ CHOOSE THE RIGHT ANSWER

Below are four evaluative statements for the cognitive explanation of gambling. Which **one** of the statements is **false**? (Tick **one** box only.)

The cognitive approach has led to effective treatments using CBT.	☐
Research supports the idea that cognitive biases are involved in gambling.	☐
The cognitive approach can effectively explain all types of gambling.	☐
The cognitive approach is limited as it does not take into account biological factors.	☐

Answers on page 372

🧩 MATCH THEM UP

Match the cognitive bias with the example.

The gambler's fallacy	John bets on a horse which comes second; however he believes that if he bets again, his horse will win next time, because he nearly won this time.
Illusions of control	Joseph remembers the time he won £500 on the National Lottery and therefore continues to play, despite the fact he has not won anything for the last two years.
The 'near miss' bias	James tosses a coin and gets two heads in a row. He now believes that his next two coin tosses will be tails, to balance the outcome.
The recall bias	David believes that he is very skilled at roulette and when he bets, his is likely to win because of his experience at the roulette table.

Answers on page 372

⚙ APPLYING YOUR KNOWLEDGE

Abdul is playing a fruit machine. While playing he gets two 'wins' and a number 7 (see picture).

He says out loud, 'I'm only putting in £1 in next time, because I know that I won't win and this will fool the machine.'

Using your knowledge of the cognitive approach, explain why Abdul is likely to continue gambling.

Identify the psychology	Link to Abdul

Answers on page 372

An idea 👍

You have now examined two explanations for nicotine addictions and two for gambling addictions. Draw a revision table to highlight the strengths/limitations of these four explanations. You should aim for at least **two** strengths and limitations for each.

	Strengths	Limitations
Nicotine: Brain neurochemistry		
Nicotine: Learning theory		
Gambling: Learning theory		
Gambling: Cognitive theory		

Possible essay question …

Outline and evaluate drug therapy as a way of reducing addiction. *(16 marks)*

Other possible exam questions …

+ Briefly explain and give **one** criticism of drug therapy as a way of reducing addiction. *(6 marks)*

 Exam tip

It is worth nothing that the specification simply says 'drug treatments' and therefore you are not required to have knowledge of any specific drugs; you just need to know how the drugs work. Of course, knowing the name of at least one drug treatment for nicotine and gambling addictions would certainly help.

MUST know…

Drug treatments for addiction

Drugs interact with receptors or enzymes in the brain, to reduce cravings or a particular behaviour (gambling).

Drug treatments for nicotine addiction

Nicotine replacement therapy (NRT) gradually releases nicotine into the bloodstream to help an individual control their cravings for a cigarette, improve their mood and help prevent relapse.

Drug treatments for gambling addiction

It is worth noting that no drug has been approved in the UK for the treatment of gambling. However, drug treatments can reduce the urges and cravings to gamble and also reduce symptoms of depression and anxiety that may trigger a gambling addiction.

 One strength of using drug therapies for nicotine addiction comes from…

…research support for NRT.

- *E* – **Stead et al. (2012)** investigated the effectiveness of NRT compared to a placebo, in the treatment of nicotine addiction, in 150 different trials.

 However, one issue with using drug therapies for nicotine addictions is…

…the questionable conclusions of NRT research.

- *E* – **Mooney et al. (2004)** found that, of 73 double-blind placebo controlled NRT trials, only 17 had actually conducted blinding assessment, where they asked the participants whether they believed they were receiving nicotine.

 One issue with using drug therapies for gambling addictions is…

…the concerns over how the drugs work.

- *E* – *Naltrexone* (an opioid antagonist) works by blocking the brain's reward system, when a person engages in gambling behaviours.

SHOULD know…

Examples of drug treatments used

Two prescription drugs have been approved by the NHS for nicotine addictions, including: *Champix* and *Zyban*. *Zyban* works by inhibiting the re-uptake of dopamine and has been effective in the treatment of smoking addictions **(Hughes et al., 2004)**.

Two drugs have been examined in relation to gambling addictions: opioid antagonists and antidepressants. Opioid antagonists bind to opioid receptors in the body, which causes the blocking of these receptors. This prevents the individual experiencing the reward response they associate with gambling. **Kim et al.** (2002) found that *naltrexone* (an opioid antagonist) was effective in reducing the frequency and intensity of gambling urges.

- *E* – They concluded that all of the different types of NRT (e.g. patches, gum and inhaler) were effective in helping people kick their nicotine addiction, and were 70% more effective than a placebo.
- *L* – This shows that drug therapies for treating nicotine addictions are highly effective.

- *E* – The researchers found that in these 17 studies, almost two-thirds of the placebo condition were 'confident' that they had not received a real nicotine patch.
- *L* – This matters because the conclusions about the effectiveness of drug treatments are less certain than originally claimed.

- *E* – This is a fairly crude mechanism which could also stop patients from feeling pleasure in other areas of life (e.g. playing sport, having sex, etc), while they are on the drug.
- *L* – This matters because these potential side-effects may stop patients from taking their medication, which therefore reduces the effectiveness of this treatment.

 FURTHER EVALUATION

 P – **Another issue with the use of drug therapies for gambling addictions is…**

…the questionable validity of the research.
- *E* – **Blaszcynski and Nower (2007)** argued that the research is characterised by small sample sizes, high dropout rates and a low number of female participants.
- *E* – Furthermore, much of the research fails to include a control group.
- *L* – This means that it is difficult to draw meaningful conclusions about the use of drug therapies for gambling addictions.

P – **However, research support for the use of drug therapies for gambling comes from….**

…studies using anti-depressants (SSRIs).
- *E* – **Grant and Potenza (2006)** gave 13 gambling addicts an SSRI for three months. At the end of the three months, some continued with the treatment, while others received a placebo.
- *E* – For those who received the placebo, their gambling and anxiety returned.
- *L* – This provides some support for the use of SSRIs for the treatment of gambling.

CHOOSE THE RIGHT ANSWER

Which **two** of the following statements are **false**? (Tick **two** boxes only.)

A Research support for drug therapies has strong validity, due to the use of blind control groups. ☐

B Research support for drug therapies is limited because of small sample sizes. ☐

C Research support for drug therapies is limited because of high dropout rates. ☐

D Research support for drug therapies can be generalised to both males and females. ☐

Answers on page 372

An idea 👍
On a separate piece of paper, draw a flow chart to outline how two of the key drug therapies work, including: Opioid antagonists for gambling and Zyban (bupropion) for nicotine.

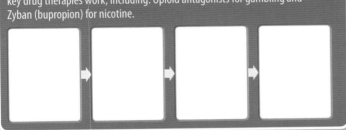

 WRITE YOUR OWN EVALUATION POINT

Grant and Potenza (2006) can be used as support for the use of SSRIs. However, their sample consisted of only 13 participants and Blaszcynski and Nower (2007) claim that research studies into the effects of drug therapies are questionable due to their limited sample sizes. Write an evaluation paragraph, where you use Blazcynski and Nower's criticism as a counter argument for Grant and Potenza.

Point	Support for the effectiveness of drug treatments for gambling comes from Grant and Potenza (2006).
Evidence	[Insert method and results]…
Explain	This shows…
Evaluate	However, Blaszcynski and Nower (2007) argue that…
Link	Therefore…

Answers on page 372

 APPLYING YOUR KNOWLEDGE

Identify the psychology

Link to Tyeisha

Tyeisha is keen to give up smoking. She has tried to stop several times but gets horrible withdrawal symptoms and cravings. She has recently started a new job and everyone disapproves of her smoking addiction.

Outline two biological treatments that will help Tyeisha give up smoking.

Answers on page 372

KEY TERMS

- Aversion therapy
- Behavioural interventions
- Covert sensitisation

Possible essay question …

Outline and evaluate the behavioural interventions used to reduce addiction. *(16 marks)*

Other possible exam questions …

+ Explain what is meant by the terms 'aversion therapy' and 'covert sensitisation' in the context of addiction reduction. *(2 + 2 marks)*

+ Briefly explain and give **one** criticism of aversion therapy as a way of reducing addiction. *(4 marks)*

+ Briefly explain and give *one* criticism of covert sensitisation as a way of reducing addiction. *(4 marks)*

★ Exam tip

Essay questions on the topic of reducing addiction can be specific (e.g. drug therapy and/or covert sensitisation) or more general (e.g. behavioural interventions). Make sure you know how to structure these different types of essay.

MUST know…

Aversion therapy

Therapies based on the behavioural approach try to replace the pleasant consequences associated with nicotine and gambling, with unpleasant consequences, so that the individual is no longer motivated to smoke or gamble.

This can be achieved in two ways, either by introducing a real association, known as **aversion therapy**, or by introducing an imagined unpleasant association, known as **covert sensitisation.**

Aversion therapy

Aversion therapy is based on the principles of **classical conditioning** – an individual learns to associate an aversive stimulus with something they have previously enjoyed. For example, an electric shock with pictures of gambling related items.

 One strength of using behavioural therapies for the treatment of addiction comes from…

…research support for aversion therapy.

- **E** – **Smith and Frawley (1993)** examined 600 patients being treated for alcoholism using aversion therapy.

 However, one issue with using behavioural therapies as a treatment of addiction comes from…

…ethical concerns raised over the use of aversion therapy.

- **E** – Some forms of aversion therapy used in the treatment of problem drinking cause extremely uncomfortable consequences (e.g. vomiting).

 Another strength of using behavioural therapies is…

…research support for covert sensitisation.

- **E** – **Kraft and Kraft (2005)** used hypnotic suggestion to associate feelings of nausea with problem behaviours such as smoking, alcoholism and chocolate addiction.

SHOULD know…

Covert sensitisation

Covert sensitisation; works in a very similar way to aversion therapy, however the unpleasant stimulus is only imagined by the individual.

Therefore, the consequences (or unpleasant stimulus) must be vivid enough so that the individual experiences significant discomfort or anxiety, when they imagine themselves engaging with their addictive behaviour. By associating these unpleasant sensations with the addictive behaviour, this leads to a decreased desire to engage with, and avoidance of the addictive behaviour in the future. For example, an individual might imagine themselves drinking alcohol, but then vomiting all over themselves and being publically humiliated as a result.

- **E** – The researchers contacted the patients 12 months after the completion of the treatment and found that 65% were totally abstinent from alcohol at this point.
- **L** – This provides support for the use of behavioural therapies as a treatment for certain types of addiction (e.g. alcohol).

- **E** – These consequences could lead to poor compliance with the treatment and high dropout rates.
- **L** – This matters because these side-effects may decrease the positive impact of the treatment and cause patients to relapse. Furthermore, some critics argue that this form of treatment is morally objectionable.

- **E** – Kraft and Kraft concluded that covert sensation is a rapid and effective form of treatment in 90% of cases.
- **L** – Therefore, not only is covert sensitisation an effective treatment but it also overcomes many of the ethical/moral issues associated with aversion therapy.

 P – Another strength of behavioural therapies such as covert sensitisation is…

…that they are considered more ethical.

- **E** – Aversion therapy has been criticised for being unethical, where covert sensitisation has not.
- **E** – Individuals are not required to engage with their problem behaviour, simply imagine it.
- **L** – This matters because it reduces the possibility of harm as the person does not have to engage with their addictive behaviour, nor experience any negative consequences.

P – However, one issue with behavioural therapies for the treatment of addiction is…

…that they fail to take into account psychological factors.

- **E** – Behavioural treatments fail to address psychological factors (e.g. irrational thoughts) that might drive addictive behaviours.
- **E** – Therefore, failure to address these underlying issues may mean that the treatment is doomed to fail.
- **L** – This matters because it may leave an individual at risk of developing another addiction, even once their original addiction has been treated.

✓ CHOOSE THE RIGHT ANSWER

Which **one** of the following statements is **false**? (Tick **one** box only.)

A Aversion therapy is seen as morally questionable.	☐
B Aversion therapy is based on the principles of classical conditioning.	☐
C Covert sensitisation is based on the principles of operant conditioning.	☐
D Cover sensitisation requires patients to have a vivid imagination.	☐

Answers on page 372

✓ A MARKING EXERCISE

Read this student answer to the following exam question:

Briefly explain and give **one** criticism of aversion therapy as a way of reducing addiction. *(4 marks)*

> One issue with aversion therapy is that it is very unethical. For example, making someone sick in order to overcome their addiction is wrong.

What mark do you think this would get?

YOUR MARK

AO1

Hint
A hint to help you decide:
How many critical points have been covered?
How much detail is there?

Write an improved answer here…

Answers on page 372

⚙ APPLYING YOUR KNOWLEDGE

Winnifred is desperate to give up her chocolate addiction and one of her friends who studies psychology, Tommy, suggests that she should try aversion therapy.

Describe aversion therapy, using an example of how aversion therapy might work for Winnifred.

Identify the psychology	**Link to aversion therapy/ Winnifred**
Aversion therapy is based on the principles of…. ➡	*Elaborate…*
Insert example of how aversion therapy… ➡	*How would this work?*

Answers on page 372

💡 DRAWING CONCLUSIONS

A researcher examined the effectiveness of aversion therapy and covert sensitisation for nicotine addicts and gambling addicts. The bar chart below shows the findings.

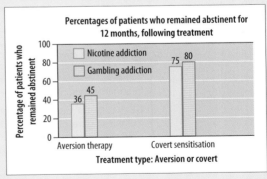

What does the bar chart show about the effectiveness of behavioural therapies?

Answers on page 372

311

KEY TERM

- Cognitive behaviour therapy (CBT)

Possible essay question …

Outline and evaluate cognitive behaviour therapy as a way of reducing addiction. *(16 marks)*

Other possible exam questions …

+ Briefly explain and give one criticism of cognitive behaviour therapy as a way of reducing addiction. *(6 marks)*

+ Explain how cognitive behaviour therapy might be used to reduce either nicotine or gambling addiction. *(4 marks)*

 Link

While revising it would be advisable to review your knowledge of Cognitive Behaviour Therapy (CBT) for the treatment of depression, that you encountered in the Psychopathology topic in Year 1. See Year 1/AS Revision and Exam Companion, page 116.

MUST know…

Cognitive behaviour therapy (CBT)

Cognitive behaviour therapy (CBT) is based on the assumption that addictive behaviours are the results of a person's thoughts.

The 'cognitive' aspect of the therapy aims to identify and alter the way individuals think about their gambling and the 'behavioural' aspect aims to change what they do.

CBT and gambling addiction

CBT can be used to identify the problem behaviour, challenge irrational thoughts and find ways of coping. Cognitive errors, such as the belief that an individual can control an outcome, play an important role in gambling addictions. CBT attempts to correct these errors and reduce the urge to gamble.

 One strength of using CBT as a treatment for addiction comes from…

…a wide-range of research support.

- ***E*** – **Migill and Ray (2009)** conducted a meta-analysis of CBT trials and found that CBT was effective for both alcohol and drug addictions.

 Another strength of CBT comes from…

…research examining patients with internet addictions.

- ***E*** – **Kim et al. (2012)** examined 65 adolescents before and after a form of CBT treatment, known as CBT-IA. Various measures were taken, including: severity of internet use and life satisfaction.

 Another strength of CBT comes from…

…the advantages of CBT in comparison to other treatments/therapies.

- ***E*** – Firstly, the development of more positive ways of thinking means that individuals no longer feel overwhelmed by everyday circumstances and are less likely to engage in addictive behaviours.

SHOULD know…

Three stages of CBT

CBT usually takes place over ten one-hour sessions and there are three key components:

1 **Identifying and correcting cognitive biases** – clients are not always aware of their cognitive biases and therefore the therapist will bring these to the surface and educate the client.

2 **Changing behaviour** – after cognitive restructuring has taken place, the client will practise these changes in their daily life, for example, by visiting a casino.

3 **Relapse prevention** – the client will identify and avoid risky situations (e.g. problem places), feelings or other difficulties that might prompt their gambling behaviour.

- ***E*** – Furthermore, research has found that CBT is more effective than 'Gamblers Anonymous' for gambling addicts **(Petry et al., 2006)**.
- ***L*** – This suggests that CBT is an effective treatment for a range of different addictions, making this treatment more universal.

- ***E*** – After therapy, those who were subjected to CBT-IA scored higher on life satisfaction and lower on internet addiction, compared to those who did not receive CBT-IA.
- ***L*** – This provides further support for CBT, and its ability to increase positive outcomes, as a result of changing unhealthy thinking patterns.

- ***E*** – Secondly, after CBT individuals have an enhanced ability to resist peer pressure, as they learn new behaviours that make them more confident to resist peer pressure.
- ***L*** – This highlights the strengths of CBT in comparison to other treatments, as patients are provided with tools that prevent relapse.

 P – However, one issue with CBT is…

…the over-emphasis on irrational thinking.

- ***E*** – CBT fails to acknowledge the role of stressful environments, which may perpetuate addictive behaviours.
- ***E*** – These stressful environments (e.g. demanding job) continue to exist beyond the therapy and reinforce problem behaviours once the therapy has ended.
- ***L*** – This suggests that CBT should be considered as part of a wider form of intervention which addresses the social environment.

P – A final issue with CBT is…

…whether or not individuals can make the transition from use to non-use.

- ***E*** – Patients with a long history of substance misuse often experience other challenges, such as unemployment, family difficulties, etc.
- ***E*** – Therefore, while being treated the patient is asked to give up their addiction and culture/lifestyle.
- ***L*** – This matters because the individual may not have the skills/resources to adjust to a new way of life, making the CBT less effective.

CHOOSE THE RIGHT ANSWER

Which **one** of the following statements is correct? (Tick **one** box only.)

A	CBT uses aversion therapy and covert sensitisation. ☐
B	CBT is based on behaviourist principles. ☐
C	CBT is based on cognitive principles. ☐
D	CBT aims to identify and correct irrational thoughts. ☐

Answers on page 373

 FILL IN THE BOXES

In each box below write one sentence describing each stage of CBT.	In each box below expand the content on the left, giving an example.
Identifying and correcting cognitive biases is where…	For example…
Changing behaviour is where…	For example…
Relapse prevention is where…	For example…
OPTIONAL: A diary is used to…	Why is the diary useful?

Answers on page 373

 APPLYING YOUR KNOWLEDGE

Chris has an internet addiction. He believes that he must always be available on Snapchat and Whatsapp. He thinks that if he doesn't reply to a friend instantly they will think he is being rude and no longer hang around with him.

Using your knowledge of CBT, explain how Chris could be treated.

Identify the psychology	Link to Chris

Answers on page 373

 A MARKING EXERCISE

Read this student answer to the following exam question:

Explain how cognitive behaviour therapy might be used to reduce a nicotine or gambling addiction. *(4 marks)*

CBT could be used to reduce a gambling addiction by identifying cognitive biases, changing the person's behaviour and ensuring that they have strategies to prevent relapse.

What mark do you think this would get?

YOUR MARK

AO1

Hint
Hint to help you decide:
How many critical points have been covered?
How much detail is there?

Write an improved answer here…

Answers on page 373

KEY TERM

- Theory of planned behaviour

Possible essay question …

Outline and evaluate the theory of planned behaviour as it relates to the reduction of addiction. *(16 marks)*

Other possible exam questions …

+ Briefly explain the theory of planned behaviour. *(3 marks)*
+ Outline **one** limitation of the theory of planned behaviour. *(2 marks)*
+ Outline the findings of research into the theory of planned behaviour as it relates to the reduction of addiction. *(4 marks)*

 Think

The theory of planned behaviour is a model that can be used to explain why addictions form, as well as the factors that can help with treatment. Therefore, it is both an explanation of addictive behaviour and a model for treatments at the same time.

MUST know…

The theory of planned behaviour

The theory of planned behaviour (TPB) suggests that an individual's decision to engage in a particular behaviour can be directly predicted by their intention to engage in that behaviour. Furthermore, the theory suggests that there are three factors that influence our attitude:

1 **Behavioural attitude:** An individual's personal views towards a behaviour.
2 **Subjective norms:** These are the product of social influence; for example, we might believe that heavy drinking is socially accepted and widespread.
3 **Perceived behavioural control:** The extent to which an individual believes they can actually perform a particular behaviour, such as giving up an addictive behaviour.

 One criticism of the theory of planned behaviour is…

…that it is too rational.
- ***E*** – The TPB fails to take into account emotions, compulsions and/or other irrational determinants of human behaviour.

 Another criticism of the theory of planned behaviour is…

…that it fails to take into account group variables and self-determination.
- ***E*** – **Topa and Moriano (2010)** suggest that group variables, such as identification, could play a mediating role in relation to nicotine addiction.

 Another criticism of the theory of planned behaviour comes from…

…the methodological issues when examining attitudes and intentions.
- ***E*** – According to **Albarracin et al. (2005)** the attitudes and intentions that are reported in questionnaires may be a poor representation of real-life attitudes and intentions.

SHOULD know…

Using the TPB to reduce addiction

The TPB can be used as a means to understand prevention and treatment.

Changing behavioural attitude

Slater et al. (2011) reviewed the effectiveness of a US campaign to lower teenage marijuana use and attributed the success to the influence on attitudes.

Changing subject norms

Anti-drug campaigns often use actual data about the percentage of people engaging in risky behaviour, in order to influence/change subjective norms.

Perceived behavioural control

Godin et al. (2002) found that perceived behavioural control was the most important predictor of behaviour in people giving up smoking.

- ***E*** – When completing a questionnaire, people might find it impossible to anticipate the strong desires and emotions that compel their behaviour in real life.
- ***L*** – This matters because the TPB fails to take into account these important factors which may play an important role in addictive behaviours.

- ***E*** – Furthermore, **Klag (2006)** found that recovery was consistently more successful in individuals who decided to give up, rather than those who were coerced.
- ***L*** – This matters because it suggests that the self-determination theory is preferable to the TPB, because it emphasises the importance of self-motivation.

- ***E*** – A person may report negative attitudes towards cigarettes when answering a questionnaire; however their actual intention and behaviour may be different when they are with a group of heavy smokers.
- ***L*** – This suggests that the research examining the TPB may not provide a valid representation of attitudes and intentions in everyday life.

 ***P* – Another criticism of the theory of planned behaviour is…**

…that it predicts intention to change and not actual change.
- ***E*** – **Armitage and Conner (2001)** conducted a meta-analysis which found that the model was successful when predicting intention, but not actual behaviour.
- ***E*** – This suggests that the TPB is an account of intention rather than specific processes involved in the behaviour.
- ***L*** – This matters because the TPB is unable to make a distinction between motivation and behaviour, which are important factors when trying to treat addiction.

***P* – A final criticism of the theory of planned behaviour is…**

…that it fails to take into account the influence of alcohol or drugs.
- ***E*** – Attitudes and intentions tend to be measured when sober, whereas risky behaviours such as gambling may be performed when intoxicated.
- ***E*** – Therefore, the attitudes being measured when sober may be different to the attitudes experienced in real-life situations.
- ***L*** – This suggests that the TPB may not provide a valid account of actual intention and behaviour.

COMPLETE THE DIAGRAM

Label the diagram for the TPB, using the key words below.

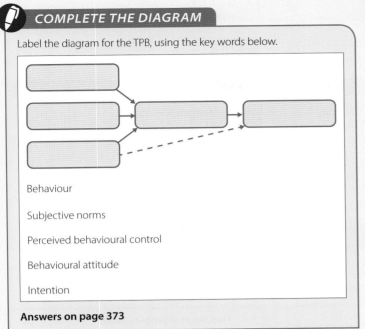

Behaviour

Subjective norms

Perceived behavioural control

Behavioural attitude

Intention

Answers on page 373

 MATCH THEM UP

Match the elements of the TPB with the examples.

Behavioural attitude	I know that my parents dislike my smoking habit and want me to stop.
Subjective norm (injunctive norm)	I know that I could give up smoking if I wanted to.
Subjective norm (descriptive norm)	All of my friends smoke, therefore it's fine.
Perceived behavioural control	I smoke because it makes me feel less stressed after a long day at work.

Answers on page 373

✓ **CHOOSE THE RIGHT ANSWER**

According to the TPB, which **one** of the follow components is the most important? (Tick **one** box only.)

Behavioural attitude	☐
Subjective norms	☐
Perceived behaviour control	☐
Intention	☐
Behaviour	☐

Answers on page 373

⚙ **APPLYING YOUR KNOWLEDGE**

Identify the psychology

Ali smokes 20 cigarettes a day and is growing increasingly concerned with the health risks of smoking.

Everyone at her work wants her to quit; however she does not believe she has the will power to actually give up.

Using your knowledge of the TPB, explain whether Ali is likely to be successful in her attempts to give up smoking.

Link to Ali

Answers on page 373

KEY TERM

- Prochaska's six-stage model

Possible essay question …

Outline and evaluate Prochaska's six-stage model of behaviour change. *(16 marks)*

Other possible exam questions …

+ Briefly explain **one** stage of Prochaska's six-stage model of behaviour change. *(2 marks)*

+ Briefly outline and give **one** limitation of Prochaska's six-stage model of behaviour change. *(4 marks)*

⭐ Exam tip

Watch out for the number of marks questions are worth in this section. While there are six stages to Prochaska's model, if the question is only worth 4 marks, you do not need to outline all six stages.

MUST know…

Prochaska's six-stage model

Prochaska's six-stage model suggests that overcoming an addiction comes about through a subtle and complex progression through a series of stages.

Stage theories emphasise the gradual nature of change and assume that an individual must move through a series of discrete stages.

According to Prochaska, the first three stages represent variations in a person's intention to change their behaviour (pre-action) and the latter three stages represent the duration of change (post-action).

Individuals move through these stages in order; however, on occasions they may relapse and revert to an earlier stage, before repeating the cycle again.

 One strength of the six-stage model is…

…its application to the treatment of addictive behaviours.

- **E** – The six-stage model suggests that the most effective strategy in reducing addictive behaviours is to determine the current stage the individual is in.

 However, one limitation of the six-stage model is…

…the lack of empirical support for behavioural outcomes.

- **E** – **Whitelaw et al. (2000)** claimed that much of the research evidence has focused on 'softer' indications of effectiveness, such as stage progression.

Furthermore, another limitation of the six stage model comes from…

…issues with the research support.

- **E** – **Whitelaw et al. (2002)** highlighted other issues with the research support, including the lack of control groups and self-selected samples.

SHOULD know…

The six stages of change

1 **Precontemplation:** The individual has no intention to change his/her behaviour in the near future.

2 **Contemplation:** The individual is aware that a problem exists, but has yet to make a commitment to doing anything about it.

3 **Preparation:** The individual combines their intention with actual behavioural change.

4 **Action:** The individual modifies their behaviour to overcome their problems.

5 **Maintenance:** The individual works to consolidate the gains they have made and prevent relapse.

6 **Termination:** The individual is no longer tempted to revert back to their previous behaviour.

- **E** – **Haslam and Draper (2000)** found that women further along the cycle of change were more convinced about the dangers of smoking during pregnancy.
- **L** – This suggests that the six-stage model can be used to provide tailored treatments based on the individual's particular stage of change.

- **E** – However, according to Whitelaw, stage progression does not necessarily equate to subsequent behaviour change. It may be the intention to quit smoking that changes and not the behaviour itself.
- **L** – Therefore, Whitelaw concluded that the popularity of the model had 'little to do with its scientific support'.

- **E** – Furthermore, other studies have used a variety of interventions as part of the treatment. For example, **Steptoe et al. (1999)** used NRT and behavioural counselling.
- **L** – This matters because it becomes difficult to disentangle the specific 'stages of change' from other interventions and therefore the effectiveness of this model remains unknown.

FURTHER EVALUATION

 P – In addition, another limitation of the six-stage model comes from…

…recent research into the effectiveness of staged interventions.

- **E** – **Baumann et al. (2015)** randomly allocated problem drinkers to an intervention experimental group and a control group.
- **E** – The researchers found no significant difference in the beneficial effects between staged intervention and the control group.
- **L** – This suggests that the advantages of the six-stage model may be overstated.

 P – A final limitation of the six stage models is…

…that it fails to acknowledge the importance of social norms.

- **E** – **Daoud et al. (2015)** found that in Arab cultures, the social norm of smoking in social situations makes it difficult to quit.
- **E** – In their research, they found that 62% of male smokers were still at the precontemplation stages.
- **L** – These findings suggest a lower readiness to quit smoking as a result of social norms, which are not taken into account in the six-stage model.

COMPLETE THE DIAGRAM

Using the following key terms, label Prochaska's six-stage model.

Contemplation	Precontemplation	Behavioural intention
Action	Preparation	Behaviour
Maintenance	Termination	

Answers on page 373

 CHOOSE THE RIGHT ANSWER

Which **one** of the following statements does **not** represent the precontemplation stage? (Tick **one** box only.)

A An individual has no intention to change their behaviour. ☐

B An individual is unaware that their behaviour is a problem. ☐

C An individual may only seek help because of the pressure from others. ☐

D An individual may be aware that a problem exists but has yet to make a commitment. ☐

Answers on page 373

MATCH THEM UP

Cover the left-hand side of your book with a blank sheet of paper. Then match up the stages of Prochaska's six-stage model with the descriptions.

Precontemplation	The individual is aware that a problem exists, but has yet to make a commitment to doing anything about it.
Contemplation	The individual has no intention to change his/her behaviour in the near future.
Preparation	The individual is no longer tempted to revert back to their previous behaviour.
Action	The individual modifies their behaviour to overcome their problems.
Maintenance	The individual works to consolidate the gains they have made and prevent relapse.
Termination	The individual combines their intention with actual behavioural change.

Answers on page 373

APPLYING YOUR KNOWLEDGE

Identify the psychology		Link to Aiden

Aiden says that he would like to give up smoking. He tells his classmate that he will only buy 10 cigarettes this week, instead of his usual 20.

With reference to Prochaska's model of change, outline which stage(s) Aiden is at and why.

Answers on page 373

Topic 1 Describing addiction

Explain what is meant by the terms 'physical dependence', 'psychological dependence', 'tolerance' and 'withdrawal'. *(2 marks each)*

Physical dependence is evident when an individual needs to take a drug in order to feel 'normal'. It can be demonstrated by the presence of withdrawal symptoms, if the individual abstains from the drug.

Psychological dependence occurs when a drug becomes a central part of an individual's thoughts, emotions and activities, resulting in a strong urge to use the drug.

Tolerance means that an individual no longer responds to a drug in the same way, with the result that larger and larger doses are needed in order to experience the same effects as before.

Withdrawal can occur when a drug on which an individual is physically dependent is discontinued. In such situations, withdrawal symptoms, such as shaking and anxiety, can occur, as the body attempts to deal with the absence of a drug's effects.

Marks awarded: 8 (2 marks each)

Examiner's comments: The answer has achieved full marks as each definition is clearly defined and elaborated.

Examiner's comments

This is purely a definition question and the answer has provided a very clear definition of every key term. Furthermore, each definition is elaborated with further description and/or an example.

Topic 2 Risk factors: Genetics, stress and personality

Outline the role of genetic vulnerability as a risk factor in the development of addiction. *(4 marks)*

Genetic vulnerability refers to inherited characteristics that are passed from parents to their children and some people appear to be born with a genetic vulnerability to substance abuse.

Vike et al. (2005) examined 1,572 Dutch twin pairs and found that 44% of smoking initiation was explained by genetic factors. Furthermore, Slutske et al. (2010) found that MZ twins had a higher rate of both twins being pathological gamblers. Male MZ twins had a heritability estimate of 49% compared to just 21% for DZ twins.

These results show that there is a genetic component to both smoking and gambling that puts individuals at risk of becoming addicts. However it also highlights that environmental factors also play a role, which may explain why the heritability in MZ twins is not 100%, despite sharing all of their genes.

Marks awarded: 4

Examiner's comments: AO1: It is typical for questions on genetics to require research as part of the knowledge (AO1), in order to demonstrate understanding. This answer has provided a definition of genetic vulnerability, described two studies accurately and made an explicit link to the question.

Examiner's comments

Questions exploring genetics require research to demonstrate knowledge, as this answer has clearly demonstrated.

Topic 3 Risk factors: Family influences and peers

Discuss risk factors in the development of addiction. *(16 marks)*

Examiner's comments

There are numerous risk factors involved in the development of addiction, including: family, peers, genetics, stress and personality. This answer will focus on family, stress and personality.

> A good introduction, although not entirely necessary.

According to social learning theory, behaviours are learned through observation of people that we have social contact with, including family and peers. Parents can influence addictive behaviours in two ways: firstly, they act as a social model for their offspring and secondly, through their parenting style. Authoritative parents help their children to develop resilience to addictive behaviours.

> Good knowledge of parental influences is shown.

Support for the idea of family influences comes from Bahr et al. (2005) who found that tolerant parental attitudes were strongly associated with an increased prevalence of binge drinking, smoking and drug use. Furthermore, they also found that adolescents with parents who were tolerant, were more likely to interact with peers who smoke, drank and/or used illicit drugs. This suggests that family and peer influences are two risk factors which are not independent and in fact interact with one another.

> This is a good evaluation point; however it would have been better if the answer had discussed peers in the AO1 section previously.

Stress is a risk factor which is often associated with substance abuse. People often deal with stressful life events by engaging in a variety of behaviours that make them feel better or forget their stress, for example alcohol. The self-medication model suggest that individuals intentionally use different forms of pathological behaviour (e.g. alcohol or drugs) to 'treat' psychological symptoms they experience, because of everyday stressors.

> Excellent knowledge of stress, using specialist terminology well.

The idea that stress is a risk factor has been supported through research. Matheny and Weatherman (1998) found a strong relationship between use of coping resources and the ability to maintain abstinence from smoking, once they had given up. This suggests that if addiction is a consequence of stress, then effective coping strategies should reduce the need for addictive behaviours. This highlights the positive application of stress coping resources (such as problem solving and tension control), as a tool for reducing addictive behaviour.

> Two reasonable evaluation points here, although further elaboration is required to make these effective. The answer should link this evaluation to the question of risk factors.

Finally, personality also appears to play an important role in predicting the development of addiction and traits like sensation seeking and impulsivity are commonly associated with addiction. Furthermore, research has found a relationship between addiction and personality disorder. Verhheul et al., (1995) found an overall prevalence of personality disorders which was 44% in alcoholics and 70% for cocaine addicts.

> Good knowledge presented.

> Reasonable use of research for knowledge, but not linked explicitly to the question.

Support for the idea of personality as a risk factor comes from longitudinal research by Labouvie and McGee (1986). They found that adolescents who progressed to heavier levels of alcohol abuse tended to score higher on impulsivity. Furthermore, they also found that impulsivity was linked to a wide range of other health-risk behaviours (e.g. illicit drug use). This provides support for the idea that personality is a risk factor for addictive behaviours.

> Good use of research support to provide evidence for personality.

Level 3 (9–12 marks)

Examiner's comments: AO1: The structure of this essay is interesting, as the answer outlines and evaluates each of the factors separately. While this is a good structure, it highlights the limited number of evaluation points. The knowledge is generally well-detailed and accurate. AO3: The evaluation is generally very good, however, it is limited in terms of the number of points. In total there are only three evaluation points, one for each factor and therefore further evaluation should have been included to demonstrate a depth of knowledge. This could have been achieved by including some general evaluation points about risk factors at the end, or by including counter-arguments.

Topic 4 Explanation for nicotine addiction: Brain neurochemistry

Outline and evaluate the brain neurochemistry explanation of nicotine addiction. *(16 marks)*

Examiner's comments

The brain neurochemistry explanation of nicotine addiction focuses on the role of dopamine and the brain's reward pathways.

Nicotine is the main active ingredient in tobacco and can have a range of different effects. Nicotine attaches to neurons in the ventral tegmental area (VTA). These neurons trigger the release of dopamine from the nucleus accumbens (NAc). Nicotine also stimulates the release of glutamate, which triggers the release of even more dopamine. Dopamine produces pleasure and a desire to repeat the behaviours again, contributing to an addiction.

> An example of the effects would have been useful here.

> The explanation of dopamine is generally well detailed and accurate.

The reason why dopamine levels remain high after the nicotine stimulus ends can be linked to the role of glutamate and GABA. Glutamate speeds up the activity of neurons, whereas GABA slows down neuron activity. Nicotine causes glutamate to speed up dopamine release, but it also prevents GABA from slowing it down after the dopamine levels have raised. This combination amplifies the effect of dopamine and the rewarding properties of nicotine, further contributing to the addiction.

> The role of glutamate and GABA are both explained accurately and in detail.

There is a range of research support for the neurochemical explanation of nicotine addiction, including research examining drugs for epilepsy and research on patients with Parkinson's disease (PD). Paterson and Markou (2002) found that GVG (an epilepsy drug) reduces the surge of dopamine in the NAc that occurs after taking nicotine. This reduces the addictive tendencies of nicotine and other drugs that boost dopamine levels in the brain. This research highlights the link between dopamine and nicotine and provides a method of treating nicotine addiction which has fewer side effects than most smoking treatments. Furthermore, PD is characterised by a gradual loss of dopamine producing nerve cells, causing symptoms of PD to appear. Research suggests that smokers are less likely to get PD, suggesting that nicotine may have a neuroprotective function against the development of PD. This provides further support for the link between nicotine and dopamine, while also providing some insight into possible treatments for PD.

> An effective evaluation point, using research support from epilepsy drugs.

> Further effective evaluation, using evidence from patients with PD.

Further support for the neurochemical explanation comes from animal research. D'Souza and Markou (2013) blocked the transmission of glutamate which resulted in a decrease in nicotine intake in rats, which is consistent with the role of this neurotransmitter. This is because glutamate enhances the dopamine-releasing effects of nicotine, so blocking it would decrease the effects of dopamine for longer. This highlights the link between glutamate and nicotine, allowing researchers to potentially devise treatments based on blocking the transmission of this neurotransmitter.

> Very effective evaluation, using research from animal studies.

Despite the research support, the neurochemical explanation is unable to explain the different effects found in men and women. Cosgrove et al. (2014) studied the brains of men and women using PET scans, while smoking. For women there was a strong dopamine effect in the dorsal put a men, whereas men had a strong effect in the ventral striatum. These results suggest that men and women smoke for different reasons, men for the nicotine effect and women to relieve stress. Furthermore, if men and women smoke for different reasons this highlights a cognitive factor which is not taken into consideration in the neurochemical explanation.

> An interesting criticism of the neurochemical explanation, plus further evaluation highlighting other explanations.

Level 4 (13–16 marks)

Examiner's comments: AO1: An accurate and well-detailed outline highlighting the role of dopamine, glutamate and GABA, using specialist terminology consistently. AO3: A thorough and effective evaluation, drawing on a range of research support and highlighting the limitations from research evidence and other explanations.

Topic 5 Explanation for nicotine addiction: Learning theory

Outline and evaluate the learning theory explanation of nicotine addiction. *(16 marks)*

Examiner's comments

The learning theory of addiction attempts to explain the initiation, maintenance and relapse of smoking (nicotine addiction).

Social learning theory can explain why young people start smoking, through the observation of social models who smoke (e.g. family and peers). Furthermore, vicarious reinforcement causes young people to expect positive consequences from smoking, thus leading to the initiation of a smoking addiction. Furthermore, as nicotine is immediately rewarding, people are then positively reinforced (e.g. by feeling less stressed) for smoking, which encourages them to continue smoking further.

> A detailed outline of the initiation of smoking is presented, with a good use of specialist terminology.

Operant conditioning then continues to reinforce a person's nicotine addiction, through positive and negative reinforcement. A person may continue smoking to 'look cool' (positive reinforcement) or to provide them with relief from unpleasant withdrawal symptoms (negative reinforcement).

> A good explanation of the maintenance of smoking through reinforcement.

Finally, classical conditioning can explain why a person who tries to quit smoking might relapse, as regular smokers associate specific moods, situations and environmental factors with the rewarding effects of nicotine and therefore these cues can trigger a relapse.

> Finally, a good explanation of relapse in terms of classical conditioning.

The learning theory is a comprehensive explanation of smoking addiction and has received a wealth of support from a range of research, examining the initiation, maintenance and relapse of smoking. For example, Karcher and Finn (2005) found that if a person's parents smoke they are 1.88 times more likely to smoke. However, this figure rose to 2.64 times for siblings and 8 times for close friends. This suggests that the closer the social model, the higher the chance of initiation, supporting the idea that social learning is implicated in the initiation of smoking.

> This is an effective evaluation point, supporting the role of SLT, using relevant research.

Research has also provided support for the idea of classical and operant conditioning involved in the relapse of smoking. Shiffman and Waters (2004) found that a sudden increase in negative moods, rather than a slow change in stress levels, was associated with relapse. Furthermore, there is even evidence that changes in negative moods can increase nicotine cravings. This suggests that negative reinforcement contributes to the maintenance and relapse of smoking, as people are more likely to smoke when they experience a negative mood, to remove these unhappy feelings (negative reinforcement). In addition, Wiers et al. (2013) found that smokers showed a significant approach bias towards smoking related cues, compared to ex-smokers and non-smokers. This approach bias was positively correlated with their cravings scores, which was not the case for ex-smokers and non-smokers. This suggests that smoking cues are present in heavy smokers and that classical conditioning plays a significant role in the relapse of nicotine addiction.

> This is a very effective evaluation point, clearly explaining support for the role of negative reinforcement in the maintenance of smoking.

> Further support for the role of classical conditioning has been presented effectively.

Despite the wealth of research support, the learning theory is unable to explain the different patterns of smoking behaviour found in men and women. Lopez et al. (1994) found that women tend to start smoking later than men. Other research has found that women are more likely to light up in stressful situations and experience withdrawal effects sooner than men. This matters because the learning theory of addiction is unable to account for these differences and therefore other factors must also be involved in smoking addiction. For example, cognitive explanations which examine the underlying thought processes involved in smoking, may be able to explain these differences.

> The answer has provided a weakness and explored the possibility of other explanations effectively.

Level 4 (13–16 marks)

Examiner's comments: AO1: This answer provides a very detailed account of the initiation, maintenance and relapse of smoking, using specialist terminology throughout. AO3: A range of strengths based on research support have been outlined in addition to an effective criticism which explores other explanations.

Topic 6 Explanations for gambling addiction: Learning theory

Outline and evaluate the learning theory explanation of gambling addiction. *(16 marks)*

Examiner's comments

There are many different aspects to the learning theory of gambling. However, the main ideas are based on the ideas of operant conditioning and reinforcement.

Griffiths (2009) suggests that gamblers may become addicted because of different types of rewards (positive reinforcement), including: physiological rewards (e.g. the buzz from winning); psychological rewards (e.g. the near misses); social rewards (e.g. peer praise); as well as financial rewards if they win. However, as gamblers generally lose, their behaviour can be explained in terms of partial reinforcement. Casinos use a form of partial reinforcement, called variable reinforcement. Gambling machines use variable-ratio reinforcement, where wins occur after an unpredictable number of responses and it's this unpredictable nature, which keeps people gambling.

> The key ideas of Griffiths (2009) are presented, with clear examples linked to gambling.

> Excellent of use of specialist terminology, linked explicitly to gambling.

Finally, there are two other theories related to the learning theory: the 'big win' hypothesis – where gamblers will continue to gamble to repeat a 'big win' they have previously experienced and the 'near miss' hypothesis – the idea a near miss creates a brief moment of excitement that can also encourage further gambling.

> Further knowledge presented with key terminology.

While aspects of the learning theory of gambling have received support, including the big win hypothesis and the idea of partial reinforcement, other aspects of the theory have received criticism.

Horsley et al. (2012) tested the idea of partial reinforcement, among high- and low-frequency gamblers, using either partial or continuous reinforcement. They found that after partial reinforcement, high-frequency gamblers continued to respond to a gambling situation for longer, in comparison to low-frequency gamblers. This supports the idea that partial reinforcement is likely to contribute to the maintenance of gambling, especially in high-frequency gamblers. Furthermore, Sharpe (2002) claimed that the placement of an early 'big win' could lead to irrational thoughts about gambling machines. For example, an early big win may give the gambler the belief that they can control the outcome of the machine and win. This supports the idea of 'big wins' and shows that the overestimation of winning and underestimation of losing, encourages persistent gambling.

> Effective use of evidence to support the idea of partial reinforcement.

> Further evaluation embedded to support the 'big win' hypothesis.

However, one issue with the learning explanation of gambling is that it can't explain all forms of gambling. The principles of operant conditioning are difficult to apply to different types of gambling, for example scratch cards and sports betting. Scratch cards have a short time period between the behaviour and consequence, whereas sports betting has a much longer period. Consequently, learning theory is unable to explain why both types of gamblers continue to gamble, despite these differences in reinforcement. Furthermore, the learning explanation of gambling can't explain why relatively few people become addicts. While many people may gamble at some time during their lives and experience reinforcement, relatively few become addicts. If the learning explanation was the only cause of gambling, then it would be reasonable to assume that a higher proportion of people may become addicts. This matters because it suggests that there must be other factors involved in the formation of gambling addictions.

> Excellent evaluation, highlighting the limitation of the learning theory.

> A related and further evaluation point is presented effectively. However, an exploration of the 'other factors' would have improved this section.

Level 4 (13–16 marks)

Examiner's comments: AO1: The knowledge is presented in detail and with excellent use of specialist terminology. AO3: The evaluation is generally thorough and effective, although there was a missed opportunity to explore other factors in the final section of this essay.

Topic 7 Explanation for gambling addiction: Cognitive theory

Outline the findings of **one** study relating to the cognitive theory explanation of gambling addiction. *(4 marks)*

Griffiths (1994) examined the thinking (cognitions) of regular and non-regular gamblers. Griffiths found that the regular gamblers believed they were more skilful than they actually were and made more irrational statements. Furthermore, in subsequent interviews 26 out of 30 gamblers believed that the game was due to skill, in comparison to none of the non-regular gamblers.

These findings support the cognitive explanation of gambling as they demonstrated the idea of irrational beliefs and distorted thinking through the irrational statements. Furthermore, they also demonstrated 'illusions of control' as they overestimated their personal ability, by believing that they were more skilful.

Marks awarded: 4

Examiner's comments: AO1: Students often struggle with these types of question and provide details of the aim and method. However, the question will only be awarded marks for the findings and an explanation of these findings (conclusion). This answer clearly outlines the findings of Griffiths (1994) and explicitly links these findings to the cognitive explanation.

Examiner's comments

It is worth noting that the first sentence is not required as the question only asks for the findings.

Topic 8 Reducing addiction: Drug therapy

Briefly explain and give **one** criticism of drug therapy as a way of reducing addiction. *(6 marks)*

One drug therapy that is often used for nicotine addiction is nicotine replacement therapy (NRT). NRT gradually releases nicotine into the bloodstream to help an individual control their cravings for a cigarette, improve their mood and help prevent relapse. NRT comes in many different forms, including: patches, gum, inhalators, nasal spray, etc.

However, one issue with NRT is that the research findings are often questionable. Mooney et al. (2004) found that out of 73 double-blind placebo controlled NRT trials, only 17 had actually conducted blinding assessment, where they asked the participants whether they believed they were receiving nicotine or not. The researchers found that in these 17 studies, almost two-thirds of the placebo condition were 'confident' that they had not received a real nicotine patch. This matters because the conclusions about the effectiveness of NRT are inconclusive due to the lack of a 'real' control condition.

Marks awarded: 6

Examiner's comments: AO1: This answer has provided a good outline of NRT and used examples to supplement the description. Furthermore, the answer has outlined one criticism of research examining NRT effectively, embedding research evidence to support their criticism.

Examiner's comments

As there isn't a lot to say about NRT, this answer has provided some examples effectively.

Topic 9 Reducing addiction: Behavioural interventions

Briefly explain and give **one** criticism of aversion therapy as a way of reducing addiction. *(4 marks)*

Examiner's comments

Aversion therapy is based on the principles of classical conditioning, where an individual learns to associate an aversive stimulus with something they have previously enjoyed, namely smoking. For example, in smoking, one approach is called 'rapid smoking' where a smoker is required to take a puff every few seconds to make smoking unpleasant.

The answer has provided a good example of aversion therapy (rapid smoking) to highlight knowledge of specific techniques.

However, one of the major criticisms of aversion therapy is its unethical nature. Some forms of aversion therapy used in the treatment of problem smoking/drinking cause extremely uncomfortable consequences, e.g. nausea, sickness, etc. These consequences could lead to poor compliance with the treatment and high dropout rates. This matters because these side effects may decrease the positive impact of the treatment and cause patients to relapse.

Marks awarded: 4

Examiner's comments: AO1: This answer has provided a good description of aversion therapy and included a smoking specific example, which is excellent. AO3: Furthermore, the answer has provided one effective and elaborated criticism of aversion therapy.

Topic 10 Reducing addiction: Cognitive behaviour therapy

Explain how cognitive behaviour therapy might be used to reduce **either** nicotine **or** gambling addiction. *(4 marks)*

Examiner's comments

There are three key steps to cognitive behaviour therapy (CBT) that could be used to help reduce a gambling addiction: Firstly, the therapist and client would identify the client's cognitive biases. The therapist will bring these cognitive biases to the surface and educate the client, about why they are irrational. For example, the therapist would make the client aware of the low odds associated with winning. Secondly, the client and therapist will create a strategy to change the client's behaviour. The client will practise these changes in their daily life, for example, by visiting a casino and not betting. Finally, the therapist and client will try to prevent relapse from occurring. The client will identify and avoid risky situations (e.g. problem places, feelings or other difficulties) that might prompt their gambling behaviour and know how/when to identify these problems to ensure they don't cause the individual to relapse in the future.

Not only has the answer outlined the steps, but also provided an explicit example in relation to each step, which is excellent.

Marks awarded: 4

Examiner's comments: AO1: This is a well-detailed and accurate answer describing CBT. This answer is particularly strong because it has related every step of CBT back to gambling, demonstrating an explicit understanding in relation to this question.

Topic 11 The theory of planned behaviour

Briefly explain the theory of planned behaviour. *(3 marks)*

The theory of planned behaviour (TPB) suggests that an individual's decision to engage in a particular behaviour can be directly predicted by their intention to engage in that behaviour. The theory suggests that there are three factors that influence our attitude. Firstly, the person's behavioural attitude, which is an individual's personal view towards a behaviour. Secondly, the subjective norms, which are the product of social influence, for example, we might believe that heavy drinking is socially accepted and widespread. Finally, there is the person's perceived behavioural control, which is the extent to which an individual believes they can actually perform a particular behaviour, such as giving up an addictive behaviour.

Marks awarded: 3

Examiner's comments: AO1: This is a very detailed answer and arguably too detailed for a 3-mark question. One exam skill is knowing how much to write for different types of questions and while this answer would achieve top marks, could the time have been better spent answering another question in more depth?

Examiner's comments

All three aspects are well explained. No examples are required as this is only a 3-mark question.

Topic 12 Prochaska's six-stage model of behaviour change

Briefly outline and give **one** limitation of Prochaska's six-stage model of behaviour change. *(4 marks)*

Prochaska's six-stage model suggests that overcoming an addiction comes about through a subtle and complex progression, through a series of stages. According to Prochaska, the first three stages represent variations in a person's intention to change their behaviour (pre-action) and the latter three stages represent the duration of change (post-action).

However, one limitation of Prochaska's six-stage model comes from recent research into the effectiveness of staged interventions. Baumann et al. (2015) randomly allocated problem drinkers to an intervention experimental group and a control group. The researchers found no significant difference in the beneficial effects between staged intervention and the control group. This suggests that the advantages of the six-stage model may be overstated.

Marks awarded: 4

Examiner's comments: AO1: This is an excellent answer which has avoided writing too much for AO1 (especially as it's only a 4-mark question). The answer provides a good general outline of Prochaska's six-stage model and one effective evaluation point, drawing on research evidence.

Examiner's comments

Rather than explaining all six stages, this answer has wisely provided a brief summary, as it's only worth 2 marks for the outline.

Section A Social influence

1 *C*

2 *C*

3 *Milgram's investigations into obedience were renowned for challenging the idea that certain types of personalities or cultures affected obedience, and instead demonstrated the importance of situational factors. The high level of control in Milgram's experiments meant this could be determined with some certainty. However, it was this high level of control that also brought limitations. The context of the experiments meant situations were seen as artificial which in turn may have impacted on the ecological validity of any findings. Also, given the social context of obedience, using samples that were only made up of American men could be seen as biased. It is possible that women and other cultures would show different levels of obedience meaning that Milgram's results may have been over-generalised.*

4 *Proximity is a situational variable that affects obedience levels. Research shows that people are more likely to obey an order that harms another if they do not have to witness the consequences of their actions. If they are harming someone who is present, this is more likely to lead to defiance. One theory is that people are more aware of their actions if they are directly exposed to them whereas under other circumstances they may be able to convince themselves that the outcome is different.*

5 *One criticism of this explanation is that it is contradicted by evidence that suggests that people can be influenced to obey or disobey. A dispositional explanation would argue that obedience is a relatively fixed trait that is not easy to change yet people's tendency to obey seems to depend on the situation they are in. At the very least, a dispositional explanation ought to recognise there is an interaction between personality and the context in which a person finds themselves.*

Examiner's comments

1 A straightforward question testing knowledge but it is reminder that you need to know the key details of any research named on the specification.

2 Again – a question testing knowledge but one where you may have to stop and think more which is a reminder that multiple choice questions are not always that straightforward. The options were all responses that Milgram commented on but the question is which one gave him his actual measure of obedience.

3 This question assesses AO3 skills only by focusing straight away on evaluation of research. There is no need to describe details of the research and you can assume the examiner knows about the investigations as they are listed on the specification.

Although not a necessity, this answer considers both positive and negative points as part of its evaluation, giving the responses a good balance. Each point is pertinent to the study and well explained. Note how the points are not generic and are clearly applied to the investigations in question. This answer easily earns the four marks available.

4 This question gives you a choice so you would want to choose a variable that you can explain the effect of in enough detail to earn the three marks on offer. There is an inherent mark for knowing a situational variable but thereafter marks would be awarded for some level of explanation in terms of its effect on obedience.

This response gets a mark for identifying a relevant variable and then a further one for explaining whether obedience increases and/or decreases as a result. One further mark is earned for offering some explanation of the effect. Three marks would be awarded overall.

5 This question is challenging in the sense that you need to identify a criticism that can be described in enough detail to access three marks – so you would need to think through the options. You would have to be careful to elaborate on the point you decide to make, rather than repeating yourself by making the same kind of point again and again.

This answer chooses an obvious criticism which recognises the main alternative explanation for obedience. A key feature of the dispositional explanation is identified to help make the point, and the answer ends with a suggestion for improving the dispositional explanation which ties in appropriately with the criticism. This is an effective way of expanding on the point to secure full marks.

6 (a) *Gina demonstrates compliance by going along with her fellow managers even though she does not agree with them. She is possibly doing this because she doesn't want them to disapprove of her especially since she has to work closely with them.*

(b) *Oliver demonstrates internalisation by not only accepting the influence of others but also adopting their views on the policy as his own. This might be because he trusts their views especially as they know the company better than he does.*

7 (a) *The Mann-Whitney test could be used. This is because the design is unrelated as two different age groups are compared. The level of data is at least ordinal as scores were collected. However, it is unlikely that two participants' with the same score are equally conformist so it is not interval data.*

(b) *The critical value he should select is 138. This is because 0.05 is the conventional level of significance and it needs to be used for a one-tailed test as the psychologist is predicting the direction of results – younger people will conform more than older people.*

8 *One explanation focuses on personality characteristics and specifically looks at a characteristic known as 'locus of control'. The term refers to how much a person perceives they have personal control over their own behaviour. It is measured on a scale of 'high internal' to 'high external' with most people being somewhere in between. A high internal locus of control is associated with the belief that we have control over events in our life. People with an internal locus of control believe that what happens to them is largely a consequence of their own efforts and ability. They are also more likely to demonstrate independence in thought and behaviour. Because they tend not to depend on the opinions of others, they are better set up to resist social influence. People with an external locus of control tend to believe that what happens to them is determined by outside factors, including the influence of others. Research into the features of 'high internal control' have identified the following as being common; high internals are active seekers of information that is useful to them and so are less likely to rely on the opinions of others; high internals tend to be more achievement-oriented and consequently more likely to become leaders rather than followers; high internals are better equipped to resist coercion from others.*

Examiner's comments

6 These questions have the same focus – you need to apply your knowledge to the information provided in the item. To earn the initial mark you would need to identify the type of conformity which requires careful reading of the item. The second mark is for more than an explanation of that type of conformity – it also needs to incorporate the situation described in the item.

Both responses are of a high standard and follow a similar format. The correct type of conformity is identified, and then there is a detailed explanation of why it occurs which also includes a clear and feasible reference to the item. Both responses would earn two marks.

7 (a) This is a question that assesses your understanding of research methods as well as your mathematical ability. The first thing to get right is the test. However, even if you are not sure of this it is still possible to earn the other marks for knowing the level of data and for knowing the type of design used. It is not enough to just state this – to earn full marks there needs to be a clear link back to the study.

This answer earns all three marks. The test selected is the most obvious one to use and the reasons for choosing it are correct. Offering two reasons is enough for securing a second mark but for full marks it is important to explain these in the context of the study. This shows that it is more than just guess work!

7 (b) This is a question that assesses your understanding of research methods as well as your mathematical ability. There is a mark for identifying the correct critical value – it can't just be any one of them and of course it is checking you don't make the mistake of choosing something else from the table. Think about research you have done yourself and how you go about locating your critical value normally – it would depend on the number of participants (which is given), the significance level and the direction of the hypothesis.

This answer earns both marks. The critical value is the one we would expect and, more importantly, the reasons for selecting it are clear and valid.

8 Again there is a choice here. You'd want to choose an explanation that you can describe in some detail but also one that is relatively easy to summarise as the command word says 'outline' and only four marks are on offer for a whole explanation. Using the specification, the choice is essentially between social support as an explanation or locus of control.

This response outlines locus of control in good detail offering both breadth and depth. This answer rightly concentrates on the personality associated with resistance to social influence which is what the question is about. Although the response essentially has to describe the personality type, it does so using a range of information. All four AO1 marks would be awarded for this.

Section B Memory

9 **(a)** *Sensory register*

(b) *Long-term memory*

10 (a)

A scattergram to show the relationship between time spent rehearsing information and recall in a memory test

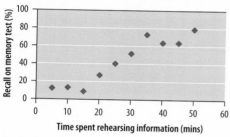

(b) *The psychologist could conclude that the longer the time spent rehearsing information, the higher the score on the recall test. This is supported by the scattergram which shows a strong, positive correlation.*

Examiner's comments

9 Two straightforward knowledge questions which test recall. Hopefully you know your stuff but you should know that you only have three stores to choose from anyway so it is always worth a guess!

One mark for the first response as the other stores use other types of coding as well modality specific coding. One mark for the second response as the other stores have limited capacities.

10 (a) This is a question that assesses your understanding of research methods as well as your mathematical ability. When asked to sketch a graph, remember it does not have to be as neat and precise as if you were constructing one outside of the exam – however, it needs to be clear enough to be assessed. Not all of the marks are for just plotting the data – a mark is reserved for a title and one is also reserved for labelling axes. But as there is quite a lot of data to plot there are two marks available for this. If there are some inaccuracies in plotting only one of the two marks would be awarded. Too many errors, then both marks are lost. Of course, if you make the mistake of sketching the wrong kind of graph then it would be difficult to earn any marks.

This response earns all four marks. The title is clear and includes both variables – one mark. The axes are accurately and clearly labelled (as per table) – one mark. All points are plotted and in the right place – two marks.

10 (b) This is a question that assesses your understanding of research methods as well as your mathematical ability. It asks about a correlation so therefore any conclusion should not refer to or imply cause and effect – phrase any conclusion carefully. Also, a conclusion is a summary of the findings not an explanation of them. Referring to the scattergram is important as this provides the evidence for the conclusion. Indeed, you would have used the graph to come up with a conclusion so it's only right that you get a mark for stating what it is you were looking at!

One mark for recognising the graph shows a positive correlation (as opposed to just a correlation). One mark for a conclusion that describes a positive correlation in the context of the study.

11 *One explanation of forgetting is interference. This is when information is blocked or distorted by similar information held in the memory. This could explain why Lily forgot most of the Spanish she had revised because similar information – the French she had revised – was interfering with her recall. More specifically, this would be an example of pro-active interference where older, well-rehearsed information interferes with newer information.*

Research, such as McGeoch and McDonald's (1931) experiment, has shown that if participants are presented with two very similar word lists and asked to recall one, the words from the other are also recalled – an effect of interference. However, critics argue that interference is much more common under these artificial conditions where it is almost primed to happen through use of highly contrived material. If such findings do lack ecological validity then it is questionable how well they apply to real-life scenarios such as Lily's. Indeed, if she has chosen to study two languages she is likely to be an able linguist who knows her languages as well and so will not perceive them as similar. This is of course an issue for this theory – 'similarity' is a subjective concept which is not easily tested.

An alternative explanation is retrieval failure. This when information is potentially accessible – so not distorted – but cannot be retrieved at that point in time due to an absence of cues. Cues can be external or internal and, if present, will allow the information to be accessed. Lily may be in a different 'frame of mind' than when she revised so is lacking internal cues – however, her Spanish revision appeared to be quite stressful and she may feel anxious in the exam so this should actually aid recall. It is more likely to be down to an absence of external cues. The sights, sounds and smells of the library are absent and so when she is sat in the exam hall – in a different context – there is nothing to help trigger the material she has revised. This is idea is supported by Abernathy (1940) who showed that when students are tested in the same room they have done their learning in then they recall more than students tested in a different room from their classroom. Of course, this theory assumes that information is there to be retrieved but it may be that it is unavailable.

In Lily's case, it may be that the Spanish material is unavailable. She did not get to revise it for as long as the French material so it may be that forgetting is due to lack of rehearsal. Rehearsal strengthens learning traces in memory but if these are weak then recall is more difficult. However critics argue that recall is more to do with meaning rather than rehearsal. Lily did spend some evenings revising and, assuming this was effective, traces should be quite strong. It is possible that Lily does not really understand or enjoy Spanish as much as French which is why she finds recall of material difficult.

It may even be the case that Lily dislikes Spanish – especially given short notice of the exam and having to revise under pressure. There is a theory that says events are forgotten if they are particularly traumatic because they end up being repressed into memory. It may be that the Spanish revision was so stressful that Lily has since repressed it and cannot access it when the exam comes around. This is the most unlikely explanation, particularly given the lack of scientific support for this theory. It is of course impossible to investigate the unconscious mind as people are not aware of what is held in it.

In conclusion, it is possibly too reductionist to look for one key factor that explains Lily's problems with recall in the Spanish exam. Giving the likely breadth and variety of what she has revised (and subsequently forgotten) it may be that different factors explaining forgetting of different types of material or that different factors are interacting to explain such a significant failure of memory.

Examiner's comments

11 This essay invites you to use two or more explanations of forgetting – but there are two explicitly named on the specification (interference and retrieval failure) so that should be enough. Indeed, if you attempted to include others then there is a danger that the response would have breadth but lose depth. The explanations have to relate to the item but again the item would have to take into account the two you have to learn – as it does. Don't just describe relevant explanations (which will address the six AO1 marks on offer) but make sure you use them to explain what Lily has experienced – this addresses the four AO2 marks on offer for application. The remaining six marks are AO3 marks which are awarded for evaluation which includes criticising explanations, use of evidence and also considering how well a theory explains what is happening in the scenario.

This response does include more than two explanations – although this is not necessary. This does mean each explanation is covered quite briefly but there is enough detail to demonstrate the candidate's understanding and it is easy to award six AO1 marks for this. Each of the four explanations is applied to Lily and this is done with clarity in every case so all four AO2 marks should be awarded. Each explanation is evaluated whether in terms of its validity as an explanation or through use of evidence. There is also coherency within the discussion through comparison of different explanations which results in a neat conclusion. This makes it easy to award all six AO3 marks. The marks suggest a Level 4 response and this is further supported by a well-structured, well elaborated response with a high quality of written communication. The essay is worth 16/16.

Section C Attachment

12 (a) *The study is an example of a natural experiment because the independent variable is not manipulated by the experimenter himself. Whether someone has experienced separation from their carer is not under the control of the experiment and happens regardless.*

(b) *One extraneous variable that may occur in this study is the occupation of the participants. If these are not matched in some way, it may be that one group has significantly more people who have stressful jobs and this could be impacting on their mental health.*

(c) *One limitation of a using a volunteer sample is that it is often unrepresentative as only certain types of people tend to come forward for psychological studies and this partly depends on what the study is about. In the case of this study, people with severe mental health problems may be missing from the sample because it will not be a priority for them to take part in an investigation. Or people that have experienced separation from a carer but have not coped well with it may not come forward to be questioned about it. With both of these examples, the extent of the effect of separation may not be truly represented in the findings.*

13 (a) *Lorenz (1935) used a very simple procedure to investigate the process of imprinting. He took a clutch of gosling eggs, dividing them into two groups. One lot of eggs were left with their natural mother while the other lot of eggs were placed in an incubator. When the incubator eggs hatched the first moving thing they saw was Lorenz. He marked the two groups to distinguish them and placed them together. Both Lorenz and their natural mother were present.*

Lorenz found that the goslings quickly separated into two groups, one following their natural mother and the other group following him instead. Lorenz's brood seemed not to recognise their natural mother. Lorenz therefore concluded that a new born animal imprints on the first moving object it sees. Lorenz also noted that this process is limited to a very definite period of the young animal's life – a critical period. Lorenz also found the effects of imprinting are irreversible and long lasting. Lorenz described how one of the geese who imprinted on him used to sleep on his bed every night!

(b) *One limitation of animal studies is when we try to generalise to humans. Critics say that other animals are too different from humans for research to be useful. One good example of this is that human beings make conscious decisions in a way that other animals do not. For example, a human being may at least partially decide to whom it wants to attach.*

Examiner's comments

12 (a) This is a question about research methods where you first have to know what a natural experiment is and then you have to apply this knowledge to the item for a further mark. Although this can be expressed in one sentence it is often better to separate the two marks out by making two separate statements.

This answer earns both marks. It essentially starts with a definition of a natural experiment and then goes on to explain how this study matches this definition.

12 (b) This is another research methods based question. When asked for an extraneous variable, you need to start by looking at the DV – is this case, whether someone has poor mental health or not. You then ask yourself what could affect this but be careful not to identify the IV itself. Any feasible factor should get the first mark. The second mark would come from explaining the relationship between your chosen EV and the findings of the study.

This answer earns a mark for a feasible extraneous variable. It also earns a second mark for explaining how it relates to mental health.

12 (c) This is a final research methods question. You should know about the strengths and limitations of different sampling techniques from lessons, but here you need to go one step further and also apply it to the study in the item.

This answer earns its first mark for a general limitation of volunteer samples. The second mark comes from a very detailed consideration of how this would manifest itself in this particular study.

13 (a) This question essentially asks you to describe a study but note how there is a reference to procedure and findings. You would normally expect to cover both of these in a good answer anyway but this would suggest that there needs to be some kind of balance between the two. This may affect your choice of study – it needs to be one where there is enough to write about in terms of what was done and then what was found out. Your obvious choices are the work of Lorenz and Harlow (who are both named on the specification).

This answer has just enough detail to earn all six marks. The first paragraph details the procedure and there is just enough information here – including the aim, the sample and the set up. The second paragraph, again, has just enough detail – including an immediate finding, a longer term finding and a general conclusion (which counts under findings). The answer is also appropriately balanced.

13 (b) This question could be answered in generic terms as it relatively easy to expand on a point about the generalisability of animal studies, or problems of inference, or ethical issues. However, there is a reference to investigating attachment in the question so it is important to bring this into the answer too.

This response explains the problem of generalisability well and the reference to conscious decision making helps with the elaboration. However, crucially, there is a link to attachment at the end which helps to secure both of the marks for this answer.

14 *Children with insecure-avoidant attachments tend to avoid social interaction and intimacy with others, while children with insecure-resistant attachments tend to resist this. This means that insecure-resistant children tend to be very distressed when separated from caregivers whereas insecure-avoidant children show little response. When reunited with caregivers, insecure-avoidant children again hardly react while insecure-resistant children display conflicting desires for and against contact. If separated and then in contact with strangers, insecure-avoidant children continue to have a limited emotional response whereas insecure-resistant children resist strangers and get very distressed in their presence.*

15 *The 'Strange Situation' is reliable in the sense that the situation is very structured so that infants go through the same process of separation, being reunited, etc. so that comparisons can be made between attachment types to identify similarities and differences in responses. However, the responses are open to interpretation as infants are obviously not able to communicate so it is a case of observing behaviour. Also, infants show only a little range of behaviours – so at what point do we decide whether an infant is very distressed as opposed to mildly distressed? There is definitely the potential for observer bias where researchers see what they expect to see depending on the type of attachment they assume a child has.*

16 *Bowlby proposes that infants attach to just one primary caregiver – which is what monotropy refers to. Critics argue that this is an outdated view which partially reflects the time in which Bowlby was writing. More recent evidence suggests that multiple attachments are common and that infants have the capacity to integrate these into one single internal working model. The idea of multiple attachments makes sense, particularly if we accept that attachments are more learned than instinctive.*

A second criticism relates to Bowlby's idea that there is a critical period for attachments to happen in. Research suggests that attachments can happen outside of the critical period even though Bowlby said they could not. However, it does seem attachments are more difficult to form later on which suggests there is something important about those first few months. Current thinking is that there is a sensitive period for attachments, i.e. a better time to form them rather than a crucial time.

Examiner's comments

14 It is tempting to answer this question by outlining one type of attachment and then the other – however, this would only show the implicit differences. This question goes beyond basic knowledge and understanding and encourages some level of comparison. Therefore, a good answer would refer to both types of attachment alongside each other.

This answer shows knowledge of both attachment types as well as understanding by comparing the attachment types on a number of dimensions. Indeed three dimensions are covered – children's reactions to separation from caregiver, their reaction to being reunited and their reaction to strangers. This is an effective way of ensuring three marks can be awarded – which is what happens here. However, they key point is that the differences are made explicit for the examiner.

15 This question needs careful interpretation. It is not quite asking for an evaluation of Ainsworth's research but more of her technique for studying attachment types. For example, this means that comments about her middle class sample of children would not be relevant but that comments around actual procedures would be. It might be appropriate to draw on your knowledge and understanding of research methods to help you to answer this question.

This response is worth all three marks. Although not essential, it is good that is offers positive as well as negative evaluation points. The points are clearly explained and, importantly, in the context of studying attachment types which takes the answer beyond a generic commentary on observations and experimentation.

16 Although this question carries AO3 marks, with a focus on criticisms, it is acceptable to identify features of Bowlby's theory as part of your answer – otherwise how does the examiner know what you are criticising? However, do not spend a lot of time describing Bowlby's ideas – make it clear what is wrong with them. Of course, each criticism needs some level of explanation as we assume there are two marks on offer for each one. Make it clear what your two criticisms are – perhaps by using separate paragraphs, or heading them up as 'first criticism' and 'second criticism'.

This response offers two clear and distinct criticisms focusing on different aspects of Bowlby's monotropic theory. It is obvious what is being criticised and how through effective expansion. All four marks would be awarded here.

Section D Psychopathology

17

Symptom of depression	Characteristic
Sleep disruption	Behavioural
Pessimistic view of the world	*Cognitive*
Feeling worthless	*Emotional*
Loss of appetite	*Behavioural*

18 *One biological explanation of OCD focuses on genetics. The theory is that individuals inherit specific genes from their parents that are related to the onset of OCD. One such gene is the COMT gene – a gene which regulates the production of dopamine. Dopamine is a neurochemical that has been linked to OCD in other research. Another gene associated with OCD is the SERT gene. This gene affects the transport of serotonin – another neurochemical associated with OCD. In general, this explanation suggests that OCD is a relatively fixed behaviour as it is innate.*

19 *One strength of using drugs on OCD is that they are cost effective compared to alternative treatments for OCD such as CBT.*

One limitation of using drugs is that they do not provide a lasting cure for OCD – for example, patients relapse within a few weeks if they stop taking SSRI's or similar.

Examiner's comments

17 Although you may not have specifically covered all of the symptoms listed as part of your own studies, you should know the difference between behavioural, emotional and cognitive characteristics so that you are able to apply your knowledge in questions like this.

Three correct responses – 'view' implies cognition, 'feeling' implies emotion, and eating is a behaviour – so three marks.

18 This question, like others, offers a choice. Note that the question only requires a brief description, so it is worth choosing an explanation that can be summarised quite succinctly. Using the specification, the choice is between genetic and neural explanations (although they are both linked by the biological approach anyway). Remember that for higher marks, you will need to relate it to OCD rather than giving a very general description which could apply to other psychological disorders.

This response focuses on the genetic explanation but is also able to bring in some of the ideas from the neural explanation by referencing neurochemicals. Indeed, it is the reference to neurochemicals that makes the answer about OCD. There is enough detail here for three marks – a general statement about the heritability of disorders plus two details about specific genes implicated in OCD.

19 This question is not very demanding in the sense it only requires a brief point for each as only one mark is on offer for the strength and for the limitation. Make sure it is clear which is which – don't assume it is obvious. You also need to make it specific to OCD even though the pros and cons of drugs are often the same whatever the disorder.

One mark for the strength. Cost effectiveness is a valid consideration and it is made relevant to OCD by comparing drugs with a feasible alternative used to treat the disorder. One mark for the limitation as ideally treatments should effect a cure. Again, it is made relevant to OCD by referring to drugs used for the disorder.

20 *A behavioural approach to phobias essentially argues that the disorder is acquired through a learning experience. This clearly fits with Keshina's case as she can relate her phobia of cats back to a 'learning experience' involving a neighbour's cat. Of course, the problem with a theory that only looks at learning is that this ignores the role of biology in the development of phobias. There is an argument that we have a natural preparedness to fear certain objects or situations more than others because they were a danger to our ancestors. It may be we have evolved a fear of animals like cats as, in the past, animals like them (especially large, wild cats) threatened our survival. It may be the incident was not as bad as she remembered, but was enough to trigger a fear which was essentially innate.*

If it was this incident that caused the phobia, then the behavioural approach would begin by explaining it in terms of classical conditioning. Classical conditioning occurs when a neutral stimulus (NS) is paired with an unconditioned stimulus (UCS) where the latter produces an unconditioned (natural) response (UCR). Because the response occurs at the same time as the NS being present, this two may become associated so that the NS is no longer neutral and now produces a conditioned response (CR) so becomes a conditioned stimulus (CS). The UCR and CR are the same kind of response but now the CS triggers it alone. This process can be applied to the development of phobias, where the UCR and CR are always a fear response, and the CS is the object or situation which is feared. Looking at Keshina, it was natural for her to be scared when she was caused pain from the scratches on her leg – the UCS was pain and the UCR was fear. However, the presence of the cat (the NS) means the fear is associated with the cat – the cat becomes the CS with fear being the CR. Indeed, due to a process known as stimulus generalisation, the fear generalises to all cats, producing a phobia.

One of the issues with classical conditioning is that it assumes people are very passive in their learning experiences. We are essentially conditioned with no cognitive intervention. Critics argue that the bad experience is only part of developing a phobia and that the behavioural approach ignores the thinking behind phobias. This would explain why other people may have had similar experiences to Keshina yet do not have a phobia. The argument is that Keshina has thought irrationally about her bad experience with the neighbour's cat. The bad experience was the starting point but the reason Keshina has a phobia could be because she believes this kind of event will happen again and again when, in reality, it is unlikely to.

Assuming phobias are a result of a bad experience, classical conditioning only explains the acquisition of phobias. The behavioural approach uses operant conditioning to explain why phobias are maintained. Operant conditioning is learning by consequences – if outcomes are positive, a behaviour will increase, if outcomes are negative then a behaviour will diminish. In the case of phobias, facing your fears is punishing because it causes so much anxiety – so this rarely happens. However, avoiding a feared situation avoids this anxiety which is reinforcing – so this avoidance behaviour continues. For example, every time Keshina crosses the road to avoid a cat she will feel relieved (this is rewarding) and she escapes a fearful situation (negative reinforcement). Of course, if conditioning is a valid explanation for the maintenance of phobias then it follows that phobias can be counter-conditioned. Behavioural therapies have some success in treating phobias but this is not always the case. Where phobias have are resistant to counter-conditioning, it may mean they are innate. If Keshina's cat phobia is really a result of conditioning, then it should be open to treatment – this would be an effective way of investigating its origins.

A general problem for behavioural explanations is that they are seen as deterministic and do not acknowledge free will. It may be Keshina has more control over her phobia than she thinks. Behavioural explanations also tend to be reductionist so it might be a number of factors that combine to cause a phobia. For example, Keshina may have a genetic predisposition which interacts with environmental experiences including witnessing other people being afraid of cats. Finally, a behavioural explanation may be too nomothetic, not recognising that a unique set of factors may contribute to each individual's phobias, including Keshina's.

Examiner's comments

20 This essay assesses all three skills from Psychology. There would be up to six AO1 marks for demonstrating knowledge and understanding of the behavioural explanation of phobias, up to four AO2 marks for applying it to the case of Keshina, and six AO3 marks for analysis of the explanation and its application. As with any extended response, it is worth planning. A good essay would integrate the three skills throughout the response rather than dealing with one at a time.

This response demonstrates sound understanding of the behavioural approach with a strong, technical description of the two types of conditioning proposed by the theory. Each of these is applied to Keshina in clear and coherent way which demonstrates a deeper understanding – for example, the UCS, UCR, NS, etc. are correctly identified from the information in the item. It is impressive how the essay incorporates all three skills in each paragraph – outlining an aspect of the approach, relating it to Keshina, and then evaluating this aspect of the approach (often still with Keshina in mind which is particularly sophisticated). The essay ends well, with a paragraph which draws in some wider debates but still considers the specific demands of this essay. Add to this the fact that the essay is well written and well-constructed, and the candidate definitely deserves 16/16.

Section A Approaches in psychology

1 (a) *C*

(b) *D*

(c) *One defence mechanism is displacement. This is used to reduce anxiety by unconsciously redirecting thoughts and feelings (usually hostile ones) away from the person that causes them and onto an innocent other.*

2 (a) *Identification occurs where an individual adopts the attitudes or behaviour because they want to be associated with a particular person. In this case, Olivia identifies with Princess Sapphire as she aspires to be like the cartoon character.*

(b) *Olivia demonstrates vicarious reinforcement in the sense she expects to get rewarded in the same way as the princess – by having her dreams come true – and this, therefore, is her motivation for wanting to be kind to others; she has observed someone else being reinforced for it.*

3 *One of the most basic assumptions of humanistic psychology is that we all have free will. In other words, people have full conscious control over the direction of their lives and are not open to coercion. Even when people believe they have been made to do something, the reality is they have chosen to allow others to influence them. This contrasts with most other approaches in psychology that tend to support some degree of determinism. This is the idea that thoughts and behaviour are subject to either external or internal forces. For example, the biological approach contends that many of our behaviours are pre-determined by our genetic make-up or that others are under the control of neurochemicals rather than being open to conscious control. This is supported by evidence that shows patients overcoming their depression through the use of drugs rather than anything more cognitive. However, counselling (which is based on humanistic principles) has had some success in tackling depression by getting people to understand themselves better and changing their perceptions of their situation. This is only possible due to the existence of free will. The existence of free will is notoriously difficult to evidence.*

Examiner's comments

1 (a) A reasonably straightforward question with C being the right answer. Just remember that the exam board may not define a concept exactly how you would – as in 'represents our moral code' – this is why it is important you have enough understanding to be able to interpret the meaning of statements. Sometimes, it is less about Psychology and more about literacy.

1 (b) Again – a straightforward question with D being the right answer. Obviously, it is not enough to just be able to name stages – you need some knowledge of what happens in each stage and how they differ.

1 (c) The first mark is earned for simply naming a defence mechanism – 'displacement' in this case. The second mark requires an outline so it is important to choose one that you understand. It is tempting to re-use the name of the defence mechanism (displacement, repression, denial, etc.) in the outline but this response does not do that and instead redefines it through a clear and detailed description. Two marks would be awarded.

2 (a) This response is straightforward to mark. It starts with a definition of identification which earns an AO1 mark for knowledge and understanding. The concept is then applied to the item to earn an AO2 mark. It says just enough to make the link between identification and Olivia's beliefs. Be careful not to write more than is needed otherwise an examiner may decide you are not being selective enough and therefore don't really know what you are looking for in an item.

2 (b) This is a different approach to this question. Rather than the AO1 and AO2 being addressed distinctly from each other, the answer demonstrates understanding of the concept while essentially applying it at the same time. Although a little trickier to mark, the two skills are evident and there is enough detail here to earn two marks.

3 This essay is a well-structured and well written response. Rather than describing a series of assumptions and then moving into the discussion, the answer uses each paragraph (apart from the last) to introduce and outline a different assumption of humanistic psychology and this is where the AO1 marks are earned. The candidate also 'plays safe' by using assumptions listed in the specification which are therefore bound to get credit. For each assumption, there is a clear discussion around issues such as strengths, criticisms, evidence and, most importantly, how the approach compares with the biological approach. This is an explicit requirement of the essay and, if not addressed, the mark awarded would have to be capped. This is also a reminder that you can be asked to compare any pairing of approaches so it is worth being prepared by knowing about ways in which approaches are similar and different. The discussion that makes up the bulk of each paragraph easily accesses the remaining ten AO3 marks for the breadth and depth

For example, if a person is challenged to demonstrate their free will by walking out of a meeting, the argument is that they have only done this because they have been challenged and therefore the response has be determined by something else. Humanist psychologists would argue that it is not important to 'prove' free will exists as this is just an effort to subject the concept to scientific investigation. They would argue that free will and human behaviour should not be studied in this way – we are too complex and individual for this. However, the biological approach would argue that it is appropriate to study human behaviour scientifically – hence their use of experimentation.

Another assumption of humanistic psychology is that human beings are driven to self-actualise. Self- actualisation describes the situation where people experience extreme inspiration and ecstasy which enables them to forget their doubts and fears. Some critics suggests that this is an over-generalisation – especially for an approach that concerns itself with individual's uniqueness. Others favour this assumption on the basis that it results in a positive and optimistic way of viewing human beings but, of course, for some it is too unrealistic. Biological psychologists would argue that we are much more driven by instincts that enable us to survive and reproduce. Not only is this a more reductionist view of human behaviour but also one that can at least explain our more negative and destructive behaviours.

The concept of congruence is another humanistic assumption that relates to the idea of self-actualisation. Self-actualisation is more likely to happen when an individual's self-concept and their ideal self are closely aligned (congruent). If there is a large gap between the two this leads to feelings of low self-esteem as an individual's perception of their self is far from where they would like it to be. Although intuitively this makes sense, once again it is hard to find evidence for. Concepts such as the self-concept and ideal self, by their very nature, are highly subjective. Of course, humanists would argue that understanding private thoughts and feelings is what allows us to understand each individual. The biological approach would question the validity of such an approach – preferring much more objective methods of study. For example, it believes it is possible to observe the brain and identify structures and activity that explain human responses. Studying the brain does not rely on self-report in the same way, and because a number of researchers can observe the same brain and agree on what they are seeing this leads to highly reliable findings. It is this degree of reliability that establishes validity rather than simply arguing, as humanist psychologists do, that the truth lies within the person.

One final humanistic assumption to consider is the idea that people can only truly self-actualise when they are offered unconditional positive regard. Humanistic psychologists are concerned that, too often, individuals are subject to conditions of worth where they only feel valued by others when they say, do or believe certain things. This is why counsellors attempt to be genuine, non-judgemental and empathetic in their relationships with clients. Indeed, these features seem central to counselling successes suggesting the assumption has some validity. Counselling is also about focusing on the individual and this is another area where humanistic psychology and the biological approach differ. The biological approach believes that humans are more similar than different (especially when we look at their physiological make up) and therefore it is appropriate to aim to discover general laws and patterns that allow us to understand and deal with people in the same way. For example, prescribing people with anxiety problems the same drugs is both more efficient and more cost effective than seeking to treat each person as a separate case. For humanistic psychologists, this very nomothetic approach is not showing individuals the respect they deserve.

To conclude, humanistic psychology lacks the scientific rigour of other approaches such as the biological approach. However, this is not an issue for humanistic psychology itself as it rejects the scientific study of human beings, preferring a more holistic, idiographic approach to understanding our thoughts and behaviour.

Examiner's comments

of its commentary. As the concluding paragraph states the discussion is primarily around how scientific humanistic psychology is (or is not!). However, the candidate cleverly breaks this down into a number of smaller issues which are considered separately in each of the main paragraphs. This is an answer which earns full marks.

Section B Biopsychology

4 *'Excitation' happens when a neurotransmitter binds to receptors and increases the likelihood that an excitatory signal is sent to the postsynaptic cell. 'Inhibition' happens when a different type of neurochemical binds to receptors – these are neurochemicals normally responsible for calming the body. This means that cells are more likely to fire as a result of excitation compared to inhibition.*

5 *The fight-or-flight response is an instinctive reaction to a situation which is perceived as threatening. In this case, Huw's friends jumping out on him is the potential threat. The response has evolved to ensure an individual's survival – either leading to them attacking the source of the threat (fight) or escaping the danger (flight). Either way, the sympathetic nervous system (SNS) needs to be triggered to prepare the body for action. This starts with a part of the brain called the amygdala which sends a distress signal to another part – the hypothalamus – which controls the activity of the SNS. Huw's heavy breathing is a sign that he was taking in more oxygen to prepare for activity. It seems as though his response was to fight (rather than flee) as he was about to hit his friends.*

6 .

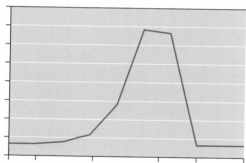

(a) *01:00*

(b) *12:00–14:00 = 2 hours*
07:00–12:00 = 5 hours
2 + 5 = 7 hours

(c) *False.*

7 *Functional magnetic resonance imaging (fMRI), like other scanning techniques, has the advantage that it is non-invasive as it does not involve the insertion of instruments into the body. In addition, it does not expose the brain to potentially harmful radiation unlike some other scanning techniques. Compared to self-report, fMRI offers a more objective and reliable measurement of psychological processes. It does not rely on people's insight or ability to articulate their experiences. However, since fMRI measures changes in blood flow in the brain, it's not a direct measure of neural activity in particular brain areas. This means it is not a truly quantitative measure of mental activity. Critics also argue that fMRI overlooks the networked nature of brain activity, as it focuses only on localised activity in the brain. Critics claim that it is communication among the different regions that is most critical to mental function and that fMRI is not useful in this sense.*

Examiner's comments

4 This response effectively targets the three marks. It shows understanding of excitation earning the first mark, and then understanding of inhibition earning the second mark. These are also described in the context of synaptic transmission (e.g. through references to neurotransmitters and receptors). It's important to note that the question wants some explanation of the difference between the two so there needs to be an explicit comparison between the two. This comes in the final sentence which is where the third mark is earned.

5 This response shows knowledge of the fight-or-flight response and a good understanding of the biology behind it. This earns the two AO1 marks on offer. The answer also integrates information from the source in order to illustrate the concepts and process, and this is done in enough detail to earn the two AO2 marks on offer for application.

6 **(a)** Since the question asks for an estimate, there will be some flexibility on the answer. On this basis, you should not be too anxious about being that precise. Here, the x-axis only gives time of day by the hour so it makes sense to give an estimate to the nearest hour. This is accurate enough for the one mark on offer.

6 **(b)** One mark for the correct answer: 7 hours. The working is not particularly difficult but still needs to be shown. Here, it also acts as evidence that the candidate is able to read and interpret the graph. Both marks would be awarded.

6 **(c)** This question is testing understanding of standard form and also that you understand the use of the symbol '>' (greater than). The main thing to understand here is that the negative sign before the 12 makes a pictogram very small i.e. 0.000000000001 grams (which is clearly much smaller than 1g).

7 A higher tariff question like this is marked in terms of levels. This is a high level, full mark response due to its substance and quality. There is a good balance of strengths and weaknesses which is preferable when the command is to 'evaluate'. It's also good that points are expanded on. Although not all of them relate specifically to use of fMRI, given the challenge of the question, they are appropriate as they are still about scanning as a method. It also helps that, throughout the answer, the candidate is clear about what other methods fMRI is being compared with.

8 *Sperry (1968) carried out his split brain research using participants who had already undergone hemisphere deconnection to reduce severe epilepsy. Using a piece of apparatus called a tachistoscope, Sperry tested the participants on a number of visual and tactile tasks.*

Participants viewed images on a screen with one eye covered – however, regardless of which eye is used, information on the left of the screen (the left visual field) is processed to the right hemisphere of the brain and vice-versa for the right visual field. With these participants, Sperry found that images shown in one visual field could only be recognised again if shown to the same visual field rather than the other. In other words, there was no transfer of memories across the hemispheres. Images presented to the right visual field could be described in speech and writing but if the same images were presented to the left visual field, the participants claimed they either did not see anything or that there was just a flash of light on that side of the screen. However the participant could point to a matching picture presented along with other pictures. If different figures were presented simultaneously to different visual fields – the participant could only draw the figure in the left visual field but would report seeing the figure in the right visual field.

There were similar findings with tactile tasks where unseen objects were put into the hands of participants just beyond the screen. Any objects placed in the right hand (which sends information to the left hemisphere) could be described in speech or writing (with the right hand). However, if the same objects were placed in the left hand (sending information to the right hemisphere) then participants tended to guess what they were (and get it wrong) or sometimes even seemed oblivious to the fact they were holding anything. Objects felt by one hand were only recognised again by that same hand. In other words, objects first touched by the right hand couldn't be retrieved by the left hand. Research like this shows that although the two hemispheres mirror each other, they also have their own functions. However, in a 'normal' brain these two hemispheres are able to communicate with each other to provide unity in conscious awareness – something people with split brains do not necessarily have.

A strength of this piece of research is that it used both quantitative and qualitative data, with the former offering some level of reliability in terms of establishing patterns in the split brain participants' responses. However, the latter data offered more validity in terms of understanding the experiences of the patients.

One major weakness was the size of the sample – there were only 11 split brain patients available to be tested. This made it hard for Sperry to make any reliable generalisations about the experiences of split brain patients. Indeed, to use this size of sample to go on to make assumptions about how the 'normal' brain functions may not be valid at all.

Finally, because of the experimental set-up of the study, there were some concerns about the ecological validity of any conclusions. For example, in a real life situation, it is unlikely that an individual with disconnected hemispheres would be using one eye to view something. Indeed, using both eyes would potentially be a way to compensate for the damage to the brain. However, without testing in this way, it becomes difficult for researchers like Sperry to isolate the functions of different parts of the brain.

Examiner's comments

8 This question is biased towards description with the clue being the use of 'briefly' before the command 'evaluate'. In this sense, the response as the right distribution of skills with a detailed description of Sperry's research study (AO1) with some evaluation points (AO3) added at the end. Having said this, there is still a good range and balance of evaluation points and they are well explained too. The description itself is accurate and clear. This response needs to be assessed holistically and in terms of bands. With its very good quality of expression (including appropriate use of psychological terminology) and coherent structure, alongside highly relevant content, it easily qualifies for the top band and full marks.

Section C Research methods

9 *There will be a significant difference in the number of participants who say they will donate money to a charity depending on whether they have been exposed to an emotion-based campaign or an information-based campaign.*

10 *The researcher may have taken the 50 names of her participants and placed them into a hat. Then she could have drawn out 25 names one after the other and these would be the participants she uses for her first condition. The names that remain in the hat make up the other condition.*

11 *One strength of using an independent groups design is that it reduces order effects. In this particular experiment, if a participant was exposed to both campaigns, it would not work. The second campaign could not have an effect alone – it may add to what has already been seen. For example, it might be the combination of emotion and information that convinces someone to donate money.*

One limitation of the design is that any differences between conditions could be due to participant variables. For example, because participants are randomly allocated, by chance people who are more generous or more easily persuaded may end up being in one condition rather than another and this is why they say 'yes' to donating money rather than because of what they have been exposed to – they may have donated money regardless of the campaign.

12 *One other extraneous variable is the length of time participants are exposed to the campaign. For example, if the emotional video was shorter because it had less information then it may not be enough time to persuade participants to donate money.*

Examiner's comments

9 This hypothesis invites you to write either a directional or non-directional hypothesis – this response opts for the latter. The examiner will be looking for a clear statement which predicts a difference (as opposed to a correlation). On this basis it is a prediction of difference, for full marks, both conditions of the IV should be stated and the DV should be fully operationalised. This statement does include both conditions of the IV as both campaigns are named, and the DV (although simple) is still fully operationalised (we know what data is being collected and how). Add to this the fact that it is a statement which is easy to make sense of, and the answer earns all three marks.

10 This is a maths based question so it is important to have some numbers and mathematical processes in the answer – we have that here. It is also important that it is specific to this study so the reference to the number of participants and the fact equal numbers are needed in each condition is important here. There are other ways of answering this question – for example, names could be drawn out and allocated to alternating conditions, or participants could draw a condition from a hat – but the key thing is that the outcome should be the same. In this answer, it would be easy for the candidate to forget to refer to the remaining names and the second condition but of course they do not. In reality, a psychologist is probably likely to use a piece of software to allocate participants – but actually using the example of 'names in a hat' probably makes it easier to illustrate the maths behind it. This answer has all the necessary elements – the technique being used, the starting point, and how the conditions end up with 25 participants each – so all three marks are earned.

11 This is a well-structured response which clearly targets the marks on offer. Both the strength (reduced order effects) and limitation (participant variables) are clearly identified in generic terms. Then the response puts each in the context of the actual experiment. The excellent explanation in each case shows that the candidate understands the implications of using this design in this particular study.

12 When looking for an extraneous variable you need to ask yourself what might affect the DV besides the IV itself – in this case, what might affect whether someone donates to charity or not besides the nature of the campaign? The answer starts with a relevant variable (worth one mark) and then does a good job of explaining its potential effect (worth a second mark). Two marks in total.

13 (a) A bar graph to show the number of people who said they would or would not donate money to a charity

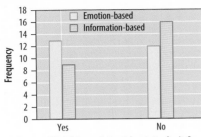

Would the participant donate to charity?

(b) *(13 + 9) = 22 = number that would donate*

22/50 = 0.44

0.44 x 100 = 44%

44% of participants said they would donate to charity.

14 *The level of data is nominal. This is because each participant is placed in a category (whether they would or would not donate to charity) rather than being scored in some way.*

15 *For Cell C $(O - E)^2 / E = (12 - 14)^2 / 14$*

$= -2^2 \div 14 = 4 \div 14 = 0.28571428571$

$= 0.29$ (to 2 d.p.)

Examiner's comments

13 (a) The first thing to get right here is to spot that a bar graph that is the appropriate graph to use as the data is in categories. Failure to spot this means no marks. This clearly is a bar graph, and therefore there is one mark available for graph itself, one for labelling and one for a title. This response earns full marks – one for accuracy (the bars go to the right height, one for correct labelling of the two axes and the bars (see key) and one for a clear title which includes the two key variables.

13 (b) This is clearly a question designed to assess maths skills and so calculations count as well as the right answer. One mark for getting the correct answer (44%) and then two further marks would be awarded for the details of how that answer is reached.

14 There is only one possible answer for the level of data – and the candidate gets it right for one mark. The justification does more than define the level of data and links it to study itself – as is required to earn the second mark.

15 This is another question testing mathematical ability. There are four marks available here because there are a number of things to get right to arrive at the correct answer. This also means that even if the final answer is wrong, marks can be awarded for getting other stages of the calculation right. Here, the candidate earns all four marks. The formula is applied to the correct set of numbers, then the first part of the calculation is correct (e.g. they know how to square a negative number), then the second part is correct in terms of the division that gives the long decimal number. The last mark is for the final answer expressed to two decimal places (the candidate knows what this means and how to round up in this case).

Mock exam: Paper 2 Suggested answers

16 *This is likely to lead a Type I error. This is because the researcher is prepared to accept a 10% chance of her results occurring by fluke which means she may end up retaining her hypothesis when there is no real difference between the two conditions.*

17 (a) *Method*
  (b) *Results*

18 (a) *'Peer review' happens when a report on the psychological investigation is reviewed by a group of psychologists (who were not involved in the investigation) before it is published.*
  (b) *Peer review is a way of checking the reliability of a study – both in terms of its procedures and the conclusions it draws. The idea is that if independent psychologists agree with the content of a report this suggests it is more objective rather than subjective. They may also suggest improvements to the report. For this study, a successful peer review would mean that there is strong evidence for any conclusions drawn about the effects of different campaigns on charitable donations.*

19 *Replicability refers to the extent to which a piece of research can be repeated. In this study, the research is highly controlled which makes it easier to do it again by closely following the procedure. Replication does not necessarily involve doing exactly the same investigation again – this is almost impossible in psychology – but a similar piece of research should ideally produce a similar set of findings. If it does not, we begin to question the validity of both pieces of research. Of course, if we exactly replicated a piece of research, we would be looking for high rates of reliability. This is a very scientific way of establishing validity – the more something happens, the more likely it is to be true. To conclude, the importance of replicability is that it allows research to be tested again to ensure any conclusions can be validated.*

Examiner's comments

16 This question is not asking about any kind of methodological error and the clue is the reference to the significance level ($p \leq 0.1$) in the opening sentence. This means the choice is between a Type I or Type II error. The candidate chooses the correct one to earn the first mark and then, for a second mark, goes on to give a clear and accurate explanation as to why. Note how the explanation does not have to relate that specifically to the study in this case.

17 (a) There is only one possible answer here and this is the right one. This shows that it is important to know the detail of what is written about in different sections of a report on psychological investigations.

17 (b) This is the obvious answer and earns one mark. Although tables of data can also be presented in something called the Appendices, this is not on the specification and so the examiner would not expect you to know this necessarily.

18 (a) The response addresses who peers are in this case (other psychologists) and what is being reviewed – good enough for the mark.

18 (b) This response earns full marks. The key purpose of peer review included (establishing reliability) as well as the value of this. As the question uses the phrase 'in this study', there also needs to be some reference back to the experiment which happens at the end of the answer.

19 With this question, there is not a requirement to relate to psychology particularly … although it might be strange to start writing about physics or chemistry. There are marks reserved for knowing what 'replicability' is as this is not given in the question, however the focus should primarily be on its importance in scientific investigations. This is a good response which makes effective use of key psychological concepts such as reliability and validity. The candidate demonstrates sound understanding of complex ideas and links between them. This leads to a coherent answer which ends by clearly addressing the question that has been asked. Full marks would be awarded.

20 *I would use a stratified sample for my experiment by dividing my population in terms of sex (male or female), age (four age categories) and income (high, medium or low) as I think these three factors could impact on whether people donate to a charity or not. For example, I would calculate the percentage of women who are 65+ and on a high income in the population and make sure this percentage is the same in my sample. This would be done by randomly selecting people from that sub-group until I had the right number. I would also make sure that I randomly divided this sub-group so that there were the same number in each condition – either reading an article or watching a video.*

One thing that would need to be controlled is the charity that was being used for the experiment. It would have to be the same charity for both conditions otherwise one might be more appealing or relevant to people than another. So, I would choose in international aid charity and find written material on it and a video about it. I would also want to make sure that the same details were included in each of these – if one had more details about the work of the charity then it might lead to higher donations.

The inferential test I would use to analyse the data is the Mann-Whitney U test. This is because it tests for a difference – in this case, the difference in charitable donations depending on the medium used. The design is also unrelated as independent groups are being used in my experiment – participants either read the article or they watch the video. The level of data is at least ordinal – as each participant will essentially have a score – how much money they actually donate. Although money follows an interval scale (each pound is worth the same as the next), I would still categorise the donations as ordinal as, for example, £10 might be worth more to one participant than another.

One ethical issue is confidentiality as participants may not want others to know how little or how much they are willing to donate to a charity. Therefore, any donations will be made anonymously – I'd only need to know what condition they were in, not who they are. Participants may feel more pressured to donate because of the experimental set up which may take away some of the freedom of choice they feel they have in real-life. Therefore, I would allow a 'cooling off' period where participants could withdraw their donations if they wanted to.

Examiner's comments

20 This is a standard question in the exam, and one that assesses your understanding of research methods by getting you to apply it to a novel situation. It will tend to follow on from the study you have already answered questions on but you need to be careful not to 'borrow' too much from this and produce a response which shows some independent thought and planning. As you're being asked to design something, the mark scheme needs to be quite 'open' to reflect this. Not much will be stipulated. If you look at this question then you will see you have a choice of sampling techniques you can write about, a choice of ethics to consider, and a choice of controls you could refer to. There are even some options on the inferential design depending on the experimental design you select. However, some tests would not get credit as the investigation is already set up to be an experiment and there is some detail on how the DV will be measured (affecting the level of data).

This answer is a top band response which earns full marks. Firstly, and importantly, all four elements listed have been addressed. Even if three or fewer are done really well, addressing all four is a requirement for being awarded a top band mark. Suggestions are generally well detailed and practical, and show sound understanding of the sampling, controls, inferential testing and ethical considerations. A response is judged as being very good if there is sufficient information for most aspects of the study to be implemented with success – that is the case here. Overall, the answer is clear and coherent with specialist terminology used effectively.

Section A Issues and debates in psychology

1   *A*

2   **(a)** *Dr Mudima believes in biological reductionism. She believes that all behaviours – however complex – can be simplified down to the activity of biological factors such as genes and biochemistry. In this case, she is talking about reducing autistic behaviour down to the presence of a single gene – put simply, if it's present then autism occurs and if it's not, then autism does not develop.*

   (b) *Dr Young believes in environmental determinism. This is the belief that behaviour is not only determined and out of our control, but that it is determined by factors external to us which we simply respond to. In this case, Dr Young believes the responses add up to a behaviour which we call 'autism' and therefore the disorder is learned not innate.*

3   **(a)** Identical twins ✔

   (b) *The conclusion is saying that intelligence is not down to just genes or learning alone but that the two factors work together to decide IQ level. For example, a person's genes may determine the range of their intelligence but whether they end up at the top or bottom of the range depends on what they experience through the environment.*

Examiner's comments

1   You need to take care with questions like this one where the options are closely linked – especially A. B and C in this case. Knowing precise definitions is important. The answer is 'alpha bias' as 'beta bias' is the opposite i.e. sex differences are underplayed. 'Androcentrism' is a more general idea and also implies a male bias whereas alpha bias could favour either sex. 'Ethnocentrism' is related to culture rather than sex.

2   **(a)**   The candidate has interpreted the item accurately and identified the right type of reductionism and this is worth a mark in itself. The other two marks are for demonstrating an understanding of biological reductionism and also doing this in the context of the doctor's comments – making a clear link between both skills. All three marks would be awarded.

2   **(b)**   The candidate, again, identifies the right type of reductionism. Here the concept is accurately explained for a further mark and then related back to the doctor's comments for a final mark. All three marks would be awarded here too.

3   **(a)**   This question requires you to do some maths. 22/34 = 11/17. This means, with12/17, identical twins do have a higher proportion of twins whose IQ scores were closely matched.

3   **(b)**   It is good that this response takes the terms 'heredity' and 'environment' and attempts to redefine them as part of the answer. It does the same with the idea of 'interaction' where it explains how this process would work in relation to intelligence. The answer demonstrates understanding of all aspects of the conclusion and earns both marks as a consequence.

4 (a) *A normal distribution is when data follows a particular pattern – the most common scores are those in the middle of the data set with the frequency of scores decreasing as we go to the extremes. The distribution is also fairly symmetrical. So in this study, we can see that an average rating of 5 is where the distribution peaks and then it drops off either side as it heads to the high and low scores – in other words, very few people believe they have no free will or complete free will.*

   (b) *Free will is essentially a subjective construct which exists within the person. Therefore a questionnaire is wholly appropriate as it allows people to describe their thoughts and feelings. Free will is not something we can really observe so self-report offers a way to access it. One of the problems with self-report methods, such as questionnaires, is that they rely on people having insight and it may be people are not able to reflect on their own free will well enough to articulate what it is like. It may be people are too embarrassed to share this kind of information about themselves – however, it is easy to make questionnaires confidential which partly addresses this problem.*

5 *One strength of a nomothetic approach is that it allows generalisation to be made as it involves selecting large samples of participants and looking for patterns in their behaviour. For example, it may that people with depression suffer a similar set up symptoms which suggests they can be treated with the same drugs. However, critics are concerned that the nomothetic approach is in danger of making over-generalisations. For example, not all people with depression will necessarily respond to drugs in the same way.*

   Another strength is that a nomothetic approach is often seen as more objective and reliable. This is because it tends to deal with large amounts of data and therefore emerging patterns are likely to be fact rather than opinion. Patterns themselves suggest some level of reliability in findings. Other psychologists would argue that we should not be looking for patterns but recognising that each individual is unique so we need to understand each person in their own right and emphasise the subjective over the objective.

   A further strength is that the approach recognises that people (or certain types of people) have more in common than they have differences between them, and this is what allows general rules and principles to be generated. Without accepting these general laws and principles, it is hard to make any predictions about human behaviour. For example, imagine a large group of people were investigated to show that lack of sleep causes irritation then it should be possible to predict that other people will show similar behaviours if deprived of sleep. Of course, those psychologists that support humanism would argue that, due to free will, people are completely unpredictable so there is no point to establishing general laws. They argue that their view is supported by the fact that so many individuals are 'exceptions to the rule' and, worse still, you can't predict who these individuals are.

   To conclude, a nomothetic approach would largely be supported by psychologists who aim to be scientific because of the ability to collect more quantitative data leading to objectivity and generalisability. Those psychologists who argue that people are too complex and too unique to be subjected to scientific study would prefer to adopt an idiographic approach.

Examiner's comments

4 **(a)** This is a question which assesses maths rather than the content of Issues & Debates. This answer earns the first mark for a clear description of the pattern that a normal distribution follows. It also earns the second mark for explicitly relating to the data on people's beliefs about free will. Obviously, if you did not know what a normal distribution is, you are unlikely to earn the second mark without the first.

4 **(b)** Holistically, this is a good answer and deserves to be in the top band. It is well structured, coherent and shows a depth of understanding. The content is strong and addresses a number of strengths as well as a key weakness. Although not balanced between strengths and weaknesses, it nonetheless considers a range of points and, importantly, these are discussed in the context of the study. A full mark response.

5 This question focuses on your ability to evaluate the nomothetic approach in psychology rather than describe it. The question obviously refers to strengths but the command 'discuss' directs you to weigh up these strengths which essentially means you will be including limitations too. This answer is expertly structured, starting with a strength as suggested by the question but then ending the paragraph by considering how this strength could be perceived as a weakness as well. This pattern continues throughout the response meaning a number of strengths are discussed. It is a nicely balanced answer which finishes with an appropriate conclusion which places the discussion in the debate around whether psychology should adopt a scientific approach or not. The quality of communication matches the excellent content of the answer, meaning it scores full marks and sits in the top band.

Chapter 1 Research methods

Topic 1   Content analysis

Choose the right answer: B

Match them up: 1G 2I 3D 4A 5C 6E 7B 8F 9H

Applying your knowledge: For example, (a) females or males with long hair, dancing, using weapons. (b) Choose which Disney films, choose coding categories by watching one film, watch all the films and tally the occurrences of each coding category. (c) The decisions about behaviours may be subjective. The categories should be clearly operationalised and examples given, so that different observers can code behaviour in the same way. (d) People in different cultures may be portrayed with different hairstyles and this may not be gender stereotyping. Categories should be chosen which are not culturally relative, such as height, bicep diameter, length of eyelashes. (e) Examples would be collected, such as screenshots, to illustrate the categories, instead of counting.

A marking exercise: Robbie's answer would receive 1 out of 4 marks because he only mentions creating a checklist and also ticking these off, and his answer is unclear. Anne's answer receives 3 out of 4 marks because she explains where the coding categories came from and also adds some examples of the categories that might be used. Pierre's answer receives 0 marks because he has focused on what he might do with the results rather than *how* the content analysis would be done.

Topic 2   Case studies

Choose the right answer: C

Research issues: Researchers should keep checking that HM was happy to continue with tasks and stop if he wasn't. Ask next of kin for consent. Ask other experts to monitor research independently to make sure it wasn't likely to distress HM.

Applying your knowledge 1: (a) For example: Quantitative: Age, amount of time spent on Netflix, closed questions such as Likert scales exploring preferences. Qualitative: open questions in interview or questionnaire, quotes from focus group discussion, video diaries.
(b) She could find some secondary published data relating to the questions she was asking teenagers. She could then see if her data matched the findings of previous research. Alternatively, she could send out a questionnaire to teenagers in other youth clubs around the country, and compare results of her group with the others.

Applying your knowledge 2: Case study advantage: A detailed description of migrants' personal lives will catch people's attention and induce an empathetic response. Disadvantage: The family he chooses may not have interesting stories to tell, or may not speak very good English, or may not be telling the truth. Statistical data advantage: Gives an overview of the migrant situation in Calais, which is useful for policy makers. Disadvantage: May be biased or incomplete data as aid organisations and police have different political interests in the situation.

Topic 3   Reliability

Match them up: 1C 2A 3B 4F 5D 6E 7G

Research issues: (a) The scores for 4 out of 5 behaviours are different for the two observers. The scorevs for observer 1 are higher than observer 2 for most of the behaviours. There are large differences particularly for behaviours D and E. (b) They could calculate a correlation coefficient, and could test the significance of the correlation. (c) The behavioural categories may not be clearly operationalised. Observer 1 may be more biased against particular politicians and notice aggressive behaviours

more than observer 2. (d) They could make sure the behavioural categories are clear and independent, without any overlap, and with examplars. They could train the observers to make sure they are consistently interpreting behaviours.

Applying your knowledge: (a) For example: 'How many hours a day do you spend doing your homework?' (b) 'How do household responsibilities affect your attendance at school?' (c) By test-retest method. She could ask a few of the girls the same questions a second time, a week later, to see if their answers are consistent. (d) If the reliability is low, the girls may not have really understood the questions or may not have felt able to be honest, so the results will also lack validity. (e) She could make sure the questions are in simple, clear English so they are not ambiguous. She could collect data by interviewing the girls rather than just giving them a questionnaire to complete, so that she can explain the questions or explore further to make sure the girls have understood.

Topic 4   Validity

Choose the right answer: D

A marking exercise: Lucy – 3 marks. Ian – 1 mark. Too much focus on assessing validity rather than improving.

Applying your knowledge: Hypothesis: Children will perform better in the game when the music is playing than when it is not. Validity issues: If the children are aware they are being studied, it might make them try much harder than normal (demand characteristics). Whether the music is 'annoying' is subjective – some children may love it. This is an extraneous variable as the music may affect children differently depending on their reaction to it.

Topic 5   Features of science

Choose the right answer: A

Applying your knowledge 1: No, she should not take it seriously. For example: Scientific theory should be based on empirical research – the quiz is based on stereotypes rather than evidence. Scientific evidence should be objective – the quiz comes up with percentages which sound scientific but are probably based on subjective views of 'typical' male and female responses. Scientific theory should lead to testable hypotheses – the quiz gives a percentage but what does this mean? Which 72% of Rachel's brain is male? This appears untestable, and therefore unfalsifiable, and so lacks scientific validity.

Applying your knowledge 2: For example: Psychology is based on empirical research – A level psychology involves learning evidence for and against each theory. Empirical data should be objective – A level psychology focuses on evaluating how objective the research is, or whether it is biased. Psychological theories are built on empirical evidence and tested scientifically by coming up with testable hypotheses – A level psychology includes practical research where you will come up with hypotheses based on existing theory, and test them using experiments.

Topic 6   Probability

Match them up: 1F 2D 3B 4E 5C 6A

A marking exercise 2: Sam – 0 marks – The probability should be less than 5%. The explanation does not add anything beyond the 'false positive', which is a description of a Type I error, not an explanation. The results being significant does not tell you anything about the likelihood of an error. Alex – 3 marks. Correct probability, as 5% = 0.05 = 5/100. The explanation is clear and accurate.

Complete the table:

Key study	Null hypothesis	Alternative hypothesis
Bandura	There is no difference in aggressive behaviour between children who observe aggressive or non-aggressive models.	1C, 2K, 3G, 4E, 5I, 6A, 7M, 8B, 9D, 10J, 11L, 12N, 13F, 14H
Asch	There is no difference in conformity between participants in groups with different numbers of confederates (or different levels of unanimity, or different difficulties of task).	There is a difference…
Harlow	There is no difference in the amount of time the baby monkeys spend on the wire or cloth mothers.	There is a difference…

Applying your knowledge: (a) Null: there is no difference between cats and dogs in their puzzle-solving ability. Alternative: Cats solve the puzzle more quickly than dogs. Or a non-directional alternative: Cats and dogs differ in their time taken to solve the puzzle. (b) Null: Rats and lizards are equally affectionate. Alternative: Lizards demonstrate different numbers and types of affectionate behaviours from rats.

Topic 7 Statistical tests

Match them up: 1C, 2K, 3G, 4E, 5I, 6A, 7M, 8B, 9D, 10J, 11L, 12N, 13F, 14H

Complete the table: Sign test: nominal – difference – repeated measures. Pearson's r: interval – parametric – association – correlational. Spearman's rho: ordinal – non-parametric – association – correlational. Related t-test: interval – parametric – difference – related (repeated measures/matched pairs). Unrelated t-test: interval – parametric – difference – independent groups. Wilcoxon: ordinal – non-parametric – difference – related. Mann-Whitney: ordinal – non-parametric – difference – independent groups.

Choose the right answer: A

Applying your knowledge: Pearson's r. Both variables are interval data. The data is probably normally distributed, therefore parametric. We are looking for a correlation between two variables.

Topic 8 Non-parametric tests of difference

Choose the right answer: C (data can be ordinal or interval)

Complete the table:

	Wilcoxon	Mann-Whitney
Level of measurement	At least ordinal	At least ordinal
Experimental design	Related (repeated measures or matched pairs)	Unrelated (independent groups)
Test statistic	T	U
How to calculate test statistic	The sum of the ranks of the less frequent sign	Use the formula, putting in the smaller rank total and the value of N that goes with it

Applying your knowledge 1: (a) People remember more concrete words than abstract words. (b) The data is at least ordinal (numbers of words recalled), it is a test of difference (concrete or abstract words) and it is a related design (same participants in both conditions, repeated measures). (c) Yes. The calculated value (37) is less than the critical value (53) ($N = 19$, $p < 0.05$, one-tailed) so it is significant. (d) The alternative hypothesis is supported – people remember more concrete words than abstract words.

Applying your knowledge 2: (b) 96 (c) 41.5

Topic 9 Parametric tests of difference

Choose the right answer: D

Maths skills: (a) with hint 94 seconds, without hint 99.7 seconds. (b) −65, 16, 32, 6, −29, 74 (c) $\Sigma d = 34$ $\Sigma d^2 = 11858$ (d) yes

(e) $t = \dfrac{34}{\sqrt{(6 \times 11858 - 34^2)/5}} = 0.395$ (f) no

(g) The null hypothesis must be accepted: There is no significant difference between participants' time taken to solve the puzzles with or without a hint.

Research issues: (a) Repeated measures. Order effects – participants may do better in the second condition due to practise (or worse due to fatigue). (b) She could counterbalance the order of the conditions, so half the participants solved puzzles first with hint then without, and the other half did it the other way round. (c) Her sample size was small so this will have affected the calculation of t. A larger sample may have shown a significant difference between the conditions.

Applying your knowledge: For example: Give students tests in each subject after a week of normal working times, and after a week of later school days. IV = early or late. DV = test results. Hypothesis: Students will achieve better test results after a week of starting school later than a normal week. Repeated measures. Related t-test, because data is interval (test scores) and related, looking for a difference, and we assume it meets the parametric criterion of normal distribution. (This study could alternatively use an independent groups design, then you would use the unrelated t-test.)

Topic 10 Tests of correlation

Choose the right answer: B

Maths skills: (a) $rho = 1 - \dfrac{708}{3360} = 0.789$. Significant (critical value = 0.521, $p < 0.01$) (b) $rho = 1 - \dfrac{3846}{6840} = 0.438$. Significant at $p < 0.05$ (critical value = 0.391) but not at $p < 0.01$ (critical value = 0.460)

Drawing conclusions: (a) There is a weak positive correlation between the two variables. As openness to experience increases, liking for sci-fi films also increase. There is a broad range of variability of liking for sci-fi films, but less variability of scores for openness to experience. (b) The correlation was significant at a stringent p level of 0.01, so there is less than 1% chance of a Type I error. The students can be 99% sure that the correlation is not just a chance effect in this sample, but represent a real effect in the population. (c) They are testing for correlation rather than difference, and the data is non-parametric as scores from a Likert scale are ordinal. The data is related as each participant provides two scores. (d) The correlation between agreeableness and liking for comedy films is also weak and positive, but as it is not significant we cannot reject the null hypothesis. We have to conclude that there is not a significant correlation between these variables.

Topic 11 Chi-squared test (χ^2)

Maths skills: Chi-Squared = 12.142. This is significant at $p < 0.05$ ($df = 2$)

A marking exercise: (a) 2 marks. The categories need to be explained: two genders and four coffee types. The association comment is correct. The data is independent but this means that each person only appears in one cell – it is not just because people are in one gender group or the other (independent groups design), but also that each person only chooses one coffee preference. (b) 0 marks. This is a non-directional hypothesis. A directional hypothesis would be: more males will prefer espresso or Americano, and more females will prefer latte or cappuccino. Alternatively, a hypothesis of association would be fine; there will be an association between gender and coffee preference, such that males will prefer espresso or Americano to latte or cappuccino, and females will have the opposite preferences.

Choose the right answer: A and C

Match them up: 1D 2E 3C 4F 5A 6B 7H 8G

Topic 12 Reporting investigations

Match them up: 1D 2C 3E 4H 5J 6F 7B 8G 9A

Fill in the boxes: (References go in a separate section at the end, with citations in the text)

Abstract	Research aims
	Hypotheses
	Procedures
	Results
	Conclusions
	Implications
Introduction	Previous research
	Reason for the study
	Research aims
	Hypotheses
Method	Experimental design
	Sampling
	Questionnaire
	Instructions
	Materials
	Ethical issues
Results	Means or medians
	Standard deviations
	Table of findings
	Scattergram
	Inferential statistics
	Themes and examples
Discussion	Conclusions
	Implications
	Applications
	Future research
	Critical evaluation

Applying your knowledge: For example: This study aimed to test whether innate personality characteristics of individuals are the cause of aggressive behaviour in prisons. In a controlled observation, we investigated the behaviour of student volunteers randomly allocated to roles as guards or prisoners in a simulated prison over a 2-week period, and were de-individuated by the use of uniforms, numbers and sunglasses. 'Guards' rapidly took an aggressive role, while 'prisoners' initially tried to resist but were controlled by increasingly harsh psychological means by 'guards'; two 'prisoners' became distressed and were removed early and the observation was aborted after six days. These findings support our hypothesis that situational factors determine behaviour more than innate individual differences. There are implications for the operation of prisons, as guards should be trained to keep order without abusing prisoners.

Chapter 2 Issues and debates

Topic 1 Gender in psychology: Gender bias

Choose the right answer: E

Match them up: 1C 2B 3A 4E 5D

Applying your knowledge: Asch's sample only contained men yet his conclusions in relation to conformity are applied to explain conformity of both sexes. This is an example of androcentrism as Asch views the world from a male centred point of view and the findings of his study (based only on males) are used as the standard or norm to explain psychological experiences of both sexes.

Furthermore, there is also the possibility of beta bias, as Asch has minimised (ignored) the differences between males and females and assumed there was no need to use female participants, when in fact females may conform differently to males.

Topic 2 Culture in psychology: Cultural bias

Choose the right answer: D

Match them up: 1C 2D 3A 4 B

Research issues: There are a range of suitable ethical issues which could be mentioned here, including: informed consent, privacy, confidentiality, right to withdraw, etc. For example, one issue that Mead would need to consider is informed consent. Mead could deal with this ethical issue by providing all of the people who she intended to observe with an informed consent form, which outlines the aim and method of her research. She could also inform the participants that they have the right to withdraw at any stage in the experiment, up until the publication of the results.

Applying your knowledge: Limitation: Mead was judging and assessing the different cultures from a different perspective, for example how she viewed aggressive behaviour was influenced by her own cultural norms and this could have distorted and exaggerated the differences between the cultures that she was studying. Strength: However, Mead also demonstrates cultural relativism as she immersed herself in the culture which she examined and tried to understand the way in which different cultures/tribes see the world.

Topic 3 Free will and determinism

Choose the right answer: A

Fill in the boxes:

In each box below write one sentence describing each type of determinism.	In each box below expand the content on the left, writing another 20 words.
Biological determinism is … the idea that our behaviour is determined by genes.	Hill *et al.*, (1999) who found that a particular gene was responsible for high intelligence.
Environmental determinism is … the idea that our behaviour is caused by previous experience.	An example of environmental determinism comes from…behaviourists who argue that behaviour is learnt through classical or operant conditioning.
Psychic determinism is … the idea that our behaviour is caused by innate drives and early experiences.	Freud who argued that behaviour was shaped by early childhood experiences and innate drives.
OPTIONAL: Free will is… the view that humans have complete control over their behaviour.	An example free will comes from… humanistic psychologists who would argue that humans have the ability to make significant personal choices.

A marking exercise: This answer is likely to receive 2 out of 3 marks. While the answer has made a distinction between hard and soft determinism, they have not provided an example. Answer: Hard determinism is the idea that our behaviour is predicted and we have no free will, whereas soft determinism allows some element of free will. For example, hard determinism would suggest that violence is caused by aggressive genes and some people will always be violent, whereas soft determinism suggests that people may have an aggressive gene, but it is their choice whether to engage in violence or not.

Applying your knowledge: Identify the psychology: Adenola's behaviour maybe the result of environmental determinism (classical and/or operant conditioning) because he has learned his aggressive behaviour from his older brother who was excluded for hitting another student. Link to Adenola: Furthermore, Adenola's behaviour may be caused by biological determinism, as an aggressive gene may run in his family, as his older brother is also aggressive.

Topic 4 The nature–nurture debate

Choose the right answer: D

Match them up: 1D 2F 3E 4C 5A 6B

Drawing conclusions: The results appear to support the nature side of the nature–nurture debate. This is because the concordance rate is strong in MZ twins (69%), where there is a greater genetic relatedness (100%). However, the results also highlight the role of nurture, as the concordance rate is not 100% (only 69%).

Applying your knowledge: Identify the psychology: There are different reasons you could suggest here. Firstly, despite having the same genes, Rainbow and CC might have different diets and therefore nurture may be one reasons for the differences found between these two cats. Link to CC: Furthermore, epigenetics may also play a role and CC's life experiences (her diet) may switch on/off a gene for metabolism which causes the differences seen in these two cats.

Topic 5 Holism and reductionism

Match them up: 1C 2B 3A

Fill in the boxes:

In each box below write one sentence describing each type of reductionism.	In each box below expand the content on the left, writing another 20 words.
Biological reductionism is… the reduction of complex behaviours to the actions of neurons, hormones, etc.	An example of biological reductionism is…the biological explanation of schizophrenia, which suggests that too much dopamine causes schizophrenia.
Environmental reductionism is…the reduction of complex behaviours to simple stimulus-response links.	An example of environmental reductionism is…the behavioural explanation of attachment, based on classical and operant conditioning.
Experimental reductionism is…the reduction of complex behaviours to isolated variables.	An example of experimental reductionism is…the experimental approach, where variables are operationalised.
OPTIONAL: Holism is… the view that we need to understand the whole experience.	An example of holism is… Gestalt psychology which focuses on perception.

A marking exercise: This answer would be lucky to achieve 1 mark and would most likely get 0. Firstly, the answer has not explained what is meant by levels of analysis and secondly the description of the highest and lowest levels is incorrect.

Answer: The levels of explanation are part of the reductionist approach and explain what aspects of behaviour are taken into consideration at three different levels. The highest level takes into account cultural and social explanations; the middle level takes into account psychological explanations of behaviour; while the lower level takes into account biological explanations of how hormones and genes affect behaviour. The lower level is the most deterministic.

Topic 6 Idiographic and nomothetic approaches to psychological investigations

Choose the right answer: A

Applying your knowledge: An idiographic approaches focuses on individuals and emphasises uniqueness. The psychologist who conducted a case study on Jack is using an idiographic approach to gather qualitative data, to develop an understanding of Jack's behavioural difficulties. A nomothetic approach seeks to formulate general laws based on the study of groups. The psychologist who examined the entire student population is using a nomothetic approach to gather quantitative data, to develop a theory which can be generalised.

Research issues: There are many ethical issues that should be considered here, although they need to be suitable for this case study. Informed consent is not suitable, although parental consent is. Privacy should be considered in terms of the interviews, to ensure that Jack and the teachers are in control of the information they provide. Furthermore, confidentiality should also be considered and any data from the observations should be coded to ensure that Jack, the teachers and the other pupils remain anonymous.

A marking exercise: This answer has provided two reword to: correct point and would therefore receive 2 marks, although both of the points could be elaborated, to include further knowledge, or an example.

For example: The nomothetic approach tries to develop general laws in relation to behaviour and is based on the study of groups. This approaches generally studies large numbers of people, in order to make generalisations.

The biological and behavioural approaches both take a nomothetic approach. For example, the biological approach seeks to formulate general laws about how the body and brain work.

Topic 7 Ethical implications of research studies and theory

Fill in the boxes:

In each box below write one sentence describing each part of the research process	In each box below expand the content on the left, writing another 20 words, related to **social sensitivity**
The research question is… a question/statement which psychologists wish to answer.	This links to social sensitivity because… it could add credibility to a prevailing prejudice.
Conduct of research and treatment of participants refers to… how the participants are treated during and after the research.	This links to social sensitivity because… the research should ensure confidentiality of the information collected during the experiment.
The institutional context refers to… where the research takes place and who is funding the research.	This links to social sensitivity because… the researcher must ensure that the data obtained during the experiment is not misused.
The application of findings refers to… how the research is applied to every day life and its implications.	This links to social sensitivity because… the findings should not be used to the detriment of anyone, following the research.

Match them up: 1D 2I 3A 4C 5G 6F 7J 8H 9B 10E

Applying your knowledge: Research findings suggest that children at the comprehensive school were not as intelligent as those from independent schools. If published this could have much wider implications for the wider community. The researcher should therefore not identify the type of schools used.

A further issue is that of debriefing & protection from psychological harm for those students who were found not to be very intelligent. This would need to be carried out in a sensitive manner and ensure confidentiality and anonymity of all data..

Research issues: 1 Nominal. 2 Nominal data is an unsophisticated measure. This is because it does not provide any information about each of the participants, it simply places them into one of three categories (not very intelligent, moderately intelligent, not very intelligent). Therefore, we do not know the differences between individual participants.

Chapter 3 Relationships

Topic 1 Evolutionary explanations for partner preferences

Choose the right answer: A

Match them up: 1C 2B 3D 4A

Applying your knowledge: Identify the psychology: According to evolutionary theory, Ashiakia will start dating Tim and not Reuben because Tim has a job, which means that he may have more resources to invest in her and any potential offspring. Link to Askiakia: Furthermore, the resources may also mean that Tim is able to protect Ashiakia and any potential offspring, which makes him a more sensible choice.

Topic 2 Physical attractiveness

Choose the right answer: D

Drawing conclusions: The results suggest that males place a greater emphasis on physical attractiveness and youth, whereas females place a greater emphasis on resources and other factors. Evolutionary explanations would support this trend, as males are interested in characteristics that are a sign of fertility, whereas females are interested in characteristics like resources, which can be invested in her and her potential offspring.

Research issues: One methodological issue with questionnaires is that participants might answer in a socially desirable way and therefore the data gathered would not be a valid representation of partner preferences in everyday life. Furthermore, one ethical issue that the researcher would need to consider is confidentiality and ensure that the participants' personal details are not recorded and cannot be linked back to their individual results.

Applying your knowledge: John supports the idea that males rate physical attractiveness as an important quality. He is happy about the fact that other guys are jealous of his girlfriend. However, he also claims that they have no secrets and this supports the idea that females are attracted to qualities like trustworthiness and someone who is likely to be faithful, which could explain why Rachelle is maintaining this relationship.

Topic 3 Self-disclosure

Choose the right answer: B

Match them up: 1B 2D 3C 4A

A marking exercise: This is not a great answer. Although the student has defined self-disclosure, they have not linked their answer to its importance in romantic relationships. For example: Self-disclosure is where a person reveals intimate personal information about themselves to another person. Collins and Miller (1994) found that people who engage in intimate disclosure tend to be liked more than people who disclose at lower levels. Furthermore, they also found that the relationship between disclosure and liking was strong if the recipient believed that disclosure was shared only with them, rather than with others. This suggests that self-disclosure is an important role in the development and maintenance of romantic relationships.

Applying your knowledge: Bobby is engaging in a lot of personal disclosure and research suggests that people should only engage in moderate personal self-disclosure in the early stages of a relationship. Chelsea may feel that Bobby discloses information indiscriminately with everyone. Chelsea on the other hand is engaging in neutral self-disclosure and Bobby may not feel like his disclosure is being reciprocated and that she is not interested in him. This would explain why both Chelsea and Bobby do not want to see one another again.

Topic 4 Attraction: Filter theory

Choose the right answer: D – It should be people who have 'complementarity needs'.

Fill in the boxes:

In each box below write one sentence describing each of the filters	In each box below expand the content on the left, writing another 20 words.
Social demography is … factors which determine the likelihood of individuals meeting in the first place.	For example… age, social background and location.
Similarity in attitudes is … the psychological characteristics, and whether or not people agree.	For example… attitudes, basic values, moral principles, religion, etc.
Complementarity of needs is … how well two people fit together as a couple.	For example… the need to be caring and the need to be cared for.
OPTIONAL: Levinger *et al.* (1970) found … no evidence that either similarity of attitudes or complementarity of needs influenced progress towards permanence in relationships.	This suggests… that the filter theory is not a valid representation of relationship development.

Applying your knowledge: Tommy's social demography has now changed and therefore his range of potential partners is now restricted to his new school, or in this case his new psychology class. Should Tommy starting dating someone, the second filter 'similarity of attitudes' would determine whether the relationship will become more stable. If Tommy and his new girlfriend have similar attitudes the relationship might become more stable. Finally, for the relationship to work Tommy and his new girlfriend would have to have complementarity of needs and provide each other with mutual satisfaction.

Topic 5 Social exchange theory

Choose the right answer: D

Drawing conclusions: The bar chart supports social exchange theory. It shows that when people are in happy relationships their comparison to alternatives is low, which suggests that they are either not seeking an alternative or the benefits of their current relationship are significantly higher than an alternate relationship. Consequently, the happy people are committed and satisfied. However, for the people in unhappy relationships, the reverse is true, their comparison to alternatives is high, suggesting that they will receive more benefits in a new relationship, in comparison to their current relationship.

A marking exercise: This answer lacks many key details and has only really named a study and outlined one key finding, which is clearly not enough for a 6-mark question. Answer: One study that examined social exchange theory was conducted by Sprecher (2001). Sprecher conducted a longitudinal study of 101 dating couples. The results revealed that the presence of alternatives was negatively correlated with both commitment and relationship satisfaction for males and females. In other words, in a relationship where the comparison level for alternatives was high, commitment to, and satisfaction with the current relationship tended to be low. This supports the social exchange theory and the idea of the CLA, suggesting that individuals continually weigh up the costs and benefits of maintaining a relationship. Individuals who

think that the benefits of entering a new relationship outweigh their current relationship, have low levels of commitment, suggesting that they are considering ending the relationship for these new benefits.

Topic 6 Equity theory

Choose the right answer: C

Match them up: 1E 2C 3B 4A 5D

Write your own evaluation point: Point – One strength of the equity theory comes from research on primates by Waal (2003). Evidence – Waal (2003) studied female capuchin monkeys and found that they became very angry if they were denied a reward. If another monkey unfairly received a reward instead, the capuchins grew angry and threw food at the experimenter. Explain – This shows that the perception of inequity has ancient origins and supports the findings of research in human studies. Evaluate – However, there are issues with using animal studies to explain human behaviour. For example, some psychologists argue that human and animal relationships are very different and that we may be unable to extrapolate the findings from animals to humans. Link – Therefore, although this study provides from support for the origins of equity theory, it may not apply to human relationships and further research is required to support this theory in humans.

Applying your knowledge: According to Schafer and Keith (1980) women often feel under-benefited during the child-rearing years and therefore it is expected that satisfaction will dip. However, usually during the empty-nest stage (when children have left home) husbands and wives should perceive their relationship to be equitable. Furthermore, now that they are both retired Emmanuela would expect Chris to take an equal share of the chores which he has not and therefore she feels under-benefited, which explains her growing dissatisfaction.

Topic 7 The investment model of relationships

Complete the diagram:

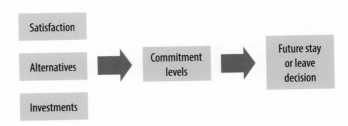

Match them up: 1D 2B 3A 4C

Drawing conclusions: The results support the investment mode because it shows that all three factors are correlated with relationship satisfaction. As expected, quality of alternatives is negatively correlated. As the individual believes that their needs will be better fulfilled in an alternate relationship, their satisfaction with the current relationship declines. However, commitment and investment size are positively correlated. As the investment size increases the desire to stay in the current relationship also increases, because of the potential loss if the relationship ended.

A marking exercise: While this is a reasonable attempt at this question, both of the points could have been elaborated further, to ensure that the answer gains full marks.

For example: One issue with the investment model is that it is difficult to measure the different factors e.g. commitment levels. For example, terms like satisfaction and commitment are hard to measure objectively and quantify and most measures simply use questionnaires which also have issues of social desirability. Another issue is that it doesn't consider future investments and some psychologists argue that relationships may persist due to the belief that something better might occur in the future.

Activities: suggested answers

Topic 8 Relationship breakdown

Choose the right answer: C

Match them up: 1D 2C 3E 4A 5B

Research issues: There is a whole range of ethical issues that the research should consider here, including: privacy, confidentiality, right to withdraw, protection from harm, informed consent. One issue the researcher would need to consider is privacy. The participants should control the flow of information that is given during the interview and not feel pressured to answer questions – especially on this sensitive topic. Furthermore, the research should consider protection from harm, as this is an emotional topic. The researchers should let the participant know that at any stage of the experiment they can withdraw.

Applying your knowledge: Tola has experienced the dyadic phase where she confronts her partner to discuss her feelings of discontentment. However, as Tamer didn't listen, Tola moved onto the social phase where she confides in her best friend and makes her distress public. Abena has taken Tola's side which is likely to speed up the dissolution, as she agrees with Tola's disappointment.

Topic 9 Virtual relationships in social media

Choose the right answer: C

Write your own evaluation point: Point – Support for virtual relationship comes from research examining the biological basis of self-disclosure. Evidence – Tamir and Mitchell (2012) found increased MRI activity in two brain regions that are associated with rewards, the nucleus accumbens and ventral tegmental area. Explain – These findings suggest that the human tendency to share our personal experience with others over social media, may arise from the rewarding nature of self-disclosure. Evaluate – However, one problem with the use of brain scans is that the results are correlational and therefore we do not know if sharing information causes activation in the nucleus accumbens and ventral tegmental, as there could be other factors. Link – Therefore, although these results appear to support the biological basis of self-disclosure we must be cautious when using this evidence, as other factors may also play an important role.

Applying your knowledge: There are two factors that could contribute to Deon's improved confidence and success online. Firstly, there is the absence of gates, which are barriers that limit his opportunities as a shy male. Furthermore, he may feel like he can reveal more intimate and personal information online and control the information he provides about himself, which may provide him with an opportunity to 'stretch the truth' in an effort to project a self that is more socially desirable. It is for these reasons why he finds it easier to conduct his relationships online.

A marking exercise: While this answer has correctly defined self-disclosure, their second sentence is vague. Self-disclosure is when a person reveals intimate information about themselves. Self-disclosure in the virtual world allows an individual to present an 'edited' version of themselves to others. People feel more secure with disclosing intimate and sensitive information in private online and the anonymity of internet interactions greatly decreases the risk of self-disclosures, because people can share their inner thoughts and feelings with much less fear of disapproval and social sanctions.

Topic 10 Parasocial relationships

Choose the right answer: A

Match them up: 1Cii 2Bi 3Aiii

Fill in the boxes:

In each box below write one sentence describing each procevss of the absorption addiction model.	In each box below expand the content on the left, writing another 20 words, by providing an example.
Entertainment-social is … where fans are attracted to their favourite celebrity.	For example, …they will watch, read and learn about their celebrity.
Intense-personal is … where an individual has intensive and compulsive feelings about their celebrity.	For example, … they may love to talk about their celebrity or only hang around with people who admire their celebrity.
Borderline-pathological is … where an individual overidentifies with their celebrity and has uncontrollable behaviours.	For example, … they may believe that they actually know their celebrity and that he/she would greet them if they met.

A marking exercise: While the addiction model does have three levels, this answer is very vague and lacks clarity and details. Answer: For example, Giles and Maltby (2006) identify three levels in the absorption addiction model: Firstly, fans are attracted to their favourite celebrity and will watch them, keep up with them, and learn about their celebrity for entertainment purposes. Secondly, the fans become involved in a deeper level of involvement and experience intensive and compulsive feelings about the celebrity. Finally, the fan over-identifies with the celebrity and has uncontrollable behaviours and fantasies about their lives.

Chapter 4 Gender

Topic 1 Sex-role stereotypes and androgyny

Choose the right answer: D

Research issues: (a) Self-report scales are easy to administer and to score, and can be very reliable. The BSRI has good test-retest reliability, as tested by Bem in the 1980s, who found a correlation of up to .94 over four weeks. However, the scale may lack validity as there can be intervening variables which affect the validity of the scores, and it has been suggested that self-esteem is being measured by the BSRI rather than androgyny. In addition, the items are all oriented the same way (positive = high score) so a positive response bias will affect the total scores for each subscale of femininity and masculinity. (b) The internal reliability can be improved by removing items which do not correlate with the other items. The external reliability can be improved by making sure that items are clear and unambiguous, so they cannot be interpreted in different ways.

Applying your knowledge 1: For example: Snow White shows a girl cleaning a house for seven males and being praised → girls identify with same-sex model, vicarious reinforcement → girls imitate the behaviour → they are praised, which is direct reinforcement, so the behaviour is maintained. OR boys don't identify with the female model → boys don't think cleaning is for them and don't imitate the behaviour. If they do, they may be mocked by other boys → punishment, which reduces the likelihood of the behaviour being repeated.

Applying your knowledge 2: Identify the psychology – people learn sex-role stereotypes from parents or society. Link to Robin – Robin has been protected her/his parents from stereotypes about behaviour and clothes, and therefore enjoys a variety of typically 'boy' and 'girl' toys. Identify the psychology – many people think it is healthy to teach boys and girls stereotyped behaviour. Link to Robin – Robin is free to explore all sorts of toys and clothes and play with boys and girls, so according to Bem, Robin will be more psychologically healthy as he/she will grow up more androgynous.

Topic 2 The role of chromosomes and hormones in sex and gender

Match them up: 1B 2D 3C 4A 5F 6E

A marking exercise: Mark 4 out of 6. Comment: Primary and secondary characteristics are not explained. Testosterone and oestrogen are correctly linked to male and female secondary sexual characteristics in puberty, but the student implies that females do not have any testosterone, which is incorrect. The example of AIS is correct, and makes the link between testosterone and development of male genitals.

Drawing conclusions: The sex chromosomes would normally be XX or XY. In this case they are XXY. This is the atypical pattern of Klinefelter's syndrome.

Applying your knowledge: Biopsychology: Turner syndrome is a lack of one X chromosome, giving XO. Females with Turner syndrome don't develop normally at puberty and are infertile, but generally have normal intelligence and can be highly fluent verbally. It affects about 1/2000 females. Link to Jolanta: As Jolanta is short and has no sign of developing secondary sexual characteristics, the doctor suspects she may have Turner's syndrome. The doctor may have spotted other physical signs such as short neck, low set ears, etc. The doctor will have to do a chromosome test to find out. It may be too late to treat Jolanta with growth hormone, but she could be given oestrogen replacement therapy so she develops female characteristics and this will protect her bones and heart too.

Topic 3 Cognitive explanations of gender development: Kohlberg's theory

Match them up: 1C 2A 3B

Choose one answer: A

Drawing conclusions: a) Boys: 7/27 = 25.9%, girls 13/27 = 48.1% b) Boys: 4, girls: 5. c) The children may have seen boys and girls playing football, so the football question would not be a good measure of adherence to gendered behaviour. There were different numbers of boys and girls in each age group, for example there were eight 2-year-old boys but only four 2-year-old girls, so this is an unrepresentative sample. The children may be answering as they think the researcher expects them too (demand characteristics) or may be in a 'pretend' mode, answering questions based on this rather than what they really think about human gender. Children may see women dress like men more than seeing men dress like women, so this could affect their answers to the questions.

Applying your knowledge: Identify the psychology: According to Kohlberg's theory, children only become aware of gender-appropriate behaviour once they have acquired gender constancy at about age 6, and understand that their gender will not change. They then pay more attention to same-sex models. Link to Jason: As Jason is only four, he has not reached the stage of gender constancy, so may not realise that his behaviour is unusual for a male. He will probably change his tastes in clothes as he grows up and sees that men do not wear fairy dresses. If he is given opportunities to observe men fighting he may well imitate this behaviour as he learns to identify with men.

Topic 4 Cognitive explanations of gender development: Gender schema theory

Choose the right answer: C

Applying your knowledge: Identify the psychology: Gender schemas are acquired from other children, adults, books, TV and films. They organise information about appropriate behaviours for males and females. They are resistant to counter-stereotypical information, as shown by Martin and Halverson, who found that children mis-remembered pictures which were inconsistent with gender schemas. Link to Oli: Oli has acquired his schema from films or stories or from other families in which the father goes out to work and mother stays at home and carries out domestic tasks. He sees a power drill as a 'boy toy' because of advertising or other factors, like the labelling of loud, powerful objects as masculine. He sees his mum and dad contradicting these gender schemas in their behaviour, but his schemas stay intact, and he answers according to the schemas rather than his observations.

Drawing conclusions: (a) The children remembered more of the firefighters and chemists as male, and more of the teachers and nurses as female. The greatest difference was for nurses, where all of the female nurses were correctly remembered as female, while only a very few male nurses were correctly remembered. The difference was least for chemists, where a lot of children got the gender of male chemists wrong too. (b) Gender schemas are learnt from observation in real life and via the media, and these tend to show males and females in traditional roles. These schemas then distort new memories, which can be adjusted to fit the expectations of the schema. So children who saw a male nurse, for example, fitted that image into a schema which says that nurses are female, and remembered the nurse as being female

Topic 5 Psychodynamic explanation of gender development

A marking exercise: Mark: 3 Comment: Correctly uses some terms; identification, penis envy. Switch of desire from mother to father to wanting to have a baby is clear. However, no mention of internalisation of mother's gender identity, and unclear explanation of why she switches desire to her father.

Research issues:

Issue	Elaboration
Based on case studies	For example, Freud's case of Little Hans: can't be generalised, and data collected very subjectively and mostly via Hans' father.
Gender bias	Freud claimed he 'didn't understand women': alpha bias – women seen as inferior to men.
Unfalsifiable	Findings in case studies are interpreted retrospectively, hypotheses cannot be tested in controlled experiments.
Lack of predictive validity	Predictions from the theory are not supported by evidence, e.g. children of same-sex couples develop sexual identities normally.
Non-experimental methods	Data suggests an association between childhood experiences and later sexual behaviour, but this is correlation not causation.

Applying your knowledge:

Little Hans	Freud's interpretation
Interested in his 'widdler'	Phallic stage age 3–6, libido focussed on the genitals/pleasure
Mother threatened to cut it off	Castration anxiety
Phobia of horses	Horse represented his father, who he wished was dead (a rival for his mother's love). General anxiety from repressing his wish to kill his father.
Wanted to cuddle his mother in bed	Sexual desire for his mother
His father objected	Reinforced the rivalry

Choose the right answer: B

Topic 6 Social learning theory as applied to gender development

Match them up: 1D 2E 3A 4B 5C 6H 7F 8G

Fill in the boxes:

Aspect of theory	SLT	GST	Freud's theory
Identification	Same-sex role models	Gender labelling: identify with ingroup	Same-sex parent
Internalisation	Learning appropriate behaviour by observation	Schema construction	Same-sex parent's gender identity and behaviour
Imitation	If reinforced (vicarious + direct)	Ingroup	After internalisation
Cognitive aspects	Mental representations	Gender schemas, affect attention and memory	Unconscious Electra/Oedipus complex, castration fear/penis envy
How behaviour is maintained	Vicarious and direct reinforcement	Evaluations enhance self-esteem	Resolution of conflict of phallic stage
Key figures	Parents, peers, media	Ingroup	Father and Mother
Nature/nurture?	Mainly learnt = nurture	Learnt = Nurture	Innate drive = nature
Free will/deterministic?	'Environmental determinism' + self-direction	Schemas are resilient (mainly deterministic)	Deterministic

Choose the right answer: C

Applying your knowledge: Identify the psychology: Modelling from peers, vicarious reinforcement vs. direct tuition from parents. Self-direction in older children. Mediational processes – expectation of future outcomes. Annabelle: receives direct tuition from parents, 'should wear a skirt', and also direct punishment – the criticism 'not being ladylike'. However, she also receives modelling from peers of wearing jeans, and vicarious reinforcement as they seem to be having fun. Conflict between these two influences; she is old enough to make her own choice and weigh up the likely punishment from her mother vs. the expectation of reward she has gained from observing peers.

Topic 7 Cultural and media influences on gender roles

Match them up: 1A 2C 3D 4G 5B 6E 7F

Research Issues: Researcher bias: Mead may have been looking for particular evidence and ignoring other evidence due to confirmation bias and the subjective nature of observational research, particularly with only one observer. Demand characteristics: the people may have guessed what answers would please her, and answered accordingly rather than truthfully. Historical validity: cultural norms of behaviour have probably changed, both in the UK (affecting researcher variables and expectations) and in Papua New Guinea (meaning that these findings are no longer relevant and the studies cannot be replicated).

Drawing conclusions: (a) Decide on a sample, e.g. TV advertisements on ITV over one weekend. Carry out a pilot observation the previous weekend to decide on behavioural categories. Make a tally chart, watch the advertisements, code the behaviours.

(b)
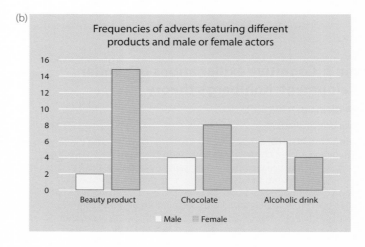

(c) Males are slightly more likely to start a conversation than females, but much more likely to give information than females. Females were shown expressing emotion quite often, whereas males didn't at all. The most common behaviour for males (the mode) was giving information, whereas for females it was expressing emotion.

Applying your knowledge: (a) 90/2.5 = 36 seconds (b) 90 × 60 = 5,400 seconds male talking time. 36 × 40 = 1,440 seconds female talking time. 5,400 + 1,440 = 6,840 seconds total student talking time. Percentage female = 1,400/6,840 ×100 = 20.5% (c) Female time = 1,400 × 3 = 4,200 seconds. Percentage female = 4,200/6,840 × 100 = 61.4%. (d) Why: The female instructor 'had an inspiring effect' on the female students, as she was a counter-stereotypical role model, a confident professional woman who took a lead and talked to the class a lot. As the instructor, she would probably be talking more than the students. Effects: This challenges stereotypes of female reticence of shyness, and enables female students to identify with her and imitate her behaviour. In contrast, male students may identify less with a female instructor and therefore be quieter. Also, there is the possibility that the female instructor was deliberately encouraging female students to talk, by targeting them with questions or by direct tuition, telling them that they need to practise talking to be successful lawyers.

Topic 8 Atypical gender development

Match them up: 1D 2C 3A 4B

Fill in the boxes:

Abnormality	What is it?	Who?	Hormonal effects	Result
Klinefelter's syndrome	XXY	1/1,000 males	Reduced testosterone	Less masculine appearance, infertile
Turner's syndrome	XO	1/2,000 females	Reduced oestrogen	Short, underdeveloped ovaries
CAH	Congenital adrenal hyperplasia	XX females	Prenatal high androgens	External male genitalia
AIS	Androgen insensitivity syndrome	XY males e.g. Batista family	Lack of testosterone receptors	No external male genitalia at birth – may develop at adolescence
'Transexual gene'	Longer version of androgen receptor gene	MtF transsexuals	Reduced sensitivity to testosterone	Suggested under-masculinisation of brain
Boys whose mothers were exposed to dioxins	Environmental pollutant	Boys	High oestrogen exposure prenatally	Feminised play
Girls whose mothers took drugs containing androgens	(Berenbaum and Bailey, see page 100)	Girls	High testosterone exposure prenatally	More tomboyish behaviour and interest in male-type activities

Choose the right answer: A

Applying your knowledge: Identify the psychology: Gender stereotypes are societal expectations about 'masculine' and 'feminine' behaviour. Can be explicit or implicit. Gender dysphoria is the feeling of discomfort with the assigned gender. Not fitting the stereotypes could make someone feel that they are in the wrong body. Application: Carol desperately wanted to be a boy, and felt she was better at 'boys stuff' than her brothers. She still describes herself as 'not girly', i.e. not fitting stereotypes of feminine behaviour, although she became reconciled to being a girl at puberty. Becks similarly 'never felt properly feminine', and even doubted her reproductive function because her personality and height fitted masculine stereotypes rather than feminine. And Adam experienced bullying for being a boy with stereotypically feminine attributes. He points out that the stereotypes should be fought, implying that this would help people to be comfortable with a range of personality traits that don't necessarily fit the stereotypes.

Chapter 5 Cognition and development

Topic 1 Piaget's theory of cognitive development

Choose the right answer: D

Fill in the boxes: Schema: Definition: Schemas are mental structures that represent a group of related concepts. Example: Recognising a human face. Assimilation: Definition: The process of incorporating new information into an existing schema. Example: When a baby is given a new toy car to play with, they may grasp it in the same way they grasped a rattle. Accommodation: When an existing schema is adapted to understand new information that doesn't seem to fit into existing knowledge. Example: Learning that things which have four legs and a tail include 'cats' as well as 'dogs'. Equilibration: Definition: Experiencing a balance between existing schemas and new experiences. Example: The balance that comes after accommodating new information about cats, such as Manx cats don't have a tail, but are still cats.

Complete the diagram: In descending order: An inbuilt sucking reflex. Using the sucking reflex with other objects. Seeking mental balance. Dealing with experiences by assimilation. Modifying the sucking reflex with other objects.

Match them up: 1B 2D 3C 4A

Applying your knowledge: (a) The child has a schema that humans who are bald on the top of their head and have long frizzy ginger hair on the side are 'clowns'. When the child sees someone with that appearance, assimilation occurs. The child incorporates this new information into its existing schema. (b) Mark could explain to this toddler that Girish is not a clown, even though part of his appearance suggests he is. Girish is not wearing a clown's costume and isn't doing things that make people laugh. The toddler would be able to change his schema to accommodate what a clown is – has funny hair, wears a costume, makes people laugh.

Topic 2 Piaget's stages of intellectual development

Choose the right answer: C and D

Drawing conclusions: (a) Nominal level. (b) 2 x 2 Chi-Squared test. The data are at the nominal level, and the researcher is looking for a difference. Additionally, an independent groups design has been used. (c) The results indicate that significantly more pre-operational children are able to solve the class inclusion task if it is presented in a different way than usual (i.e. the researcher's hypothesis has been supported). The null hypothesis can be rejected at $p < 0.05$.

Fill in the boxes: 1 Sensori-motor – 0-2 years – The child learns that an object remains present even if they cannot see it (object permanence). 2 Pre-operational – 2-7 years – The child can only see the world from their perspective. 3 Concrete operational – 7-11 years – The child can conserve number, volume, and mass. 4 Formal operational – 11+ years – The child can solve problems in an abstract way.

Match them up: 1B 2D 3C 4A

Applying your knowledge: This activity is based on a study conducted by McGhee (1976). Concrete operational children recognise that it doesn't matter if the pizza is cut into six or eight pieces, the amount of pizza doesn't change. Pre-operational children lack these conservation skills.

Thus, the concrete operational child finds what Rona said funny while the six-year-old does not.

Topic 3 Vygotsky's theory of cognitive development

Choose the right answer: A

Drawing conclusions (a) See scattergram

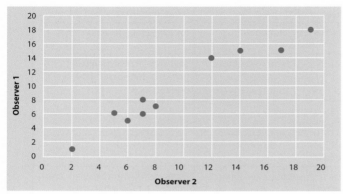

(b) Inter-observer reliability (c) Pearson's *r* (d) Spearman's rho (e) One reason for low inter-observer reliability is that the behavioural categories have not been operationalised clearly enough, so one observer might interpret a phrase used by a mother differently from another observer. Making behavioural categories clearer and/or giving observers more practice in using the behavioural categories can both improve the reliability of observations.

Applying your knowledge: Scaffolding is how an expert helps a learner through the zone of proximal development. It is a temporary support that aims to help a learner only when necessary, and will be gradually withdrawn as the learner masters the task and is able to work independently. In this case, Beth's mum is the expert and she creates a 'scaffold' to help Beth make cakes. As Beth didn't know how to make cakes at the beginning, Beth's mum had to give her lots of help with things like scales. She also gave more explicit, clear instructions about what she had to do. As Beth mastered the task, she became more successful and so her mother gave fewer explicit instructions and eventually Beth had learned how to make cakes on her own.

Topic 4 Baillargeon's explanation of early infant abilities

Choose the right answer: D

Match them up: 1C 2A 3B

Fill in the boxes: In descending order: A way of studying object permanence. Whether infants will express surprise when witnessing an impossible event. Infants expressed surprise when a tall object failed to appear in a short window. Infants do possess object permanence. The infants were only three-months-old.

Research issues: This is done to avoid the mother unconsciously communicating cues to the infant about how it should react to the stimuli which may affect the results.

Applying your knowledge: This fictitious example illustrates violation of expectation. Violation of expectation research suggests that infants will show surprise when they see an impossible event. In this case, the infant expected to see the lemmings fall off the cliff, so she looked only very briefly. Then, she got bored and stopped looking. However, when Larry the Lucky Lemming remained suspended in mid-air, this violated her expectation (that he was going to fall) and so she looked at it for longer.

Topic 5 The development of social cognition: Selman's theory

Choose the right answer: A and D

Fill in the boxes: Stage 0: Undifferentiated perspective-taking – Children can distinguish between self and others, but are largely governed by their own perspective. Stage 1: Social-informational perspective-taking – Children are aware of perspectives that are different to their own. Stage 2: Self-reflective perspective-taking – Children can now view their *own* thoughts and feelings from someone else's perspective. Stage 3: Mutual perspective-taking – Children can imagine how they and others are viewed from the point of view of a third, impartial, party. Stage 4: Societal perspective-taking – Personal decisions are now made with reference to social conventions.

Drawing conclusions: (a) Group A mean: 6.3 Group B mean: 3.3 (b) Group A median: 6.5 Group B median: 3 (c) Group A mode: 5 Group B mode: 3 (d) The standard deviation is a measure of dispersion, and tells us how much variation there is around the mean score. The larger the standard deviation, the more variable performance is. The standard deviations indicate that there is some variability in the performance of both groups, but slightly more in Group A. (e) Mann-Whitney U test (or Unrelated t-test). (f) The researcher is looking for a difference, and an independent groups design has been used. Additionally, the data are at least at the ordinal levels of measurement.

Applying your knowledge: Frank is nine-years-old, so he is at the self-reflective perspective-taking stage. This means he can view his own thoughts and feelings from another person's perspective and recognise that others can do the same. So Frank thinks that the boy's father will not be angry once he realises the boy's perspective, i.e. that he ran down the road to catch a thief (not for fun). Lisa is 13-years-old and so she is at the societal perspective-taking stage. This means that her personal decisions are made by referring to social conventions, including the idea that stealing is wrong. This means Lisa understands that the reason the boy's father won't be angry is because the boy wants to catch a thief, since stealing is conventionally wrong in our society.

Topic 6 The development of social cognition: Theory of mind

Drawing conclusions:

(a)

	Non-autistic children	Autistic children
Successful at the task	23	4
Unsuccessful at the task	4	16

(b)

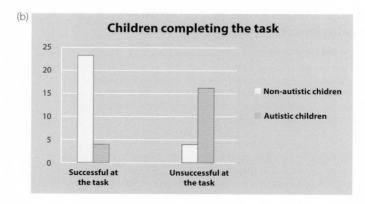

(c) 2 × 2 Chi-Squared test (d) The data are at the nominal level, and an independent groups design has been used. Additionally, a difference is being looked for. (e) A Type I error occurs when the null hypothesis is rejected when it should have been accepted. (f) Since the significance level was set at $p < 0.05$, there is a 5% chance that a Type I error has been made.

Match them up: 1C 2A 3D 4B

Research issues: The Down's syndrome participants were included as kind of 'control' group to ensure that any differences between the non-autistic and autistic children was not a result of differences in intelligence. The mental age of the autistic children was higher than that of the non-autistic children, so poorer performance was independent of differences in intelligence and must be specific to autism.

Applying your knowledge: Given that ToM usually develops around the age of four, we might expect Kirsty's three- and six-year-old sisters to differ in their responses. If the six-year-old has a ToM, and understands that Dad won't know the tube is full of buttons, she will say 'Smarties'. However, if the three-year-old doesn't have a ToM, she will not be able to put aside her knowledge that the tube does not have Smarties in it, and so will say 'buttons' because she cannot appreciate that Dad has a separate belief to her.

Topic 7   The development of social cognition: The mirror neuron system

Choose the right answer: D

Research issues: (a) One ethical issue is informed consent. Electrodes were implanted in the epileptic patients' brains, based on purely clinical criteria – they were being used to identify seizure foci for potential surgical treatment. The researchers took advantage of this and used the same electrodes to 'piggyback' their research. However, they sought the patients' consent before doing this. (b) As with research into 'split-brains', the participants were all suffering from intractable epilepsy. It could be argued that the epileptic brain is somehow different from the non-epileptic brain, and therefore that the participants were not a representative sample.

Drawing conclusions: (a) 12/184 = 6.5% (b) 39/87 = 44.8% (c) 12/39 = 30.8%

Match them up: 1B 2D 3C 4A

Applying your knowledge: Your answer to this needs to make reference to mirror neurons (MN). Paresh observed a player being kicked on the knee. When Paresh saw this, mirror neurons reacted, and enabled him to experience the action as if it was happening to him. Presumably, Paresh's observation-response link was 'online' and he repeated the behaviour immediately. This caused his leg to react as though he had been kicked, which caused his pizza to go flying through the air.

Chapter 6 Schizophrenia

Topic 1   Classification of schizophrenia

Choose the right answer: C and E

Fill in the boxes (1):

	Definition	Example
Hallucinations	Perceptual distortions or exaggerations in any of the senses	Auditory hallucinations include hearing a voice (or voices) telling the person how to behave or commenting on their behaviour
Delusions	Firmly held, but erroneous, beliefs caused by distortions of reasoning, or misinterpretations of perceptions or experiences	Paranoid delusions involve the belief that a person is being conspired against (e.g. being followed by MI5)

Fill in the boxes (2):

	Definition	Example
Speech poverty	Deficits in verbal fluency and productivity, a less complex syntax	Producing fewer animal names as non-schizophrenics in the same time period
Avolition	A reduction of self-initiated involvement in interests and desires, as well as an inability to begin and persist with tasks	Sitting in the house for hours every day, doing nothing

Complete the table: Criterion A – symptoms, delusions, hallucinations. Criterion B – dysfunction, social and/or occupational functioning. Criterion C – duration, six months continuous duration.

Applying your knowledge: This classic example is taken from Bleuler (1911). It is an excellent example of disturbances in the *form* of schizophrenic thought (as opposed to its *content*) and illustrates loose associations (or derailment). The individual shifts from topic to topic as new associations arise, and fails to form coherent and logical thoughts. As a result, language is often rambling and disjointed. 'Poverty of content' refers to schizophrenic language which, while being grammatically correct, conveys or communicates very little, as is the case in the letter.

Topic 2 Reliability and validity in diagnosis and classification

Choose the right answer: C

Match them up: 1B 2C 3A 4D

Fill in the boxes:

	Explanation	Elaboration
Co-morbidity	The extent to which two or more conditions occur simultaneously in a person.	Conditions that are co-morbid with schizophrenia include substance abuse, anxiety, and obsessive-compulsive disorder.
Culture bias	Culture has an influence on the diagnostic process since there is a significant variation between culture in the diagnosis of schizophrenia.	When asked to diagnose a patient, British and American psychiatrists have been shown to differ significantly (Copeland, 1971).
Gender bias	Gender bias occurs when the accuracy of a diagnosis depends on a person's gender.	American clinicians equated mentally healthy 'adult' behaviour with mentally healthy 'male' behaviour, meaning that women tended to be perceived as less mentally healthy.
Symptom overlap	This occurs when the symptoms of one disorder occur in another disorder.	Some of the symptoms in schizophrenia occur in depression, bipolar disorder, and dissociative identity disorder.

Drawing conclusions: (a)

	Genuinely schizophrenic	Not schizophrenic
Schizophrenia diagnosed	23	14
Schizophrenia not diagnosed	12	6

(b) 35/55 = 64% (c) 12/35 = 34% (d) 6/20 = 30%

Applying your knowledge: It has been argued that a bias in diagnosis exists with schizophrenia. It is believed that psychiatrists are much more reluctant to diagnose people from their own social class as 'schizophrenic'. This is because of the stigma that schizophrenia brings to families, which is argued to be greater amongst the 'established' middle class. If this bias does exist, then it clearly raises important issues about how valid diagnosis is, which seems to be Chrissy's concern.

Topic 3 Biological explanations for schizophrenia

Choose the right answer: B and C

Fill in the boxes (1):

	One finding that suggests genetics are involved	One finding that challenges the view that genetics are involved
Family studies	Gottesman (1991) found that a person's risk is higher the closer their degree of genetic relatedness to a schizophrenic.	Findings from family resemblance studies are limited by the fact that families typically share environments as well as genes.
Twin studies	Joseph (2004) found a 40.4% concordance for MZs, but only 7.4% for DZs.	It is widely accepted that MZs are treated more similarly than DZs in several ways, such as how other people treat them. Therefore, it is difficult to assess the relative contribution of genes and environmental factors.
Adoption studies	Tienari et al. (2000) found that 6.7% of children whose mothers were schizophrenic developed the disorder compared with 2% whose mothers weren't.	Adoption studies assume that adoptees are not 'selectively placed'. However, parents who adopt children of schizophrenic parents differ from those who adopt children of non-schizophrenic parents.

Fill in the boxes (2):

	The cause of schizophrenia	One finding which supports the hypothesis	One finding which challenges the hypothesis
The original dopamine hypothesis	The positive symptoms are caused by an excess of dopamine.	Effective antipsychotic drugs are dopamine antagonists, and reduce activity in the neural pathways that use dopamine.	Hallucinations and delusions are present in people *despite* their dopamine levels being normal.
The revised dopamine hypothesis	The positive symptoms are caused by an excess of dopamine in the *mesolimbic pathway*, while the negative and cognitive symptoms are believed to be due to a deficit of dopamine in the *mesocortical pathway*.	PET scans of dopamine levels in schizophrenics indicate low levels in the prefrontal cortex.	Anti-psychotic drugs do not alleviate hallucinations and delusions in about one-third of people experiencing these symptoms.

Research issues: The major issue here would appear to be one of generalisation. As Boksa (2007) has observed: 'I agree that we will never be able to model the complete disorder of schizophrenia in a rat — there is no such thing as a schizophrenic rat or even an animal model of (the whole of) schizophrenia.' Nonetheless, Boksa believes that animal studies are a useful way of trying to understand schizophrenia's causes. You can read about her defence of using non-humans to study the causes of schizophrenia here: http://www.ncbi.nlm.nih.gov/pmc/articles/PMC1764543/

Applying your knowledge: One way around the issue of shared environments is to look at the concordance rate for schizophrenia in identical twins that have been separated at (or shortly after) birth and reared in completely different environments. Under these circumstances, Gottesman and Shields (1982) found a concordance rate of 58%. However, the main issue with this sort of study is that of sample size. In this kind of study, the chances of someone being an identical twin, who was separated at birth, and then went on to develop schizophrenia, is bound to be small. Gottesman and Shields' study is based on a sample size of only 12, which is hardly big enough for any firm conclusions to be drawn.

Topic 4 Psychological explanations for schizophrenia

Fill in the boxes:

	Double bind	Expressed emotion
Basic outline	Parents predispose their children to schizophrenia by communicating with them in contradictory ways. Such contradictions invalidate each other, and prevent the child developing an internally coherent construction of reality, and schizophrenia develops.	Expressed emotion (EE) is a family communication style in which a schizophrenic's family members talk about them in a critical or hostile manner (high EE) or a non-critical or non-hostile manner (low EE).
One strength	Berger (1965) found evidence of more double bind statements in families of schizophrenics than non-schizophrenics.	High EE levels are associated with high relapse rates in schizophrenics.
One weakness	Liem (1974) reported no differences in communication patterns in families of schizophrenics and non-schizophrenics.	Not all schizophrenics are equally vulnerable to high levels of EE in the family environment. For example, Altorfer *et al.* (1998) found that 25% of schizophrenics showed no physiological responses to stressful comments from relatives.

Drawing conclusions: (a) High EE is 196/4 = 49%. Low EE is 61/4 = 15.25%. (b) Relapse is much more likely if participants came from high EE families. All four studies show the same thing, and so the finding is reliable. (c) The ranges are very similar to the high and low EE participants. This suggests similar variability in relapse rates (even though the means are very different). (d) The means for the two continental European groups combined is 45% for high EE and 10.5% for low EE. This has the effect of making the mean relapse rate the lowest for the British, American and European high EE participants (even though Milan on its own has the highest high EE relapse rate). The rankings of the British, American and European participants low in EE remains the same.

Applying your knowledge:

	Description	Cognitive explanation
Hallucinations	Perceptual distortions or exaggerations in any of the senses.	Explaining a *self-generated* auditory experience to an *external source*.
Delusions	Firmly held, but erroneous, beliefs caused by distortions of reasoning, or misinterpretations of perceptions or experiences.	Relating *irrelevant information* to the self and drawing a false conclusion.
Anhedonia	A loss of interest or pleasure in all or almost all activities, or a lack of reactivity to normally pleasurable stimuli.	Having low *expectations* of pleasure.

Topic 5 Drug therapy

Choose the right answer: D

Fill in the table:

	Typical antipsychotics	Atypical antipsychotics
The drug works by...	binding to dopamine receptors, but not stimulating them	blocking dopamine receptors, but rapidly dissociating from them, allowing normal dopamine transmission
An example of the drug is...	chlorpromazine	clozapine
The drug significantly reduces...	the positive symptoms of schizophrenia	both the positive and negative symptoms of schizophrenia
One side effect of the drug is...	extrapyramidal effects, such as tardive dyskinesia	weight gain

Drawing conclusions: (a) IV = Antipsychotic drug (A, B, C, and D). DV = Amount of improvement as measured by a 7-point rating scale. (b) The researcher's colleague's observations might be biased given his familiarity with antipsychotic medication. (c) We do not know to what extent the schizophrenics would have shown an improvement if they had been given no medication. For example, if there was no improvement whatsoever in those schizophrenics given no medication, then a case could be made for claiming that each drug was to varying degrees 'effective'. (d) The Mann-Whitney U test could have been used. The researcher is looking for a difference, an independent groups design has been used, and the data are at the ordinal level of measurement.

Applying your knowledge: One way in which the problem could be addressed is through the use of *active placebos*. An active placebo is designed to produce the same side effects as the actual drug without, of course, having the drug's therapeutic effects. The aim of this is to convince the person being tested that they are receiving an actual treatment and to make it difficult for an assessor to know whether the person has received the treatment or not.

Topic 6 Cognitive behaviour therapy

Choose the right answer: C

Research issues: One of the things that meta-analysis fails to take into account is a study's quality. In good quality research looking at CBTp's effectiveness, participants are randomly allocated to treatment conditions. However, in many studies participants were not allocated in this way. Therefore, conclusions drawn from meta-analytic studies should be treated with extreme caution.

Complete the diagram: *Assessment:* The person's current symptoms and their origins are discussed with the therapist. *Engagement:* The therapist empathises with the person's distress. The **ABC** model: Ellis' approach is used to challenge the person's beliefs. *Normalisation:* This involves placing the person's own psychotic experiences on a continuum with normal experiences. Critical **collaborative** analysis: Gentle questioning is used to help the person understand their false beliefs, in an empathic and non-judgemental way. Developing **alternative** explanations: This involves enabling the person to produce healthier explanations for their behaviour.

Applying your knowledge: The aim of CBTp is to identify and correct distorted beliefs. The stimulus material is based on a study reported by Chadwick *et al.* (1996). They showed a patient video recordings of people talking and asked him to predict what would be said next. In 50 attempts, the patient failed to make any correct predictions, which appeared to be sufficient to change his belief that he did not have this ability after all.

Topic 7 Family therapy

Choose the right answer: C

Match them up: 1C 2D 3B 4A

Drawing conclusions: (a)

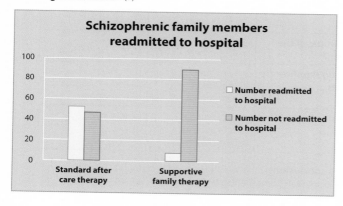

(b) 2 × 2 Chi-Squared. The researcher is looking for a difference and the data are at the nominal level of measurement. Additionally, an independent groups design has been used. (c) 5%. (d) The calculated value of Chi-Squared is actually 45.3, and the result is significant beyond the 5% level. The table indicates that significantly fewer schizophrenics are readmitted to hospital following supportive family therapy than standard after care therapy.

Applying your knowledge: One practical issue is that attending family therapy sessions makes demands on family members. These include time, motivation, energy, and even transport (and its associated costs). A second practical issue is the lack of preparation and specific training of therapists. A third practical issue is the lack of availability of this form of therapy within the mental health system. Other practical issues that are relevant include the need to understand the culture in which the family lives, and the cost-effectiveness of family therapy.

Topic 8 Token economy and the management of schizophrenia

Choose the right answer: C and D

Match them up: 1C 2A 3D 4B

Drawing conclusions: (a) The calculated value of 'S' is 2. 'S' is the number of times the least common difference occurs. There is one instance of the number of target behaviours remaining the same, eight of an increase in the number of target behaviours, and two of the number of target behaviours decreasing. (b) The value of N is 10. The tabled value at $p < 0.05$ is 1. Since the calculated value is greater than the tabled value, the difference is not significant at $p < 0.05$. (c) The introduction of the token economy system did not lead to a significant increase in the number of target behaviours performed. (d) Related t-test (e) Accepting the null hypothesis when it is false (i.e. concluding there is no difference or correlation when there is). (f) Parametric tests are more powerful than non-parametric tests, that is, they are more likely than non-parametric tests' to detect a difference or correlation.

Applying your knowledge: A reinforcer is defined in terms of its effect on behaviour. Anything that increases a behaviour is a reinforcer. A reward, by contrast, does not necessarily increase the probability of a behaviour it follows. Since Simon's 'reward' card makes him more likely to go to one petrol station in preference to any other, it could, as Matt suggests, be referred to as a 'reinforcement' card.

Topic 9 An interactionist approach

Choose the right answer: D

Match them up: 1B 2C 3D 4A

Applying your knowledge: Adrian has medium biological vulnerability and is experiencing stress. However, he is not schizophrenic. Barry has high biological vulnerability and is experiencing stress. He is schizophrenic. Chris has low biological vulnerability and is experiencing a lot of stress. However, he is not schizophrenic. Dave has moderate biological vulnerability and is experiencing some stress, but he is not schizophrenic. However, subsequent stressors impact on him and Dave develops schizophrenia.

Chapter 7 Eating behaviour

Topic 1 The evolutionary explanation for food preference

Choose the right answer: D

Fill in the boxes:

In each box below state one evolutionary food preference.	Then explain the adaptive advantage of each chosen food preference
Food preference 1: Fatty food	Fatty food would have provided our ancestors with a source of energy, to stay alive and find their next meal.
Food preference 2: Meat	Meat is full of nutrients and provides a catalyst for the growth of the brain, which helped humans to evolve into intelligent creatures.
Food preference 3: Sweet foods	Sweet foods provide vitamins and minerals that are necessary for bodily functions and growth, which were valuable to our ancestors in the EEA.
Taster aversion is… a learned response to eating toxic, spoiled or poisonous food.	This prevented our ancestors from eating poisonous foods more than once, helping to keep them alive.

Applying your knowledge: Abigail is experiencing food neophobia, which is characterised by a reluctance to consume new or unusual foods, especially animal products. However, as she became ill after trying the frogs' legs she is now experiencing taste a version which is a learned response to eating a food which made her ill.

Topic 2 The role of learning in food preference

Choose the right answer: C D

Drawing conclusions: The graph shows that the effect of advertising has a strong influence on the food preferences of all children. However, the results also show that males are significantly more influenced in comparison to females, although the females were more likely to desire unhealthy food, even when they were not exposed to any advertisements.

Applying your knowledge: Identify the psychology: One way in which Jamie Oliver could influence the eating behaviour of children would be to educate families. By educating families, he could make parents aware that their behaviours are often observed and copied by their children. Therefore, if the parents want their children to eat healthy food, they would need to engage with eating healthy foods themselves. Link to Jamie: Furthermore, Jamie could try and restrict the advertising of unhealthy foods, as the media has a major impact on what people eat and their attitudes towards foods. Therefore, if he can target advertising during children's television programmes he may be able to influence the eating behaviour of children.

A marking exercise: Unfortunately, this answer has not outlined cultural influences and has infact outlined social influences and would therefore be unlikely to receive any marks.

For example: Two cultural influences include the media and the growing reliance on takeaway food. Social learning can explain the role of television and other media on food preferences. The media may have a major impact on what people eat and their attitudes towards certain types of food, especially if advertising is focused on unhealthy food. In certain societies, like the US and UK, the desire for convenience foods is growing increasingly common and people learn to rely on takeaway meals as a way of feeding themselves.

Topic 3 Neural and hormonal mechanisms

Complete the diagram:

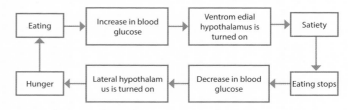

Choose the right answer: A

Match them up: 1B 2A 3D 4C

A marking exercise: This is a six-mark question; however, the answer only really contains two points and would therefore receive a maximum of 2 marks. The answer needs to develop the explanation of these hormones and their function. For example: There are two main hormones involved in the control of eating: ghrelin and leptin. Ghrelin is realised in the stomach and stimulates the hypothalamus to increase appetite. Ghrelin levels determine how quickly we feel hungry, as they go up drastically before we eat and then down for about three hours after a meal. Leptin is a hormone that plays a crucial role in appetite and weight control. It is normally produced by fat tissue and secreted into the bloodstream, where it travels to the brain to decrease appetite.

Topic 4 Biological explanations for anorexia nervosa

Choose the right answer: A

Match them up: 1Cii 2Ai 3Biv 4Diii

Write your own evaluation point: Point – One issue with the serotonin explanation of AN is that drug treatments involving serotonin are ineffective. Evidence – Ferguson *et al.* (1999) found no difference in the symptom outcomes for patients with AN, for those taking SSRIs and those who were not. Explain – This suggests that the serotonin explanation of AN does not provide a valid account of AN. Evaluate – However, there are numerous advantages with the biological explanation, for example explanations based on biological approach challenge the belief that AN is somehow the patients fault. Furthermore, they also offer the possibility of treating AN by regulating the brain areas involved in the behaviours associated with the disorder. Link – Therefore, although not every aspect of the biological approach is supported, the biological approach has helped improve the lives of many individuals suffering from AN.

A marking exercise: While this is a reasonable start to this answer, it only provides two key points and further elaboration is needed. For example: There are two neural explanations for AN, including serotonin and dopamine. Bailer *et al.* (2007) measured serotonin activity in women recovering from different types of anorexia, in comparison to healthy controls. They found higher levels of serotonin in women recovering from binge-eating/purging type anorexia, compared to the other two groups. Furthermore, Kaye *et al.* (2005) used PET scans to examine dopamine activity in patients recovering from AN. They found over activity of the dopamine receptors in the basal ganglia which is implicated in AN.

Topic 5 Family system theory and anorexia nervosa

Choose the right answer: D

Match them up: 1E 2C 3A 4D 5B

Research issues: While there are a range of ethical issues you could outline here, there are some which are more suitable to this particular experiment. For example: The researcher would need to consider privacy, as this is a particularly sensitive topic involving patients with AN. He/she would need to ensure that the patient and their family members control the flow of information from the interview and do not feel as though they have to answer any particular question(s).

Furthermore, the researcher would need to consider confidentiality and ensure that the data and information gathered remains anonymous and could not be traced back to the individual participants. Furthermore, any transcripts from the interviews must be coded or destroyed, following the interview process.

Applying your knowledge: There are two factors that might have contributed to Demelza's AN. Firstly, she has an enmeshed family, who are overly-involved with each other. For example, her mother insists on knowing everything about her children and will even read their diaries. This over-involvement might have stifled Demelza's ability to cope with everyday stressors and contribute to her AN. Secondly, her father is showing a high degree of control and over protectiveness, which may affect Demelza's belief about the amount of control she has in her own life. Consequently, Demelza may be rebelling against this control by refusing to eat.

Topic 6 Social learning theory and anorexia nervosa

Choose the right answer: C F

Drawing conclusions: The results suggest that the media has resulted in a decrease in BMI for both males and females, although the effect is larger in females than in males. There is a 2.7 decrease for females, in comparison to a 1.6 decrease for males.

The standard deviation is useful as it shows the variability in the scores. For example, the results reveal the spread of scores in 1998 were much more varied, suggesting that the media does not affect everyone equally.

Draw a graph:

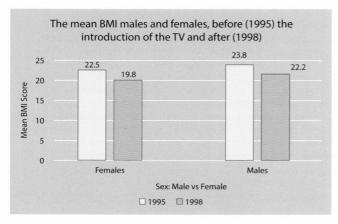

Applying your knowledge: There are two key influences that might be affecting Denise's behaviour. Firstly, she is reading lots of fitness magazines and therefore the media may have an impact on her body image and desire for thinness, especially if she has low self-esteem. Secondly, Denise's behaviour is being positively reinforced by her boyfriend who keeps telling her how great she looks, which will motivate her to continue skipping meals and going to the gym seven days a week.

Topic 7 Cognitive theory and anorexia nervosa

Choose the right answer 1: C

Choose the right answer 2: B

Research methods (calculations): 1) Time taken for food-related words mean score 3.26. Time taken for non-food words mean score 1.65. 2) The results suggest that patients with AN take longer to solve food-related words in comparison to non-food words, because of their cognitive preoccupations. Their attention is drawn to the food-related word which causes them to take longer when responding in the Stroop test.

A marking exercise: This is a very good answer which is likely to achieve 3 marks. Further elaboration is required to add to the definition.

Topic 8 Biological explanations for obesity

Choose the right answer: C (Hypothalamus not hippocampus)

Drawing conclusions: 1) The bar chart shows that obesity levels have increased in both males and females over a 20-year-period. Furthermore, the results show that obesity levels have gone up slightly more in males in comparison to females. 2) Here you could outline any two biological explanations for obesity, including genetics, neural (both leptin and the hypothalamus) and/or evolutionary explanations. For example: One biological explanation of obesity is that of genetics which suggests that we inherit obesity. Maes *et al.* (1997) conducted a meta-analysis and found heritability estimates for BMI of 74% in MZ twins and 32% in DZ twins, highlighting a large genetic component, as the more genes we share the more likely we are to inherit obesity. Another biological explanation of obesity comes from the role of the hormone leptin. Leptin is a hormone secreted by fat cells and acts to decrease feeding behaviour and promote energy expenditure. Leptin inhibits food intake and Bates and Myers (2003) found that disruption to leptin signalling, can result in obesity.

Key terms:

Key term	Key point	Key point
Genetic: Twin studies	Maes *et al.* (1997)	74% MZ twins, 32% DZ twins
Genetic: Adoption studies	Stunkard *et al.* (1986)	Strong relationship between weight of adopted individuals and biological parents
Neural: Hypothalamus	Arcuate nucleus	Malfunction leads to overeating
Neural: Leptin	Secreted by fat cells	Inhibits food intake
Evolution	The 'thrifty gene' hypothesis	Adaptive advantage

Research has identified a part of the hypothalamus called the arcuate nucleus which appears to play a role in appetite and obesity. Any malfunction in the area can lead to overeating.

Applying your knowledge: There are two key biological explanations that could support Daniel's view that his weight problem is inherited. Maes *et al.* (1997) conducted a meta-analysis and found heritability estimates for BMI of 74% in MZ twins and 32% in DZ twins, highlighting a large genetic component. Furthermore, Stunkard *et al.* (1989) examined 540 adult adoptees. They found a strong relationship between the weight category of adopted individuals and their biological parents, but no significant relationship with their adoptive parents, also suggesting a strong genetic link. These two studies highlight a genetic component with obesity and support Daniel's claim that his weight problem 'is not his fault'.

Topic 9 Psychological explanations for obesity

Choose the right answer: C – they are less sensitive

Drawing conclusions 1: The participants who weren't on a diet (the unrestrained eaters) ate less of the ice cream if they had already had the milkshake (the preload), prior to the ice cream tasting. However, participants who were on a diet (i.e. restrained eaters) reacted differently. Those who had not had the milkshake were very restrained when tasting the ice cream. However, those who had already had the milkshake ate more ice cream. In fact, the bigger the preload, the more ice cream they ate.

Drawing conclusions 2: The data in Table 1 shows that restrained eaters clearly eat more dishes than unrestrained eaters. The boundary model would argue that restrained eaters have a higher biological satiety level. Furthermore, the preload may have taken them beyond the 'what the hell effect' at which point they continued eating until they feel satiated. The unrestrained eaters are more full after their preload and simply have to eat less to become satiated.

Applying your knowledge: According to the boundary model, Joseph, who is trying to be restrained may have a higher biological satiety level. Furthermore, once he starts eating he goes through his self-imposed boundary and experiences the 'what the hell effect' and continues to eat the entire bag, before feeling satiated.

Topic 10 Explanations for the success and failure of dieting

Choose the right answer: D

Match them up: 1D 2C 3A 4B 5E

Applying your knowledge: Jasmine's diets are likely to fail because she is getting bored. According to Redden, people like experiences less the more they repeat them, so as she becomes accustomed to each diet, they're more likely to fail. For a diet to work Jasmine must focus on the particular details of a meal, rather than considering the meal as a whole, this will stop her from getting bored and help her to maintain her diet.

Chapter 8 Stress

Topic 1 The physiology of stress

Choose the right answer: A D and F

Match them up: 1D 2A 3E 4B 5C

Drawing conclusions: (a) It is primary data because it has been collected from participants directly (or 'first-hand'), rather than gathered from reports of previous research. (b) One strength of primary data is that first-hand data can be controlled, whereas secondary data may have been gathered under differing conditions. Other explanations include less peripheral/redundant information, and the fact that the data gathered is more likely to be focused on the purpose of the research. (c) The scattergram shows a positive correlation. As scores on the adrenaline measure increase, they tend to increase on the perceived stress measure. (d) Spearman's rank order method or Pearson's 'r' method. Both are tests for a correlation between two variables. Spearman's is appropriate to use with data that are at least ordinal in nature. Pearson's is appropriate when the data are at least interval in nature. (e) Just because two variables are correlated, it does not necessarily mean that a change in one is causing a change in the other (i.e. causality cannot be inferred on the basis of correlation alone).

Applying your knowledge: The stimulus would have activated the sympathomedullary pathway, and the sympathetic branch of the viewer's autonomic nervous system would have been activated, causing the fight-or-flight response. The viewer would probably have perceived this most in terms of elevated heart rate. The adrenal medulla would have released adrenaline and noradrenaline into the bloodstream, which would have targeted her key organs including her heart. When the stimulus was terminated, the parasympathetic branch of the autonomic nervous system would have dampened down the reaction, and returned the body to its normal state. However, this does not occur immediately, so the viewer would have continued to experience a heightened state of physiological arousal for a while afterwards (as can clearly be seen in the video!).

Topic 2 The role of stress in illness

Choose the right answer: C and E

Match them up: 1D 2B 3A 4C

Research issues: (a) The hypothesis was directional. The researcher clearly specified the direction the difference would take ('wounds would take *longer* to heal'). (b) The researcher was looking for a difference and an independent groups design was used. Additionally, the data were at least at the ordinal level of measurement. (c) Independent t-test. (d) A Type I error occurs when the null hypothesis is rejected when it should have been accepted (i.e. the researcher concludes that there is a significant difference/correlation when there isn't). We are told that the difference was significant at $p < 0.05$, so the probability of a Type I error being made is 5/100 (5%). (e) The researcher has concluded that caring for relatives is the causal factor affecting wound-healing time. However, we do not know to what extent other consequences of caring for a relative with dementia (such as sleep disturbances) affect the immune system's functioning.

Applying your knowledge: Kirkup and Merrick (2003) propose that losing a home game may lead to anger, frustration, or depression among supporters. All of these are known to increase the risk of heart attacks and strokes. Stroke rates are also known to be higher in association with mental stress, particularly depression. The lack of an effect on women might reflect differences in interest in football between men and women. Kirkup and Merrick say that home defeats are widely accepted to be the worst result for a team. Supporters have lower expectations away from home, but are predisposed to anticipate a victory in a home game. The article on which this activity is based can be found at: http://jech.bmj.com/content/57/6/429.full.

Topic 3 Sources of stress: Life changes

Choose the right answer: A and D.

Fill in the boxes:

Life changes can be defined as. events that require major adjustment in some aspect of our life, and are believed to be significant sources of stress.	An example of a life change is... marriage (or any of the other 42 events on the SRRS).
The researchers who devised the SRRS are... Holmes and Rahe (1967).	The number of life changes on the SRRS is... 43.
A life change unit is... a number assigned to each life change to represent how stressful it is judged to be.	The life change which has the highest life change unit is... death of a spouse (100 life change units).
An alternative to the SRRS is... the Schedule of Recent Experiences (SRE).	Researchers who used this scale in their study are... Rahe *et al.* (1970).

Research issues: (a) There is a positive correlation between scores on the SRRS and estimated number of days taken off through sickness in the previous year. (b) Internal validity refers to how accurately a test or measuring instrument measures what it says it measures. (c) Volunteer sampling (d) One limitation of this sampling method is that the sample is likely to be non-representative, making the findings difficult to generalise. (e) The study is looking for a correlation, and the data collected is at least at the ordinal level of measurement. Additionally, the test is suitable for pairs of scores, and there is a linear relationship between the scores. (f) Pearson's 'r' (g) The table for Pearson's 'r' can be found on page 31 of the Complete Companion Student Book. For a directional hypothesis (one-tailed), at the p < 0.05 level, with N = 12, the tabled value is .475. There is *not* a significant correlation between the two variables. With Pearson's 'r', the reported correlation (.27) must be *equal to or greater* than the appropriate tabled value (.475). Since it isn't, the null hypothesis cannot be rejected.

Applying your knowledge: Munya's first evaluation point ('It's too simplistic.') relates to the fact that the SRRS ignores the possibility that the same life change may be more (or less) stressful for some people than others, and that a better measure of life changes would take individual differences in the perception of stressors into account. His second point ('It doesn't apply to students like us.') echoes Lazarus's (1990) point that major life changes are relatively rare for most people, and the additional point that at least some of the changes on the SRRS are unlikely to have been experienced by students (e.g. 'jail term', 'divorce', 'retirement'). A scale which might be more appropriate for students such as Munya and Nadia is the 'College Student's Stress Event Checklist', which can be found at: https://eoss.asu.edu/sites/default/files/StressChecklist_0.pdf

Munya's third point ('It relies on you having a really good memory.') refers to the fact that respondents have to recall events that have happened to them, and that the memory is sometimes fallible. That said, research (e.g. Hardt *et al.*, 2006) indicates that reliability for retrospective reports of life events actually are reliable.

Topic 4 Sources of stress: Daily hassles

Choose the right answer: C D

Match them up: 1A 2C 3D 4B

Research issues: (a) Content analysis is a method for analysing various kinds of qualitative data. Categories can be established and observations falling into the categories can be counted (qualitative). Alternatively, data can be analysed in terms of its themes (qualitative). (b) One approach would be to watch some of the recordings from the head-cams and identify instances of instances that could be described as 'hassles'. These could include things like 'finding the canteen has run out of sandwiches', 'having to queue to enrol', and so on. The two researchers would have come to an agreement on what counted as a 'hassle' and then watched the twenty recordings, counting the number of hassles each student experienced. (c) Two ways in which reliability could be intra-rater reliability (test-retest reliability) and inter-rater reliability. Since there are two researchers watching the recordings, they could content analyse them independently and then compare their observations. If their observations are reliable, then a strong positive correlation should be found. (d) The prediction is non-directional since the researchers are predicting that that there will be a difference in the number of hassles experienced by males and females without specifying the direction the difference will take. (e) One non-parametric test is the Mann-Whitney U test. It is a test for a difference and can be used with an independent groups design. Additionally, the data is at least at the ordinal level of measurement. (f) The difference is significant at p<0.02. The probability of a Type I error (rejecting the null hypothesis when it is true) is less than 2 in 100. (g) The table for Spearman's rho can be found on page 30 of The Complete Companion Student Book. For a non-directional hypothesis (two-tailed), at the p<0.02 level, with N = 10, the tabled value is .648. With Spearman's rho, the reported correlations must be *equal to or greater* than the appropriate tabled value of .648. For males (.66) it is, and therefore the correlation is significant. However, for females (.63) it isn't, and therefore the correlation is not significant.

Applying your knowledge: You need to find a way of summarising the findings from research into daily hassles and uplifts, namely that daily hassles have been shown to be negatively correlated with psychological and physical well-being whereas uplifts have been shown to be positively correlated with psychological and physical well-being. One example is: '@Liza Research shows daily hassles are negatively, and daily uplifts positively, correlated with psychological and physical well-being.' This tweet has 135 characters!

Topic 5 Sources of stress: Workplace stress

Choose the right answer: D

Research issues: In this kind of study, the most obvious ethical issue is confidentiality. Participants, and the data gained from them, must be kept anonymous *unless* they give their full consent for their names to be used. The questionnaire included questions about extremely sensitive issues (e.g. sabotage). Researchers have no legal obligation to disclose criminal acts, and have to determine which is the most important consideration – their duty to the participants vs. their duty to the wider community. Any decision to disclose information has to be set in the context of the aims of the research. (Other ethical issues could be chosen and would be valid.)

Research methods: (a) Low degree of control mean = 65/10 = 6.5. High degree of control mean = 34/10 = 3.4. (b) There is a very low score in the low degree of control group (the rating of 1), which makes the mean artificially low for that group. (c) Median and mode (d) Standard deviation (or range) (e) Independent t-test (f) Mann-Witney U test (g) The rating scale is at least at the ordinal level.

Applying your knowledge: Homer is experiencing work overload. Because the type of work is too hard for him, it is called *qualitative work overload*. Moe finds his job too easy, and is experiencing *qualitative work underload*. Lenny is experiencing work overload. However, he has too much work to do and not enough time to do it. This is called *quantitative work overload*. Karl doesn't have enough work to do, so he is experiencing *quantitative work underload*. Note that Moe makes reference to 'being his own boss', so he has a high degree of control, which the other three, as employees, might not.

Topic 6 Measuring stress: Self-report scales and physiological measures

Choose the right answer: A C

Fill in the boxes:

Scale	Total number of items	How the scale is completed	One strength of the measure	One weakness of the measure
SRRS	43	The respondent identifies which of the changes has occurred within some specified time period.	It has some predictive validity, and correlates, to some extent, with the likelihood of future illness.	It does not take into account individual differences in the perception of stressors.
HSUP	252	The respondent rates each of the items on a 3-point scale with reference to a specific time period.	Like the SRRS, it has some predictive validity, and correlates, to some extent, with psychological and physical dysfunction.	The scale is time-consuming to complete, since it has 252 items for participants to respond to.

Drawing conclusions: (a) The teaching staff (b) The administrative staff (c) The administrative staff (d) Marks would be awarded here for correctly labelled axes, an appropriate title, and an accurate bar chart. (e) The teaching staff appears to be the most stressed, since they have the highest hassles score and lowest uplifts score. The students appear to be the least stressed, since they have the lowest hassles score and highest uplifts score. The administrative staff are mid-way between the teachers and students. Other conclusions are possible. For example, the hassles score for the teachers is twice that of the students, and the students have an uplifts score four-and-a-times that of the administrative staff.

Applying your knowledge: Mizti's slogan is helping her to remember that test-retest (intra-test) is one way of assessing reliability; if a measurement is reliable then more-or-less the same score should be obtained when participants complete the test at Time 1 and again at Tiime 2. Her slogan also helps here to remember that a measure's validity can be assessed by correlating score on it with scores on a test which is known to measure the variable in question. This is called *concurrent validity*.

Topic 7 Individual differences in stress: Personality

Choose the right answer: C and E

Key words:

Personality type	Key term 1	Key term 2
Type A	Time pressure, competitiveness, anger	Higher risk of CHD
Type B	Easy going and relaxed	Lower risk of CHD
Type C	Suppress negative emotions	Possibly linked with cancer

Possible answer: The Type A personality is characterised by time pressure, competitiveness, and anger. By contrast, the Type B personality is easy-going and relaxed. Research shows that Type A personalities are at significantly higher risk of developing some form of CHD compared with Type Bs. Type Cs experience negative emotions, but unlike other personalities they suppress those emotions. Whereas Type A behaviour has been linked with CHD, some research suggests that Type C personality is possibly linked with cancer.

Drawing conclusions: Amongst other things, the findings suggest that Type As are more likely than Type Bs to suffer from some sort of CHD (heart attacks, recurring heart attack, and fatal heart attacks). Type As are nearly three times more likely than Type Bs to suffer fatal heart attacks, and over three times more likely than Type Bs to suffer recurring heart attacks. Type As are twice as likely as Type Bs to suffer a single heart attack.

Applying your knowledge (a) Ben (b) Oliver (c) Sanya (d) Oliver (e) Sanya (f) Ben

Topic 8 Individual differences in stress: Hardiness

Choose the right answer: B and D

Research methods: (a) The hypothesis is two-tailed since the direction of the association has not been specified. (b) There is no association between participants' scores on the 3Cs and the companies concern or otherwise about their absenteeism. (c) Nominal (d) The mode (e) A Chi-Squared test (2 x 2). (f) One disadvantage is social desirability responding (especially given the sensitive nature of the topic being studied!). Participants may give the answer they believe will make them appear in a 'good light'. (g) Deception. This could be dealt with at the end of the study by debriefing participants as to the real purpose of using the questionnaire.

Applying your knowledge 1: After the costs of absenteeism have been deducted, the company is left with £900,000 profit. If the expert can guarantee a saving of at least 50%, then the company's loss to absenteeism would be reduced to £50,000, leaving it with a profit of £950,000. Subtracting the £25,000 cost of the training course leaves a total profit of £925,000. This leaves the company £25,000 better off than it would be given the budget officer's decision. Therefore, he made the wrong decision.

Applying your knowledge 2: The first lecturer is low in challenge and sees change as a threat ('Next year they want me to teach a subject I've never taught before.'). The lecturer is also low in commitment (he is not willing to work outside his contracted hours) and has a low degree of control (he doesn't get a choice in which classes are taught). The second lecturer scores highly on the 3Cs. He would 'jump at the opportunity' to teach a new course (challenge), 'wants the college to be the best' (commitment), and is allowed to 'just get on with my job' (control). The second lecturer is clearly the hardier of the two.

Topic 9 Managing and coping with stress: Drug therapies

Choose the right answer 1: C and E

Choose the right answer 2: A and E

Research issues: A demand characteristic is a cue that makes participants unconsciously aware of the aims of a study or helps participants work out what the researcher expects to find. An investigator effect is anything that an investigator does that has an effect on a participant's performance in a study other than what was intended. Clearly, if the participant knows that she has been given the drug that is being investigated, her behaviour is likely to change. Equally, if a researcher knows that the participant has been given the drug her behaviour is likely to change as well. RCTs overcome both of these issues. When neither the participant nor

Activities: suggested answers

researcher are aware of whether the participant has been given the drug or a placebo, the term 'double blind control' is used.

Fill in the boxes: Reading downwards for BZs: Yes No Yes Yes Yes Yes Reading downwards for BBs: Yes No No No Yes Yes

Applying your knowledge: How you answer this depends on the value you place on the 'yes' and 'no' answers. For example, while the finding that the drugs are effective is a strength of drug therapy, the fact that drugs only address the symptoms of stress is a weakness. However, does the strength outweigh the weakness? Being able to argue this kind of issue is necessary for your AO3 to be credited as effective. BBs would appear to have advantages over BZs, but the issue about only addressing the symptoms is also a weakness for BBs!

Topic 10 Managing and coping with stress: Stress inoculation therapy

Choose the right answer: B and D

Fill in the boxes 1: Skill acquisition, rehearsal, and consolidation; Conceptualisation; Conceptualisation; Application and follow-through; Skill acquisition, rehearsal, and consolidation; Application and follow-through.

Fill in the boxes 2: Reading downwards: Yes Yes No No No No

Applying your knowledge: The advice given will depend (a) on whether BZs or BBs are chosen, and (b) the weight you assign to each of the strengths/weaknesses. For example, SIT and BBs are both effective, do not lead to biological dependence, and do not have unpleasant side effects. However, SIT requires time/effort whereas BBs do not. BBs are also widely available and relatively inexpensive compared with SIT. SIT addresses the causes of stress whereas BBs do not.

Topic 11 Managing and coping with stress: biofeedback

Choose the right answer: C and D

Drawing conclusions: One finding is that more people who received biofeedback training showed a reduction in physiological activity (36) than showed no change or an increase (14). Biofeedback would therefore seem to be effective for at least some people who are trained in its use.

Fill in the boxes: Reading downwards: Yes Yes No No No Yes

Applying your knowledge: As in the previous chapter, the advice given will depend (a) on whether BZs or BBs are chosen, and (b) the weight you assign to each of the strengths/weaknesses. All three therapies are effective and (if BBs have been chosen) none lead to biological dependence or have unpleasant side effects. However, BBs do not address the causes of stress, which the other two do. BBs do not require time/effort which the other two do. BBs and biofeedback are widely available and relatively inexpensive compared with SIT. Chris will need a table just like the one you have constructed in this activity to make an informed judgement!

Topic 12 Gender differences in coping with stress

Choose the right answer: D

Fill in the boxes: Problem-focused coping style: This can be defined as a way to cope with stress by tackling the factor(s) causing the stress, often in a practical way. An example is doing something, such as providing money. The gender this is typically seen in is men. Emotion-focused coping style: This can be defined as a way to cope with stress by tackling its symptoms. An example is focusing on the anxiety a person is feeling. The gender this is typically seen in is women.

Match them up: 1C 2A 3D 4B

Research issues: Validity refers to whether something measures what it says it measures. Self-report scales typically involve retrospective recall of information and are liable to social desirability responding. Both of these seriously threaten the validity of self-report scales.

Applying your knowledge: Charlie is showing the typical male response to stress in which adrenaline, noradrenaline and testosterone levels rise, leading to aggression. Kitty, by contrast, is displaying the typical female tend-and-befriend response, possibly as a result of unsuppressed oxytocin production.

Topic 13 The role of social support in coping with stress

Choose the right answer: C

Fill in the boxes: Emotional support: This involves focusing on the anxiety a person is feeling, and trying to reduce it. An example is offering advice. Esteem support: This involves increasing a person's sense of self-worth. An example is making a person feel better about themselves. Instrumental support: This involves offering direct aid and material resources. An example is providing money.

Research issues: (a) Since this is a partial replication of Nabi *et al's* (2013) study, a one-tailed hypothesis can be justified. (b) The scattergram shows a weak positive correlation. (c) Pearson's 'r' assumes that the data are at the interval level of measurement, the populations are assumed to have a normal distribution, and the variances of the samples are assumed to be the same. (d) Spearman's rho. (e) The sample size is 13 and the hypothesis is one-tailed. At the $p < 0.05$ level, the tabled value is .484. Since the calculated value (.30) is smaller than the table value, the null hypothesis cannot be rejected. On this occasion, then, the student has failed to replicate Nabi *et al's* findings.

Applying your knowledge: Based on Bailey and Dua's (1999) research, we might expect to find that Bruce (an Australian) would seek instrumental social support, whereas Ravi (an Indian) would seek emotional support. Based on Lucknow *et al's* (1998) research, we might expect Sally to seek emotional support, while Steve might be expected to seek instrumental support. However, we don't know to what extent culture and gender interact, so Sally (as a woman from an individualistic culture) and Ravi (as a man from a collectivist culture) are, perhaps, the more difficult to predict.

Chapter 9 Aggression

Topic 1 Neural and hormonal influences

Choose the right answer: A D

Research issues: There are several strengths of longitudinal studies. One is that they are ideal for conducting research on developmental trends. Unlike cross-sectional studies, in which different people with the same characteristics are compared, longitudinal studies track the same people. Consequently, any differences seen are much less likely to be the result of cultural differences across age groups. However, longitudinal studies also have weaknesses. One is that they require a large amount of time to collect all the data that is needed. They also suffer from 'drop out', which reduces the data that can be used.

Drawing conclusions: (a) Volunteer sampling (b) One limitation is that because people self-select, the sample could be biased and the results would be difficult to generalise to the population from which the sample was drawn. (c) Random allocation is used as a way of trying to distribute participant variables evenly across the two groups (although this cannot be guaranteed, of course). (d) Being given a drug that suppressed testosterone so that all participants had similar levels for the study. (e) Mann-Whitney U test (or Unrelated t-test). An independent groups design was used, and the researcher was looking for a difference. Additionally, the data are at least at the ordinal level.

Applying your knowledge: Determinism is the view that an individual's behaviour is controlled by either internal or external forces. Free will refers to the belief that people are capable of self-determination and can therefore freely choose their actions. At first sight, Whitman would appear to be a case of biological determinism. His case is a good one to use for the free will and determinism debate.

Topic 2 Genetic factors in aggression

Choose the right answer: D

Drawing conclusions : (a) There are five MZ twin pairs and three are concordant for aggression. Therefore, the concordance rate is 3/5 or 60%. (b) There are five DZ twin pairs and two are concordant for aggression. Therefore, the concordance rate is 2/5 or 40%. (c) Both types of twin share environments. However, MZs share all of the genes whereas DZs do not. The higher concordance rate in MZs suggests that genetic factors at least play a role in aggressive behaviour.

Applying your knowledge: (1) Families typically share environments as well as genes. (2) More than one gene usually contributes to a given behaviour. (3) Genes and environment may interact with each other. Genetic factors may affect which environmental factors have an influence, and *vice versa*.

Topic 3 The ethological explanation of aggression

Choose the right answer: C

Match them up: 1D 2A 3B 4C

Drawing conclusions:

(a)

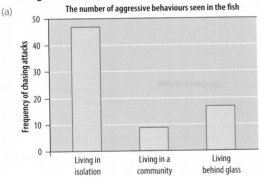

The number of aggressive behaviours seen in the fish

Frequency of chasing attacks (y-axis, 0–50)

Living in isolation / Living in a community / Living behind glass

(b) Aggression was lowest when the fish were with other fish in a communal tank, and highest when they were kept in isolation from other fish. An intermediate amount of aggression was seen when the fish were kept behind a glass screen that allowed them to see fish in the other section of the tank. (c) It is possible that action-specific energy increased in the isolated male. Because this energy needed to be released, the male became aggressive towards the female sharing the tank with him.

Applying your knowledge: Unwittingly, Tom has given Duncan an evaluation point about ritualised aggression. The culture in question (actually the Dani of New Guinea) do not lack an ability to use their knowledge in a practical way. What is likely is that they are practising a form of 'arms limitation' (Marsh, 1978); they are well aware that putting flights on to arrows would result in more deaths of rival group members. However, if they use flights, then their opponents will do the same, and more members of their own group will be killed. By 'fighting' in this ritualised way, neither group will suffer as badly as would otherwise be the case.

Topic 4 Evolutionary explanations of human aggression

Choose the right answer: D

Research issues: (a) Given the socially sensitive nature of the MRI, issues of anonymity and confidentiality would need to be addressed before the study began. (b) One limitation of the MRI is that respondents may not give truthful answers (for whatever reason). Researchers must assume that respondents are answering truthfully, when they may be answering in a socially desirable way.

Drawing conclusions: (a) There will be no positive correlation between how violent gang members are as assessed by self- and peer-ratings and their status within the gang (and any correlation there is reflects the operation of chance factors). (b) One-tailed. The hypothesis states the direction the correlation will take (positive). (c) The researcher predicted a correlation and the data are at least at the ordinal level. (d) The correlation is significant. The tabled value (see page 31 of the Complete Companion book for the Critical Value Table) for a one-tailed test at p < 0.05 is .564. Since the calculated value (.61) is greater than the table value, the null hypothesis can be rejected. (e) Just because two variables are correlated, it does not necessarily mean that a change in one causes a change in the other. Just because the more violent the gang members were, the higher their status within the gang, this does not mean that being more violent causes this status increase. Correlations do not permit us to infer causality.

Applying your knowledge: The scenario suggests that evolutionary explanations of aggression might not be true. Aggressive behaviour may not always be adaptive, and may actually be maladaptive. Rather than being accepted as a mate for behaving aggressively, aggression may lead to a male being rejected as a potential mate. In this case, Nicholas' attempt at behaving aggressively, by starting a fight with other men, has led to him being rejected by Denise. This challenges the claims made by evolutionary explanations that aggressive displays will attract a mate.

Topic 5 The frustration–aggression hypothesis

Choose the right answer: D

Research issues: The confederate directed sarcastic comments towards the children at the same time he frustrated them. It is possible that the comments provoked anger, and it is therefore impossible to determine whether the children in the frustration group later demonstrated greater aggression against the confederate than those in the control group because of his frustrating actions, his comments, or both of these factors.

Drawing conclusions: (a) The hypothesis was one-tailed. The researcher specified the direction the difference would take ('People who were second in line would feel *more* aggressive than those who were twelfth in line.'). (b) One strength is that field experiments tend to have higher external validity (greater 'mundane realism'). One limitation is that field experiments tend to have lower internal validity, since it is more difficult to control extraneous and confounding variables. (c) Mann-Whitney U test. The researcher is looking for a difference and an independent groups design has been used. Additionally, the data are at the ordinal level at least. (d) Peer review is the process by which psychological research papers, before publication, are subjected to independent scrutiny by other psychologists working in a similar field who consider the research in terms of its validity, significance and originality. (e) The aim of this study was to test the frustration–aggression hypothesis. A male research assistant was instructed to push in front of a person who was either second or twelfth in line. This was done ten times in each condition. After each person had bought their ticket, they were asked to rate how aggressive they felt towards the research assistant on a 7-point scale, with a higher value indicating more aggression. The average rating was 5.9 for the second in line group and 2.4 for the twelfth in line group. It was concluded that how close a person is to reaching their goal has a strong effect on how much frustration they experience, and that this is reflected has an effect on how aggressive they feel.

Applying your knowledge: This activity relates to Pastore's (1952) research. Pastore found that people said they would be angrier if a bus they were waiting for simply didn't stop (unjustified) than if it didn't stop but had an 'out of service sign' clearly displayed (justified). Reasons for train delays that people see as being justified (e.g. a passenger being taken ill) are less frustrating, and produce less aggression, than those that people see as being unjustified (e.g. 'strong sunlight' or the 'wrong kind of snow').

Topic 6   Social learning theory (SLT)

Choose the right answer: C

Research issues 1: Safety: The stated aim of Bandura *et al*'s study was to increase aggressive tendencies in young children by exposing them to aggressive role models. Modern codes of ethical conduct would consider this 'mental harm'. Consent: According to Bandura, consent was only obtained from the children's teachers. Consent should have been sought from parents or guardians. Confidentiality: The participants were children, so all information should have been kept confidential. However, videos of the experiment were published and widely circulated, violating standards for consent (and, indeed, privacy).

Research issues 2: In Bandura *et al*'s study, researchers pre-tested the children for how aggressive they were. This was done by observing them in the nursery and judging their aggression on four 5-point scales. This enabled the researchers to match the children in each group. Using inter-rater reliability, the reliability of two or more observers' ratings was assessed by measuring the correlation for 51 of the children. The correlation coefficient was .89, indicating strong agreement between the observers about the children's behaviour.

A marking exercise: The answer received 0 marks because it is an outline of one limitation of Bandura *et al*.'s study rather than SLT as an explanation of human aggression. A better answer would have drawn on knowledge from the first year course, when SLT was studied as an approach in psychology. An appropriate answer might be the following: SLT makes little reference to the role of biological factors in behaviour. In Bandura's own studies, it was found that boys were often more aggressive than girls regardless of the nature of the experiment. This could be explained by hormonal factors, such as differences in testosterone, a hormone that is present in greater quantities in boys than girls and which is linked to increased aggressive behaviour.

Applying your knowledge: When we imitate someone's behaviour because we have seen them being rewarded for it, it is called vicarious reinforcement. In football, players are often seen arguing with the referee and 'getting away with it', which is rewarding, so the behaviour is vicariously reinforced. Whereas in rugby, players do not question the referee's decision, even if they know it is wrong, for fear of being immediately sent off the pitch. Being sent off is a punishment and so if they see someone else being sent off, they are less likely to repeat the behaviour themselves.

Topic 7   De-individuation

Choose the right answer: B E

Research methods: The calculated value of Chi-Squared is 9.67. (a) There will be a difference in the extent to which warriors who change their appearance and those who do not kill, torture, or mutilate their victims. (b) At $p < 0.05$, for a two-tailed test, and with one degree of freedom, the tabled value of Chi-Squared is 3.84. Since the calculated value (9.67) is bigger than the tabled value, the null hypothesis can be rejected at the $p < 0.05$ level. (c) Warriors who change their appearance are significantly

more likely than warriors who do not change their appearance to engage in high levels of killing, torture, and mutilation.

Drawing conclusions: For example: Finding 1: 8% of children stole something when they were alone and identifiable compared with 21% who were alone but anonymous. Conclusion 1: Stealing was nearly three times more likely when a child is alone but anonymous. Finding 2: 57% of children stole when they were anonymous and in a group, compared with 21% who were in a group but identifiable. Conclusion 2: Being anonymous and in a group led to the highest amount of stealing.

Applying your knowledge: Aveni (1977) points out that approaches to the study of crowds have tended to focus attention on the individual level of behaviour and to ignore group-level behaviour. Aveni's found that people celebrating a football victory were in *groups* (i.e. with friends). This finding challenges Zimbardo's belief that being in a large crowd gives people a 'cloak of anonymity' that diminishes any personal consequences for their actions. It is hard to be anonymous with your friends! According to Aveni, more research should be done on group-level phenomena in the conceptualisation of 'crowd behaviour'.

Topic 8   Institutional aggression in prisons

Choose the right answer: D

Fill in the boxes:

	Factors influencing aggression	First example of a factor	Second example of a factor	Main reason for prisoner aggression
Deprivation model	Prison specific variables	Loss of liberty	Loss of autonomy	Coping with the need for respect and fairness
Importation model	Dispositional characteristics	Anti-social personality	Impulsivity	Using violent pasts as coping mechanisms

A marking exercise: The second paragraph was awarded no marks because it is not true. There *is* evidence that supports the situational explanation. There are also several limitations of the situational explanation, such as the following: One limitation of the situational explanation is that it has not always been supported by research. For example, Harer and Steffenmeier (1996) collected data from American prisons, including importation variables, such as race, and deprivation variables, such as security levels. They found that only the importation variables were significant predictors of prison violence. This shows that the deprivation model may not be an adequate predictor of institutional aggression.

Applying your knowledge: One 'very good reason' is that if most violence occurs in overheated, noisy and overcrowded environments, then decreasing these factors should reduce aggression. This is what Wilson (2010) did at HMP Woodhill and found a large reduction in assaults on prison staff and other inmates. These findings suggest that situational variables are at least one cause of prison violence, and can be successfully applied to reduce prison violence.

Topic 9   Media influences on aggression

Choose the right answer: C

Research issues: One strength of content analysis is that it has high ecological validity. The method involves analysing samples of *real* artefacts from things like TV programmes, songs, and so on. One weakness of content analysis in studies of media influence is that different researchers may interpret the meanings of material and the behavioural categories or coding systems differently, due to observer bias. Therefore, content analysis may lack reliability and internal validity.

Match them up: 1B 2D 3A 4C

Drawing conclusions: (a) Students who played the violent video game responded much more aggressively than those who played the non-violent video game on all three dependent variables (thoughts, feelings and actions) did. (b) Mann-Whitney U test (c) An independent groups design has been used, and a difference is being looked for. Additionally, the data are at least at the ordinal level.

Applying your knowledge: This activity relates to Przybylski *et al.*'s (2014) research. They found that aggressive behaviour may be due to the player's frustration and failure during a game, rather than the violent storyline. Apparently, 'Super Hexagon' (iOS, 2013) is one of the hardest games ever, the aim simply being to survive for as long as possible. It could be that the brother playing this game is finding it difficult to master, and that this is leading to frustration and aggression.

Topic 10 Explanations of media influences

Choose the right answer: C E

Research issues: One ethical issue that arises with this method is that participants are led to believe that they are delivering electric shocks to another participant. Thus, the method uses deception. One way in which this issue can be dealt with is by debriefing participants after the study is over. They should be told about the deception that was used and why it was necessary to use it.

Fill in the boxes:

	Definition	Application
Desensitisation	Media violence may lead to aggression by removing anxiety about behaving aggressively. The more violence that is watched, the more acceptable aggression becomes.	Long-term
Disinhibition	Watching or playing violent media may change our usual standards of what is considered acceptable behaviour. Exposure to violent media can legitimise the use of violence because it undermines usual inhibitory social sanctions.	Short- and long-term
Cognitive priming	Constant exposure to violent media activates aggressive thoughts/ideas about violence, which then 'prime' other aggressive thoughts through their associations in memory pathways.	Short-term

Match them up: 1B 2A 3D 4C

Applying your knowledge: The study appears to offer support for desensitisation theory. It could be argued that playing violent games desensitised the players to the violent images, and this is reflected in the smaller brain response as compared with those who played the non-violent game. The study was originally done by Engelhardt *et al.* (2011). They found that participants showed a reduction in the P3 component of the event-related brain potential to violent images, and that this is evidence of a neural marker which can at least partially account for the causal link between violent game exposure and desensitisation.

Chapter 10 Forensic psychology

Topic 1 Defining and measuring crime

Choose the right answer 1: A

Choose the right answer 2: C (This would be a breach of contract, which is a civil offence not a crime)

Research issues: (a) The people who took part may have more time available to answer questions, or be more keen to support the law. (b) 75/100 x 50,000 x 2.3 = 86,250 people. 80% of 86,250 = 69,000 aged 16 and over (c) Murders and manslaughters (as the victims are dead) OR victimless crimes such as shoplifting (d) Domestic abuse may not be mentioned if the abuser is present OR victims who feel ashamed such as rape victims may keep their experiences secret. (e) It is not representative of the population as, for example, homeless people may be especially vulnerable to crimes such as violence and rape, but are not included.

Drawing conclusions: (a) 5,532 / (5,532 + 29,819) x 100 = 15.6% (b) (348 + 546 + 2,522) / (348 + 536 + 2,522 + 5,021) x 100 = 40.5%

(c)

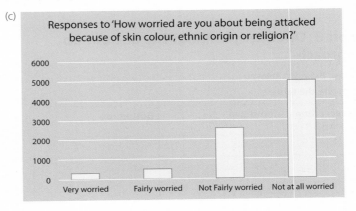

(d) The data collected is only gathered from households and so does not include the views of homeless people. This means that people such as refugees and migrants (who may be worried about crime) are not included in the survey and so the data collected is not a true observation of the fear of crime.

Topic 2 Offender profiling: The top-down approach

Research issues: Potential offenders might be able to read the articles and find out how to mislead investigators by leaving confusing clues. This creates an ethical dilemma; should forensic psychologists keep this information out of the public domain?

Applying your knowledge 1: Identify the psychology: Collect all details of the crimes and scenes, no matter how trivial. Look for patterns using intuition and experience. Classify as organised or disorganised. Construct a profile of the offender. Use to assess the crimes, reconsidering the profile as new evidence or suspects emerge. Link to the investigation: Saga and Henrik should collect every detail of all the crimes, and look for patterns, such as the staging of the bodies. They will use their experience and intuition to help them, but try not to get fixed on a particular suspect and miss other possible explanations. This murderer is likely to be an organised type, as the bodies were staged after death. A profile might suggest the likely background, habits and beliefs of the offender and will help them develop a strategy for catching the offender.

Drawing conclusions: (a) Both groups rated the profile as highly accurate (4 = neutral on a 7-point Likert scale), and there was no difference between the mean accuracy ratings. However, there was a greater standard deviation in scores in Group B, so there was more variation in scores of accuracy of the fabricated offender, showing that police had more varied opinions about the accuracy in this group. (b) The police were not able to match the genuine offender any better than the fabricated one, despite differences in their characteristics, so these profiles may not be very useful for identifying an offender. (c) As the median is 6 it suggests that the bulk of the scores are high but that a few extreme low scores skew the mean (5.3) and result in a negative skewed distribution.

Applying your knowledge: 2(a) Luke could identify behavioural categories that would match each group's profile, for example organised offenders move the body away from the crime scene; disorganised offenders tend to leave evidence like blood or semen. He could then read the transcripts and tally the different behaviours, and see how they match the two different profiles, or whether some contain behaviours from both types of profile. (b) The criminals may not be honest, or may not remember details correctly because of the passage of time or mental illness or drug or alcohol use at the time of the crime, whereas the court and police reports were written at the time of the crime's investigation so may be more accurate.

Topic 3 Offender profiling: The bottom-up approach

Choose the right answer: C

Complete the table:

Aspect of the approach	Top-down	Bottom-up
Developed by	FBI agents in the US	Psychologists in the UK
Starts with	All details about crime scene, no info about suspects	Statistical analysis of similar crimes
Research basis	Interviews with 37 imprisoned serial killers	Court and police records of hundreds of prisoners
How the profile is developed	Experience and intuition of the profiler	Predictions based on empirical data
Assumptions	Offender's characteristics match characteristics of the crime: organised/disorganised	Spatial mindset Interpersonal coherence Forensic awareness Categories of offenders identifiable from data
Usefulness	Police think it is useful, but unreliable judgments of accuracy	Can be useful in hard-to-solve cases
Criticisms	Classifications are not mutually exclusive and not supported by evidence	May not give any more information than traditional methods
Conclusion relating to both approaches	Can narrow down suspects, BUT may lead to police focussing on he wrong suspect	

Drawing conclusions: (a) 6 (b) Validity increases the more crime sites are available for analysis. Validity is poor when there are few crime sites. (c) A commuter commits crimes at a different location from their residence; this model assumes that they live within the area that the crimes were committed.

Applying your knowledge: Identify the psychology: Geographic profiling – CGT, jeopardy surface. Bottom-up profiling: data about similar crimes. Link to this investigation: Saga and Henrik could use a CGT map to see where the offender was most likely to live in the Malmö or Copenhagen region, based on the crime sites; this would narrow down search areas. They could look up research findings about similar serial murders where bodies were staged, to see if there are useful themes that could help them narrow down suspects. They will also be taking into consideration that the murderer may have some experience of police techniques and is leaving deliberate clues or misleading evidence.

Topic 4 Biological explanations of offending behaviour: A historical approach

Choose the right answer: B

Research issues: (a) Strengths: large sample size; objective measurements of physical features; Limitations: no control or comparison group; only studied males (b) He attempted to use empirical observations to collect data and studied actual criminals. (c) His conclusions were based on assumptions which were ethnocentric (certain physical characteristics being less evolved) and androcentric (women being less evolved). He also ignored the possibility of free will, that people may decide to commit crimes based on cognitive reasoning.

Match them up: 1D 2C 3E 4A 5B 6F

Applying your knowledge: Atavistic means throwback to ancestral type, ape-like. Lombroso identified peculiarities of ears, nose, jaw, chin, arms etc. Dracula's massive eyebrows, bushy hair, protruding lips, coarse, broad hands and hairy palms are ape-like qualities. The aquiline face was characteristic of murderers, according to Lombroso. Overall, the description is atavistic as it implies that a murderous person must the appearance of a lower primate, and the description of Dracula contains some of these features.

Topic 5 Biological explanations of offending behaviour: Genetic and neural

Match them up: 1C 2A 3D 4F 5B 6G 7E

Choose the right answer: B D

Research issues 1: (a) There are genetic factors in delinquency, as the concordance rate for MZ is higher and they have identical DNA whereas DZ only have 50% the same DNA. However, there are other factors involved too as the concordance rate for MZ twins is not 100%. (b) MZ twins may be treated more similarly because they look the same, and will always be the same sex, so there is greater environmental similarity for MZ twins too. (c) Early studies classified twins by appearance, so some may have been wrongly classified; DZ twins may look extremely similar. Now it is possible to use DNA testing so mistakes can't be made.

Research issues 2: (a) If children spend some time with their biological parents, they might experience abuse, neglect or social learning (environmental influences) from them. This means that the similarities with biological parents are not just due to heredity. (b) Families may have similarities in culture, education, ethnicity, religious beliefs etc.; this means that shared environmental factors make it more difficult to separate out biological and environmental influences. (c) Children may be traumatised by breaking an attachment to the birth mother, or they may have been neglected and have attachment disorders which mean they find it difficult to form healthy relationships with their adopted parents.

Applying your knowledge: Identify the psychology: Faulty MAOA gene leads to low serotonin and occurred in 28 Dutch men studied by Brunner; combination with faulty CDH13 gene found in Finnish offenders makes it hard to resist violence. However, Caspi showed that the interaction with childhood maltreatment was important. The gene alone does not determine violent behaviour. In adoption studies, 80% of boys with biological parents who were criminals did not become criminals themselves. Link to Alan: He may have inherited genes such as MAOA or CDH13 variants, but even if he has, this does not mean he will become a murderer. Childhood experiences are also important. Alan has not been brought up with his father so has not received social influences from him. As Alan has not suffered maltreatment as a child he would be unlikely to become a criminal despite his genes.

Topic 6 Psychological explanations of offending behaviour: Eysenck's theory

Match them up: 1C 2A 3F 4E 5B 6D

Research issues: (a) The same participants take the same test after an interval of time, such as a week later. The two sets of results are compared by correlation. High correlation means good reliability. (b) Some items may need to be removed or rewritten to make them less ambiguous. (c) The scores match those from a previously validated scale. (d) The correlation between scores from both scales was high, so the new scale is measuring the same traits as the original one. (e) Face validity. The items on the scale should be considered to see whether they are obviously related to the traits of extraversion, neuroticism and psychoticism. (f) The questions are forced-choice so there is no possibility of answering 'sometimes', which may be a more valid answer as people behave differently in different situations. There may be social desirability effects where people answer as they think is socially acceptable rather than being honest about their negative behaviours, so they are not truthful.

Applying your knowledge: Luca probably scores high on extraversion, as he loves partying and is the class clown, and he gets bored easily, so seeks external stimulation like climbing things. He is high on neuroticism, as he feels low and anxious when he is alone. He is also high on psychoticism, as he is rude to the teacher and doesn't seem to care what people think. Extraverts become involved in dangerous risk-taking behaviour, which Luca is starting to do. Neurotics are unstable and can overreact, which Luca does by being stroppy to the teacher. All three traits seem to be leading him into anti-social behaviour.

Topic 7 Psychological explanations of offending behaviour: Cognitive

Choose the right answer: C
Match them up: 1B 2A 3C

Applying your knowledge 1: (a) Hostile attribution bias – assuming their partner would refuse to comply, or would respond negatively. No recognition that using force may be a poor way to achieve things. (b) Encouraging them to reflect on their thinking, challenging negative, irrational thoughts. (c) If more students graduate from high school, they will be able to earn more, pay more taxes, be less dependent on state support. If they commit fewer crimes, they will cost less to the economy via the justice system.

Applying your knowledge 2: (a) (i) His wife needs it so he should steal it as long as he thought he wouldn't get caught. (ii) He is doing the right thing to help his wife, even if he has to break the law. (iii) The principle of care for the sick is more important; the chemist was wrong to refuse to give the drug to Heinz, therefore Heinz was justified in stealing it. (b) The scenarios are imaginary, and people may behave differently in real life. The participants were young males who would not have experienced marriage or life-threatening illness so could not imagine how they would respond. The sample is all male so cannot be generalised to females, whose moral principles may be different.

Topic 8 Psychological explanations of offending behaviour: Differential association

Match them up: 1D 2A 3B 4C 5E
Choose the right answer: A

Applying your knowledge: Differential association theory proposes that offending behaviour is learned from other people, particularly peers and the local community. Lauren is hanging out with girls who have been excluded from school, so Lauren is learning norms, attitudes to crime, and methods from them through observation and direct reinforcement. According to Sutherland, the frequency, length and personal meaning of social associations determine their degree of influence; Lauren is spending a lot of time with these girls and she didn't have friends in the area before, so they are important to her at a vulnerable time after her parents' divorce and the house move.

	Eysenck's theory	Cognitive	Differential association	Psychodynamic
Consists of:	Personality traits – genetic + learned	Cognitive distortions + levels of moral reasoning	Social learning	Maternal deprivation or superego problems
Link to criminal behaviour	High E/N/P lead to criminal behaviour, biologically mediated	Hostile attribution bias, minimalisation. Pre-conventional level	Learned attitudes towards crime and methods of crime	Affectionless psychopathy. Underdeveloped or overdeveloped superego
Applications	Treatment by modifying socialisation experiences of high E/N children	CBT for treatment of cognitive distortions	Improving social environments to reduce crime	Protecting early attachments, providing emotional care
Research support	Zuckerman – twin studies. Dunlop – E/P predicted delinquency	Schonenberg – violent offenders misattribute aggression. Kennedy – sex offenders minimalise crimes	Akers – peers main influence on substance abuse	Bowlby's 44 thieves – separations associated with affectionless psychopathy and delinquency
Criticisms	Personality may not be consistent, self-report tests not valid	Kohlberg's theory based on scenarios, not real choices, and only in males	Can't account for all crimes, ignores biological factors	Bowlby's findings not causal. Gender bias in Freud's theory

Activities: suggested answers

Topic 9 Psychological explanations of offending behaviour: Psychodynamic

Match them up: 1F 2E 3D 4C 5B 6A

Complete the table: (see below)

Research issues: (a) Opportunity sampling. May not represent other offenders, and the young people may not have had a choice about participating. (b) Researcher bias: his observations which led to his diagnosis may have been biased due to knowing which were thieves and which were controls. (c) Their memories may not have been accurate. Or they may have been responding to what they thought Bowlby wanted to hear – demand characteristics.

Topic 10 Dealing with offending behaviour: custodial sentencing and recidivism

Match them up: 1Biii 2Civ 3Ev 4Aii 5Di

A marking exercise: The depression point is well explained. The psychological effects of overcrowding are not mentioned, making this point ineffective. This overcrowding leads to stress and aggression as well as more illness.

Drawing conclusions: (a) 0.48 x 3,948 = 1,895 (b) 100 – 81 = 19% (c) Almost twice the percentage of women as men had psychotic symptoms, and more than twice the percentage of women had attempted suicide than men, which is a sign of depression. Also women were twice as likely to have experienced abuse which is likely to lead to psychological problems.

Applying your knowledge: Custodial sentencing can worsen depression and there are high rates of self-harm and suicide in prison. Brigitte is vulnerable to depression already and imprisonment may make it worse for her. Children with a parent in prison are affected financially and psychologically. Brigitte has a young baby and imprisoning her is likely to separate her from her baby, which will cause anxiety for both of them, and possibly long-term damage to the baby. Other types of sentencing such as community service can be more effective for non-violent and first-time offenders. Brigitte needs support rather than punishment, and a community sentence could be more effective.

Topic 11 Dealing with offending behaviour: Behaviour modification in custody

Choose the right answer: 1A 2B 3D 4E

A marking exercise: 3 marks. They could give more details of the findings and compare with the control group.

Research issues: (a) IV = before and after token system, DV = number of behaviours in each category (b) The boys in one cottage were not included in the token system, and were used as a control – this was a naturally occurring group and they were not randomly allocated. (c) So reliability could be calculated by comparing their tallies of behaviours for each boy, and to make sure all behaviours were observed. (d) Train the supervisors better, or make sure they are not trying to carry out other tasks at the same time as recording observations, such as dealing with behavioural issues. (e) The supervisors were busy doing other things, and became less consistent in monitoring behaviour and issuing tokens, so the token economy system became less effective and got dropped. (f) Operant conditioning requires a schedule of reinforcement, otherwise the stimulus-response link is extinguished. The boys will no longer have this when they are released. When the boys are in the real world, they would have different environments and some of the behaviours, like walking in a straight line, would no longer be relevant. However, young offenders did maintain some learning in Cohen and Filipcjak's study, and

re-offending rates were decreased, so Hobbs and Holt's participants may have some generalisation of learned behaviours like following rules.

Applying your knowledge: It needs to be carefully planned. Mrs Cole should decide what the key aims are, then agree with staff and student representatives what hierarchy of behaviours and rewards the staff will use. All the students must be aware of the new system, and what tokens they will get for each behaviour and what rewards will be available. The rewards should be extra treats, not essential items like lunch as this would be unethical. All the staff must be trained so they remain consistent. This would be expected to improve pro-social behaviour and reduce anti-social behaviour of students as long as the reinforcements continue consistently and the rewards are things the students' value. Token economy can improve behaviour short-term and improve life in the institution for staff and students.

Topic 12 Dealing with offending behaviour: Anger management

Choose the right answer: C E

Drawing conclusions: (a) S = 2 (b) Yes. N = 16, critical value of S = 4 at p < 0.05. Calculated value is less than critical value so it is significant, and in the expected direction. (c) They are young people who have shown some willingness to change, as they have signed up for the course. They are otherwise similar, living in the same environment etc. (d) The calculated value of S for the control group is 6, N = 14, Critical value (p < 0.05) S = 3, so this decrease in anger is not significant. The control group shows that the change is due to the anger management course, not some other changes that are going on at the secure training centre, as the group who completed the programme decreased their anger ratings but the control group did not have a significant decrease. (e) The self-report measure is not very objective, and may be affected by demand characteristics; the young people may want to be helpful and say that they are less angry than they were, the 'hello–goodbye' effect. Or an improvement in anger ratings may get them other benefits like early release.

Applying your knowledge: Stress inoculation therapy is a CBT model, three stages: cognitive preparation, skill acquisition, application training. Aims are: cognitive restructuring, regulation of arousal, behavioural strategies. Dexter should be offered SIT. It is important that he agree to this and is willing to change, as readiness to change reduces dropout and improves the success of the treatment. He will learn about anger generally and analyse his own patterns of anger and triggers, for example going to clubs and bars. He will acquire skills to regulate his emotional and physiological state of anger in those situations, such as breathing and relaxation, and alternative strategies like walking out of the bar when he is feeling angry, or talking in a calm voice. He will then practise these skills with other group members in role play, who will give him feedback about how he's coming over, then he will try them in real-world situations. Hopefully he now has better self-awareness and control, and some useful strategies to stop him getting angry.

Topic 13 Dealing with offending behaviour: Restorative justice programmes

Choose the right answer 1: C

Choose the right answer 2: D

Applying your knowledge 1: Anwar could set up a peace circle. It will need a 'keeper', or facilitator, which needs to be someone respected by people from different sections of the community, maybe Anwar himself. The keeper is there to maintain an atmosphere of respect. Community members, including victims and offenders, will be invited to take part. Everyone will get a chance to express their views, experiences and fears, and to listen to each other. This will hopefully generate more understanding between different groups, like the residents and the young men who are carrying out the crimes. The offenders could be asked to carry out service in the community as a form of compensation and recognition of their responsibility of their crimes. This in turn will hopefully lead to a reduction in crime.

Drawing conclusions: (a) 90% (b) 45% (c) 20 (d) 6,941

Applying your knowledge 2: Purpose: rehabilitation of offenders, atonement for wrongdoing, victim having a voice and understanding the offender's reasons for offending. It could benefit Craig by hearing Nick's distress about losing his brother, which will reduce the chance of him committing a similar crime in the future. He also had the chance to express his remorse and say sorry. Nick was helped to understand that Craig realised he had made a mistake, and that Craig deserved a second chance in life.

Chapter 11 Addiction

Topic 1 Describing addiction

Match them up: 1A 2C 3D 4B

Choose the right answer: B

Applying your knowledge: Joseph is clearly showing withdrawal symptoms because he starts to feel nauseous and anxious when the effect off the caffeine wears off. Furthermore, he is also demonstrating tolerance because he now needs more coffee in order to feel the same effect and stay awake, which could be the result of metabolic tolerance.

Topic 2 Risk factors: Genetics, stress and personality

Choose the right answer: B

Maths skills 1: 1) Mean score for Group A 67.9; Mean score for Group B 19.8. 2) The mean is the most appropriate measure because it takes into account all of the scores for Group A and Group B. As there are no outliers, the data will not be distorted, which is why this measure is the most appropriate.

Maths skills 2:

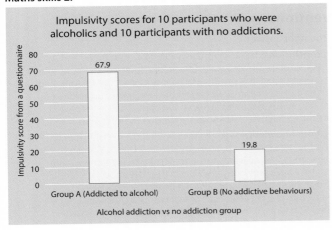

Impulsivity scores for 10 participants who were alcoholics and 10 participants with no addictions.

Applying your knowledge: First, it is possible that Chris has a genetic vulnerability to smoking. It could be that Chris has inherited a dopamine receptor gene (as both of his parent's smoke) which causes him to suffer from abnormally low levels of dopamine and the smoking activates the dopamine receptors in the brain creating strong feelings of euphoria. Secondly, it could also be that Chris is using smoking to deal with his stressful job as the smoking may make him feel better or help him to forget the stress.

Topic 3 Risk factors: Family influences and peers

Choose the right answer 1: D

Choose the right answer 2: B

A marking exercise: This is not a great answer. Firstly, the answer simply states three reasons without explaining them and secondly, the final point about authoritative parenting style is not accurate (due to its lack of explanation).

Improved answer: Parents can influence addictive behaviour in two ways. Firstly, they act as a social model for their offspring and secondly, through their parenting style. Authoritative parents help their children to develop resilience to addictive behaviours. In addition, social learning theory can also explain the role of family, as children can learn through people they have extensive social contact with, including parents and siblings.

Applying your knowledge: Tola is being indirectly influenced by peers and a desire to fit in with a popular group at school. Social identity theory could explain why Tola smokes, as she wants to be socially accepted with the 'ingroup' (who smoke) and therefore adopts their behaviour.

Furthermore, the lack of parental influence may also contribute to Tola's addiction. Stattin and Kerr (2000) suggest that a lack of parental monitoring may result from adolescents disclosing too much information about their substance abuse. Therefore, her parents' inability to deal with this information may cause them to stop monitoring Tola which therefore contributes to her addiction.

Topic 4 Explanation for nicotine addiction: Brain neurochemistry

Complete the diagram:

Dopamine reward pathway

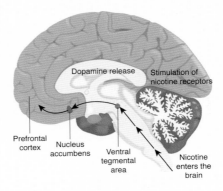

Choose the right answer: A

A marking exercise: This is a good start to this question, however the answer needs further points to gain full marks. The answer has outlined one good point and made an effective link, but it requires evidence to support the claim. For example: One problem with the neurochemistry explanation of nicotine addiction is the fact that nicotine has a different effect on men and women. Cosgrove *et al.* (2014) studied the brains of men and women using PET scans, while smoking. These results suggest that men and women smoke for different reasons, men for the nicotine effect and women to relieve stress. This means that the reason why men and women smoke is different, which is not taken into account in this neurochemical explanation.

Topic 5   Explanation for nicotine addiction: Learning theory

Complete the diagram:

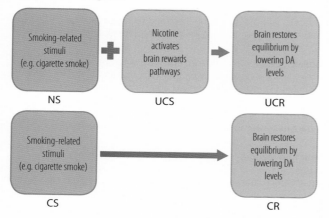

Choose the right answer: E

Match them up: 1D 2E 3C 4B 5A

Applying your knowledge: There are two key answers here. Firstly, Nico associates leaving his work building with smoking (a smoking-related cue) and the rewarding effects of smoking, which therefore contributes to his urge. Furthermore, he also finds that the urges are stronger when he has a stressful day and therefore he is craving the negative reinforcement (removal of the stress) which he is used to experiencing through smoking.

Topic 6   Explanation for gambling addiction: Learning theory

Choose the right answer: D

Match them up: 1C 2A 3E 4B 5D

Applying your knowledge: There are two key reasons which could explain why Gareth had become addicted. Firstly, he finds the gambling environment very exciting and therefore the betting shop has become a condition stimuli and the excitement a conditioned response, which will prompt him to continue returning. Secondly, he has had several early wins, which could be explained by the 'big win' hypothesis, as Gareth will continue to gamble to try and repeat these wins.

Write your own evaluation point: Point – One strength of the learning explanation of gambling comes from Horsley *et al.* (2012). Evidence – Horsley *et al.* (2012) tested the idea of partial reinforcement, among high- and low-frequency gamblers, using either partial or continuous reinforcement. They found that after partial reinforcement, high-frequency gamblers continued to respond on a gambling situation for longer, in comparison to low-frequency gamblers. Explain – This supports the idea that partial reinforcement is likely to contribute to the maintenance of gambling, especially in high-frequency gamblers. Evaluate – While many people may gamble at some time during their lives and experience reinforcement, relatively few become addicts. Link – Therefore, if the learning explanation was the only cause of gambling, then it would be reasonable to assume that a higher proportion of people may become addicts. This matters because it suggests that there must be other factors involved in the formation of gambling addictions.

Topic 7   Explanation for gambling addiction: Cognitive theory

Choose the right answer: C

Match them up: 1C 2D 3A 4B

Applying your knowledge: Firstly, Abdul has experienced a 'near miss' and because he has got two 'wins' and a number 7 this may provide him with motivation to continue gambling, because he sees this as 'nearly winning' and not losing. Secondly, Abdul is also experiencing an illusion of control, because he believes that he can trick the machine which is an irrational statement and a clear example of a cognitive bias.

Topic 8   Reducing addiction: Drug therapy

Choose the right answer: A D

Write your own evaluation point: Point – Support for the effectiveness of drug treatments for gambling comes from Grant and Potenza (2006). Evidence – They gave 13 gambling addicts an SSRI for three months. At the end of the three months, some continued with the treatment, while others received a placebo. They found that for those who received the placebo, their gambling and anxiety returned. Explain – This shows SSRIs are effective in the treatment of gambling addictions, because the participants who did not continue with their treatment relapsed. Evaluate – However, Blaszcynski and Nower (2007) argue that research investigating drug treatments is characterised by small sample sizes. Link – Therefore, despite the fact that Grant and Potenza (2006) appear to support the use of SSRIs in the treatment of gambling, their support is questionable due to their very limited sample size. Therefore, further research should be conducted to assess the reliability of their findings.

Applying your knowledge: There are two treatments that would be suitable for Tyeisha. Firstly, she could use a NRT, like patches or gum. This would gradually release nicotine into her system to help her control the cravings and improve her mood (by reducing the horrible withdrawal symptoms). Furthermore, Tyeisha could use a drug like Zyban (a type of bupropion), which stops the re-uptake of dopamine and reduces cravings and any withdrawal symptoms.

Topic 9   Reducing addition: Behavioural interventions

Choose the right answer: C

Drawing conclusions: The key with questions involving the interpretation of graphs is to use all of the information. For example: the bar chart reveals that covert sensitisation is a more effective treatment for both nicotine and gambling addictions in the long term. Furthermore, the results also reveal that all behavioural therapies (both aversion and covert) are more effective on gambling addicts in the long term.

Applying your knowledge: Identify the psychology: Aversion therapy is based on the principles of classical conditioning. Link to Winnifred: This is where an individual learns to associate an adverse stimulus with something they have previously enjoyed, in this case chocolate. Identify the psychology: Winnifred might be given an electric shock every time she sees a picture of a chocolate bar, or reaches for a chocolate bar. Link to Winnifred: Therefore, Winnifred would associate these unpleasant electric shocks, with chocolate, which should eliminate her addiction.

A marking exercise: Although the student has correctly identified one issue of aversion therapy, their example is not very strong and they have not elaborated their answer. This is a 4-mark answer and therefore they should aim to write four key points. Model answer: One issue with aversion therapy is that it is has been criticised for being unethical. Some forms of aversion therapy used in the treatment of problem drinking cause extremely uncomfortable consequences, e.g. vomiting. These consequences could lead to poor compliance with the treatment and high dropout rates. This matters because these side-effects may decrease the positive impact of the treatment and cause patients to relapse.

Topic 10 Reducing addiction: Cognitive behaviour therapy

Choose the right answer: D

Fill in the boxes:

In each box below write one sentence describing each stage of CBT	In each box below expand the content on the left, giving an example
Identifying and correcting cognitive biases is where…a therapist will bring cognitive biases to the surface and educate their client about these biases.	For example…an individual might believe that they can predict the outcome on a slot machine and the therapist will make the client understand that slot machines are due to chance.
Changing behaviour is where…the client practises the changes from part 1 in their everyday life.	For example…a gambler may be asked to visit a casino or betting shop and not bet.
Relapse prevention is where… the patient identifies and avoids risky situations that can trigger the addiction.	For example…they might identify places (e.g. casinos or betting shops), feelings or other situations that might prompt gambling.
OPTIONAL: A diary is used to…record the triggers related to their problem behaviour.	This enables the patient to record their progress in overcoming their addiction.

Applying your knowledge: The first stage of CBT is to identify and correct Chris's irrational thoughts. He believes that if he doesn't reply to a friend instantly, that they will hate him. The therapist will bring this thought to the surface and educate Chris to make him understand that this thought process is irrational. Secondly, Chris will be encouraged to change his behaviour, this could involve setting aside two hours a day (or longer) where he doesn't use the internet. Finally, Chris will be given strategies to prevent relapse and avoid risky situations that might make him return to the internet.

A marking exercise: This is quite a good answer in terms of outlining the three stages correctly, however the answer lacks depth, which could have been achieved with examples. For example: CBT could be used to reduce a gambling addiction by identifying cognitive biases (for example, a gambler might believe that they can predict the outcome of a fruit machine, which is clearly irrational); changing the person's behaviour (for example, asking them to visit a casino and not gamble) and ensuring that they have strategies to prevent relapse (for example, by identifying situations which might prompt relapse, e.g. casinos boredom, etc.).

Topic 11 The theory of planned behaviour

Complete the diagram:

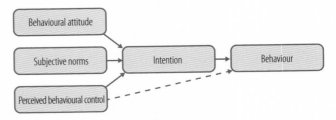

Choose the right answer: C

Match them up: 1D 2A 3C 4B

Applying your knowledge: Ali has a positive 'behavioural attitude' to stop smoking, as she is worried about the health risks involved in smoking. Furthermore, she has the support of her colleagues which provides her with 'positive subjective norms' in order to help her quit. However, she does not have the 'perceived behavioural control' as she does not believe that she could actually give up smoking. According to the TPB the perceived behavioural control is an important aspect and therefore, if she does not believe that she can give up, she may be unlikely to succeed.

Topic 12 Proschaska's six-stage model of behavioural change

Complete the diagram:

Choose the right answer: D

Match them up: 1B 2A 3F 4D 5E 6C

Applying your knowledge: Aiden is aware of his problem and therefore might be at the contemplation stage, however he has made a plan to buy fewer cigarettes and therefore could be in the preparation stage, where he combines his intention with actual behaviour. If Aiden follows through his plan and only buys ten cigarettes, then he will be at the action stage.

Training yourself to be an examiner (page 9)

Training task 4

Description: Level 4 – accurate and well-detailed.

Evaluation: Level 3 – mostly effective.

Application: Level 2 – application is only partial

Organisation: Level 3 – mostly clear and organised

Specialist terminology: Level 4 – used effectively

Final level: 3

Final mark: 11/16

The Research Methods Companion

- Written by leading Psychology author, Cara Flanagan.

- Practical, activity-based Student Book covers everything you need to know for the research methods part of AS and A Level Psychology.

- Designed for use with all A Level Psychology courses.

- Developed to boost your confidence and provide you with the skills, knowledge and understanding you need to get to grips with this challenging part of the course.

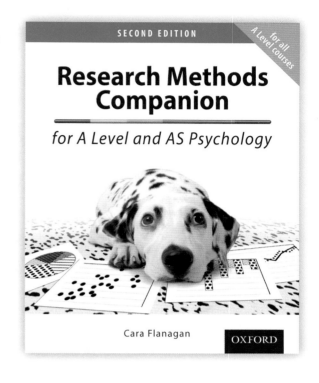

SECOND EDITION

for all A Level Courses

Research Methods Companion

for A Level and AS Psychology

Cara Flanagan

OXFORD

Order your copy now: 978 019 835613 4

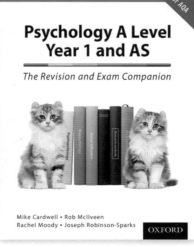
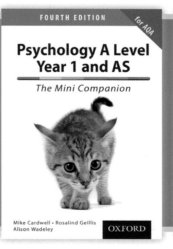
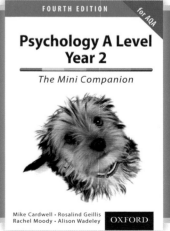